WRITING FOR PRINT
AND DIGITAL MEDIA

WRITING FOR PRINT AND DIGITAL MEDIA

MICHAEL RYAN

UNIVERSITY OF HOUSTON

JAMES W. TANKARD JR.

UNIVERSITY OF TEXAS, AUSTIN

Boston   Burr Ridge, IL   Dubuque, IA   Madison, WI   New York
San Francisco   St. Louis   Bangkok   Bogotá   Caracas   Kuala Lumpur
Lisbon   London   Madrid   Mexico City   Milan   Montreal   New Delhi
Santiago   Seoul   Singapore   Sydney   Taipei   Toronto

Higher Education

WRITING FOR PRINT AND DIGITAL MEDIA
Published by McGraw-Hill, an imprint of The McGraw-Hill Companies, Inc., 1221
Avenue of the Americas, New York, NY 10020. Copyright © 2005. All rights reserved.
No part of this publication may be reproduced or distributed in any form or by any
means, or stored in a database or retrieval system, without the prior written consent of
The McGraw-Hill Companies, Inc., including, but not limited to, in any network or other
electronic storage or transmission, or broadcast for distance learning.

This book is printed on acid-free paper.

1 2 3 4 5 6 7 8 9 0 DOC/DOC 0 9 8 7 6 5 4

ISBN 0-07-286735-3

Editor in Chief: *Emily Barrosse*
Publisher: *Philip Butcher*
Sponsoring Editor: *Philip Butcher*
Signing Representative: *Janet Taborn* and
Paul Moorman
Editorial Assistant: *Francoise Villeneuve*
Marketing Manager: *Leslie Oberhuber*
Developmental Editor: *Laura Lynch*
Production Editor: *Holly Paulsen*

Manuscript Editor: *Joan Pendleton*
Design Manager: *Preston Thomas*
Text and Cover Designer: *Yvo Riezebos*
Art Editor: *Katherine McNab*
Illustrators: *Katherine McNab* and *Ayelet Arbel*
Photo Research: *Natalia Peschiera* and *Judy Mason*
Production Supervisor: *Randy Hurst*
Media: *Nancy Garcia* and *Christie Ling*

Composition: *11/13 Minion by Precision Graphics*
Printing: *PMS 314, 45# New Era Matte, R. R. Donnelley, Crawfordsville, Ind.*

Cover: (clockwise from top left) © Royalty-Free/Corbis, © Image Source/Corbis, © PictureArts/Corbis,
© PhotoDisc, © Colin Anderson/Corbis, © Digital Vision.

Credits: The credits section for this book begins on page C-1 and is considered an extension of the
copyright page.

Library of Congress Cataloging-in-Publication Data
Ryan, Michael
   Writing for print and digital media / Michael Ryan, James W. Tankard Jr.
     p. cm.
   Includes bibliographical references and index.
   ISBN 0-07-286735-3
   1. Journalism—Authorship.   2. Report writing.   I. Tankard, James W.   II. Title.

PN4775.R93 2004
808'.06607—dc22
                                 2004058158

The Internet addresses listed in the text were accurate at the time of publication. The inclusion of
a Web site does not indicate an endorsement by the authors or McGraw-Hill, and McGraw-Hill
does not guarantee the accuracy of the information presented at these sites.

www.mhhe.com

For Janet, Sara and Kevin Ryan

For Lanie, Amy, Jessica and Margaret Tankard

ABOUT THE AUTHORS

Michael Ryan, a professor of communication at the University of Houston, has taught media writing, public relations, editing, feature writing, research methods, precision journalism and theory at the University of Houston, Temple University and West Virginia University. He worked as a news reporter for the *San Angelo* (Texas) *Standard-Times* and for the Long News Service, an Austin news bureau that serves Texas newspapers and radio stations. He has won two School Bell awards from the Texas State Teachers Association for op-ed pieces in the *Houston Chronicle*.

Ryan has co-authored two books and published more than 100 scholarly and professional articles. His work has appeared in *Journalism & Mass Communication Quarterly, Journalism & Mass Communication Monographs, Public Relations Review, Public Relations Quarterly, Journalism & Mass Communication Educator, Feedback* and the *Journal of Communication,* among others.

James W. Tankard Jr. is a retired professor from the School of Journalism at the University of Texas at Austin. During his 34-year academic career, he taught newswriting, reporting, editing, feature writing, computer-assisted reporting, Web publishing, literary journalism, communication theory and communication research methods. He worked as a reporter for The Associated Press and the *Raleigh* (N.C.) *Times,* and as a guest editor of the *Lampasas* (Texas) *Dispatch Record.*

He is the author of *The Statistical Pioneers;* the co-author with Werner Severin of *Communication Theories,* which has been translated into four languages and is now in its fifth edition; and a co-author with Pamela Shoemaker and Dominic Lasorsa of the recently published *How to Build Social Science Theories.*

CONTENTS IN BRIEF

CONTENTS

PART V   APPENDICES

PREFACE

Mass media are among the most exciting, important and dynamic institutions in communities around the globe. Careers in mass communication provide opportunities for those so inclined to have positive, profound impacts on social, political, cultural and economic conditions wherever they live. The responsibilities of journalists and public relations practitioners are great, but the rewards are, too.

WRITING

This book is designed to assist readers who want to make the most of these opportunities. *Writing for Print and Digital Media* helps students develop the superb writing skills they'll need to succeed as media professionals. We're not talking only about a writer's knowledge of grammar, spelling, punctuation and style, although these fundamentals are critical.

Our vision of writing is much broader and much deeper than that. Stated most simply, good writers produce copy that is accurate, compelling, fair, balanced, complete, clear and concise—and they do that within laws, professional standards and ethical codes of conduct that inform *all* of their work. They have mastered a complex array of skills and know how to apply them, often under difficult circumstances. Here are some of the characteristics that we hope readers of this book will develop as they study and apply the concepts outlined here and by their teachers:

- Good writers are critical thinkers who can effectively use the research tools discussed in this book to analyze problems and find solutions. If they want to know, for example, whether a community's police department is unfairly targeting minorities in a traffic control program, they know how to do a systematic study of records. If they need information on which to construct a public relations campaign and they can get it only by doing a social science study, they know how to do that. They have the critical thinking skills necessary to analyze, to synthesize and to interpret information so that it makes sense to them and to their audiences.

- Good writers try to adopt the objective approach and all that entails. They are, for example, skeptical of authority; dedicated to accuracy, completeness, precision and clarity; creative; consistent in making strategic decisions; fair and impartial; unwilling to support any political, social, cultural or economic interests that conflict with public or professional interests; ethical in their professional and personal lives; and honest about their own preferences and idiosyncrasies.

■ Good writers understand the social, political, legal, economic and cultural contexts within which they work. They realize that nothing is more important to a free society than the free flow of accurate and useful information and that journalists and public relations practitioners are responsible for protecting that free flow against those who would limit or pollute it.

■ Good writers understand the communication context within which they work and try to minimize the worst aspects of mass communication while maximizing the best aspects. Journalists need to understand how the drive for profits influences the media for which they work, and public relations practitioners need to understand that the interests of their organizations and of society will occasionally conflict, sometimes in fundamental ways.

■ Good writers are interested in *everything,* from politics to farming to science to art to poetry and all things between and beyond. They want to know how the powerless get by when times are tough and how the powerful exercise their power; why some public school children don't learn and why some do; how language shapes our lives and determines our futures. They have the skills to find answers to these and thousands of other questions.

■ Good writers strive to rise continuously and relentlessly to new levels of competence and creativity. This requires that they read constantly and that they write constantly. It takes practice, practice, practice. A good teacher helps.

■ Good writers can write for any medium and any purpose using any format, for they have mastered the fundamentals, and those don't change—regardless of medium or purpose. Good writing is good writing, whether one is producing a novel, a news release, a documentary film, a feature story, a love letter or anything else. A writer who knows the fundamentals can produce copy for a newspaper, a public relations agency, a Web site or a broadcast outlet. The format differences are easy to master.

SELF-EDITING

Many bad writers just bang out stories and then turn them in without reading them over—good writers don't do that unless they are working under extreme deadline pressure. Media writers turn their copy over to editors when they are done, but that doesn't mean they aren't editors—or that editors cannot profit from the principles outlined in this book.

The best writers are good self-editors. That means they finish first drafts and then go to work on them all over again. They make sure that the mechanics are right and the style rules are used correctly; that the lead is clear, concise, compelling and to the point; that the story is organized well; that the facts are complete and accurate; and that they have attributed carefully.

We have included sections about self-editing in chapters 3, 4 and 5, but even where we have not incorporated a separate section, it's important to think in terms of self-editing, for the ability to self-edit effectively and efficiently is one of the things that separates mediocre writers from good writers.

It's possible to hang on to a story too long, of course. A good rule of thumb is for a writer to turn in the story when he or she starts editing sentences that have already been edited.

RESEARCH, THEORY AND OTHER WRITINGS

Writing for Print and Digital Media contains many references to some of the latest (and some of the classic) research, commentary and theory in mass communication. Media professionals can learn a great deal from the critical theorists' analyses of power and the media; the social scientists' studies of media effects; the cultural theorists' investigations of the media's portrayals of marginalized groups; and the media professionals' descriptions of tough assignments they've handled.

This body of knowledge, accumulated over several decades, is important to those who want to understand how communication works (and doesn't work), who want to change mass media for the better and who want to be better professionals.

This book does contain chapter endnotes. Some may object on principle to notes in textbooks, and readers can ignore them if they so choose. But we hope they won't. We try to cite literature that is easy to find (we frequently cite more than one source for important information) and that elaborates on points we can cover only superficially. The notes are here not only to document assertions but also as suggested readings. These valuable materials really will expand horizons and help make readers better writers and better citizens.

We hope this book, in combination with the classroom teachers who are working hard to teach writing, will help students change the ways they view the world and their places in it. We hope, too, that each reader becomes a better writer.

STRUCTURE

This book is designed primarily for a semester-long class in beginning media writing with lecture-laboratory format. The class meets for six to eight contact hours each week for roughly 16 weeks. Experience shows the book works well with this format.

However, mass communication programs schedule courses in many different ways and in many different formats (semester versus quarter system, for example). Further, some teachers cover information collection before writing fundamentals, and some cover writing before information collection. There are many other variations.

We have organized *Writing for Print and Digital Media* to maximize flexibility. If a program schedules writing in one term and information collection in another, the book would fit that format. A teacher could assign chapters 1–7 in the first term and chapters 8–12 in the second term. Chapters 13–15 could be assigned in either term. If a teacher wants to discuss attribution and quotation before lead writing, he or she can assign Chapter 7 before Chapter 5.

All of this is probably obvious. Our point is simply that we have tried to arrange the book so that it can fit conveniently into almost any format. We hope it works for yours.

STYLE

Style, in this context, refers to the standards of language usage that a medium adopts as it tries to ensure consistency in everything it publishes or broadcasts. A medium's editors, for example, must decide whether courtesy titles (Mrs., Mr., Ms.) will be used in the stories they print or air. When the style is decided, all writers and editors follow that style, and readers and listeners become accustomed to that format. Literally hundreds of decisions are made as editors develop their style sheets.

The Associated Press Stylebook and Briefing on Media Law is the standard in the news industry. Many newspapers, Web sites, magazines, public relations offices and broadcast outlets use the style manual and nothing else. Others incorporate many of the rules into their own style manuals—but with some changes.

We have mostly followed The Associated Press' style in preparing this book because AP style is so widely used. We have made one alteration, however. The names of newspapers, magazines, television programs, books, films and similar content are set in italic type, as are court cases. The Associated Press does not use italic type for technical reasons, but italic type is used by most media. We decided to use it here whenever it would ordinarily be used in a textbook.

ACKNOWLEDGMENTS

We are grateful to the following for reading parts or all of the manuscript:

Ted Stanton, Les Switzer and Shawn McCombs, University of Houston

Jay Black, University of South Florida St. Petersburg

Robert Brown, Salem State College, Massachusetts

James A. Crook, University of Tennessee

Bruce Garrison, University of Miami

W. Wat Hopkins, Virginia Tech

Annette Johnson, Georgia State University

Sharon Murphy, Bradley University, Peoria, Ill.

Raul Reis, California State University, Long Beach.

We are grateful also to Lisa Peck, a University of Texas at Austin journalism student, for research assistance.

And we wish to thank all the supportive professionals on the publishing team at McGraw-Hill: Phil Butcher, publisher; Laura Lynch, developmental editor; Marcella Tullio, editorial assistant; Holly Paulsen, production editor; Joan Pendleton, copy editor; Leslie Oberhuber, marketing manager; Preston Thomas, design manager; Katherine McNab, art editor; Natalia Peschiera, photo research coordinator and Nancy Garcia and Christie Ling, media producers.

PART I

CONTEXT

CHAPTER 1

SOLUTIONS

Communication Is Critical

Individuals and societies have little hope of solving their problems and achieving meaningful change if they don't have accurate, complete and unbiased information on which to base their tough decisions. Knowledge is critical as societies decide which pollution control plans to adopt, whose taxes to cut or which wars to fight. And information is crucial as an individual decides which candidate to support, what doctor to visit, which movie to attend or what car to buy.

Journalism, public relations and World Wide Web professionals are essential cogs in the development of culture, which is expressed in music, literature, film, dress, automobiles, theater, politics, photographs and other objects, images, practices, ideas and narratives that give meaning to life. Their job is unique in that they process and disseminate the news and information that help readers, listeners and viewers recognize cultural trends; understand how those trends affect individuals and society; and make sound political, economic, cultural and social decisions.[1]

DEMOCRACY'S FOUNDATION

Freedom to communicate is the foundation for any democratic entity or institution, whether a nation, a city, a public university, a volunteer organization or a family. Some of the classic arguments for a free flow of information are outlined in John Milton's *Areopagitica* and in John Stuart Mill's *On Liberty*. Milton argued that society is best served when different views are presented freely in a marketplace of ideas and that the truth emerges through a self-righting process.[2] Mill said that suppressing any opinion was robbing humanity of an opportunity to find the truth.[3] A more recent affirmation comes from Judge Learned Hand, who said the First Amendment "presupposes that right conclusions are more likely to be gathered out of a multitude of tongues, than through any kind of authoritative selection."[4]

Inclusion Versus Exclusion

If society and democracy are to work well, professional communicators must be inclusive, not exclusive. They must seek out information, ideas and opinions that might not surface otherwise (Chapter 3). Society is threatened when the opinions of marginalized groups (the poor, for instance) are excluded because the media fail to take aggressive steps to discover and communicate them. And it is threatened when a government is allowed to avoid the normal channels of accountability by operating in secrecy.

Many observers criticized media coverage of the Pentagon's plans to invade Iraq, plans that were extraordinarily detailed and that might have helped Saddam Hussein prepare a military defense.[5] The reports, however, stimulated a necessary debate about the wisdom and perils of launching military strikes against Iraq. The debate most certainly would not have been as intense had those invasion plans not been leaked. Democracy worked well during this emotional and turbulent period.

Salon.com and other media made sure the powerless were heard in Florida when they complained that the Republican secretary of state hired a company with Republican ties to strike from the voter rolls thousands of alleged felons. Most of those purged were not, in fact, felons, but members of minority groups.[6] "In all, some 200,000 Floridians were either not permitted to vote in the November 7 election on questionable or possibly illegal grounds, or saw their ballots discarded and not counted. A large and disproportionate number were black."[7] The media did not stop the purging of minorities from Florida's voter lists, but they did give voice to those who claimed they were treated unfairly.

None of this means that freedom of speech is absolute—or should be. In the absence of any laws, a media professional could publish or broadcast anything, including obscenity, defamation and advocacy of the violent overthrow of the government. Absolute freedom does not exist in the United States because of laws that regulate libel, obscenity, treason and sedition (Chapter 13).

Professionals encourage *responsible*—not just *legal*—communication, because messages that are perceived as irresponsible invite broad censorship. Many Americans are convinced that television programs and movies contain excessive sex and violence and that such content is partly responsible for a general moral decline. Some of these critics would impose severe restrictions on the First Amendment rights of television producers and filmmakers. Deciding what is *responsible*, of course, is not without risk or controversy—primarily because someone must define *responsibility,* and people don't always agree about who is competent to do that (Chapter 14). Media professionals must be part of the discussion, however, and they must ensure that all reasonable voices are heard.

Quality of Life

At their best, communication professionals contribute substantially to a better quality of life for everyone, as in these four examples:

- A 16-month-old girl was admitted to Denver's Children's Hospital on Oct. 16, 1996, after she drank a smoothie containing Odwalla apple juice. She suffered cardiac, kidney and respiratory problems before dying three weeks later of hemolytic uremic syndrome, a complication of *E. coli* poisoning. Meanwhile, public health officials in Vancouver, Canada, and in the states of Washington and California were dealing with dozens of cases of *E. coli* poisoning. Health officials had by late October found a common thread: Odwalla apple juice.[8]

  Odwalla, notified of the link on Oct. 30, issued within 24 hours a voluntary recall of all potentially dangerous beverages and was cooperating fully with health officials. The recall included both the pure apple juice and 12 other Odwalla products that contained apple juice. Officials announced the following day that vegetable and carrot juices also were part of the recall. Company officials detailed plans to ensure that manufacturing plants were clean, reported findings that juice from one of its plants tested positive for *E. coli,* launched a Web site to respond to questions about the recall and to outline the company's responses, created a Nourishment and Food Safety Advisory Council to recommend ways to improve safety throughout the industry and joined with other juice manufacturers to promote safety.

  Odwalla eventually paid a $1.5 million fine after pleading guilty to selling tainted food. The company was not a good citizen when it manufactured its product in unsanitary conditions, but it was forthcoming and responsible in its response, a response that was not perfect (Odwalla did not apologize for its behavior), but that did serve the company and its publics reasonably well.

- The *Detroit Free Press* heard from Michigan educators in 1998 that scores on the state's standardized tests could be influenced by factors (poverty, for example) that were beyond the schools' control. The issue is important in many states because important decisions are based on standardized test scores: Principals can be reassigned or fired; some parents will move so their children can attend "high performing" schools; and property values, school funding and educational resources all can be affected.[9]

  Heather Newman and her colleagues at the *Free Press* relied heavily on the Internet and other electronic resources to determine how the scores were being used in elementary schools and whether individual schools were solely responsible for student performance. Results from the six-month investigation suggested that "Most of the differences between scores in urban and suburban districts can be statistically explained by factors outside of the district's control, ranging from poverty to unemployment to parental education."[10]

Radio is awful, according to Salon.com's *well-documented investigative report, because stations frequently play the music that recording companies pay them to play, and that's not necessarily the music that listeners most want to hear.*

What happened at home seemed to have more impact than what happened in the classroom.

■ Dale Russell of WAGA-TV in Atlanta launched a six-month investigation after he discovered that minority travelers were searched more frequently and more thoroughly than others by U.S. Customs Service agents at Hartsfield International Airport.[11] Most passengers "randomly selected" for pat-downs, X-rays and strip searches were black and almost none constituted threats to anyone.

Congress investigated racial profiling at the nation's airports, in part because WAGA-TV's report caught the attention of Rep. John Lewis, D-Ga., who launched the probe. U.S. Customs Service policies and procedures were tightened to prevent racial profiling and to improve safety. Russell's report, "Singled Out," won a prestigious George Foster Peabody Award for broadcast news excellence.

■ Eric Boehlert exposed in *Salon.com* the sordid relationship between record producers, radio stations and "indies," the independent record promoters who are paid by recording companies to get their songs played on radio stations across the country. Indies are paid hundreds of millions of dollars by recording companies, and they in turn "align themselves with certain radio stations by promising the stations 'promotional payments' in the six figures."[12]

Recording companies target roughly 1,000 of the nation's 10,000 commercial radio stations to turn their songs into hits so they can sell records. "Each of those 1,000 stations adds roughly three new songs to its playlist each week. The indies get paid for every one: $1,000 on average for an 'add' at Top 40 or rock stations, but as high as $6,000 or $8,000 under certain circumstances."[13]

Boehlert and *Salon.com* were not the first to publish stories about corruption in the recording industry, but the story was unusual in that it was exceedingly well-documented and it situated the indies problem within a larger context—contemporary practices of radio stations nationwide.

MEDIA PROBLEMS AND PRESSURES

Most media professionals recognize the important service they perform for society, and they try to do their best each day. But critics are right when they suggest that professionals too often fail, sometimes with negative consequences. At their worst, media professionals can indeed pass along biased, distorted or inaccurate news and information, making it exceptionally difficult for society to make the right choices. Critics cite many reasons for breakdowns in communication processes.

Consolidation Trends

Politics and society in the United States were transformed between roughly the 1830s and the 1920s, when a technological revolution made it possible for mass-circulation newspapers to saturate urban neighborhoods. This news saturation helped to broaden participation in elections and to stop the rigid separation of society by class. At the same time, the number and variety of alternative newspapers, newsletters, pamphlets and magazines—including a vigorous socialist press—directed toward working-class, ethnic and non-English-speaking immigrant audiences increased dramatically. The poor, the powerless and the marginalized—long excluded from the political, social and economic mainstream—began to find they were included.[14]

These voices were gradually muted, however, as radio, television, cable, telephones, satellites and the Web joined the communication mix. The news gradually was homogenized to attract wider audiences and to improve profit margins. America's broadcast, newspaper, magazine, Internet, public relations, advertising, film, publishing and cable industries did not escape the consolidation trends that have characterized the business scene for decades. Most news media were independently owned 40 or so years ago. No longer. Most are part of conglomerates, many of which have holdings having nothing to do with communication. Bigger typically means more profit.

The Walt Disney Co., for example, is the third largest international media conglomerate. Its holdings include ABC News, 10 television stations, 27 radio stations, the Disney Channel, the History Channel, *Discover* magazine, Disneyland, Walt Disney World and other companies (Figure 1.1 shows a partial list of companies completely or partially owned by Disney).[15]

Critics fret about the concentration of power Disney wields over news in the United States. While conglomerate owners claim each medium is independent, that claim rings hollow when one remembers who signs the media professionals' checks.

Do financial considerations determine how news departments treat their parent companies? Will ABC News, for instance, treat a story about problems at Disneyland as it would if Disney were not its owner? Will ESPN (owned jointly by Hearst and Disney) treat the Mighty Ducks the same way it treats other teams? Would the Disney-owned television stations treat the sinking of a Disney Cruise Line vessel the same way they would treat the sinking of a Carnival Cruise Line vessel? It's difficult to answer such questions. There may be no conflict of interest. But it certainly appears there could be, given the financial stakes typically involved.

News as Commodity

Most news media are similar in fundamental respects to any other corporation or industry in which the primary goal is to make money. The commodity of the

FIGURE 1.1 SOME COMPONENTS OF THE DISNEY EMPIRE

■ Television

- ABC News
- ABC Sports
- ABC Daytime
- ABC Kids
- ABC Family
- Television stations: 10
- Disney Channel
- SOAPnet
- ESPN (partial)
- A&E Television Networks (partial)
- The History Channel
- Lifetime Entertainment Services (partial)
- E! Entertainment Networks (partial)
- TOON Disney
- Japan Sports Channel
- TV Sport of France

■ Internet Companies

- ABC.com
- ABCnews.com
- Oscar.com
- Disney.com
- Disneyauctions.com
- Family Fun.com
- ESPN.com
- Movies.com
- NFL.com
- NBA.com
- NASCAR.com
- Soccernet.com (partial)
- Infoseek (partial)
- Toysmart.com (partial)
- DisneyVacations.com
- DisneyStore.com
- Toontown Online (partial)

■ Film & Television Production, Distribution

- Walt Disney Pictures
- Walt Disney Television
- Walt Disney Feature Animation
- Walt Disney Television Animation
- Touchstone Pictures
- Touchstone Television
- Hollywood Pictures
- Caravan Pictures
- Miramax Films
- Buena Vista International
- Buena Vista Home Entertainment
- Buena Vista Television

■ Theme Parks, Resorts

- Disneyland Resort
- Walt Disney World Resort
- Tokyo Disneyland Resort (partial)
- Disneyland Resort Paris (partial)
- Hong Kong Disneyland
- Disney-MGM Studios
- Disney Regional Entertainment
- Disney Cruise Line

■ Radio

- ABC Radio
- Radio Stations: 62
- Radio Disney
- ESPN Radio

■ Book, Magazine Publishing

- Disney Publishing
- Hyperion Books
- Miramax Books
- Buena Vista Magazine Group
- *ESPN The Magazine*
- *FamilyFun* magazine
- *Disney Magazine*
- *W.i.t.c.h.* magazine
- *US Weekly* (partial)
- *Discover* magazine

■ Sport Franchises

- Mighty Ducks of Anaheim

■ Theatrical

- Buena Vista Theatrical Group
- Disney Theatrical Productions

■ Music Companies

- Buena Vista Music Group
- Hollywood Records
- Lyric Street Records
- Walt Disney Records

media professional is not hardware or hair spray, but news and information. And while news and information have more social importance than pencils or soft drinks, they still are commodities for sale.[16] The profit motive can have a negative effect on content, for as Eric Alterman writes:

> Any remotely attentive consumer of news has noticed, in recent years, a turn away from what journalists like to term "spinach," or the kind of news that citizens require to carry out their duties as intelligent, informed members of a political democracy, toward pudding—the sweet, nutritionally vacant fare that is the stock in trade of news outlets. The sense of a news division acting as a "public trust" ... has given way to one that views them strictly as profit centers.[17]

Jane and Steve Aker, for example, produced for a Fox television station a story about Florida's governor and secretary of state, who illegally struck from the voter rolls the names of thousands of potential Democratic voters, a move that had a critical impact on the 2000 presidential election. Fox wanted to kill the story without creating a huge journalistic flap. According to Jane Aker, "Fox's general manager presented us with an agreement, crafted by Fox counsel, that would give us a full year of our salaries and benefits worth close to $200,000 in no-show 'consulting jobs' with the same strings attached: no mention of how Fox covered up the story and no opportunity to ever expose the facts Fox refused to air."[18] The Akers did not take the deal and were fired.

In his analysis of the Gannett chain, Philip Weiss says that the best journalism has a fierce commitment to the community, but that Gannett offers only generic front pages. Gannett publishes primarily in one-newspaper towns, where it "serves as chief interpreter and informer about society—and does so unsustained by ideals of independence or thoroughness."[19]

Even more disappointing, 40 percent of nearly 300 journalists surveyed by the Pew Research Center for the People and the Press admitted softening the tone of some stories or avoiding some altogether to protect their organizations. Approximately 33 percent said they sometimes skip stories to avoid embarrassing advertisers or threatening the financial integrity of their own organizations. Market pressure was named as one cause for this behavior.[20]

News consumers evidently aren't pleased about the consolidation of media ownership into fewer hands, according to a 2003 public opinion poll commissioned by the First Amendment Center in Nashville, Tenn., and the *American Journalism Review*. In that poll, 52 percent of the respondents said the concentration of ownership has led to a decreased number of viewpoints in the media; 53 percent said the quality of news coverage has declined because of consolidation; 78 percent said media owners influence newsgathering to a "fair" or "great" degree; and only 4 percent said owners don't tamper with news collection or dissemination.[21] These results are not encouraging for anyone concerned about the flow of news in the United States.

Ivy Lee, frequently called the father of modern public relations, said organizations must earn public confidence by disseminating honest, complete and accurate information.

A Public Relations Quandary

The public relations industry started in roughly the 1920s to become a serious player in the information dissemination process when Ivy Lee, an industry pioneer, noted that a professional could tell clients either what they wanted to hear or what they needed to hear.[22] Ultimately, "Lee embraced the idea that an informed public was society's best safeguard against social ills. He aggressively demonstrated to the managers of a variety of major organizations how they could win public support over time by consistently providing the public with accurate information."[23]

But most public relations professionals, like their journalism colleagues, work for organizations that must show profits or raise funds, and they sometimes are faced with the unhappy choice of serving conflicting interests: Serving an organization's interest sometimes harms the public's interest.

Public relations professionals are expected to make their organizations look good because too many bosses think that doing so will protect their bottom lines or their ability to get donors to give money or time. While it is shortsighted and ultimately harmful to the organization, it is not unusual for a public relations writer to omit relevant, important information from a news release or annual report because the information might embarrass the organization.

Dow Corning's efforts to protect its profit margins during the silicone breast implant debacle illustrate what can happen when a company adopts that strategy. Dow Corning sold the implants even though company officials knew they could potentially damage women's health. The first lawsuit was filed in 1977, and there still is no evidence that the implants are dangerous.

Dow Corning, relying on this lack of scientific evidence, was consistently antagonistic to the media and the government. The company, to divert public attention, attacked the Food and Drug Administration when it requested internal documents; refused to release information to the media or to allow interviews with top executives; and provided misleading information on an implant hot line that was supposed to provide safety information to women (the FDA shut the hot line down). Dow Corning ultimately filed a bankruptcy reorganization plan.[24]

Another example is the corporate response to global warming. Burson-Marsteller Public Relations, for example, created in 1989 the Global Climate Coalition, an industry group composed of powerful corporations like Chevron, the American Petroleum Institute, the National Association of Manufacturers, Ford, Exxon, Texaco, Dow Chemical and the American Forest and Paper Association.

The goal was to generate so much confusion, the public would not know that global warming is viewed by reputable scientists as serious. An uninformed public was less likely to demand action.[25]

Part of the effort was the Heidelberg Appeal, a petition circulated by S. Fred Singer's Science and Environmental Policy Project. The petition, signed by 4,000 scientists and 72 Nobel laureates, is cited frequently as evidence that scientists do not support the global warming theory. The petition advises "the authorities in charge of our planet's destiny" against making decisions that "are supported by pseudo-scientific arguments or false and non-relevant data."[26] But it is simply a statement of support for science and rational behavior. It does not even mention global warming.

As the world struggled to understand global warming, some public relations professionals tried to muddle the issue to protect their clients' interests.

Many public relations professionals try to convince their organizations and clients that it is good business—and ethical—to ensure that the organization's interest is consistent with the public interest, but research suggests many are not central players as organizations try to institutionalize ethics. One study suggests that less than 7 percent of today's institutional ethics officers have public relations training and that less than 12 percent of ethics committees have public relations representation.[27] (See the box "Antagonism Does Exist" for a discussion of the conflict between journalism and public relations.)

Trivialities

Journalists and public relations professionals often fuss too much about the wrong things—about what athletic coach is going to be hired or fired next, what the jury is thinking during a sensational trial, what politician is going to run for president four years hence, what voters are thinking on Election Day.

In politics, for example, too many public relations professionals want to find and publicize that little dab of dirt about the opposition, rather than focus on issues. And too few journalists are willing or able to ask good questions or to explore substantive problems. "The subtle but sure result is a stream of daily messages that the real meaning of public life is the struggle of Bob Dole against Newt Gingrich against Bill Clinton, rather than our collective efforts to solve collective problems."[28]

Two days before the Nov. 8, 1994, election that swept Republicans to congressional power, *The Washington Post* published its "Crystal Ball" poll. Fourteen "experts" predicted the number of seats each party would win in Congress and in state governors' races. "One week later many of these same experts would be saying on their talk shows that the Republican landslide was 'inevitable' and 'a long time coming' and 'a sign of deep discontent in the heartland.' But before the returns were in, how many of the fourteen experts predicted that the Republicans would win both houses of Congress and that Newt Gingrich would be speaker? Exactly three."[29]

ANTAGONISM DOES EXIST

Journalists and public relations professionals do not always get along well.

Professionals in both groups would laugh hysterically at that statement, for it is so obvious. It doesn't take a week for a new newsreporter to learn that many public relations professionals view journalists in general as irresponsible characters who are interested only in digging up dirt about the individuals or organizations the public relations writers work for—and very likely respect. Many view journalists as too preoccupied with the trivial, with bad news, with personalities, with scandal and gossip, and as too little concerned about issues and problems. Journalists, many believe, will do absolutely anything to get a story.

For their part, many journalists likewise view public relations professionals negatively. A journalist surveyed in one study cited one reason when he said, "Practitioners apparently are concerned too often about their own needs or those of their organizations and not about the journalist's need for clear, concise, accurate information. Failure to supply timely information or to understand other needs of journalists undoubtedly leads to antagonism."[30] In this context, it is not helpful that public relations professionals are instructed by the Public Relations Society of America's code of ethics (Chapter 14) to put their organizations' needs first.

Research suggests that blanket statements that journalists and public relations writers dislike each other profoundly, and that they have good reasons for doing so, are not altogether true. One study, for instance, suggests that journalists and public relations professionals view lying in similar ways.[31] Other studies suggest that they define news similarly.[32] Still another study suggests that journalists who think little of public relations as a field may have good opinions of some individuals they know. It's not clear whether public relations professionals who dislike *journalism* in general like *individual journalists*.[33]

What does all this mean? One interpretation is that professionals who are ethical, considerate, sensitive and competent will enjoy the respect of other professionals—regardless of the specific work they do.

Media organizations—whether journalism or public relations—must decide how they will use their precious time and space. These are ethical decisions. If one decides to devote the space and time to trivia, the result is a mediocre product that does not serve its audience well. The audience gets predictions that require little effort or thought and that frequently are wrong; it gets empty feature stories about meaningless but marginally interesting topics; it gets bombarded with stories about a relatively routine murder case that is splashed across America because its principal is prominent; it is exposed to a parade of violent incidents, but with little analysis that would indicate what lies behind those incidents; it is exposed to news releases that contain no news. Is it ethical to decide to use precious time and space for such content? That question is not often debated, but it should be.

Partisanship

Partisan groups from the left and the right sometimes try to pressure institutions, organizations or media outlets to stop disseminating information that the groups view as offensive or dangerous. Censoring groups and individuals can complain through telephone calls and letters (some of which they expect to be published) to editors, government officials or corporate officers about individuals who write or broadcast ideas they condemn; establish foundations to "monitor" and subsequently condemn "unacceptable" information disseminated by media, organizations and corporations; and circulate petitions condemning individuals and organizations.[34]

Some Americans judged it unpatriotic or worse for anyone to question the United States' use of military strikes in its war against terrorism or to suggest alternatives. When the media did publish or air dissenting voices, they typically were criticized severely. University of Texas professor Robert Jensen, for example, received roughly 2,500 electronic mail messages in response to his commentary raising questions about the Sept. 11, 2001, terrorist attacks,[35] and the American Council of Trustees and Alumni compiled a list of 117 "anti-American statements" made on college campuses.[36] One comment was by Joel Beinin, a Middle Eastern history professor at Stanford, who was quoted as saying, "If Osama bin Laden is confirmed to be behind the attacks, the United States should bring him before an international tribunal on charges of crimes against humanity."[37] The statement does not seem to be "anti-American," but part of a rational discussion of alternatives.

News organizations must avoid relying too heavily (and carelessly) on partisan sources. *The New York Times* published in May 2004 a "note" explaining that some of its stories about Iraq's alleged weapons of mass destruction were inaccurate, largely because they were based on information from partisan sources whose veracity was not questioned sufficiently. The articles, which overstated the Iraqi threat, "depended at least in part on information from a circle of Iraqi informants, defectors and exiles bent on 'regime change' in Iraq, people whose credibility has come under increasing public debate in recent weeks." The accounts frequently were "verified" by partisan U.S. officials "convinced of the need to intervene in Iraq."[38] *The Times* promised to do better, but the damage was already done.

Efforts by groups and individuals to ensure their voices are heard by and expressed in the media must not be condemned, for they too are exercising their free-speech rights. But when individuals and groups try to silence dissent or mislead the public, they should be condemned, for that is most unfortunate in a democracy. It is even more unfortunate when such efforts succeed.

Personal Loyalties

Critics from both the left and right condemn media professionals whose personal loyalties seem to be to themselves or to ideologies they care about. This can mean that some information is not released because it is not ideologically acceptable or that a report or release is slanted—sometimes unknowingly—to reflect the writer's political, social, cultural or economic biases. The information also can be slanted or hyped in ways designed to help writers get ahead.

William McGowan, who argues that journalists too often allow their personal ideologies and feelings to intervene as they produce news reports, cites a CBS News story as one example.[39] Ed Bradley of *60 Minutes* did a segment about the highly controversial Partial Birth Abortion Ban Act of 1997, which would ban third-term abortions. Bradley focused on the sensational and exceptionally rare tragedy of a third-trimester fetus whose brain was growing outside its head, claimed that third-trimester abortions are rare and cited a doctor who said physicians would not abort a healthy fetus in the third term. Bradley's focus on a single case might have been misleading.

A subsequent investigation by *The* (Bergen, N.J.) *Sunday Record* showed that 1,500 partial birth abortions were performed annually in New Jersey alone and that few were performed to save a mother's life or to abort a deformed fetus.[40] A national investigation by *The Washington Post* reported similar findings and suggested that, contrary to claims of those opposing the ban, the aborted fetus did feel pain.[41]

In a different case, a *New York Times* report about the impact of the U.S. Supreme Court decision upholding a ban on gays in the Boy Scouts—a ban that *The Times* opposed—noted that dozens of United Way organizations nationwide had cut off funding for the Scouts; that San Jose, Chicago and San Francisco closed their schools, parks and other facilities to the Scouts; and that Chase Manhattan Bank, Merrill Lynch and other corporations had cut off hundreds of thousands of dollars in support.[42]

The Times ran a correction a week later stating that Chicago did not ban the Scouts, but would charge for use of public facilities, and that San Francisco would not allow use of facilities during school hours.[43] Both decisions were announced before the U.S. Supreme Court acted. San Jose did not rescind the Scouts' privileges because of the ban, but because their activities interfered with school activities. Roughly a dozen United Way organizations cut off funding, not dozens, and Chase Manhattan Bank and Merrill Lynch said they would continue to fund the Scouts.

Those who produced the *60 Minutes* report were biased in favor of abortion, McGowan argues, and *The New York Times'* writers and editors were biased against the Boy Scouts' ban. As society tried to decide about third-term abortions, *60 Minutes* gave viewers a sensational, misleading report that did little to help Americans find the right path, McGowan argues, and as Americans grappled with the rights of private organizations to exclude individuals who hold views contrary to their own, *The New York Times* offered up a report that inaccurately detailed the consequences of one such ban.

ROY PETER CLARK ON PLAGIARISM

- Plagiarism is a form of deception.

- Plagiarism is a violation of language. Linguists, like Noam Chomsky, emphasize the essential creativity of all language. Almost every sentence is unique. If you don't believe that, apply this test: Count all the sentences in all the stories in the *New York Times* for any given year. How many are identical? Plagiarism is a crime against the nature of language.

- Plagiarism is a substitute for reporting. A reporter who assumes the accuracy of information in the clips or in wire stories or in textbooks is living in Cloud Cuckoo Land. Of course, reporters consider the source of information and are always fighting the clock. But to the extent that they depend upon the work and words of others, they distance themselves from events and people and create an environment for inaccuracy.

    Important mistakes, especially when they turn up in usually reliable sources of information, become fossilized in the clips. "What you get," says Mel Mencher, "is this installation of inaccuracy in the record."

- Plagiarism is a substitute for thinking. "Writing is discovery," says Donald Fry, professor of English at the State University of New York, Stony Brook. "Plagiarism is secondhand thinking."

- Plagiarism poisons the relationship between writer and reader. "What readers want to believe," says Fry, "is that they're listening to a real voice conveying his own thought."

Source: Roy Peter Clark, "The Unoriginal Sin: How Plagiarism Poisons the Press," *Washington-Journalism Review*, March 1983:42–47, p. 46.

Roy Peter Clark, a senior scholar at The Poynter Institute for Media Studies, has worked as a writing coach at the *St. Petersburg* (Fla.) *Times*.

Nobody really knows why Jayson Blair and Jack Kelley, reporters for *The New York Times* and *USA Today*, respectively, would fabricate information and plagiarize other writers' work, but investigations by their news organizations suggest they did so.[44] Their loyalties evidently did not lie with *The Times, USA Today* or to the public. Both writers (and top editors) resigned in the wake of disclosures about some of their stories. (See the box "Roy Peter Clark on Plagiarism.")

Blair filed dispatches from several states, including Maryland, West Virginia and Texas, when he was actually in New York City. After an exhaustive in-house investigation, *The Times* found that Blair had made up quotes, fabricated scenes and plagiarized materials from other news media. *The Times'* investigators found problems in 36 of 73 stories published between October 2002 and May 2003. *The Times* concluded that "The widespread fabrication and plagiarism represent a profound betrayal of trust and a low point in the 152-year history of the newspaper."[45]

A team of reporters spent seven weeks reviewing 720 stories written by Kelley between 1993 and 2003. The team eventually focused on 56 stories that cited anonymous sources, were based on eyewitness accounts or offered human-interest accounts of human suffering. The team interviewed dozens of people, prowled through files on Kelley's laptop computer, examined his hotel and telephone records, and ran stories through software designed to detect plagiarism. The team "found strong evidence that Kelley fabricated substantial portions of at least eight major stories, lifted nearly two dozen quotes or other material from competing publications, lied in speeches he gave for the newspaper and conspired to mislead those investigating his work."[46]

Mistakes

The *British Medical Journal* published in its 1999 "joke" issue a study purporting to show that martinis that are shaken, rather than stirred, contain useful antioxidant properties that are effective against cancer, heart disease and other maladies.[47] References to James Bond, Ian Fleming's fictional British agent, and his fondness for martinis should have been sufficient warning that the "research" was not serious. It wasn't. The Associated Press, Reuters, UPI and Scripps Howard all transmitted stories to their clients. More than 100 publications—including *The New York Times,* London *Financial Times, Milwaukee Journal Sentinel, Forbes, Playboy* and *The Seattle Times*—played the bogus story as serious news.[48]

NBC's Lisa Myers interviewed Linda Lay shortly after Enron's collapse. Her husband, Kenneth Lay, had received more than $100 million in cash payments during 2001. Lay told Myers that the couple was trying to avoid bankruptcy, that they had nothing left, that everything "mostly was in Enron stock" and that everything they owned—other than their home—was for sale. Myers accepted Lay's assertions, which turned out to be lies. Only two of the couple's 18 properties were for sale, and they held at least $10 million in other stocks.[49] Myers made a big-league mistake in not checking the facts.

The media that treated the martini story seriously made a mistake, but the mistake is not as grievous as Myers' story about Linda and Kenneth Lay's financial situation, which gave a misleading impression of a key figure in Enron's collapse. Neither mistake is as bad as deliberately misleading the public or plagiarizing others' work. Still, they contributed a great deal of pollution to the daily stream of news and information.

AN OBJECTIVE APPROACH

The difficulties media professionals encounter as they process and disseminate news and information can be mitigated or avoided if they will try to use an objective approach. Objectivity has been criticized for decades, but media professionals can get into serious trouble when they abandon the principles of objectivity, as did those working for *60 Minutes, The New York Times* and Dow Corning. Communication professionals best serve society, their organizations and themselves when they try always to use an objective approach to news and information dissemination.

Professionals who reject objective approaches are not perceived as credible by their audiences, and without trust, effective communication is impossible. As increasing numbers of journalists have abandoned the quest for objectivity, audience confidence in the news media has dipped dramatically. And confidence in public relations has plunged as Americans have discovered the efforts of some professionals to obscure the truth.[50]

The best media professionals seek to disseminate news and information that describes reality as accurately as possible. They assume the existence of a "real" world about which human beings can be right or wrong, an assumption not shared by everyone, particularly critics who believe all knowledge is socially constructed. Professionals who accept the tenets of objectivity believe it is possible to produce a reasonably accurate description of the world.[51] They do not guarantee their descriptions are accurate in every respect, claim that they have no underlying values and opinions that could affect their work or assert that absolute objectivity is attainable. They claim only that they have used a professional process that allows them to produce a description that is more accurate and fair than any other process allows. (See the box "Jack Fuller on Objectivity as an Approach.")

The objective approach requires that communicators try to be impartial and to adhere to professional norms.[52] Strategic decisions (a journalist's selection of sources, for instance) are not based on a writer's personal preference (say, for a source who cannot adequately clarify or defend an "unapproved" position), but on professional norms; that is, the writer consistently seeks the most informed, qualified and forthcoming source available to address each side.

Definition

An objective approach is characterized by accuracy, completeness, precision and clarity in information collection and dissemination. Those who adopt this approach are (1) receptive to new information and alternative explanations; (2) skeptical toward authority figures, the powerful and the self-righteous; (3) creative (in finding ways, for example, to uncover information); (4) imaginative and consistent in making strategic decisions (in selecting information to disseminate and details to emphasize) and in presenting information in compelling ways; (5) fair and impartial; (6) unwilling to serve or to support any political, cultural, social or economic interests; and (7) honest about personal idiosyncrasies and

JACK FULLER ON OBJECTIVITY AS AN APPROACH

"Objectivity," the word we once used to naively define journalism's aim, is really not best thought of as an attribute of the story at all, still less an attribute of a hopelessly subjective human being who writes it. ... Of course, it is impossible for subjective individuals, locked within the prison of their own perceptions, to produce objective accounts of reality. But it is possible for subjective individuals to use rigorous methods, just as subjective scientists do. And it works. We might not be able to say what the truth is, but we can reach deep into space, play billiards with subatomic particles, and manipulate the very helix of life.

Another way of putting it is that, while we might all agree that it is epistemologically naive to think we can know and communicate The Truth, some accounts of reality are closer approximations than are others. Seen this way, what journalists do is to arrive at their judgments in a careful and disciplined way and make their claims confidently but provisionally, subject always to revision.

Source: From Jack Fuller, "Making Truth an Idea that Journalists Can Believe in Again: 'Every Journalist Knows That Truth Can Make Nonnegotiable Demands,'" *Nieman Reports,* Summer 2001: 8. Fuller is responding to Bill Kovach and Tom Rosenstiel, *The Elements of Journalism: What Newspeople Should Know and the Public Should Expect* (New York: Crown, 2001).

Jack Fuller is the president and chief executive officer of the Tribune Publishing Company and author of *News Values: Ideas for an Information Age* (Chicago: University of Chicago Press, 1996).

preferences (information is not evaluated, for example, on the basis of the professional's personal beliefs).[53]

None of this means that professionals who adopt this approach cannot use analytical and interpretative skills in collecting and disseminating information. On the contrary, they cannot avoid applying these skills; they can't, for example, fulfill the mandate for completeness if they can't interpret and analyze information during information collection. They must remain true to the norms of objectivity, however.

Communication professionals who accept these norms make every effort to ensure that all relevant information is obtained and disseminated, even that which they or powerful interests might prefer to see suppressed. They gather facts and opinions that conflict, verify information carefully and seek to determine why accounts conflict and which most accurately reflect reality. And they are accountable to their audiences, to the highest ethical and professional standards of their

Journalists find it hard to use an objective approach when information is tightly controlled, as it was when the Pentagon insisted that journalists be embedded with military units during the invasion of Iraq. Journalists shown here gather in Kuwait as they prepare to join the units.

field and, finally, to their employers. They never assume that their employers, and not themselves, bear the ultimate moral responsibility for their behavior.

Any communication professional may encounter a situation in which it is difficult to meet the standards of objectivity, but public relations writers may encounter difficulties more frequently than others. Professionals who adopt the objective approach refuse to allow powerful interests to control the information they disseminate. But for public relations professionals, those powerful interests usually are their bosses. They either hide information or find other jobs. Journalists find themselves in this situation less often, because such behavior is contrary to journalistic norms. But it does happen.

There is no good option when an organization demands that a professional violate the tenets of objectivity. A professional can simply do as he or she is told and disseminate misleading or inaccurate information, or move to a more responsible organization. These are tough personal choices. It is well to remember always, however, that writers who follow the objective approach are fundamental to a free society. This is particularly true at a time when the number of information sources, many of which are unreliable or biased, is expanding at an almost incomprehensible rate.

Critiques

Critics have attacked objectivity for a wide range of sins, which seem to fall into at least six broad categories.[54] Some of the criticisms apply primarily to journalism, because the objective approach typically is discussed in the context of journalistic practice, but some apply to all communication. It is necessary to understand the criticisms if one is to understand and appreciate the approach.

Objectivity as Myth

Mass communication has not escaped the influence of the relativists, who argue that evaluations of truth are intertwined with cultural values and that absolutes do not exist in knowledge or morals. Consequently, they conclude, objectivity is not achievable and it is not a useful goal.[55] Mass communicators, like everyone else, are conditioned by many factors (gender, economic circumstance and education are examples), which, when coupled with the need to be selective in deciding what information to report, make it impossible for professionals to be objective.[56]

Response   One need only read James Weldon Johnson's *The Autobiography of an Ex-coloured Man* to understand that reality can be and is socially constructed.[57] But critics who argue that objectivity is a myth miss two important points:

- An observer who tries to use the objective approach—who recognizes personal and environmental influences and limitations and tries to transcend them— can describe reality with reasonable accuracy.

- An observer who adopts the objective approach will reconstruct reality more accurately than one who allows a personal agenda to influence strategic decisions. An observer who rejects the objective approach might well construct a "perceived reality" that has little to do with real life.

Disengagement

An objective approach means a professional presents only two sides of an issue or event without assessing the veracity of each side, some critics argue. Those who are committed to the approach, they suggest, are spectators in political, social, cultural and economic affairs; they must be disengaged from the vital issues because they are expected to be disinterested observers.[58]

The problem seems exacerbated by the organizational context within which professionals work. The Commission on Freedom of the Press said mass communication provides an essential service, but it noted that "the element of personal responsibility, which is of the essence of the organization of such professions as law and medicine, is missing in communications. Here the writer works for an employer, and the employer, not the writer, takes the responsibility."[59] The situation may be worse in, for instance, corporate public relations, where a professional may have little control over his or her work.

Response   Professionals who employ the objective approach need not be moral spectators. In journalism, in fact, the objective approach requires a professional to collect and to disseminate the information a community needs to make sound decisions. These writers evaluate the veracity of all information, and they do reveal the superior sides of issues (when one side is, in fact, superior). It is a cliché, but facts do speak for themselves. If one side is more compelling, that is apparent from the report of a writer who uses the objective approach. It is not necessary or desirable for the writer to become an advocate for that position.

Journalists who use the objective approach—whether they work for newspapers, magazines, broadcast outlets or Web sites—do not permit their employers to assume responsibility for their news reports or actions, as the Commission on Freedom of the Press asserted. They feel an ethical obligation to disseminate reports that describe reality as accurately as possible, and they are true to the highest standards of the objective approach—regardless of their employers' views.

Many public relations writers are actively engaged in the issues of the day as they try to provide information that society needs to make decisions about health care, education, the environment and countless other issues. Many of these professionals try to use the objective approach, for they know the consequences (decreased credibility, pollution of the information stream, jail time) if they do not. In general, however, public relations professionals—particularly those who work for corporations or agencies—are more tightly controlled than are journalists.

Status Quo

Professionals who try to use the objective approach in effect help the powerful maintain order and establish behavioral standards because their approach insulates the system—whether a nation, a university, a corporation or a not-for-profit organization—from pressures for change, some critics argue. "So long as 'both sides' are presented, neither side is glorified above the other, and the status quo remains unchallenged."[60]

For journalists, truth can be obscured also by source selection. The objective approach ensures that information flows from bureaucracies, through the media, and to the public by introducing a bias toward sources who supply information most steadily.[61] "Reporters do not seek independent confirmation or use a critical method to test the statements issued by officials. ... There is no real attempt to balance the official version against the contextual evidence."[62]

Response   The powerful fear proponents of the objective approach, for they cannot be manipulated. They present all sides of a story, and if information suggests one side is superior, that is clear from their stories. These writers don't shout, "This side is superior," as some critics seem to suggest they should, but the superiority is apparent. It is simply not accurate to argue that the status quo is not challenged by journalists who subscribe to the objective approach. (See the box "Cooke on Murrow on McCarthy.")

COOKE ON MURROW ON MCCARTHY

The objective approach has been used for decades as a scapegoat for many of journalism's ills. Critics argue that the objective approach was one reason why journalists did not challenge many of the false assertions made by Sen. Joseph McCarthy, R-Wis., during the senator's attempt to find communists in the United States. Leaders in the media, the artistic and intellectual communities and the government were too intimidated to speak out against a campaign that ruined or damaged so many lives.

Edward R. Murrow of CBS News devoted an entire half-hour news program to McCarthy, and he did it using the objective approach—he simply let McCarthy be McCarthy. British journalist and social critic Alistair Cooke described Murrow's actions in March 1954 this way:

Last Tuesday night Mr. Murrow gave over his whole half-hour to a pictorial analysis of "McCarthyism" by projecting visual excerpts from the Senator's speeches and sessions of his [congressional] subcommittee. It was McCarthy exposed by McCarthy, and Mr. Murrow added only the sparest narrative comment. But at the end, after the huge audience for this programme had seen McCarthy merciless, McCarthy jocular, McCarthy cunning, McCarthy sentimental, Mr. Murrow looked his audience in the eye and ended with these words:

"This is no time for men who oppose Senator McCarthy's methods to keep silent. Or for those who approve. We can deny our heritage and our history but we cannot escape responsibility for the result. There is no way for a citizen of the Republic to abdicate his responsibilities. ... We proclaim ourselves—as indeed we are—the defenders of the free world, or what's left of it. We cannot defend freedom abroad by deserting it at home.

Edward R. Murrow, one of the most prominent journalists of his time, exposed the false and misleading assertions made by Sen. Joseph McCarthy, R-Wis., during a campaign that damaged many innocent people.

"The actions of the junior Senator from Wisconsin have caused alarm and dismay among our allies abroad and given comfort to our enemies. And whose fault is that? Not really his. He didn't create the situation of fear, merely exploited it, and skillfully. Cassius was right: 'The fault, dear Brutus, is not in our stars, but in ourselves.'"

These words were spoken with the blessing of the Aluminum Corporation of America, which has obviously a lot to lose by taking this stand. The response, however, of televiewers across the country has been a stunning endorsement of Mr. Murrow. So far the comments, by telephone, telegram, and letter, are running about fifteen to one in his favour. Hence the surprising rally of candour in public men who have stayed astutely silent for three years. Hence President Eisenhower's relieved approval of Senator Flanders [who criticized McCarthy's tactics]. Hence a morning chorus of suddenly uninhibited newspaper columnists praising Murrow for "laying it on the line. ..." Mr. Murrow may yet make bravery fashionable.

Source: Alistair Cooke, *America Observed: The Newspaper Years of Alistair Cooke* (London: Reinhardt, 1988): 67–68.

Nor is it accurate to suggest that the status quo is never challenged by public relations writers who try to use the objective approach. Some professionals working within the tobacco industry, for example, argued for more complete disclosure about the risks of smoking. Such dissent does not necessarily make its way into the public domain, but advocates of the objective approach have produced some positive changes within their organizations.

The objective approach is less responsible for poor source selection in journalism than are deadline pressures, source or document unavailability, laziness and confusion. Even journalists who endorse the objective approach and who recognize the need to obtain information from dissenting sources encounter difficulties. Dissenting sources may not be available; they may refuse to talk; or there may be too little time to contact them.[63]

It also is difficult at times to know to whom one should talk. Who is, in fact, the leader of a marginalized group? Some black individuals argue that the media should not give the Rev. Al Sharpton space or air time because he does not speak for the black community;[64] others argue that he is a legitimate, though flawed, black leader.[65] Anyone, whether an advocate of the objective approach or not, would find such a situation confusing.

Deception

In journalism, professionals occasionally conclude during their investigations that official findings (about the guilt or innocence of a murder suspect, for example) are "wrong" and that they, the journalists, have found the "right" answers. Those who respect the tenets of objectivity, critics argue, then try to find sources to state the journalists' opinions. Such journalists deceive themselves into thinking they have written their stories based solely on the facts (or evidence), the critics argue, and they deceive their audiences into thinking they have used an objective approach.[66]

In public relations, professionals and the organizations for which they work might conclude they have the right answers and others are wrong, as did those who created the Global Climate Coalition. The GCC did recruit "experts" to attack the view that greenhouse gas emissions were a problem and that something needed to be done. The public relations professionals were using the "cloak of objectivity" to deceive, some critics argue.

Response This criticism about journalism is odd: A journalist who suspects that official findings or actions are "wrong" (police have arrested the wrong person) has no business rushing into print or onto the air with his or her opinion. The journalist must seek evidence. This is not deceptive—this is how good journalists work, as journalism students at Northwestern University demonstrated when their research helped free a death row inmate.[67] The students, appropriately, contacted sources whom they knew or suspected had information about the inmate's case; it would have made little sense for them to contact individuals who were ignorant about the case.

The criticism about public relations can be true when the writer uses an "expert" simply to attack the opposition or to muddle the discussion—pretending all the while to be using an objective approach. But it is not deceptive to use real, objective experts to help an organization make a case. The credentials of these experts and details of any agreements must be fully disclosed or they will have no credibility.

Self-preservation

The objective approach is simply a ruse that professionals have devised to protect themselves from legal actions and criticism. In public relations, critics argue, professionals try to appear to use the objective approach as they release information because that will protect them against subsequent lawsuits or criticisms. If they are blatantly one-sided, as the tobacco industry was for many years, they put themselves at risk.

In journalism, a professional "can claim objectivity by citing procedures he has followed which exemplify the formal attributes of a news story or a newspaper," says sociologist Gaye Tuchman. For example, "the newsman can suggest that he quoted other people instead of offering his own opinions."[68] Thus, objectivity is a strategic ritual that protects journalists from the risks of their trade.

Response This charge is beside the point. Proponents of the objective approach, when asked, tell how their information was obtained. Yes, writers are on solid legal, professional and ethical ground if they have tried to follow the tenets of objectivity, but this seems analogous to airline mechanics who follow proper procedures and do excellent work; does it really matter whether they do good work to protect passengers or to protect themselves? The result either way is a safer aircraft. Certainly, though, one would hope that professionals try to use the objective approach (or protect passengers) because that is the right thing to do.

Build Audiences

The objective approach demands that professionals, to build their audiences, seek information from sources who are close to the political, cultural, economic and social center and ignore individuals who articulate the more extreme positions. The convention of objectivity "resembles a strategy on the part of the media to present a centrist position in the ideological spectrum in order to appeal to the middle of the road audience and increase their market share."[69] Marginalized groups, individuals and ideas are essentially ignored because they are at the extremes and communication professionals don't want to risk losing audience members by reporting their views.

Response   The objective approach may build audiences, although that assertion is questionable in light of the anecdotal evidence. Huge audiences are attracted daily to sensational, biased or clearly untrue "news" reports and programs, and to radio and television talk shows that reflect definite biases.

   If the objective approach does build audiences, this is an incidental outcome. It is unlikely that critics could produce a single proponent of the objective approach who says he or she ever heard a boss say it is important (1) to be objective because objectivity increases audience share or (2) to ignore the views of marginalized groups because reporting their opinions might mean a loss of audience. It is more likely that dedicated news and information consumers lose confidence in media that abandon this approach.

Implementation

Critics who argue that the objective approach is responsible for many of mass communication's failures, documented earlier, are not paying attention. The real problem is that too many professionals reject the approach—and for many reasons.

- Many communication professionals view a science-based objective approach as rigorous and difficult.[70] Professionals in all fields find it is far easier to simply slap their opinions together to produce a story, a news release, a Web page or an annual report, than to exert the effort to find out whether those opinions are based on solid information. It is easy to avoid the hard work required by the objective approach when the climate of opinion is against it (and we have seen that it is) and communication professionals do not feel obligated to adopt its norms.

■ Many media writers are ill-prepared, as Phyllis Kaniss's study of local news in Philadelphia suggests. Most professionals choose media careers because they have reasonable verbal skills, not because they have strong quantitative skills.[71] It is hard to employ the tenets of objectivity when one doesn't understand technical information. Web professionals and public relations professionals can't snicker too much about Kaniss's observation because it applies just as well to many of them.

■ Many professionals evidently agree that the objective approach "has become too staid, dull, pallid, and noncommitted for the new generations of audience members being raised in a climate of instant confrontation, dissent, and permissiveness."[72] In short, the objective approach does not sell, and so it is not practiced.

ALTERNATIVES TO AN OBJECTIVE APPROACH

Critics have tried for decades to redefine the objective approach to resolve one or more of the problems they attribute to that approach. The alternatives are discussed in the context of journalism, but the principles can be applied beyond journalism. Two current, and widely discussed, alternatives are public journalism and existential journalism, which have weaknesses of their own, but which contain philosophical constructs one can use to clarify and to improve the objective approach.

Public, or Civic, Journalism

Public journalism allows, or even requires, journalists to participate in social, cultural, political and economic processes, to help Americans reconnect to the public life from which many have become disengaged.[73] Journalists and other mass communicators are inextricably bound up with public life, whether they like it or not or acknowledge it or not, and they are critical to efforts to revitalize public life.[74]

Public journalism does not necessarily mean professionals must start taking sides or privileging particular issues or groups.[75] Public journalism "begins with a consideration of what will improve the public life, rather than what will make a good story, and it implies a commitment to solving community problems beyond the publication of one story or series."[76]

Public journalism can accomplish the goals set for it by its advocates in several ways. Communication professionals uncover problems and motivate citizens to seek solutions, but without being led by official policy-makers; report research relating to public problems and issues; monitor official responses to various alternatives; and help initiate and sustain public discussions about community problems, even if that means convening participants.

Existential Journalism

Existential journalism is difficult to define because existentialism is so complex and can manifest itself in so many ways (it can be moderate or extreme).[77] In general, moderate existential journalism is extremely personal, requiring its practitioner to be independent, creative, passionate, committed, responsible and subjective. It permits, or even requires, its practitioner to promote the freedom and welfare of others and to define what "freedom" and "welfare" mean in various cultural, social, political and economic contexts.

Existential journalism makes no *a priori* assumptions about journalistic practice. "It is mainly an orientation of being 'true to one's self,' however trite this may sound," rather than to corporate or organizational interests.[78] The existential journalist is an autonomous moral agent who must accept moral responsibility and take the "right" or "responsible" actions, as he or she defines them, not the easy, safe or most profitable actions.[79]

Finally, existential journalists "thrust themselves into the social maelstrom, seeking to harmonize their own self-interest with the wider public interest of society."[80] They do not worry about the commercial impact of their work, but about whether they have behaved ethically, tried to become better journalists, promoted freedom and the general welfare and examined their own subjective reactions to events and issues. "This means that ethical decision making begins with a recognition of one's biases, weaknesses, and background."[81]

Existential journalism is subjective, but it does not ignore the objective world: "It is just that the *perception* of this objective world is emphasized, with substantial attention given to the journalist as the creator of the verbal or symbolic world that reflects the real world."[82]

A Serious Difficulty

Students should know there are alternatives to the objective communication approach so that they eventually can make their own decisions about various alternatives and can better understand how the objective approach fits into the larger communication mosaic.

The alternatives have been criticized, just as the objective approach has been criticized, but for a different reason. The alternatives require direct ideological intervention, meaning that a professional's political, cultural, economic or social views drive the information collection and dissemination process.[83] This is problematic because the communicator could select primarily that information which supports his or her view and present contrary information in a bad light. This is good neither for the communicator nor the audience.

MEDIA CONVERGENCE

Media professionals traditionally have been locked into a single news delivery system (airwave or print), and each system has distinct advantages and disadvantages. Television reporters cannot cover complex science stories well because they don't have enough space (minutes) to tell the story. Newspaper writers might have 2,500 words to tell the story, magazine writers 5,000 words—and television writers 300 words. Television is further constrained by its relatively small screen, which prohibits the kinds of complex graphics that can make a story infinitely easier to tell— and to understand. Conversely, print writers can't convey the horror of a train wreck or the excitement of a basketball game as effectively as television because they cannot "show" human joy or suffering. Much has changed in the past decade in the face of media convergence.

Definition

Convergence in journalism typically is seen as a merger into one newsroom of television, radio, newspaper and Web newsrooms. This means a journalist might write a story for a newspaper, then for a Web site and then for television or radio. The writer might even read the news on radio or television.

For public relations, convergence means a writer might produce several versions of the same news release: One would be posted on the organization's Web site, one would be distributed to print journalists (newspapers, magazines), one would go to Web sites and one might be taped so that an audiotape or videotape could be sent to broadcast media and Web sites.

For media professionals, changing technologies mean they need to be adaptable and to learn a variety of skills. A newspaper writer might eventually have to appear on camera, reporting live from a dramatic scene for the benefit of Web or television viewers. A television journalist might have to write a long story for a newspaper or Web site, in addition to the televised report. Many broadcast outlets and newspapers refer their readers and viewers to Web sites for additional information.

An estimated 50 television news operations are converging with newspapers, and hundreds of television stations and newspapers are relying on Web sites as part of their daily operations.[84] (See the box "Convergence in Orlando, Fla.")

The Arizona Republic's reliance on television, print and online resources to cover a breaking event is typical. In its coverage of terrifying wildfires, *The Republic*'s Web site was updated frequently to provide new details and to show new photo packages; newspaper writers worked with KPNX-TV journalists to report breaking news; television journalists relied on newspaper experts to add depth to on-air reports; and all stories referenced information on the other platforms (television, Web site or newspaper).[85]

Tragic events lend themselves well to multimedia coverage, certainly, but the *Lincoln* (Neb.) *Journal Star* demonstrated that convergence can work also when media professionals need to cover tough social issues. When the University of Nebraska Medical Center disclosed in 2000 that researchers were using cells from aborted fetuses, the public and its leadership needed information as they formed opinions about this relatively new issue.

The *Journal Star,* with financial support from the Pew Center for Civic Journalism, took a multimedia approach. "The main components of the project were (1) a

CONVERGENCE IN ORLANDO, FLA.

Florida Today at Brevard has a television news operation in the middle of its newsroom. The experiment in convergence merges television, Web and print journalism into one. The television station is WKMG-TV, a CBS affiliate, in nearby Orlando. The goal, Derek Osenenko, executive editor of *Florida Today*, says, is "to make *Florida Today* a true multimedia operation, delivering news with greater immediacy and depth on three platforms: print, online and television."[86]

Florida Today created a multimedia department to help develop broadcast and Web capabilities and to promote interdepartmental cooperation in collecting and delivering news. The move to convergence required that some job descriptions be rewritten. One writer reports and posts news as it breaks throughout the day; those stories are published in the next day's newspaper. A copy-desk position became an online-content editor's position, and the library and online staffs were merged. *Florida Today* staffers work with WKMG to cover Brevard County with greater immediacy—and broadcast from the *Florida Today* newsroom. Here are just a few examples from Osenenko of how convergence works in Orlando:

- *Florida Today* provides beat reporters to discuss news stories and ongoing issues on the air. For example, our space reporters are used along with a WKMG reporter to provide shuttle launch coverage from Kennedy Space Center.

- We collaborate with Channel 6 on every major project. Generally, our broadcast partner develops segments on its newscast that augment special reports. For instance, the station did its own reporting on a special report investigating the rising number of accidents on Interstate 95. Using the findings in our report, the station developed its own interviews and field footage to advance the Sunday section.

- A *Florida Today* columnist produces a video version of his weekly column called Bill Cox's Florida. ...

- Because the library staffers now have a greater ownership of the Web site, they have been great contributors to content enhancements, such as finding Web links and archiving stories and video or audio to use on the site.[87]

statewide public opinion survey [Chapter 12]; (2) a series of depth pieces in the *Lincoln Journal Star* on four Sundays; (3) Web pages; and (4) a two-hour forum broadcast on educational and commercial television stations. The four main areas of research covered were gene therapy, xenotransplants, cloning and stem-cell research."[88] Experts were called upon during the broadcasts to clarify issues or to comment as needed.

"Those who watched ordinary people discussing these issues on TV got the message that these issues belong to us all, not just the experts," *Journal Star* editor Kathleen Rutledge said. "Those who read the newspaper and Web site reports were given enough information to formulate their own views."[89]

A public relations professional needs to know how to use all information delivery systems. He or she might write (and record) public service announcements for broadcast, news releases for the local media or copy for an annual report or brochure, all in an afternoon. Or the professional might prepare and post graphics and stories to a company Web site.

The lines separating job functions have blurred or, in some cases, disappeared, meaning that television, for example, can tell that complex science story by reporting the primary facts on the nightly news and referring viewers to a Web site for more information. Newspapers can refer readers to Web sites to watch streaming video shot at the scene of that horrific train wreck or to review highlights of the latest game.

Problems Remain

It's important to avoid making too much of such changes, however, because convergence, for a number of reasons, does not solve all problems and can well lead to others.

- Television journalists remain stuck in a land of superficiality. *The Washington Post* publishes approximately 100,000 words in a typical issue, for instance, compared to a paltry 3,600 words in an *NBC Nightly News* broadcast.[90] Broadcasters can refer viewers to Web sites, but many will not or cannot go to those sites. Newspapers can refer readers to streaming video coverage of last night's football game, but many will not visit the site. This will change as technologies improve and become more available.

- The reason why a media company merges its components is important. If a company merges all of its components into one newsroom to improve the quality of journalism, that is admirable. But if it merges components so it can sell its product (information) better, that's problematic because it may mean the quality of journalism drops.

  Robert Haiman tells the story of one of the nation's best education journalists, who, when his newspaper merged with television, found he had to report on camera. "This magnificent education reporter who reports like a buzz saw and writes like a dream unfortunately is more than a little fat, more than a little bald, and speaks with more than a slight lisp."[91] The writer got special dispensation; he doesn't have to read news. But who replaces him when he retires? Haiman is concerned those who "look good" will get jobs and those who "write well" will not.

YOUR RESPONSIBILITY IS . . .

- To understand the social, political, cultural and economic context in which mass communication is practiced.

- To study and to learn to appreciate the importance of free and responsible journalists and public relations professionals to the success of a democratic society and to individuals in their daily lives.

- To learn why you cannot assume that the problems of media consolidation, the profit motive and conflicting loyalties will not affect you and to understand why you cannot ignore these issues and problems.

- To learn how and why partisanship, plagiarism and other problems pollute the information stream and make life harder for media professionals (including you) and for everyone else.

- To try to develop a genuine sensitivity to the powerless so you will understand why it is so important that their voices are reflected in the media.

- To learn how an ethical media professional recognizes the powerless, hears their concerns and ensures their voices are represented.

- To study the objective approach and alternatives to it; to investigate the critiques of the objective approach and its alternatives; and to try to decide which approach is best for you, for your profession and for society.

- To study and understand what convergence means (and what it doesn't mean) for you and for your profession and what implications convergence has for you.

- To start thinking about why you want to be a mass communicator and about whether this is the profession for you.

NOTES

1. Les Switzer, John McNamara and Michael Ryan, "Critical-cultural Studies in Research and Instruction," *Journalism & Mass Communication Educator,* 54:3 (1999): 23–42.
2. John Milton, *Areopagitica* (New York: Grolier Club, 1890).
3. John Stuart Mill, *On Liberty* (New York: Appleton-Century-Crofts, 1947).
4. Learned Hand, "The Self-interests of the Newspaper Industry Are Not Conclusive," in Harold L. Nelson (ed.), *Freedom of the Press from Hamilton to the Warren Court* (Indianapolis: Bobbs-Merrill, 1967): 367–376, p. 373. Excerpt is from *U.S. v. Associated Press,* 52 Federal Supplement 362.

5. David Warren, "Sooner or Later," *DavidWarrenOnline*, July 8, 2002. Downloaded on June 21, 2003, from <www.davidwarrenonline.com/Comment/Jul02/index70.shtml>.

6. Gregory Palast, "Florida's Flawed 'Voter Cleansing' Program," *Salon.com*, Dec. 4, 2000. Downloaded on Aug. 21, 2002, from <archive.salon.com/politics/feature/2000/12/04/voter_file>; and Eric Alterman, *What Liberal Media? The Truth About* Bias *and the News* (New York: Basic Books, 2003): 177.

7. John Lantigua, "How the GOP Gamed the System in Florida," *The Nation*, April 30, 2001:11–12, 14–17, p. 11. Available at <www.thenation.com/doc.mhtml?i=20010430&c=1&s=lantigua>.

8. Steven R. Thomsen and Bret Rawson, "Purifying a Tainted Corporate Image: Odwalla's Response to an E. Coli Poisoning," *Public Relations Quarterly*, Fall 1998: 35–46.

9. Heather Newman, "Test Results Can Be Skewed by Many Outside Factors," *Detroit Free Press*, May 7, 1998: B-3; and Christopher Callahan, *A Journalist's Guide to the Internet: The Net as a Reporting Tool*, 2nd ed. (Boston: Allyn and Bacon, 2003): 79–80.

10. Newman, "Test Results Can be Skewed": B-3.

11. "FOX5's I-team Win Peabody," Fox Television Stations, undated. Downloaded on Aug. 22, 2002, from <www.fox5atlanta.com/iteam/Peabody.html>.

12. Eric Boehlert, "Pay for Play," *Salon.com*, March 14, 2001. Downloaded on May 23, 2003, from <archive.salon.com/ent/feature/2001/03/14/payola>.

13. Ibid.

14. T. J. Jackson Lears, "From Salvation to Self-realization: Advertising and the Therapeutic Roots of the Consumer Culture, 1880–1939," in Richard Wightman Fox and T. J. Jackson Lears (eds.), *The Culture of Consumption: Critical Essays in American History, 1880–1980* (New York: Pantheon, 1983): 1–38; Holly Allen, "Gender, the Movement Press, and the Cultural Politics of the Knights of Labor," in William S. Solomon and Robert W. McChesney (eds.), *Ruthless Criticism: New Perspectives in U.S. Communication History* (Minneapolis: University of Minnesota Press, 1993): 122–150; and Jon Bekken, "The Working-class Press at the Turn of the Century," in Solomon and McChesney, *Ruthless Criticism*: 151–175.

15. Compiled from *Annual Report 2002*, "Walt Disney Co.," undated. Downloaded on July 24, 2003, from <www.disney.com/investors>; "Who Owns What: The Walt Disney Co.," *Columbia Journalism Review*, undated. Downloaded on July 29, 2003, from <www.cjr.org/owners/Disney.asp#>; and "The Walt Disney Company," Public Broadcasting Service, undated. Downloaded on Nov. 7, 2002, from <www.pbs.org/wgbh/pages/frontline/shows/cool/giants/disney.html>.

16. This is an old, continuing story, as suggested by Gerald J. Baldasty, "The Rise of News as a Commodity: Business Imperatives and the Press in the Nineteenth Century," in Solomon and McChesney, *Ruthless Criticism:* 98–121; Ben H. Bagdikian, "The Best News Money Can Buy," *Human Behavior*, October 1978: 63–66; John H. McManus, *Market-driven Journalism: Let the Citizen Beware?* (Thousand Oaks, Calif.: Sage, 1994); Benjamin M. Compaine and Douglas Gomery, *Who Owns the Media? Competition and Concentration in the Mass Media Industry*, 3rd ed. (Mahwah, N.J.: Erlbaum, 2000); Christopher H. Pyle, "Irresponsible Journalists Are Jeopardizing Serious Investigations by the Press," *The Chronicle of Higher Education*, Jan. 7, 2000: B-9, B-10.

17. Alterman, *What Liberal Media?*: 24.

18. Jane Akre, "The Fox, the Hounds, and the Sacred Cows," in Kristina Borjesson (ed.), *Into the Buzzsaw: Leading Journalists Expose the Myth of a Free Press* (Amherst, N.Y.: Prometheus, 2002): 37–64, p. 49.

19. Philip Weiss, "Invasion of the Gannettoids: The Clones That Ate American Journalism," *The New Republic*, Feb. 2, 1987: 18–20, 22, p. 18.

20. The Associated Press, "Media Poll: Many Admit Softening Stories," *Houston Chronicle*, May 1, 2000: A-6.

21. "State of the First Amendment 2003," report of the First Amendment Center, Nashville, Tenn., July 2003. Downloaded on Aug. 4, 2003, from <www.firstamendmentcenter.org/about.aspx?item=state_of_First_Amendment_2003>.

22. Mark P. McElreath, *Managing Systematic and Ethical Public Relations* (Madison, Wis.: Brown & Benchmark, 1993).

23. Ibid., p. 9.

24. Katie LaPlant, "The Dow Corning Crisis: A Benchmark," *Public Relations Quarterly*, Summer 1999: 32–33.

25. Sheldon Rampton and John Stauber, *Trust Us, We're Experts: How Industry Manipulates Science and Gambles With Your Future* (New York: Jeremy P. Tarcher/Putnam, 2001): Chapter 10.

26. Ibid., p. 277; "The Heidelberg Appeal," Science and Environmental Policy Project, 1992. Downloaded on Aug. 25, 2002, from <www.sepp.org/heidelberg_appeal.html>.

27. Kathy R. Fitzpatrick, "The Role of Public Relations in the Institutionalization of Ethics," *Public Relations Review*, 22:3 (1996): 249–258.

28. James Fallows, "Why Americans Hate the Media," *The Atlantic Monthly*, February 1996: 45–48, 50–52, 55–57, 60, 62–64, p. 50.

29. Ibid., p. 55.

30. Cited in Michael Ryan and David L. Martinson, "Journalists and Public Relations Practitioners: Why the Antagonism?" *Journalism Quarterly*, 65:1 (1988): 131–140, p. 140.

31. Michael Ryan and David L. Martinson, "Public Relations Practitioners, Journalists View Lying Similarly," *Journalism Quarterly*, 71:1 (1994): 199–211.

32. Lynne M. Sallot, Thomas M. Steinfatt and Michael B. Salwen, "Journalists' and Public Relations Practitioners' News Values: Perceptions and Cross-perceptions," *Journalism & Mass Communication Quarterly*, 75:2 (1998): 366–377; Patricia A. Curtin and Eric Rhodenbaugh, "Building the News Media Agenda on the Environment: A Comparison of Public Relations and Journalistic Sources, *Public Relations Review*, 27:2 (2001): 179–195; and Lillian Lodge Kopenhaver, David L. Martinson and Michael Ryan, "How Public Relations Practitioners and Editors in Florida View Each Other," *Journalism Quarterly*, 61:4 (1984): 860–865, 884.

33. Ryan and Martinson, "Journalists and Public Relations Practitioners."

34. Rampton and Stauber, *Trust Us, We're Experts*, Alterman, *What Liberal Media?*; David Brock, *Blinded by the Right: The Conscience of an Ex-conservative* (New York: Crown, 2002).

35. Robert Jensen, "U.S. Just as Guilty of Committing Own Violent Acts," *Houston Chronicle*, Sept. 14, 2001: A-33.

36. Jerry L. Martin and Anne D. Neal, "Defending Civilization: How Our Universities Are Failing America and What Can Be Done About It," report of the American Council of Trustees and Alumni, Washington, D.C., November 2001.

37. Emily Eakin, "On the Lookout for Patriotic Incorrectness," *The New York Times*, Nov. 24, 2001: Arts 15, 17, p. 15.

38. "From the Editors: The Times and Iraq," *The New York Times*, May 26, 2004: A-10.

39. William McGowan, *Coloring the News: How Crusading for Diversity Has Corrupted American Journalism* (San Francisco: Encounter Books, 2001).

40. Ruth Padawer, "The Facts on Partial-birth Abortion: Both Sides Have Misled the Public," *The* (Bergen, N.J.) *Sunday Record*, Sept. 15, 1996: RO-1, 4.

41. David Brown, "Late Term Abortions: Who Gets Them and Why," *The Washington Post*, Sept. 17, 1996: Health 12–14, 17, 19.

42. Kate Zernike, "Scouts' Successful Ban on Gays Is Followed by Loss in Support: Gifts Are Cut and Public Property Use Is Limited," *The New York Times,* Aug. 29, 2000: A-1, 16. Also cited in McGowan, *Coloring the News:* 118–122.

43. "Corrections," *The New York Times,* Sept. 6, 2000: A-2.

44. Blake Morrison, "Ex-USA Today Reporter Faked Major Stories," *USA Today,* March 19, 2004. Downloaded on June 15, 2004, from <www.usatoday.com/news/2004-03-18-2004-03-18_kelleymain_x.htm>; "Times Reporter Who Resigned Leaves Long Trail of Deception," *The New York Times,* May 11, 2003: A-1, 20–23, p. A-1; and Richard Cohen, "Blind Spot at the N.Y. Times," *The Washington Post,* May 13, 2003: A-19.

45. "Times Reporter Who Resigned": A-1.

46. Morrison, "Ex-USA Today Reporter."

47. C.C. Trevithick, M.M. Chartrand, J. Wahlman, F. Rahman, M. Hirst and J.R. Trevithick, "Shaken, Not Stirred: Bioanalytical Study of the Antioxidant Activities of Martinis," *British Medical Journal,* 319:7225 (1999): 1600–1602.

48. Rampton and Stauber, *Trust Us, We're Experts:* 307–308. A sample story is Eric Nagourney, "Recipe for Health: Shaken, Not Stirred," *The New York Times,* Dec. 21, 1999: F-8.

49. Felicity Barringer, "Did NBC Let Lay's Wife Get Around Hard Issues?" *The New York Times,* Jan. 30, 2002: C-7; Frank Rich, "State of the Enron," *The New York Times,* Feb. 2, 2002: A-19; and Alterman, *What Liberal Media?:* 136.

50. Davis Merritt, *Public Journalism and Public Life: Why Telling the News Is Not Enough* (Hillsdale, N.J.: Erlbaum, 1995): xv; Christine D. Urban, *Examining Our Credibility: Perspectives of the Public and the Press* (Reston, Va.: American Society of Newspaper Editors, 1999); and "PR Pros Are Among Least Believable Public Figures," *O'Dwyer's PR Services Report,* August 1999: 1, 24.

51. Michael Ryan, "Journalistic Ethics, Objectivity, Existential Journalism, Standpoint Epistemology, and Public Journalism," *Journal of Mass Media Ethics,* 16:1 (2001): 3–22.

52. Everett E. Dennis, "Journalistic Objectivity *Is* Possible," in Everette E. Dennis and John C. Merrill, *Basic Issues in Mass Communication: A Debate* (New York: Macmillan, 1984): 111–118.

53. Noretta Koertge, "Feminist Epistemology: Stalking an Un-dead Horse," in Paul R. Gross, Norman Levitt and Martin W. Lewis (eds.), *The Flight from Science and Reason* (New York: The New York Academy of Sciences, 1996): 413–419; and Meera Nanda, "The Epistemic Charity of the Social Constructivist Critics of Science and Why the Third World Should Refuse the Offer," in Noretta Koertge (ed.), *A House Built on Sand: Exposing Postmodernist Myths About Science* (New York: Oxford University Press, 1998): 286–311.

54. Meenakshi Gigi Durham, "On the Relevance of Standpoint Epistemology to the Practice of Journalism: The Case for 'Strong Objectivity,'" *Communication Theory,* 8:2 (1998): 117–140; Jane Rhodes, "The Visibility of Race and Media History," *Critical Studies in Mass Communication,* 10:2 (1993): 184–190; Jay Rosen, "Beyond Objectivity: It Is a Myth, an Important One, But Often Crippling and It Needs to be Replaced With a More Inspiring Concept," *Nieman Reports,* Winter 1993: 48–53; Michael Schudson, *The Power of News* (Cambridge, Mass.: Harvard University Press, 1995); and Kevin Stoker, "Existential Objectivity: Freeing Journalists to Be Ethical," *Journal of Mass Media Ethics,* 10:1 (1995): 5–22.

55. David L. Altheide, *Creating Reality: How TV News Distorts Events* (Beverly Hills, Calif.: Sage, 1976); Helen E. Longino, *Science as Social Knowledge: Values and Objectivity in Scientific Inquiry* (Princeton, N.J.: Princeton University Press, 1990); Pamela J. Shoemaker and Stephen D. Reese, *Mediating the Message: Theories of Influences on Mass Media Content,* 2nd ed. (White Plains, N.Y.: Longman, 1996).

56. John C. Merrill, "Journalistic Objectivity Is *Not* Possible," in Dennis and Merrill, *Basic Issues in Mass Communication:* 104–110.

57. James Weldon Johnson, *The Autobiography of an Ex-coloured Man* (New York: Vintage, 1927).

58. J. Herbert Altschull, *Agents of Power: The Role of the News Media in Human Affairs* (New York: Longman, 1984); and Theodore L. Glasser, "The Puzzle of Objectivity I: Objectivity Precludes Responsibility," *Quill,* February 1984: 12–16.

59. The Commission on Freedom of the Press, *A Free and Responsible Press: A General Report on Mass Communication: Newspapers, Radio, Motion Pictures, Magazines, and Books* (Chicago: University of Chicago Press, 1947): 77.

60. Altschull, *Agents of Power:* 128.

61. Robert A. Hackett, "Decline of a Paradigm? Bias and Objectivity in News Media Studies," *Critical Studies in Mass Communication,* 1:3 (1984): 229–259.

62. Tom Koch, *The News as Myth: Fact and Context in Journalism* (New York: Greenwood, 1990): 174–175.

63. Jane Delano Brown, Carl R. Bybee, Stanley T. Wearden and Dulcie Murdock Straughan, "Invisible Power: Newspaper News Sources and the Limits of Diversity," *Journalism Quarterly,* 64:1 (1987): 45–54.

64. Hugh Pearson, "Enough of Al Sharpton's Masquerading as Leader," *Houston Chronicle,* Feb. 29, 2000: A-21.

65. Jack E. White, "Big Al's Finest Hour: Sharpton Emerges as the Voice of Black Outrage," *Time,* March 6, 2000: 28.

66. Stoker, "Existential Objectivity": 11.

67. Pam Belluck, "Death Row Inmate Freed After 16 Years: Investigation by Professor, Five Journalism Students Key to Release," *Houston Chronicle,* Feb. 6, 1999: A-3.

68. Gaye Tuchman, "Objectivity as Strategic Ritual: An Examination of Newsmen's Notions of Objectivity, *American Journal of Sociology,* 77:4 (1972): 660–679.

69. Ekaterina Ognianova and James W. Endersby, "Objectivity Revisited: A Spatial Model of Political Ideology and Mass Communication," *Journalism & Mass Communication Monographs,* 159 (1996): 1.

70. Walter Lippmann, *Public Opinion* (New York: Free Press, 1922).

71. Phyllis Kaniss, *Making Local News* (Chicago: University of Chicago Press, 1991).

72. John C. Merrill and Ralph L. Lowenstein, *Media, Messages and Men: New Perspectives in Communication,* 2nd ed. (New York: Longman, 1979): 214.

73. Don H. Corrigan, *The Public Journalism Movement in America: Evangelists in the Newsroom* (Westport, Conn.: Praeger, 1999); Edmund B. Lambeth, Philip E. Meyer and Esther Thorson (eds.), *Assessing Public Journalism* (Columbia: University of Missouri Press, 1998); Peter Parisi, "Toward a 'Philosophy of Framing': News Narratives for Public Journalism," *Journalism & Mass Communication Quarterly,* 74:4 (1997): 673–686.

74. Merritt, *Public Journalism and Public Life:* 5.

75. Lewis A. Friedland, "Bringing the News Back Home: Public Journalism and Rebuilding Local Communities," *National Civic Review,* Fall 1996: 45–48.

76. Paul S. Voakes, "Civic Duties: Newspaper Journalists' Views on Public Journalism," *Journalism & Mass Communication Quarterly,* 76:4 (1999): 756–774, p. 759.

77. John C. Merrill, *Existential Journalism* (Ames: Iowa State University Press, 1996).

78. Ibid., p. 28.

79. Stoker, "Existential Objectivity."

80. John C. Merrill, *The Dialectic in Journalism: Toward a Responsible Use of Press Freedom* (Baton Rouge: Louisiana State University Press,1989): 149.

81. Stoker, "Existential Objectivity": 16.

82. Merrill, *The Dialectic in Journalism:* 147.

83. Ryan, "Journalistic Ethics"; Ralph D. Barney, "A Dangerous Drift? The Sirens' Call to Collectivism," in Jay Black (ed.), *Mixed News: The Public/Civic/Communitarian Journalism Debate* (Mahwah, N.J.: Erlbaum, 1997): 72–90; and Hanno Hardt, "The Quest for Public Journalism: A Review Essay," *Journal of Communication,* 47:3 (1997): 102–109.

84. Anne Saul, "API Workshop Focuses on Successful Convergence Partnerships; Gannett's Online Training Program Explained to Participants," *News Watch,* July 2002. Downloaded on May 23, 2003, at <www.gannett.com/go/newswatch/2002/july/nw0712-1.htm>.

85. Paul Maryniak, "Specialized Training, Planning Ahead Aid Phoenix in Fire Coverage," *News Watch,* July 2002. Downloaded on May 23, 2003, from <www.gannett.com/go/newswatch/2002/july/nw0703-1.htm>.

86. Derek Osenenko, "Florida Today Expands Its Reach in Print, on the Web and on TV," *News Watch,* June 2002. Downloaded on May 23, 2003, from <www.gannett.com/go/newswatch/2002/june/nw0614-1.htm>.

87. Ibid.

88. Kathleen Rutledge, personal communication with the authors, Aug. 12, 2003.

89. Ibid.

90. Leonard Downie Jr. and Robert G. Kaiser, "Good News Needed: Why Newspapers Must Continue to Set the Media Agenda," *Editor & Publisher,* Feb. 18, 2002: 30.

91. Robert J. Haiman, "Can Convergence Float?" speech to a "Smart Conference," The Poynter Institute for Media Studies, Feb. 28, 2001. Downloaded on June 13, 2002, from <www.poynter.org/centerpiece/022801haiman.htm>.

NEWS

What It Is and What It's Not

News is information, but information is not necessarily news. A public relations professional in a medical research laboratory, for example, may have important information about the most effective way for women to conduct self-examinations for breast cancer. The writer may produce a useful and accurate description of the procedure and post that to a World Wide Web site or publish it in a brochure, where it can be read by those at risk for the disease.

The information becomes "news" when a researcher discovers evidence that the self-examination process is flawed or can be improved. The discovery is timely and, therefore, is news. The public relations writer prepares a news release or a video for journalists, updates the information for the Web site and perhaps arranges a news conference so journalists can interview the researcher. Journalists may also hear about the new development on their own and then investigate and present the information through newspaper, magazine, Web or broadcast news stories.

Millions of events occur every day, and editors must determine which events are important enough to cover. One definition of news is that it is whatever an editor says it is. While this may be largely accurate, it is not very helpful to a beginning writer. Another definition of news—from television anchor Dan Rather—is that news is information judged to be important, interesting or both.[1]

This narrows it down a bit, but it begs the question of who gets to decide. Interest and importance are relative: What is important and interesting in Omaha, Neb., may not be in Manchester, N.H. Furthermore, the direct answer to "who gets to decide?" is, "those who own the media." It is tempting for media owners to focus more on interesting (or entertaining) news, for that can mean bigger profits as audiences gravitate toward interesting stories.

But media critic Nat Hentoff and others emphasize that audiences frequently need to know things they might rather not know if they are to participate meaningfully in the democratic process and to cope with their own lives. Writers, he says, "owe it to our readers—and our own self-respect—to also tell them what they *need* to know, and in a way that will impel them to want to read it."[2] Good writers try to strike a balance between what audiences *want* to know and what they *need* to know, but, in the end, they make sure audiences have the information they *need*.

What audiences need, some critics argue, is a definition that emphasizes news that (1) helps educate readers, viewers and listeners so they can help democracy work; (2) helps them cope with their daily lives; and (3) focuses on real problems and issues so they can be resolved. This means the definition is inclusive and not exclusive: The views of the powerful and the powerless are valued; all ideas are open to discussion; and the producers of news accounts represent various components of the social order.[3]

Some news definitions, however, give some political, social, cultural or economic practices priority over others and reinforce the social order to the point that there appear to be no alternatives. Definitions that would challenge or question the existing order are simply not considered.[4] Some news definitions also focus almost exclusively on ritual or ceremony, personalities, official actions and pronouncements, human frailty, spectacle, conflict, crisis and almost anything else that will entertain the masses—essentially undermining the democratic potential of the mass media (Chapter 1).[5] (See the box "What's the Story?")

Editors often define campaign news almost exclusively in terms of what James Fallows calls "the pure game of politics—the struggle among candidates interested mainly in their own advancement." Journalists seldom are overly concerned with the impact of legislation, proposals, position papers and politics on everyday lives.[6] Some campaign public relations professionals want to see substantive issues defined as news, but most are satisfied with definitions that emphasize personality and the game.

Disagreements about what is and is not news were pronounced during the Anglo-American invasion of Iraq in 2003, when Arab news definitions were sometimes quite different from those of American editors. Arab editors showed the obligatory news conferences, news from the front, interviews with Anglo-American soldiers and presidential statements. "But they also show charred bodies lying beside gutted cars. Cameras linger over dead allied soldiers and bandaged Iraqi children. Mourning families wail, and hospitals choke with bleeding and burned civilians."[7] At the same time, the U.S. media defined the news in a way that gave primacy to the official view of the war. The focus was on comments from Pentagon brass, retired officers and troops at the front.[8]

The way news about the invasion was defined had political consequences, some critics charge, just as other news can have political consequences. "As images of civilian casualties and Iraqi resistance fill their TV screens, support for Iraq and animosity toward the United States grows and hardens among Arabs."[9] Editors must not define news with eyes toward political, economic, social or cultural consequences. The *context* in which news is defined is as important as *how* it is defined.

WHAT'S THE STORY?

Human beings started telling each other stories just as soon as they learned to communicate with hand signals and grunts, and they started archiving those stories on cave walls as soon as they learned that one rock would make an interesting (and important) mark on another rock.

Though they did not think in those terms, those early communicators passed on "news" and "information." The news might have been the number of animals killed on the latest hunt, while the information might have been about how to sharpen a tree limb to make a spear.

There are many names for stories: Narratives, myths, legends, ballads and tales are some. And there are many kinds of stories: Fiction/nonfiction and verbal/nonverbal are a couple of broad categories. Features, documentaries, spot news stories, news releases, commentaries and editorials are more specific.

"Story," as used in this book, is a nonfiction account of news that is prepared by a newspaper, magazine, broadcast or online journalist, or by a public relations professional. Students who learn the fundamentals—which have evolved over hundreds of years and are still evolving—can successfully prepare stories in a variety of media. The skills also are useful in completely different domains, such as fiction writing.

Middle Eastern and Anglo-American editors often defined news about the invasion of Iraq in markedly different ways. Scenes of bodies and fighting that appeared in Arab media did not make the news in the United States.

NEWS VALUES

All the disagreement aside, media professionals must find ways to define news. Most journalists and public relations professionals use a set of guidelines, called news values, to help them. Writers use news values to help them decide what information should be used in the lead (Chapter 5); what should come second, third and fourth; and what should be left out altogether. Editors use them to decide what stories to cover and how to play them (whether to lead a newscast or to end a newscast).

The news values discussed in this book—timeliness, proximity, prominence, impact, magnitude, conflict, human interest and visual potential—are first described as they might be used by a public relations or journalism editor in judging the importance of a given news event or issue. In the next section of this chapter, we shall see how the eight values can help writers determine which bits of information they should emphasize.

Some editors may apply other values in judging the importance of news, and the values described here might be labeled differently by other media professionals or scholars (impact, for example, sometimes is called consequence). However, a great deal of research has been conducted on news values, and those listed here have been found to be important in the selection and writing of news.[10]

Timeliness

Communication professionals are expected to report events as soon as possible after they happen. In general, the older a story is, the less valuable it is as news. Broadcast news media and news sites on the Web are expected to report events the day they happen. Public relations professionals whose employers are involved in crises and other news must have facts and statements ready to disseminate immediately. Newspapers are expected to report events no later than the next day.

This eagerness to report the latest news is evident in election night coverage, particularly during presidential elections. In the 2000 presidential election, the television networks were so eager to report a winner that they announced that George W. Bush had won and then had to retract the report.

School board meetings, city council meetings, sports results, speeches by prominent figures, major accidents or crimes—all these are expected to be reported in the news media as soon as possible. Public relations professionals often are expected to produce releases about these events and to help journalists gather facts and statements so they can meet their deadlines.

Proximity

Defined as a news element concerning people, events or institutions in the immediate coverage area, proximity is one of the more important of the news values. Most readers, listeners and viewers want to know what's happening in their own communities, to find out what their neighbors are doing and to see their names and the names of their friends and relatives in the news.

Rarely is a state, national or international story as important to an editor as a local story. Editors think individuals are most interested in what happens in their own communities (and to residents of those communities), and they try to give their audiences that news. Even for important state, national and international stories, editors look for local angles, which usually are played up.

When an airplane crashes, a disaster occurs or a group holds its annual convention, someone from the local area might be involved, and the activities and reactions of that individual receive extensive coverage. When a state law is passed providing more money for the state's college and university system, a broadcast or newspaper editor will likely send a writer to a nearby university or college to find out how its share of the money will be spent.

When a school district's public relations officer writes a release or an annual report summarizing student performance on statewide standardized tests, he or she highlights the local scores (proximity) and breaks scores down by school so that students and parents within each school's boundaries will know how that school performed. When a writer posts a report to the Web, he or she includes a hyperlink to each school's test results.

Prominence

Prominence comes into play in a story or release that involves people, institutions or issues well known because of past publicity or position in the community. Some people are more prominent than others, and, for better or worse, they get more space and better play than people who are not well known.

A story about a relatively unknown man who hired someone to murder his wife, for example, might not even appear in a city or state magazine. If the man is a well-known attorney, doctor, city official or criminal, however, the murder could be the cover story in that same magazine. A public relations professional for an activist organization is more likely to cite testimonials or statements of prominent supporters than those of supporters who are not prominent.

Many public officials—including the president, members of Congress, governors, mayors and judges—are automatically prominent. They are more likely to make the news and to get more extensive coverage when they do.

Some criminals are so infamous, so prominent, that books and movies are produced about them. Hundreds of thousands of words have been written about Unabomber Theodore Kaczynski, serial killer Jeffrey Dahmer, bank robbers Bonnie Parker and Clyde Barrow, Oklahoma City bomber Timothy McVeigh, Houston child killer Andrea Yates and hundreds of ordinary people who have committed extraordinary crimes. Millions of words are written also about good people such as Mother Teresa.

Celebrities also have a kind of automatic prominence and tend to receive a great deal of coverage. Bono, the lead singer of the rock group U2, has received considerable coverage for his political activities; an average citizen doing the same things does not get such coverage. Media professionals let us know when actor Nicolas

Cage and Lisa Marie Presley, the daughter of Elvis, got married; when *Friends* star Courtney Cox Arquette became pregnant; and when film star Jennifer Lopez may or may not have married salsa singer Marc Anthony.

Some critics have suggested that American media are obsessed with celebrities and spend too much time and space reporting their doings while neglecting more important news. Bob Steele and Roy Peter Clark of The Poynter Institute for Media Studies (an independent journalism think tank and training organization) have even suggested that celebrity-hood by itself has become a news value, and that this is not a good thing.[11]

Prominence also extends to buildings (the Empire State Building), retail stores (McDonald's, Wal-Mart), charitable organizations (the March of Dimes) universities (Harvard), government agencies (the Centers for Disease Control and Prevention), corporations (Microsoft, General Motors) and issues (taxes, abortion, a Palestinian homeland).

Impact

A story has impact if the event reported has a major effect, usually on a large number of people, now or in the near future. The term implies an effect or consequence that can either damage or enhance some aspect of many individuals' lives. The following examples are events with the element of impact:

- The World Trade Center attack on Sept. 11, 2001, which killed approximately 3,000 people
- An earthquake in Gujarat, India, on January, 26, 2001, which killed 20,003 people
- A severe economic recession that forces thousands of people out of jobs
- President Bush's 2003 invasion of Iraq, which cost taxpayers billions of dollars

An event can also have impact on one or a few people and therefore be newsworthy. In a small town, any fatal car accident will be a major news story. Similarly, local roads undergoing construction may not seem like a big deal, but they are reported in the news media because they affect people driving to work and other places.

Magnitude

Magnitude refers to large quantities or numbers. The larger the numbers or amounts involved, the greater the magnitude and the more important the story is. Demonstrations against the World Trade Organization meeting in Seattle drew tens of thousands of protesters. Police arrested almost 600. These large numbers contributed to the perceived importance of the event.

Several other kinds of magnitude were reflected in a story from South Africa about an elephant with a toothache. The animal had a cavity the size of a man's fist (magnitude) in one molar. Seventeen (magnitude) dentists, doctors, veterinarians and technicians drilled the tooth and filled the hole with $200 (magnitude) worth of amalgam. They used enough anesthetic to kill 70 (magnitude) people.

The Woodstock Music and Art Fair was set apart from other folk festivals of the 1960s because of the massive number who attended—approximately 400,000. If 500 persons had attended, the story wouldn't have received the national and international coverage it did get. Since that time, additional music festivals at Woodstock have also attracted large crowds—and scored high in magnitude.

Magnitude, however, is relative. A hundred people demonstrating is not big news in San Francisco. But if 100 persons demonstrated in Enid, OK, the story would have great magnitude there.

Conflict

Conflict refers to verbal or physical clashes or confrontations among peoples, nations, groups, animals or other living things—or to conflicts between any or all of these and nature. Anyone who doubts the importance of the conflict news value should spend a few days reading a collection of daily newspapers and newsmagazines and watching network and local newscasts. It is even apparent in some news releases prepared for activist organizations. Conflict is clearly evident in the emphasis on accidents and disasters, crimes, differences of opinion within and among various groups, local political squabbles and demonstrations that might lead to violence.

It matters little what the story is or who is involved. If conflict is present, the story is news, and it probably will get time or space. The kind of play it receives, however, depends to some extent on the prominence of the persons involved (attacks against the media by prominent people, for instance, are given greater play than attacks by people who are less prominent) and the magnitude of the story (a strike by teachers in one school in a district will receive less play than a strike by all the teachers in the district because fewer pupils and teachers are involved).

Some activist or advocacy groups have learned to take advantage of the conflict news value to get media coverage. If they can provoke the police into making arrests, this greatly increases the likelihood of media coverage. Some politicians attack the powerless (gays and lesbians, for instance) to galvanize their supporters and to raise money during elections.

Human Interest

Some news is important or interesting because it is high in human interest value. Human interest stories typically stress oddity or emotional appeal. Odd behaviors or events are more than simply unusual. They typically have strange, abnormal or unpredictable twists; the behaviors or events are the opposite of what one might expect. Emotional appeals stress such human emotions as anger, fear, joy, admiration and sadness.

The best human interest stories often contain elements of both oddity and emotional appeal. A mother cat who plunges into a burning building to save her litter is doing something many human beings would consider exceptional or odd.

If she were badly burned as she saved her kittens, her story would be broadcast nationwide because of its inherent emotional appeal. As happens frequently, the story would generate hundreds of offers to adopt the cat and her kittens.

A story about a 9-year-old bank robber in New York was published widely because it was such an unusual occurrence. The lead (the first sentence of a story), provided by the New York Daily News Service, stated:

> New York City's smallest desperado, a 9-year-old boy accused of sticking up a midtown
> Manhattan bank two days ago, gave himself up to authorities Friday.

The boy is reported to have taken $100 in $5 bills from a teller and then run out the door, saying, "Thanks a lot. Goodbye."

Visual Potential

Print media professionals try to illustrate many stories with compelling, accurate and attractive graphics and with strong photographs. The digital revolution has made it possible for newspaper and magazine professionals to do things they could not have even considered doing only a couple of decades ago. Still, print editors can and do pursue news that has little potential for high-quality visuals. Visual potential is not always as high on the list of news values for print editors and writers as other news values are. Indeed, print professionals often select a story and *then* decide how to illustrate it.

Public relations writers typically value visual potential more highly than newspaper editors do. They "publish" through their hyperlinks far more graphics and photographs than newspapers and magazines publish on their printed pages; they can add streaming video to the list of options; and visuals are important components in the speeches and presentations they prepare. The visual potential is an important consideration for most stories.

Visual potential is *very* high on the list for television editors and most online writers. (See the box "Sharyl Attkisson and Don Vaughan on Writing to Video.") Jonathan Dube emphasizes the importance of visual potential when he writes, "Before you start reporting and writing a story, think about what the best ways are to tell the story, whether through audio, video, clickable graphics, text, links, etc.— or some combination."[12]

If there is no visual element, a television journalist typically does not cover a story. Rightly or wrongly, most television journalists believe the "talking head" is the fastest way to turn away viewers. Looking at it more positively, a strong visual element makes an event much more newsworthy for television editors. The event has got to have other news values, certainly, but the visual potential is often primary.

It is important for media professionals to worry about the package for news, but as Dube says, "Don't forget the fundamentals of journalism. Facts still have to be double- and triple-checked; writing still needs to be sharp, lively and to the point; stories should include context; and ethical practices must be followed. Don't let the 24/7 speed trap and the new tools distract you from these basics."[13]

SHARYL ATTKISSON AND DON VAUGHAN ON WRITING TO VIDEO

People who aren't used to writing to video mistakenly write their stories in a vacuum. They construct a script with no specific images in mind, as if they were writing a newspaper article. They then leave it up to a videotape editor or producer to figure out how to cover all of the words with pictures (videotape). The result is often a confusing or uninteresting story with videotape that doesn't support or match the words.

Catherine Harwood, a former local television news director, and a one-time reporter in Orlando, Florida, and Houston, Texas, tells about words of wisdom she got about matching video and graphics to the copy:

The most memorable writing advice I ever got came from one of my college professors who taught the concept of cognitive dissonance: the proven theory that

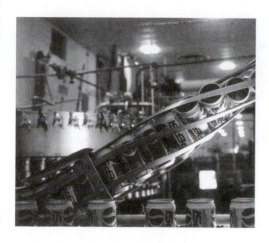

people generally can't digest and retain a story if you show pictures of one thing while describing something else. It impairs communication. That simple lesson came back to me so many times when I was sitting at a computer struggling to make sense of a complicated story. The pictures and graphics must reasonably match what you're talking about. It's a simple lesson that seems more appropriate than ever as the television screen is filled up with multiple bits of information competing for attention.

PepsiCo "wrote to video" when it showed part of a bottling plant in a video news release designed to convince the public that its products were safe. The release was part of PepsiCo's response to charges that its products were tampered with.

Source: Sharyl Attkisson and Don R. Vaughan, *Writing Right for Broadcast and Internet News* (Boston: Allyn and Bacon, 2003): 144.

Sharyl Attkisson has worked for PBS, CNN and CBS. Don Rodney Vaughan teaches at Mississippi State University.

Combinations

Some events may reflect several of the news values. This occurrence of multiple news values often appears with some of the biggest news stories. Research indicates that stories containing several news values are most likely to be selected for front page play in newspapers.[14] For example, consider this lead:

> WASHINGTON—Sen. Hillary Rodham Clinton sought an invitation Thursday to Crawford
>
> to spend some time with the Republican who replaced her husband in the White House.

This lead has strong elements of prominence, with a current president and a former first lady; conflict (Clinton is a Democrat and Bush is a Republican); and oddity (the idea of Hillary Clinton surrounded by her Secret Service entourage wandering out into the woods to cut brush with President Bush, surrounded by his Secret Service entourage). This news item probably originated with a skilled public relations professional who knew it was unlikely that Bush would invite Clinton, but who also realized the story would receive wide coverage because of the strong combination of news elements.

The story about the elephant receiving a filling, described in relation to magnitude, is also high in oddity. The occurrence of multiple news values also makes this event especially newsworthy.

Another example of using the news values in combination is reflected in the lead of this release from the National Aeronautics and Space Administration:

> Two eagle-eyed NASA spacecraft—the Mars Global Surveyor (MGS) and Hubble
>
> Telescope—are giving amazed scientists a ringside seat to the biggest global dust storm
>
> seen on Mars in decades.

This lead is high in the news values of oddity (seen in decades) and magnitude (biggest global dust storm). It works in the name of the prominent organization (NASA) early, and it gives a favorable picture of the Hubble Telescope, an instrument that received some negative press earlier when it was discovered that the lens had been manufactured improperly. The writer also did a good job of writing the lead in familiar and colorful language (eagle-eyed, ringside seat) when it could have easily been overloaded with highly technical language.

PEGS AND ANGLES

Beginning writers often find it helpful to think about news in terms of news pegs and news angles, both of which are discussed in this section.

News Peg

A news peg is a development that a writer can "hang a story on." Sometimes a media professional will hear about an interesting situation, but there isn't enough specific information to make it a solid story. The writer needs a news peg. The peg

ROBERT ENTMAN ON THE NEED FOR SAVVY NEWS CONSUMERS

Because most members of the public know and care relatively little about government, they neither seek nor understand high-quality political reporting and analysis. With limited demand for first-rate journalism, most news organizations cannot afford to supply it, and because they do not supply it, most Americans have no practical source of the information necessary to become politically sophisticated. Yet it would take an informed and interested citizenry to create enough demand to support top-flight journalism. ...

The nature of both demand and supply cements interdependence and diminishes the press's autonomy. On the demand side, news organizations have to respond to public tastes. They cannot stay in business if they produce a diverse assortment of richly textured ideas and information that nobody sees. To become informed and hold government accountable, the general public needs to obtain news that is comprehensive yet interesting and understandable, that conveys facts and outcomes, not cosmetic images and airy promises. But that is not what the public demands.

Source: Robert M. Entman, *Democracy Without Citizens: Media and the Decay of American Politics* (New York: Oxford University Press, 1989): 17, 18.

Robert Entman is a professor of communication studies, journalism and political science at Northwestern University.

typically is an element that is timely and proximate and that reflects at least one other news value.

For instance, a newspaper writer on the education beat hears that administrators of a particular school are being harassed—possibly by a student. Hate letters have been sent to newspapers and churches with one of the administrator's names at the bottom. A bill for abortions and venereal disease treatment was sent to the office of a lawyer who worked with the school district. Reports that administrators had pornographic files on their computers were sent to the school superintendent.

School administrators are sure the fake letters are the work of a student who lost a civil rights suit filed against the school, but the administrators will not reveal the student's name. The situation is interesting, but so far the reporter does not have a news peg to hang a story on. If the school brings harassment charges, or a lawsuit, against the student, the writer would have a news peg—and a firm basis for a story.

Sometimes an anniversary can provide a news peg. In Austin, Texas, in 1992, a "Save Our Spring" movement, known as SOS, was aimed at preventing development that would pollute Barton Springs, a popular recreational area. In the summer of 2002, the 10th anniversary of the movement gave journalists an opportunity to review the SOS movement and the effects it might have had. The anniversary became a news peg for stories with headlines such as "Ten years later, Austin still working to save its springs" (*Austin American-Statesman*) and "Did SOS Matter?" (*The Austin Chronicle*).

Public relations writers must keep in mind always that the main complaint by newspaper, Web and television editors who process public relations releases is that too many lack news pegs. Releases that report no news are not published or aired, regardless of how well an organization serves its community. Here is the lead on a release that would not be used:

> The Handicapped Students Services Office supplied 32 students with wheelchairs and 67 students with special computer equipment so they could get to their classes and do their work last semester, Director Joanna Earles said today.

The release might be used if it were rewritten to incorporate a news peg—such as a computer company donating equipment *this week*.

Public relations writers tend to stress conflict and human interest less than journalists do, but this is not to say that their reports never contain these news elements. They typically must produce a release when their organization has lost an important court case (conflict), for example. And sometimes they will want to stress human interest, as The Home Depot did when it ran commercials featuring employees who were on Olympic teams. A rescue organization stresses conflict with nature and human interest when it tries to raise funds for victims of floods, earthquakes and other natural disasters.

News Angle

The news angle is different from the news peg in that the latter refers to the new information on which the story hangs, and the former refers to the approach the writer takes in a particular story. Writers almost always can approach a story (abandoned horses) from one of several angles (what happens to them now, why they were abandoned, who abandoned them?), just as a photographer can approach a basketball game from several angles.

A television reporter notices, for instance, that the Methodist Church has dug a large hole in its front lawn and is beginning to pour the foundation for a new Sunday school building. The church has also bought two houses next to its property and is tearing them down to build a new administration building. The church has some prominence in the community because several well-known people are members and because it has been there for decades.

The reporter realizes that a story about this new development could be approached from several angles and that some decent video of construction and of sources interviewed in interesting settings would be available to illustrate and add interest to the story:

- The expansion of the congregation. Are the new buildings needed because church membership is increasing? This could be a good angle, because church attendance is decreasing in many parts of the country. The reporter would talk to church administrators and try to gather statistics about church membership and attendance over a number of years. The reporter might also try to gather data about national trends in church attendance to put the local situation into a context. The report might open with video of a packed church on Sunday and of crowded Sunday school classes.

- The response of neighbors to the construction project. Are they bothered by the noise and by the constant presence of workers and heavy machinery? How do they feel about the church taking over another part of the neighborhood? Neighbors might be interviewed with construction and heavy equipment as a backdrop.

- The reactions of church members, particularly those who have been around for a while, to the changes. Some of them may have liked the large, open lawn at the front of the church and may not be happy to see part of it filled with a large building. This piece could develop into a historical feature, talking about the church in the old days and how it has changed through the years. Old photographs and stories about how the church used to be could make interesting visuals.

A public relations writer for the church might take yet another angle in a story for the annual report: how the new facilities will help the minister and the congregation accomplish their Christian mission.

PURPOSES OF NEWS

Communication professionals and scholars have devoted considerable time and money to finding out how consumers use the news available to them and what needs are gratified by that news.[15] This research suggests that media usage habits are enormously complex. Consumers use the news media for several purposes.

Daily Account of Events

Individuals are unable personally to monitor more than trivial portions of their environments, so they rely on media reports for news and information beyond their personal grasp. But even the media can report only a small part of each day's events, and some of their decisions about what to cover and what not to cover are criticized by those who believe they are failing to fulfill their public trust adequately.

Still, a number of media outlets are dedicated to supplying daily accounts of what's happening. Readers and viewers can stay abreast of events when they monitor newsmagazines (*Time, Newsweek*), television broadcasts (*60 Minutes, The News*

Hour with Jim Lehrer, BBC World news), mainstream newspapers (a local newspaper, the *Los Angeles Times,* the London *Financial Times*, all of which are available online); corporate, not-for-profit and government Web sites (Centers for Disease Control and Prevention, Susan G. Komen Breast Cancer Foundation); alternative broadcast outlets (National Public Radio, Public Broadcasting Service); bloggers (talkingpointsmemo.com, kausfiles.com); alternative newspapers (*The American Reporter, The Village Voice*); and minority newspapers (*The Indianapolis Recorder, El Heraldo de Maryland*).

Bloggers, by the way, write for blogs, online journals called Web logs (or blogs for short). Blogs, which typically are updated frequently, address just about every topic one can think of. Like personal journals, they are filled with personal experiences, thoughts, links and whatever else a blogger wants to post. Some information is accurate; some is not. Because blogs are so personal, content can be exceptionally varied—or not. Some blogs focus on single topics (politics, the local police force or religion, for instance).

Watchdog Function

Media professionals who function as watchdogs typically are viewed as part of a kind of fourth branch of government. Without the watchdogs (in the media and other institutions), government doors are closed, corruption is unchecked and democracy suffers (see the box "Murrey Marder on Failed Watchdogs"). "When the government begins closing doors, it selectively controls information rightfully belonging to the people," Judge Damon J. Keith wrote for the 6th U.S. Circuit Court of Appeals in a 2002 ruling that said the Bush administration illegally held hundreds of secret deportation hearings. "Selective information," Keith wrote, "is misinformation."[16]

In one of American journalism's most famous examples, *The Washington Post* won a Pulitzer Prize for its role in uncovering the Watergate scandal, and, more recently, WAGA-TV won a Peabody Award for exposing racial profiling during airport security checks. Some public relations professionals, though certainly not all, are watchdogs, too. The Sierra Club, for example, monitors environmental regulations and laws that are proposed by governments at all levels. The group has posted details about President George W. Bush's plans to roll back standards for air conditioner efficiency, logging on government lands and dumping mining waste into rivers and streams.[17] The Drudge Report is one of the more famous, or infamous, Web sites that specializes in exposing official corruption.[18]

News for Decision Making

The most obvious way citizens in a democracy participate in government is through elections—to choose candidates for public office and to make decisions about such issues as school bonds and the building of nuclear power plants. Professionals spend a good deal of time and effort in covering (and, in the case of public relations,

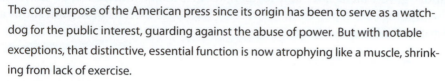

MURREY MARDER ON FAILED WATCHDOGS

The core purpose of the American press since its origin has been to serve as a watchdog for the public interest, guarding against the abuse of power. But with notable exceptions, that distinctive, essential function is now atrophying like a muscle, shrinking from lack of exercise.

When it has been true to its heritage, the press has sounded the alarm if public rights were being impaired. It marshaled public opinion to act against city, state, or federal authorities, or against any other group, public or private, found to be misusing the public trust.

How could such a vital function fall into widespread disuse? By not admitting that it has deteriorated. By pretending that it is being pursued. By focusing on minor abuses of power and avoiding the greater abuses. By making superficiality the norm for news coverage. ...

During the 2000 campaign, literally thousands of reporters walked right past the biggest story of the presidential election—the humiliating inadequacy of the voting equipment not just in Florida but across the nation. Where precincts used the antiquated ballot-punching machines, the error rate was a well-known disgrace glossed over by election managers until it crashed over the nation's head. The lesson: News exists everywhere in the power structures that surround us. No reporters or editors worth their press passes would ever say, "There's no news today."

Source: Murrey Marder, "Press Failure to Watchdog Can Have Devastating Consequences: Every News Organization Should Monitor the Powerful in the Public Interest," *Nieman Reports,* Summer 2001: 21.

Murrey Marder, a former correspondent for *The Washington Post*, created the Watchdog Journalism Project at the Nieman Foundation in 1997.

scheduling) public meetings, speeches and other events. Local media outlets might offer accounts, for example, of a city council meeting to discuss widening a road through a residential area or a school board meeting in which controversial textbooks are being considered. Citizens can participate in these kinds of decisions only if they are well-informed about the issues and the personalities.

Broadcast outlets supply the airtime for public debates, and newspapers provide space for candidates to outline their platforms; and both try to provide news and information that will help citizens decide how to vote (such as explaining how the complex Electoral College works when a presidential election appears dead-locked). Public relations professionals provide details about candidate positions to reporters, who then produce stories. The American Association of Retired Persons monitors government laws and regulations that affect individuals 55 and older, and its findings are reported in *AARP The Magazine*. Dozens of organizations are engaged in similar activities.

News for Every Day

People demand a great deal of specific information in their daily lives, including weather reports; announcements of births, deaths and marriages of people they know; reports of changes in tax or public utility rates that affect their pocketbooks; secrets for getting a red wine stain out of a sofa; public school schedules that affect their children's lives directly; and announcements of upcoming entertainment or sports events they may wish to attend.

A reader can learn what to do with that stain by reading "Hints from Heloise," how to run faster miles by reading *Runner's World* or how to care for a cockatiel by reading *BirdTalk*. Many newspapers and broadcast outlets also provide information about products and prices (automobile reviews), and many news and public relations organizations provide consumer hot lines (or hot sites) that respond directly to requests for help with day-to-day problems. The Web is a particularly good vehicle for fulfilling this function: A Web designer who is in touch with his or her audience can establish all sorts of links that provide helpful information.

Continuing Education

Media also help people no longer in school keep up with new ideas and new developments in culture, the arts, international relations, science, medicine, health, technology and many other fields. Reports about the usefulness of dental floss in preventing tooth decay or the relationship between lack of exercise and heart disease fulfill this function, for example. So do stories about a new novel by John Grisham, a new movie by Steven Spielberg or a new album by Metallica. The media are for many people the main sources of contact with the world of ideas.

The media, particularly the magazine industry, are even helpful to Americans who want to keep up with their own fields. In communication, several magazines meet this need: *Public Relations Quarterly, Information Week, Columbia Journalism Review, American Journalism Review, ADWEEK, Publishers Weekly* and *Broadcasting & Cable*. The Web is even more helpful—to the point that it can provide too much information (Chapter 8). If one types in *first amendment* during a Google search, he or she will be overwhelmed. Still, there is a good deal of useful information.

Entertainment

The comics in newspapers, talk and political confrontation shows in broadcasting (CNN's *Crossfire*), and games and chat rooms on the Web are obviously there for

Media professionals keep up with their fields by reading professional journals and magazines, as this promotional photograph for PRWEEK suggests.

their entertainment value. But the entertainment value of other content is important, too, although that information may have other purposes. That other content includes sports reports, feature stories, brites (short, humorous features), advice columns, crossword puzzles, editorials and opinion pieces.

TYPES OF CONTENT

Few media professionals try to meet all of society's varied information needs. It would be quite difficult for a single professional to give an account of daily events, to monitor government, to supply information that is helpful in daily life, to provide continuing education *and* to entertain. A single medium, however, might undertake such a task (a newspaper, say, might employ many professionals to supply the sort of news and information society requires). Here are some of the kinds of content that professional communicators supply to meet society's needs.

Straight, or Spot, News

Straight news (sometimes called hard or spot news) is a report, absent the writer's opinion, of timely events and issues that are judged by journalists and public relations writers to be important or interesting. Straight news—typically reported in a print or broadcast news story, on the main page of a Web site or in a news release—usually takes as its starting point an event, a definite happening in time and space. Straight news reports convey as many relevant details as possible, within limitations of time and space.

The media typically rely heavily on straight news to give a daily account of what is happening in the world; straight news makes up most of the content of most news outlets, and it is an important foundation for decision making. Straight news can also be used to entertain or to provide news to use, but that is less common. Much of the content produced by the wire services (The Associated Press, Reuters) falls into the straight news category.

Investigative, or Precision, Writing

Investigative reporting, once known in journalism as muckraking, is an important vehicle for monitoring government and other public bodies.[19] It is similar to straight news reporting except that its practitioners go far more deeply into their topics, and they may use more sophisticated techniques (systematic computer studies of records, for example). One finds investigative professionals in all media and all occupational classifications.

Donald L. Barlett and James B. Steele, two of America's best-known investigative journalists, analyzed for *Sports Illustrated* the federal money lavished on Utah to support the 2002 Olympic Games. They found that $1.5 billion was spent and that no federal official or agency monitored the spending. Much of the cash went into the pockets of already-wealthy business leaders. The lead on the story suggests that investigative journalism does not have to be dull:

Is this a great country or what? A millionaire developer wants a road built, the federal government supplies the cash to construct it. A billionaire ski-resort owner covets a choice piece of public land. No problem. The federal government arranges for him to have it. Some millionaire businessmen stand to profit nicely if the local highway network is vastly improved. Of course. The federal government provides the money.

How can you get yours, you ask? Easy. Just help your hometown land the Olympics. Then, when no one's looking, persuade the federal government to pay for a good chunk of the Games, including virtually any project to which the magic word *Olympics* can be attached.[20]

Features

Features emphasize human interest and de-emphasize timeliness.[21] Typically, when a professional is told to do a feature story about a person, place, thing or idea, the article is being done because the subject is interesting and there is not a sense of urgency about completing the report for the next edition, news release, Web update or broadcast. Features are particularly important for public relations professionals, who use them to add interest to their internal and external newsletters and magazines and to their annual reports. The personality profile can be especially useful.

Timeliness is more important when one produces a news-feature, which gives feature treatment to some aspect of a current news event. During a long and newsworthy murder trial, an editor might assign a reporter to write a news-feature about the growing acceptance of DNA test results in American jurisprudence. The report could be aired almost any time during the trial. (See also the box "Janice Hui and Craig LaMay on Hard and Soft News.")

Opinion

Personal or *institutional opinion* is common in the mass media, and it typically is designed to help citizens participate in the democratic process or to monitor public, institutional behavior.[22] Public relations professionals are not called upon often to contribute opinion to democratic discussion and debate, although those who work for advocacy groups may well do that. Many communicators do express their views, however, and in a variety of formats.

News analyses give more than the who, what, when and where of news. They typically include background information and the professional's opinions, interpretations and predictions. So that it can be distinguished from straight news, news analysis usually is labeled or described as such. News analyses often are produced by "national correspondents" or "special correspondents" who have many years of experience.

Editorials express the official opinions of a newspaper, magazine, Web site, employee newsletter or broadcast outlet. In larger media, editorial boards decide (with guidance from the owners) what the medium's opinion is, and editorials usually are written or produced by the editorial board members, who specialize in that form of analysis and commentary. On smaller newspapers, reporters are sometimes encouraged to submit editorials, but that is not their primary job.

Most newspapers and broadcast outlets try to follow an old rule: Opinion appears only on the editorial page or in an editorial segment and never in news reports. Public relations writers seldom produce editorials, unless their advocacy organizations publish newsletters or magazines, so this seldom is an issue. Web practice is evolving, but those sites that want to disseminate credible news and information should consider keeping editorials and news separated.

Commentaries are not editorials, but they may look like editorials. They typically are published on a newspaper's op-ed (opposite-editorial) page, on a dedicated magazine page or Web link or near the end of a television or radio newscast. In many newspapers and some magazines, commentaries are contributed by people who think they have something to say. The *Houston Chronicle,* for example,

JANICE HUI AND CRAIG LAMAY ON HARD AND SOFT NEWS

In the effort to cut costs and attract audience, television has shifted away from hard news toward more entertainment-driven "soft" news. These are stories that have no clear connection to public affairs or policy issues and that are selected for their capacity to entertain rather than inform. The softening of news is especially pronounced in the morning news programs and prime-time news magazines, but has also become a major factor on the networks' signature evening newscasts. NBC revamped its "Nightly News with Tom Brokaw" in 1997 by trimming hard news and adding more lifestyle and soft features. It has been the dominant and most profitable newscast ever since.

"Soft news" has also become an important staple of local television newscasts. ... While soft news may grab people's attention initially, it may be hastening the overall decline in news audience. A recent survey by political scientist Thomas Patterson found that two-and-a-half times as many people said they prefer hard news to soft news, and those who prefer hard news are much heavier consumers of news. But the survey found that hard news consumers are not happy with the product they are getting, and as a result, are paying less attention to news than in the past. Patterson said this suggests that soft news may actually be diminishing the overall level of interest in news. ...[23]

Yet hard news strategies are not always successful. Two years ago Chicago's WBBM-TV experimented with a no-frills 10 o'clock newscast anchored by respected journalist Carol Marin. The goal was to offer viewers hard-hitting reports without sensationalism or fluff. While it was widely praised, the program was poorly rated. Among viewers between the ages of 25 and 54—a group coveted by advertisers—the show dropped from a 3.8 rating to a 1.8. WBBM pulled the plug on the experiment after eight months.[24]

Source: Janice Hui and Craig L. LaMay, "Broadcasting and the Public Interest," in Cynthia Gorney, *The Business of News: A Challenge for Journalism's Next Generation* (New York: Carnegie Corporation, 2002): 29–60, pp. 47–48.

Janice Hui is a research associate at the University of California at Berkeley, and Craig L. LaMay teaches in the Medill School of Journalism at Northwestern University.

publishes only 18 of the roughly 350–400 commentaries that are submitted every week. Television and broadcast stations more commonly *invite* commentary from interested citizens. Some of the commentaries are supplied by public relations writers (often under their bosses' bylines), particularly those who work for advocacy organizations or think tanks.

Columns are produced regularly by professionals who have designated space or time in a newspaper, magazine, employee newsletter, news broadcast or Web site. Columnists express their opinions about a wide variety of topics—from politics to wine stains to advice to the lovelorn.

Columns can be written or produced locally or they can be syndicated, in which case they are written somewhere else and then circulated nationally by a feature service. Columns can offer humor (Andy Rooney of CBS), report on local life and people (Eric Zorn and Dawn Turner Trice of the *Chicago Tribune*) or deal with some specialty such as finance (Scott Burns of the Universal Press Syndicate). The most popular topic for columns is politics and government. Columnists writing in this area span an ideological spectrum—from the politically conservative (Charles Krauthammer, a nationally syndicated columnist based in Washington, D.C.) to the moderate (E.J. Dionne Jr. of *The Washington Post*) to the liberal (Maureen Dowd of *The New York Times*).

SPECIALIZATION

Newspaper and magazine journalists discovered long ago the value of specialization in covering news and information; broadcast, Web and public relations writers learned the same lesson as their professions matured later. This specialization takes many forms.

Content

Entire publications, Web sites, public relations agencies and broadcast programs are devoted to only one kind of content. *Hispanic Business* and *Oregon Business* magazines, PBS's *Nightly Business Report* and *Bloomberg.com* all specialize in business news; *Arizona Highways* and *National Geographic Traveler* magazines specialize in travel; Bell Pottinger Public Affairs in the United Kingdom specializes in political and regulatory issues; and the Smart Choices Web site provides links for students needing information about drinking and alcohol abuse. Literally thousands of other publications, programs and Web sites are devoted to single topics.

Specialization also is common *within* media. Discrete sections often focus exclusively on specific kinds of news and information. Television news broadcasts typically are divided into news, sports and weather, for example. Major American daily newspapers and Web sites devote entire sections to sports, business, opinion, home and garden, local news, national and international news, real estate, travel, the arts, entertainment and lifestyles, as well as other topics. Individual pages are devoted often to science and health, obituaries, education and technology.

News Beats

Writers frequently are assigned to cover "news beats," or specialized content areas like education or science. Most news media and many public relations organizations divide groups, organizations, government agencies and other information sources into beats, although television newsrooms typically rely less heavily than newspapers on the beat structure.[25] Beats were invented by journalists in part to ensure that knowledgeable writers cover specialized news and to facilitate information collection.[26] Specialization can work well for public relations writers, too.

Journalism

Journalists debate beat structures, and some even argue that beats should be eliminated altogether; but most new reporters are likely to find themselves assigned to a beat and they have to know everything that happens on that beat.[27] (See also the box "Robert Brown on the Imperfection of Beats.") Some common beats are city, county and state government; science and health; education; the military; public safety; courts; business and finance; sports; entertainment; and weather (Appendix A). Some beats (affirmative action and minority rights, for example) slice across all other beats.

A writer who covers municipal government, for example, might have the local zoning commission on the beat and would know all members of the board, the public affairs officer, all the clerks and secretaries and the complex and confusing zoning laws. A writer who does not cover a zoning board regularly might well be lost during the first several meetings and might not recognize the problem when a zoning commission approves a variance allowing a biotechnology company to build a level-four containment facility in a residential area. That oversight would be quite serious.

A writer who covers a local university's physics department might have no difficulty translating into everyday English a speech by theoretical physicist Stephen Hawking, because the writer will have a formal science background or will have acquired a background through self-study. A newcomer to the beat might find the task daunting, if not impossible. The result might be a story that is embarrassingly bad.

A writer who covers problems and issues relating to the disabled might find he or she must cooperate with a municipal beat reporter. A city council, for example, might find that drivers who don't need to park in spots reserved for the disabled are using temporary permits to hog those spots long after any need has passed. The council might deliberate an ordinance that would increase the fine for parking illegally in spots for the disabled and tighten procedures for getting special parking permits.

In this case, two different reporters from two different beats would have useful experience and expertise, and they should work together to produce better stories.

Public Relations

Professionals who work in large agencies, companies or organizations sometimes are required to specialize. A writer in a large university, for example, might be assigned to cover news from the physics, engineering and biology departments.

ROBERT BROWN ON THE IMPERFECTION OF BEATS

Beats are popular in part because editors can assign specialists to write about the complex problems and issues that characterize most beats. Specialists are expected to have greater insight and knowledge, and to produce better stories than generalists. This is not always the case, however. Problems can also arise when an editor assigns a specialist in medical writing to cover a story about physics.

At a local academic institution, a public relations writer with a medical-reporting background ran into near disastrous problems trying to gain access to and to develop a relationship with a number of visiting astrophysicists. Despite the fact that the frazzled writer's aim was public relations-oriented coverage of the physicists for an internal publication, her e-mails to the scientists went unanswered, and there soon developed a toxic atmosphere of mutual distrust. A veteran medical reporter with high-profile clips in national publications, the frustrated publicist was utterly out of her depth in trying to cover the physicists' research, largely because of severely limited access to standoffish sources and the handcuffing effects of organizational politics.

These roadblocks of organizational behavior and communication play a crucial role in determining success or failure for publicists, reporters and their organizations. Access is not only a challenge for reporters; it can be a crisis for internal PR staff, particularly when editors and managers fail to provide strong, consistent political "cover" for them—leaving them to twist in the wind, to the embarrassment of the publication's staff top to bottom. Such failures damage the delicate relationship between publication staffers and their internal sources.

Source: Robert E. Brown, personal correspondence with the authors, Aug. 25, 2003.

Robert E. Brown is a professor in the communications department at Salem State College.

Another might be assigned to cover communication and journalism, English and history. Still another might be assigned to cover music and theater. Each would be expected to develop expertise in his or her respective area and to get to know students, faculty and staff in those areas.

Public relations professionals also need to understand they may be important contacts for journalists covering their organizations. They frequently are the first individuals contacted when journalists need information. They need to get to know the journalists well, to develop reputations for cooperation and reliability and to supply complete information in timely fashion. Professionals who do these things serve their organizations extremely well—and they make journalists very happy.

YOUR RESPONSIBILITY IS . . .

- To understand that news and information are not necessarily the same thing. You must, as a media professional, learn how to recognize what is news (and what is *not* news), or you cannot be a success.

- To learn the news values and, more important, know how to apply them in the real world. You must understand the importance of visual potential for broadcast and Web news and learn to recognize that potential.

- To learn how to identify the news peg and how to sift through the potential angles for each story and to identify the most effective approach each time.

- To recognize the various functions of news so that you can write to your audience and so that you can decide which aspect of communication truly interests you and which one you might be best at.

- To understand the different kinds of media content (editorials, straight news) and how they relate to each other, to audience preferences and to political, social, cultural and economic processes.

NOTES

1. John Aeilli, interview with Dan Rather, *Eklektikos*, KUT-FM, Austin, Texas, May 17, 2002.
2. Nat Hentoff, "Getting It Right: The Future of News," *Editor & Publisher*, May 6, 2002: 26.
3. Les Switzer, John McNamara and Michael Ryan, "Critical-cultural Studies in Research and Instruction," *Journalism & Mass Communication Educator*, 54:3 (1999): 23–42; and James Fallows, *Breaking the News: How the Media Undermine American Democracy* (New York: Vintage, 1996).
4. Switzer, McNamara and Ryan, "Critical-cultural Studies."
5. Fallows, *Breaking the News*; Robert W. McChesney, *Rich Media, Poor Democracy: Communication Politics in Dubious Times* (Urbana: University of Illinois Press, 1999).
6. Fallows, *Breaking the News*, p. 22.
7. James Poniewozik, "What You See Vs. What They See: The Arab Networks Are Not Without Bias, But They Often Fill in Missing Pictures From the War," *Time*, April 7, 2003: 68–69, p. 69.
8. Ellen Hale, "Arab Media Focus on Another Side of Conflict: News, Images Feed Animosity Toward War, United States," *USA Today*, March 31, 2003: A-10.
9. Ibid.

10. Definitions of news values used here are based on work described in L. Erwin Atwood, "How Newsmen and Readers Perceive Each Others' Story Preferences," *Journalism Quarterly,* 47:2 (1970): 296–302; Robert W. Clyde and James K. Buckalew, "Inter-media Standardization: A Q-analysis of News Editors," *Journalism Quarterly,* 46:2 (1969): 349–351; Lynne M. Sallot, Thomas M. Steinfatt and Michael B. Salwen, "Journalists' and Public Relations Practitioners' News Values: Perceptions and Cross-perceptions," *Journalism & Mass Communication Quarterly,* 75:2 (1998): 366–377; and Dennis M. Corrigan, "Value Coding Consensus in Front Page News Leads," *Journalism Quarterly,* 67:4 (1990): 653–662.

11. "Coverage of the Kennedy Crash: The Crisis of Celebrity Journalism: A Conversation Between Bob Steele and Roy Peter Clark," The Poynter Institute for Media Studies, July 1999. Downloaded on June 20, 2003, from <http://www.legacy.poynter.org/research/compcred/point/kennedy.htm>.

12. Jonathan Dube, "Writing News Online," in Jan Winburn (ed.), *Shop Talk & War Stories: American Journalists Examine Their Profession* (Boston: Bedford/St. Martin's, 2003): 201–205, p. 201.

13. Ibid., p. 205.

14. Corrigan, "Value Coding Consensus."

15. Werner J. Severin and James W. Tankard Jr., *Communication Theories: Origins, Methods, and Uses in the Mass Media,* 5th ed. (New York: Longman, 2001).

16. Adam Liptak, "A Court Backs Open Hearings on Deportation: Secrecy May Be Sought Case by Case, It Says," *The New York Times,* Aug. 27, 2002: A-1,12.

17. "Politics & Issues Watch: Keeping Tabs on the President's Environmental Moves," Sierra Club, May 14, 2003. Downloaded on Aug. 27, 2002, from <www.sierraclub.org/wwatch>.

18. The Drudge Report, from <www.drudgereport.com>.

19. David Spark, *Investigative Reporting: A Study in Technique* (Boston: Focal, 1999).

20. Donald L. Barlett and James B. Steele, "Snow Job: Thanks to Utah Politicians and the 2002 Olympics, a Blizzard of Federal Money—a Stunning $1.5 Billion—Has Fallen on the State, Enriching Some Already Wealthy Businessmen," *Sports Illustrated,* Dec. 10, 2001: 78–84, 87, 90–92, 94, 96, 98, p. 80.

21. Peter P. Jacobi, *The Magazine Article: How to Think It, Plan It, Write It* (Cincinnati, Ohio: Writer's Digest Books, 1991).

22. Conrad C. Fink, *Writing Opinion for Impact* (Ames: Iowa State University Press, 1999).

23. Thomas E. Patterson, "Doing Well and Doing Good: How Soft News and Critical Journalism Are Shrinking the News Audience and Weakening Democracy—And What News Outlets Can Do About It," report of The Joan Shorenstein Center on the Press, Politics and Public Policy, Harvard University, 2000. Available at <www.ksg.Harvard.edu/presspol/publications/pdfs/softnews.pdf>.

24. Robert Feder, "Channel 2 Lets the Ax Fall on Marin Newscast: Abysmal Ratings Signed Death Warrant," *Chicago Sun-Times,* Oct. 31, 2000: A-3.

25. Lee B. Becker, "Print or Broadcast: How the Medium Influences the Reporter," in James S. Ettema and D. Charles Whitney (eds.), *Individuals in Mass Media Organizations: Creativity and Constraint* (Beverly Hills, Calif.: Sage, 1982): 145–161; Dan Berkowitz, "Refining the Gatekeeper Metaphor for Local Television News," *Journal of Broadcasting & Electronic Media,* 34:1 (1990): 55–68; and David H. Weaver and G. Cleveland Wilhoit, *The American Journalist in the 1990s: U.S. News People at the End of an Era* (Mahwah, N.J.: Erlbaum, 1996).

26. Lee Becker, Wilson Lowrey, Dane Claussen and William Anderson, "Why Does the Beat Go On? An Examination of the Role of Beat Structure in the Newsroom," *Newspaper Research Journal,* 21:4 (2000): 2–16.

27. Ibid.

CHAPTER 3

ACCURACY

To Err Is Awful

Good editors are intolerant of errors in news disseminated by their organizations, and they are more than happy to chew on writers who make mistakes. They demand that each writer be committed absolutely to accuracy: "Anything less and you're a sloppy, lazy reporter who stains the reputation of your profession."[1] Editors who have a choice between a writer who can produce sparkling, but inaccurate, prose and one who can produce accurate, but merely competent, prose will opt for accuracy every time. The world of journalism was shocked in the spring of 2003 when it was revealed that Jayson Blair, a reporter for *The New York Times,* had fabricated portions of dozens of articles. There can be no greater sin against accuracy than the making up of facts.

A MEDIA SCOURGE

Errors are a scourge in part because they are out there for everyone to see. A few members of every audience delight in pouncing on errors and making sure the entire world knows about them. Professionals who work for broadcast or the Web are marginally better off than their colleagues who write for magazines, newsletters and newspapers. They typically don't have to process nearly as much information, and their errors disappear quickly into cyberspace—assuming the Web site is updated frequently. Readers and viewers who don't catch the error the first time are unlikely to get a second chance. Those who write for print know their errors may be copied, passed around and discussed in electronic mail messages, telephone conversations and, worst of all, letters to editors.

Consequences of Error

Many errors are fairly innocuous, though none is unimportant. *Newsweek* magazine, for example, had to correct a story about women who are presidents of major universities. Donna Shalala, Health and Human Services secretary in the Clinton administration, was identified as the president of Miami University, which is in Oxford, Ohio. In fact, she is president of the University of Miami, which is in Florida.[2]

Some errors are more serious, such as CNN's inaccurate report that hoof-and-mouth disease—which can decimate a herd of hoofed animals (cattle, goats or sheep) and destroy an entire industry—was reported or suspected in New Zealand and Australia.[3]

Other errors can have more widespread consequences. *The New York Times,* for example, reported in a Page One article that individuals can risk exposure to the West Nile virus through organ transplant or blood transfusions. *The Times'* failure to report that blood donors do not risk exposure if equipment is sterile could have had a serious impact on blood donations.[4]

Writers and editors suffer mightily when they make errors of any magnitude, but they can suffer more than hurt feelings. Most audiences are forgiving and understand that humans make mistakes. But if errors are chronic, an organization's credibility suffers. That is a very serious proposition, since credibility is an organization's most important asset in news dissemination.[5] It is exceptionally difficult to regain lost credibility. Accompanying the loss of credibility is a loss of audience, advertisers, influence and prestige.

Public relations professionals who consistently make errors in news releases also find their information has little value: Nobody believes what they say and their releases are not published, posted or broadcast. The lost credibility is hard to recover (see the box "*O'Dwyer's* on Public Relations' Low Credibility Mark").

Another concern is that a medium can be sued for libel because of an error. Consider the case of a television news report that describes an accident in which a gasoline truck, traveling in the wrong lane, collides with a moving van on the freeway, igniting the gasoline in a fire that burns six hours. A reporter broadcasting live from the scene might make this erroneous statement: "The driver of the moving van was traveling south in the wrong lane."

Such an error is serious because the story assigns fault in an accident before a court determines who is to blame and before charges are even filed. The assignment of blame is worse here because the broadcast reporter has the wrong truck traveling in the wrong lane. The broadcast journalist might get lucky and dodge a libel suit, as some do every single day, but a journalist shouldn't rely on good luck.

Public relations professionals can be sued for libel, just as journalists can, but they run another risk. A writer who reports inaccurate information that causes the value of a stock to double within hours is likely to be in trouble with the Securities and Exchange Commission, which has strict laws about what can and cannot be released (Chapter 13).

O'DWYER'S ON PUBLIC RELATIONS' LOW CREDIBILITY MARK

The public believes PR pros are slightly more credible than either celebrities or TV/radio talk show hosts. That's the only bit of good news for PR people in PRSA Foundation's credibility survey. An impeached President Clinton scores a higher ranking than PR. PR pros tell us the low ranking is because the public is unaware of what they do. They describe their role in a Machiavellian fashion. We operate "behind-the-scenes," they say. That, however, is the problem. PR should be done in the open. The "profession" should stand for sunshine, not darkness. How can PR attract the best and the brightest, if the public holds it in such low regard?

Source: "PR Deserves Its Low Credibility Marks," editorial, *O'Dwyer's PR Services Report,* August 1999: 6. The credibility survey referenced is in the same issue: "PR Pros Are Among Least Believable Public Figures," *O'Dwyer's PR Services Report,* August 1999: 1, 24.

Avoiding Error

Writers and editors are preoccupied with accuracy because accurate information is a valuable commodity, as novelist Michael Crichton explains: "But what if somebody offered me a service ... in which all the facts were true, the quotes weren't piped, the statistics were presented by someone who knew something about statistics? What would that be worth? A lot. Because good information has value. The notion that it's filler between ads is outdated."[6]

Organizations that are in the information business try very hard to eliminate inaccuracy. Public relations writers and journalists are expected to submit error-free copy (see the upcoming section, "Self-editing" and Chapter 4). Those who make too many errors ultimately are fired. A main function of editors in all media organizations is to ensure that copy is accurate, and all organizations maintain libraries of useful reference materials (Chapter 9).

Reputable magazines spend considerable money on research departments that check every single fact in every single bit of copy. *Forbes* magazine, for instance, employs four research librarians to help editors and writers in all of its departments check for accuracy. A key part of the process, of course, is selecting reliable reference sources. The research staff meets each week to decide how (and whether) to use each new reference work purchased. *Forbes* rarely uses other magazines, Web sources or newspapers to verify information, for they are not considered accurate enough.[7]

Correcting Error

For all this, errors slip through, and most media outlets correct mistakes scrupulously. Most publications and Web sites have a section in which corrections are

One of the great errors in journalism history was the Chicago Daily Tribune's *Page One declaration that Thomas E. Dewey defeated Harry Truman in the 1948 election.*

posted or published as necessary. Broadcasters correct their errors on the air or on their organization's Web site. The corrections typically include an apology for the error and, sometimes, a brief explanation of how the mistake happened.

The Washington Post, MSNBC.com, *The New York Times* and other media employ professionals to hear and to evaluate complaints. *The Post* calls its professional an ombudsman (the post is held now by a man), and *The Times* calls its representative a public editor. Other media call their professionals audience (reader, viewer, listener) advocates or representatives. By whatever name, audience representatives attempt to do the following:

- Provide a mechanism whereby reader complaints can be investigated and evaluated by a knowledgeable professional
- Allow the medium to correct the record when it publishes an inaccurate story
- Provide editors and writers with useful criticism that can help improve the editorial process
- Constitute an effective public relations tool for an organization, which can demonstrate daily its dedication to accuracy and fairness—and also have a platform from which to explain its position when a complaint is unjustified

The sort of thoughtful self-criticism that can lead to better writing is provided by Michael Getler, *The Washington Post*'s ombudsman. *The Post* received several complaints in early 2002 about its coverage of the Palestinian suicide bombings against Israeli citizens. Getler analyzed *The Post*'s coverage and discussed specific stories in some detail. He concluded, in part:

> The Post has done a good job of reporting these bombings, but it has done less well in capturing the impact of these attacks on Israeli families and society. At the same time, The Post has reported powerful stories about Palestinian suffering from the Israeli offensives taken in response to these and other attacks, and this sharpens the contrast with the lesser focus on the effect of such bombings on Israel's Jewish citizens.[8]

Some readers had complained that *The Post* inadequately reported the reason why the Israeli military intercepted Palestinian ambulances—a highly controversial action—as they transported wounded civilians. The newspaper should have been more forceful in reporting that Palestinian terrorists had moved explosives by ambulance, they said. Getler did not find support for the complaint, and he tried to show how difficult it is to report about that terrible conflict.

Media professionals are right to be preoccupied with errors, for they occur too frequently. Most organizations correct some errors each day. Systematic studies of news have shown that many news sources perceive inaccuracies in stories citing them. Studies of perceived errors in newspapers, television and newsmagazines have shown, for example, that approximately half contain substantive (more than typographical) errors.[9] The number of perceived errors is greater when the reporting is about social, scientific or technical issues.[10]

Errors can be broken down into two general types: objective, or errors of verifiable fact, and subjective, or errors of interpretation or meaning.[11]

OBJECTIVE ERRORS

Objective errors should be the easiest to avoid, for they are misstatements of fact. Writers should be able to avoid spelling, numerical and typographical errors by carefully verifying all facts before they submit their work to editors. Here are two examples of objective errors:

- A *Good Morning America* report about an executive order to freeze the assets of organizations suspected of having terrorist ties said some charities in the United States were accused of sending money to Osama bin Laden. It mentioned the Holy Land Foundation for Relief and Development, the Islamic Relief Agency, the Global Relief Foundation and the Al Kifah Refugee Center. ABC News reported later that the organizations had not been accused and that the Holy Land Foundation for Relief and Development is an Islamic group based in Richmond, Texas.[12] Incredibly, the correction itself was wrong. The foundation is based in Richardson, not Richmond.

■ *Newsweek,* in a story about the 2002 Olympic ice-skating scandal, identified World Wrestling Federation star Triple H as Triple X. The reference was a sarcastic barb that had nothing to do with the story.[13]

Sources of objective error are many, and writers must be exceptionally careful, for they can introduce inaccuracy or distortion in dealing carelessly with biased sources, in using loaded words and in dealing with hoaxes.

Source Error

Sources typically are highly involved in issues or events, and they usually want a story written in the most favorable manner possible. The CEO whose company accidentally dumped thousands of barrels of crude oil into the local lake would prefer to see media attention focused on the company's efforts to remove the crude oil and to save the wildlife and not on the environmental impact of the mistake. The CEO (against the advice, one would hope, of the company public relations officer) might mention that 200 white egrets were saved by volunteers, but neglect to mention that 400 died and 200 others were endangered.

Writers sometimes accept an official source's analysis of a situation and ignore the views of those who see things differently. Writers give these sources too much weight, in part because official sources typically are available and willing to comment. It is too often true that "Reporters do not seek independent confirmation or use a critical method to test the statements issued by officials. ... There is no real attempt to balance the official version against the contextual evidence."[14]

A 2001 study of the nightly news by Media Tenor tried to determine what percentages of stories cited nonwhite sources. Race could not always be established, but the German firm found that 92 percent of the sources were white and 7 percent were black. Only 0.6 percent were Arab-Americans; 0.6 percent were Hispanic; and 0.2 percent were Asian-Americans. Only one Native American was cited.[15]

That official sources can mislead is suggested by President Bush's effort in 2002 to rally support for the invasion of Iraq. During a meeting with British Prime Minister Tony Blair, the two cited a 1998 report by the International Atomic Energy Agency, which is affiliated with the United Nations, that supposedly said Saddam Hussein could have nuclear weapons within six months. "I don't know what more evidence we need," Bush said. "We owe it to future generations to deal with this problem."

But the IAEA report did not say Iraq could have a nuclear capability *within six months of September 2002,* as Bush suggested. It said Iraq could have had a nuclear capability *within six months to two years at the time of the Persian Gulf War in 1991.* Iraq lost its enriched uranium and plutonium, required for a nuclear device, and its nuclear infrastructure following that war. In fact, the IAEA said it had found *no* evidence that Iraq had the capacity to develop a nuclear weapon.[16]

Some writers gave special weight to Mr. Bush's views, but some rejected the lazy approach—in which they might simply have reported Bush's statements. They checked the accuracy of Bush's interpretation of the IAEA report and found it misleading.[17] The White House acknowledged the report was misrepresented.

CHARLES SHEEHAN ON SPELL-CHECK

How might you drag a good writer's work down to the level of a lesser scribe? Try the spell-check button.

A study at the University of Pittsburgh indicates spell-check software may level the playing field between people with differing levels of language skills, hampering the work of writers and editors who place too much trust in the software.

In the study, 33 undergraduate students were asked to proofread a one-page business letter— half of them using Microsoft Word with its squiggly red and green lines underlining potential errors.

The other half did it the old-fashioned way, using only their heads.

Without grammar or spelling software, students with higher SAT verbal scores made, on average, five errors, compared with 12.3 errors for students with lower scores.

Using the software, students with higher verbal scores reading the same page made, on average, 16 errors, compared with 17 errors for students with lower scores.

Dennis Galletta, a professor of information systems at the Katz Business School, said spell-checking software is so sophisticated that some have come to trust it too thoroughly.

"It's not a software problem, it's a behavior problem," he said.

Microsoft technical specialist Tim Pash said grammar and spelling technology is meant to help writers and editors, not solve all their problems.

The study found the software helped students find and correct errors in the letter, but in some cases they also changed phrases or sentences flagged by the software as grammatically suspicious, even though they were correct.

For instance, the letter included a passage that said, "Michael Bales would be the best candidate. Bales has proven himself in similar rolls."

The software—picking up on the last "s" in "Bales"—suggested changing the verb from "has" to "have," as if it were a plural. Meanwhile, the spell-check ignored "rolls," which should have been "roles."

Richard Stern, a computer and electrical engineer at Carnegie Mellon University specializing in speech-recognition technology, said grammar and spelling software will never approach the complexity of the human mind.

"Computers can decide the likelihood of correct speech, but it's a percentage game," he said.

Source: Charles Sheehan, "Spellcheck Dumbs Down Good Writers," The Associated Press, March 20, 2003. Reprinted with permission of The Associated Press.

Charles Sheehan is a writer for The Associated Press.

A writer can produce an accurate report even when a source provides biased or inaccurate information by verifying important facts, statements and opinions with other sources; making a source personally responsible for all statements through careful attribution; and thoroughly identifying all important sources (Chapter 7).

Loaded Words

Loaded or emotion-charged words typically are used for one of three reasons: (1) they permit a lazy or uncreative writer to add an element of excitement to a lead paragraph or a report without much effort; (2) they allow a writer to interject bias into a report in a subtle manner that may not be noticed by a careless editor; and (3) their potential to distort is not recognized.

Said is a simple and direct word of attribution that should in no way influence the perceptions of a reader, nor indicate a writer's position relative to problems and issues described. *Said* should be used in a story about Mayor Shirley Roselle's decision to ask for a 10 percent increase in the city wage tax before the end of her term. Here is one possible neutral approach:

> Mayor Shirley Roselle said today that she will seek a 10 percent increase in the city wage tax beginning in January. The mayor said last year that taxes would not be raised during her administration.

Another report of the mayor's position might state:

> Mayor Shirley Roselle today broke her campaign promise not to raise taxes when she announced that she will ask for a 10 percent increase in the city wage tax beginning in January.

The phrase *broke her promise* is charged with emotion and indicates clearly the writer's feelings about the mayor's position. The proposed tax increase might also be described this way:

> Mayor Shirley Roselle today changed her mind about raising city taxes and announced that she will seek a 10 percent increase in the city wage tax beginning in January.

Changed her mind is less emotion-charged than *broke her promise*, but it is a loaded phrase, nevertheless. *Contended, denied, charged, asserted, boasted, quipped* and similar words all are loaded, and all can be used to give a distorted picture of a source's words or statements.

Writers also must guard against using loaded words in other contexts. Adverbs such as *only* and *regularly* and verbs such as *struggled* (rather than tried) or *controlled* (rather than coordinated) must be used with great care, for they can be used to inject inaccuracy or bias. Consider these sentences:

- The school district reduced property taxes only 1.5 percent.
- Safety expert Robert Douglas controlled the recovery effort.

MICHAEL SHERMER ON ANALOGIES AND EMOTIVE WORDS

Emotive words are used to provoke emotion and sometimes to obscure rationality. They can be positive emotive words—*motherhood, America, integrity, honesty.* Or they can be negative—*rape, cancer, evil, communist.* Likewise, metaphors and analogies can cloud thinking with emotion or steer us onto a side path. A pundit talks about inflation as "the cancer of society" or industry "raping the environment." In his 1992 Democratic nomination speech, Al Gore constructed an elaborate analogy between the story of his sick son and America as a sick country. Just as his son, hovering on the brink of death, was nursed back to health by his father and family, America, hovering on the brink of death after twelve years of Reagan and Bush, was to be nurtured back to health under the new administration. Like anecdotes, analogies and metaphors do not constitute proof. They are merely tools of rhetoric.

Source: Michael Shermer, *Why People Believe Weird Things: Pseudo-science, Superstition, and Other Confusions of Our Time* (New York: MJF, 1997): 55.

Michael Shermer publishes *Skeptic* magazine and directs the Skeptics Society.

The first sentence implies inappropriately that the district's tax reduction was too small. The second suggests that Douglas was heavy-handed in coordinating the recovery effort. An unbiased (or more professional) writer would have dropped *only* and changed *controlled* to *directed* or *coordinated.* (See also the box "Michael Shermer on Analogies and Emotive Words.")

Hoaxes

Professional hoaxer Alan Abel has been fooling the news media for more than three decades. Yes, he tries to get writers to report his goofy—but seemingly plausible— activities. He runs an organization called Citizens Against Breast-feeding, which protested at the 2000 Republican National Convention and which has its own Web site at <www.banbreastfeeding.org>. In late August 2002 Abel did four radio interviews about the dangers of breast-feeding. Although exposed as a hoax, Abel says he still gets requests for interviews.[18]

Binjamin Wilkomirski described in his book, *Fragments,* his life in Hitler's concentration camps and in an orphanage in Krakow, Poland. Even Holocaust survivors were impressed by the way Wilkomirski captured the Holocaust experience in his 1995 book. Swiss journalist Daniel Ganzfried discovered several years later

Benjamin Wilkomirski's story of his experience in Nazi concentration camps was an award winner. But it was all a hoax and his book, Fragments, *was discredited.*

that Wilkomirski was, in fact, Bruno Doessekker, a musician and instrument maker who never was in a concentration camp. The book was denounced as a fraud and was recalled.[19]

The professional hoaxer is rare, but writers must be on guard nevertheless, for some individuals think it is great fun to trick the media.

SUBJECTIVE ERRORS

Subjective errors are more difficult to nail down because an *error* to one observer may not be an *error* to another. Some critics claim a writer has made an error when a story is perceived as too short or too long; a source allegedly is quoted out of context; definitions or explanations supposedly are incorrect or omitted; or some aspects of the report seemingly are overemphasized or underemphasized. In each instance, the error is in the eye of the beholder. That does not mean the critic is wrong, just that he or she is not *necessarily* right.[20]

One example is a report by *Media Reality Check*, which is prepared weekly by the conservative Media Research Center to document alleged distortions in the news media. MRC charged that ABC's *World News Tonight* presented a one-sided view of the debate about a possible war with Iraq. "Rather than showing both sides, ABC's 'Road to War?' series has stressed claims [that a] U.S. military effort would have damaging consequences, but has not explored the costs of U.S. inaction or the benefits of ousting Saddam." MRC said that "All of these anti-war arguments are news, of course, but an unbiased series would have also focused its investigative efforts on Saddam's murderous history and the danger he still poses. It's called balanced reporting."[21]

The MRC complaints were matters of opinion, which made them neither valid nor invalid, and those holding different views might argue that ABC's coverage was balanced. The difficulty for ABC and other media outlets is that it is nearly impossible to defend against charges that subjective errors were made, for there is no standard that everyone will accept. ABC's position was made more difficult because the Bush administration had not as of September 2002 provided the evidence that Hussein was a threat. MRC demanded that ABC report evidence that it did not have, evidence that could come only from government sources.

Some individuals charge that reports are distorted simply to protect their own interests. These sources want to protect themselves or to advance their own social, cultural, economic, ideological or political agendas. A policewoman named in a story as having abused a citizen, for instance, might attempt to take the pressure off herself by charging that a story was distorted because it began with a description of the crime. Individuals who advocate war with Iraq might charge media coverage is distorted simply to influence the media to slant reports to reflect the critics' views.

Subjective errors can distort a report by leaving a false or misleading impression, but few media professionals intentionally mislead or lie—if only because they are likely to get caught and because their editors will not allow it. Distortions typically occur because writers hype reports to get more space or time or better positions relative to other reports; sensationalize to attract larger audience shares; or just make mistakes. These behaviors are unprofessional, but they do not constitute bias.

Subjective error can creep in at many points in the writing process. Problems can arise as editors decide which stories to cover, which to ignore and which to give favored treatment (some lead a newscast and some don't). Writers are sometimes criticized for how they select and order details.

Selecting, Playing Content

Communication professionals are criticized almost daily for the reports they choose to cover and those they choose to ignore. A medium that fails to cover a campaign speech, a garden club meeting, a crime or disaster, a rent strike or demonstration or any of a hundred other events might be accused of bias. A public relations writer who does not issue a news release detailing a company's financial status might be charged with a cover-up. A medium or professional who does report the events or information might also be accused of bias—but by different groups. Broadcast journalists are particularly vulnerable to charges that they are biased because they have so little time for news and must omit so much.

Because time and space are limited, an editor must decide carefully what information will and will not be disseminated. Society can suffer greatly when journalists or public relations professionals consistently give important stories no play while focusing on inconsequential stories.

The news media were agog when Newt Gingrich, Republican majority leader of the House, and President Bill Clinton announced a $1 billion "Say-No-To-Drugs" advertising campaign. The mainstream media were paid millions to develop articles and advertisements that convinced Americans to *say no* to drugs. The media increased their wealth at taxpayer expense, but an investigation by journalist Michael Levine showed that nobody—including the Partnership for a Drug Free America, under whose auspices the program was run—had done research to determine whether such a campaign would be effective.

"In fact, according to psychological studies conducted by neuro-linguistic experts, a growing body of evidence indicated that the ads weren't just ineffective, they actually increased drug use."[22] The media did not serve society well by failing to select and disseminate this news.

Error also can be introduced by the way a story is played. An editor who likes Mayor Susan Moore better than her opponent in the next election might put Moore stories (under four-column, two-line headlines in 42-point type) on Page One and the opponent's stories (under two-column, one-line headlines in 24-point type) on Page 17.

Selecting, Ordering Details

Writers can distort their reports as they decide which details to emphasize and which to omit. A report on a corporate Web site about an oil spill that kills hundreds of egrets could reflect an effort by a public relations writer to put the best face on the bad news. A writer could emphasize the cleanup effort (below, left) rather than the costs of the spill (below, right):

EnvirAmerica has organized dozens of volunteers from local Boy Scout troops, churches and environmental groups to help rescue hundreds of egrets injured when the company accidentally emptied crude oil into Lake Placid. CEO Sam Gantry has announced that cleanup efforts have already begun and that all oil should be out of the lake soon.	Hundreds of egrets died when EnvirAmerica accidentally dumped 2,500 gallons of crude oil into Lake Placid over the weekend, and more are dying. Dozens of volunteers have organized to save as many birds as they can, EnvirAmerica CEO Sam Gantry has announced.

The superintendent of a local school district also has a vested interest in convincing the public that schools are safe. Consider the first few paragraphs of two accounts of opening day at a troubled, urban school district:

It was a calm day Monday in Atlanta schools, with 81 percent of students attending first-day classes, school officials said.	Two Pasadena Park High School students were arrested in separate incidents Monday during the first day of classes in Atlanta's school system, school officials said.

No major incidents were reported, although two Pasadena Park High School students were arrested in the morning. A 16-year-old female student was arrested for disrupting a school assembly, and a 17-year-old male was arrested for marijuana possession.
 	
    Forty-one students—a "relatively normal number"—from all schools were suspended for infractions ranging from smoking in school to disruptive classroom behavior, Superintendent Pat Smith said.
	A 16-year-old female student was arrested for disrupting a school assembly, and a 17-year-old male was arrested for marijuana possession.
	
	    Forty-one students from all schools were suspended for infractions ranging from smoking in school to disruptive classroom behavior, Superintendent Pat Smith said.
	
	    Eighty-one percent of students attended classes.

The two versions give different impressions of opening day because of the way details are organized. The version on the right omits the statement by school officials that the 41 suspensions reflected a "relatively normal" day, while the version on the left reports that statement. The selection of details and the ways in which those details are ordered obviously can determine how a report is received.

CONSCIOUS SLANTING

Writers who deliberately slant their stories are biased, and that is the worst sin professionals can commit. But media professionals seldom slant their reports intentionally. Good writers, in fact, try to analyze their own personal preferences, attitudes and values and ensure that those views do not influence what they produce (Chapter 1). To do otherwise is unprofessional, but there are other reasons to avoid deliberate slanting:

- A media outlet, or public relations department or agency, that seeks to serve a general audience will lose its credibility if it consistently disseminates biased reports. It will soon find that its audience has diminished to the point where the organization is left only with individuals who agree with its slant.

    Some specialized media outlets need not worry about slanting their reports, for slanting is accepted—or even demanded—by their audiences. Indeed, such organizations argue their reports are true *because* they are biased, and their audiences accept such assurances. Conservative talk show host Rush Limbaugh, for example, makes no pretense to fairness or objectivity, and yet millions listen to his program. Heather MacDonald wrote for the *National Review Online* a commentary charging that news media are prejudiced against police officers and that the resulting coverage endangers their lives. She demonstrated her own bias as she tried to document media bias.[23] This kind of bias is demanded by some audiences. Some media would lose their audiences and advertisers if

A CASE OF CONSCIOUS SLANTING

President George H.W. Bush's nomination of Clarence Thomas to the U.S. Supreme Court unleashed a debate that continues to this day. Liberals saw Thomas as a mediocre judge who was soft on civil rights and who did not deserve a seat on the nation's highest court. Conservatives viewed Thomas as a strict constructionist who would help reverse *Roe v. Wade* and other "liberal" rulings in the past.

Into the maelstrom stepped Anita Hill, who charged during the Senate confirmation hearings that Thomas had sexually harassed her when he was her boss at the Equal Employment Opportunity Commission. Thomas was confirmed, but his supporters, to ensure Thomas' legitimacy as a Supreme Court justice, continued to discredit Hill long after the Senate hearings.

David Brock, a partisan conservative writer, wrote *The Real Anita Hill* as part of the campaign to discredit Hill. Conservatives who knew Thomas assured Brock that Thomas had not asked Hill for dates, had not made questionable remarks and had not read and viewed pornography, all of which had been charged. "Already conditioned to think the best of Thomas and the worst of Hill, I did nothing to test these sources or question their motives. ... My incompetence was compounded by an uninformed bias, by the grip of a partisan tunnel vision that was by now such a part of my nature that it distorted my work, disabling me from finding the truth, without my even knowing it."[24] Brock later admitted that his case against Anita Hill was not only wrong and false, but "almost precisely opposite of the truth."[25]

The Real Anita Hill was reviewed favorably by *The New York Times* and other publications; was on best-seller lists for months; and was a finalist for the *Los Angeles Times'* book prize. Brock suggests the book was well received because it *looked* like good investigative journalism and because "The argument I made was logically sound, and it seemed to fit the available evidence to those who had not studied it or reported on the case themselves."[26]

they failed to meet these expectations and desires. These specialized media are not the focus of this book, however.

■ Good writers understand they serve society best when they use an objective approach (Chapter 1). If a public relations, Web or journalism writer's interpretations about an issue are sound, the information upon which those interpretations are based should sway an intelligent (or even a not-so-intelligent) viewer, listener or reader. If the audience is not swayed by a fair and accurate presentation, the writer's interpretations may be faulty. It certainly does not serve society well to impose those interpretations on an audience when they are not supported by the facts. (See the box "A Case of Conscious Slanting.")

■ A writer who thinks an audience needs help in understanding a complex issue can ask that an editorial be written, suggest additional reports or recommend the preparation of a story or series labeled *news analysis* or *news interpretation,* in which more—though not unlimited—freedom to interpret the facts often is allowed. A public relations professional can seek additional information from organizational experts.

SELF-EDITING

The only sure way for writers to avoid error is to edit carefully and critically everything they produce—from grocery lists to electronic mail messages to term papers to news reports to books to video scripts. They make sure their work is complete, verify every fact, make no assumptions, attribute carefully, consult published documents, leave out doubtful information and verify the accuracy of every comma, every spelling and every fact.

This is not easy for all students. It's difficult to know when sources are making judgments when writers don't know what a judgment is (Chapter 7). It's hard to know whether a libel case is from a court of original jurisdiction or from an appellate court if writers don't know what those courts do. And it's hard to ensure that nouns agree with their antecedent pronouns when writers don't know what a noun is (Appendix B). It's even difficult for some students to be skeptical about what they hear in class because they have not developed the critical thinking skills that 21st-century communicators must have.

What do students do if they don't have broad knowledge or critical thinking skills? If they slept through high school, they have some catching up to do. If they don't sleep through their college classes and if they read and understand this book, they will have a sound foundation on which to build effective self-editing skills.

Completeness

Communication professionals must try always to ensure that their reports are complete, that all relevant questions are adequately answered and that all relevant sources have been contacted. A report about standardized tests in public schools is not complete if a journalist, for example, has not talked to classroom teachers. A report about intercollegiate football is not complete if a writer has not consulted the report of the Knight Foundation Commission on Intercollegiate Athletics.[27]

It is not always easy to ensure that reports are complete. Most communication professionals work under deadline pressures, some of which are extreme and generate considerable stress. For journalists dealing with fast-breaking news, there may be no time to ask all the questions, or even to think of all the questions. Public relations professionals work under the same constraints when their companies are faced with sudden, catastrophic events, such as a factory explosion. The public wants answers, and there is not always time to get a complete picture.

It's hard to produce a complete report also when information sources—or, in the case of public relations, corporate managers—refuse to supply the information a professional needs to understand an issue or event.

Media writers must do the best they can within these constraints: They must try to understand what has happened, to determine who is involved and who is affected and to produce a report that is reasonably complete under the circumstances. A writer who is dedicated to getting all the information will succeed more often than one who is not. Techniques for getting complete information are discussed in later chapters.

Inclusion

A good writer makes sure all voices are heard in every story. The marginalized and the disenfranchised, however, are sometimes not heard. A good self-editor would do well to consider these guidelines—based on the work of Marie Hardin, Ann Preston, Valerie Hyman and others—as he or she checks to be sure nobody is left out.[28]

- Make sure that the marginalized (gays, the disabled, ethnic minorities, the homeless) are represented in most stories. This does not apply *just* to "disabled" stories, for example, but to *all* stories. Voices of the marginalized deserve to be heard on a variety of topics, just as all other voices deserve to be heard. When government officials debate extending health benefits to the partners of gay and lesbian employees, the views of gays and lesbians must be reported.

- Consult with advocacy groups, foundations, government agencies and media for the marginalized to find out their views about issues affecting their clients and constituents. (See the box "Diversity and the Rainbow Sourcebook.") These groups typically are able to recommend knowledgeable, articulate sources and to help writers uncover information they might not find on their own. County employees who run health centers for the poor often are excellent sources of information about the impact of budget cuts on their clients, for instance, and they can recommend clients who are articulate and willing to speak out.

- Try to see the world through the eyes of the marginalized. One may have no idea what it's like to be a paraplegic or homeless, but one can talk to the homeless and the disabled to find out how they see the world and how they think the world sees them. One writes better when one sees the world through the eyes of sources—whether a city mayor or a vagrant. A writer can produce a much better story about the impact of budget cuts on the poor if he or she will spend many hours, or even days, talking to and observing those immediately affected.

- Try to see the homeless and the disabled through the world's eyes and to understand how professional communicators contribute to the world's view. "When journalists focus on how someone deviates from the norm and when

DIVERSITY AND THE RAINBOW SOURCEBOOK

The Rainbow Sourcebook, a national database created and maintained by the Society of Professional Journalists, helps media professionals locate sources whose views are not always sought by mainstream writers. Most of the sources are women, gays, lesbians, people of color and people with disabilities. The database can be searched using news topics. To begin, go to <www.spj.org/rainbowsourcebook>.

The Sourcebook's "Diversity Toolbox" is particularly useful, as it provides links to frequently ignored sources who can help a writer broaden his or her perspective. The essays about diversity and the links to other resources make it easier to ensure diversity in news and information.

Areas of expertise include affirmative action, aging, biotechnology, civil rights, crime, disability issues, domestic violence, gay and lesbian issues, hate crimes, immigration, law, native rights, poverty, prison, public health, race and technology. The Diversity Toolbox is available at <www.spj.org/diversity_toolbox.asp>.

Undocumented immigrants frequently are the subjects of stories about the disenfranchised. Here they hide in Las Piedras because Border Patrol agents don't want to enter the contaminated waters.

they 'pull on heart strings' to add drama to content, they may send a message of pity and tragedy to their audience," Beth Haller writes.[29]

The Pulitzer Prize–winning feature story of 2001 chronicled the decision of Sam Lightner, a teenager with a severe facial deformity, to have surgery.[30] Haller suggests that some stories might focus on the reasons why Sam Lightner thought he should have surgery. "To me, this problem that society has with difference in appearance, not Sam's face, should be the focus of a prize-winning series."[31]

Verification

The most common way to ensure accuracy is to verify every fact. Most news media did not do this before reporting statements by President Bush and Prime Minister Blair about the report of the International Atomic Energy Agency. They should have.

In its purest form, the principle of verification requires that every element of a story be checked. Information is not always verified because media writers are sometimes under extreme deadline pressure and because, incredibly, some don't think it's important. Dennis Dible, *Beaver County* (Pennsylvania) *Times* editor, is quoted as saying, "Rampant in this industry is the expectation that other people will pick up your mistakes. ... As they enter the newsroom for the first time, reporters go through what I call a lobotomy arch and forget everything they promised to do. They say they won't take the attitude of 'I'm a reporter and I won't look up names in the phone book.' But three months after they're here, that attitude is pervasive."[32]

Those writers who verify everything frequently use the two-source rule, popularized by Bob Woodward and Carl Bernstein of *The Washington Post* as they investigated the Watergate scandal.[33] The two-source rule requires that any allegation be confirmed by two independent sources before it is disseminated. If they are government sources, for example, both cannot work for the FBI.

Writers also can check facts quickly on the Web. One who needs to verify that Triple H really is Triple H can find out in moments by visiting <www.wwe.com>. One who needs to know which university Donna Shalala heads can find out through a Google search. And one who wants to determine whether President Bush summarized the International Atomic Energy Agency report accurately can find out at <www.iaea.org>.

General reference books, telephone books, city directories, maps and state handbooks—many of which are available on the Web—can be used to verify facts. Writers should develop the habit of using reference books to verify facts, spellings and dates (Chapter 9, Appendix G). They are important allies in the war against inaccuracy.

Writers also need to check all numbers. They must know how the numbers were generated (whether poll results are based on random samples, for example) and whether numerical analogies make sense, percentages are computed accurately and decimal points are in the right places. Professionals can't argue they are writers and not statisticians; they have got to verify that every number is right (Chapter 12).

Assumptions

The classic illustration of why writers must assume nothing occurred in 1948 when public opinion polls showed Thomas Dewey ahead of Harry Truman in the presidential election. The *Chicago Daily Tribune,* which is still remembered for its monumental error, did not wait until the results were in before printing its early edition. It ran as its Page One banner headline "Dewey Defeats Truman." That would not have happened had the editors obeyed the cardinal rule: Assume nothing.

A more recent example is coverage of Al Gore's trip down the Connecticut River in New Hampshire during his 2000 presidential campaign to demonstrate his commitment to protecting the environment. *The Washington Times* reported that "local authorities had granted Gore a special favor when they released nearly four billion gallons of water from a nearby dam into the drought-stricken river in order to keep the vice president's boat afloat; alleged cost: $7 million."[34]

The damaging story about Gore's campaign (this friend of the environment wasting precious water for political purposes) was picked up by major media, including CNN, *The Washington Post, Newsweek* and *The New York Times.* The story was untrue. Gore did not even ask for the water release. Many reporters assumed the story was accurate merely because it was published.[35]

Some mistakes are less spectacular than those about Truman and Gore, but they still must be avoided. A writer should not take it for granted, for instance, that a name is spelled the "usual" way. A writer who submits a story about professional baseball player Jeff Blum is going to be in trouble. Blum's first name is Geoff. Other names that can cause problems are Jon (John), Sara (Sarah), Luci (Lucy), Daryl (Darryl), Cathy (Kathy) and Josef (Joseph). The meticulous writer verifies the spelling of *all* names and assumes nothing.

Another source of potential error is a town name. A writer who is told by a source that a murder was committed in Miami might assume the source was referring to Miami, Fla., when the source might actually be talking about Miami, Ohio. Most states have a Lake View, a Cushing and a Columbus. It's important to know which "Columbus" a source is talking about.

Some news media attach so much importance to the correct spelling of names that they require writers to check them all and to write "all names verified" at the top of each article or write "cq" or "sic" above each name.

Doubtful Information

Many professional writers disagree with James O'Shea, a *Chicago Tribune* editor, who was quoted as saying, "We're in a new world in terms of the way information flows to the nation. ... The days when you can decide not to print a story because it's not well enough sourced are long gone."[36] The justification for such behavior typically is that unverified information already has been disseminated or soon will be. That makes the practice okay.

But disseminating unverified information is not okay, for the news might turn out to be wrong. A professional's final recourse when he or she has unverified information is simply to leave the material out. Although it's important to produce reports that are complete, it's more important to ensure that all information is accurate. Then perhaps the information can be verified and published or aired at a later time.

Sensitivity

It's relatively easy for a writer to be sensitive to the concerns of those in his or her social, political, economic and cultural group. It's not so easy when a source resides outside that group. It's important in self-editing to ask whether the story is sensitive to marginalized and disenfranchised sources. The work of Hardin, Preston and Hyman is helpful in making that determination:[37]

- Writers must treat sources from marginalized groups just as they would any other sources. To do otherwise is patronizing, disrespectful and, well, stupid. Particularly when speaking with the disabled, writers should maintain appropriate eye contact, speak in a normal voice (one doesn't need to shout at the blind) and treat the sources with respect.

- Writers must not harp on the characteristics that place individuals into any marginalized group. Writers wouldn't describe a source as "pretty" (if they value their jobs), and they wouldn't describe a source as black, disabled or gay, unless that were relevant to the story. If a paraplegic climbs Mount Everest, the disability is relevant to the story. If a paraplegic becomes the chief executive officer of a huge conglomerate, it's not. Writers never use words like *queer, deformed, crippled, deaf and dumb* or *honey,* unless they want to be perceived as insensitive buffoons—or worse. (See the box "Tom Arviso Jr. on the Power of Words.")

- Even when an individual's disadvantage or disability is relevant, a writer doesn't emphasize it excessively. A lesbian who works for a city that provides health benefits to the spouses of married employees—but not to the partners of gay and lesbian employees—must be identified as a lesbian. The emphasis in the story must not be on the lesbian lifestyle, however, but on the hardships created by the city's policy.

- Writers must avoid suggesting—particularly when writing about the disabled—that an accomplishment is surprising or unusual. Theoretical physicist Stephen Hawking, who is severely handicapped with amyotrophic lateral sclerosis (Lou Gehrig's disease), writes important books, gives speeches and participates in scholarly activities. No writer should congratulate Hawking for overcoming his disability to accomplish great things, and he or she should not suggest that this is unusual.[38]

TOM ARVISO JR. ON THE POWER OF WORDS

The field of journalism is a colorful one, especially when it comes to covering the people and cultures of the world. Here in the United States, the culture that seems to be the most misunderstood by reporters and editors is the Native American people. That's because what most of these journalists learned and know about Native Americans probably came from watching old John Wayne Westerns on television. This is evident in the choice of words and terms used when writing stories about Native Americans.

The most offensive term, used to address Native American women, is "squaw." This word came from French fur trappers and means female genitalia. Another is "redskin," which is the equivalent of using the "n-word" when addressing a person of Native American ancestry. The word "chief" is often misused when addressing tribal leaders—a chief is a person who has earned his or her distinguished honor by displaying strong leadership skills within his or her specific tribe. But not all Native tribes have chiefs. Some tribes have a chairman or chairwoman, president and principal chief. It is disrespectful and insulting to call someone a "chief" when he or she is not.

It is most appropriate and respectful to identify a Native American person by his or her particular tribe, band or pueblo. I am of Navajo heritage and would rather be known as, "Tom Arviso Jr., a member of the Navajo tribe," instead of "Arviso, a Native American or American Indian." This gives an authentic description of my heritage, rather than lumping me into a whole race of people just like African-American, Asian-American or Hispanic, which is too broad of a term and not generally used to identify someone unless absolutely necessary.

Also, the use of American Indian and Native American are both basically correct, as Native people use both. American Indian is the more modern term used but the Native American Journalists Association endorses the use of Native American as being the most appropriate, especially when covering a story.

It is important to always be aware and respectful of a person's culture and heritage when you are writing. If you are not, then your story or broadcast is basically untrue and inaccurate, and you are adding to the longstanding ignorance of non-Native media as well as perpetuating stereotypes of Native Americans. Most importantly, though, you will lose the respect of the Native person you are writing about as well as those who are aware of your ignorance.

Source: Tom Arviso Jr., "Watch Your Language: Words Have Power," Society of Professional Journalists, undated. Downloaded on May 23, 2003, from <www.spj.org/diversity_toolbox_words.asp>.

Tom Arviso Jr. is publisher and editor of *The Navajo Times*.

- Writers should show that the marginalized are part of a broader world, but without taking a "Wow, look at that" approach or unduly emphasizing the characteristic that makes them part of a marginalized group. "Showing" Stephen Hawking talking with colleagues is one way to accomplish this.

- Writers must not compromise the standards of objectivity in writing about the marginalized. They should not, for example, de-emphasize accurate, relevant information that is not consistent with what members of a marginalized group are telling them. Just like everyone else, the marginalized have self-interests to protect. It's important not to accept without question a marginalized group's worldviews.

- Writers must cover the negative aspects of a marginalized group as well as the positive. Everyone has weaknesses. Writers must remember that always, even if they are branded as "insensitive" because they write about those weaknesses.

YOUR RESPONSIBILITY IS . . .

- To develop a loathing for errors. You must see any error as a challenge never to make another error. You will be frustrated if you develop this attitude, for you, like everyone else, will make mistakes. But if you truly hate errors, you'll be a better writer.

- To understand the danger of shortcuts. You should use with great care computer programs that check spelling or grammar; you should never assume information or sources are accurate; and you should understand that no fact is too trivial or too obvious to check.

- To appreciate the difference between objective and subjective errors, for some subjective "errors" are not mistakes at all.

- To understand the consequences of mistakes, large and small, in news and information dissemination and to understand why news media take such pains to avoid and to correct all errors.

- To understand who and what the primary sources of error are and to learn to be cautious when using those sources.

- To learn the strategies for minimizing errors and to learn how to use them automatically. Style rules, for example, should flow automatically from your fingertips to your keyboard. You must know the rules so well, you don't need to ask whether *California* is abbreviated when it follows a town name.

- To learn how to edit your own copy carefully because you can't be sure an editor will catch your errors.

NOTES

1. Dave Griffiths, "To Err Is Human: Accuracy Falls Victim to Lost Redundancy, Ineffective Copy Systems," *Quill,* April 1994: 35–36, 38, p. 35.

2. Barbara Kantrowitz and Pat Wingert, "The Group: A New Generation of Women Is Running Some of the Country's Most Important Universities," *Newsweek,* July 1, 2002: 52–53.

3. "A Correction," CNN, March 19, 2001. Downloaded on Sept. 8, 2002, from <www.cnn.com>.

4. Lawrence K. Altman, "West Nile Cases Raising Questions Over Transplants: No Test to Screen Blood," *The New York Times,* Sept. 2, 2002: A-1, 12.

5. Christine D. Urban, *Examining Our Credibility: Perspectives of the Public and the Press* (Washington, D.C.: American Society of Newspaper Editors, 1999); and Radio and Television News Directors Foundation, *2003 Local Television News Study of News Directors and the American Public* (Washington, D.C.: Author, 2003). Available at <www.rtndf.org/ethics/2003survey.pdf>.

6. Michael Crichton, "The Mediasaurus: Today's Mass Media Is Tomorrow's Fossil Fuel," *Wired,* September/October 1993: 1–4.

7. Linda Stinson, "Fact-checking 101 (Forbes Magazine's Information Center)," *Searcher,* January 1999: 60–66. Downloaded on May 23, 2003, from <www.findarticles.com/cf_0/m0DPC/1_7/53657083/print.jhtml>.

8. Michael Getler, "The Shadow of the Bombers," *The Washington Post,* April 2, 2002: B-6.

9. Mitchell V. Charnley, "Preliminary Notes on a Study of Newspaper Accuracy," *Journalism Quarterly,* 13:4 (1936): 394–401; Fred C. Berry Jr., "A Study of Accuracy in Local News Stories of Three Dailies," *Journalism Quarterly,* 44:3 (1967): 482–490; Michael W. Singletary and Richard Lipsky, "Accuracy in Local TV News," *Journalism Quarterly,* 54:2 (1977): 362–364; and Larry L. Burriss, "Accuracy of News Magazines as Perceived by News Sources," *Journalism Quarterly,* 62:4 (1985): 824–827.

10. James W. Tankard and Michael Ryan, "News Source Perceptions of Accuracy of Science Coverage," *Journalism Quarterly,* 51:2 (1974): 219–225, 334; Michael Ryan and Dorothea Owen, "An Accuracy Survey of Metropolitan Newspaper Coverage of Social Issues," *Journalism Quarterly,* 54:1 (1977): 27–32; D. Lynn Pulford, "Follow-up Study of Science News Accuracy," *Journalism Quarterly,* 53:1 (1976): 119–121; and Eleanor Singer, "A Question of Accuracy: How Journalists and Scientists Report Research on Hazards," *Journal of Communication,* 40:4 (1990): 102–116.

11. Berry, "A Study of Accuracy," and Michael Ryan, "A Factor Analytic Study of Scientists' Responses to Errors," *Journalism Quarterly,* 52:2 (1975): 333–336.

12. "Correction: A Note About Our Broadcast," ABC, Oct. 1, 2001. Downloaded on Sept. 8, 2002, from <www.abcnews.com>.

13. Sharon Begley, "Our Sport Has Gangrene," *Newsweek,* Feb. 25, 2002: 38–41, 43–45.

14. Tom Koch, *The News as Myth: Fact and Context in Journalism* (New York: Greenwood, 1990): 174–175.

15. Ina Howard, "Power Sources: On Party, Gender, Race and Class, TV News Looks to the Most Powerful Groups," *Extra!,* May/June 2002. Downloaded on June 21, 2003, from <www.fair.org/extra/0205/power_sources.html>. See Eric Alterman, *What Liberal Media? The Truth About Bias and the News* (New York: Basic Books, 2003): 114–115.

16. Robert Windrem and Norah O'Donnell, "Study: Iraq Could Arm Nukes Quickly," MSNBC, Sept. 9, 2002. Downloaded on Sept. 12, 2002, from <www.msnbc.com/news/802167.asp>.

17. Ibid.

18. Alan Abel, "How I Found Deep Throat and Fooled the FBI," *U.S. News & World Report,* Aug. 26–Sept. 2, 2002: 34.

19. Victoria Pope, "A Case of Past Imperfect: An Award-winning Holocaust Memoir Was Not What It Seemed," *U.S. News & World Report,* Aug. 26–Sept. 2, 2002: 60, 62; and Benjamin Wilkomirski, *Fragments: Memories of a Wartime Childhood* (Carol Brown Janeway, trans.) (New York: Schocken, 1996).

20. Gary C. Lawrence and David L. Grey, "Subjective Inaccuracies in Local News Reporting," *Journalism Quarterly,* 46:4 (1969): 753–757.

21. Rich Noyes, "Is ABC's 'Road to War?' Really Anti-war?" *Media Reality Check,* Sept. 3, 2002. Downloaded on Sept. 6, 2002, from <www.mediaresearch.org/realitycheck/2002/fax20020903.asp>.

22. Michael Levine, "Mainstream Media: The Drug War's Shills," in Kristina Borjesson (ed.), *Into the Buzzsaw: Leading Journalists Expose the Myth of a Free Press* (Amherst, N.Y.: Prometheus, 2002): 257–294, p. 287.

23. Heather MacDonald, "A Cop's Life: The Media Takes Sides and Endangers Lives," *National Review Online,* July 23, 2002. Downloaded on Sept. 6, 2002, from <www.nationalreview.com/script/printpage.asp?ref=comment/comment-macdonald072302.asp>.

24. David Brock, *Blinded by the Right: The Conscience of an Ex-conservative* (New York: Crown, 2002): 99.

25. Ibid., p. 114.

26. Ibid., p. 116.

27. "A Call to Action: Reconnecting College Sports and Higher Education," report of the Knight Foundation Commission on Intercollegiate Athletics, Miami, Fla., June 2001. Downloaded on Aug. 12, 2002, from <www.ncaa.org/databases/knight_commission/2001_report>.

28. Marie Hardin and Ann Preston, "Inclusion of Disability Issues in News Reporting Textbooks," *Journalism & Mass Communication Educator,* 56:2 (2001): 43–54; and Valerie Hyman, "Getting More Diversity in Content," The Poynter Institute for Media Studies, March 1996. Downloaded on Feb. 14, 2003, from <www.media-awareness.ca/eng/issues/minrep/journl/poynter.htm>.

29. Beth A. Haller, "Confusing Disability and Tragedy," *The* (Baltimore) *Sun,* April 29, 2001: C-1, 4.

30. The first article in the series is Tom Hallman Jr., "The Boy Behind the Mask: Part One: At a Certain Age, Nothing Is More Important Than Fitting In," *The Sunday* (Portland) *Oregonian,* Oct. 1, 2000: A-1, 8–9. See also Tom Hallman Jr., *Sam: The Boy Behind the Mask* (New York: G.P. Putnam's Sons, 2002).

31. Haller, "Confusing Disability and Tragedy": C-4.

32. Griffiths, "To Err is Human": 38.

33. Carl Bernstein and Bob Woodward, *All the President's Men* (New York: Simon and Schuster, 1974).

34. Alterman, *What Liberal Media?:* 162.

35. Eric Boehlert, "The Press vs. Al Gore: How Lazy Reporting, Pack Journalism and the GOP Spin Machine Distorted Gore's Character and Helped Cost Him the Election," *Rolling Stone,* Dec. 6–13, 2001: 53–54, 57.

36. Joan Didion, "Clinton Agonistes," *The New York Review of Books,* Oct. 22, 1998: 16, 18, 20, 22–23, p. 18. Available at <www.nybooks.com/articles/article-preview?article_id=699>.

37. Hardin and Preston, "Inclusion of Disability Issues"; and Hyman, "Getting More Diversity in Content."

38. Stephen W. Hawking, *A Brief History of Time: From the Big Bang to Black Holes* (Toronto: Bantam, 1988); and Stephen W. Hawking, *The Universe in a Nutshell* (New York: Bantam, 2001).

PART II

WRITING

CHAPTER 4

STYLE

A Multimedia Approach

The ability to write well is the single most important attribute editors look for in potential new employees. A professional communicator who can write well is likely to succeed—for a radio or television station, magazine, public relations agency, newspaper, film production company, World Wide Web site, book publisher or anything in between. The good news is that almost anyone who is willing to work and to learn can develop competent writing skills. The outlook is even brighter for those who have some natural talent.

The goal is simple: to produce copy that is accurate, compelling, clear and concise. The hard part is achieving that goal. It is difficult, for example, to produce copy that sparkles. That difficulty is compounded when a writer must ensure that every fact, every word and every letter is correct. A writer who can produce compelling, sparkling text, but who cannot guarantee that text is accurate, is not a good writer.

Students sometimes charge that writing teachers in mass communication want to force them to write in only one—uncreative—way. It's true that the primary function of mass communication is to convey accurate information efficiently, not to entertain with ambiguous prose. If Abraham Lincoln had been trained as a modern media writer, his Gettysburg address (below, left) might have come out quite differently (below, right):

Fourscore and seven years ago, our fathers brought forth upon this continent a new nation, conceived in liberty and dedicated to the proposition that all men are created equal.	We meet today to dedicate a part of this Civil War battlefield as a cemetery for the soldiers who died during the Battle of Gettysburg.
Now we are engaged in a great civil war, testing whether that nation—or any nation, so conceived and so dedicated—can long endure.	It is appropriate that we honor those who gave their lives to preserve this nation, which was created 87 years ago to ensure liberty and equality for all.
We are met on a great battle-field of that war. We are met to dedicate a portion of it as the final resting place of those who have given their lives that that nation might live.	
It is altogether fitting and proper that we should do this. ...	

Lincoln would not have written the version at the right even if he had been trained to use modern media writing techniques, for speeches and news reports have different demands and purposes. But if he had delivered the version at the right, the Gettysburg address would have been remembered for maybe 30 minutes, not honored for centuries. The point is, simply, that modern media writing style differs from news styles used in earlier eras and from other writing forms (speeches and novels, for instance). Neither form is more important than the other.

Novelists, politicians and essayists use different styles in part because they rarely have the severe space problems media writers do and because the primary function of the media writer—unlike that of the essayist, politician or novelist—is to inform readers, listeners and viewers quickly and efficiently. Few members of any audience are inclined to spend more time on a report than they think it's worth. If they can't understand a report right off, they likely will skip to something else—or switch to a medium they can understand more easily.

FUNDAMENTALS

In a sense, those who argue that students are crammed into a box to write only one way are right. Students need to acquire basic skills, just as soccer players or ballet dancers must learn the fundamentals. If they don't, they'll never achieve their potential. The editor who does not insist that writers master fundamental skills will not produce a good magazine—just as the coach or choreographer who does not teach the fundamentals will never produce a strong team or a good dance troupe. Writing skills can be broken down into two broad categories: conceptual and mechanical.

Conceptual Skills

Writers must develop critical thinking skills that will help them to analyze and interpret a mass of information, to figure out what it means and to determine how that information fits into a larger context. An important step is to understand the nature and power of the mass communicator's primary tool—the language itself. Some critics argue that language is unstable and that meanings constantly shift, which can leave mass communicators wondering whether the language they use has shared meanings—whether audiences use terms in the same ways they do.[1]

If language is unstable, who has the power to decide what words mean, and how do they exercise that power? When the United States launched a war against terrorism, the *war* was unlike any America had fought before. Many Americans questioned whether it really was a war. President George W. Bush solved the problem by calling the war against terrorism a *new kind of war*. As president, he had the power to assign new meaning to an old term, and the media embraced the change.

Attorney General John Ashcroft described germ weapons expert Steven Hatfill as a *person of interest* in the FBI's anthrax investigation, but he refused to say what that phrase meant, and many observers assumed the worst—to the point that Hatfill was fired from his job and spent considerable money defending himself. Hollywood has for years portrayed Arabs as crooks and terrorists.[2] This is an exercise of power that assigns meaning to and marginalizes an entire minority group.

Many women have felt marginalized, in part because of the way language is used. A professional who writes that "the group will elect a new chairman" precludes the possibility that a woman might be selected and subtly suggests that a woman would not be suitable for the job. A journalist might write a feature story about a state's office of governor and use the personal pronoun *he* exclusively, as in "When a new governor is sworn in, he has to have his legislative agenda already planned." This language is structured in a way that precludes women from the job, and the writer exercises power when he or she assigns meaning to the term *governor*.[3]

Linguist Ferdinand de Saussure saw all languages as systems of binary signs, in which words have meaning in opposition to other words—as in black versus white, man versus woman, terrorist versus freedom fighter, profane versus sacred. The list is as endless as the language.[4] News reports are grounded in this world of binary signs, where control of language confers power.

In reality, the truth is most often found somewhere between these binary signs. Writers have a responsibility to seek that truth—to find out what words really mean in the context of a story and to determine whether the words truly describe what people think they describe.

Writers who don't understand the complexity of language have a hard time developing critical thinking skills. They don't know what questions to ask or even whom to ask; they cannot see critical relationships among people and groups; they cannot understand how power is exercised, by whom and over whom; and they certainly can't write well because they can't think well.

An example of the lapse in critical thinking is media coverage of the Credit Research Center at Georgetown University. Many debtors, the center charged in one of its reports, are using bankruptcy laws to avoid paying their bills, a study that credit card companies and banks cited widely in their campaign to get Congress to change the law to make it more difficult to file for bankruptcy.

Public relations writers for banks and credit card companies—and many journalists—stressed the Georgetown connection, for that conferred some legitimacy on the study. But many did not say the center is funded by the credit industry and the study was supported by MasterCard International Inc. and Visa USA. Many news outlets, including *The Washington Times,* published or aired stories without identifying the center adequately.[5]

Integral to critical thinking is research technique. A writer who doesn't have solid information simply cannot produce good, credible copy, for it will be inaccurate, incomplete or misleading. A writer who consistently fails to find the necessary information is simply not going to be successful. This does not mean information

Many Americans, such as these commuters on a train to Connecticut from New York, relied heavily on newspapers for information about John F. Kennedy's assassination in 1963. A wider array of media sources is available in the 21st century.

will always be available. It won't. Nobody has found evidence, for example, of a second assassin the day President John F. Kennedy was killed. But when information is available and relevant, it must be found and used.

When TWA Flight 800 crashed into the Atlantic in 1996, some observers speculated that it was brought down by a bomb or a missile, particularly when residue from explosives was found in the debris. The residue came from a training exercise for a bomb-sniffing dog on that plane a few weeks earlier, government investigators said, and almost everyone accepted the explanation. One journalist, David E. Hendrix of *The* (Riverside, Calif.) *Press-Enterprise,* discovered the training exercise was carried out on a different airplane, not on the one that became Flight 800. The information about the training exercise should have been verified. The cause of the crash was never proved.[6]

Mechanical Skills

The mechanics of style and language usage are the easiest things to learn, and they are in some ways the most important. Writers cannot invent their own styles as they go or use whatever grammar rules appeal to them at the moment. All good media organizations have style manuals, the most common one being *The Associated Press Stylebook and Briefing on Media Law,* which is used by thousands of newspapers, magazines, broadcast stations and public relations offices around the world. When you apply for a job and take a media organization's diagnostic test, chances are good that your knowledge of AP style will be tested. Some of the most common AP rules (Appendix C) must be memorized.

Inconsistencies interrupt thought and the smooth flow of even well-written sentences. A reader accustomed to seeing the word "through" may, for example, be distracted if it appears as "thru." A reader whose daily newspaper never uses "Mr." may wonder why someone merits special attention when "Mr." is used. Variations in style focus reader attention on style, not where it should be—on content.

Established rules also help writers save time and eliminate the necessity of making a dozen small but important decisions about style in every single report. The writer knows, for example, that a *$3 million budget* will be called a *$3 million budget.* A conscious decision is not required—*three million dollar budget* is incorrect. And a journalist writing about an accident at *305 N. City Line St.* knows not to use *305 North City Line Street.* No time is wasted: *305 N. City Line St.* flows automatically.

Style rules, which are designed also to save precious space or time, help a professional write more concisely. AP style rules, for example, demand the use of *Jan. 6,* not *January 6,* with a date of the month; *Blvd.,* not *Boulevard,* in a specific address; and *N.Y.,* not *New York,* when used with the name of a town or city. Each rule helps conserve space.

As they must adhere to style rules, writers also must know grammar, spelling and punctuation fundamentals (Appendix B). Editors insist that writers know the rules so that language is used consistently throughout their publications, Web sites, news releases and broadcasts. A consistent style is helpful to both audience and writer.

Those who can't master the mechanics are destined to remain poor, unsuccessful writers. Every culture has a dominant language, and mass communicators must master the dominant language.

BEYOND THE BASICS

In focusing on the fundamentals, students may produce boring writing that only a parent would want to read. That is okay initially, but beginners must learn that it's not enough to know the rules, for as journalism student Ana Mantica said, "A school can teach you every rule in the book, but that doesn't mean you'll be a good writer."[7]

Media writers face a most difficult creative challenge: to communicate information in a compelling way. Just producing a solid first sentence is hard, because one must capture the heart of a problem or issue, find just a few words to summarize the facts and put all that into a package that is attractive and even gripping. Some writers seem to have fingers of gold; everything they write sparkles. This does not mean writing is easy for them, just that, in the end, people want to read what they produce.

The rest of us must develop this skill. It helps to read, and read, and read and read some more, and to write, and write, and write and write some more. Reading and writing are useless, however, when writers fail to bring critical thinking skills to the process and when they don't have good critics to tell them when their work is not good. Not everyone can be James Fallows, Joan Didion or Truman Capote, but everyone—with hard work and adequate guidance—can learn to produce copy that people want to read.

One skill that all good writers eventually learn is to show (or describe), rather than tell. It is not enough to simply *tell* that a dog show contestant is not feeling the pressure. A good writer will *describe* that. Literary journalist Mark Kramer says that *show, don't tell* means to excite the senses, and a writer can do that by describing a scene or a person. "A site isn't a story," Kramer is quoted as saying. "A person isn't a story. A story is a place of strong emotion. What subjects are bothered about is the center of their interests."[8] Writers often find those centers when their subjects are doing routine things: Kramer would "prefer to see a surgeon scrub than cut, a baseball star buy shoes than steal third."[9] To describe that happy dog show contestant, a writer might say:

> Dolly tore off across the parking lot, chasing the soccer ball as if it were a living thing running for its life. When she pounced on it, she shook the ball until it was flat, leaped into the air and flung it away. She charged back across the lot in search of more prey.

A broadcaster who wants to let listeners know how happy a defendant is after he is acquitted of a crime might say:

> Donovan, grinning for the first time in days, absorbed the verdict, kicked his chair over as he jumped up from the defense table and threw both fists into the air. He turned to his lawyer, who disappeared for half a minute into a bear hug, and then went over to the jury box to work the panel until everybody had gone home.

SHOW; DON'T *TELL*

Leo Tolstoy, the author of *War and Peace,* said, "I don't tell; I don't explain. I show; I let my characters talk for me."

Writers are often given the advice to "show; don't tell." Writing that *shows* (or *describes*) uses language that is specific, definite and concrete. It is the kind of language that helps the reader see a picture.

A study of sentences that described versus those that showed indicated that all the *show* sentences were rated as more interesting than their *tell* counterparts. Describing rather than telling is a proven way to make writing more gripping.[10]

Consider the following "show" and "tell" versions of the same sentences identified in the study ("tell" versions are on the left and "show" versions are on the right):

The trees by the water are filled with birds frantically looking for insects.	The budding maples and birches overhanging the brook are alive with yellow-rumped warblers darting from twig to twig in a search for early insects.
The local playground is in disrepair.	At the local playground, weeds poke through cracked concrete and children climb over collapsed, rusted swing sets.
Suddenly I awoke, frightened.	Suddenly I awoke in a drenching sweat, my heart racing.

The writers showed a happy hound and an ecstatic defendant. This kind of description obviously is not appropriate in all situations. But sometimes it is, and a writer needs to be able to *show*, rather than *tell*, when it is appropriate (see the box "*Show;* Don't *Tell*").

SELF-EDITING

Good writers understand that self-editing (revising) is as important as producing a first draft, although revision may be somewhat less difficult. Media writers first check copy to ensure it is accurate (Chapter 3). The next step is to ensure they avoid grammar, spelling, style and punctuation errors. This is critical because it is unlikely that anyone who cannot master these fundamental writing tools can ever succeed.

Writers cannot assume editors will catch their errors, particularly as deadlines approach. Grammatically correct sentences have got to spring from their fingertips automatically, for they don't have time to look up a couple of style rules and four or five grammar rules. Good writers memorize and use the English usage rules in Appendix B and the style rules in Appendix C. Their fingers should be unable to type, for example, "1012 West Elm Street" or "Each child brought their book." If their fingers can type such phrases, they are not good self-editors.

A good self-editor also needs to check copy to ensure the writing is clear and concise. Indeed, a writer who cannot communicate clearly and concisely in everyday language will not reach many viewers, listeners or readers.[11] This section is devoted to helping students acquire the skills they need to ensure their writing meets professional standards.

Sentence, Paragraph Length

Media writing isn't fancy. Good writers avoid long, complex sentences, preferring instead short, declarative sentences—and for good reasons:

- Audiences tend to avoid confused, obscure writing and to seek more easily understood material. If they see confusing sentences on a Web site, for instance, they will change sites.

- Writers often can create feelings of immediacy and drama through the effective use of short sentences and paragraphs, particularly for television or radio.

- Reports written in short sentences and paragraphs are more attractive when set in type, distributed in a news release or posted on a Web site. Long sentences and paragraphs appear as imposing blocks of gray type that are hard to read. It also is easier to understand simple sentences when they are spoken by broadcasters.

Consider the following versions of the same report:

Amy Shannon, former Valera Township police sergeant, who was dropped from the force in 1999 for failing to appear at a departmental hearing, has won an out-of-court settlement in a libel suit she filed in June 1997 against *Style Magazine,* which, it was charged, published "false and malicious statements" in an article (published in the March 1996 issue) that linked Shannon and half a dozen other officers to an illegal silver smelting business.

The suit was filed in 23rd Superior Court, and no settlement amount was

Amy Shannon, former Valera Township police sergeant, has won an out-of-court settlement in a libel suit she filed in June 1997 against *Style Magazine.*

The suit in 23rd Superior Court charged that "false and malicious statements" were published in an article published in the March 1996 issue.

The article linked Shannon and half a dozen other officers to an illegal silver smelting business.

No settlement amount was announced because of a confidentiality agreement.

announced because of a confidentiality agreement. Allegations that Shannon took kickbacks were dropped in 1998 and removed from her record.	Shannon was dropped from the force in 1999 for failing to appear at a departmental hearing. Allegations that she took kickbacks were dropped and removed from her record.

The first sentence at the left is so long and confused that many readers would refuse to read it the two or three times it would take to decipher its meaning. They wouldn't even get the chance if a radio journalist afflicted them with this account, and they probably wouldn't want to hear it twice even if they had the chance. The version at the right is much easier to understand and is aesthetically more pleasing because it is not a mass of unbroken, gray type.

Efforts to keep sentences short should not be carried to extremes. A series of short sentences without smooth transitions can produce an irritating staccato

Writers in CNN's Washington bureau fight deadline pressure to produce stories that are accurate, complete, concise and compelling.

effect, particularly in writing for print. No story should read more like a first-grade primer than an article for adults.

Long sentences, furthermore, don't necessarily *have* to be incomprehensible. Long sentences—as Saul Pett, William Faulkner and others have shown—can be comprehensible and colorful. Sometimes a long sentence can convey information more effectively than several short ones. But long sentences must be handled carefully, and inexperienced media writers should avoid them.

A good rule of thumb for the inexperienced writer is to deal with only one idea in each sentence and to include only one sentence in each paragraph. If the audience has to read or hear a sentence twice to comprehend it, the sentence should be rewritten (and perhaps divided into two sentences.)

Sentence Structure

Media professionals worry about each sentence they write, for if each sentence is the best it can be, the rest of the copy is likely to be strong, too. Writers rely on simple sentences and start each sentence with the most important information.

Subject-verb-object

Media writers prefer the simple to the complex, and sentence structure is no exception. Simple declarative sentences, with predicates following subjects, are the rule. Simple structure is used partly because a sentence written in that form is easier to understand, as indicated in the following examples:

After being charged with first-degree murder in the stabbing death Wednesday night of 22-year-old John H. Galvin outside a Main Street store, two youths from Galena Park were freed on $25,000 cash bail today.	Two Galena Park youths were freed today on $25,000 cash bail after they were charged with first-degree murder in the stabbing death Wednesday night of 22-year-old John H. Galvin outside a Main Street store.

Contrast the sentence at the left, which begins with a prepositional phrase, with the sentence at the right, in which the subject and predicate are placed near the beginning of the sentence. The version at the right flows more smoothly and is easier to understand, particularly if the report is directed toward a radio or television audience.

Competent writers also ensure that their sentences make sense. Here are two that don't (below, left), with revisions (below, right):

An electrical fire in the home of Sandra C. Frick was extinguished today before any serious damage was done by the Clear Brook Fire Department.	An electrical fire in the home of Sandra C. Frick was extinguished today by the Clear Brook Fire Department before the blaze did any serious damage.

| The Mingo County Museum's calendar of events says the exhibit of American sculpture of the 1990s will be conducted Jan. 14 through March 14. Eighty-seven works will be displayed by 54 American sculptors, all executed since 1990. | An exhibition of 87 American sculptures completed in the 1990s is scheduled for Jan. 14 through March 14 at the Mingo County Museum. Fifty-four sculptors will be represented. |

A journalist implied that the firefighters would damage Frick's home if they did not get that fire out in a hurry, and a public relations writer implied that all 54 sculptors had been executed, which seems pretty unlikely.

Best Information First

Writers also are concerned about putting the most important information at the first of their sentences and the least important information at the last (Figure 4.1). This model requires that writers view their reports as four parts, each of which is composed of one sentence containing an independent clause with dependent clauses and phrases, which is the way most sentences are written.[12]

It helps for students to *see* each paragraph as three lines long with each sentence element a line and a half long. Three lines is a good length, and this rule of thumb can help beginners keep their sentences short as they learn to apply a few thousand concepts and rules in their own writing.

Good writers put their most important and interesting material into the first paragraphs of their reports, which is Part 1 of the model. While a novelist might save the most important or interesting material for the end (the climax), a media writer does not. The first part of the first paragraph (1-A) might, for example, note that an anti-abortion exhibit has opened on a college campus despite efforts of the administration and pro-abortion activists to stop it (Figure 4.2). Writers frequently put an attribution into Part 1-B.

Part 2 in the model (Figure 4.1) often is reserved for background material a reader, listener or viewer needs to understand a story (2-A) and for identification of sources or other persons mentioned (2-B). In most instances, Part 2 will be only one paragraph of background material, but it can be composed of two or three paragraphs if an issue is particularly complex. The writer of the report about the anti-abortion display (Figure 4.2), for example, needs only one background paragraph (Part 2) to explain that the university lost a court battle to stop the exhibit and then dropped its appeal to a higher court. A new source is introduced in 2-B.

Part 3 typically follows up on material in Part 1-A. The first phrase of a story (1-A) summarizes what has happened, and Part 3 supplies more details, frequently in a direct quotation. In the abortion protest story, the writer quotes an anti-abortion activist who tries to explain what the university's decision means (3-A). The source is cited in the second part of that sentence (3-B).

FIGURE 4.1   A MODEL FOR SENTENCE ORGANIZATION

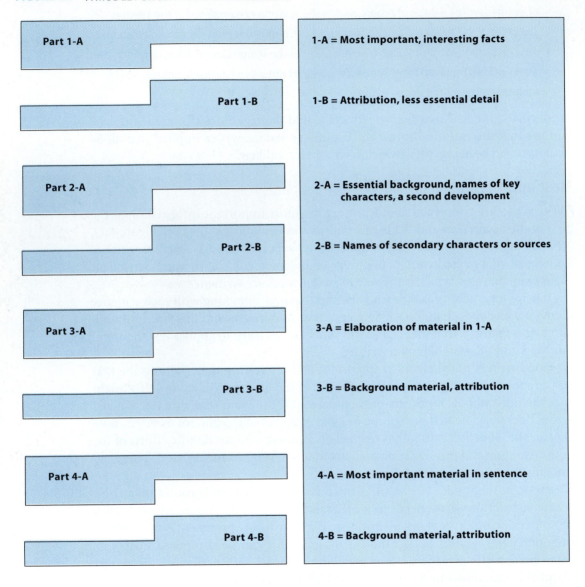

Part 1-A

Part 1-B

Part 2-A

Part 2-B

Part 3-A

Part 3-B

Part 4-A

Part 4-B

1-A = Most important, interesting facts

1-B = Attribution, less essential detail

2-A = Essential background, names of key
characters, a second development

2-B = Names of secondary characters or sources

3-A = Elaboration of material in 1-A

3-B = Background material, attribution

4-A = Most important material in sentence

4-B = Background material, attribution

Part 4 represents all the rest of the paragraphs. In the anti-abortion display story, the writer uses two Part 4 paragraphs to describe events leading to the court fight and the results; the views of students, faculty and staff toward the display; and information about how long the display will be up.

In *every* sentence in *every* part (1, 2, 3 and 4), the most important and interesting information is placed first (1-A, 2-A, 3-A and 4-A). This nearly always means background material and attributions are placed in the second parts of the sentences

FIGURE 4.2 ANTI-ABORTION DISPLAY STORY

(1-A) An anti-abortion display that features huge photographs of aborted fetuses will open Monday on Smith Plaza despite legal efforts by the administration and pro-abortion activists to stop it, **(1-B)** Steven Miles, head of the group sponsoring the display, said today.

(2-A) The University lost its suit last month in 34th District Court to have the display moved to Jones Plaza on the edge of the campus and has decided not to appeal, **(2-B)** University spokesman Stan Hathaway said today.

(3-A) "This is an important victory for all students and faculty who cherish free speech and for those who oppose abortion," **(3-B)** Miles, head of University Lions, said.

(4-A) The university decided not to appeal the court decision because it was too costly, **(4-B)** Hathaway said.

(4-A) The suit was filed initially because of complaints by students and faculty that the color photographs—which were six-feet square and showed bloody, aborted fetuses—were not appropriate for display in such a prominent part of campus, **(4-B)** Hathaway said.

(1-B, 2-B, 3-B and 4-B). The subject of the sentence ordinarily is placed first, although writers can disagree about what is most interesting and important, as in this example:

Gov. Shirley West has abandoned her plan for aid to higher education, accepting the approach advanced by the Legislature and agreeing to double the appropriation she had called for last month, the governor announced today.	The Legislature's plan for aid to higher education has been accepted by Gov. Shirley West, who abandoned her plan and agreed to double the appropriation she called for last month, the governor announced today.

In the version at the left, the writer felt the most important noun in the story was *Gov. Shirley West,* which was the subject of the sentence. The most important noun, from the second writer's perspective, was *the Legislature's plan,* and that was the subject of the sentence—and therefore holds the preferred position in the sentence. Writers must make decisions constantly about which nouns are most important and interesting and place them in the preferred position (1-A).

The decision about how to order the facts frequently is a no-brainer. A public relations writer, for example, has not used the model if he or she produces a first paragraph like the version at the left (below) rather than the version at the right:

John Dodson, vice president of sales and marketing for Midwest Airlines, announced Thursday the installation of machines in Des Moines, Cincinnati, Cleveland and Kansas City that issue boarding passes directly to customers.	Midwest Airlines has installed machines in Des Moines, Cincinnati, Cleveland and Kansas City airports that dispense boarding passes directly to customers, John Dodson, vice president of sales and marketing, announced Thursday.

The version at the left is upside down: The most important information is not where it must be—in the first phrase of the first paragraph—as in the version at the right.

Good writers seldom start sentences with attributions to sources already mentioned or with background material many readers already know. This does not mean, of course, that a writer should not start a sentence with an attribution when failure to do so would confuse a reader. Writers must be flexible in using this model.

A Caveat for Broadcasters

Radio and television news writers profit from learning to apply the model described here, but they need to make some concessions to the human ear: Some sentences are easier to follow when they are *read* than when they are *heard*, and so the sentences need to be recast. To make a sentence easier to *hear*, broadcast writers typically do the following:[13]

- Use a somewhat less formal writing style than do most print writers. This means using more contractions, the occasional sentence fragment, very short sentences, less formal words (kids versus children) and few pauses. This produces copy that is easier to understand and that is more dramatic. Most broadcast journalists try to achieve this breathless, staccato effect because they think viewers and listeners find it compelling.

- Use fewer details about sources and others mentioned in news reports. Broadcast writers sometimes do not even use the name of a source when the title is the important information and most people would not recognize the name anyway. Identification is not unimportant in broadcast writing; it is simply less important than other information.

- Put attributions at the beginnings of sentences, rather than at the ends. While they end up with the most boring material at the front, this format is more direct and requires no pauses. The version at the left (below) requires no obvious pauses, while the version at the right does:

The President of the Monroe County Volunteer Fire Department Jorge Castillo said today the department will have to go out of business if the county doesn't kick in more money.	The Monroe County Volunteer Fire Department will go out of business if the county does not kick in more money, Jorge Castillo, president of the department, said today.

The version on the left also gives a listener, who likely is distracted by an oncoming bus or any of 15 other things, a chance to register "Jorge Castillo," "Monroe County" or "Volunteer Fire Department"; to decide whether any of that is of interest; to establish a frame of reference if it is; and then to listen to the news in the rest of the sentence.

- Use actualities (in which sources are viewed or heard speaking), rather than direct quotations. Although they use direct quotations in similar ways and for essentially the same reasons as print writers, broadcast journalists plug in audio or video at the appropriate points in their stories. If they don't have actualities, but they have to quote sources on the air, they typically use paraphrases.

- Use some redundancy to ensure listeners and viewers get the story. This is why an anchor typically gives the gist of a story as a lead-in to a field writer's account. These are comparable to headlines in print writing, although they typically are more detailed. This is why broadcast journalists frequently sum up the gist of a story at the end, just in case a listener decides a little late that he or she is interested in the story. Here, for example, is how a radio writer might begin a story about President Bush's statements about Saddam Hussein of Iraq:

Anchor: The White House said today the president was wrong when he told the American people during his State of the Union address that Iraq tried to obtain uranium in Africa.	Reporter: Presidential spokesman Ari Fleischer said the president relied on false information in forged documents when he said Saddam Hussein had tried to purchase uranium from Niger to jumpstart his nuclear weapons program.

Active, Passive Voice

Verbs are written in active or passive voice to indicate whether the subject performs the action (active voice) or receives the action (passive voice) of the verb. The passive voice always is a verb phrase, rather than a single verb as in the active voice—the auxiliary of the phrase is a form of *to be* followed by the past participle. "The mayor fired (active) the assistant who took payoffs" is an example of the active voice, in which the subject performs the action. "The assistant who took payoffs was fired (passive) by the mayor" is an example of the passive voice, in which the subject experiences the action.

The active voice generally is preferred to the passive voice; it is more forceful and more immediate, and it takes less space. Passive voice may be better when the subject is not important or not known or when the subject is obvious, as in the following example:

Passive	**Active**
Mayor Paula Stone was elected by one of the largest majorities in the city's history.	The voters elected Mayor Paula Stone by one of the largest majorities in the city's history.

Citizens know who elects the mayor, and the passive voice is more natural than the active voice in this case. The passive voice might also be used when it allows the writer to better emphasize an important noun, as in this example:

Passive	Active
Two Northeast High School cheerleaders were honored Friday by their parent-teacher association.	The parent-teacher association honored two Northeast High School cheerleaders Friday.

Since the story mainly concerns two Northeast cheerleaders and not the school's parent-teacher association, the most important noun is *cheerleaders,* which is the subject of the sentence in the passive voice and an object in the active voice.

Writers should not use the passive voice when it weakens the emphasis on an important noun or pronoun. For example:

Passive	Active
A national health care plan to insure all Americans was outlined today by President George W. Bush.	President George W. Bush today outlined a national health care plan to insure all Americans.

Since several health care plans have been proposed in recent years, the reader should know immediately that *this plan* was prepared by the president. The president's plan obviously carries more weight because it is, well, the *president's* plan.

Finally, writers should avoid shifts from one voice to another, because such shifting results in an awkward and confusing sentence, as in the following example:

Shift to Passive	Active Throughout
Republicans supported Jones, Democrats supported Smith and Flagship was supported by Independents.	Republicans supported Jones, Democrats supported Smith and Independents supported Flagship.

Figures of Speech

A media writer can add color to copy by using figures of speech, but he or she must use them with great care. Figures of speech include similes, metaphors, hyperbole and other literary devices. These kinds of phrases may be more commonly used in feature stories, reviews or opinion pieces, but occasionally they are appropriate in news. Nobody has used more of them than Dan Rather of CBS News did in his coverage of Election Night 2000 (see the box "Ratherisms").

Technical, Bureaucratic Terms

The Vietnam War brought such phrases as *incursion, protective air strike* and *terminate with extreme prejudice* into public discourse. Watergate added its share of bureaucratic euphemisms, including calling burglars *plumbers* and clarifying a contradictory statement by a presidential news secretary by saying the earlier statement

RATHERISMS

Dan Rather of CBS News attracted attention during his coverage of the 2000 presidential election returns with his colorful figures of speech. It is difficult to tell whether he was driven to these phrases by the excitement of the moment or whether he wrote out a bunch of catchy expressions before the telecast and tried to work them all in. Some critics argue Rather overdid the use of dramatic, and sometimes quaint, expressions. But viewers might have enjoyed his eccentric commentary during a long evening of reporting that would otherwise have been mostly numbers. Or it may be that Rather, who is from Wharton, Texas, is just a good ole boy who uses these phrases naturally.

But they'll be doing backflips in Nashville, because Gore almost positively had to have Pennsylvania.

If Gore had lost Florida, you might be saying sayonara to his hopes.

Seldom is heard a discouraging word for any Republican in the Southwest.

Dan Rather, shown here during election night 2000, is famous for his colorful figures of speech. They have even earned a name: Ratherisms.

They're playing what amounts to a sudden-death overtime in Pennsylvania; it's that close.

But the way this night is going, wild and wooly as it is, who can say?

His lead has evaporated and melt—been melted faster than ice cream in a microwave.

The—the presidential race is crackling like a hickory fire here.

Bush has had a lead since the very start, but his lead is now shakier than cafeteria Jell-O.

Al Gore may be as cross as a snapping turtle about this Tennessee situation because it's his home state.

Bush is sweeping through the South like a tornado through a trailer park.

(continued)

RATHERISMS *(continued)*

Governor, you just didn't tumble off the turnip truck [to Gov. Tom Ridge of Pennsylvania].

And you can bet the rent money that down in Austin, they're watching Pennsylvania very carefully, those 23 votes.

And for the first time tonight, mark it if you will, if you're in the kitchen, Mabel, come back in the front room: 145 for Gore, 130 for Bush; 270 needed to win.

Gore got Florida. That put him in the hunt early [later proven to be wrong].

In Rhode Island, four electoral votes—Little Rhody goes for Gore.

These returns are running like a squirrel in a cage now, and one can get a little confused.

And it was as hot and squalid as a New York elevator in August [about the Hillary Clinton–Rick Lazio Senate race].

Bush has run through Dixie like a big wheel through a cotton field.

You can bet that they're smiling like a cat in a creamery down in Austin.

Another look at the electoral vote count. Can't get a cigarette paper between them: 185, Bush now that he's picked up Ohio and Tennessee—he goes to the front; 182 for Gore.

As Gov. Bush's father, President Bush, once said in another context, "This is tension city."

It's cardiac arrest time in this presidential campaign.

Well, we've said it many times, if—if a frog had side pockets, he'd carry a handgun."

Source: CBS News Election Night 2000, CBS News transcript, Nov. 7–8, 2000.

was *no longer operative.* More recently, authorities use *a person of interest,* which nobody seems to know how to define. But an individual identified as *a person of interest* could see his or her life changed dramatically. These phrases make the writer's job difficult because they sound like explanations, but they are not. They cloud, rather than clarify, thought.

Anyone who is close to a technical field or topic knows the technical and bureaucratic terms (jargon), and they may begin to think everyone else knows them. Anyone who works for the Federal Reserve Board, for example, knows what *prime rate* means and will assume everyone else knows. Anyone who works for the Gallup Organization of Princeton, N.J., knows what *margin of error* and *standard error* mean and will assume everyone else knows. Some public relations professionals who work for technical organizations and some journalists who cover them have the same knowledge and will make the same assumptions. They shouldn't.

Media writers who can't translate complex terminology—jargon—into simple language might as well scrap their stories, and if they can't learn how to translate jargon they might as well scrap their media writing careers. Educators, economists, attorneys, scientists and politicians understand the technical jargon of their own professions, but most lay readers, viewers and listeners don't. Those technical words and phrases must be replaced with less complex language or they must be adequately explained. Here is an example of untranslated jargon, which sounds like gobbledygook:

> After hitting a new high of business activity in October, the seasonally adjusted index of Nevada business activity dropped 4.5 percent in November, the Coleman-Talpa University Business Research Bureau has reported.
>
> Even with the general drop, however, the reading was 10 percent above last November's and the highest November value on record, according to Dr. Cheryl Flood, consulting statistician of the BRB.
>
> Business activity for the first three quarters of this year also was high, and a gain of 9 percent was recorded this year over the same year-ago period. A cyclical downturn that might alter this pattern during the final quarter of the year is unlikely, Flood said.

An economist, merchant or industrialist might understand the three paragraphs, but the average reader wouldn't. What, for instance, is a *seasonally adjusted index of business activity*? What business activity is included in the term *business activity*? And what is a *cyclical downturn*?

Jargon can be used to hide the truth or mislead, making it especially important for a writer to translate it. (See the box "George Orwell on Bureaucratic Euphemism.")

Jargon sometimes isn't translated because even the writer doesn't understand the technical terms or phrases. A lazy writer will merely quote the incomprehensible passages directly and attempt to sneak them by editors. But a good writer will ask knowledgeable colleagues or consult qualified sources for help. The good writer will substitute a more common word or phrase for the technical term or explain what the technical term means, as in this Associated Press lead:

> WASHINGTON—A study that found adult blood stem cells were unable to transform themselves into other types of tissue raises new doubts about whether they could be used to reinvigorate ailing organs.
>
> The finding supports the view that embryonic stem cells offer the most promise for treating such conditions as heart disease, spinal injury, diabetes and Parkinson's disease, some researchers say.

The story does not tell readers what *adult blood stem cells* are, in part because the stem cell controversy is a few years old and readers who have not lived on Pluto almost surely have read prior stories. But the second paragraph does bring the story

GEORGE ORWELL ON BUREAUCRATIC EUPHEMISM

In our time, political speech and writing are largely the defense of the indefensible. Things like the continuance of British rule in India, the Russian purges and deportations, and dropping of the atom bombs on Japan, can indeed be defended, but only by arguments which are too brutal for most people to face, and which do not square with the professed aims of political parties. Thus political language has to consist largely of euphemism, question-begging and sheer cloudy vagueness. Defenseless villages are bombarded from the air, the inhabitants driven out into the countryside, the cattle machine-gunned, the huts set on fire with incendiary bullets: this is called *pacification*. Millions of peasants are robbed of their farms and sent trudging along the roads with no more than they can carry: this is called *transfer of population* or *rectification of frontiers*. People are imprisoned for years without trial, or shot in the back of the neck or sent to die of scurvy in Arctic lumber camps: this is called *elimination of unreliable elements*. Such phraseology is needed if one wants to name things without calling up mental pictures of them.

Source: George Orwell, "Politics and the English Language," *The New Republic,* June 24, 1946: 903–904, p. 903.

George Orwell, author of *1984*, analyzed bureaucratic euphemism in 1946 in a classic essay for *The New Republic,* from which this excerpt is taken.

into focus by tying the latest information to embryonic stem cells and explaining what stem cells can do. In effect, the writer explained the context and did it early enough (Part 2) for the reader to understand the story from the beginning.

Pretentious Phrasing

This category might also be called, "It sounds good, but what on earth does it mean?" Pretentious phrasing typically is used by individuals who like to use big, flashy words to show the world how intelligent and well-educated they are or by people who find it difficult to translate big words into everyday language. Writers not only must avoid passing along their own pretentious phrases but also must avoid using other people's pretentious phrases. An example of pretentious phrasing comes, ironically, from a convention paper discussing the difficulties of writing clearly about medical research:

> Society does not require, and we do not expect, that adults should try to explain differential equations to first graders just learning that two plus two invariably is four. The

> level of comprehension is just not there; we do not make the attempt because we have
> no words with meaning for such an audience. Yet the medical writer essays an equal
> translation problem when he reports the cutting edge of research—areas at the far lim-
> its of existing knowledge.
>
>   The task is impossible on a prima facie basis. And those who forge the paths into the
> terra incognita of knowledge cannot really assist much. Their thoughts are expressed in
> the lingua franca of the frontier. They have forgotten the language of the stay-at-homes.
> And worse, they don't realize they have forgotten it.

This is not a parody. It was part of a presentation at a technical writers' convention by a director of scientific reports for a federal office. The pretentious use of the word *essays* in the third sentence hints at the problems coming in the next paragraph. There are three Latin phrases in a passage discussing the importance of using clear language.

Another example comes from the speech of a university president:

> Now we are engaged in testing whether this University can long endure as a university
> of the first class in an egalitarian society where all political and social pressures are
> toward damming the rivers, filling up the valleys, and leveling the peaks to the end of
> establishing an academic peneplane that will undulate featurelessly and lie as an anti-
> monument to the mediocrity of all that is second-best in the American culture.

This 73-word sentence starts out as a paraphrase of some famous statesman (Abraham Lincoln, perhaps) and ends up in a hopelessly complex geological metaphor that few persons could comprehend. A journalist covering the speech or a public relations professional writing the speech would have to translate it into English. These are some pretentious words to avoid:

accommodations (rooms)   parsimonious (tight)
annihilate (destroy)   petite (small)
arduous (difficult)   resolve (decide)
circumvent (go around)   superfluous (unnecessary)
covert (secret)   utilize (use)
endeavor (try)   vacillate (waver)
expedite (hurry)   vanquish (defeat)
fatigued (tired)   vivacious (active)
ignominious (bitter)   vocation (job)
indolent (lazy)   worsted (defeated)

Unnecessary Words

Good writers hate *fat* sentences, those that have an extra word or two in them that contribute nothing—and that may in fact interfere with comprehension. Good writers eliminate, with a few exceptions, all unnecessary words, as in the following examples.

Cutting the Fat

The group held a meeting for the purpose of electing a new chair-person.	The group met to elect a new chair-person.
Bobby Clawson scored from a distance of 35 feet out.	Bobby Clawson scored from 35 feet.
The fact that Harris did not succeed in defeating Kentwell did not do serious harm to the Democratic Party.	Harris didn't defeat Kentwell, but the Democratic Party suffered no harm.
The group picketed at the corner of Fifth Avenue and Market Street downtown.	The group picketed at Fifth and Market.
Our present city officials simply aren't providing the kind of moral leadership needed.	City officials aren't providing necessary moral leadership.
The present budget is a total of $3.57 million over last year's budget.	The budget is $3.57 million more than last year's.
The meeting, which is scheduled for 2:30 p.m. on Saturday afternoon, will be held in the auditorium.	The meeting is scheduled for 2:30 p.m. Saturday in the auditorium.
The painter fell off of the 50-foot scaffold, but she miraculously was unhurt.	The painter was unhurt when she fell from a 50-foot scaffold.
A car, which was yellow, was completely destroyed by the blast.	The blast destroyed the yellow car.
Flagship was present at the meeting and argued for more money for schools.	Flagship argued for more school money.
His secretary said that McGuillicutty would be unavailable for comment.	McGuillicutty is unavailable for comment.

Clichés, Trite Expressions

Thoughtful writers are as careful to avoid clichés as they are to avoid unnecessary words—primarily because clichés are inexact. They often camouflage poor observation and sloppy thinking. A pitcher described as *rifling the ball* is made to seem exactly like all the other pitchers who have been described as *rifling the ball*. Careful observation should suggest some differences in the way this pitcher throws the ball.

Those differences make the pitcher unique, and they are the kinds of details that make a story interesting. But a writer must observe that kind of detail to report it. The writer who doesn't notice detail or isn't willing to expend some energy in finding ways to describe a person or situation is likely to use well-worn phrases that aren't interesting or descriptive.

Such phrases as *rifle the ball, bolt from the blue, dangerous departure* and *pay the piper* come from a writer's memory, not from a scene to be described. In that sense, clichés weaken writing because they tell less about the scene than they do about the writer's memory of trite phrases. They cast doubt on a report's accuracy. A statement that someone was caught in *a hail of bullets* leaves the audience wondering how much the writer has exaggerated the real situation.

Clichés also can irritate an audience. Good writers try to know what words and phrases are overworked long before an audience does. They keep up with what appears in a wide variety of sources—books, newspapers, magazines, newscasts and employee newsletters. Here are some clichés that are best avoided:

achieve closure	hale and hearty
across the board	honest as the day is long
at this point in time	iron out difficulties
average man or woman	Lady Luck
ax to grind	level playing field
back to square one	looks like a winner
been there, done that	long and short of it
blanket of snow	no uncertain terms
blind as a bat	pearls of wisdom
blue ribbon (panel, group)	point with pride
bone of contention	pretty as a picture
bottom line	push the envelope
bull in a china closet	reign of terror
busy as a bee	resounding victory
caught red-handed	the rest is history
checkered career	ribbon of concrete (highway)
conventional wisdom	riot of color
do lunch	sea change
don't go there	smell a rat
face time	sober as a judge
few and far between	take to task
food for thought	tender loving care
goes without saying	third degree
the good news and the bad news	to be sure

throw the hat in the ring	where the rubber meets the road
time immemorial	whole new ball game
tired expression	wide-eyed innocent
up for grabs	word to the wise
water over the dam	worse for wear
water under the bridge	worth its weight in gold

What if a news source uses a cliché in a statement that a writer wants to quote? The writer has several choices. If the quotation is more vivid and helps to make a point with the cliché, the writer might decide to include it in a direct quote. Sometimes it might actually be the writer's point to show that an individual talks in clichés. If the cliché detracts from or weakens the quote, however, another option is to switch to quoting the speaker indirectly (without quotation marks) and omitting or replacing the cliché (Chapter 7).

Colloquialisms, Slang

Colloquialisms are expressions—words, phrases and idioms—typically used only in familiar conversation and informal writing, not in formal speech and writing. Colloquialisms, which tend to find their way into common usage and endure for long periods, are not necessarily incorrect or undesirable words. Good writers typically avoid colloquialisms, although such expressions, when properly used, can provide verbal impact unduplicated by more formal words.

They include popular words, abbreviations for longer words (*prof* for *professor*) and learned words used in popular ways (*alibi* for *excuse*). Such contractions as *doesn't, it's, didn't, don't, I'll, they'll* and *he'll* are colloquialisms, and some editors have policies against their use. However, such colloquialisms are widely accepted; a writer may use them when they are appropriate and policy allows. Here are some colloquialisms best to avoid:

aggravate (annoy)	heap (many, much)
around (approximately)	hold on (wait)
auto	into something (interested in)
awfully (very)	kind of (sort of)
back of (behind)	lit (literature)
bust (raid, failure)	lots of (many)
darn	lousy
doggone it	mighty (very)
folks (persons, people)	okay
funny (odd, unusual)	over (more than)
gumption (shrewdness, courage)	phone
hang in there (persevere)	poli sci (political science)

prof (professor)	show (movie)
psych (psychology)	sure (certain, certainly)
run (manage)	terribly (very)

Slang—typically considered to be colloquialisms that are outside the realm of standard or conventional usage—often develops from an individual's attempt to find a colorful, cute, dramatic, funny or brand-new expression. Slang words usually are old words used in new ways. Slang expressions often are taken from the specialized vocabularies of certain pastimes or occupations. *A-OK* is from the vocabulary of the space program; *brass* and *goldbrick* are military expressions; *poker face* is card players' jargon; *bummer* and *downer* stem from hallucinatory drug use; and *behind the eight ball* is the jargon of billiards.

Slang words typically flourish for a brief period only, until overuse robs them of color, cuteness or drama, and then they die. Some slang words, however, survive. *Mob, blurb, debunk* and *hoax,* for example, once were considered to be slang expressions, but now they are widely accepted for use even in formal writing. Such words as *bum, show* (film), *phone, taxi* and *auto* once were classified as slang but now are viewed by many as colloquialisms.

Writers should recognize two fundamental drawbacks to the use of slang and colloquialisms. First, it is easy to rely too heavily on such words and expressions and to substitute them for more precise terms that would produce crisper, more accurate prose. Second, some slang words aren't well known. One of the worst writing sins is to communicate in such a way as to be misunderstood. If the use of *the man* for *official* or *bad* for *good* is confusing, the expressions should not be used.

YOUR RESPONSIBILITY IS . . .

- ■ To understand that different writing forms (speeches, news, novels) may require somewhat different approaches and formats, but that good writing principles and fundamentals are common to all forms.

- ■ To learn that different media use different formats and have different ways of preparing copy for publication or broadcast. You must not be intimidated by those differences. The more formats you master, the better writer you will be.

- ■ To study, practice and master mechanical skills of writing. If you can't master grammar, style, punctuation and spelling fundamentals, you won't be much of a writer.

- ■ To develop conceptual skills. You must have critical thinking skills and learn how to gather complete, accurate information, for only then will you perform competently in virtually any job in any medium, from broadcast to Web.

■ To accept that a story is not acceptable if each word and each sentence in that story is not the best you can make it.

■ To develop higher-level writing skills—you must know how to "show" (or describe) rather than "tell," for instance.

NOTES

1. The work of French philosopher Jacques Derrida and the deconstructionist movement has sought to undermine the view that language is stable and capable of fixed meanings: Jacques Derrida, *Of Grammatology* (Gayatri Chakravorty Spivak, trans.) (Baltimore: Johns Hopkins University Press, 1976). See also Ferdinand de Saussure, *Course in General Linguistics* (Charles Bally and Albert Sechehaye, eds.; Wade Baskin, trans.) (New York: Philosophical Library, 1959).

2. Jack G. Shaheen, *Reel Bad Arabs: How Hollywood Vilifies a People* (New York: Olive Branch, 2001).

3. Arthur Asa Berger, *Narratives in Popular Culture, Media and Everyday Life* (Thousand Oaks, Calif.: Sage, 1997); and Dennis K. Mumby, (ed.), *Narrative and Social Control: Critical Perspectives* (Newbury Park, Calif.: Sage, 1993).

4. Ferdinand de Saussure, who had enormous impact on the work of scholars in disciplines ranging from anthropology to literary studies, is a pioneer in a field called structural linguistics: de Saussure, *Course in General Linguistics*.

5. Sheldon Rampton and John Stauber, *Trust Us, We're Experts! How Industry Manipulates Science and Gambles With Your Future* (New York: Jeremy P. Tarcher/Putnam, 2001): 15.

6. David E. Hendrix, "Coal Mine Canaries," in Kristina Borjesson (ed.), *Into the Buzzsaw: Leading Journalists Expose the Myth of a Free Press* (Amherst, N.Y.: Prometheus, 2002): 151–174.

7. Ana Mantica, "Shoptalk: The J-School Blues: Even the Best Programs Can't Take the Place of Work in Real World," *Editor & Publisher,* April 29, 2002: 38.

8. William Kirtz, "Show, Don't Tell, the Secret Story: Take Readers in Hand, Excite Their Senses, Says Literary Journalism Practitioner," *Quill,* September 1996: 28–29, p. 29.

9. Ibid.

10. James Tankard and Laura Hendrickson, "Specificity, Imagery in Writing: Testing the Effects of 'Show, Don't Tell,'" *Newspaper Research Journal,* 17:1–2 (1996): 35–48.

11. Help for the student weak in English usage is available from the following sources: Lauren Kessler and Duncan McDonald, *When Words Collide: A Media Writer's Guide to Grammar and Style,* 5th ed. (Belmont, Calif.: Wadsworth, 2000); William Strunk Jr. and E. B. White, *The Elements of Style,* 4th ed. (Boston: Allyn and Bacon, 2000); Brian S. Brooks, James L. Pinson and Jean Gaddy Wilson, *Working With Words: A Handbook for Media Writers and Editors,* 5th ed. (Boston: Bedford/St. Martin's, 2003); Paul J. Hopper, *A Short Course in Grammar: A Course in the Grammar of Standard Written English* (New York: Norton, 1999); Paula LaRocque, *Championship Writing: 50 Ways to Improve Your Writing* (Oak Park, Ill.: Marion Street Press, 2000); and Joseph M. Williams, *Style: The Basics of Clarity and Grace* (New York: Longman, 2003).

12. Michael Ryan, "The Use of a Writing Model for Print or On-line News," *Journalism & Mass Communication Educator,* 49:4 (1995): 74–77; and Michael Ryan, "Models Help Writers Produce Publishable Releases," *Public Relations Quarterly,* Summer 1995: 25–27.

13. Ted White, *Broadcast News Writing, Reporting, and Producing,* 3rd ed. (Boston: Focal Press, 2002); Bob Dotson, *Make It Memorable: Writing and Packaging TV News With Style* (Chicago: Bonus Books, 2000).

CHAPTER 5

LEADS

That Most Formidable Challenge

The lead (aka lede)—the beginning of a newspaper or magazine article, broadcast story, Web news item or public relations release—is intended to "lead" readers, listeners or viewers into the rest of the story. One of the most important jobs of the lead is to grab or hook the audience and pull it into the story. When editors or writers talk about a lead being a "grabber," they are referring to this characteristic.

The summary lead was the workhorse of news writing for most of the 20th century. A summary news lead is associated with the inverted pyramid form of writing (Chapter 6), which places the most important and interesting information at the top, or wide part, of the inverted pyramid and then relates the remaining information in order of descending importance.

One of the strengths of inverted pyramid structure is that it is an extremely efficient way to convey information. For decades, news reports were written almost without exception in inverted pyramid structure, with a strong summary news lead at the beginning. Other types of leads—question leads, quotation leads, and narrative leads—were usually limited to feature articles. But in the past 30 years, other types of leads have begun to appear on news stories and releases in print and digital media. It is increasingly common to see narrative leads on articles that are clearly news stories and releases.

FIVE W'S AND THE H

Before writing a lead, a writer must decide what information is important, what isn't important and what angle is best. The five W's and the H of news writing—who, what, where, when, why and how—and the news values (see Chapter 2) can help a professional make the necessary decisions.

Who

A writer must know precisely who is involved in every story. It's important to obtain the correct spelling of all names, record all addresses accurately and, if possible, obtain the ages of the people involved if they seem relevant.

A writer must decide whether the names of the people involved should be placed in the first sentence or in the second or third sentences and whether names should be in the first part of the first sentence (1-A) or in the second part (1-B). If the individuals are prominent, the names typically appear in the first part of the first sentence. Imagine, for example, placing the names of the following people in sentences other than the first or later in the sentence instead of at the beginning:

> Sen. Hillary Clinton defended her and her husband's request for $3.5 million in taxpayer money to help pay legal bills from the Whitewater investigation, saying other presidents got similar bailouts.

> Former Attorney General Janet Reno, who is challenging fellow Democrat Bill McBride for the right to face Florida Gov. Jeb Bush in November, has booked rock superstar Elton John to sing at a fund-raising concert.

> Tony Blair, the prime minister of Great Britain, was last night given his starkest warning yet of the growing scale of mainstream Labour opposition to war with Iraq and distrust of President Bush.

> The loyalist, Gerald Kaufman, who has backed recent conflicts against Iraq and the Taliban and military action in Kosovo and the Falklands, told Blair of "substantial resistance" in the Parliamentary Labour Party.

All people mentioned in the leads are prominent by virtue of the offices they hold (Clinton, Bush, Blair, Kaufman), the offices they have held or are aspiring to (Reno) or their celebrity status (Elton John). *Who* is a definite part of the angle or approach each writer took for each story. Had the individuals not been prominent, the *who* might not have been emphasized and the stories might have been approached from slightly different angles.

A specific *who* doesn't appear in the first sentence of every news story, particularly when the inclusion of a name makes an awkward sentence. Consider the following lead:

> JEFFERSONVILLE, Ga.—Two local men awaiting trial on burglary charges filed suit in U.S. District Court in Macon Wednesday to close the 74-year-old Twiggs County jail. Jesse Day, 17, and James D. Hill, 18, named Sheriff Earl Hamerick, Jailer James Hamerick and the five-man Board of County Commissioners as defendants in the suit.

It would have taken a good deal of space in the first sentence of the story, which appeared in *The Atlanta Journal-Constitution,* to identify the two young men. Naming them in Part 1-A also would have detracted from the real point of the story—that an effort was being made to close a 74-year-old jail. If the two men had been sons of the mayor or the state's governor, however, the names definitely would have appeared in the first sentence.

It is important to determine not only whether the *who* should be included in the first paragraph, but also whether the *who* should be the subject of the sentence. The subject, the most important and prominent part of any sentence, should contain the story's most important noun.

Public relations writers sometimes struggle under constraints that other professionals do not. One of these may be a standing order to put the name and title of a CEO in the first part (1-A) of every release. That can lead to this:

> Sam Waterstein, president and chief executive officer of U.S. Information Network, said today that the company will begin offering next fall high-speed Internet service for $12.95 a month.

That's a pretty boring start for a newsworthy, and fictitious, release. The upside-down sentence needs to be turned over so the most interesting and important material ($12.95 Internet service) is in Part 1-A.

What

What in lead writing refers to the happening or occurrence that makes an item worth reporting. The *what* might be the election of a public official, the issuance of an injunction by a court, an automobile accident, a fire, a legislative or congressional action, a crime or any number of events that occur every day and that are judged to be important or interesting.

A *what* is virtually always in the news lead. And writers often must decide just how to play a given *what*, particularly when a story contains a large number of *what* elements. Consider, for example, how a writer might handle a story that contains the following elements:

Who	Dr. Ruth Love Holloway, director of the Department of Health, Education and Welfare's Right-to-Read program
What	Released a special report on schoolchildren
What	Report showed 4.8 percent illiteracy among schoolchildren
What	Nationwide, a million children 12–17 can't read at fourth-grade level
Where	Report released in Washington, D.C., at the National Center for Health Statistics

A *what* is the most important element of the story, but the question is which *what* to use first. The fact of the release really tells the reader little, so that leaves the 4.8 percent figure and the million figure. Both have impact, because many students, parents, educators and politicians must be affected by the results.

Freelance writer-photographer Arthur "Weegee" Fellig wrote his leads in the early decades of the 20th century from the back of his car, which doubled as a newsroom and darkroom. The equipment Fellig would need to do the same jobs today would fit into an attaché case.

The million figure also has another obvious news value—magnitude. The 4.8 percent figure implies great magnitude, but the million figure clearly specifies great magnitude. Compare the following two-paragraph leads that a public relations writer might produce for a news release:

Approximately 1 million U.S. schoolchildren aged 12–17 can't read at the fourth-grade level, according to a special government study released today.

The four-year testing program conducted by the Department of Health, Education and Welfare found that 4.8 percent of schoolchildren studied were illiterate.

Results of a special government study suggest that illiteracy among U.S. schoolchildren is unexpectedly widespread.

A four-year testing program conducted by the Department of Health, Education and Welfare found that 4.8 percent of the youths were illiterate. Projected nationwide, that would mean about a million children 12–17 can't read at fourth-grade level.

The lead on the left is nearly a dozen words shorter than the one on the right, but, more important, the impact and magnitude news values are merely implied in the lead on the right, not clearly stated as in the one on the left. The less precise lead doesn't satisfy the reader's curiosity as quickly because the wrong material is specified in Part 1-A. Because the impact and magnitude values aren't as clearly stated, the lead at the right is less likely to capture an editor's attention or to draw a reader into the story.

A great deal of news involves a prominent person saying something. In these cases, the writer has to decide which to put first—the speaker's name and identification (the *who*) or *what* the speaker said. For instance, an Associated Press reporter decided that the person (the *who*) was important enough to come first (in Part 1-A) in this lead:

> National Security Adviser Condoleezza Rice said in a speech Thursday that freedom is the equal birthright of Palestinians as well as Jews, pledging that the United States would stand by Israel but continue to call for a Palestinian state.

A different writer might have decided to play up (in Part 1-A) what was said:

> Freedom is the equal birthright of Palestinians as well as Jews, National Security Adviser Condoleezza Rice said in a speech Thursday. She pledged that the United States would stand by Israel but continue to call for a Palestinian state.

A public relations writer must keep in mind always that a *who* is not important simply because the *who* is the boss, unless the boss mandates that his or her name must come first.

Where

Where an event or problem happens is an important part of any story. Is it in the news consumer's back yard, or is it 2,000 miles away? The following lead from the *Las Vegas Review-Journal* indicates that several locations are important to the story. (Linda Sue Miller is not the suspect's real name.)

> For the past two weeks, Las Vegas authorities have been trying to connect one slaying in Las Vegas and another in California to occult rituals or Satanism.
>
> According to a Las Vegas police search warrant, police are examining whether Linda Sue Miller—a suspect in the slayings of her mother and husband—could have relied in part on books about the occult or Satanism to carry out the crimes.

This report incorporates the *where* elements well, but the beginning is less compelling than it might be because the sentences are upside down. The writer started each sentence with boring information that should have gone into parts 1-B and 2-B.

It's an important axiom that a story that occurs locally—which has high proximity—takes precedence over a story that occurs outside a medium's listening, viewing or circulation area—other parts of the stories being equal. A writer, then, should indicate early that a story is in fact local. This lead from the *Wisconsin State Journal* in Madison establishes the place in the first sentence:

> Restaurateurs who oppose changes in Madison's smoking regulations asked Monday night what's next: Will Madison police greasy food?
>
> "I think that (the city is) infringing on the most important right—freedom of choice," said Otto Dilba, marketing manager for Angelic Brewing Co. in Downtown Madison.

The following lead from the Albany, N.Y., *Times Union* provides several indications of location, or *where:* a dateline (BLENHEIM), a city that a man is from (Albany) and the place where a body was found (a Schoharie County field):

> BLENHEIM—A charred corpse, believed to be that of a 40-year-old Albany man, was found inside a minivan that was discovered parked and burning in an isolated Schoharie County field Sunday evening, police said.

A writer often must be more specific in identifying the location of an event or other occurrence than simply stating that it happened locally. It's not enough to say, "the mayor was picketed today for her stand on abortion." It should be made clear in the first sentence precisely where the pickets were located: in the mayor's office, outside city hall or in front of the mayor's home. The location should be stated precisely in the case of a crime, fire, disaster or accident.

A *where* element seldom is the subject of the first sentence, but in some cases the place where the event occurred is worthy of the most prominent position, particularly when the location is odd, as in the following example:

> A bawdy house [an odd *where*] was the scene Tuesday of a gun battle that left two patrons slightly injured and the house's owner in jail.

Since no one was severely injured or killed, the *where* could appropriately receive the most prominent play by being the subject of the sentence.

A Web writer must pay particular attention to a *where* element and give it prominent play since Web sites can be accessed from any computer in any geographic location. A weather site dedicated to disseminating news about local and national weather, for example, must ensure that readers can easily distinguish between national weather reports and local weather reports. Site visitors must be able to move quickly and easily to the appropriate local links.

When

One of the most important of the seven news values is timeliness. Writers, therefore, strive for fresh news or a new angle on old news. Because timeliness is so prized, writers usually specify the day and/or time when something occurred in the first sentence of their stories, as in the following example:

> Fifteen blind children and two other people were injured Monday when a bus in which they were riding went out of control and hit a pole and a tree on East River Drive just above Midvale Avenue in East Falls.

When news is more than a few days old, a writer may de-emphasize that fact by using *recently* or a similar vague phrase in the lead. In these examples, the time peg deliberately is not emphasized: "Mayor Saunders recently purchased a $200 ash tray for her office"; "Dritsas has been pardoned by the governor." Some writers, in handling old news, never specify the exact time when an action was taken or an event occurred. Others specify the precise time far down in the story, thereby admitting they were late getting the news.

It is the role of broadcast news to report *today's* news, and many broadcast news reports will include the word *today*. If broadcast writers have to report an event that happened yesterday, they are likely to look for a new angle that is happening today to give the story some freshness. Public relations professionals should follow the same practice: Editors usually are not interested in old news, so a release should not be written. But when information is timely, it should be reported.

Why and How

The *why* news element refers to the cause, reason or purpose behind an event's occurrence, and the *how* refers to the means by which something happened. Writers sometimes know *how* something was done, but not *why*, or *why* something was done, but not *how*. In the *why* lead, the writer states the reasons for an action or a happening, as in the following example from *The Daily Texan*, student newspaper at the University of Texas:

> The drastically rising number of reported rape cases in Austin has led to creation of a Rape Crisis Center, sponsored by the University's Women's Affairs Committee.

A *how* element might also be more important in some stories than any of the other news elements, and in that case it may receive top play in the first sentence. Consider, for example, a story in which the *how* contains an oddity news value. The writer might have the following information:

Who	Mr. and Mrs. James Dorsey, both 26, 1405 N. Riverside Ave. (a local address)
What	Involved in an automobile accident—no one injured
When	8:05 a.m. Monday
Where	11th and Sawdust
Why	Brakes failed
How	Went off the road to Homer's Mountain, went through a pile of hay in a field, bounced back onto the highway, struck three cars, knocked over a fire plug and finally ran into the window of Gilbert's Furniture Store

Because no one was injured in the accident, and because the *how* does contain an element of oddity, the lead might be written this way:

> A car went off Homer's Mountain road early Monday, plowed through a haystack, bounced back onto the highway, struck three other cars, knocked off a fire plug and finally plunged into the window of Gilbert's Furniture Store at 11th and Sawdust.
>
> Neither driver James Dorsey nor his wife, both 26, of 1405 N. Riverside Ave., was injured in the accident, which was caused when the brakes of the Dorsey car failed.

Had someone been injured in the accident, the story would have been written differently.

SUMMARY LEAD

Despite the increasing popularity of narrative leads, the summary lead is still the primary tool of news writing for journalism, Web and public relations professionals. The summary news lead has two tasks to accomplish: It needs (1) to capture the interest of the reader, as does any lead, and (2) to tell the essence or gist of the event, problem or issue. Ideally, it needs to do both of these things in one sentence. Strong summary news leads quickly satisfy a news consumer's need and desire for information and attract a consumer to the rest of the story. Neither task is easy, and a news writer is faced with many hard decisions in constructing a lead. Following are examples of the summary lead:

> A local couple was awarded $2 million in damages Tuesday in Crawford County Court for injuries suffered in a traffic accident last March.

> Gary Kinnear, a school crossing guard at Kennedy Elementary School for 32 years, died Thursday at his home at 312 Enfield Road.

Each summary lead gets to the point of the story in Part 1-A (see Figure 4.1 on page 100) so the reader has no difficulty understanding the news. The less important and interesting information is in Part 1-B in each lead. The strength of the summary news lead is its ability to convey important information quickly and efficiently.

Enticing a reader to finish a story is much more difficult than quickly satisfying the need and desire for information. A complicated or dull lead reduces substantially the probability that someone will read further. But if a lead is straightforward and bright and holds a promise of interesting and worthwhile things to come, the probability is high that more of the story will be read or heard.

The problems of lead writing are compounded by limitations on the length of every lead sentence. Ninety-five percent of Associated Press leads are one-sentence paragraphs.[1] Research on leads of six wire services found that the Washington Post News Service had the longest leads at 39 words. The Associated Press and United Press International scored similarly at 30 words. Scripps-Howard News Service had the shortest leads at 25 words.[2] Reading expert Robert Gunning has suggested 20 words as an appropriate length for readers with at least 12th-grade educations.[3]

Squeezing the gist of a complex story into a short, readable lead sentence is one of the great creative challenges. The difficulty of the task is illustrated by the fact that *The New York Times* hires writers who specialize in lead writing.

A REALLY CONCISE LEAD

When James Thurber worked for the New York *Evening Post*, the editors demanded that news leads be as tight as possible. On his next story, Thurber obeyed with the following lead:

> Dead.
>
> That was what the man was the police found in an areaway last night.

Source: Burton Bernstein, *Thurber: A Biography* (New York: Dodd, Mead, 1975): 154.

At The Tampa Tribune, *a WFLA-TV camera located next to the copy desks is used when reporters need to broadcast stories written for the newspaper. The multimedia desk is the center of* The Tampa Tribune's *state-of-the-art newsroom. Broadcast, online and print editors and producers work side by side as they cover the news.*

Traditional Lead

The first step in writing a traditional summary lead is to pick out the most important or interesting element. It may help to list the five W's and the H on paper and look them over. The list might include several *what* elements. Often one of the *what* elements (what happened?) will be the most important, as in this example:

What	A three-alarm fire
What	Apartment building gutted
Where	El Campo Apartments at 1912 Nueces St.
Who	Nine residents escaped
Who	Fire Department Battalion Chief Harry Evans
What	Evans said the firefighters' main concern was to keep the fire from spreading to an apartment complex 30 feet to the south.
What	No injuries reported
What	All residents left homeless
When	Monday night
How	Fire started in attic and spread through the entire structure

A writer might look over this list of elements, particularly the *whats*, and pick several to combine in the lead:

> A three-alarm fire gutted an apartment building Monday night, leaving nine residents homeless.

The writer has also inserted a *when*, which normally is included in most leads because it adds only one or two words. After the writer makes a first try at writing a lead, he or she will usually read it carefully to determine whether it can be improved. This lead is fairly short, at 14 words. The reporter might decide that the where (the El Campo Apartments at 1912 Nueces St.) can be inserted:

> A three-alarm fire Monday night gutted the El Campo Apartments at 1912 Nueces St., leaving nine residents homeless.

Note that the when (Monday night) has been moved to an earlier point, so it doesn't get lost at the end of a longer sentence.

A different writer might emphasize a different *what* in Part 1-A, the premier part of the lead:

> Nine residents were left homeless Monday night when a three-alarm fire gutted the El Campo Apartments at 1912 Nueces St.

After the lead sentence or lead paragraph is written, it is important to back it up in the second sentence or paragraph. Suppose a news article started with the following lead:

> First lady Laura Bush told a group of 2,500 students at Texas A&M University Wednesday that individuals can become heroes in many different ways, including reading to children or joining the USA Freedom Corps.

If the next sentence were the following, it would not be supporting the lead with further details:

> After her lecture, Bush received several gifts, including a Texas A&M T-shirt, from Cadet Sean Cullen.

The following sentence, if it came directly after the first sentence, would do a much better job of supporting the lead:

> "I urge you to use the energy you have at this time in your life to help someone else," Bush said.

It sometimes helps to think of the lead as more than one paragraph. Many writers who use multiple Part 1 paragraphs see their leads as units, and the lead is not finished until the unit is complete. For example:

> Consumer activists welcomed the Fairfield Town Council's decision last night to demolish a row of condemned houses and to move a cemetery to make way for a modern shopping complex in this rapidly growing retirement community.
>
> The action was condemned by people who live in the historic row houses, who have relatives buried in the cemetery and who say they want to preserve Fairfield's history.

This lead must be viewed as a unit because the story is unbalanced if the writer does not mention in the second paragraph (a second Part 1) that the action by the town council was condemned by some residents. Thinking of the lead as a unit helps a writer to avoid a one-sided report and to distribute information in a reasonable way.

Less Formal Lead

Leads for broadcast journalism and the Web generally follow the principles outlined here, although they sometimes are less formal than leads for public relations, magazines or newspapers, and they don't always try to compress all the important information into one sentence. Broadcasters frequently slide into a story gradually. Thalia Assuras, anchor of the *CBS Morning News*, began a newscast this way:

> Looking again at our top stories, Monica Lewinsky is expected back before Kenneth Starr's grand jury today. Prosecutors want to compare her previous statements with the president's testimony given Monday. Lewinsky has reportedly told friends she is upset with the president's public characterization of their relationship.

And anchor John Roberts of the *CBS Evening News* reported Lance Armstrong's fourth Tour de France victory this way:

> American supercyclist Lance Armstrong has done it again. He easily sped to his fourth straight Tour de France title today, finishing the three-week, 2,000-mile course more than seven minutes ahead of his closest competitor. Armstrong says he hopes to race at least two more years, and if he wins both times, he would make biking history with six straight victories.

A direct address lead is another kind of less formal summary lead. Here is an example from *Reader's Digest:*

> You may remember the grapefruit diet, or the cabbage-soup regimen. These weren't merely diets; they were magic. They offered negative calories: The more you eat, the more you lose. They don't, of course, work as advertised.

This article starts with a highly involving *you* because the editors know this is a powerful way to draw readers into unfamiliar subjects. The informal, chatty first sentence is typical of broadcast reporting. Broadcast news writers are able to ease into stories in a way that newspaper, public relations or magazine writers usually cannot, as in this broadcast news lead:

> If you are waiting for your new driver's license to arrive in the mail, you aren't the only one. The Department of Public Safety is switching to a new kind of driver's license with computer-generated digital photo images of the driver. The new cards are more difficult to duplicate, and they should cut down on consumer fraud.

Notice the direct address to the listener—more common in broadcast news than newspaper, public relations, magazine or wire service writing—the absence of a *when,* and the absence of attribution. These are all elements of the more informal—and dynamic—style commonly used in broadcast news writing.

Web writers also adopt this chatty tone on occasion, and they try to play up a catchy aspect to capture that rapidly scanning reader. *The Daytona Beach News-Journal's* online edition included on its front page this lead sentence:

> After a round of all-night negotiations, baseball players and owners reached a tentative agreement on a labor contract that averted a walkout threatened today.

The lead has the directness of a newspaper lead, the conversational style of broadcast news and a conciseness that works well on the Web.

The following news item from *Salon.com,* a Web magazine, uses more casual language than most print writing and also includes some intriguing elements (what is the "dishy little item"?):

> On Thursday, Fox News ran a dishy little item with the headline "Al and Tipper Wouldn't Pony Up for the Boss." The piece quoted anonymous sources who allegedly are close to

JONATHAN DUBE ON REMEMBERING THE AUDIENCE

Write and edit with online readers' needs and habits in mind. Web usability studies show that readers tend to skim over sites rather than read them intently. They also tend to be more proactive than print readers or TV viewers, hunting for information rather than passively taking in what you present to them.

Think about your target audience. Because your readers are getting their news online, chances are they are more interested in Internet-related stories than TV viewers or newspaper readers, so it may make sense to put greater emphasis on such stories. Also, your site potentially has a global reach, so consider whether you want to make it understandable to a local, national or international audience, and write and edit with that in mind.

Source: Jonathan Dube, "Writing News Online," in Jan Winburn (ed.), *Shop Talk & War Stories: American Journalists Examine Their Profession* (Boston: Bedford/St. Martin's, 2003): 201–205, p. 201. Originally a column for the Poynter Institute for Media Studies.

Jonathan Dube is the technology editor for MSNBC.com and founder of CyberJournalist.net, which helps media professionals cope with the Web.

the Gores and rocker-poet-icon Bruce Springsteen who claimed Al and Tipper tried to hit up the Boss for free tickets to the Aug. 10 show at the MCI Center in Washington.[4]

Leads on Web news articles may eventually become even more casual as they are influenced by the informal style already found on much of the Web. (See also the box "Jonathan Dube on Remembering the Audience.") A good place to sample some of this style is in the many blogs, or Web logs, found on the Web. Recall from Chapter 2 that a blog is a site on which an individual (blogger) posts experiences, thoughts, links, opinions or news. One blog, Scott Rosenberg's "Links & Comment," on *Salon.com,* featured this item:

It turns out that beer is probably just as effective, or more effective, than red wine in protecting you from heart attacks, raising the "good" cholesterol in your blood, and so on— according to today's Wall Street Journal. Moderation matters, of course; one or two beers a day seems to be the happy medium, with emphasis on "happy."[5]

NARRATIVE LEAD

Narrative leads often are associated with "soft" news or features that emphasize human interest elements like oddity and emotion. While summary leads get to the point immediately, narrative leads do not. Writers of narrative leads begin their stories with direct quotations, scene setters and anecdotes.

The narrative lead typically begins with a kind of mini feature story. The mini features, usually called anecdotes or vignettes, describe in sometimes vivid language a sequence of ongoing events, much as a fiction story does, and they stress interest over importance almost all the time.

The lead may begin with a specific scene or a specific individual in the act of doing something. Narrative leads have been used for decades in *Reader's Digest, The Atlantic, The New Yorker* and other popular magazines. But narrative leads have become common in recent years in the news columns of newspapers, too, and even on the front pages—something that would not have been the case 30 years ago. Television, Web and public relations writers also have discovered that narrative leads are useful ways to interest readers.

Narrative Technique

A narrative lead usually describes one or a few individuals prominent in an event, issue or problem. Here is the same news event presented with a summary news lead and a narrative lead from the Norfolk *Virginian-Pilot* (the individual's name was changed):

Narrative Lead	**Summary Lead**
VIRGINIA BEACH—Standing on a sidewalk near Pembroke Mall, a mother gripped her 2-year-old son's stroller Thursday afternoon and waited for a light to change.	VIRGINIA BEACH—A 2-year-old boy was fatally injured Saturday when an out-of-control car jumped the sidewalk and hurled the boy and his stroller into a traffic pole.
Suddenly, two cars collided. One spun out of control, jumped the sidewalk and hurled the boy and the stroller into a traffic pole.	
The boy, Michael Hammer of Virginia Beach, suffered a head injury and was declared dead at 2 p.m. at Sentara Norfolk General Hospital.	

The *Reader's Digest,* the second largest circulation magazine in the world, used this narrative lead on a story about the transplant of a dead infant's heart into a 5-month-old boy suffering from a rare heart defect:

The call came at 11 a.m., three days before Christmas. Marguerite Brown, R.N., donor coordinator for Stanford University Medical Center's transplant program, took it at her desk. There had been a crib death in Fargo, N.D. The four-month-old infant's heart had been resuscitated, but the brain had not survived.

Television journalists frequently tell their stories through the eyes of individuals who are part of a problem or situation. NBC's Tom Aspell used a beauty salon operator to illustrate how business is making a comeback in Kabul, Afghanistan (video shows women getting makeovers in the salon):

> Nazaneen has opened a beauty salon in Kabul—unthinkable during Taliban rule, when women were largely confined to their homes and banned from working or attending school.
>
> Brides and wedding guests, Nazaneen's specialty, spend up to $5 each for a makeover.

Aspell used this narrative lead as a springboard to a larger discussion of the return of normal business practice in post-Taliban Kabul.

Public relations and Web writers also use narrative leads that seem to capture a moment or a problem. Here is an approach that a public relations or Web writer might use to start a story about a rodeo:

> These thoroughbreds know what it's all about. Their ears prick and their snouts press the starting gate when they hear the familiar tune warning that a race is about to start.
>
> These aren't thoroughbred horses trying to win the roses, but potbellied pigs trying to win cookies.
>
> The porker handlers at the County Pig Races at the County Livestock Show and Rodeo get the pigs to run faster by showing them cookies. "The winner gets the cookie; the loser gets the crumbs," the announcer tells the audience matter-of-factly. "That's the way it is in life, and that's the way it is at Ham Hock Downs."

Narrative leads can be humorous, but they don't have to be, as in this classic from *Time* magazine:

> A smooth bar of soap, wrapped neatly in a white handkerchief and tucked safely in the breast pocket of a faded leather jacket, is all that keeps George from losing himself to the streets. When he wakes each morning from his makeshift bed of newspapers in the subway tunnels of Philadelphia, he heads for the rest room of a nearby bus station or McDonald's and begins an elaborate ritual of washing off the dirt and smells of home-lessness: first the hands and forearms, then the face and neck and finally the fingernails and teeth. Twice a week he takes off his worn Converse high tops and socks and washes his feet in the sink, ignoring the cold stares of well-dressed commuters.[6]

The article described in vivid detail and with heavy reliance on anecdotes the problems homeless people face on the streets of Philadelphia.

Popularity

Research on changes in newspaper style over the past 50 years has shown a dramatic increase in the use of narrative leads. A study of the *Los Angeles Times*, the

Time *magazine used the narratives supplied by individuals interviewed for a story about the plight of Philadelphia's homeless to make the story human and compelling. Narrative leads are increasingly common, but they must be used carefully, for narrative leads don't always work well.*

Chicago Tribune and *The New York Times* found the percentages of narrative leads on front pages rising from 7 percent in 1950 to 36 percent in 2000 (Figure 5.1).

The use of narrative leads in newspaper writing has become popular for several reasons. One is that newspapers have been facing a decrease in readership and subscriptions in recent years. The use of narrative leads is part of an effort to make newspapers more interesting and appealing. Furthermore, newspapers are finding it increasingly difficult to compete with broadcast news outlets and Web news sites in conveying the news quickly. Often a news event has been covered so heavily by radio, television and Web news outlets that newspapers have to find a different approach.

A narrative lead and narrative structure (often with a focus on one person) is one way of doing this. Newspapers are also drifting away from printing hard news, which has often been reported by other media by the time the newspaper comes out, to longer interpretative stories, analytical pieces and features—often based on the news events that drew the earlier coverage. These forms are particularly well suited to narrative leads. In addition, research has shown that many newspaper readers prefer articles written in a narrative form to those written in inverted pyramid form.[7]

Broadcast, Web and public relations professionals use narrative leads for similar reasons. Competition for viewers and readers in Web and broadcast journalism is intense. The drop of a few percentage points in audience share for a television news

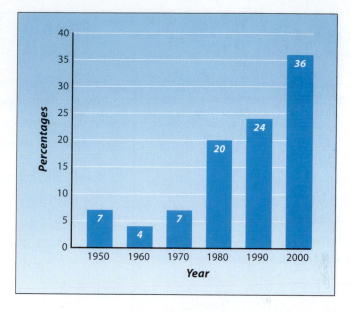

FIGURE 5.1 PERCENTAGES OF NARRATIVE LEADS ON THREE NEWSPAPERS' FRONT PAGES, 1950–2000
Source: Hoon Shim, "The Professional Role of Journalism Reflected in Press Reportage from 1950 to 2000" (Ph.D. dissertation, University of Texas at Austin, 2002).

program, for instance, can mean hundreds of thousands of dollars of lost revenue. If the number of hits on a Web site drops, advertisers might decide to go elsewhere. And public relations professionals must compete for time and space with dozens of other organizations.

A Caveat

Narrative leads do not always work well. Some readers and listeners, particularly those who surf the Web for news, don't want to wade through a long, anecdotal lead. They want the news up front and they will seek writers who report the news that way.

Some editors are suspicious when a public relations release begins with a narrative lead; they fret that there really is no news in the release and that a writer is trying to hide that fact with clever writing. And some stories just don't lend themselves to narrative leads, but writers tack them onto their stories anyway. Writers need to understand that narrative leads do have some disadvantages, particularly when they are overdone by an individual writer or medium. The box "Types of Leads" gives examples of different types of leads one might use for one story.

SELF-EDITING

Writers must self-edit their leads in the same way they self-edit for accuracy and for content. Here are six pitfalls they can guard against: the say-nothing lead, the lead with the wasted beginning, the say-everything lead, the tasteless lead, the inaccurate-tone lead and the sensational lead.

TYPES OF LEADS

Summary: Summarizes as quickly as possible the most important and interesting aspects of a story in an accurate, direct, compelling way.

Question: Poses a question, which involves a reader or listener more directly than some other kinds of leads. Usually used for features, and often avoided because it invariably delays the news, frustrating some readers and listeners.

Direct Address: Involves the reader directly in a story by using "you." Primarily used for features, particularly in broadcast and Web stories. Too informal for many purposes.

Anecdote: The workhorse of the narrative lead. An anecdote is a mini feature story that captures the emotion, or human interest, of an event or issue. Writers must be careful to avoid favoring one side of an issue or event over another by focusing too much on one side.

A Coleville man filed suit today in district court against Clearview Hospital for allegedly giving him an overdose of a painkiller that sent him into cardiac arrest.

Does a hospital patient have the right to refuse medication to kill pain he says he doesn't have?

You might want to talk to John Hill before you decide to stay overnight at your local hospital.

John Hill told the night nurse he was feeling fine and didn't need the Dilaudid that the nurse wanted to give him to ease his pain.

Hill says he told the nurse that he had received Dilaudid—which is eight times more potent than morphine—only two hours earlier and that he was not supposed to get another dose for at least two more hours.

The first thing Hill remembers seeing after he watched the nurse plunge the needle into the IV tube was a crowd of people around his hospital bed and a doctor pounding on his chest. That was 30 minutes later and he still doesn't know what happened during that period.

First Person: Typically used when a writer is part of the story—either by intent or because he or she accidentally becomes part of a news event. Seldom used, but sometimes extremely effective. Some critics argue that journalists should never be part of the stories they cover. This kind of story would carry an editor's note explaining the circumstances.

Scene Setter: Another workhorse of the narrative approach. If the scene is unusual or particularly germane to the story, the scene setter can be effective. A danger is that such a lead can unfairly privilege one side of a story over another.

Direct Quotation: The story begins with the exact words of a news source or personality. These are not often used because few people talk in "leads" and they almost always are one-sided.

I know I was sound asleep because I remember I was surprised when the nurse woke me up to give me the Dilaudid, a powerful painkiller that I had gotten twice before that same day.

I told him I was not in pain and that I had two milligrams of the stuff only two hours earlier. I watched him inject the medication into the IV tube.

The next thing I remember was a crowd around my bed and a guy sitting on me and pounding my chest. That was about 30 minutes later, and I felt like somebody was sucking my brain out the back of my head.

It was 2 a.m., but the dark hospital floor was bustling with only two nurses trying to meet the needs of a floor crammed with demanding patients. One was sitting on the call button demanding attention.

John Hill was sleeping in his hospital bed when a nurse woke him up to give him Dilaudid, a pain reliever that is eight times more potent than morphine.

Hill was groggy, but he told the nurse he didn't need the medication. He had no pain and he had two milligrams only two hours earlier.

"It felt like somebody was sucking my brain out of the back of my head after the hospital gave me an overdose of painkiller. That's why I filed my lawsuit today. I don't want to see somebody else get hurt."

Say-nothing Lead

Virtually every news story has some important element that can be emphasized in the lead. If an event has no news potential, an editor wouldn't assign a writer to cover it in the first place, and he or she certainly would not use a release or a news story with no news. The writer's job is to get the most important element into the lead and to avoid the kind of say-nothing lead that can turn readers away. This sort of lead must be avoided:

> First lady Laura Bush focused on volunteerism and education in an address to more than 2,500 people at Texas A&M University Wednesday.

This lead just tells what Mrs. Bush talked *about*, rather than reports what she *said*. The fact that Mrs. Bush spoke about volunteerism and education is somewhat predictable. It would be more useful to readers or listeners if they were told something specific that she said. The following lead conveys more of what she said:

> The legacy of last year's terrorist attacks is that America has become a more compassionate nation, first lady Laura Bush said Wednesday, renewing her husband's call for people to participate in public service.

The following lead also does not convey as much information as it could:

> The number of traffic accidents for the last year was released by Chief of Police Ralph O'Brien at a news conference in his office Tuesday.

The number is known by the journalist or public relations writer. It must be in the lead. There's no point in withholding that information. Here is another lead that holds back on the news:

> Startling statistics on the relationship between the number of legal executions and the crime rate in this country were reported Thursday night by Theodore L. Sendak, attorney general of Indiana.

The lead is delaying the real news—what the relationship is. Here is a more informative lead:

> Statistics showing the crime rate has gone up as legal executions have decreased were reported Thursday night by Theodore L. Sendak, attorney general of Indiana.

Lead With a Wasted Beginning

It is important to put the most important information in the first sentence when a writer uses inverted pyramid structure, and it is equally important to put meaningful information at the *beginning* of that sentence (Part 1-A). Some writers waste the beginnings of their leads—which is the point of greatest emphasis in the sentence—by using it to state the time or some other minor element. Here is an example of a lead with a wasted beginning:

> Meeting at noon Friday, the Lions Club heard Gov. Ann Crowder defend her tax program.

This is an upside-down sentence. "Meeting at noon Friday" needs to be in Part 1-B, and "noon" doesn't need to be reported at all. This would be a better lead:

> Gov. Ann Crowder defended her tax program Friday at a meeting of the Lions Club.

This is even better:

> A modest hike in the general sales tax will balance the state budget and stimulate the economy, Gov. Ann Crowder said Friday as she defended her tax program at a meeting of the Lions Club.

The following lead also wastes its beginning:

> According to the College and University Personnel Association, University of Columbus faculty salaries are equal to, and often exceed, national averages.

This lead is better:

> University of Columbus faculty salaries are equal to or higher than national averages, the College and University Personnel Association reports.

A public relations writer has wasted a lead when he or she begins this way:

> Sally M. Oglethorpe, president and CEO of Bong International, reported today that the company will not meet its fourth quarter earnings target.

The sentence is upside down.

Say-everything Lead

Almost as bad as the say-nothing lead is the lead into which the writer packs every bit of important information—a say-everything lead:

> Morris Hughes, 36, 912 W. 11th St., sustained head injuries and Mr. and Mrs. Michael Berger, both 46, 1205 N. Grandview Ave., were treated for cuts and bruises as a result of an automobile accident at 8:04 p.m. Thursday near Burris Funeral Home at the corner of Cherry Blossom Road and 17th Street. Police said Berger apparently lost control of his car when the brakes failed on a hill and his car crossed the center line, where the Berger and Hughes cars collided.

Some readers or listeners might not be discouraged by the excessive detail, but many would not read on unless they knew the victims. A better lead would have the W's and H better distributed through the first few paragraphs:

> Three people were injured—one seriously—in a two-car collision Thursday near the Burris Funeral Home, located at Cherry Blossom Road and 17th Street.
>
> Morris Hughes, 36, 912 W. 11th St., sustained severe head injuries and Mr. and Mrs. Michael Berger, both 46, 1205 N. Grandview Ave., were treated for cuts and bruises.
>
> Berger, the driver of one car, apparently lost control when his brakes failed on a hill and crossed the center line, police said, where the Berger and Hughes cars collided.

More examples of cluttered news leads were discussed in a report by a committee of the Associated Press Managing Editors association.[8] This is one of the leads the committee members said could have been improved:

> General Motors Corp., hit by a 67-day strike which began Sept. 15, lost $135 million in the fourth quarter last year, dropping the giant corporation's earnings from $1.71 billion last year to $609 million this year.

The lead presents too many combinations of numbers. The result might be that some readers will simply forgo the effort of figuring out what the writer is saying. Here's another cluttered news lead identified by the APME committee:

> Stocks of tuna now on American markets are below the government-set danger level for mercury content, with the equivalent of roughly 15 million eight-ounce cans having been recalled or held off the shelves as a result of a six-week testing program by the Food and Drug Administration and the tuna industry, FDA said.

A lead shouldn't be so complex that it requires two readings. Many in the audience won't bother. Readers or listeners might also wonder why there is a problem (and a story) if the mercury content is *below* the government's danger level. (See the box "Paula LaRocque on Grabbing the Audience.")

Tasteless Lead

Clever or cute lead sentences should not be used when a story contains an element of tragedy, as in the following:

> A light aircraft from Roberts Field apparently lost power today and crashed onto the top of the Fairgate Insurance Building downtown. The plane was perched precariously before it toppled from the building, hit a deserted window-cleaning scaffold on the way down and crushed a streetcar that just minutes ago was full of passengers.
>
> Brothers John and Sam Bergfeld of Northwest City died in the crash.

The rather lighthearted—or lightheaded—first paragraph would not have been in poor taste had no one been injured or killed. But because the second paragraph reported that two persons were killed, the first paragraph is tasteless and inappropriate. This is a better lead:

> Brothers John and Sam Bergfeld of Northwest City died today when the light plane they were in crashed onto the top of the Fairgate Insurance Building downtown.

Inaccurate-tone Lead

Lead sentences can give a reader or listener the wrong impression about a story without necessarily being in poor taste. Suppose a state senator introduced a bill

PAULA LAROCQUE ON GRABBING THE AUDIENCE

Journalism seems always in the grip of one writing trend or another—especially for that all-important lead. Right now, the tension is between the summary news lead and the "story-telling" narrative lead. Suddenly summary is *passé*; the narrative is style *du jour*.

This bandwagon tootling on the "best" way to begin a story is so much hot air. Neither the summary nor the narrative lead is better. We need both, and more. We need whatever there is.

A good newswriter's repertoire should include something besides what it now seems to contain—which is chiefly the five W's, the scene-setter, and the anecdote. Each can succeed as a lead, but none ensures success. That's because compelling leads are as individual as writing—and writing, in turn, is as individual as thinking. More than technique, we need intelligence and understanding, inventiveness and imagination. We need to connect, extend, associate, allude.

Writing is not much different from thinking—the better we think, the better we write. And to think well, we need room and intellect. Formulas not only narrow our room, they also constrict reason and imagination. Stories are infinitely various; so are the best writers. Accordingly, they write for this occasion, this story, only.

Source: Paula LaRocque, "Hooking the Reader Depends on a Variety of Well-written Leads: Writer's Success Hinges Not on One Style But Several," *Quill,* July/August 1995: 41.

Paula LaRocque, a columnist for *Quill,* is an assistant managing editor and writing coach at *The Dallas Morning News.* She is the author of *Championship Writing: 50 Ways to Improve Your Writing.*

outlawing the killing of jackrabbits in a state in the Southwest. A writer might produce a lead like this:

> The state's jackrabbit population has a new friend in Sen. John Goldman, I-Jacksboro, who has introduced a bill that would make the killing of the furry critters illegal.

This lead sets an inaccurate tone. Jackrabbits eat a great deal of grass, and an uncontrolled jackrabbit population could reduce the amount of grass available to cattle. Ranchers might face economic hardships and consumers might have to pay higher beef prices because fewer cattle could be grazed per acre. A cute approach about an action that has serious implications is inappropriate. Here is a different approach:

> A bill that would outlaw the killing of jackrabbits was introduced today by Sen. John Goldman, I-Jacksboro.

Sensational Lead

Media compete for audience attention, and writers compete for prominent play within the limited space or time of their own media. To win the struggle for space or time, some writers hype a lead to make the story appear more important, interesting or sensational than it really is. Then they attempt to restore the story's proper perspective lower in the article, after they have given a misleading impression.

A writer who hypes a lead simply selects as an angle the most sensational aspect of a story, sometimes taking an aspect out of context or (worse) exaggerating or distorting an aspect of a story. A writer who hypes a lead and creates a false or misleading impression may see the story published on Page One, but the problems caused by the sensationalism could be substantial.

A study of science writing found that sensational leads caused problems in several stories. A report about a research team's efforts to find a treatment for psoriasis was reported under the headline, "Psoriasis Cure Breakthrough Seen," and the lead said:

> University of —— scientists Wednesday announced a breakthrough in treating psoriasis, the skin disease which causes misery for about 6 million Americans.

The head of the research team, objecting to the sensational use of the word breakthrough in the lead and the headline, said:

> We prepared a carefully written story for —— news information service. Nowhere in that writeup nor at the meeting was the word breakthrough used. [The] last sentence of our writeup said cure of psoriasis is probably 50 years away. Yet the title of this article you sent says "Psoriasis Cure Breakthrough Seen." All I can say is, "for Christ's Sake!"[9]

The sensational approach had several negative results, for as the source said:

> I will not speak to a reporter in the future nor will I prepare a release. I have the phone ringing every five to 10 minutes with patients from all over the world. I have received several thousand letters which I can't answer (having only one secretary). I had to have an unlisted phone put in to conduct usual business. Regular phone tied up. This is a total disaster. Our work is key and we are working on a treatment, as paper says. Whether this is a breakthrough and whether we have a "cure" will be known in no less than five years and only in retrospect. I recommend you advise experienced scientists of what they can be in for when tangled up with the newspapers.[10]

The point is not that writers must prepare leads of which their news sources approve, but that care should be exercised when material is taken out of context for use in a lead sentence. In the case of the research on psoriasis, writers may have lost forever a potentially important information source. The writer unnecessarily raised false hopes for many psoriasis sufferers and caused unnecessary delays in the research program by forcing the researcher to devote valuable time to answering anxious inquiries about his research. A public relations writer who made this mistake might well be looking for a new job.

It isn't enough for a writer to sensationalize a lead and then explain what was really meant further down in the story. Some audience members won't read or listen that long, and some who do see the explanation will recall the material in the lead and forget the explanatory material.

Here is a different kind of sensational lead from The Associated Press, and it would be criticized by many readers for being too graphic:

> BOSTON (AP)—An insurance executive was charged with tearing out his wife's heart and lungs and impaling them on a stake in a fight about overcooked ziti.

The story also added this news: "Laura Rosenthal, 34, had been slit with a butcher knife from her throat to her navel, and her organs had been placed on an 18-inch stake in a nearby garden." This lead is less sensational:

> A Boston insurance executive was charged today with murdering and mutilating his 34-year-old wife, apparently because she overcooked his ziti.

YOUR RESPONSIBILITY IS . . .

- To learn to appreciate the complexity and difficulty of writing leads for anything—news stories and releases, term papers, books, documentary films, editorials or magazine articles.

- To learn how to use the five W's and the H to help you decide what information to use in your lead and how to order it.

- To know how and when to write different kinds of leads (summary and narrative are only two) and to understand that the most important thing is to use the *best* approach, not simply the easiest or most familiar, for each story.

- To practice long hours to learn how to write compelling and accurate leads that capture the heart of the story at hand.

- To avoid the pitfalls (say-everything lead, for example) of lead writing.

- To learn how to apply the fundamentals of lead writing, in this age of media convergence, to a variety of tasks in a variety of media under a variety of circumstances. The 21st-century writer who is unable to do this will not be as successful as the one who can.

NOTES

1. Kevin Catalano, "On the Wire: Six News Services Are Exceeding Readability Standards," *Journalism Quarterly,* 67:1 (1990): 97–103.

2. Ibid.

3. Ibid.

4. Anthony York, "Gore, Fox and the Boss," *Salon.com,* Aug. 9, 2002. Downloaded on Aug. 13, 2002, from <archive.salon.com/politics/feature/2002/08/09/gore/index_np.html>.

5. Scott Rosenberg, "Hop High," *Salon.com,* Aug. 13, 2002. Downloaded on July 7, 2003, from <http://blogs.salon.com/0000014/2002/08/13.html>.

6. Jon D. Hull, "Slow Descent Into Hell," *Time,* Feb. 2, 1987: 26–27, 29, p. 26.

7. "The Readers & the Results," *Ways With Words: A Research Report of the Literacy Committee* (Reston, Va.: American Society of Newspaper Editors, 1993): 18–23.

8. *Writing, Editing, Headlines: 1971 Report* (New York: Associated Press Managing Editors Association, 1971): I–Z.

9. Michael Ryan and James W. Tankard Jr., "Problem Areas in Science News Writing," *Journal of Technical Writing & Communication,* 4:3 (1974): 225–235, p. 233.

10. Ibid.

CHAPTER 6

ORGANIZATION

Structures, Unity and Background

A logical structure is important for any story because effective organization makes writing easier, and it makes any writing easier to read or hear. After struggling with the lead, a professional communicator can choose from a number of structures that will help him or her organize the rest of the story. Structures that are frequently used are the inverted pyramid, chronological order, suspended interest and block (or chunk) structures. Writers also combine some of these forms to create various hybrid structures.

INVERTED PYRAMID

The inverted pyramid model places great emphasis on the first few sentences of the story (Figure 6.1). The model demands that the most important elements of a story be placed at the beginning (or at the wide end of the inverted pyramid) and that the least important information be placed at the end (or at the lower point of the inverted pyramid). Other information is distributed throughout the story according to interest and importance.

Advantages

The inverted pyramid form is frequently used for two good reasons:

- It is the most efficient means of transmitting information. Most newspaper readers spend 30 minutes a day or less reading their newspapers. Many people read only the first sentence of some articles before deciding they are of little interest and importance to them. They will read several paragraphs of other stories and then stop after they obtain all the information they want. And

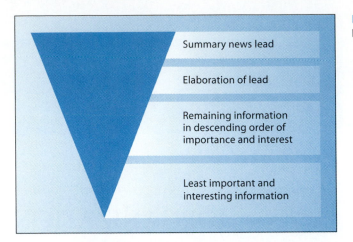

FIGURE 6.1 INVERTED PYRAMID MODEL

they will read other stories completely because the subject matter interests them greatly.

Readers, listeners and viewers of other media have similar habits. While lead writing for the Web is evolving, it would seem the inverted pyramid is the perfect model for an effective Web writer, for research indicates that people prefer to scan information and that a lead needs to be short, concise, simple, intriguing or catchy to snag the reader who is skimming rapidly. Scanning is made easier by the inverted pyramid format, with its demand for short sentences, paragraphs and articles and for a concise writing style.

Good public relations writers also use the inverted pyramid model, for they understand that the editors who decide whether to use their releases want to know *immediately* what the news is. Editors scan enormous numbers of releases, and they will not linger on a release that doesn't make its point in a hurry—and neither will the audience for which the editor makes selections. Broadcast journalists, who compete with a dozen distractions for audience attention, also have to get to the point quickly and in an interesting way.

The inverted pyramid structure is a kind of shared code between listeners, viewers, readers, writers and editors of all media. Writers use the form to serve their audiences, members of which learn, perhaps unconsciously, to expect the most important and interesting information at the beginning of a story and the least important and interesting information at the end.

Readers who want to find out the news quickly are sometimes frustrated with the narrative leads and other kinds of delayed leads that are used on some stories and releases. Consider the following lead from the front page of a newspaper:

Beau Armstrong is visibly uncomfortable.

It's not just because he's standing in the sun in a white shirt and tie on a cloudless August day with the temperatures nearing 90.

By the time they read the third paragraph, some readers may be getting irritated with a story that is obviously holding back information.

■ Dealing with limited space and time is always a problem. When a print story must be shortened, it's more easily edited if the least important elements are in the last few paragraphs. An editor can cut a well-written story from the bottom up without damaging the article. Important facts might be dropped from a story not written in the inverted pyramid format by an editor who, working under deadline pressure, cuts from the bottom up.

Public relations and Web writers also understand that their articles might be cut. A newspaper editor may have a four-inch hole to fill with a release that is eight inches long. If the release is written in the inverted pyramid format, the least important material will be cut. And a Web writer might discover that a story is too long to fit on a Web page without forcing a reader to scroll down. To avoid the problem, the piece is cut from the bottom. A news release from General Motors, for example, began with this lead:

> CHARLOTTE, N.C.—General Motors Corp. today announced a new, multi-million dollar campaign to promote the use of corn-based ethanol fuel E85 as an alternative to gasoline.
>
> The public awareness effort is a 2-year partnership with the non-profit National Ethanol Vehicle Coalition (NEVC) focused on increasing ethanol use in flexible fuel vehicles. Flexible fuel vehicles are designed to use either ethanol or gasoline; E85 Flexible Fuel Vehicles can be powered by gasoline or a mixture of 85 percent ethanol and 15 percent gasoline.
>
> According to Phil Lampert, executive director of the NEVC, "The limited number of ethanol fueling stations available—about 140 in 22 primarily Midwestern states—make it a challenge for people to utilize this alternative fuel source. We believe this effort will help increase the use of ethanol, which will benefit the environment and help reduce the nation's dependency on foreign oil."[1]

The release noted that the campaign was part of a partnership with the National Ethanol Vehicle Coalition; what ethanol is and how it is produced; and the reasons why it is good to promote ethanol. An editor could kill several of the following paragraphs (mostly about other fuel-saving technologies and about General Motors) and still provide a reader or listener with the real news.

Ordering Facts

Writers don't wait until they are sitting at a computer to start ordering facts. They begin to organize even as they are collecting information. For example, many broadcast, newspaper, magazine and Web journalists start writing their stories in their heads as they gather facts. They think about what will go in the lead, what will come second and so forth. This planning of stories as they are interviewing sources

The New York Daily News *picked out* the *most important fact about the 1928 execution of Ruth Snyder: She was DEAD! The photographer strapped the camera to his ankle to get the forbidden picture. Many readers and journalists condemned the Page One photograph.*

or witnessing events—or possibly driving back to the office—means that journalists can usually sit down at their computers and quickly write two- or three-page stories. This is a valuable skill for writers working on deadline. Most public relations practitioners, who certainly are not strangers to deadlines, use a similar process.

Writers often go through their notes and number sections, putting them in the inverted pyramid order in which they will use them, or they list the major points that should be covered and then number the points in the order in which they will appear. Many writers break the information down by who, what, when, where, why and how. A writer taking this approach might come up with the following pieces of information:

Who (source)	Randy Sijansky, regional director for the State Department of Emergency Management
Who	At least *four people* were killed. *Thirteen others* were injured and *an unknown number* were missing.
Where	The causeway connecting South Padre Island and Port Isabel
When	2:30 a.m. Saturday
What	A barge hit the Queen Isabella Causeway.
What	The barge knocked out a 100- to 200-foot-long section of the bridge, causing the roadway to fall into the water.
What	Between five and nine cars fell into the water.
What	At least four people were killed.
What	Thirteen people were injured and an unknown number of people were missing.
What	The accident also knocked out telephone service to South Padre Island because the telephone line was strung along the causeway.
What	Ferries from Port Aransas were moved down the coast to take people back and forth between South Padre Island and Port Isabel.
What	Barges with cranes were being used to pull cars out of the water.
What	Divers were searching for missing persons.
Background fact	The causeway is the longest bridge in Texas.
Relevant fact	The water is between 12 and 15 feet deep in that part of the lagoon.

The event reflects a number of different whats, and the writer must decide which ones are important enough to put in the lead. The four deaths should be in the lead, since death is high in impact and consequence and is almost always a

USING THE INVERTED PYRAMID

Four people were killed Sunday morning when a barge knocked out a 100- to 200-foot-long section of the Queen Isabella Causeway, sending several automobiles into the water, officials said.

The accident on the bridge connecting South Padre Island with the mainland left 13 people injured and an unknown number of people missing.

Between five and nine cars fell into the water, Randy Sijansky, regional director for the State Department of Emergency Management, said. The water is between 12 and 15 feet deep at that section of the causeway.

Barges with cranes were being used to pull cars out of the water, Sijansky said. Divers were searching for missing persons.

The accident also knocked out telephone service to South Padre Island because the telephone line was strung along the causeway.

Ferries from Port Aransas were moved down the coast to take people back and forth between South Padre Island and Port Isabel.

The causeway is the longest bridge in the state.

The deaths, the most important element in the story, are played up, not only by putting them in the lead, but also by putting them at the very beginning of the lead. A *when* is easy to insert with two words (Sunday morning). The sentence is attributed to a source with the two words at the end, "officials said."

Starting the second sentence with "the accident" forges a strong linkage to the first paragraph. The second sentence tells what happened to other people, a major point of interest for most readers.

The third paragraph continues to give details about what happened. It also names and identifies the source of the information.

This paragraph reports more of what happened—the *what* element.

This paragraph reports an additional *what*, but one that is less important than the loss of human life.

This paragraph looks to the future and answers the question, "What are people going to do?"

This is an interesting fact, but probably the least important detail in the story.

significant element when it is present. The lead should also tell how the people were killed and when the event occurred. After producing the lead, the writer includes the remaining information in decreasing order of importance and interest (see the box "Using the Inverted Pyramid").

Members of the media and onlookers survey the damage caused to the Pentagon on Sept. 11, 2001, when a commercial aircraft slammed into the building. The terrorist attack will be the subject of retrospectives for decades to come.

OTHER STRUCTURES

The inverted pyramid is not always the best model for a story. Other structures are chronological order, suspended interest, block (or chunk) structure and hybrids.

Chronological Order

When a report is written in chronological order, the elements appear in the same sequence in which they occurred in time. The minutes of a city council meeting or of a stockholders' meeting usually are written in chronological order. A common fault in inexperienced writers' accounts of meetings is that they sound more like boring minutes than interesting stories or releases. Most stories about meetings should be written in inverted pyramid structure with the most important item at the beginning of the story, no matter when it happened during the meeting.

Chronological order is probably used most often with feature stories—particularly those that recount first-person experiences or adventures. But even a straight news report or release can contain a mixture of inverted pyramid structure and chronological order. A story by Bob Lewis of The Associated Press, a news-feature focusing on the one-year anniversary of the Sept. 11, 2001, terrorist attack, illustrates this technique (see the box "Using Chronological Structure.")

Reporter Mark Bowden of *The Philadelphia Inquirer* used chronological order to organize his highly successful account of a U.S. combat mission in Somalia that turned into a disaster. The piece begins with a dramatic action lead:

> Staff Sgt. Matt Eversmann's lanky frame was fully extended on the rope for what seemed too long on the way down. Hanging from a hovering Blackhawk helicopter, Eversmann was a full 70 feet above the streets of Mogadishu. His goggles had broken, so his eyes chafed in the thick cloud of dust stirred up by the bird's rotors.[2]

Bowden's series in *The Inquirer* in late 1997 became a book, *Blackhawk Down*, a detailed narrative account of a single episode in the United States' participation in the military action in Somalia in October 1993 through the eyes of young U.S. soldiers. *Inquirer* editors put the series on the newspaper's Web site, with links to video clips, audio recordings, maps, photographs and a reader response feature. *Blackhawk Down* became a dramatic example of media convergence, appearing as a newspaper series, a Web site, a television documentary, a commercial videotape, a hardcover book, a paperback book and a Hollywood feature film.[3]

Suspended Interest

Sometimes a writer deliberately withholds an important element until the end of a story to heighten interest. This creates a structure that is basically the opposite of the inverted pyramid form.

One kind of story that frequently uses suspended interest order is a bright (or brite), a short (two- or three-paragraph) item written to entertain readers or listeners. Magazine, Web and newspaper brights—which frequently are boxed—are convenient for layout because they can be put in small holes in a page. Broadcast brights often appear at the ends of newscasts or segments. The media use brights to help them balance the more serious news. The following brights depend on suspended interest for much of their effect:

> LIVERMORE, Calif. (AP)—Mrs. Arlene Higuera thought her 18-year-old dog was getting to be unusually sluggish in walking about, so she took the canine to a veterinarian.
>
> The doctor operated and removed 267 marbles from the dog's stomach.

> CINCINNATI, Ohio (AP)—Attorney Jerry O'Dowd, appointed by the court to defend a man accused of burglary, has been granted permission to withdraw from the case.
>
> When O'Dowd went to the jail to interview the suspect, he found that the man was accused of breaking into a law office—O'Dowd's.

USING CHRONOLOGICAL STRUCTURE

Alan Wallace had 1.5 seconds from the time he saw American Airlines Flight 77 bearing down on the Pentagon one year ago to run before impact.

A dramatic lead, starting with a moment of danger and presented with suspense.

He got all of about 20 feet before the searing heat of a jet fuel fireball sent him sprawling onto the asphalt tarmac of the Pentagon heliport. He believed his clothing was on fire and his life near an end.

On Wednesday, Wallace stood with fellow firefighters from Arlington and elsewhere in northern Virginia who responded to the terrorist attack that killed 184 people in the Pentagon and on the airplane, not counting the five terrorist hijackers.

The second paragraph continues with a chronological account; then the third paragraph makes a transition to the news peg, an anniversary gathering on Wednesday.

They talked to one another. They talked to Gov. Mark Warner and other state and federal dignitaries there to mark the anniversary. They talked to reporters. They talked freely.

For most, it seemed to help, especially Wallace.

Two paragraphs about the current happening, the ceremony marking the anniversary. But it is clear that this is just a news peg—the story is really about the experiences these firefighters had a year before. The last phrase, "especially Wallace," smooths the transition back to the chronological account.

He had taken the first of what was to have been several fire trucks to the Pentagon from Fort Myer, just two miles away. They were to be there, arrayed by the heliport, for the arrival of President Bush later that day.

"I was walking beside the truck and I looked across and saw the plane, and it was already over the Pentagon property," he said. He screamed a warning to two fellow firefighters and began running from the building.

Beginning of a long chronological account about Alan Wallace and other firefighters.

The chronological account is told partly through direct quotes from Wallace and others and partly through indirect quotation or paraphrase.

(continued)

USING CHRONOLOGICAL STRUCTURE *(continued)*

"I ran 'til I thought I was on fire and that I'd done about as much as I could do for myself, so I hit the ground," Wallace said. "I went down face first, just like Pete Rose used to slide into base."

Had he not hit the ground, it's likely he would have died. The fireball mushroomed upward, and he got up, looked at the flaming hole gouged into the bottom floors of the Pentagon's western face and went to find his buddies.

"We asked each other if they were all right, and everybody said yeah, they were OK, so we went back and started helping people," said Dennis Young, a Fort Myer firefighter who was on the truck with Wallace that morning.

They ran to a window near the impact point where people inside the Pentagon were screaming for help. The three firefighters reached through the shattered window, burning their shoulders and arms on its simmering metal frame, as they pulled people to safety.

"It was so hot and the smoke was so thick. I thought, 'I've got to get away from here and get some air,'" Wallace said.

Within minutes, he said, the number of hands helping people from the building doubled, then tripled and quadrupled as police officers, volunteers off the street and military personnel from other parts of the massive building joined them in leading people out of harm's way.

Wallace's remark about sliding like Pete Rose is an effective simile and therefore a good choice for a direct quote.

The author writes a sentence of vivid description beginning with "The fireball mushroomed upward." Some of these descriptive words may have come from the firefighters but some of them probably came from the writer.

The chronological account continues with a direct quote from Dennis Young, another firefighter. It takes some planning on the writer's part to keep the chronological account moving forward, but the feature includes dramatic direct quotes from several sources.

What bothers Wallace and others to this day is the people trapped in the inferno who were unable to make it to that window. Neither he nor Young likes to ponder it.

"If people couldn't get themselves to that window, then ... well, there just wasn't anything we could do for them," he said.

Later that day, Wallace and the other firefighters were treated for their painful burns and for cuts, bruises and abrasions. And when they were done, they put their fire gear back on and returned to the Pentagon. ...

The story returns briefly to the ceremony and the current thoughts of some of the participants.

The article ends by picking up the chronology again and bringing it to a finish. This ending reinforces the underlying structure— the story is fundamentally a chronological account.

Source: Bob Lewis, "Just 140 Feet From Impact Point, Fort Myer Fireman Survived," The Associated Press, Sept. 11, 2002. Downloaded on Feb. 27, 2003, from <web.lexis-nexis.com/universe/doclist?_m=c83bce55949300d93297b30527dbb9da&wchp=dGLbVzb-1S1zV&_md5=ee5186f6a9410ffd86410d503caf397f>. Reprinted by permission of The Associated Press.

Block (Chunk)

Writers use the block, or chunk, structure when they want to keep sets (or blocks) of facts together—but separate from other blocks of facts. The facts within one block relate specifically to each other; the facts that comprise that block relate more generally to all other blocks in the story. A fact in one block may even be more important than the facts in blocks that appear earlier in the story.

In a story about disease, for instance, a writer might use an anecdotal lead (block one), a description of the disease (block two), efforts of health professionals to stop the disease (block three) and what individuals might do to protect themselves (block four). Each block would almost certainly be several paragraphs long.

The block, or chunk, structure is well suited for information that can easily be divided into sections. In fact, writers use some variation of this structure for almost every story they produce, regardless of the overall structure, for it's always a good idea to keep similar facts together. It just makes sense, for example, to describe a disease before moving on to any other information.

Bob Thomas of The Associated Press used the block structure effectively in an obituary about film actor Charles Bronson, who died in 2003 (see the box "Using Block Structure"). Some of the chunks can be on other pages of a Web site. A Web

USING BLOCK STRUCTURE

LOS ANGELES—Charles Bronson, the Pennsylvania coal miner who drifted into films as a villain and became a hard-faced action star, notably in the popular "Death Wish" vengeance movies, has died. He was 81.

Bronson died Saturday of pneumonia at Cedars-Sinai Medical Center with his wife at his bedside, publicist Lori Jonas said. He had been in the hospital for weeks, Jonas said.

A summary lead (block) focuses, as obituaries do, on the *main* thing Charles Bronson accomplished. The accomplishment is contrasted with Bronson's background. Cause of death often is part of the initial block.

During the height of his career, Bronson was hugely popular in Europe; the French knew him as "le sacré monstre" (the sacred monster), the Italians as "Il Brutto" (the ugly man). In 1971, he was presented a Golden Globe as "the most popular actor in the world."

Like Clint Eastwood, whose spaghetti Westerns won him stardom, Bronson had to make European films to prove his worth as a star. ...

At age 50, he returned to Hollywood a star.

A three-paragraph background block explains more about Bronson's career—how it developed and who knew him best. Readers should by now recall who Bronson was.

His early life gave no indication of his later fame. He was born Charles Buchinsky on Nov. 3, 1921—not 1922, as studio biographies claimed—in Ehrenfeld, Pa. He was the 11th of 15 children of a coal miner and his wife, both Lithuanian immigrants.

Charles' father died when he was 10, and at 16 Charles followed his brothers into the mines. He was paid $1 per ton of coal and volunteered for perilous jobs because the pay was better.

Drafted in 1943, he served with the Air Force in the Pacific, as a tailgunner on a B-29. Having seen the outside world, he vowed not to return to the squalor of Scooptown.

An interesting block, or "small story," about Bronson's life before acting. The impact on his life of his military service and his pay of $1 per ton of coal are interesting highlights.

He was attracted to acting not, he said, because of any artistic urge; he was impressed by the money movie stars could earn.

As Charles Buchinsky or Buchinski, he played supporting roles in "Red Skies of Montana," "The Marrying Kind," "Pat and Mike" (in which he fell victim to Katharine Hepburn's judo), "The House of Wax," "Jubal" and other films. In 1954 he changed his last name, fearing reaction in the McCarthy era to Russian-sounding names.

His status grew with impressive performances in "The Magnificent Seven," "The Great Escape," "The Battle of the Bulge," "The Sandpiper" and "The Dirty Dozen." But real stardom eluded him, his rough-hewn face and brusque manner not fitting the Hollywood tradition of leading men.

His most controversial film came in 1974 with "Death Wish." As an affluent, liberal architect, Bronson's life is shattered when young thugs kill his wife and rape his daughter. He vows to rid the city of such vermin, and his executions brought cheers from crime-weary audiences.

The character's vigilantism brought widespread criticism, but "Death Wish" became one of the big moneymakers of the year.

"He was attracted to acting" is a good transition phrase to a block about the films Bronson made. The block is made more interesting by personal notes, such as Katharine Hepburn's judo and the different spellings of his name.

An interesting block about Bronson's controversial and popular *Death Wish* films. The connection to the "real world" ("crime-weary audiences") is interesting.

(continued)

USING BLOCK STRUCTURE   *(continued)*

Bronson's first marriage was to Harriet Tendler, whom he met when both were fledgling actors in Philadelphia. They had two children before divorcing.

In 1966 Bronson fell in love with the lovely blond British actress Jill Ireland, who happened to be married to British actor David McCallum. Bronson reportedly told McCallum bluntly: "I'm going to marry your wife."

The McCallums were divorced in 1967, and Bronson and Ireland married the following year. She co-starred in several of his films.

Ireland lost a breast to cancer in 1984, and died of the disease six years later.

Personal information that might not be of great interest to most readers. Putting that information in the final block is appropriate.

Source: Bob Thomas, "Action Film Star Bronson Dies at 81," The Associated Press, Sept. 1, 2003. Available at <www.sltrib.com/2003/Sep/09012003/nation_w/88789.asp>. Reprinted by permission of The Associated Press.

writer, for instance, could link to a list of Bronson's films or to photographs of the star. Writers need to give careful thought to links to blocks of information, however, for research suggests that readers don't respond well to all kinds of links.[4]

The *Rocky Mountain News* of Denver used a block structure effectively for a story about three candidates for superintendent of Denver schools. The article began with this lead:

> A Denver finance manager, the former head of Colorado's community college system and a California school superintendent are vying for the chance to lead Denver Public Schools.

The writers followed the lead with a few general paragraphs about the candidates and the situation that led to a search for a new superintendent. Then the story turned to separate sections about each candidate clearly separated by subheads giving each candidate's name.

A block structure is often a good choice for feature stories. Many features are basically a collection of anecdotes, or little stories. The structure of these stories is essentially a block structure, with each anecdote constituting a block. The transition from one block to the next can be made with phrases such as "on another occasion," "one time" or even "once." The block relating to Charles Bronson's *Death Wish* films is one example of a little story within a larger report.

Writing in screen-sized chunks is a good way to write for the Web. Each screen is a self-contained unit, and the reader can proceed to the next unit by clicking on a "next page" or "Part 2" button at the bottom of the page. Some Web sites also list an index or table of contents to the side of the main text. This index lists other pages (chunks) that the reader can also visit.

Atlas, the Web magazine, for example, ran a photo feature titled "Patrolling Despair" that dealt with people illegally crossing the border from Mexico to the United States.[5] Each Web page of the story had a "next" button at the bottom, but every page also had an index at the top (with the numbers 1 through 25 in buttons) so that a reader could skip to any of the 25 pages by clicking on its number. A reader could choose a linear path by clicking the "next" button repeatedly or jump immediately to any other page.

Hybrids

One common hybrid structure is the article that starts off with a narrative lead and then follows this with a general discussion of some issue. The narrative lead often focuses on one person who illustrates a particular problem or situation. This technique is often used to humanize a story that might otherwise be a dry statistical report or a discussion of abstract legal issues. One problem with the approach is that often the person mentioned in the first few paragraphs is never mentioned again in the story. Another is that a single individual might not really represent others facing the same problem or situation.

The technique of using the humanizing beginning for a story dealing with abstract issues is illustrated by the first several paragraphs of a story by Reynolds Holding of the *San Francisco Chronicle.* Holding begins with a lead that sets the tone:

> It's chilly out there on the Internet.
>
> Phil Ostroff, an Australian bloke transplanted to Texas, found out how chilly after he launched his Web site five years ago.

The next part is the kind of background block that one often associates with stories written in the inverted pyramid format:

> It's called IntelHawk.com, a sweaty male kind of place with photos of helicopters, bomb-scarred landscapes and children mangled by battle. It's about war, weapons and military intelligence. Hence the name: "Intel" for "intelligence" and "hawk" for, well, "something that flies over and sees everything," explains Ostroff.
>
> It is definitely not about computers.

Holding begins to suggest in the next block, or chunk, what Ostroff's problem is with Intel:

> But don't tell that to Intel.
>
> At the end of January, an attorney for the giant chipmaker accused Ostroff of poaching the sacred Intel trademark. People would confuse the site with the company, the attorney huffed in an e-mail, and so Ostroff must, in the unnerving language of the law, cease and desist.

The next block reports Ostroff's reaction to Intel:

> "I thought it was a practical joke," recalls Ostroff. "Then I thought I could be in real trouble."
>
> Fortunately, a co-worker steered him to the San Francisco-based Electronic Frontier Foundation and then to a legal clinic at the University of San Francisco, where third-year law student Katy Little assured Ostroff that Intel was probably blowing smoke.

Holding uses the following paragraph as a transition to the rest of the story:

> But, as Little explains, he may be the exception, one of the few Internet small-fries not chilled from speaking freely by the intimidating tactics of a corporate bully.
>
> The cease-and-desist letter has become the weapon of choice for companies that take perverse delight in charging Web site operators with copyright or trademark violations.[6]

The article never returns to Ostroff. The purpose of introducing him was mostly to give the article an interesting beginning, but readers might like to know how he fared against the corporate giant.

Meetings

Meeting stories often are hybrids of the inverted pyramid, chunk and chronological structures. They frequently begin with a lead and several paragraphs about the most important thing that happened at a meeting, as in this example:

> Tacoma police officers will get a 6.6 percent salary increase starting in July, Tacoma City Council decided today.

Subsequent paragraphs focus on how the increases would be financed, what the raises could mean for public safety and what raises other city employees might expect in the coming year.

After the pay raises are thoroughly discussed, the story is a chronological account introduced by the phrase, "In other action, council. ..." If there are five other actions, there will be five chunks, each reporting one action. Each chunk might be a single paragraph or several paragraphs. Writers nearly always group into individual chunks all facts relating to the same topic. Stories get confusing when writers bounce back and forth between and among topics.

Broadcast Hybrids

Radio and television writers tend to use the same organizational structures that other writers do, although they have to make accommodations for extreme space limitations and for the verbal nature of the medium.

In using the inverted pyramid, for example, radio and television writers superimpose a kind of label (comparable to a headline in a magazine or on a news release) at the top. The label may be read by an anchor in a studio or by the on-air personality as a kind of lead-in. The label is followed by a summary or narrative lead similar to those one sees in other media.

While print writers put the least important information at the ends of their stories, broadcast writers frequently will restate at the end the news reported at the top of the story. There is a good reason for this seeming redundancy: A listener who does not hear the news at the top of the story, but who is interested nevertheless, gets one last chance at the end.

STORY UNITY

Effective writing has unity. That is, all the material in a story is related to one purpose, and the relevance of each element to that purpose is clear. The purpose may be to inform, to analyze, to background, to describe or to entertain. But in any case, no material in the report should make the reader wonder, "Why is this in the story?" Some story structures—particularly inverted pyramid and chronological structures—by themselves provide a great deal of unity for a piece of writing. Other tools for bringing unity to a piece of writing are repetition, transitional phrases and nut grafs.

Repetition

One of the most effective techniques for achieving unity is repetition of a key idea or term. Notice how Judy Stark's story from the *St. Petersburg Times* achieves unity through repetition of the keyword "code":

> Hurricane Andrew revealed shoddy construction and inadequate building inspection that led to new statewide requirements to produce more hurricane-worthy homes.
>
> Ten years later, one thing is clear: If you are buying a newly constructed home, it will cost you thousands of dollars more because of Andrew-prompted building **code** changes.
>
> What isn't clear is whether those changes will make homes any safer. The building industry persuaded the Legislature to delay implementing the new **code** from July 2001 to March, then pulled thousands of permits under the old **codes** at the end of February.
>
> The new **code** is supposed to eliminate a patchwork of building regulations across the state. But each community can interpret it differently. Confusion abounds.

"We used to have 467 building **codes**," said Jack Glenn of the Florida Home Builders Association: "Now we have one **code** with 467 interpretations."

After Andrew, the state began enforcing rules that had been on the books since 1986 but had been overlooked. Sturdier foundations. Hurricane straps instead of clips. More reinforcing bars. Concrete to hold masonry blocks in place. Nails instead of staples in roofs.

Glenn said his phone has been busy with builders seeking clarification.

"But two of every five calls about 'something new' in the **code** are really about something that's been in the **code** for 10 years, and one of every five is about something that's been in there for 15 years," he said.[7]

Transitional Words, Phrases

Story unity can be more of a problem with a long, complicated report, particularly one dealing with several situations, several time periods or several locations. With that kind of story, the writer must pay more attention to showing how parts of the story relate to one another. One of the main techniques for doing this is skillful transition.

A good transition—a smooth change from one topic to another—lets the reader or listener know that a change in subject matter has occurred and tells what the change is. Transitional words or phrases are used to help keep the reader or listener oriented in a story that might involve different locations or different times.

Phrases

When Secretary of State Colin Powell traveled to India and Pakistan after the terrorist attacks of Sept. 11, 2001, the weekly Arab political magazine, *Ain-Al-Yaqeen*, reported about his trip. The writer used several transitional phrases to make clear when and where Powell made various comments (see the box "Using Transitional Phrases").

A problem frequently facing a writer covering a meeting is that the group takes a number of very different actions. This can make it difficult to produce a unified story. One way to handle these situations is to discuss one action fully at the beginning of the story and then use a transitional phrase such as "in other action" to change to another topic or topics. Here is an example from *The Modesto (Calif.) Bee:*

In other action, the City Council will again be asked to double sewer fees during the next four years to fund an expansion of the city's sewage plant.

A writer can face a similar problem in covering a speech. When a writer obtains quotes from a speaker's public speech or remarks and from an informal interview later, he or she must make clear what was said in each instance. Phrases such as "in an interview later" or "in his main address" help ensure effective transition.

USING TRANSITIONAL PHRASES

In New Delhi Colin Powell told his Indian counterpart that the American-led fight against terrorism includes all terrorism, including that faced by India.

The phrase *In New Delhi* makes Powell's location clear.

Speaking at a press conference following talks with Indian External Affairs Minister Jaswant Singh, Secretary Powell said he held important talks with India's Prime Minister and Foreign Minister covering the new strategic framework which U.S. President George Bush suggests for the bilateral relations between Washington and New Delhi.

The prepositional phrase beginning with *Speaking* gives the precise setting for Powell's remarks.

Powell said: "We deplore terrorism wherever it exists, whether on September 11 or on October 1 in Srinagar.

"The United States and India stand united against terrorism and that includes terrorism directed against India as well," Powell added. ...

Lack of quotation mark shows quotation continues, which helps transition.

Earlier, Powell said in Islamabad that he has held discussions with Pakistani officials on "our mutual interest in a stable Afghanistan."

Earlier indicates a transition to a previous time. *In Islamabad* indicates a transition to a different place.

Sometimes a phrase is useful for indicating the switch from one speaker in one setting to another speaker in another setting. The following example is from a story reporting about the need for better supervision of contracts in the Department of Energy. The phrase "in an interview" is used to switch from remarks by Energy Secretary Spencer Adam to a comment from Bruce Carnes, another department official:

In an interview, the department's chief financial officer, Bruce Carnes, said, "We are serious. We are changing the tires on this car while it's driving 60 miles an hour."

In a story based on a single speech or interview, a prepositional phrase can be used to show a change of topic. The following example is from a press conference in which President Bush talked primarily about the administration's war against terrorism:

> On the topic of corporate corruption, Bush said, "I think, by far, the vast majority of CEOs in America are good, honorable, honest people who have nothing to hide and are willing to let the true facts speak for themselves.

This is a smoother transition than the phrase "When asked about," which sometimes appears in stories. The "when asked about" device is wordy and draws unnecessary attention to the writer.

Words

Often a single word can provide an effective transition. Some common transition words follow:

once	later	however
before	afterward	nevertheless
earlier	meanwhile	nonetheless
previously	instead	moreover

An article reporting CIA estimates of North Korea's nuclear capability used the word "previously" to signal a shift to background information from an earlier time:

> Previously, it had estimated that North Korea probably extracted enough plutonium from a nuclear reactor to build one or two weapons.

An article about the Department of Homeland Security used the word "meanwhile" to introduce a shift from one problem—bringing a number of government agencies together—to another problem—lack of funding:

> Meanwhile, the new department faces another pressing need—money.

In the example below, the word "however" is used to show a shift from arguments on one side of a case to arguments on the other side:

> However, Neal Sonnett, a defense attorney, said the fact that some witnesses had never testified indicated that the material witness statute was being used as a ruse.

Nut Graf (or Graph)

The nut graf actually is composed of multiple paragraphs that summarize a story and suggest why readers or viewers should continue. The nut graf typically is a bridge (or transition) from a narrative lead to the rest of the story. Consider this anecdotal lead from the box in Chapter 5, "Types of Leads":

> John Hill told the night nurse he was feeling fine and didn't need the Dilaudid that the nurse wanted to give him to ease his pain.

> Hill says he told the nurse that he had received Dilaudid—which is eight times more potent than morphine—only two hours earlier and that he was not supposed to get another dose for at least two more hours.
>
> The first thing Hill remembers seeing after he watched the nurse plunge the needle into the IV tube was a crowd of people around his hospital bed and a doctor pounding on his chest. That was 30 minutes later and he still doesn't know what happened during that period.

The writer could use this nut graf as a bridge from the anecdote to the rest of the story:

> Hill today filed suit in 24th District Court against Clearview Hospital because of that blast of Dilaudid, which he claims sent him into cardiac arrest and caused permanent heart damage.
>
> The suit claims Hill went into Clearview on Jan. 10, 2004, because of the "excruciating pain" caused by a kidney stone. Two milligrams of Dilaudid were administered at 8 p.m., at midnight and at 2 a.m. He suffered cardiac arrest at 2 a.m.
>
> The recommended dosage for Dilaudid administered through an IV tube, Hill claims, is 2-4 milligrams every four to six hours, and it must be injected very slowly.

This nut graf is a transition to the rest of the story. The hospital's response would be reported in the next block, or chunk.

BACKGROUND

Media writers must put background information into virtually every story they produce so that readers or listeners can follow as the story unfolds. When background material is omitted, readers and listeners struggle to figure out what a writer is saying. Many won't bother: They will switch to another story, another Web site or another channel. An editor who is trying to decide whether to use a news release likely will trash one that is not easy to understand. Background information must be in every story, and it must be in the right place.

Consider this lead on a story by The Associated Press about stem cell research:

> WEST ORANGE, N.J.—New Jersey became the second state to allow stem cell research on Sunday as Gov. James E. McGreevey signed a law he said will "move the frontiers of science forward."

Readers would have had a hard time making sense of all the facts without this second, background paragraph:

> Stem cell research, which has been strongly opposed by anti-abortion groups and the Roman Catholic Church because it involves the use of fetal and embryonic tissue, is also permitted in California and bills are pending in Illinois and New York.

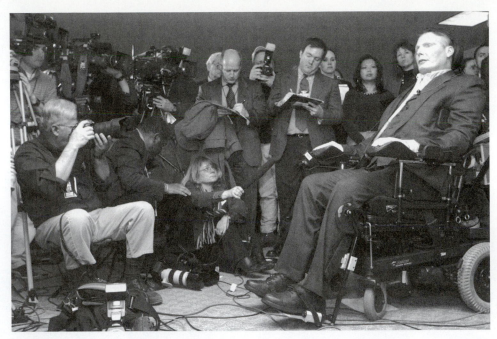

Journalists should mention an individual's handicap only when it is directly relevant to a story. Christopher Reeve's handicap is relevant in stories about his efforts to get Congress to support medical research. Reeve is shown here speaking to reporters prior to his testimony before a Senate committee.

AP writer Krista Larson also reported the crucial information that researchers want to use stems cells, which are created during the first days of pregnancy, to fight disease and to grow replacement organs.

Background information should be brief, but it must be complete enough to help a reader or listener who has insufficient knowledge of the situation or problem. Sometimes a writer places background in a separate sentence or paragraph as in the stem cell story, but a writer sometimes inserts the background within a phrase or clause in a sentence, as in this example from a story about actor Christopher Reeve:

> Reeve, 49, who was paralyzed from the neck down in a horseback riding accident in
> 1995, said he had regained some movement in his fingers.

The clause starting with *who* reminds the reader of the circumstances of Reeve's injury years earlier.

A good rule of thumb is to use background information the moment an audience needs it to understand a story. Regardless of the story's structure (inverted pyramid, suspended interest), an audience should not be denied the knowledge it needs to understand any part. A writer should never leave a reader or listener hanging.

YOUR RESPONSIBILITY IS . . .

- To learn how to use the inverted pyramid format, for this is the most common structure in all writing areas. You must practice constantly.

- To learn about the other structures (chronological order, suspended interest, block and hybrids) and how to use them. You should not be locked into a single structure and use that constantly just because it is familiar. Different stories can require different structures.

- To understand the relationship between the structure you select and the kind of lead you write. Read the leads on all sorts of stories with a critical eye, for this will help you learn.

- To learn how to unify your stories—to ensure all information is relevant and that your copy flows smoothly and gracefully from one topic to another. Effective transitions are essential if you want to avoid writing stories in which sentences clunk gracelessly from one topic to another.

NOTES

1. General Motors Corp., "GM Partners With National Ethanol Vehicle Coalition to Advance the Use of E85: Campaign Aimed at Increasing Alternative Fuel Use," news release dated Feb. 25, 2003. Downloaded on Feb. 28, 2003, from <www.gm.com/cgi_bin/pr_display.pl?3416>.
2. Mark Bowden, "Chapter 1: The Combat Begins," *The Philadelphia Inquirer*, Nov. 16, 1997: A-1, 20–21, p. A-1. Available at <www.inquirer.philly.com/packages/somalia/nov16/default16.asp>.
3. Cindy Royal and James W. Tankard Jr., "The Convergence of Literary Journalism and the World Wide Web: The Case of *Blackhawk Down*," paper presented at the conference on "Expanding Convergence: Media Use in a Changing Information Environment," University of South Carolina, Nov. 16, 2002.
4. Karen Vargo, Carl Schierhorn, Stanley T. Wearden, Ann B. Schierhorn, Fred F. Endres and Pamela S. Tabar, "How Readers Respond to Digital News Stories in Layers and Links," *Newspaper Research Journal*, 21:2 (2000): 40–54.
5. Olivier Laude, "Patrolling Despair," *Atlas Magazine*, Summer 1996. Downloaded on Feb. 26, 2003, from <www.atlasmagazine.com/photo/laude_despair/laude_d08.html>.
6. Reynolds Holding, "Intel It's Not," *San Francisco Chronicle*, March 17, 2002: D-3. Available at <www.sfgate.com/cgi-bin/article.cgi?file=/chronicle/archive/2002/03/17/IN202466.DTL>.
7. Judy Stark, "New Building Code Brings Cost, Confusion," *St. Petersburg Times*, Aug. 19, 2002: A-1, 6. Available at <pqasb.pqarchiver.com/sptimes/doc152343321.html?MAC=716f5e93fac6e7a292ebe76f748>.

CHAPTER 7

SOURCES

Quotation and Attribution

A writer works with several kinds of information sources (some written, some human) in composing stories. Deciding which of these sources should be used and how they should be cited is an important part of writing the body of an article. Three elements basic to the process are quotation, attribution and identification. Writers also need to know how to categorize statements as reports, inferences or judgments.

QUOTATION

One of the many decisions a writer has to make is when to use direct quotations and when to use indirect quotations.

Direct Quotations

Material that appears as a direct quotation is enclosed in quotation marks or is in a sound bite—a video or audio recording of a person making a statement. Basically, the writer is saying, "This is exactly what the person said." Any statement enclosed within direct quotation marks should be the *exact* language of the person or document cited. There may be rare exceptions to this rule, but changing a quotation is an editor's decision. And it should not be done lightly.

Using Direct Quotations

Direct quotations are more effective in some situations than others. Here are some guidelines for getting and using direct quotations.

- When a person says something controversial. In this situation, the writer must make absolutely sure there is no misrepresentation of what a speaker

President Bill Clinton asserted in January 1998 that "I did not have sexual relations with that woman, Miss Lewinsky." This incident suggests that even highly placed sources should not always be trusted, for Clinton was, at the very least, stretching the truth.

says. The best way to do that is to use a sound bite or to quote the exact words spoken. On Jan. 26, 1998, President Clinton ended a news conference by replying to accusations that he had had an improper relationship with White House intern Monica S. Lewinsky. Here are his exact words:

But I want to say one thing to the American people. I want you to listen to me. I'm going to say this again: I did not have sexual relations with that woman, Miss Lewinsky. I never told anybody to lie, not a single time—never. These allegations are false.[1]

Many news organizations reported the entire quotation because of the scandalous nature of the unfolding Lewinsky story and because many people probably believed Clinton had been involved with Lewinsky. Most news organizations reported the president's remarks, but some raised the question of what they really meant. (See also the box "It's All in the Language.") For instance, the *St. Louis Post-Dispatch* reported:

Clinton's fresh denial did not put the issue to rest. Reporters asked Mike McCurry, the White House press secretary, exactly what sex acts Clinton would include under the term "sexual relations." McCurry replied testily, "I'm not going to dignify that question."

■ When a writer wants to make it clear that the words are the source's and not the writer's. *The* (Norfolk) *Virginian-Pilot* used this lead for its story about the historic vote in 1998 on Clinton's impeachment:

President Clinton said Wednesday that House members should "cast a vote of principle and conscience" on an impeachment inquiry today.

IT'S ALL IN THE LANGUAGE

Political scientist Richard D. Anderson Jr. notes that President Clinton could have worded his denial about having had sexual relations with Monica Lewinsky in any number of ways:

> We didn't have sex.
>
> We didn't have sexual relations.
>
> She and I didn't have sex.
>
> Monica and I didn't have sex.
>
> Ms. Lewinsky and I didn't have sex.
>
> That woman and I didn't have sex.
>
> I didn't have sex with her.
>
> I didn't have sexual relations with her.
>
> I didn't have sexual relations with Monica.
>
> I didn't have sexual relations with this woman.
>
> I didn't have sexual relations with that woman.
>
> I did not have sexual relations with Ms. Lewinsky.
>
> I did not have sexual relations with that woman (pause, gaze averted) Ms. Lewinsky.[2]

In choosing the last sentence (using "Miss" instead of "Ms."), says Anderson, Clinton was selecting the wording that created the maximum linguistic distance between himself and Lewinsky. Not every reader or listener will analyze a president's remarks as thoroughly as Anderson did, but even the average person can probably sense the distancing created by Clinton's choice of language.

■ When a speaker says something that is colorful, well-said or otherwise "quotable." Sometimes a source will use figures of speech such as similes or metaphors in a kind of "poetry of the streets." When President Bush delivered an address in Cincinnati outlining the reasons a military strike against Iraq might be necessary, he said:

We cannot wait for the final proof—the smoking gun—that could come in the form of a mushroom cloud.

This statement may come perilously close to being a mixed metaphor, but it is a dramatic and colorful expression nevertheless.

A United Nations official who was part of the weapons inspection team sent to Iraq in November 2002 said about an offer of help from the United States: "We're happy for the handshake, but we don't want the hug." This statement would lose all its effectiveness if it were not reported precisely.

■ To give the flavor of an individual's speech. An obvious use of direct quotation is to show the way a person talks. For instance, Lillian Ross, in her famous "Portrait of Hemingway," captured the writer's exact speech. Ross tells of Hemingway shopping for a coat in Abercrombie and Fitch and saying to the clerk, "I think I still have credit in this joint," and, a minute later, "Want to see coat."[3] Some critics said Ross was trying to show how ridiculous Hemingway was, but others praised Ross for presenting an honest portrait.

■ Any other time the exact words of a speaker are important. For instance, a story might deal with the question of whether a speaker used profanity or threatened someone. The exact words would be crucial.

■ To help build credibility. A reader or listener probably would not trust a report that was presented entirely in indirect quotation. Direct quotations, whether in sound bites or within quotation marks, help to authenticate a story. (See also the box "Shirley Biagi on Using Direct Quotations.")

Special Problems

A writer should never use quotation marks when guessing about what a speaker's exact words were. A writer who is unable to verify a quotation has a couple of alternatives. One is partial quotation, in which quotation marks are placed around some but not all of the words. For instance, a story about a possible shortfall in a state budget contained this sentence:

> A press secretary for the governor's office said it is "foolish" to guess about a shortfall before hearing revenue expectations.

The second technique is to use the words the writer does remember, but leave the quotation marks off. This is indirect quotation, which is discussed in the next section.

A writer must remember: The overriding principle in using quotation marks is that they should enclose words actually spoken (or written) by the person quoted. Additional guidelines for using quotation marks follow:

■ When two people are quoted one immediately after the other, a writer should start a new paragraph for the second speaker. Every time there is a change of speaker, there should be a new paragraph.

■ If a quotation runs several paragraphs long, the closing quotation mark is omitted at the end of each paragraph except the last one. This shows there is

SHIRLEY BIAGI ON USING DIRECT QUOTATIONS

A [direct] quotation is unfiltered talk. The writer moves out of the way and says to the reader, "Here is my interviewee. Listen." A quotation shows someone's thinking. You should use a direct quote only when it shows someone's thoughts better than you can—more characteristically, more succinctly, more authoritatively or more emphatically.

When you use quotes, you ask the reader to briefly listen in on your interview. Comments in quotations belong to the interviewee, not to the reporter. The reader hears the interviewee through the quotation without the reporter as an interpreter.

The people who talk in your stories should be worth hearing. Quotation marks bring attention to words. Because the words stand out, the quotations should be important to the reader. So you should be very selective about what you quote.

Source: Shirley Biagi, *Interviews That Work: A Practical Guide for Journalists,* 2nd ed. (Belmont, Calif.: Wadsworth, 1992): 138.

Shirley Biagi is chair of the journalism department at California State University, Sacramento. She is the author of *Interviews That Work.*

more quoted material to follow. A quotation mark is placed at the beginning of each paragraph of a quotation that is several paragraphs long.

- Except for quotations of more than one paragraph in length, there should be a closing quotation mark for every opening (or beginning) quotation mark. Inexperienced writers sometimes forget to close their quotations.

- If a direct quotation is several paragraphs long, only one attribution to a source is needed, and it should appear in the first paragraph of quotation.

- Single quotation marks should be used to indicate a direct quotation within another direct quotation. Sometimes an apostrophe is used as a single quotation mark, as in this example:

"J. Edgar Hoover was a narrow conservative who fiercely believed the words, 'My country, right or wrong,'" Anderson said.

- Newspaper, public relations and Web writers try to avoid brackets and parentheses, although few editors ban their use altogether. Magazine writers tend to use them more frequently. English teachers demand, appropriately, that brackets be used to include within a direct quotation clarifying information that the source did not speak. Most media writers use parentheses instead. Parenthetical material must be used to clarify the quotation, not to change it. For example, "he" is changed in the following example to "Sheriff Ashley Beal" simply to clarify the sentence:

"The search party found the escaped prisoner, but (Sheriff Ashley Beal) went into the house alone to talk to the armed man," Deputy Sheriff Phil Pitts said.

Writers sometimes use a parenthetical word or phrase after a word whose meaning is unclear or imprecise, as in this sentence:

"The man pointed the weapon (an assault rifle) at Ashley, but he didn't fire," Pitts said.

Broadcast writers obviously cannot use parentheses, so they avoid using direct quotations (actualities) that are unclear or imprecise. When they must use such a quotation, they typically explain the imprecision before airing the actuality.

- Ellipses, which indicate that part of a direct quotation has been omitted, are rarely used by newspaper, magazine and Web writers. Broadcast writers obviously can't use them at all. It is risky to drop words from direct quotations, for writers run the risk of changing the speaker's meaning. Readers also may wonder what material was dropped—and why.

  Ellipses are used, if at all, primarily in quotations taken from documents and other written materials. Writers must remember always that an ellipsis is three periods only. If punctuation is required (at the end of a sentence, for instance) it must be added, as in this example:

  "Home environment has a greater impact on standardized test scores than teaching technique … ," the researchers wrote.

- Quotation marks should not be put around clichés. Consider this example:

  The new executives have created hardly a "ripple on the pond" of the business community.

  Either the phrase should be strong and clear enough that quotation marks are not necessary, or it should be dropped and a better one found. In the example above, "ripple on the pond" is so trite that another phrase should have been used.

Partial Quotations

Print, Web and public relations writers sometimes put only two or three words of direct quotations inside quotation marks, as in this example:

Redrawing congressional districts is "far more important" than reforming the school finance system, the governor said today.

Partial quotations are appropriate in only a few circumstances:

- When a writer is certain about the meaning and accuracy of the main portion of a direct quotation, but not about a less important part of the quotation.
- When a writer wants to emphasize the main point stated in a direct quotation, as in the example above.
- When a writer wants to emphasize that he or she is reporting the source's *exact* words, even if it is only two or three of those words.

Partial quotations tend to be used too frequently, and they sometimes are misused. Writers generally should *not* use partial quotations, for they seldom add to a sentence in any meaningful way.

Partial quotations can cause readers to wonder why only a few words were quoted directly and to question why the entire quotation was not used. They may even wonder whether a writer deliberately used the words out of context. This does not enhance credibility. Some writers also use partial quotations to question in a subtle way the credibility of a source, as in this sentence:

> The student, in her address to the discipline committee, "claimed" that the paper was her own work and that she had not copied it from the Web.

The writer obviously has decided the student cheated and does not believe the "claim."

Broadcast News

Direct quotations in broadcast news have to be handled somewhat differently from those in print, since people can't "hear" quotation marks. It's best to use sound bites whenever possible, but when that is not feasible, broadcasters have a couple of options:

- Alert the listener that a direct quotation is coming up by using the word "quote," as in the following example:

  > At one point he said, quote, "Basically, I got on a plane with a bomb. Basically, I tried to ignite it."

  A broadcast story can also introduce a direct quotation with a phrase like "in his words" or "in her words," as in the following example:

  > One of the passengers aboard this Air India flight from Heathrow headed to JFK Airport has a name that is, in the words of an FBI official, "similar to or very close to the name of someone who is on an international terrorist watch list."

- Use mostly indirect quotation. Writers of broadcast news stories often avoid the problem of direct quotation by using mostly indirect quotation, as in the following example:

  > Daugherty says the information is false and that he has the documentation to prove it.

Indirect Quotations

Indirect quotation is reporting a statement without quotation marks, but attributing it to a source. Material that appears as indirect quotation must be an accurate reflection of what a speaker said, but it is not claimed to be the speaker's exact words. Indirect quotation is also referred to as paraphrase. Many summary news leads are made up of indirect quotations because the device lets the writer put the words in the form that will make the lead most effective. Consider this lead sentence:

> Towns of 1,500 to 4,000 will not have hospitals in three to five years, a rural Texas physician said Tuesday night to the West Texas Press Association.

It paraphrases the exact words of the speaker:

> I believe, and many in my profession believe, that within three to five years there will be no more one-doctor hospitals such as mine in Seagraves. Towns of 1,500 to 4,000 population simply will not have any medical care available.

When should a writer use indirect quotation? The following are some guidelines:

- When the speaker uses jargon, bureaucratic euphemism or gobbledygook (Chapter 4). In these cases, the speaker's words would not be clear to the reader, and little purpose would be served by quoting them directly. The following is an example of bureaucratic euphemism from a press briefing at the Pentagon by Gen. Tommy Franks, commander, U.S. Central Command:

> Let me be quick to say that you also find, however, a very uneven situation in Afghanistan. There are places in Afghanistan that I think are very, very secure, and of course those become magnets to a lot of nongovernmental activity. I mean, if we're more secure, then that's a place where we feel like we can take NGOs and do a lot of work. The places where security is less sure, then there is a bit more reluctance—and it's probably obvious to everyone—to go into those areas to do the work which some of us would say is necessary to rebuild the infrastructure and so forth, in order to permit the security to improve.[4]

This answer was so convoluted that Franks himself said, "Reasonably circuitous answer to a very good question." The word "infrastructure" is a typical bureaucratic term—it sounds impressive but no one is quite sure what it means. A writer would have to struggle with this statement to come up with a meaningful indirect quotation.

A public relations writer must be certain that simple, clear, concise quotations make it into news releases, annual reports and all other materials. It's difficult to do that when the writer's client or boss is speaking directly to the media, as Franks was, but it's certainly possible to ensure clarity when the

Gen. Tommy Franks, commander of the U.S. Central Command (shown here in 2003), took obfuscation to a new level during an October 2002 news conference about the military situation in Afghanistan.

writer is disseminating a quotation from someone in his or her organization. A military public affairs officer, for instance, might have summarized Frank's statement this way:

Some parts of Afghanistan are secure and nongovernmental organizations are allowed to work in these regions, Franks said.

■ When a speaker or piece of information is unnecessarily wordy. Another one of Franks' answers illustrates this problem:

With regard to why I'm in Washington, actually, every week or two I'll come to Washington in order to talk to the secretary; talk to him about my region, which certainly includes Iraq; talk to him about what we have going on with everything from the International Security Assistance Force in Afghanistan to what we're doing in Operation Enduring Freedom. And so that was the purpose of this trip up here. I just got back from the region last week, and he asked that I come up and share the insights that I'd gained during that trip.[5]

That same public affairs officer might have used the following indirect quotation to summarize Franks' rambling statement:

Franks said he comes to Washington every week or two to brief the Secretary of Defense on developments in Afghanistan and Iraq.

It would have been helpful if military public relations officers had worked with Franks to help him express himself more clearly and concisely. It's not easy to learn to speak publicly, but it's worth the effort—particularly for someone who was in Franks' position.

- When a writer isn't sure of the speaker's exact words. Suppose a writer interviewed the victim of a shark attack and upon returning to the office to write the story found this hastily written sentence in the notebook:

I hollered to my wife to get back in the boat and I started —— toward the boat.

This would make a good direct quotation, but unfortunately the writer knows something was left out between "started" and "toward" and doesn't remember what. The best guess is that it is "swimming," since the attack occurred in deep water and the person couldn't have been wading. But the missing word could have been "paddling," "scrambling" or "hightailing it." The safest way to use such information is to check with the source to find out what the exact words were or to use an indirect quotation, such as this:

Daniels said he yelled to his wife to get back in the boat and started swimming toward the boat.

Notice that putting the information in the form of an indirect quotation also requires some other changes. The word "I" must be changed to "he" because, in the indirect quotation, the writer is speaking, not the source. Similarly, "my" has to be changed to "his" or it will sound as if the writer were involved in the incident. Finally, most journalism and public relations writers would prefer "yelled" to "hollered" in a passage of indirect quotation because "hollered" is colloquial.

ATTRIBUTION

Full and accurate writing requires that information obtained from a source be attributed carefully to that source, whether it is a person or a document. A writer must attribute information carefully for three reasons:

- The process forces the professional to substantiate and verify all material. One who is committed to careful attribution is likely to commit fewer mistakes than one who is not. A writer who uses information without citing a knowledgeable, fair source is looking for trouble.
- It is a means of assigning responsibility for misinformation when a source lies or misleads. A writer who does not cite a source for information, or who uses

an unnamed source, must accept all blame if the information turns out to be wrong. The unfortunate writer who wrote the following for the *Houston Chronicle* assumed all the blame when it turned out the man was not the Dallas Cowboys' star receiver:

> Former Dallas Cowboys wide receiver Gordon "Golden" Richards, now a Metro bus driver, was arrested in Houston on Tuesday on charges of parole violations dating to 1996.
>
> Richards, 48, employed by the Metropolitan Transit Authority since February, was arrested by Metro police about 9 a.m. at 801 N. San Jacinto.

■ Readers, listeners and viewers can trust material that is carefully attributed more than that which is not, and they can trust organizations that have reputations for careful attribution more than those that do not. Many understand when a writer is feeding them moonshine—such as trying to pass off a personal judgment as "real" information—and many don't like it. A vague attribution can create a suspicion that information didn't come from a qualified source at all, as in this example:

> Mayor Leon Bradley gave his mistress a $34,000 a year job with the city and helped her get a city-subsidized apartment in St. John's Place, a source in city government said today.

This pseudo-attribution, which is not an attribution at all because the source is not named, is too vague to be of much use to a viewer who wants to evaluate the information. The viewer might even ask: Is this really from a qualified source, or is this the writer's own opinion? If it is the writer's opinion, why should I believe it? Why did the qualified source not want to be identified? Is this stuff true or a fabrication?

Placement

Though the beginning of a sentence is typically not the best place for an attribution, one can be placed there, as in the following lead:

> Noted linguistic scholar and political radical Noam Chomsky said Sunday on campus that a pending conflict in Iraq will not rid the world of terrorism but will only make things worse.

Or an attribution can be placed at the end of a sentence, using a device known as dangling attribution:

> A pending conflict in Iraq will not rid the world of terrorism but will only make things worse, linguistic scholar and political radical Noam Chomsky said Sunday on campus.

A dangling attribution is not an error of sentence construction, like a dangling participle, but rather a useful means of emphasizing a quotation by placing it at the beginning of a sentence. The dangling attribution was invented by print writers because *who* is saying something is usually not as important as *what* is said. The dangling attribution rarely is used by broadcast writers.

After a source has been identified in a print story (and sometimes even on first mention), it is almost always best to give less emphasis to later attributions by placing them within or at the ends of sentences. In general, each sentence in a story should begin with the most important information in the sentence; rarely is the name of an already-identified source important enough to merit placement at the beginning of a sentence.

Dangling attribution is not appropriate in certain situations. Sometimes a source is important enough to emphasize at the beginning. Or, in a story containing more than one source, a writer may have to begin some sentences with attributions to avoid confusing readers.

Unobtrusive, Smooth Attribution

Skillful writers use attributions smoothly and unobtrusively. They vary attribution by putting a source's name at different positions in different sentences, by switching between the name of the source and the personal pronoun (he or she) and by finding ways to reduce the numbers of attributions they use. One useful technique is to start a paragraph with a direct quotation that has a dangling attribution at the end. Then another direct quotation can be added immediately after it in the same paragraph, as in this example:

> "I was never the cheerleader at school," Bjork said. "I was always the kid at the back of
> the class with the spiders in her pockets."

The writer attributes two direct quotations while naming Bjork only once.

Another device for smooth attribution is to vary the verb used. The writer should avoid the temptation to find numerous synonyms for the basic verb "said," however. "Said" can be used many times in a story or release without becoming irritating. Students may worry that they are repeating "said" too frequently, but actually it becomes like a punctuation mark. Neutral synonyms, such as "added" and "continued," are the best substitutes for "said." One of the weakest substitutes is "according to," which is longer and carries a slight connotation of doubt. "According to" might be a good choice when a writer is quoting from documents or other nonhuman sources for which "said" is not quite appropriate. (See also the box "Roy Copperud on Verbs Used in Attribution.")

Special Problems

Media professionals must be exceptionally careful as they attribute information to sources and personalities in the news, for there are many pitfalls awaiting the careless writer:

- Verbs such as "feels" or "thinks" and phrases such as "is afraid of" should not be used as attributions. The writer cannot know what a person feels, thinks or is afraid of, but a writer can know what a person says. Weak attributions such

ROY COPPERUD ON VERBS USED IN ATTRIBUTION

According to. Best avoided because it casts a shadow, however slight, on the credibility of the speaker. The raising of such a doubt may be desired, and then, of course, *according to* is suitable, conveying "that's what *he* thinks." Often *according to* is just a roundabout and careless displacement of *said.*

Admitted. See *pointed out.*

Advised. A common gaucherie when it displaces *said.* As an intransitive verb, it is best saved for the sense *counsel, give advice:* "They advised on marital relations." Sentences like "Small-craft warnings have been posted, he advised" are journalese.

Affirmed. "Stated positively; asserted as valid or confirmed." Close to *declared,* but implies reiteration of a previous statement or position.

Alleged. "Declared as if under oath but without proof; brought forward as a reason or excuse." Used mostly by reporters with the hope of getting themselves off the hook in police stories. Contrary to a fairly widespread assumption, *alleged* does not give immunity from suit for libel, but it may be useful to establish absence of malice.

Announced. "Made known publicly; proclaimed."

Asseverated. Too bookish for news contexts, and seldom seen any longer, though it was once favored (like *averred*) as a variant of *said.* It means "to affirm or aver positively or earnestly." Thus it implies some special emphasis, and is unsuitable (like most of the expressions listed here) as a random variant of *said.*

Averred. "Verified or proved to be true in pleading a cause; declared positively." This too implies some emphasis; further, it is not common parlance.

Cited the fact that. See *pointed out.*

Commented. Strictly, made an observation on something. Thus unsuitable for attribution of an offhand statement.

Conceded. See *pointed out.*

Contended. One of the most disagreeably misused words in the lexicon of attribution. It denotes controversy or disagreement, and when those conditions are absent, *contended* should be too. Webster gives *maintain, assert* as synonyms, but both these words imply, if they do not denote, perseverance in a view against opposition. The raunchier reporters drop *contend* in at random where *said* or something similarly colorless is called for.

(continued)

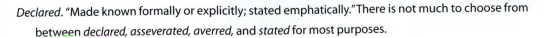

ROY COPPERUD ON VERBS USED IN ATTRIBUTION *(continued)*

Declared. "Made known formally or explicitly; stated emphatically." There is not much to choose from between *declared, asseverated, averred,* and *stated* for most purposes.

Disclosed. See *revealed.*

Explained. Students often use it to attribute commonplace remarks that are not explanations; that is to say, not clarifications of something that has gone before. This inescapably brings to mind Ring Lardner's "'Shut up,' he explained."

Maintained. "Upheld in argument; contended for; asserted, declared." The word should be used in reference to a statement backing up a previously defined position, or at least one made with some emphasis. For purposes of attribution, it is more or less interchangeable with *contended* or *affirmed.* ...

Mentioned. "Referred to; cited by name." The commonest error here is not mistaking the meaning but using *mentioned* as an intransitive verb: "The book was poorly written," he mentioned. *Mention* requires an object: "He mentioned *that the book was poorly written. Mention* is suitable only if the reference is brief or casual.

Noted. See *pointed out.*

Observed. "Uttered as a remark." Suitable, like *remarked,* for a casual statement.

Pointed out. Implies truth, or factualness. Thus it must be used with care lest the writer (and the newspaper) unwittingly associate themselves with what is only speculation or opinion, and thus give the effect of editorializing. *Admitted, conceded, noted,* and *cited the fact that* all similarly imply factualness.

Remarked. "Took notice of; observed." The connotation is offhand, casual.

Reported. "Gave an account of; told what happened; narrated; related." The word is also used to convey doubt of authenticity, or absence of verification: "He was reported to have fled the country." This example, however, is not direct attribution, as in "The coast is clear, he reported."

Revealed. Like *disclosed,* suitable only in reference to what has been concealed. Often misused where *announced* would be appropriate.

Said. The all-purpose word for attribution. As has been noted, the writer should not be afraid to repeat it, nor should he use another word without carefully considering whether it fits the occasion.

Stated. "Set forth in detail or formally declared." A great favorite, but too stiff for most contexts. Most *stated*s should be replaced by *said*s. The word is used habitually by young reporters with an impulse to make their stuff sound portentous, and by old ones who have never acquired a sensitivity to stereotypes.

Vowed. This also gives too much emphasis for most news contexts; furthermore, it has a quaint flavor. *Promised* is usually preferable. The solemnity that *vow* connotes is often inappropriate.

Wrote. Sometimes misused in reference to what has been published: "as the Daily Bladder wrote in its issue of Dec. 18." Writers write, publications publish. In the example, *said* should have been used, or perhaps *reported*.

Source: Roy H. Copperud, "Editorial Workshop: The Tone of the Talk—I," *Editor & Publisher,* Jan. 13, 1973: 22; and Roy H. Copperud, "Editorial Workshop: The Tone of the Talk—II," *Editor & Publisher,* Jan. 27, 1973: 22.

Roy H. Copperud was a longtime columnist for *Editor & Publisher* magazine.

---

as "it is reported" and "reliable sources said" should also be avoided. They are not attributions at all; they are pseudo-attributions. They appear to cite a source, but they do not.

- Some professionals argue that adverbs such as *reportedly, allegedly* and *apparently* should never be used in media writing. They have a point. Such words certainly do not protect a writer who is charged with bias (Chapter 1) or libel (Chapter 13). Adverbs can be useful, however, when they are used carefully, as in this sentence:

The woman charged with embezzling $500,000 from her employer in July allegedly bought a $200,000 yacht during the same month, Police Chief Ronnie Birch said today.

If Birch is not sure the woman bought the yacht, the use of "allegedly" is appropriate. That usage alone will not save a publication from a libel suit, but it is not a good idea to say with seeming certainty that she bought the yacht (as a writer would do if he or she dropped the word "allegedly").

- A writer who cites someone named in a document or on a Web site must state clearly that another writer reported the direct or indirect quotation. For example:

"The accident was caused when a defective tire blew out and the car hit the curb too hard," *Bugle.com* quoted Smith as saying.

This kind of careful attribution is important, for if it turns out Smith was misquoted, a writer (and his or her editors) will feel considerably better if he or she has cited the *Bugle.com* author. It's still an error, but at least the original mistake clearly is someone else's.

■ Broadcast and print writers must decide how much attribution should appear in a story. It is better to over-attribute than to under-attribute. The writer becomes the source for any unattributed statement. If no other authority is given, the reader or listener assumes the writer is standing behind the information. If unattributed material turns out to be wrong, the writer is solely responsible. A reader or writer cannot evaluate a source that is not identified adequately.

Good writers know, however, that it is possible to over-attribute, and they try to avoid doing that. Consider this example:

The accident victim is in good condition at Bellaire Medical Center, spokeswoman Elly Smithson, head of BMC's public affairs unit, said today.

Unless the writer has reason to think the accident victim is *not* in good condition, the long attribution is not necessary, particularly in broadcast news. Clearly, such information comes from a hospital. A "hospital spokeswoman said" is sufficient. Some writers would not even use that phrase.

IDENTIFICATION

With few exceptions, every person mentioned in a story should be carefully identified. A reader might not remember who John Ashcroft is even though his name is familiar. A complete report would identify Ashcroft as the attorney general of the United States. Broadcast writers typically use somewhat less identification material than print writers do, but they still need to use enough so listeners can evaluate sources or news personalities. Only a few superstar celebrities, such as Michael Jackson, Cher and Madonna, are likely to be perceived by writers as so famous that they do not need to be identified beyond their names.

Writers must cultivate the habit of getting first names, middle initials and last names; exact addresses; and occupations for *all* news sources and personalities, even when they aren't sure they will use all of that information. Precise information is particularly important in covering crime and police news. Media outlets lose libel cases because writers were careless in writing down basic information (Chapter 13). The best source for such information, of course, is the news source or personality. Business cards, accurate directories and public relations professionals are good alternatives.

A typical identification reports the individual's name, occupation, title or company affiliation (age and address are used less frequently). A paragraph from *The Washington Post* about a White House dinner illustrates a number of forms of identification:

The guest list of 130 included a number of prominent Polish Americans, including Baseball Hall of Famer Stan Musial (obviously a special treat for President Bush), Sen. Barbara Mikulski (D-Md.), Rep. Bill Lipinski (D-Ill.), former national security adviser Zbigniew

Brzezinski and Duke University basketball coach Mike
Krzyzewski. Other guests included Chicago Mayor Richard
Daley, Supreme Court Justice Clarence Thomas and CNN's
Wolf Blitzer, whose family comes from a village in Poland.
In addition to Musial, blasts from the past included former
secretaries of state Henry Kissinger and George Shultz.[6]

A broadcast writer likely would mention fewer names—
a list like this one would take up a huge chunk of a
broadcast news report—but the identifications would be
similar.

It is difficult sometimes to find a brief phrase that
adequately identifies a person. Ralph Nader created a
unique job for himself when he began pointing out the
dangers to the public from automobiles and other products. News organizations finally began to identify him as
"consumer advocate Ralph Nader." More recently, he is
referred to as "presidential candidate Ralph Nader" or
"consumer advocate and presidential candidate."

*A single word or title may be sufficient iden-
tification for a source like President George
W. Bush, shown here at a 2004 news conference during which he called for a constitutional amendment that would ban
same-gender marriages. That one word of
identification typically is used before the
name of a prominent person.*

Ordinary people are usually identified by job or, if no
job information is available, by address. At least giving
the address will distinguish them from other persons
with the same names. This is sometimes crucial in avoiding libel actions.

What an individual is or has done is sometimes more
important than who he or she is. *The Washington Post*
story about the White House dinner contained this paragraph:

> Also on hand: Bush "Pioneers"—Tom Foley, Jim Francis and Akin Gump's James
> Langdon—each of whom had raised at least $100,000 for Bush's 2000 presidential cam-
> paign. Francis's wife, Debbie, was seated next to the president during the dinner.[7]

The paragraph reveals the importance that President Bush attaches to big donors—
they are rewarded by being allowed to hobnob at White House dinners with some
of the most influential people in the world.

Journalists and public relations writers should avoid racial or ethnic identification. Some organizations may still identify people as blacks or Hispanic, but it is
inconsistent to do that when other people are not identified in print as Jewish,
Italian-American or Irish. Similarly, some organizations identify individuals as disabled, but many disabled people object to that reference.[8]

Many writers follow a simple rule of thumb: If disability, ethnicity, gender or
race are not relevant, don't note those characteristics. If Carroll Parrott Blue comes
to campus to talk about her book, *The Dawn at My Back,* it is important to identify
her as black, for that is central to her book.[9] If a black speaker is the head of a major

corporation, race should not be mentioned, unless the speech is about the challenge blacks face in a white corporate environment.

A person's full name should be used the first time the individual is mentioned in a story. This is called the first reference rule. After the first reference, the same person is referred to only by last name. One exception is broadcast writing, in which writers sometimes mention complete names in subsequent references when stories are long and have multiple sources. This technique can help a listener recall a source.

Identification is often necessary with organizations as well as individuals. People in the business world might assume that everyone knows what Intel is. But many members of the news audience might not, and a phrase like "the world's largest chip maker" should be included the first time the name is used. Usually an organization's complete name is given the first time it is mentioned. If there is a common acronym or abbreviation for the organization's name, the organization can be referred to subsequently by that acronym or abbreviation, as in this example:

> The American officials were to meet Wednesday with representatives of the Organization of Petroleum Exporting Countries to discuss recent spikes in the price of oil.
>
> OPEC leaders have said they cannot increase production.

Public relations professionals often face a different dilemma as they identify their organizations and attribute information to sources, whom they usually know well and for whom they sometimes work: They include too much identification and much of it is hype. Some chief executive officers like to see their resumes in every news release, but that means each release has little chance of being published or aired. Where possible, public relations writers should attribute as journalists do. This improves the chances that releases will be used.

Web writers have an important advantage over their colleagues in other areas, for they often can establish links to pages that have biographical information about persons mentioned in their stories. In a story about research conducted by three scientists, for instance, a Web writer almost certainly would establish a link to biographical information about each scientist, for most research organizations have information about people on their staffs.

Three common devices for identification are title before name, phrase in apposition and prepositional phrase.

Title Before Name

Writers identify many news figures by putting short titles before the names. Sometimes the title is an official one, as in these examples:

- Johnson County District Attorney Kimberly Owen
- Sen. Judith Zaffirini
- U.S. Sen. Elizabeth Dole
- Secretary of State Colin Powell
- Prime Minister Ariel Sharon

Sometimes a false or pseudo title is used to identify a person. False and pseudo titles, since they are not official, should not be capitalized unless they are at the beginning of a sentence. Here are some examples:

- rock star Bruce Springsteen
- writer Joan Didion
- university spokeswoman Ann Kellett
- civil rights advocate Jesse Jackson
- Nobel Prize winner Elie Wiesel

Broadcast writers nearly always put titles and other identification before names, regardless of how long that material is.

Phrase in Apposition

Sometimes it is effective to identify an individual with a phrase after the name, particularly when a title or explanatory material is more than three words or so. Here are some examples of identification by a phrase in apposition:

- Tim Connelly, assistant county attorney, said ...
- Helen L. Johnson, organizer of the exhibit, said ...
- Alberta Sanchez, a senior business major at Towson State University and a member of the Ballet Folklorico Dance Team, said ...

The last example is clearly a case in which the identification is too long to go before the name. A phrase in apposition must be set off by two commas, one before and one after. Formal titles are written in lowercase when they follow names.

Prepositional Phrase

Identification by means of a prepositional phrase is more unusual than the other two methods, but it is useful. Here are some examples:

- Laura W. Murphy of the American Civil Liberties Union argued ...
- Dr. Etienne Krug of the World Health Organization said ...
- Nancy Boswell of Transparency International said ...

Commas should not be used to set off prepositional phrases.

REPORTS, INFERENCES AND JUDGMENTS

It is important for all writers—professionals and beginners—to recognize the differences among the statements they get from news sources and personalities because different kinds of comments often are attributed in different ways. It is useful, for instance, to categorize information as reports, inferences or judgments.[10]

Reports

Reports are statements and facts that can be verified for accuracy. They exclude, to the greatest extent possible, inferences and judgments. A report might originate with a writer when something happens within the immediate environment, as when a professional writes about a murder trial that he or she has watched.

Or a report might be given to the writer by someone else. For a story about the results of all murder trials in a city in the past decade, obviously, a writer would have to rely on statistics prepared by court officials. That is a report of a report, which is not the best way to get information.

Writers cannot personally verify every report they use in every story they write. There is no time for such verification, and the effort would be to some extent wasted. If a police officer tells a journalist that a crime was committed at 12:07 a.m., the journalist doesn't have to verify that report (unless there is some reason to believe the police officer is lying or has lied in the past). The officer can be relied on to tell the truth, particularly when the officer's name is used in the story.

A writer must, however, verify any report that is of questionable validity. If a university president says that $80,000 will be cut from the history department's budget and that the cut won't hurt academic programs, the report must be verified with the head of the history department and with teachers in the department. It is necessary also to check the department's budget, which should be available in any public university.

Public relations writers usually do have to verify the accuracy of every single report, for employers typically *demand* that level of verification. It is not unusual for a draft news release to be distributed to all managers and to be read by several people. This can be irritating at times because many managers don't understand professional communication and how it can affect an organization, but the release is accurate—at least as the managerial hierarchy perceives accuracy.

Inferences

A writer who uses personal inferences or those made by others is on less firm ground than one who sticks with reports. Unfortunately, inferences—which are statements about the unknown made on the basis of known facts—are made every day, and professionals must report some of them. Suppose, for instance, an influential mayor said:

> James Taborsky, after reading a pornographic book, visiting a pornographic Web site and viewing a pornographic film, raped a young woman. One must conclude that pornography causes violent sex crimes.

The inference may or may not be accurate, since few politicians are qualified to make inferences about the relationship between pornography and sex crimes. A reporter who published the mayor's statement might be passing along false information. If the main concern is the accuracy of the inference, the comment shouldn't be published.

However, the mayor made the statement; and the accuracy of the quotation can be verified, although the accuracy of the inference cannot. The mayor's comment is reported, not because it is an accurate statement about the relationship between pornography and violent sex crimes, but because it shows the mayor thinks there is a relationship—and because the comment may indicate that a crackdown on pornography is imminent.

A professional must be particularly careful about inferring that someone is thinking a certain way simply because the known facts indicate that the person might be thinking that way. Suppose a woman speaking at a public meeting about the need for better schools pounds her fist on the table. A journalist may infer from that action that she is angry, but the inference may be incorrect. The woman may simply pound her fist for emphasis or because she is excited. She might not be angry at all.

The journalist should report that the woman pounded her fist on the table, but without saying she did it angrily, for emphasis or for some other reason. In the interest of producing a more accurate and complete report, the journalist could ask the woman at the end of the meeting whether she was angry. If the woman says she was angry, that can be used.

Judgments

A judgment is a statement (either direct or implied) of approval or disapproval of a person, institution, issue or event. As with reports or inferences, a judgment can be made by a media professional (this should never happen), or it can be made by another person and quoted by a writer.

Writers should avoid publishing someone else's judgment just because it can be legitimized by quotation marks. Some judgments are irresponsible and should be used only if failure to report them is worse than using them. A mayor who charges that two members of city council are charlatans has made a judgment. Failure to report that judgment would be acting against the public interest because the public deserves to know the mayor's feelings.

It would be better, though, to report the evidence on which the mayor bases this claim (perhaps the mayor has evidence that the two vote in ways that benefit their friends) and let the reader decide whether the two are indeed charlatans. This means a writer uses a combination of judgments and reports (see the box "S.I. Hayakawa on Snarl-words and Purr-words"). The judgment is the mayor's personal opinion. The report (the factual information) is the basis for that opinion. The judgment is important as a reflection of the mayor's state of mind, even if it is not supported by reports.

Media professionals must carefully avoid passing on their own judgments. It is far better to report the facts clearly, accurately and fairly and let the audience make the judgments (Chapter 1). Here is a case in which a public relations writer uses a judgment to hype an event:

> Metropolis will witness the most spectacular, star-studded fundraising event ever presented in the city when seven dynamic performers take over the stage at Corbitt Hall for the "Million Dollar Event" benefiting the Franklin Foundation for Cancer Research.

S.I. HAYAKAWA ON SNARL-WORDS AND PURR-WORDS

To call these judgments "snarl-words" and "purr-words" does not mean that we should simply shrug them off. It means that we should be careful to *allocate the meaning correctly*—placing such a statement as "She's the sweetest girl in the world!" as a revelation of the speaker's state of mind, and not as a revelation of facts about the girl. If the "snarl-words" about "Reds" or "fascists" are accompanied by verifiable reports (which would also mean that we have previously agreed as to who, specifically, is meant by the terms "Reds" or "fascists"), we might find reason to be just as disturbed as the speaker. If the "purr-words" about the sweetest girl in the world are accompanied by verifiable reports about her appearance, manners, character, and so on, we might find reason to admire her too. But "snarl-words" and "purr-words" as such, unaccompanied by reports, offer nothing further to discuss, except possibly the question, "Why do you feel as you do?"

Source: S. I. Hayakawa, *Language in Thought and Action,* 4th ed. (New York: Harcourt Brace Jovanovich, 1978): 39.

Semanticist S.I. Hayakawa analyzed the dichotomies of language in his famous book, *Language in Thought and Action.*

The public relations professional makes two judgments in one sentence: that the "Million Dollar Event" is the most spectacular fundraising event ever in Metropolis and that the seven performers are dynamic. It is important to avoid such judgments, for such claims are mere hyperbole designed to make organizations or personalities look good. Such judgments reduce the chances that releases will be used. The writer of the Franklin Foundation release should present the evidence on which the judgments are based.

Attributing Inferences, Judgments

Most inferences and judgments, if used at all, should be used in direct quotations and attributed carefully to named, qualified sources. It is exceptionally poor practice to disseminate inferences and judgments from unnamed sources; a writer should not give a source a soapbox from which to speak anonymously. Direct quotation and careful attribution don't absolve a writer of responsibility for an inference or judgment that turns out to be wrong. However, the person identified in the story as the source of a questionable inference or judgment must bear some of the responsibility for the inaccuracy. Furthermore, the reader, listener or viewer knows the fault for the inaccuracy isn't entirely the writer's.

The decision to use or not to use an inference or judgment usually depends on the quality or status of the source. Some sources have no idea what they're talking about. Their inferences and judgments simply aren't credible. When an inference or judgment is made by a source who doesn't seem well informed, or when an inference or judgment seems weak, illogical, inaccurate or stupid, the writer must seek other views about the validity of the first source's statements.

When the Illinois Senate passed a bill requiring women to have written consent from their parents or husbands before getting abortions, for instance, a Chicago Democrat said that the bill, if passed, "would have the effect of driving abortions underground and the abortion mills will grow in Illinois once again." That's an inference about the bill's effect that must be checked with persons on the other side of the issue. Failure to obtain the opinions of the bill's proponents would be shoddy reporting. The same is true for countless reports written daily.

PUTTING IT ALL TOGETHER

A writer builds a story by putting together the kinds of material that have been described in this chapter—direct quotations, indirect quotations, attribution and identification. Jonathan Osborne of the *Austin American-Statesman,* combines the elements effectively in a story about a proposed city ordinance (see the box "Putting the Elements Together").

PUTTING THE ELEMENTS TOGETHER

After seven months of sometimes noisy debate, downtown residents and club and business owners may have struck a deal to turn down the sound in this live music town.

The draft of a proposed noise ordinance is still mired with written notes, scribbles and chicken scratches. But that will be cleaned up if, as expected, the City Council sets a deadline today to present a final draft to the public and then to vote on it. That hearing would likely take place Dec. 5.

Story begins with a summary news lead, with the writer using a great deal of his own phrasing to pull together a series of events. Information is unattributed, but attribution does come later.

This paragraph brings out the news peg—the City Council may set a deadline today for presenting the noise ordinance to the public and voting on it. Attribution is implied with "as expected," but that must be clarified later. The information is verifiable.

(continued)

PUTTING THE ELEMENTS TOGETHER   *(continued)*

The ordinance would not affect concerts in city parks, such as Auditorium Shores. It would, however, change the rules for most indoor and outdoor venues in the city.

If the ordinance passes, owners or operators of clubs with outdoor venues, such as Stubb's or Emo's, would need to apply for a permit from the city before any acts take the stage outdoors.

"That is the most significant change," said Laura Huffman, assistant city manager. "The permit process was created so the city would have an enforcement mechanism."

City officials could yank a venue's permit if it is found to have violated the noise ordinance twice.

And under the new law, those venues will have a firm schedule for when the party's over. Concerts must end by 10:30 p.m. Sunday through Wednesday, by 11 p.m. on Thursday and by midnight on Friday and Saturday. The present law is vague on such restrictions.

There is an exception: Bands playing at outdoor venues in the Sixth Street or Warehouse entertainment districts that hold 500 or fewer can play until 2 a.m.

That exception doesn't help club owners like Frank Hendrix, who owns Emo's at 603 Red River St. Even though he says he has spent thousands of dollars on sound-deadening features around his outdoor patio, it can hold 600, meaning he would have to shut down at 10:30 p.m. during the week.

This is unattributed, but the information comes directly from the ordinance, and therefore is verifiable.

Attribution and identification of the speaker come at the end of the first direct quotation. The second quotation follows without additional attribution and provides useful background.

Three paragraphs are used without attribution, but the information obviously comes directly from the ordinance. This is good background that helps readers comprehend the story.

This is an indirect quotation from club owner Frank Hendrix, plus information about how the ordinance would apply. Hendrix's club is the address.

"That's ridiculous," Hendrix said. "Our shows don't even get started until 10:30 p.m. That would essentially put our outside shows out of business."

Instead, Hendrix said the city should go after the habitual noise ordinance violators and consider exceptions for club owners who take precautions when it comes to keeping the music in the venue and off the street.

"We've actually gone to great length ... to keep our noise in," he said. "We've never had a sound issue. It sounds like I need to go to the City Council meeting."

An upside for both indoor and outdoor facilities is that the proposed ordinance would keep the legal sound level outside a venue at 85 decibels, roughly the noise level of sport-utility vehicles whizzing down South Congress Avenue. The downside is that the proposal would expand where police can take noise measurements.

Before, officers had to take readings from the front door of a venue. Under the new ordinance, they could measure from anywhere along a property line. And between 2 a.m. and 10 a.m., any sound along the property line outside a venue would be a violation.

While lawyers clean up the technical language and prepare a final draft, city officials will begin presenting the proposed law to downtown leaders, business owners and groups. Officials don't anticipate any significant changes before the public hearing.

A direct quote from Hendrix using a dangling attribution is used at the end of the first quoted sentence followed by a second direct quotation without attribution.

The transition word *instead* shows a change to another suggested solution for the noise problem. The Hendrix direct quotation personalizes the story and provides good elaboration. The attribution "he said" is unobtrusive.

Upside and *for both indoor and outdoor* are effective transition words. This paragraph clearly is going to elaborate on what's gone before. Note the good *sport-utility* analogy.

Before serves as a transition word to more background. *Under the new ordinance* shows where the information came from.

This paragraph explains and interprets events. Attribution is to city officials; this should be more specific.

(continued)

PUTTING THE ELEMENTS TOGETHER   *(continued)*

"I think what this will do is allow us to regulate noise in a way that continues to allow Austin to be the Live Music Capital of the World but also respects downtown residents' needs," Huffman said.

The revised noise ordinance came after the city's original proposal was rejected by much of Austin's music industry last spring.

To curb noise complaints downtown, police officials had suggested simply lowering the legal decibel level for an outdoor venue to 75 decibels. Club owners and music promoters called that proposal unreasonable.

As a result, the city put together a committee of downtown residents and club and business owners in June to come up with a compromise. After 10 two-hour meetings and a Friday night field trip to the clubs, the group came up with recommendations reflected in the current draft of the ordinance. ...

Another direct quotation from the assistant city manager explains the city's goal.

Three paragraphs of background information help the reader understand the story and place it in a context.

Source: Jonathan Osborne, "City Council Close to Offering Noise Ordinance: Clubs With Outdoor Stages to Face Tougher Rules Under Proposed Law," *Austin American-Statesman,* Nov. 21, 2002: A-1, 19.

YOUR RESPONSIBILITY IS . . .

- To understand that news sources and personalities must be identified carefully and completely, with special emphasis on the reason why an individual is worth talking to about a story.

- To master through constant practice the arts of collecting and using direct and indirect quotations and of attributing information carefully to qualified sources.

- To understand that direct quotations are just that—they are the *exact* words a source or news personality spoke. Be sure that you collect direct quotations yourself and that you do not "lift" them without attribution from someone else.

- To learn how to divide direct and indirect quotations into three categories—reports, inferences and judgments—and to practice doing that. You may well use quotation marks and attributions differently for reports than for inferences and judgments.

NOTES

1. For a video clip of President Clinton's denial, go to <www.washingtonpost.com/wp-srv/politics/special/clinton/stories/whatclintonsaid.htm>.
2. Richard D. Anderson Jr., "'I Did Not Have Sexual Relations With That Woman (Pause, Gaze Averted) Ms. [sic] Lewinsky'—The Iconicity of Democratic Speech in English," paper presented to Third International Symposium on Iconicity in Language and Literature, Jena, Germany, March 29–31, 2001: 4. Downloaded on Feb. 26, 2003, from <www.sscnet.ucla.edu/polisci/faculty/anderson/Lewinsky.htm>.
3. Lillian Ross, "From 'Portrait of Hemingway,'" in Kevin Kerrane and Ben Yagoda (eds.), *The Art of Fact: A Historical Anthology of Literary Journalism* (New York: Scribner, 1997): 129–138, p. 132.
4. From a transcript of a news conference with Gen. Tommy Franks, Defense Link, Department of Defense, Oct. 29, 2002. Downloaded on Nov. 2, 2002, from <www.defenselink.mil/news/Oct2002/t10292002_t029fran.html>.
5. Ibid.
6. Ann Gerhart and Roxanne Roberts, "A Night for Polish Pride: State Dinner Honors 'Steadfast' Ally," *The Washington Post,* July 18, 2002: C-1, 4, p. C-4.
7. Ibid.
8. Marie Hardin and Ann Preston, "Inclusion of Disability Issues in News Reporting Textbooks," *Journalism & Mass Communication Educator,* 56:2 (2001): 43–54; Valerie Hyman, "Getting More Diversity in Content," The Poynter Institute for Media Studies, March 1996. Downloaded on Feb. 14, 2003, from <www.media-awareness.ca/eng/issues/minrep/journl/poynter.htm>; HolLynn D'Lil, "Being an 'Inspiration,'" *Mainstream,* November 1997: 14, 16–17; and Beth A. Haller, "Confusing Disability and Tragedy," *The* (Baltimore) *Sun,* April 29, 2001: C-1.
9. Carroll Parrott Blue, *The Dawn at My Back: Memoir of a Black Texas Upbringing* (Austin: University of Texas Press, 2003).
10. S.I. Hayakawa, *Language in Thought and Action,* 4th ed. (New York: Harcourt Brace Jovanovich, 1978).

PART III

INFORMATION

CHAPTER 8

THE WEB

Find and Evaluate Information

It is difficult to overstate the impact the home computer and the Internet have had on mass communication. Only those unfortunate souls who worked in a world without computers can begin to comprehend the magnitude of the deprivation. It was only three decades ago that Donald Barlett and James Steele conducted one of the first computer-assisted studies for a newspaper.[1] Only a decade ago, some media professionals still were writing on typewriters.

For most readers of this book, the Old World is not merely gone; it never existed. Computers, the Web, streaming audio and video, Google, electronic mail, direct satellite links, cell phones, bookmarks, broadband technology and all the rest are part of the electronic culture of the young. But many old coots are catching up—because they must.

Studies suggest, for example, that just about all public relations professionals think they have acquired the skills they need to use the Web to get their messages out, to see what individuals and groups are saying about their products and services, to engage in two-way communication with their publics, to tramp through databases, to collect information and to communicate with journalists and other publics electronically. Job applicants are not asked *whether* they can use new technologies; they are asked how *extensively* they can use them.[2]

Journalists, too, have embraced the new technologies. The trend started with journalists at the large media outlets—big metropolitan newspapers and radio and television stations. But technology has trickled down to the smaller publications—to the point that all journalists need to know how to surf the Web for information, how to use electronic mail and how to write and edit online.[3]

One of the buzzwords among journalists for years was computer-assisted reporting, meaning mainly that journalists used computers to gather and to generate

This photograph captures a scene that is replayed thousands of times daily in media offices around the world: A writer uses Google, the most widely used search service, to collect information. Writers must remember, however, that a good deal of useful information is not available on the Web and that much of what is on the Web is inaccurate.

information. It's a sign of the changing times that the term is not wholly accurate today, for all journalism is computer-centered and all journalists use computers to collect information they could not have found just a few years ago. The term applies today primarily to journalists who generate new knowledge by using computers to collate and analyze bits and pieces of information. Another, perhaps more accurate, term for the process is precision journalism.[4]

This chapter covers some fundamentals of using the Web—some or all of which some readers may already know—so that readers will have the background they need to understand fully the remaining chapters about information collection. The chapter is not simply "how to surf the Web," though there is an element of that, so please read on.

PROBLEMS

Writers can encounter some important obstacles as they try to use the Web to get information: (1) Web information must be evaluated carefully, for much of it is inaccurate and useless; (2) the Web is limited in that a good deal of information is not available online; (3) some writers are tempted to use the Web improperly; and (4) Web searches can be time-consuming. (See also the box "What Is a Search Engine Anyway?")

WHAT IS A SEARCH ENGINE ANYWAY?

A decade ago, few readers of this book would have had a clue about what search engines are. Today, most readers not only know what search engines are but are also quite skilled in their use. Search engines typically are provided by search services (such as AltaVista, Yahoo!, Excite, WebCrawler, Infoseek, Ask Jeeves, Dogpile, Google, Looksmart and others). Lycos' search engine, for instance, is called Pursuit, and Harvest uses multiple search engines. While the services do provide search engines, they also offer other services (such as electronic mail, maps and Web sites) that subscribers like to use.[5]

A search engine almost miraculously "searches" its own database of Web pages for those in which the keywords (which the user specifies) are mentioned. The engine then lists the "hits" or "strikes"; those that match the keywords most closely are indexed first. A metasearch engine sends a user's request to multiple search engines at once. It is not unusual for a search to produce thousands of hits, most of which are not remotely relevant. Type in *cedar rapids city council* and Google's search engine, for example, will return (in 2004) 168,000 hits. The *most* relevant Web site, however, is usually listed among the top five or 10.

Writers must never assume that search engines turn up everything relating to a topic, even when they see 200,000 hits. Some useful information is never posted to a Web site, and some sites are not scanned by a search engine looking for keywords. Search engines produce material that is a good starting point, however.

The most successful seekers (users) are adept at picking good keywords. A writer who types in *first amendment*, for instance, had better be prepared to be overwhelmed. Typing in *first amendment confidential sources* will narrow the search considerably—though still, perhaps, not enough. Most search engines incorporate a useful "search within results" feature. Google's engine, for example, would list 75 trillion sites under *first amendment*. A writer can narrow that by clicking "search within results" and typing *confidential sources*. The number of hits can be narrowed further by typing in *journalism* or, still later, *new mexico* and so on.

It helps to use unusual or technical words, names or phrases and to avoid common words and those with multiple meanings. Phrases, or even multiple phrases, usually produce the best results, and it sometimes helps to change the keyword or its spelling. Results for *attorney* might be somewhat different from those for *lawyer*.

If a user types in *first amendment* using some search engines, he or she will get every Web site that contains "first" and every site that contains "amendment." The

(continued)

> **WHAT IS A SEARCH ENGINE ANYWAY?** *(continued)*
>
> writer should try typing in *first and amendment*, or *"first amendment,"* using quotation marks, to get more specific results.
>
> Most search engines have an advanced search option that allows a user to search for words that are similar to the keywords in which they are most interested. If one types in *psych*, for instance, some search engines will seek psychosomatic, psychology and psychoanalysis. Most provide the option of searching only for titles or photographs, which can be useful for some communication purposes.
>
> Writers should try all of the services' search engines. Some will end up using one primarily, while some will use several different ones for different purposes.
>
> One must remember always that much of the information on the Web is incomplete, inaccurate, dated—or dead wrong. Be wary.

Evaluating Information

Much of the information on the Web is inaccurate, misleading, partisan and, in a word, useless. The now classic example of what can go wrong if a professional gets the wrong information is Pierre Salinger's assertion that TWA Flight 800 was downed by a U.S. Navy missile in 1996. Salinger, former news secretary to John Kennedy and former ABC reporter, got an electronic mail message tipping him off that the information was verified on a Web page.[6]

Salinger distributed the hot information from the Web without checking its veracity. Several media outlets distributed the false report. *The* (Phoenix) *Arizona Republic* noted, correctly, that Salinger was seduced by official-looking, but worthless, information and that "[M]ost anybody, anywhere and at any time can create an item on the Internet and make it look credible."[7] The fact that much of the information is from anonymous sources makes some Web information doubly dangerous.

Several academics and professionals have offered advice to those who would use the Web. A list based on the work of Stan Ketterer of Oklahoma State University and others would include these questions: (1) Has the source been reliable in the past? (2) Does the source have a reasonable motive for supplying information? (3) Can the source provide documentation that the information is accurate? (4) Is it possible to verify the information with other sources? (5) Is the source of any information on a site anonymous?[8]

Media professionals who are new to the Web would do well to limit their searches mainly to government, media, reference, university and research sites that, for the most part, meet Ketterer's criteria, and to use the Web primarily to verify information already in hand. Several credible and useful sites are listed in the box "Useful Professional Sites and Books" on page 202 and Appendix G. Above all, media professionals must bring the same standards to the Web that they use to verify information from all other sources.[9]

Physical Limitations

So much information is available on the Web, it is easy to forget its limitations: "Not all of the world's accumulated knowledge exists on Web servers, and probably never will. Copyright, privacy, and the expense involved in digitalizing old documents effectively keep billions of information sources offline."[10] Some American newspaper and magazine archives are a hundred years old and more, and yet most of the content from those newspapers is not available online. Most began digitalizing their archives in the mid-1980s or so. Most also charge fairly high fees to *download* or to read more than a paragraph of the materials from those archives, although the *search* typically is free.

Corporations and not-for-profit organizations have started posting massive amounts of information on their sites, and much of the information is free, but a surfer is unlikely to find a news release or annual report from, say, 1980 on most sites.

One recent study focused on completeness of Web information along the dimension of time by searching for all the years from 1900 to 2001, with "year 1900" as the form for the search term. Two search engines were used—AltaVista's and AlltheWeb's. The researchers included the word "year" to make sure they found only pages referring to or at least mentioning specific years.

The results showed a strong chronological effect. A graph of the data looked like a steep, precipitous cliff (Figure 8.1). The 10 most recent years yielded 85 percent of the Web pages found. Information dealing with the past 10 years was found to be eight times more likely to appear on the Web than information for the previous 92 years.

The lesson is that media writers—along with students, everyday users and scholars—should not become excessively dependent on the Web. Media communicators, for the near term, will not be able to dig deeply into the past using Web resources. "While teaching the wonders of the Internet, we also must emphasize the importance of archives and libraries and human beings. Tomorrow's journalists [and public relations professionals] must learn that the Internet hasn't made other research skills obsolete. It has made them more valuable—and necessary."[11]

Media professionals must supplement their Web searches by consulting standard reference works, books, documents and academic journals in conventional libraries. Instructions for evaluating information on the Web often stress that information on the Web can be inaccurate. The instructions should also warn users that information on the Web is often incomplete.

FIGURE 8.1 THE WEB HAS MUCH MORE INFORMATION FOR RECENT YEARS
THAN IT DOES FOR PAST YEARS

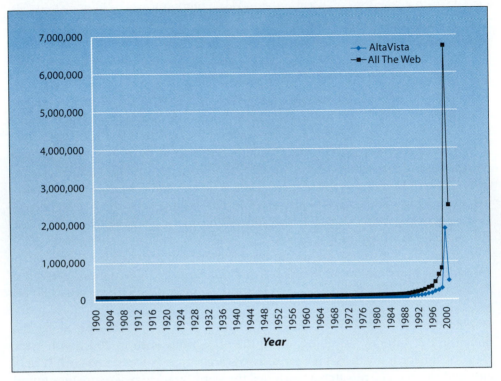

This chart plots the number of sites found by search engines analyzing each year from 1900 to 2001. It shows many more sites for recent years than for earlier years. The year 2000 shows a greater number of sites than 2001 because of all the attention given to the new millennium.
(Source: James W. Tankard Jr. and Cindy Royal, "What's on the Web—And What's Not," paper presented to the International Communication Association, San Diego, May 24, 2003.)

Avoiding Temptation

Jayson Blair, a former reporter for *The New York Times*, managed to get away with plagiarism, fabrication and lies for months before he was caught (Chapter 1). He was able to fool his readers and his editors partly because of the marvelous technological tools that can make writing easier. According to *The Times*, "His tools of deceit were a cellphone and a laptop computer—which allowed him to blur his true whereabouts—as well as round-the-clock access to databases of news articles from which he stole."[12]

Many college students have fallen into the same trap that ensnared Blair. It's just too easy and too tempting to download, for instance, the Dixie Chicks' latest album without paying for the privilege. It's too easy to download information and then incorporate it unchanged and without quotation marks or attribution into the term paper that's due tomorrow in History 1271. In fact, it's easy and tempting to download an entire paper and submit that.

Jayson Blair, who resigned from The New York Times *in part for fabricating information, said Jessica Lynch's West Virginia home was surrounded by pastures and tobacco fields. The Lynch family joked about the inaccurate portrayal.*

Not everyone uses the Web in this dishonest way, but it is one of the problems contemporary media professionals must resist. Writers can avoid trouble if they develop the habit of attributing information from the Web as they do all other information (Chapter 7). That doesn't necessarily mean writers must always give exact uniform resource locators (Web addresses), although it's not a bad idea to do so. It does mean indicating clearly which site was the source for information in a story, and giving information about that site.

Media professionals also are tempted to rely too much on electronic tools. It's easier to rely on the Web for documents and records, but a media professional who uses *only* the Web will miss a great deal of information that can't be found there. Sometimes a trip to the library is the only answer. And while it's easier to interview a source by electronic mail, that is not usually the best way to do it, mainly because personal interaction is sacrificed. An interviewer using electronic mail doesn't get to hear a source's tone of voice or see his or her gestures and other nonverbal "messages" (Chapter 10).

The Web allows individuals to disassociate from society if they want to. This may be good for hermits, but social disconnection through electronic connection is not good for media professionals, for the organizations for which they work or for a society that depends on their work.

USEFUL PROFESSIONAL SITES AND BOOKS

One of the good things about using the Web is the amount of help that is available to those who are willing to give the Internet a chance. It's almost impolite or unfair to mention any of those sources because it's impossible to mention them all, and some good organizations and individuals are left off of every list. But we'll do it anyway.

One of the best sites for resources, ideas and education is maintained by Investigative Reporters and Editors Inc. at <www.ire.org>. The IRE site offers several good features, including a frequently updated list of hot stories. The *Los Angeles Times'* series about dangerous Harrier fighter jets, which can take off and land vertically (Chapter 9), is in that file. Also useful are the tips for accessing and using databases, a math test for writers, the Net tour and links to useful databases and other sites. The site also lists information about workshops, conferences, boot camps and training programs.

Other helpful sites include

The National Institute for Computer-assisted Reporting at <www.nicar.org>

The Kansas State Library's Skyways Train Station at <http://skyways.lib.ks.us/training>

The Campaign Finance Information Center at <www.campaignfinance.org>

The American Library Association's "Toolkit for the Expert Web Searcher" at <www.ala.org/ala/litaresources/toolkitforexpert/toolkitexpert.htm>

Reporters Committee for Freedom of the Press at <www.rcfp.org>

FACSNET at <www.facsnet.org>

Some useful books are Christopher Callahan's *A Journalist's Guide to the Internet*, Bruce Garrison's *Computer-assisted Reporting*, Shel Holtz's *Public Relations on the Net*, James Horton's *Online Public Relations*, Brant Houston's *Computer-assisted Reporting,* the Radio and Television News Directors Foundation's *Wired Journalist,* Matthew Reavy's *Introduction to Computer-assisted Reporting* and Randy Reddick and Elliot King's *The Online Journalist*.[13]

A student who wants to learn how to use the Web (and all students should) needs to spend a few minutes a day poking around the Internet, looking at some of the sites mentioned throughout this book and in Appendix G. Another good way to learn to use the Web is to complete one of the online tutorials. Here are some good ones to try:

The Webwise Online Course (BBC) at <www.bbc.co.uk/webwise/course>

Net Tour (the National Institute for Computer Assisted Reporting) at <www.ire.org/training/nettour>

A Journalist's Guide to the Internet (the St. Louis Chapter of the Society of

Professional Journalists) at <www.stlouisspj.org/surf/surf.html>

Finding Information on the Internet: A Tutorial (University of California at Berkeley Teaching Library) at <www.lib.berkeley.edu/TeachingLib/Guides/Internet/FindInfo.html>

Time Constraints

Searching the Web can be terribly frustrating the first 10 or 100 or 1,000 times a media professional tries it. The frustration level doubles, triples or quadruples if a search is done under deadline pressure. Writers need to avoid that. The dangers of Web searches are obvious to those who have done them: (1) They can take inordinate amounts of time as a surfer tries to find that one fact, and (2) they can produce more information than a writer can handle.

The good news is that searches take far less time (and frustration levels recede) as professionals learn how to do them. It helps to try out some of the search services available (see the box on search engines on page 197), pick out the most useful ones, and stick with them for most searches. It's a good idea, too, to bookmark (have a computer store) links that are particularly helpful—and credible. Writers who have dozens of links bookmarked can create their own Web sites and store useful links there (Appendix G). It may seem mysterious and hard, but it's not difficult to create a Web site using the right software (Front Page and Go Live, to name only two). Other tips for surfing the Web efficiently are in this chapter. (See also the box "Useful Professional Sites and Books.")

GENERAL INFORMATION

The Web is so large and diverse it's impossible to do much more than hint at how it can help a media professional. The Web is particularly helpful for a professional who needs general background information.

Suppose, for example, that French paleontologist Michel Brunet is coming to a university to discuss the skull his team found of the earliest known hominid (or human ancestor). A university public relations professional needs some background, including assertions by critics who claim the skull is not human, for an advance story about Brunet's speech. If the information about Brunet and the topic is sparse and the time is short, a simple search should turn up plenty of information. A good first stop is at a news medium's archive, which is reasonably trustworthy and is likely to have the necessary information.

A Seattle writer who needs to know about Michel Brunet, for instance, might visit *The Seattle Times'* archive, one of the few newspaper archives that was still free in 2002. A newspaper's home page usually pops up when a user types in the newspaper's name in a search engine. The sites listed will include the newspaper's main URL (uniform resource locator, or the newspaper's Web address).

A writer seeking information about Brunet will click *The Times'* "search archive" button, which will bring up a screen that offers a "search by keywords" option (see the box "Conducting a Keyword Search"). When one types in *michel brunet*, three articles appear. A writer can learn that Brunet directs the human-paleontology laboratory at the University of Poitiers, that the skull is nicknamed Toumai (hope of life), that it was discovered in Chad, that the discovery was reported in the scientific journal *Nature,* that some scientists dispute the skull is human and many other useful facts.

A writer who needs still more information can go to <www.altavista.com>, which offers a widely used search engine, and type *michel brunet* in the appropriate box. That first search attempt would, in 2002, produce a list of nearly 8,000 Web sites that mention Brunet. To reduce that number, one can type *university of poitiers* in the appropriate slot. That produces 150 hits, including one site that provides contact information (including telephone numbers and electronic mail addresses) for Brunet and his team.

The information obtained locally and from the Web should be professionally packaged in a news release and distributed. The release should be posted on the organization's Web site and sent to the media and interested parties by regular mail, fax or electronic mail. Electronic mail is sent to journalists and other interested individuals whose addresses are on one or more of the public relations writer's electronic mailing lists. An electronic mailing list contains the electronic addresses of individuals who are interested in various aspects of an organization's activities. A single message is sent automatically to all those on that mailing list. Public relations professionals maintain multiple lists because not all individuals are interested in all of an organization's activities. (Such a list frequently is called a Listserv, but the usage is inappropriate since Listserv is a registered trademark for the L-Soft computer program that is used widely to manage electronic mailing lists.) The writer's job is not to hype the event to get people to attend. It is simply to give people information so they can decide whether that event is of interest or importance to them.

CONDUCTING A KEYWORD SEARCH

Most college students have done keyword searches using the electronic catalogs in their college libraries. The principles are much the same so this is nothing really new, whether you're using a search service like AltaVista to search the Web or the Census Bureau's search mechanism to find one of its documents.[14]

Search *engines,* like those used by Dogpile and Hotbot, typically search for Web sites or documents across a wide range of sites (external), while a search *mechanism* typically searches for documents within a site (internal). Writers are using AltaVista's search engine, for example, when they search for Web sites across the Internet. They are using a search mechanism when they search *The New York Times'* archives.

Happily, keyword searches work in similar ways whether one is using a search engine or a search mechanism. The first step is to come up with the right keywords. A writer who needs an index to Nevada government documents, for example, can type *government documents* in the box in a preferred search service and get 6 trillion hits. But a writer who types in *nevada government documents* will reduce the number of hits and increase the likelihood of finding useful information.

A keyword or phrase should be as specific as possible, as in the example above. It helps also to pick an unusual or technical word. A writer can learn the value of the unusual word by trying to find out whether he or she is mentioned in any Web site. A writer named Michael Ryan will get so many hits, he'll not find himself. But a writer named Ashley Stepenhausen will find herself—if she's there at all. It's best to go for the unusual word or phrase that *might* lead to a useful site and to try different spellings and words. Just taking an *s* off the end of a word can make a difference, as can looking under *physician* rather than *doctor.* It's good to be specific, but a writer may have more success using several keywords.

If this is all a writer has to worry about, he or she is good to go. But it's not. Some search engines and mechanisms look for sites that mention *each* of a user's search words: Nevada, government and documents. That means the user will get back a bunch of useless stuff.

Nobody can say *precisely* what to do in every situation because different search engines and mechanisms work in different ways. Some seek all sites that mention each term individually—Nevada, government and documents—but some don't. For some, one must insert *and* or + between the words, so a user is looking for

(continued)

CONDUCTING A KEYWORD SEARCH *(continued)*

nevada and government and documents. Any site that does not mention all three will not pop up. "And," by the way, is a logical operator, a technical term a user might need to know.

A writer who needs information about a specific kind of flower might use *not,* as in *roses not violets.* To learn about both kinds of flowers, a user might use *or,* as in *roses or violets.* In the first case, one would get sites dealing only with roses. In the second, one would get sites dealing with roses or violets. To search a complete phrase, one types in only the phrase for some engines and mechanisms. For others, one puts the phrase in quotation marks—some require double quotation marks, some single.

This business can get more complicated, but don't despair. Searching the Web or databases gets easier with experience. Most every search engine and mechanism comes with directions. A writer can learn from clicking on "help" that a site requires the logical operators like *and,* or that one can just put single quotation marks around a phrase and the search will be limited to sites or documents that contain that exact phrase.

For a special event, the public relations professional needs to get information about *each* participant, each participant's area of expertise (why he or she is there), the title of the event, the subject matter and general statements about what will be discussed or decided. For a news conference, it is particularly important to understand why the event is newsworthy (why journalists should be asked to attend). Much of this information is available on the Web.

DATABASES

It's helpful, in trying to understand what a database is, to know what records and documents are (Chapter 9). Documents generally are books, articles, reports, films, advertisements, letters, diaries, grocery lists, tapes and similar materials. They are prepared by governments, corporations, media, individuals, foundations and other groups for specific purposes, and they frequently summarize, analyze or merely list records and other information.

Records are discrete bits (or bytes) of information about an individual, group, organization or other entity (a city, for example). A person who pays property tax and gets a telephone has created two records. The telephone number goes into a telephone book, and the property tax record goes into the tax assessor's online database.

Databases are collections (in electronic files or written documents) of numbers, letters, articles, legal cases and other materials systematically arranged by topics and stored in a computer. The electronic index to Florida's government documents at <http://dlis.dos.state.fl.us/fgils/pubdoc.html> is a database containing records (government publications) organized around a central theme (Florida). *USA Counties* at <www.census.gov/statab/www/county.html> is an elaborate database prepared and maintained by the U.S. Census Bureau. The records (responses to census questions) are organized around one theme (the county). (See also the box "Strategies for Exploring Databases.")

All records are part of databases and all databases are contained in electronic or printed documents. However, not all documents (this book is one example) are databases.

Accessibility

Unfortunately, not all databases are easy to access. Businesses, for example, often create databases to make money, and they can be expensive to use. Private businesses also can restrict access to their databases—either because they have something to hide, because records are private or because they have a proprietary interest in keeping them secret.

Media professionals often use databases constructed by governments from records they are required by law to maintain. Since they have to collect the data anyway, governments frequently charge only for printing costs (if the databases are not available online) or for computer time or disks containing raw data. These charges typically are nominal and frequently are established by state or federal law.

Two broad categories of records are found in databases: (1) those that are generally open and available, such as property tax, police, land, incorporation, safety, campaign and some court records, and (2) those that aren't open, such as income tax, telephone and military records, and some personal letters or documents. Some sources fall into a gray area, and writers must be well versed in the law to know which sources can be closed legitimately and which cannot (Chapter 13). When a government agency refuses to permit access, it's time to file a complaint under the state or federal Freedom of Information Act. Agencies often are forced to make the data available.

Those who have access to the databases use keyword searches to find the information they need, much as students use electronic library catalogs to find books. The information in some databases (telephone books, for example) cannot be reconfigured or re-analyzed in different ways, while information in other databases can be. Media writers, for example, can re-analyze raw census data to produce tables not created by U.S. Census Bureau analysts.

Secondary Analysis

A database user who wants to examine relationships an original analyst did not must re-analyze those data (social scientists call this a secondary analysis). The great benefit of this procedure is that media professionals can conduct their own analyses of the

STRATEGIES FOR EXPLORING DATABASES

Media professionals frequently use spreadsheet and database manager programs to analyze interesting and important databases. The following are some common strategies for analyzing databases:

- *Find the biggest, smallest, highest, lowest, richest, poorest, wettest, driest, etc.*

  Which county has the highest average income in a state?

  Which city has the highest murder rate in a state?

  Which city in the United States has the highest syphilis rate?

  What is the leading cause of death among teenagers?

- *Rank things.*

  How does one city compare on some indicator—income, rate of car thefts, percentages of persons with AIDS—with other cities?

  How does one state compare in ranking on some indicator—obesity, amount spent on education, infant death rate—with other states?

- *Compare two or more time periods.*

  Is a state's budget larger or smaller than it was last year, and is there a budget surplus or deficit?

  Is the portion of the budget allocated to education larger or smaller than it was last year?

  Is the percentage of public school students who passed standardized tests larger or smaller than last year?

- *Look for trends.*

  What has been the trend in the murder rate in the United States over the past 30 years?

  What has been the trend in the rate of AIDS cases in a city over the past 10 years?

- *Search for an individual.*

  Is Barbra Streisand on the list of contributors to former President Clinton's legal defense fund?

  Did the CEO of Enron contribute to President Bush's election campaign?

- *Look for co-occurrence of names or items on lists.*

  Are any local school bus drivers also convicted felons?

  Where do individuals convicted of sex crimes live in a city?

  Did any campaign donors contribute money to both George W. Bush and John Kerry?

■ *Count.*

How many lawyers contributed money to the campaign of George W. Bush?

How many individuals in one community are home-schooling their children?

■ *Group and find the total amount for the group.*

How much money did John Kerry receive from environmentalists during his campaign for the presidency?

■ *Find an average or mean.*

What is the average salary for a professional baseball player?

What is the mean family income in one city?

■ *Compare two groups by looking at the total amount or mean for each group.*

Do men and women doing the same work receive equal pay?

Who received a larger amount of campaign contributions from the tobacco industry, George W. Bush or John Kerry?

■ *Show how something is divided into parts.*

What percentage of a city's budget is spent for police, firefighters, libraries and other purposes?

What are the sources of revenue for a state, and how much revenue comes from each source?

■ *Find a correlation.*

Is there a relationship between a city's crime rate and amount spent on police?

Is there a relationship between a county's median income and percentage of students who go to college?

■ *Illustrate data with a map.*

Which parts of a town have high crime rates and which parts have low crime rates?

Which parts of a town voted for one candidate for mayor and which parts of town voted for another candidate for mayor?

Source: Based on James W. Tankard Jr. and Dominic L. Lasorsa, "Teaching Strategies for Analysis in Computer-assisted Reporting," *Journalism & Mass Communication Educator,* 55: 3 (2000): 14–26.

Kenneth Prewitt, director of the Census Bureau, met with media professionals after announcing Census 2000 Resident Population numbers. Census Bureau databases are reliable sources for social, cultural, economic and political information.

data and reach their own conclusions. They are not dependent on experts, corporation executives or government sources to tell them what is important in the data.

The U.S. Census Bureau is one of the best sources of data that can be re-analyzed. The Bureau collects national data once a decade about population characteristics (for example, race, age, gender, marital status and relationship to the head of the household for each person in a home). Those data are readily available (Chapter 9, Appendix G).

The Bureau also prepares a long version of the standard census form; the long form is sent to sample households in the United States. Information from these samples includes country of parents' birth, income, occupation, employment status now and five years ago, schooling, number of children, mother tongue, years in present house, school or college enrollment, military status, state or country of birth, place of work and means of getting to work for each person in the household.

The easiest way to learn how to use the Bureau's raw data is to visit the Bureau's Web site at <www.census.gov>. It's not a bad idea to first visit the site's news section at <www.census.gov/pubinfo/www/news.html>. Useful news releases prepared by the Bureau's public relations personnel describe social, economic, political and cultural trends. The best part is that online releases often take writers to local sites where raw data are available for secondary analysis.

DOWNLOADING FILES FROM THE WEB

The Web is a rich repository of data files that the media professional can download and import into a spreadsheet (such as Excel) or a statistical analysis program (such as Statistical Package for the Social Sciences). It can take some perseverance to download and import a file successfully. Here are some different situations, each of which requires a different technique for downloading and importing a data file.

- *Files already available in Excel or other spreadsheet form.*

    These files are often recognizable by a file extension such as .xls that is visible on the Web page. These files are the simplest to import; a writer simply clicks on the filename or the .xls and the file should download to his or her computer as an Excel or other spreadsheet file. One can open it in Excel and proceed with the analysis.

    Example: Go to <http://www.census.gov/statab/www/freq.html>. Click on the .xls beside National Health Expenditures. The data file should download to a home computer and open in Excel.

- *Files that can be copied from a browser page and pasted into Excel.*

    Select the table or data file. Copy it. Open a blank worksheet in Excel. Click on the upper left cell and choose paste. The table or data file should paste into the cells of the worksheet.

    Example: Go to <http://www.fbi.gov/ucr/hatecm.htm>. Drag the cursor across the Web page selecting everything from "Participating States" in the upper left corner to "7,947" in the lower right corner. Choose Copy from the Edit menu. Open Excel. Click on cell A1 and paste. The rows should fill with the data from the Web. It may be necessary to widen some of the columns to make all the column headings and data visible.

- *Files that can be saved as text files and imported into Excel with the Text Wizard.*

    Select and copy the table or data file. Paste it into Word or another word processor. Some editing or cleaning up of the file may be necessary at this stage. Save the file as a text file. Open Excel, go to the File menu, select Open and try to open the file. The Text Import Wizard should appear on the screen. Follow the steps through the Text Import Wizard and the file should appear in Excel. Sometimes one needs to try the Text Import several times, choosing different options until one works.

(continued)

DOWNLOADING FILES FROM THE WEB   *(continued)*

Example: <http://www.census.gov/>

Go to subjects A–Z; choose C. Go to commuting. Double click on "Travel to Work Characteristics for the 50 Largest Cities in the United States by Population: 1990 Census" (5k). Go to the Edit menu in the browser and choose Select All. Go back to the Edit menu and select Copy. Open Word or another word processing program and go to the File menu. Create a new blank document. Paste the "Travel to Work Characteristics" table into the document. Save the page as a text file. One might call it "travel.txt." Close the file in Microsoft Word. Open Excel and then open the file travel.txt. The Text Import Wizard will present various options. One might choose to start importing at line 12 since that is where the data start. The headings can be added later, after the data are in Excel.

Step 2 in the Import Wizard lets one insert lines that will define columns on the Excel worksheet. In this table, a writer might want to insert break lines on both sides of the vertical lines that were present in the original table. Then one can eliminate these lines from the final Excel worksheet.

Step 3 lets a writer select columns that he or she does not want to import. If one put break lines around the vertical lines in the original table, one can now indicate that those vertical lines should not be imported. Hit Finish, and the data should appear in an Excel worksheet. It may be necessary to do some data cleanup, eliminating rows that don't contain data, reinserting headings and so forth.

■ *Files that download in PDF form.*
Find the target table or data file and select it with the Text Select Tool. Sometimes these tables will copy and paste into the Excel file (as with the second technique above), but sometimes they have to be converted to a text file and imported with the Import Wizard (as with the third technique above).

Example: <http://www.fbi.gov/ucr/ucr.htm>

Go to "Law Enforcement Officers Killed and Assaulted" and click on 2001. A PDF file will be downloaded to the computer. Use Acrobat Reader to open the document. Scroll through to Table 4, "Law Officers Feloniously Killed." Go to the toolbar and click on the Text Select Tool, a capital T with a small dashed rectangle beside it. Hold the mouse button down and drag the cursor across the entire table, from Table 4 to the end of the footnote at the bottom. Go to the Edit menu and select Copy. Paste the table into a blank Microsoft Word document and save it as a text file. Close the document in Microsoft Word. Open Microsoft Excel and try to import the file using the Text Import Wizard (as in the third technique above). In the first step, indicate that the importing should start at line 7. Also indicate that the data type is delimited. At step 2, click "space" under delimiters. At step 3, click on Finish.

■ *Tip.*

Often it takes a great deal of perseverance and resourcefulness to download a data file from the Web. The key is to try different techniques until one works.

Sometimes a writer can find data files on a topic by typing the topic name and .xls into a search engine. For instance, one might type "crime.xls" into a search engine and find some crime statistics ready to be downloaded as an Excel file.

A release posted on Nov. 27, 2002, reported the results of a two-year study of residential segregation trends between 1980 and 2000 in the United States. The study suggested that black people experienced declines in residential segregation, but that "despite the declines, African-Americans remained the most highly segregated group." Segregation patterns were mixed for Asians, Native Americans, Hispanics, Alaska Natives and Pacific Islanders.[15]

The next step is to figure out what kinds of census data best complement a news release or story and how to get those data. State data centers are accessible through <www.census.gov/sdc/www>.

Information in an electronic database must be "imported" into a writer's computer if he or she is going to analyze those data in different ways (see the box "Downloading Files From the Web" on page 211). It's important to understand that a writer must have the right software if he or she wants to import data successfully. Without the software, which can be expensive, nothing is possible.

Fortunately, many databases include directions (software requirements, for instance) for moving data from their file to a writer's file. The process doesn't have to be hard, but read carefully. The Investigative Reporters and Editors organization provides help to those who want to find and use raw data.

ELECTRONIC MAIL

Electronic mail is, strictly speaking, different from the Web. However, electronic mail would not work without the Internet, so it is introduced here. Corporations, businesses and individuals have embraced electronic mail so enthusiastically that it is one of the most widely used of all the digital communication technologies.[16] Media professionals must use electronic mail if only to keep up with the rest of the world. And they do.

One survey shows that 91.5 percent of newspaper journalists used electronic mail in the newsroom in 2001 and that 34.2 percent used electronic mail at home for business purposes.[17] Surveys suggest that nearly two-thirds of television journalists used electronic mail in 1997,[18] and that 95 percent of public relations writers used electronic mail in 2000.[19]

Advantages

Media professionals accumulate a great deal of good information using electronic mail. Journalists conduct formal interviews, of course, although there are problems with that approach (Chapter 10), but they also correspond with sources, superiors and colleagues; transmit stories and visual material to newsrooms; get news tips; learn when speeches, news conferences and meetings are scheduled; get official reactions and comments quickly on deadline; obtain useful background information efficiently; and subscribe to electronic mailing lists, news groups and discussion groups.[20]

Public relations writers use electronic mailing lists and other electronic messages to notify journalists of important news and to give them background for stories; to keep important publics informed; and to obtain background information and comments for news releases, annual reports, internal and external newsletters and other documents.

Electronic mail messages also are useful as information sources. A source may forward to a writer a message (not sent originally to the writer) that supports the source's version of an event (and, hence, supports the writer's story). Or electronic mail messages may be part of a huge file subpoenaed in a civil or criminal case. The material may come out at trial and be part of a permanent court record. Regardless of how they come into a writer's hands, electronic mail messages are increasingly important sources of information.

Disadvantages

Media professionals must be aware always of the difficulties associated with electronic mail. Here are some of the potential problems:[21]

- Reading and responding to electronic mail can be enormously time-consuming. The proliferation of junk electronic mail in the new century has exacerbated the problem as users find they spend increasing amounts of time deleting unwanted messages.

■ Electronic mail is less personal even than the telephone, and it is far less personal than the personal interview. An impersonal approach is not good interview strategy (Chapter 10).

■ It is sometimes quite difficult to obtain an electronic address.

■ Computer viruses are spread primarily through electronic mail, and while most organizations have virus-protection programs and firewalls (methods of preventing outside access to computers), they don't always work. It's a good idea to delete a message from an unknown and suspicious source.

■ Messages do not always remain confidential. Some are inadvertently publicized, as when someone prints a message on a remote printer and forgets to pick it up; some are read as part of an organization's internal monitoring system; some are simply stolen by hackers; and some are publicized as part of legal actions.

■ Electronic mail makes it feasible for professionals to work at home after hours, making it difficult to "leave the office behind."

■ The approach of many individuals to electronic mail (just bang it out without regard for the fundamentals of good writing) has led to an overall deterioration of writing skill and language usage.

YOUR RESPONSIBILITY IS . . .

■ To learn never to assume that any information that you find on the Web is accurate *simply because it is posted there.* A great deal of information—particularly that posted by user groups, individuals and partisan groups—is inaccurate.

■ To attribute and to verify all information carefully—preferably using at least two credible sources—in the same careful way you attribute and verify all other information.

■ To learn that useful information is not always available on the Web. You might well find the information in your library.

■ To avoid the temptation to plagiarize material from the Web, to use the Internet as a substitute for human sources or to cut corners as you collect information.

■ To make yourself an expert in using search engines, services and mechanisms and in conducting keyword searches quickly and efficiently.

■ To put aside your fear of all things numerical and to learn what a database is, how to construct one and how to analyze the information in that database (Chapter 9).

■ To understand the limitations and strengths of electronic mail and to always strive to produce your best work in electronic mail messages you write.

NOTES

1. "Court Story Built on 75,000 Facts," *The Philadelphia Inquirer,* Feb. 18, 1973: A-14. See also Donald L. Barlett and James B. Steele, "Equal Justice for All? ... Not in Philadelphia's Courts," *The Philadelphia Inquirer,* Feb. 18, 1973: A-1, 14.

2. Robert Grupp, "Public Relations Must Control the Web Site," *The Public Relations Strategist,* Winter 2000: 32, 34; Michael Ryan, "Public Relations and the Web: Organizational Problems, Gender, and Institution Type," *Public Relations Review,* 29:3 (2003): 335–349; Jeffrey P. Geibel, "How Digital Tools and Audiences Are Changing High-tech PR," *Public Relations Tactics,* November 1999: 5, 18; and Steven R. Thomsen, "Using Online Databases in Corporate Issues Management," *Public Relations Review,* 21:2 (1995): 103–122.

3. Bruce Garrison, "Computer-assisted Reporting Near Complete Adoption, *Newspaper Research Journal,* 22:1 (2001): 65–79.

4. "Q&A: Reporting With Computers: Some Doubts From a Founder," *Columbia Journalism Review,* May/June 2001: 39.

5. Barbara K. Kaye and Norman J. Medoff, *The World Wide Web: A Mass Communication Perspective* (Mountain View, Calif.: Mayfield, 1999): Chapter 2.

6. Lisa Anderson, "U.S. Denies Report TWA Jet Was Downed by Navy Missile," *Chicago Tribune,* Nov. 9, 1996: 1–3; James Coates, "Internet Is Thick With False Webs of Conspiracy," *Chicago Tribune,* Nov. 10, 1996: 1-1, 19.

7. "A Tangled Web: Internet 'News' Pitfalls," *The* (Phoenix) *Arizona Republic,* Nov. 18, 1996: B-4.

8. Stan Ketterer, "Teaching Students How to Evaluate and Use Online Resources," *Journalism & Mass Communication Educator,* 52:4 (1998): 4–14.

9. Jodi B. Cohen, "Surfing for Sources," *Editor & Publisher,* June 29, 1996: 34.

10. John Lenger, "If a Tree Doesn't Fall on the Internet, Does It Really Exist?" *Columbia Journalism Review,* September/October 2002: 74.

11. Ibid., p. 74.

12. "Times Reporter Who Resigned Leaves Long Trail of Deception, *The New York Times,* May 11, 2003: A-1, 20–23, p. A-1; and Richard Cohen, "Blind Spot at the N.Y. Times," *The Washington Post,* May 12, 2003: A-19.

13. Christopher Callahan, *A Journalist's Guide to the Internet: The Net as a Reporting Tool,* 2nd ed. (Boston: Allyn and Bacon, 2003); Bruce Garrison, *Computer-assisted Reporting,* 2nd ed. (Mahwah, N.J.: Erlbaum, 1998); Shel Holtz, *Public Relations on the Net: Winning Strategies to Inform and Influence the Media, the Investment Community, the Government, the Public, and More!* 2nd ed. (New York: Amacom, 2002); James L. Horton, *Online Public Relations: A Handbook for Practitioners* (Westport, Conn.: Quorum, 2001); Brant Houston, *Computer-assisted Reporting: A Practical Guide,* 2nd ed. (Boston: Bedford/St. Martin's, 1999); Radio and Television News Directors Foundation, *News in the Next Century: Wired Journalist: Newsroom Guide to the Internet,* 2nd ed. (Washington, D.C.: Author, 1996); Matthew M. Reavy, *Introduction to Computer-assisted Reporting: A Journalist's Guide* (Mountain View, Calif.: Mayfield, 2001); and Randy Reddick and Elliot King, *The Online Journalist: Using the Internet and Other Electronic Resources,* 3rd ed. (Fort Worth: Harcourt College, 2001).

14. Norm Goldstein (ed.), "Internet Search Tips," *The Associated Press Stylebook and Briefing on Media Law* (Cambridge, Mass.: Perseus, 2002): 131–133, and Michael L. Kent, "Don't Be Left Behind: Essential Tips for Searching the Web," *Public Relations Quarterly,* Spring 2001: 26–30.

15. "Residential Segregation of African-Americans Declines; Signals Mixed for Other Groups, Analysis Shows," news release, U.S. Census Bureau, Nov. 27, 2002. Downloaded on Jan. 9, 2003, from <www.census.gov/Press-Release/www/2002/cb02cn174.html>.

16. "E-Mail Addiction," *PC Magazine,* Sept. 4, 2001: 29. Available at <www.pcmag.com/article2/0,4149,481877,00.asp>; and Dave Haskin, "Do More with E-mail: Get More Out of Your Favorite Communications Application," *Small Business Computing,* August 2001: 49–50.

17. Bruce Garrison, "The Use of Electronic Mail as a Newsgathering Resource," paper presented to the Newspaper Division's Southeast Colloquium, Association for Education in Journalism & Mass Communication, Gulfport, Miss., March 7–9, 2002.

18. Sonye Forte Duhe and Erin Haynie, "Computer-assisted Reporting: A Nationwide Survey of Television Newsrooms," paper presented to the Radio-Television Journalism Division, Association for Education in Journalism & Mass Communication annual convention, Baltimore, Md., August 1998.

19. Ryan, "Public Relations and the Web."

20. Garrison, "The Use of Electronic Mail."

21. Ibid.

CHAPTER 9

DOCUMENTS

Directories, Records and Databases

Maj. Michael J. Ripley thundered toward a practice target in Chesapeake Bay in the hot Harrier jet that he was flying for the U.S. Marine Corps. The decorated combat pilot approached the target at a sharp angle and could not pull out fast enough to avoid crashing. Ripley, who went down on June 18, 1971, was the first of 45 Marines to die in Harrier accidents between 1971 and 2002.

The Marines coveted the Harrier, which hovers and can take off and land vertically, for the unique manner in which it provides air cover for ground troops. The Marines got their first planes from the British in 1971 and received 397 Harriers from British and American manufacturers during the following three decades. Only 154 Harriers remain in the Marines' arsenal, and the aircraft no longer is manufactured.

An exhaustive, four-part study by the *Los Angeles Times* showed the Harrier's vertical-lift capability was never used in combat and that it was dogged from the beginning by maintenance errors and mechanical failures.[1] Taxpayers lost $1.8 billion in 900 incidents and 300 accidents involving Harriers, according to the *Times*, excluding losses prior to 1980. Thirty-three wives lost their husbands; three women lost their fiancés; and 38 children (and five more on the way) lost their fathers.

Times writers Kevin Sack and Alan C. Miller knew the Harrier was a troubled and controversial aircraft long before they started the research for their series. And they knew they could not rely exclusively on interviews to tell the story. They needed solid documentation to supplement the interviews, and they turned to documents to get it.

Miller and Sack used the Freedom of Information Act (Chapter 13) to obtain Harrier accident investigation reports from the Navy's Judge Advocate General's office. They pored over the 87 reports filed between 1971 and 2001 looking for the official reasons for accidents and for trends. Information from these and other reports was used to describe what happened in the individual accidents and incidents, most of which were described in the series, and to verify information from interviews.[2]

Sack and Miller started Part 2 with an interesting narrative lead that described an October 1997 Harrier crash in an Ohio cornfield. Official investigators discovered that a "foreign object" had "ricocheted through the whirring engine, reducing compressor blades to shrapnel."[3] One of the damaged blades showed that a ball bearing was the likely culprit. The night before, three maintenance workers had used slingshots to hurl ball bearings at pigeons in the rafters. The Harrier was parked nearby and one of the ball bearings apparently had lodged in the engine, only to be shaken loose on takeoff the following day.

The *Times* also obtained under the Freedom of Information Act data from the Naval Safety Center's aviation database, which contains records about crew members and aircraft that were involved from 1980 through June 2002 in Navy and Marine accidents (records are special kinds of documents). "Comparative statistics about accident rates were provided by the Naval Safety Center and Air Force Safety Center. Harrier cost data came from the Naval Air Systems Command and the Navy Center for Cost Analysis."[4]

The 45 pilots killed in Harrier accidents were not identified by the Marines, so the *Times* searched news clippings, online databases, the National Archives and the Marine Corps Historical Center to find out who they were. Reporters interviewed at least one relative of each dead pilot, dozens of military analysts, retired and active Marine Corps officers, Harrier pilots and maintenance personnel, Pentagon officials, Boeing and Lockheed Martin personnel and members of the Federation of American Scientists, Flight International, among many others.

The *Times'* writers used direct quotations, vignettes and narrative leads to make the series compelling, but information from documents made the series credible—and difficult to refute.[5] Information collection took months, and Sacks and Miller had help from Richard O'Reilly, the *Times'* director of computer analysis, and Joel Greenberg, the *Times'* graphics reporter.

Reports that rely heavily on documents typically are illustrated with photographs, illustrations and graphs. The *Times'* series was nearly 12 complete newspaper pages long and was illustrated by 26 photographs, 77 mug shots (including photographs of the 45 pilots who died), four illustrations (including one showing how the Harrier works) and two graphs (including one that compared Harrier accident rates with those of other airplanes over three decades).

The *Los Angeles Times'* series shows what can happen when media writers put their resources into newsworthy, interesting, compelling topics and go beyond the usual process of reporting the views of sources on all sides of an issue. (The box "A Classic Study of Documents" on page 222 offers another example.)

The Los Angeles Times *used more than two dozen photographs in 2002 to illustrate its stories about the U.S. Marines Corps' troubled Harrier fighter plane (shown here). Media writers frequently use photographs and other graphics to bring to life stories based on database research.*

The investigations by the *Times* and many other organizations are commendable and important,[6] but some journalism and public relations organizations are unwilling to dedicate so much time and money to such projects. The lack of money and time isn't the only reason documents aren't used regularly. Some editors and writers simply don't recognize the potential value of documents; they don't know what kinds of sources are available; or they don't know how to access and use that information. Worse, some can't work up the initiative to find out.

A first step in learning to use documents is to know the difference between record, document and database. Recall the following from Chapter 8:

- Documents are reports, letters, books, articles, documentary films and similar materials that are prepared by corporations, media, not-for-profit organizations, governments, foundations, individuals and other groups. They often list or summarize records and other information.

- Records are discrete bits of information about groups, organizations, individuals or other entities. Arrest reports, students' academic records and driving reports are examples of records.

A CLASSIC STUDY OF DOCUMENTS

The Sun Newspapers of Omaha, a chain of weekly newspapers in Nebraska, won a Pulitzer Prize and six other national awards three decades ago for an investigation of the financial status of Father Flanagan's Boys' Home in Boys Town, Neb. More important, the investigation resulted in major changes in Boys Town's operations, fund-raising procedures and expenditures.[7]

The investigation is a classic because the reporters relied heavily on public records (a kind of document)—a rarity in those days when computers were not widely available and no records were accessible electronically. The reporters used budget records to show that Boys Town's net worth (approximately $209 million by the end of 1971) was exceeded by only 270 of *Fortune Magazine*'s "Top 500" firms, that its endowment was approximately three times the size of Notre Dame University's, that Boys Town had an annual income of roughly $25.9 million at the end of 1970 and that its elaborate mail fund-raising program was soliciting donations not needed for Boys Town's day-to-day operations.

The journalists used postal records to discover that 34 million letters were mailed from the Boys Town post office in the 1971 fiscal year, and they found out through interviews that at least $10 million in donations would be needed to justify the cost of sending out so many fund-raising letters.

Reporters and editors relied heavily on Boys Town's Form 990, a document that most nonprofit foundations and institutions must file with the Internal Revenue Service. The form lists officers and directors, their salaries and their interests in the operation, if any; assets and liabilities; sources of income; and the places money was spent during the calendar year. The net worth of Father Flanagan's Boys' Home Inc. at the end of 1970 was $191,401,421, a staggering sum in those days.

Land records showed that Boys Town's largely tax-exempt property was worth approximately $8.4 million; education records indicated that approximately 665 boys, not the 1,000 Boys Town could accommodate, lived at the home; and promotional literature from Boys Town itself showed that some publicity material was inaccurate or misleading.

Boys Town's directors stopped their fund-raising efforts, including one that was almost ready to mail; established a $30 million endowment to support treatment for children with speech and hearing defects; promised $40 million to support a center to research child development; and hired consultants to study the Boys Town program. Many changes were implemented.

■ Databases are collections of letters, legal cases, numbers and other information arranged by topics. In recent years, records typically have been stored in electronic databases, but they also can be stored in written documents. The electronic index to the *San Francisco Chronicle,* which was free to use in 2003, is an electronic database.

A second step is to understand that not all documents are available (Chapter 8). Writers generally can gain access to some kinds of records without difficulty: property tax, police, library, land, incorporation, campaign, safety and some court records fall into this category. They almost never can gain legal access to other kinds of records, including income tax, telephone and military records and some personal letters. Some sources fall into a gray area, and writers must be well versed in the law to know which sources governments can rightfully close and which they cannot (Chapter 13).

A third step is to understand that some documents are available through Web sources, but that many are not, and that many are not available in a format that a writer can use. Many documents produced before computers were widely available are not accessible online, and some recent documents are unavailable because no one has found a compelling need to make them available. Writers still need to go to the library.

Only those records, databases and documents that typically are open are discussed here. Even within this single category, no attempt is made to identify all the important sources—only those that are most helpful to beginning print, broadcast and Web writers and to public relations professionals are listed. Appendix G, Hot Web Sites, is a useful guideline only.

MEDIA DOCUMENTS

One of the joys of writing in the 21st century is the easy availability of documents (stories, editorials, annual reports, advertisements, legal notices, news releases) aired or published months or years ago by newspapers, magazines, Web sites, corporations, organizations and broadcast stations. A couple of decades ago, newspaper stories, for example, were available only from the newspapers that published them and, sometimes, on microfilm from libraries. Older public relations releases and broadcast clips and programs were nearly impossible to find.

All of that changed in the mid-1980s or so. A student assigned to write a news release about a program to reduce the incidence of alcoholic binge drinking on campus, for example, can find useful background information in a matter of minutes from a local newspaper or an organization or foundation dedicated to the prevention of alcoholism. A student can ask better questions and write a stronger release if he or she knows, for instance, that student athletes, men, fraternity and sorority members and whites are more likely than other students to be binge drinkers.[8]

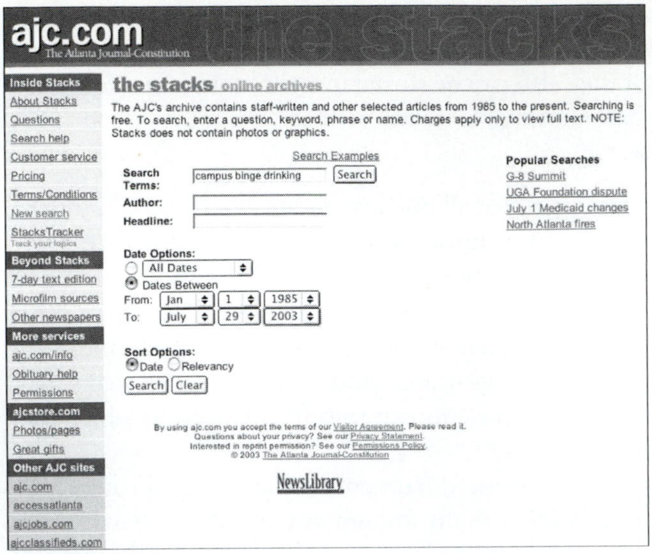

FIGURE 9.1 *THE ATLANTA JOURNAL-CONSTITUTION'S SEARCH MECHANISM*

It's easy to find information about binge drinking—and other current topics. A public relations student at an Atlanta-area university, for instance, could consult *The Atlanta Journal-Constitution*'s archives before writing and researching a news release about binge drinking. Here is one way to do it:

- Go to <www.google.com>.
- Enter *atlanta journal constitution* in the box and click Search.
- An annotated list of Web sites pops up. Click on *The Atlanta Journal-Constitution*'s home page.
- Click on Archives, which is usually part of a list on the left side of a newspaper's Web page. Newspaper, Web, broadcast station and public relations archives are databases containing virtually everything published or aired from a certain date (typically, the mid-1980s for newspapers) to the present.
- Type *campus binge drinking* in the box and click Search (Figure 9.1).

Sixty-six articles relating to campus binge drinking were listed in early 2003. Many would provide useful background to anyone writing about that critical campus problem; some would not. Since they were published in a newspaper, the articles should be substantially accurate.

Unfortunately, and perhaps shortsightedly, *The Atlanta Journal-Constitution*, like most other media sites, charges its archive users. Students pay *The Journal-Constitution* $2.95 (payable by credit card) to view 10 articles within a 24-hour period. Or anyone can pay $9.95 a month to read 100 articles during that period. Subscribers to most newspapers get to use the archives for free, although registration is required.

Another good source of newspaper and magazine content is LexisNexis, which provides online database services that are tailored to the needs of different users (direct mail marketers, students, advertisers, journalists, lawyers and corporate executives, for example). Most college libraries subscribe to this costly service. One advantage is that a user can complete a national search of newspapers or magazines very quickly, rather than visiting each medium's Web site individually. That process could take forever. But a user who wants local information is smart to visit a local site first.

DIRECTORIES

Hundreds of directories are available to help a writer track down a contact. The two most useful types are the telephone directory and the cross-reference directory.

Telephone Directory

The most common directory certainly is the telephone book. From this source a writer can check the spelling of names of people, groups, businesses, institutions and other organizations; verify the accuracy of addresses; and call every doctor, lawyer, dentist or other business or professional person in town, if necessary.

Three useful parts of the alphabetical listing of telephone numbers in the white pages (or, sometimes, the blue pages) are the sections for city, county and federal government offices. In a state capital, a section for state government offices also is listed. These sections include all the branches and departments within a government (such as the city). A writer who wants a list of all the libraries in a large city can find it under the "library" subheading in the city government listings. Similarly, all the swimming pools in town are listed under the "recreation facilities" subheading.

A writer sometimes can gather interesting information by comparing telephone directories from different years. If a suspicious investment corporation that was in the telephone directory last year is not listed this year, it might be worth finding out why.

Telephone books are generally accurate and handy tools. One problem is that not everyone is listed. Some people think the telephone is an unnecessary annoyance or that it is too expensive. Some want the telephone, but don't want their names listed. Others rely solely on cell phones, which are not yet listed in directories.

Another problem is that a writer might need the telephone directory from another town or city. This problem was solved, however, when companies started making their databases available online. A writer who knows the name and location (town or city) of a potential information source can almost certainly get a telephone number from a Web resource—unless the number is unlisted. Some good sources are Switchboard at <www.switchboard.com>; Yahoo! People Search at <people.yahoo.com>; Infospace at <www.infospace.com>; and Telephone Directories on the Web at <www.contractjobs.com/tel>. Most have Yellow Pages that are helpful in locating businesses, and they can be used to find some electronic mail addresses.

A writer who knows only the person's first initial has a decent—though not certain—chance of getting a telephone number. A writer who needs a number for M. Ryan (a co-author of this book) in Houston, for example, can open Yahoo! People Search and type in that name. There are (in 2003) eight possibilities—with telephone numbers. If the information is important, a media writer can call all eight to find the right person. Unfortunately, none of the numbers is correct. Ryan is listed not by M. Ryan, but by P. M. Ryan because his first name is Paul. If one types in *p m ryan,* one gets 11 hits, one of which is correct. Clearly, the Web has not resolved all problems.

A writer who has only a telephone number can find out to whom that number is registered by consulting Switchboard or AnyWho at <www.anywho.com/rl.html>.

Cross-reference Directory

Cole Publications Inc., headquartered in Lincoln, Neb., publishes cross-reference directories for most large U.S. metropolitan areas. Although directed primarily at business buyers, the directory provides communication users with the following:

- A reverse address book, which means a writer can find out who lives at a specific address
- Income levels of residents per home
- Percentages of homeowners and apartment dwellers in a neighborhood
- Names and telephone numbers matched to specific addresses
- Lists of elected officials, board and commission members, court officers and other public officials by name, address and telephone number for all towns, townships, boroughs and other incorporated areas in a metropolitan region
- The names and telephone numbers of tenants in major office buildings
- Telephone owners in order of number

The reverse address book can be particularly useful. The list by addresses can be used to pinpoint the location of a fire or robbery. Many newspapers and broadcast stations have police radios in their newsrooms, but police or fire department reports often state only that there is "a fire at 1800 W. First St." A reverse directory enables a writer to look up that address and find out whether a residence or business is located there. The homes and businesses located near the fire or robbery can also be identified. A writer sometimes can obtain information about the situation simply by telephoning the house across the street.

A drawback to city directories is that they are expensive.

BUSINESS INFORMATION

Writers, particularly those in public relations, frequently need information about corporations and small businesses.[9] Considerable information is available for free from directories, the office of the secretary of state and other sources, but writers sometimes have to use databases maintained by private businesses, which can charge a great deal. These sources often can be used in the reference sections of college and public libraries.

LexisNexis for the public relations industry is, not surprisingly, useful to public relations professionals and other writers interested in business affairs. LexisNexis at <www.lexisnexis.com/Prindustry> offers business and public records information, news and legal information about companies, products, services and people. The service provides access to more than 200 million state and federal court records and notifies users by electronic mail when new cases are filed or decisions are handed down. The service is expensive, but it might be available in a nearby library.

Edgar Online at <www.edgar-online.com> supplies the latest news, links to useful Web sites, financial data and information about initial public offerings, customer support, corporate sales, international business and jobs. Edgar specializes in distributing information contained in filings with the Securities and Exchange Commission.

Public business records also are available through Database Technologies' Auto-Track Plus at <www.llrx.com/features/dbt.htm>. Users can search nearly 4 billion records purchased from more than 1,000 private and public sources. While the site might be most useful for public relations writers, other communication professionals find it helpful. The use fee discourages some potential users, but this resource is available in many local libraries.

Many public relations persons, agencies and offices subscribe to the *Online Journal*, maintained by *The Wall Street Journal*. Subscribers can tailor *Journal* content to meet their specific needs. They can, for instance, build their own "news-page" so it will provide features and stories that fit the criteria they establish, list only the prices of stocks or mutual funds they own or supply news about companies that interest them. The site is at <http://online.wsj.com>.

GOVERNMENT DOCUMENTS

Federal, state and local governments are publishing documents at an unprecedented rate—a rate that makes it virtually impossible for a writer to keep up. The federal government makes many documents available in electronic form because electronic documents cost less to produce than paper documents. Many state and local governments also are embracing electronic publishing, although some are not as far down that road as others. This chapter barely scratches the surface in describing what is available, but it does suggest possibilities that can be pursued. After a writer takes the initial plunge, it becomes easier to swim through a sea of documents of all kinds.

U.S. Government

Some documents are more sensational, controversial and newsworthy than others. One of the most sensational documents the federal government has ever published is the report by Independent Counsel Kenneth Starr suggesting that former

President Bill Clinton "committed acts that may constitute grounds for impeachment."[10] Starr charged, among other things, that Clinton lied under oath, used his position to get Monica Lewinsky a job and tried to obstruct justice. The report, which contained many lurid details about the relationship between the president and the intern, was more widely distributed and read than almost any other government report.

Although the sensational or dramatic documents get most of the attention, hundreds of other documents are published each year by each branch of government. Four different kinds of documents—general, legislative, executive and judicial—are discussed here. Virtually all the sources are available in any good library, on the Web or from the Superintendent of Public Documents, U.S. Government Printing Office, Washington, D.C.

General Indices

A difficulty with using government documents lies in finding those that are relevant. The main source for locating U.S. government documents published since 1994, such as the Starr report, is the *Catalog of United States Government Publications,* available at <www.gpoaccess.gov/cgp/index.html> or, in some libraries, on CD-ROM (see Figure 9.2). For earlier documents, writers need to consult the *Monthly Catalog of United States Government Publications.* The catalog indexes print and electronic documents generated by federal agencies. Some agencies make the records on which reports are based accessible through their Web sites, and some of those data can be re-analyzed (Chapter 8).

Writers who know the names or nicknames of the documents they want might find them most easily by using a search service like Yahoo! or Lycos.[11] For example, they open <www.yahoo.com>, type *starr report* in the box, click Search and get overwhelmed. They'll have roughly a quarter million hits. But they need not worry: The complete, official report is one of the first items listed.

Congressional Sources

The *Congressional Record*—which reports the voting records of members of Congress, almost verbatim accounts of all speeches and debates on the House and Senate floors and the texts of bills—is published daily while Congress is in session.

Volumes of the *Congressional Record* since 1994 are available on the Web at <www.gpoaccess.gov/crecord/index.html>. Many libraries have volumes published before 1994. The *Congressional Record* typically is updated by 11 a.m. on days when Congress is in session. Users can view the "Daily Digest" from the previous day's *Congressional Record,* and writers often find the links to related databases useful.

Using the *Congressional Record* presents several problems, however. One is that the sheer bulk of the publication diminishes its value as an information source, although the index is helpful in overcoming that problem. A much more serious

FIGURE 9.2 SEARCHING FOR THE STARR REPORT

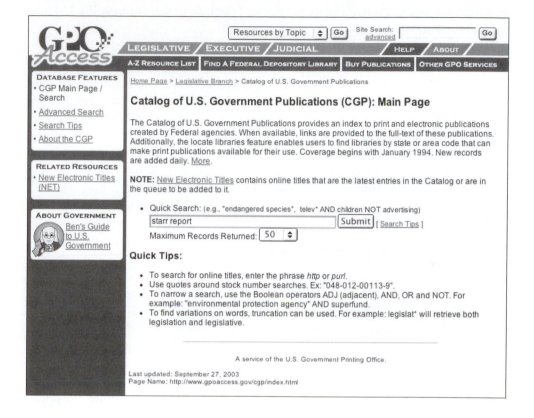

problem is that some speeches reported in the *Congressional Record* are subject to editing by members of Congress who want to make themselves look good to the voters. Still, it is useful to know the official positions of House and Senate members as they are reflected in the *Congressional Record.*

The *Official Congressional Directory,* one of the federal government's oldest working handbooks, contains information about the formal organization of Congress and committee memberships; biographical sketches of senators, representatives and other public officials; terms of service; committee memberships; government contact information; and data about the many organizations that work with Congress.

The directory is available online at <www.gpoaccess.gov/cdirectory/index.html>. Users can do keyword searches beginning with the 1995 volume. Information about congressional districts, senators and representatives is conveniently arranged by state.

Writers can visit one of the Library of Congress's pages, <thomas.loc.gov>, to find the text of congressional legislation, electronic mail addresses for members of Congress and staff members, committee assignments, congressional ethics manual, committee reports, status of bills, votes and loads of other information. Writers can even find the Declaration of Independence and the U.S. Constitution at the Thomas (as in Jefferson) site.

Executive Branch Sources

The *United States Government Manual,* revised annually, contains some information about all branches of the federal government, but it focuses primarily on the executive branch. The manual describes the creation and function of important federal agencies and bureaus and provides charts that help readers understand the operations of the more complex ones. It lists the major officials in agencies and bureaus, and it contains information about committees and commissions that aren't part of formal departments and agencies (for example, the Interstate Commerce Commission) and quasi-governmental organizations (for example, the National Academy of Science).

The manual—available in most libraries and at <www.gpoaccess.gov/gmanual/index.html>—provides a keyword search mechanism for volumes published since 1995. Search directions are clear and to the point.

The *Federal Register* is a good source of information about orders, proclamations and regulations issued by the president and by bureaus and agencies within the executive branch. The *Federal Register,* the first place to look for the complete text of orders, proclamations and regulations, is published five days a week and is indexed quarterly and annually. All items in the *Federal Register* go ultimately into the *Code of Federal Regulations.*

The *Federal Register*'s database can be searched by keyword at <www.gpoaccess .gov/fr/index.html>. Look in the *Federal Register* for local news about hospitals, military installations, waterways, corporations and power companies. A University of Maryland student used the *Federal Register* to document a story about a Pentagon proposal to tear down or sell 24 historic structures at the Walter Reed Army Medical Center. The buildings housed a women's finishing school from the late 1800s until World War II. Nicole Gill's interesting article was published in *The* (Baltimore) *Sun.*[12]

Verbatim transcripts of presidential messages, speeches, news conferences, public statements and similar materials are published in the *Weekly Compilation of Presidential Documents.* Prepared by the Office of the Federal Register, National Archives and Records Administration, the *Weekly Compilation* publishes all materials released by the White House during the preceding week. Documents from 1993 to the present are available online at <www.gpoaccess.gov/wcomp/index.html>. The site provides good guidance for a keyword search.

The American Journal, a nationally syndicated television program, relied on executive branch records to produce an important story about commercial airliners that are put back into service after they are in accidents. First, Mark Sauter and his team found from a LexisNexis search that an aircraft that tore open over Hawaii in 1989 was put back into service. This suggested that damaged planes do indeed get put back into service, so the *American Journal* team forged on.[13]

The National Transportation Safety Board ran a computer search and gave the journalists a list of commercial airliners damaged since 1985. They examined the "service difficulty reports" maintained by the Federal Aviation Administration at <www.faa.gov> and obtained the N-number for each aircraft. The reports list every problem and repair for every airplane, and the N-number is an identification number that never changes. Then the journalists went to <acro.harvard.edu/GA/search_nnr.html> to find out which planes were still in use. Roughly 100 airplanes that were in accidents were still being used commercially. The team had its story.

State Government

State governments, unfortunately, often aren't as meticulous as the federal government about keeping track of their many documents, and sometimes it is difficult to find a relevant record or document.

General Indices

Most states publish guides to their own publications, and many are available on the Web. The New Jersey State Library, for example, maintains a Web site that helps users find publications posted on New Jersey government Web pages. Writers can track down information about civil rights, casino gambling, the Legislature, local government budgets, military and veterans affairs, banking and insurance and much more. The URL is <www.njstatelib.org/NJ_Information/links/index.php>.

Similar publications and sites are available in many states. Useful information is available, for example, at <www.sos.mo.gov/library/reference/checklist>, maintained by the Missouri Secretary of State's office; at <www.nlc.state.ne.us/docs/pilot/pilot.html>, maintained by the Nebraska Library Commission; and at <find-it.lib.az.us>, maintained by the Arizona State Library. State guides can be found at <lcweb.loc.gov/global/state/stategov.html>, the Library of Congress's guide to state government information. Or one can use Google to find URLs in seconds (type in, for instance, *new york government publications*).

General Reference Books

The *Book of the States,* published annually by the Council of State Governments, contains information and summarized records about state legislatures, state officials, constitutions, trends, flowers, census data, birds, directories, mottoes, elections and other items. Writers can consult literally hundreds of tables to find out, for example, how much money each state spent on education and social services during the previous year. It's an expensive, commercial database, but it is available in many libraries.

Many states also publish each year or so an almanac or manual containing information about the state. *The New Hampshire Almanac,* for example, is available on the Web at <www.nh.gov/nhinfo>. Compiled by the state library, the *Almanac* is divided into several sections, including demographics and statistics, elections,

RECORDS AND THE POWERLESS

Systematic studies of records are particularly useful when journalists and advocacy groups want to find out how well the powerful (nursing home administrators and their staffs, for example) treat the powerless (nursing home residents). Here are some examples of reports that use records to determine the extent to which the powerful treat the powerless humanely.

- The *San Francisco Chronicle* found during a three-month investigation that California's poor, ill and elderly were forced to wait for flu shots, even though the vaccine had been ordered and the Centers for Disease Control and Prevention had recommended that high-risk health care providers and patients be inoculated first. The vaccine went first to the young and healthy who could pay more. The *Chronicle*'s report was based in part on thousands of pages of transcripts and documents obtained under the Freedom of Information Act from the U.S. Food and Drug Administration.[14]

- CBS News found during a story about the dangers of nursing home care that thousands of patients die because of simple neglect. CBS found in its analysis of nursing home inspection reports that more than 3,500 homes were cited for poor care and that almost 500 patients died or were seriously injured because of that care. Even more disturbing, records showed that some of those ill or dead patients were just fine. The CBS report noted that one patient who was described as walking around was still in a coma. Another record showed the patient received care two days after she died. CBS provides a link to the care record from its Web site.[15]

- The *Tallahassee* (Fla.) *Democrat* discovered the ballots of voters in poor counties during Florida's 2000 election campaign were more likely to be discarded than were ballots of those in affluent counties. In fact, they were more than twice as likely to be discarded in counties having large concentrations of minorities and the elderly. The link between income and disregarded ballot was much stronger than the link between discarded ballot and type of ballot, the *Democrat* found in its exhaustive study of election records.[16]

Jacob Riis' 1889 photograph of homeless children sleeping on a New York City grate was an attempt by the writer-photographer to publicize the plight of the disenfranchised. His writing and photographs appeared in many books, including his How the Other Half Lives: Studies Among the Tenements of New York.

flora and fauna, local and state government, history and people and places. Writers can find out how bills become laws, what local property tax rates are, what rare plants grow in New Hampshire, what the state constitution says and who the government officials are and how they can be contacted.

State manuals, or blue books, are available in many media offices, all libraries and, in many cases, on the Web. Most are like the *Wisconsin Blue Book,* available at <www.legis.state.wi.us/lrb/bb/index.htm>. Blue books help writers seeking information about all aspects of a state, including state emblems and symbols, all facets of state and local government, history, statistics and rankings. Blue books can be found through any search service by typing in, for instance, *north carolina blue book.*

Other Sources

State legislative bureaus and councils, public expenditure councils and legislative reference services often provide reports of legislative actions, speeches, texts of bills, political affairs and other activities each week during the session. To find these sources, users can search under *oklahoma legislature,* for example. They will find the appropriate site and there get information about pending and approved legislation, the status of bills, powers and duties of members, committee memberships, schedules and agendas, the capitol building and, for some, live broadcasts of some hearings.

Information about proclamations, speeches, veto messages, reports or statements by a state governor typically is available at the governor's Web site. Users can search under *wyoming governor,* for instance, and get where they need to go. Copies of important documents, legislation and publications usually are readily available, and there are useful links to other state agencies and documents.

A good example of a news report based on state records is David Boliek's story on North Carolina's Job Training Partnership. Boliek—of WTVD-TV in Raleigh-Durham—used the program's records to show that 86 percent of the individuals who entered the job training program left with jobs that paid less money than they would need to rise above the poverty level. Nearly half got jobs paying less than the minimum wage. Boliek got the records from the program, but he could not interpret the codes used to identify the jobs. He turned to SIC-all-codes at <www.iis.com/SIC/SIC-all-codes.html> and found the "standard industrial classifications." From that information he learned where the students were going.[17]

Boliek got another good story when he visited the Web site of North Carolina's Purchasing and Contracts Division at <www.doa.state.nc.us/PandC>. Under an entry for "birth control devices," Boliek found $150,000 was spent to purchase 2 million colored, ribbed, rainbow-colored, ultra-sensitive and mint-flavored condoms. They were distributed by North Carolina health agencies, and the story created a firestorm.[18]

The best way to get information about a court decision is to be present in the courtroom when the decision is announced. When that isn't possible, or when it is necessary to confirm what was said, a writer should consult the court clerk, whether in a court of original jurisdiction or an appellate court. Written opinions sometimes are available in the clerk's office or online.

Reports from all state appellate courts and some state courts of original jurisdiction are published privately by the West Publishing Co. in its *National Reporter System.* Many state and regional editions are published. The *North Western Reporter* contains law reports for Iowa, Michigan, Minnesota, Nebraska, North and South Dakota and Wisconsin; *California Reporter* contains law reports for the state of California; and *Southern Reporter* contains reports for Alabama, Florida, Louisiana and Mississippi. Many other editions are published. All are expensive, but they are available in many libraries.

A state's laws are compiled in a publication similar to the United States Code. Laws often are arranged by subject in volumes called revisions, compilations, consolidations, general statutes or codes (Iowa Code Annotated, for instance). When they are updated frequently, such publications are invaluable.

Indiana's code is available at <www.IN.gov/legislative/ic/code>, for instance. The site is maintained by the Office of Code Revision, Indiana Legislative Services Agency. The table of contents provides links to laws relating to elections, taxation, alcoholic beverages, tobacco, transportation, motor vehicles, police and military affairs, corrections, human services, the environment, utilities and resources, agriculture and animals, health, education, business, labor and industry, trade, consumer sales and credit, occupations, financial institutions, family and juvenile law, courts and legal procedures, insurance and probate. The Indiana site has a keyword search capability that makes it easy to find any law.

Local Government

Many city and county agencies compile statistics, write reports, keep records and churn out document after document, many of which are worthwhile to writers who know where to find them.

General Sources

One of the best sources of information about local governments is *The Municipal Year Book,* published by the International City Management Association. The book lists roughly 70,000 local government officials and contains data about laws and courts, leisure activities, salaries of municipal officials, police and fire departments in cities having populations exceeding 10,000 (including salaries, training and expenditures), community health, city planning, city legal problems, councils of government, public employee unionization, employee recruitment practices and training and many other aspects of local government. The tables and graphs generally are easy to read.

A writer who wants to find out whether the local fire department is working with less than the authorized personnel strength should consult the *Year Book.* The strength of one city's fire department can be compared with that of fire departments in cities of comparable size. Or a writer might compare the salaries paid officials in 21 major positions in one municipality with salaries paid high officials in cities of comparable size.

The *County and City Data Book,* published by the U.S. Census Bureau, contains data about all U.S. counties, metropolitan areas having more than 25,000 residents and places having more than 2,500 inhabitants. Hundreds of bits of information are available for each area, and notes and descriptions are provided to help the reader interpret the mass of records. Information is derived primarily from the population census conducted every 10 years, but data also are provided by government agencies and other sources.

The 1994, 1998, and 2000 editions are available at <fisher.lib.virginia.edu/ccdb> and the latest edition is available at <www.census.gov/prod/www/ccdb.html>. *The County and City Data Book* is available in most libraries in printed form or on CD-ROM. Writers can re-analyze census data (to create custom printouts or customized data sets) to answer questions the Census Bureau did not. The Census Bureau has taken great pains to make the data sets as user-friendly as possible.

Related useful sources are *Statistical Abstract of the United States* at <www.census .gov/prod/www/statistical-abstract-us.html>; *USA Counties* at <www.census.gov/ statab/www/county.html>; and *State and Metropolitan Area Data Book* at <www .census.gov/statab/www/smadb.html>.

Most of these books contain material that can be used to bolster features or more serious reports. From the *Statistical Abstract,* for example, a writer can learn that, of households that have pets, 32 percent have cats and 36 percent have dogs. Households run by cats are more likely to have another pet in the house, and dogs might cost a little more because they visit veterinarians more often. Eighty-five percent of the dogs in canine households visited the veterinarian in 2001 and 67 percent of the cats in feline households went.

These kinds of figures can add a good deal to a feature story about an upcoming dog or cat show or about the search for a family's lost pet. But they can also add a great deal to a story about a pet rescue group or about the horrendous numbers of pets killed each year in pounds.

Local Databases

Local governments are making more and more records available online. An example is the Miami-Dade County Property Appraiser site at <www.co.miami-dade .fl.us/pa/Property_Search/ASP/record.asp>. Writers can search the site by folio number, property address or owner name for information about private or business property.

Users can learn the exact location and type of property (single-family home), number of bedrooms and floors, lot size, square footage, year constructed, legal description, original price, date of purchase, appraised value, market value and other useful information. More important, in some cases, writers can also learn what *other* properties the owner of that house owns.

Why is any of this useful? Suppose a member of city council introduces a bill that would lower property taxes in the city and then works hard to get that bill passed. It would be interesting to check the Miami-Dade County site to learn the appraised value (the amount that is taxed) of that member's house. If he or she lives in a home appraised at $900,000 and stands to save $3,000 if the rate is reduced, voters should know that. If the same council member owns six houses worth $2.5 million and would save another $8,000, that needs to be reported.

Information is typically available from many other departments. Education departments, for example, which administer virtually all of a state's activities in local public school districts, maintain databases relating to teacher certification, desegregation of schools, federal and state subsidies to local schools, school schedules and hours, lunch programs, school budgets and construction.

Health departments enforce all state laws regarding sanitation, public water supplies, sewage disposal and communicable diseases. Records are maintained on births, marriages, deaths, adoptions, individuals who use narcotic drugs, diseases, health reports, food and water supplies and inspections of restaurants, meat markets and other places where food is sold or processed.

Houston television personality Marvin Zindler of KTRK-TV has fashioned a long, productive career in large part from restaurant reports from the local health department. Zindler finds out which eateries have slime in their ice machines, cockroaches, spoiled meat and other health deficiencies and broadcasts them on the evening news. Zindler also helps consumers resolve grievances against local government officials and business leaders. Still, the restaurant reports are the heart and soul of his program.

Justice departments furnish legal advice to the governor and all other commissions, boards and agencies in state government; represent the state in legal cases; and operate bureaus for correctional institutions, consumer protection, pardons and investigations. Records are maintained on most activities, and many are available.

Most departments of public welfare inspect state, private and sectarian hospitals and maternity homes; approve plans for construction or alterations of homes for the aged, hospitals and county homes; license and inspect nursing, convalescent and boarding homes for the aged; examine and license homes and institutions that care for homeless children; and supervise all public and private institutions for mental patients. Many records, inspection reports and other documents are available.

The chief administrator of a city (whether a mayor or city manager) prepares and submits to the council an annual city budget, reports on the fiscal condition of the city, investigates complaints about city administration, ensures that city laws and ordinances are enforced and prepares policies or ordinances. Also available are budgets of city departments; reports from city agencies; records kept by various agencies; names of people who have received city franchises and details of the franchises; and contracts between the city and private contractors, engineers and architects.

Police departments are the sources of most of the information about crimes committed in the United States. Three major sources are the police blotter, official reports of crimes and other violations and the arrest book. The police blotter contains an up-to-the-minute record of crimes and other violations of some importance. Official police reports are filed for every important automobile accident, crime and domestic quarrel, and for other matters police must investigate (Figure 9.3). Arrest books, kept by all city and county jails, typically contain an arrested person's name, address and alleged offense. These records must be checked daily by a news gatherer, but they, along with numbers and kinds of crimes reported, are compiled into cumulative reports (databases) that need to be analyzed.

Nonfederal courts in cities, counties and towns are part of state judicial systems, and they derive their powers and authority from the state. Court systems

FIGURE 9.3 A SAMPLE TRAFFIC ACCIDENT REPORT

TRAFFIC ACCIDENT REPORT

FORWARD THIS REPORT WITHIN 5 DAYS TO THE STATE DEPARTMENT OF TRANSPORTATION, BUREAU OF ACCIDENT ANALYSIS

TIME

Date of Accident (Month - Day - Year)	County	Day of Week	Hour	Check if Hit-Run
March 3, 2004	**Montgomery**	**Wednesday**	**1:30** A.M. P.M.	☐

SEVERITY	Estimated Total Damages: $ **2200**	Number Injured: **3**	Number Killed: **none**

VEHICLE . 1

Operator's Name (First, Middle, Last) ~~Mr.~~ ~~Mrs.~~ ~~Miss~~ **James J. Eberhart**	Sex **M**	Birth (Month - Day - Year) **August 18, 1968**

Address (Street, City, State, Zip Code) **926 Pleasant Street, Springtown**	Operator's No. & State **14-502-391**

Owner's Name (First, Middle, Last) Mr. Mrs. Miss **Same as above**	Year **2001**	Vehicle Make **Jeep**	Model **Cherokee**	Registration No. **8D3252**

Address (Street, City, State, Zip Code)	Estimated Damage: $ **900**

VEHICLE NO 2

Operator's Name (First, Middle, Last) ~~Mr.~~ ~~Mrs.~~ Miss **Jane D. Martin**	Sex **F**	Birth (Month - Day - Year) **October 26, 1981**

Address (Street, City, State, Zip Code) **1012 W. Cedar Street, Columbia**	Operator's No. & State **22-845-963**

Owner's Name (First, Middle, Last) Mr. ~~Mrs.~~ ~~Miss~~ **Robert M. Martin**	Year **2003**	Vehicle Make **Ford**	Model **Taurus**	Registration No. **5B1874**

Address (Street, City, State, Zip Code) **1012 W. Cedar Street, Columbia**	Estimated Damage: $ **1300**

IF MORE VEHICLES ARE INVOLVED USE EXTRA BLANK PAPER SAME SIZE AS THIS REPORT

OTHER

Pedestrian's Name (First, Middle, Last) Mr. Mrs. Miss	Sex	Age	Check One ☐ Uninjured ☐ Injured ☐ Killed

Address (Street, City, State, Zip Code)			

Name of Property Owner (First, Middle, Last) Mr. Mrs. Miss	Description of Damaged Property

Address (Street, City, State, Zip Code)	Estimated Damage: $

OCCUPANTS

NAME	Age	Seat Belts in Use Yes/No	Sex	Injury See Below	Veh #	Position In Vehicle	Injured Taken To:
Jane D. Martin	**22**	**no**	**F**	**A**	**2**	**1**	**Springtown**
Elizabeth R. Johnston	**20**	**no**	**F**	**B**	**2**	**4**	**Memorial**
Robyn L. Bandre	**22**	**no**	**F**	**B**	**2**	**3**	**Hospital**
Ruth Miller	**22**	**no**	**F**	**N**	**2**	**6**	By:
James J. Eberhart	**35**	**no**	**M**	**N**	**1**	**1**	**City ambulance**

POSITION IN VEHICLE

```
  4  1
  5  2      DRIVER
  6  3      IS NO. 1
```

A–VISIBLE SIGNS OF INJURY, BLEEDING, DISTORTED MEMBER OR HAD TO BE REMOVED FROM SCENE
B–OTHER VISIBLE INJURY, BRUISES, SWELLING, LIMPING, ABRASIONS
C–NO VISIBLE INJURY, BUT COMPLAINT OF PAIN, DIZZINESS, ETC.
D–DEAD BEFORE COMPLETION OF REPORT
N–NO INJURY

POLICE INVESTIGATED	☐ NO	X YES	If Yes, Name of Police Dept. Which Investigated Accident: **Springtown Police Department**

AA -600 (1-74)

WEATHER:			ROADWAY:			NO. LANES
	☒ RAIN	☐ SNOW		☒ WET	☐ SNOWY	**Two**
☐ CLEAR	☐ FOGGY	☐ OTHER	☐ DRY	☐ ICY	☐ OTHER	

LOCATION

CITY - BOROUGH - TOWNSHIP	COUNTY	ON: (STREET NAME OR HWY NO.)
Springtown Township	**Montgomery**	**Pleasant Street**

AT INTERSECTION WITH: IF NOT AT INTERSECTION: ☐ N   ☐ S

Newman Avenue   OF _____

FEET ☐ E   ☐ W   STATION MARKER - INTERSECTION - ETC.

INSTRUCTIONS: To properly locate accident use landmarks, highway station numbers, mile posts, the intersection of two highways, the names or numbers of bridges, railroad crossings, creeks, streams, city, borough, township or county lines, draw diagram of this accident as clearly as you can. Write down streets or highways. Draw an arrow in the circle so it points north. Show your vehicle as No. 1.

ACCIDENT DIAGRAM

Pleasant Street

Vehicle # 2

Vehicle # 1

Newman Avenue

INDICATE NORTH BY ARROW

LEGAL SPEED	**30**	MPH
ESTIMATED SPEED	**10**	MPH

Veh. 1

CIRCLE DAMAGED AREA ON EACH VEHICLE

Veh. 2

LEGAL SPEED	**30**	MPH
ESTIMATED SPEED	**45**	MPH

NARRATIVE – GIVE A DETAILED DESCRIPTION OF THE ACCIDENT (REFER TO VEHICLES BY NUMBER)

Vehicle # 1, which was heading west on Newman Avenue when it stopped for a red traffic light, started to turn left from Newman Avenue onto Pleasant Street when light turned green. Vehicle # 2 was heading south on Pleasant Street when it ran red light and struck Vehicle # 1 on right rear side. Vehicle # 2 was traveling 45 miles per hour when driver attempted to brake suddenly. Driver of vehicle # 2 sustained a broken leg, a broken left arm and head injuries; one occupant was bleeding profusely from severe head injuries; and one occupant suffered bruises of the left shoulder. Driver of Vehicle # 1 was not injured in the crash. All injured persons were taken to Springtown Memorial Hospital.

Signature _Sgt. Richard B. Stang_   Date **March 3, 2004** aren't the same in all states, and the names of the courts often differ from state to state. A district court in Texas, for instance, has roughly the same jurisdiction as a court of common pleas in Pennsylvania and a superior court in California.

Whatever the courts are called, their records and documents can be useful to media professionals. Some officials from whom records and documents may be obtained are the district or state's attorney, court clerks, chairpersons of jury selection boards or jury commissioners, registers of wills and official court reporters.

The district attorney, the chief prosecuting officer in a county, draws up indictments, investigates violations of the law and provides legal advice to city and county agencies, boards, commissions or officials. The district attorney is an important source of records and documents pertaining to criminal trials, investigations into crime and corruption (including that involving public officials), complaints by citizens of crime or corruption in the area and arrest and bench warrants issued by various courts (Figure 9.4).

Court clerks (or, in some jurisdictions, county clerks) often are the best sources of information because at one time or other they handle almost every document that passes through the court. A writer can obtain records of probate proceedings (settlements of estates after someone has died) and criminal indictments, briefs in criminal and civil cases, grand jury reports, divorce records, dockets for upcoming trials, subpoenas for defendants and witnesses, arrest warrants, costs and fines imposed by courts, bail in criminal cases, drivers' license suspensions, appeals from administrative board decisions, writs and injunctions, witness fees and court decisions.

A county clerk must attend all meetings of a county board of supervisors; keep permanent minutes of meetings; maintain permanent records of petitions and other matters considered by the board; certify and file ordinances the board passes; keep records of petitions, appeals and complaints concerning property assessments; maintain records of certified notaries public, marriages and incorporations; conduct elections and register voters; and accept nominations for elections to public offices.

A county recorder (sometimes called a register of deeds) keeps records pertaining to deeds, transfers of mortgages or real estate, releases of mortgages or real estate, leases, powers of attorney to transfer real estate, certificates of marriage and marriage contracts, decrees and court judgments, bankruptcy proceedings, births and deaths, attachments on real estate, wills admitted to probate, official bonds, corporate records, personal property mortgage records and veteran discharge papers.

Legal Sources

A writer who needs to know what an interlocutory order is (a judgment that is temporary or provisional) can find out from *Black's Law Dictionary,* which has been around for more than 100 years. *Black's* contains more than 30,000 legal definitions written clearly and accurately. The cross-referencing feature, which makes it easy to find words, and the pronunciation guide are helpful.

FIGURE 9.4   A SAMPLE BURGLARY REPORT

WEATHERFORD TOWNSHIP POLICE DEPARTMENT

CASE # __73__

BURGLARY REPORT   DATE: **Oct. 6, 2004**

INVESTIGATING OFFICER: __Lt. Peter K. Bernardo__

COMPLAINANT: __Earl F. Gallina__   PHONE: **355-7379**

ADDRESS: __1314 E. York Road; Weatherford Township__

VICTIM: __Same as above__   PHONE: ____

ADDRESS: ____

TIME & DATE DEPARTURE: __7:30 AM__ AM/PM.   RETURN: __9:15 PM__ AM/PM

METHOD OF ENTRY: __Pried off outside screen, broke window glass, unlatched__

__window through broken glass__

EXIT FROM BUILDING: WHERE: __Through rear door__

UNUSUAL ACTS BY BURGLAR: __None__

NEIGHBORS NAME: __L.P. Manning__   ADDRESS: __1316 E. York Rd.__
CHECKED:

NAME: __Julius Hackenberg__   ADDRESS: __1312 E. York Rd.__

DESCRIPTION OF SCENE: __House appeared in good order except that it appeared__

__someone had searched bedroom carefully__

EVIDENCE LEFT AT SCENE, ETC.: __A long-blade knife which thieves apparently used__

__to pry off screen and several lengths of rope were found at the scene__

WEATHER CONDITIONS: __Clear__

OFFICERS REPORT: __When Mr. Gallina returned home from a trip with his family at__

__9:15 PM, he found someone had broken into his house through a rear window. Thief__

__(or thieves) took a $500 color television set, $1900 worth of stereo equipment, $257__

__in cash, a $225 typewriter and $3500 worth of jewelry. Mr. Gallina is investigating__

__to determine whether anything else is missing. Neighbors reported a blue van in the__

__area during the day, but they saw nothing suspicious or unusual happen.__

LexisNexis (see CourtLink, DolphinSearch and Shepard's, for example) offers access to literally thousands of court records, law review articles, links to original documents, court decisions and popular articles in magazines and newspapers about legal issues and problems (and to articles about hundreds of other topics). It's expensive, but it is available in many college libraries.

The *Index to Legal Periodicals and Books* indexes articles published in hundreds of periodicals dealing with the law in the United States, Canada, Australia, New Zealand, Ireland and Great Britain. This database references judicial decisions, law reviews, symposia, articles, books, legislation, book reviews, yearbooks, scholarly work and government publications. Articles from roughly 200 periodicals from 1994 to the present are cited. The *Index* is available at <www.hwwilson.com/Databases/legal.cfm>, but it is not free. The keyword search capability is easy to use.

West Publishing Co.'s FindLaw site at <www.directory.findlaw.com> is perhaps the most complete directory of U.S. law firms and attorneys. Listing nearly 1 million firms and lawyers, FindLaw is searchable by name, legal specialization, state, city and college attended.

U.S. Supreme Court rulings are available the day they are handed down at <http://supct.law.cornell.edu/supct/>. Decisions rendered before 1990 are available at <www.fedworld.gov/supcourt/index.htm>. Full text versions of the opinions of the 11 U.S. Circuit Courts of Appeal are available through the Emory University School of Law at <www.law.emory.edu/FEDCTS>.

Writers who need to know what a specific federal law or regulation says should first try <www.gpoaccess.gov/nara/index.html>. Maintained by the National Archives and Records Administration, the site provides the text of presidential orders, public laws and laws published in the *Federal Register* and the *Code of Federal Regulations.*

The National Criminal Justice Reference Service at <www.ncjrs.org> is an excellent source of information about substance abuse, crime victims, prisoner reentry, courts, juvenile justice, hate crimes, forensic science, policy, law enforcement, crime statistics and public safety. NCJRS is federally funded and sponsored by more than a dozen federal offices and agencies. Electronic mail addresses are supplied for experts who can answer specific questions.

SYSTEMATIC STUDIES OF RECORDS

Public records can be examined in a couple of ways. They can be searched routinely, or superficially, as when a crime reporter checks the city jail's arrest record each night. Or they can be searched more systematically, in the way a social scientist might (although the social scientist would probably call the approach content analysis). In trying to make the study of records systematic, an investigator must follow several steps:

- Specify a question to guide the study.
- Define the set of records relevant to the question.

- Construct a database using information from all relevant records or from a sample of records, or use an existing database created for some other purpose.

- Present the results in an analysis (perhaps using some graphics) that allows a conclusion to be drawn. Carefully select and use a statistical test, if appropriate.

Existing Databases

Writers for the *Milwaukee Journal Sentinel* used a local government database to find out whether minorities and the poor were affected more than whites by the Milwaukee Police Department's push for safer streets. They used Wisconsin's open records law to gain access to Milwaukee's municipal court database. Data from more than 147,000 tickets were analyzed in two categories: (1) speeding and other traffic violations, jaywalking and driving unregistered vehicles, and (2) carrying concealed weapons, vandalism, playing loud music and curfew violations.

Many police officers identified Hispanics as "white," thereby inflating the number of white offenders and underrepresenting the number of Hispanic offenders. *Journal Sentinel* writers used U.S. Census Bureau data to create a list of common Hispanic surnames and then cross-checked those names with those of male offenders. This procedure increased the number of Hispanics in the study by 7 percent and reduced the number of whites by 7 percent.[19]

Dave Umhoefer's lead was, "Now in its fourth year, Milwaukee's experiment with zero-tolerance policing has changed everything—and nothing—about law, order and life on the city's streets."[20] The series reported that most tickets for speeding and jaywalking are issued to minorities in high-crime areas, that 75 percent of municipal tickets were issued to blacks and Hispanics and that 70 percent of traffic tickets went to minorities.

The *Journal Sentinel*'s investigation answered questions about Milwaukee's social experiment in a more definitive way than other approaches (such as interviewing the district attorney, who might purposely distort the situation or who might not remember it correctly) would have done.

Existing Records

The *Chicago Tribune* constructed its own database for a series about patients who die of infections in U.S. hospitals. The *Tribune* found that roughly 100,000 people die each year because of unwashed hands, unsanitary facilities and dirty instruments. Sadly, records show that U.S. hospitals have reduced cleaning staffs by 25 percent since 1995 to cut costs.[21]

The *Tribune* series, written by Michael J. Berens, was based on data from 75 state and federal agencies, internal hospital files, court documents, patient databases and health organizations around the nation. The *Tribune* relied on records from the Centers for Disease Control and Prevention, Florida's Agency for Health

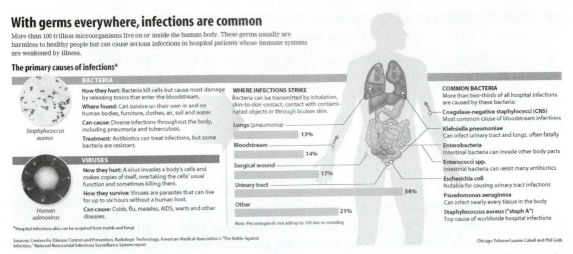

With germs everywhere, infections are common

More than 100 trillion microorganisms live on or inside the human body. These germs usually are harmless to healthy people but can cause serious infections in hospital patients whose immune systems are weakened by illness.

The primary causes of infections*

BACTERIA

Staphylococcus aureus

How they hurt: Bacteria kill cells but cause most damage by releasing toxins that enter the bloodstream.

Where found: Can survive on their own in and on human bodies, furniture, clothes, air, soil and water.

Can cause: Diverse infections throughout the body, including pneumonia and tuberculosis.

Treatment: Antibiotics can treat infections, but some bacteria are resistant.

VIRUSES

Human adenovirus

How they hurt: A virus invades a body's cells and makes copies of itself, overtaking the cells' usual function and sometimes killing them.

How they survive: Viruses are parasites that can live for up to six hours without a human host.

Can cause: Colds, flu, measles, AIDS, warts and other diseases.

*Hospital infections also can be acquired from molds and fungi.

WHERE INFECTIONS STRIKE

Bacteria can be transmitted by inhalation, skin-to-skin contact, contact with contaminated objects or through broken skin.

Lungs (pneumonia) — 13%

Bloodstream — 14%

Surgical wound — 17%

Urinary tract — 34%

Other — 21%

Note: Percentages do not add up to 100 due to rounding

COMMON BACTERIA

More than two-thirds of all hospital infections are caused by these bacteria:

Coagulase-negative staphylococci (CNS)
Most common cause of bloodstream infections

Klebsiella pneumoniae
Can infect urinary tract and lungs, often fatally

Enterobacteria
Intestinal bacteria can invade other body parts

Enterococci spp.
Intestinal bacteria can resist many antibiotics

Escherichia coli
Notable for causing urinary tract infections

Psuedomonas aeruginosa
Can infect nearly every tissue in the body

Staphylococcus aureus ("staph A")
Top cause of worldwide hospital infections

Sources: Centers for Disease Control and Prevention, Radiologic Technology, American Medical Association's "The Battle Against Infection," National Nosocomial Infections Surveillance System report

Chicago Tribune/Lauren Cabell and Phil Geib

Writers and editors frequently use informative graphics to clarify complex stories. This one was used to illustrate the Chicago Tribune's story documenting the role of poor hygiene in hospital deaths across the United States.

Care Administration, the American Hospital Association and others. The *Tribune*'s methods were similar to those used by epidemiologists.

Another complex and useful database was constructed by the Center for Public Integrity, the Center for Responsive Politics and the National Institute on Money in State Politics. The study of campaign finance practices in the states during the 2000 election cycle showed that "The transfers of unregulated soft money from federal party committees to their state counterparts confirm a commonly held perception that state parties are used to launder soft money and influence presidential and congressional elections in ways never envisioned nor intended by federal election law."[22]

Information for the year-long study came from agencies in the 50 states; they used different forms and had different filing schedules. Only 40 percent of the data were stored electronically by the states, so information from written documents had to be typed into the database.

The researchers first analyzed the states' election laws to determine standards of enforcement and disclosure for political parties and interviewed hundreds of election officials around the country. Then they analyzed records of expenditures and contributions, interest and other noncontribution income, loans, loan repayments, refunds of expenditures and contributions. Expenditures were categorized by purpose (for example, issue advertising in print media). Contributions were categorized by organization and employee.

Information about transfers from the national parties to the states also was obtained from the Federal Election Commission because state records were not always reliable. The Democratic Central Committee in Washington state, for instance, reported getting $705,040 from national Democratic Party committees, which was $6.6 million less than FEC records showed. All data were entered into an Excel file for analysis.

CONSTRUCTING DATABASES

Constructing databases is a pretty mysterious and frightening process for many writers because they have phobias about anything numerical. If they knew math, many argue, they would study physics so they could earn the big bucks. But math expertise is required of 21st-century communication professionals. They just can't do their jobs if they don't know how to use numbers (Chapter 12).

Be Fearless

The fear is misplaced anyway. It's not difficult for students and professionals to learn the mathematical fundamentals they need to succeed. Even the mysteries of analyzing information in databases can be solved. Most students have good backgrounds already because they've been tromping through databases for years. The next step—creating databases—is not that hard.

Careful thought and planning must go into database construction. A professional communicator who wants to create a database needs to decide why the database is necessary, interesting and important—in short, why the database is critical to the story he or she is preparing.

The news values described in Chapter 2 should help writers find the answers. Journalists, in particular, need to be sure their topic is newsworthy before they start the difficult, expensive, boring process of database construction. But public relations writers aren't off the hook: They must think very carefully before constructing a database that will be used to guide a campaign or to bolster a news release, report or other document.

Writers must decide next what *specific* question they want to answer. This will help them to remain focused and to avoid mistakes (such as collecting data that will not be used). Social scientists write precise research questions as they design research, and communication professionals should do the same. A Web writer who is researching standardized testing in public schools might ask, for example: What factors other than classroom instruction are related to variations in student scores on standardized tests? It's a good idea to tack that question (which may never be reported on the Web site) to the wall above the computer and refer to it constantly. This helps a writer stay focused.

The next step is to determine which variables need to be part of the database. "Variable" may seem a pretentious-sounding term, but a variable is simply a broad category into which a researcher places bits of data—records in this case. Gender (a broad category), for example, is a variable having two alternatives: male and female (bits of data). Other variables are education, income, height, grade point average, religious affiliation, occupation—just about anything a researcher can think of that relates to the research question can be a variable, although not all are useful or can be measured.

Variables must be defined carefully if a writer is to avoid wasting time or producing a weak report. A public relations professional who is preparing a news release about binge drinking, for example, needs to decide what binge drinking is.

Most scholars who study the problem define campus binge drinking as five drinks in an hour for men and four drinks in an hour for women. The definition can be found by writing *campus binge drinking* into the box on a favorite search service and hitting Search. A writer who visits some of the sites that pop up will soon find <www.edc.org/hec/pubs/factsheets/scope.html>. The report about binge drinking at this site was published by the Higher Education Center for Alcohol and Other Drug Prevention, a credible and well-known organization.[23]

The next step is to find out whether the records are maintained in electronic or written form and whether they are available. Some records are not collected or saved by any group or agency, and some that are maintained cannot be released because they were privately collected or because the law prohibits their release. It is difficult, for example, to access student records, even for legitimate research purposes.

A Hypothetical Case

Assume that a hospital administration wants to change the hospital's negative image within the community and assigns the hospital public relations department to help. Terry Smith of the public relations department is asked to develop a campaign to improve the hospital's image. The first criterion is satisfied: The negative hospital image is a serious problem and it's worth doing something about it. (Furthermore, when the boss tells a writer to do something, it gets done.)

Smith decides that an important first step in developing a strategy or campaign is to analyze complaint records (which most hospitals maintain). A Web search (*customer complaints*) turns up several articles pertaining to consumer complaints about customer service and how they might be addressed. This information provides helpful guidance.[24] Smith formulates a reasonable research question: Who is complaining about the hospital and what is the nature of those complaints? The question is a bit broad, but that's okay at this point—most important, the second criterion is satisfied.

Smith's next step is to decide which variables should be measured. An initial list might include gender, height, ethnicity, doctor, medical error or unexpected outcome, eye color, weight, family income, doctor's medical specialty, marital status, illness or injury, hair color, occupation, patient-doctor communication. The list could go on, but this is a reasonable accounting.

Some of the variables are more relevant and potentially useful than others. Eye and hair color, height and weight might be related to hospital image, but even if Smith finds they are, that is not terribly helpful. Such variables typically are not worth measuring. Smith discovers from previous studies that most complaints in malpractice cases center on doctor-patient communication. That becomes the focus, and Smith's research question is narrowed (and improved):

FIGURE 9.5   ENTERING DATA FOR ANALYSIS

pat/var	unexout	error	mislinfo	lateinfo	docacces	docname
1	1	1	3	3	3	2
2	3	3	1	4	3	1
3	3	1	4	1	2	2
4	2	1	2	1	3	2
5	3	1	1	4	3	2
6	1	1	1	1	1	5
7	1	4	1	1	1	2
8	4	2	3	1	3	2
9	1	1	1	1	1	2
10	3	1	4	1	3	3
11	3	1	4	1	3	2
12	1	3	4	1	4	4
13	2	1	1	3	2	2
14	3	1	1	1	2	2
15	1	1	1	1	1	2
16	1	1	1	1	2	3
17	3	3	3	3	2	2
18	3	1	1	1	2	2
19	4	5	2	1	1	2
20	3	1	4	1	3	2

What aspects of the doctor-patient communication process are patients complaining about most?[25]

Prior studies suggest that Smith might usefully focus on misleading information, giving information belatedly, not talking about errors or unexpected outcomes (an intestine is unexpectedly punctured during prostate surgery) and access to the doctor. In a real study, a public relations writer would include other variables, such as doctor's gender and specialty, nature of the illness and doctor's productivity (number of patients seen daily).

The next step is to determine whether the records are available. They are in most hospitals, and they are in this hypothetical hospital. Smith might enter the records for all patients who have complained in the past five years onto a form like that in Figure 9.5, which shows data entered into each field (each box is a "cell" or "field").

FIGURE 9.6   A SAMPLE CODING SHEET

Coding sheet: Complaints about doctor-patient communication

Outcome of treatment unexpected

1. No
2. Yes: Life-threatening
3. Yes: Not life-threatening
4. Yes: Unanticipated surgery required

Error

1. No
2. Yes: Life-threatening
3. Yes: Not life-threatening
4. Yes: Unanticipated surgery required
5. Yes: Heroic measures required

Doctor gives misleading information

1. No
2. Yes: Always
3. Yes: Frequently
4. Yes: Infrequently

Doctor gives information late

1. No
2. Yes: Always
3. Yes: Frequently
4. Yes: Infrequently

Doctor is accessible

1. No: Will not return messages
2. No: Will not see patient in room
3. Yes: Primarily by telephone or e-mail
4. Yes: Primarily in person

Doctor name

1. Brown
2. Green
3. Orange
4. Blue
5. Yellow

The data don't mean anything in this form without a coding sheet to explain the entries. The descriptors of the variables (at the top of Figure 9.5) are not unlike those used in any database. For technical reasons, the variable names are short and not terribly enlightening. Nobody can know what "unexout" refers to, for example, without the coding sheet. In working with databases, it's always important to get that document (Figure 9.6).

After the data are entered into a data analysis program (Statistical Package for the Social Sciences or Excel, to name only two), they can be analyzed in several different ways (Figure 9.7).

The table tells Smith some useful things, but the data are much more useful if Smith uses a cross-tabulation program to determine, for example, which doctors have the most problems communicating with their patients. Cross-tabulation means only that one variable is broken down by another (Figure 9.8).

Clearly, Smith needs to include in any public relations campaign a training session that will help the problematic doctors communicate better with patients. If the public relations person can reduce the number of times doctors (particularly Green) give misleading information, the hospital's image should improve. (In national studies, by the way, 9 percent of all doctors account for 50 percent of patient complaints.)

FIGURE 9.7   A SAMPLE TABLE

Table 1: Results of records analysis, in frequencies and percentages		
Outcome of treatment unexpected	**Number**	**Percentage**
1. No	7	35
2. Yes: Life-threatening	2	10
3. Yes: Not life-threatening	9	45
4. Yes: Unanticipated surgery required	2	10
Error		
1. No	14	70
2. Yes: Life-threatening	1	5
3. Yes: Not life-threatening	3	15
4. Yes: Unanticipated surgery required	1	5
5. Yes: Heroic measures required	1	5
Doctor gives misleading information		
1. No	10	50
2. Yes: Always	2	10
3. Yes: Frequently	3	15
4. Yes: Infrequently	5	25
Doctor gives information late		
1. No	15	75
2. Yes: Always	0	0
3. Yes: Frequently	3	15
4. Yes: Infrequently	2	10
Doctor is accessible		
1. No: Will not return messages	5	25
2. No: Will not see patient in room	6	30
3. Yes: Primarily by telephone or e-mail	8	40
4. Yes: Primarily in person	1	5
Doctor name		
1. Brown	1	5
2. Green	15	75
3. Orange	2	10
4. Blue	1	5
5. Yellow	1	5

Doctor gives misleading information		Yes	No
	Green	8	7
	Brown	1	0
Doctors' Names	Orange	0	0
	Blue	1	0
	Yellow	0	1

FIGURE 9.8   A SAMPLE CROSS-TABULATION TABLE

YOUR RESPONSIBILITY IS . . .

■ To learn how to analyze information from documents, for that information is the best kind of evidence: It is extraordinarily difficult to refute evidence drawn from documents.

■ To learn how to use the Web effectively and efficiently to get information from records, documents and databases, for that skill is increasingly important and valued.[26]

■ To learn the steps in creating databases and to learn how to apply that knowledge to real records.

■ To learn how to analyze and interpret statistical results from real-world data analyses.

■ To know how to package stories, photographs, videos and graphics attractively so readers, viewers and listeners will want to know the results of systematic studies of records.

NOTES

1. The first article in the series is Alan C. Miller and Kevin Sack, "Far From Battlefield, Marines Lose One-Third of Harrier Fleet," *Los Angeles Times*, Dec. 15, 2002: A-1, 46–48.
2. "About This Series," *Los Angeles Times*, Dec. 15, 2002: A-48.
3. Kevin Sack and Alan C. Miller, "A Staggering Abundance of Crash-causing Glitches," *Los Angeles Times*, Dec. 16, 2002: A-1, 16–18, p. A-1.
4. "About This Series," p. A-48.
5. Some critics have charged that stories based on records and documents may be perceived by readers as not credible because journalists are personally involved in analyzing data. Some assert that personal involvement is inconsistent with the tenets of objective journalism. First, the argument that journalists who base stories on data they have analyzed are not using an objective approach is dubious because analyzing, collating and reporting

information is the essence of writing; data are just another kind of information. Second, at least one study suggests such stories are as credible as stories based on information from traditional sources. See Justin Mayo and Glenn Leshner, "Assessing the Credibility of Computer-assisted Reporting," *Newspaper Research Journal,* 21:4 (2000): 68–82.

6. Recent examples of stories based on records analyses are available from the Investigative Reporters and Editors site at <www.ire.org>. Look under "hot story." A useful archive also is available.

7. Paul N. Williams, "Boys Town: An Expose Without Bad Guys," *Columbia Journalism Review,* January/February 1975: 30–38.

8. Daniel Ari Kapner, "Infofacts Resources: Alcohol and Other Drugs on Campus—The Scope of the Problem," report of the Health Education Center for Alcohol and Other Drug Prevention, June 17, 2003. Downloaded on Nov. 24, 2003, from <www.edc.org/hec/pubs/factsheets/scope.html>.

9. For a discussion of the use of commercial databases in public relations, see Steven R. Thomsen, "Using Online Databases in Corporate Issues Management," *Public Relations Review,* 21:2 (1995): 103–122.

10. The Office of the Independent Counsel, "Referral to the United States House of Representatives Pursuant to Title 28, United States Code, § 595 (c)," Sept. 9, 1998. Downloaded on Jan. 9, 2003, from <thomas.loc.gov/icreport>.

11. Most search services offer many products (news, stock reports, chat rooms), one of which is a search engine that searches hundreds of online indexes in moments and lists for the user sites that have a high probability of containing information the user wants (Chapter 8). Lycos, a search service, uses a search engine called Pursuit. Barbara K. Kaye and Norman J. Medoff, *The World Wide Web: A Mass Communication Perspective* (Mountain View, Calif.: Mayfield, 1999): Chapter 2.

12. Nicole Gill, "Walter Reed Weighs Fate of Forest Glen Buildings," *The* (Baltimore) *Sun,* Jan. 20, 1998: B-8.

13. Radio and Television News Directors Foundation, *News in the Next Century: Wired Journalist: Newsroom Guide to the Internet,* 2nd ed. (Washington, D.C.: Author, 1996): 56–59.

14. Sabin Russell, Reynolds Holding and Elizabeth Fernandez, "Waiting for Shots: Pleas to Make Vaccine Available to the Frail and Elderly Were Ignored as Flu Season Approached," *San Francisco Chronicle,* Feb. 26, 2001: A-1, 8–9. Available at <www.sfgate.com/cgi-bin/article.cgi?file=/chronicle/archive/2001/02/26/MN159567.DTL>.

15. Vince Gonzales, "The Hidden Danger: Neglect," CBS News, Feb. 28, 2000. Downloaded on Feb. 10, 2003, from <www.cbsnews.com/stories/2000/02/28/eveningnews>.

16. Nancy Cook Lauer, "Incomes, Discarded Votes May Be Linked," *Tallahassee* (Fla.) *Democrat,* Dec. 3, 2000: A-1, 2.

17. Radio and Television News Directors Foundation, *News in the Next Century:* 70–71.

18. Ibid., pp. 71–72.

19. "How We Did It," *The* (Milwaukee) *Sunday Journal Sentinel,* June 18, 2000: A-22. Available at <www.jsonline.com/Alive/news/jun00/explainer18061700a.asp?>.

20. Dave Umhoefer, "Ticket Blitz Has Winners, Losers: Minorities, Poor Affected Most by Push for Peaceful Streets," *The* (Milwaukee) *Sunday Journal Sentinel,* June 18, 2000: A-1, 22. Available at <www.jsonline.com/news/qualityoflife/june00/main18061700.asp?>.

21. The first story in the *Tribune* series is Michael J. Berens, "Infection Epidemic Carves Deadly Path: Poor Hygiene, Overwhelmed Workers Contribute to Thousands of Deaths," *Chicago Tribune,* July 21, 2002: A-1, 14, 15.

22. John Dunbar, MaryJo Sylwester and Robert Moore, "States Used as a $263 Million Back Door for Soft Money," report of the Center for Public Integrity, 2002. Downloaded on Jan. 6, 2003, from <www.statesecrets.org/dtaweb/index.asp?L1=20&L2=9&L3=10&L4=0&L5>.

23. Kapner "Infofacts Resources."

24. Kimberly Hill, "CRM Special Report: In Praise of Customer Complaints," *CRMDaily.com,* April 4, 2002. Downloaded on January 12, 2003, from <www.crmdaily.com/pert/story/ 17098.html>; and Kathy Robertson, "Local Docs Generate Higher Complaint Rate," *Sacramento Business Journal,* Nov. 22, 2002: 3, 40. Available at <sacramento.bizjournals.com/ sacramento/stories/2002/11/25/story6.html>.

25. Andis Robeznieks, "Being Open May Avoid Lawsuits: Research Shows Poor Communication and Lack of Access Lead to Malpractice Claims," *amednews.com,* June 10, 2002. Downloaded on Jan. 12, 2003, from <www.ama-assn.org/sci-pubs/amnews/pick_02/prsb0610.htm>.

26. Michael Ryan, "Public Relations and the Web: Organizational Problems, Gender, and Institution Type," *Public Relations Review,* 29:3 (2003): 335–349; and Bruce Garrison, "Computer-assisted Reporting Near Complete Adoption," *Newspaper Research Journal,* 22:1 (2001): 65–79.

CHAPTER 10

INTERVIEWS

Preparation and Problems

If mass communicators were forced to give up all but one of their many information collection tools, they would vote to keep the one that's been around longest: the personal interview.

Newspaper journalists were the first mass communicators to see the value of the personal interview roughly 170 years ago, when they started publishing verbatim accounts of court testimony to bring to life the major characters in trials.[1] It wasn't long before journalists began using the same question-answer technique that judges and attorneys used in court and that police officers used in interrogations.

With the rise of the penny press during the mid-1830s, more Americans could afford newspapers, and publishers often used human interest stories to expand circulations. The interview was an excellent way to obtain the direct quotations that could make a news personality exciting and tangible. An example of how direct quotations were used roughly 120 years ago is an interview by a writer in *The New York Herald* with a possible witness (a student) to the murder of a woman in Hackettstown. Here is an excerpt about the student's multiple stories (the entire interview was in direct quotation marks):

"What have you to say in regard to your denial yesterday of the statement that you had seen sights too horrible to describe? What did you see?"

"I saw nothing that night. I never left my room after half past nine, or about that time, on the night of the murder."

"Did you see Titus [the man he had implicated earlier] on that night after the girl returned home, on the night that she was murdered?"

"No, I did not."

"Did you get out of bed and go down stairs on the night she was murdered?"

"No."

"Did you hear any cries?"

"No."

"Did you see the girl murdered?"

"No."

"Did you see Titus with the girl?"

"No; I did not."

"Did you know that she was being murdered?"

"No; I knew nothing about it. I saw nothing—heard nothing that gave me any clew [sic] to it. I knew nothing about it until the next morning, when the body was found."

"Then, I understand you to say that you did not see any murder committed nor anything done that might implicate Titus in the murder?"[2]

Modern readers would not see an extended direct quotation like this one in their morning newspapers, for conventions have changed. But the importance of the direct quotation and other information has not changed, and the personal interview remains an indispensable tool for all mass communicators. A journalist or public relations professional who can't conduct a competent personal interview will not be as successful as colleagues who can. This chapter should help readers develop their interviewing skills so that they can succeed.

PRE-INTERVIEW RESEARCH

Writers don't want to face editors—*any* editors—if they don't have the facts or don't understand the information they got from their sources. The risk can be particularly great for a public relations writer or broadcast journalist.

A writer who interviews the chief executive officer for the company newsletter and makes a poor impression because of poor interviewing skills—or lack of knowledge about the company—might be looking for a new job. A writer who is "Live at Five" doesn't want to be embarrassed before thousands of viewers when an anchor asks a question a source could have answered—if the reporter had only asked.

The key to a successful interview—to getting the "right" information—lies in advance preparation. The initial preparation begins in college. Students need to work hard to develop the body of knowledge that is required if they want to write successfully about land commissions or vacancies, interlocutory orders, the disabled or any complex group or topic. College students who study economics and politics, law and courts, state and municipal government, science and health, education and other relevant content areas (Chapter 15) are building useful bodies of knowledge.

Newspaper, magazine, public relations and online writers typically must update these bodies of knowledge immediately before interviews if the interviews are to succeed. Broadcast journalists typically do not have as much background material

A reporter interviews a University of Oregon athlete after his victory in an event at the Pac-10 Track and Field Championships at the University of Washington's Husky Stadium.

as other communicators do for two reasons: (1) They do not have the time to conduct extensive pre-interview research, and (2) they don't have enough air time to explore issues in depth, so they have less need for extensive background material.

However, broadcast journalists must recognize that good background material can mean the difference between a good interview and a poor one, even for a short story, and they should collect as much information as practical. The World Wide Web makes it possible to obtain much more background material than was the case only a few years ago (see chapters 8 and 9). Useful information can be obtained through a laptop computer as a broadcast writer travels to an interview (with someone else driving).

Advantages

Pre-interview preparation can help media writers in a number of ways:

- Preparation shows interviewees that the writer is serious about the subject.
- Interviewers need not waste time asking for information obtained during prior research, so they can focus on more important matters. If the writer has read about the interviewee beforehand, for instance, he or she doesn't need to spend time seeking biographical or background information.
- Preparation often suggests important questions that a writer might not raise otherwise.

CLAUDIA DREIFUS ON INTERVIEW PREPARATION

Whether or not the interview will succeed will very much depend on the chemistry between the subject and the interviewer. That, in turn, depends on the level of preparation. An actor needs to know his lines, understand the motivation of his and the other characters. An interviewer needs to know all that is possible about the interviewee—through Nexis, books, clips, interviews with friends and relatives—before he or she ever turns on the tape recorder. Whenever I feel anxious about a particular interview, I combat my fears with aerobic research.

Even the toughest subjects will respond warmly to a well-prepared interviewer. The fact that I have confidence in my material makes me a strong questioner. Interviewing can be a bit like an intellectual boxing match. One had better enter the ring in top shape. ...

At the same time, the interviewer must be willing to be astonished. It is useful to come in with a line of questions and a rehearsed plan but it is important not to hold rigidly to it. If this is a play, it is an improvisational one. And just like in acting, the interviewer must be able to listen, to go with what is heard, to change course mid-interview.

Source: Claudia Dreifus, *Interview* (New York: Seven Stories, 1997): XX.

Claudia Dreifus' interviews have appeared regularly in *The New York Times* for more than a decade. She is the author of *Interview*.

- A writer who is not ignorant of the subject matter cannot be manipulated as easily by an unscrupulous or overzealous source. Public relations writers seldom run into sources who try to manipulate them, but sources might do so unconsciously. A writer needs to see gaps or inaccuracies in a chief executive officer's information before he or she talks to a journalist and before a writer distributes a news release that later embarrasses everyone.

- A well-prepared writer can recognize a significant statement or bit of information during an interview, a point the writer might miss if he or she is not so well prepared.

- The information gleaned from pre-interview research can be used to put an interviewee at ease (by briefly discussing a topic in which he or she has great interest). It can also be used by a writer who needs to decide whether to be tough, kind or sympathetic during the interview. (See also the box "Claudia Dreifus on Interview Preparation.")

Plenty of information is available as a writer prepares for an interview. A large number of sources are available on the Web (Chapter 8), in printed form in a newsroom or from a company librarian, from the public library and—sometimes—from local, state and federal agencies (Chapter 9).

A writer who wants to know about Lou Gehrig's disease for a story about Stephen Hawking, for instance, could use the Yahoo! search engine. One can type *lou gehrig's disease* into the box on the Yahoo! home page and get a list of nearly 37,000 sites, one of which is that of the ALS Association. From that organization, one can learn all about Lou Gehrig's disease, including its scientific name (amyotrophic lateral sclerosis). Perhaps most important, one can get contact information about those researching ALS. For local information, writers typically visit the archives sections of their newspapers, broadcast news Web sites, corporations or other organizations.

Public relations professionals can be important sources of advance information for journalists about an interviewee or topic. Those who want to have good relations with the news media are as helpful as they possibly can be when journalists seek to interview sources within their organizations.

Lack of preparation is inexcusable in these days of instant access to libraries and resources around the world. Indeed, the problem may be one of information overload. But that is a far better problem than having too little information. An interviewer may be justified in *not* preparing for an upcoming interview only when deadline pressures are extreme or when he or she already knows about the interviewee and the content (for example, a broadcast reporter on a *beat* or a magazine journalist who is writing in an area of special expertise).

Know the Source

The news media have been criticized, rightly, for focusing too much on such official and quasi-official sources as government bureaucrats, corporate leaders, committee chairs, elected officials or professionals (Chapter 1). This means those who exercise political, social, economic or cultural power are seldom challenged and that those who have no power typically are not heard.[3] A constant reliance on such sources makes it difficult if not impossible for communicators to describe reality fairly and with reasonable accuracy.[4]

Excessive reliance on official and quasi-official sources can undermine media credibility, turn marginalized groups away from the news media, lead to inaccurate media reports, strengthen those who wield power unwisely and militate against meaningful political, social, economic and cultural change.

But good writers do not rely exclusively on official or quasi-official sources. They try always to seek sources who are knowledgeable about the topic and have something worthwhile to say and to avoid those who merely have opinions about the topic. They also seek those who exercise power over others through their official or quasi-official positions, as well as those who may be marginalized as others exercise power over their own professional, personal or civic lives.[5]

The task is not always easy. Not all sources, particularly unofficial sources, are willing to talk or have time to talk to writers working against deadlines. It's often difficult to cut through a source's political, cultural, religious, economic or social ideology to find the truth. And it's not always easy to determine who a community leader is. The black community, for example, does not always agree about who its representatives are. Some black people argue that the Rev. Al Sharpton does not speak for their community, while others argue that he does.[6] Anyone—journalist or not—would find that situation confusing.

Public relations professionals should not assume the admonition to interview sources who represent a wide range of information and views applies to everyone but them. They must interview many sources within their organizations, not just the chief executive officer and other high officials. It is good to interview the chief executive officer about a new electric switching system, but it adds credibility and interest to a newsletter if the public relations writer interviews the engineer in charge of installing it and, perhaps, technicians who must make it work. Interviewing rank-and-file workers makes them feel part of the organization and shows that the organization is interested in their views.

Public relations professionals also must recognize they may work for the very official and quasi-official sources the critics of journalism abhor. They need not apologize for this, for the official and quasi-official sources have every right to be heard. And they need not suggest to inquiring journalists that some unofficial sources should be consulted.

However, public relations writers must understand that a good journalist will talk to unofficial sources, who often have views that are contrary to those of their organizations, and they should explain to their bosses that this is sound journalistic practice. One implication is that they need to know what the critics of their organizations are saying and to seek ways to respond meaningfully to those critics.

Planning Questions

After a writer learns as much as possible about the interviewee and topic, he or she should formulate questions carefully, as the success or failure of the interview will depend on the questions and how they are asked.

Writers must obtain specific information about their sources so they can tell their audiences why the sources are qualified to speak about the topic and why they should be believed. Occasionally, a source's credibility is self-evident. It's not necessary to tell much about a chief operating officer or the town mayor. People know who they are.

A writer needs to learn the correct name and title of most sources; the nature of the subject's work if the title doesn't make that clear—and for whom, precisely, the source works. An audience needs to know, for example, whether the source is an official who makes policy or a bureaucrat who implements policies made by others. If the story is a magazine profile about a personality in a large nonprofit agency, readers will want to know where that person "fits" in the organization. News consumers need to know precisely who a source is so they can assign credibility and assess responsibility.

Interviewers also must plan questions that will elicit interesting and important quotations that *show* what a source is thinking or feeling, for these quotations can make a good story an outstanding story. This is particularly important for broadcast journalists, for they must try to show the personal emotion of their sources. An example was coverage of the terrorist attacks against the World Trade Center. Broadcast journalists could show the emotion of the survivors in ways that print journalists never could. Planning questions that will induce the interviewee to show that emotion is frequently a major challenge for broadcast interviewers.[7]

Phrasing Questions

A communicator who carefully plans an interview thinks about how questions should be phrased, for the phrasing can be crucial. That aspect of question planning never should be ignored.

A journalist, for example, might hear conflicting reports about the cost of a house constructed for a public official who is paid $35,000 a year. The official might claim the house cost $90,000, while others might say the house cost $325,000, a high price for a $35,000-a-year employee. To find the best estimate, the reporter might consult a building contractor.

A writer who prepares questions before an interview recognizes the inadequacy of a question such as "How much did it cost to build that house?" The journalist should ask, "As a building contractor, you've constructed many houses, and you know approximately how much it costs to build certain kinds of homes. How much would you say it would cost to construct a home similar to that one? Can you tell me the average price per square foot of homes in this area?"

The writer has thought ahead and realized that the contractor probably wouldn't know how much the public official's house cost and would refuse to speculate. But the writer has placed the contractor in the role of an expert and asked how much it would cost to build a similar house. That question should get a response.

Or a writer who is preparing one of those news releases about the appointment of a new corporate executive needs to phrase questions in ways that will elicit responses that make the executive seem human and interesting. The writer could ask, "Are you going to do anything new as the head of operations?" And he or she would probably get something like "I don't know," or "Not much—but don't put that in the release."

Instead, the writer might phrase the question in a different way: "The company's talked for several years about upgrading a three-year old, and probably obsolete, computer system. We've talked about hardware and software purchases that would allow us to link the 29,000 computers in our offices around the world. Do you plan to work on upgrading our system?"

ELIJAH GOSIER ON INTEGRATING WRITING AND RESEARCH

I have always been uncomfortable with the notion that journalists dissect their job into two separate functions, reporting and writing.

My discomfort, I think, hinges on the fact that too often the reporter gathers bland facts, most of them by phone, and then the writer, more by turn of phrase than by understanding (or feel) for the material, sits down to make of them something worth reading.

We rarely bring personalities back in our notebooks. We bring "talking heads" and the quotes that will fit in here or there, often as much for typographic aesthetics as for understanding.

That tendency assures that news will continue to be a throwaway item, and that readers will keep looking to media that give them more than just the bland facts.

We tell our readers what happened and who did it, but we don't give them the reasons it happened. And for good reason: We often don't have enough understanding ourselves. We don't know the people well enough. ...

That means that the feelings surrounding an issue should be observed as surely as the brass tacks of it. That means the reporter should have as good an understanding of why something is happening as he or she does of when and where it's happening.

The reporter should know who is being affected and to what extent. ...

Source: "What Our Real Journalists Learned," *Ways With Words: A Research Report of the Literacy Committee* (Reston, Va.: American Society of Newspaper Editors, 1993): 26–31, pp. 28–29.

Elijah Gosier is a city desk reporter and columnist at the *St. Petersburg* (Fla.) *Times*. This selection appeared originally in *Ways with Words*, which describes an experiment in which some of the *Times'* writers wrote four different stories about the same event. Stories were written in four modes, including inverted pyramid and narrative formats.

This question will elicit more than a "yes" or "no" response, and the release would not be just another boring new-executive-appointed story. It might well get published widely exactly as written, for it would be newsworthy and interesting. (See also the box "Elijah Gosier on Integrating Writing and Research.")

Broadcast journalists have another reason for phrasing questions carefully. They often are on camera with their sources, so their colleagues, competitors and bosses—not to mention thousands of listeners—may hear their questions. They certainly don't want to appear unprofessional or incompetent, although many do. This public exposure of the questions they ask is becoming increasingly common for other interviewers as well, as their interviews are posted on the Web.

DIRECTIVE VERSUS NONDIRECTIVE INTERVIEWS

Interviewers, particularly novices, often are perplexed about whether to ask broad, general questions that get interviewees talking or narrow questions that elicit specific information. The decision depends primarily on what kind of information is needed and on whether the interview is directive or nondirective.

Directive Approach

In a purely directive interview, a communicator consistently asks specific questions and follows up on evasive or incomplete answers with still more specific questions. The directive interviewer also may comment on or evaluate responses and provide information to the source.

A disadvantage of the directive approach is that the source is influenced by the interviewer. The questions can suggest answers to the interviewee in ways that inhibit communication or produce distorted or inaccurate information. For example, a source may focus on the suggested answer and not think it is important to volunteer additional, important information. Narrow questions also may discourage the source from addressing new and fruitful issues.

A subject who sees that a communicator approves a view he or she has expressed may well elaborate on or overemphasize that view while withholding or even denying information that conflicts with or refutes it. On the other hand, a source who sees that a communicator disapproves a view may stop the interview, refuse to discuss the topic or de-emphasize that view.[8] Either result is bad because the story could be distorted and inaccurate.

The directive approach can cause interviews to become so formal an effective rapport cannot be established with sources. Most people respond best when they are treated warmly and informally, and an extremely businesslike approach—in which the reporter comes in, gets the information and leaves—can be a turnoff. It is difficult to get the quotations needed to make a report or release both credible and interesting if a subject is not responsive. Unresponsive sources are particularly disruptive in broadcast news, for they can absolutely ruin a report.

That's not to say, certainly, that an interviewer can never establish rapport or motivate someone to speak freely during a directive interview. Many trial lawyers use directive techniques to coax information from witnesses.[9] For example, it is sometimes useful for a lawyer who is questioning a nervous or embarrassed witness to help the respondent along by first asking questions that are easy to answer and by keeping the pace slow and deliberate. The specificity of the questions, since they concern matters that can be readily verbalized, puts the witness at ease.

In some situations, furthermore, rapport is not necessarily desirable. If an interviewee is hostile, a tough, directive interview—in which no effort is made to put the source at ease—is appropriate.

The choice of directive techniques used depends on whether the subject is hostile or cooperative. But, whichever approach is used, the first part of the interview typically is most crucial. The way in which the initial questions are asked and the content of those questions can set the tone for the entire interview. Careful planning is vital. When the directive interview is well-planned, it can be exceptionally effective.

The greatest advantage of the directive interview is that it can be conducted quickly and efficiently, and the interviewer is in control throughout, which is why most broadcast journalists rely almost exclusively on the directive approach. When a subject seems to be lying, an interviewer can bring up facts that were checked with another source (but without directly stating the suspicion that the source is lying) or other information that indicates the source's statements are untrue. An interviewer taking the purely nondirective approach would be less comfortable making such statements.

Nondirective Approach

In a purely nondirective interview, a writer avoids the kinds of specific questions that are the foundation for the directive interview. He or she rarely comments on or evaluates statements and seldom provides information to the interviewee. The nondirective interviewer encourages the source to talk freely by establishing good rapport and by showing sympathy for and understanding of what is being said.

A major disadvantage of the nondirective interview is that it can require substantially more time. A busy writer does not have the time to listen to an interviewee—even the chief executive officer he or she is interviewing for the annual report—talk about matters not relevant to the report. And few broadcast journalists can afford to spend two hours with a single source for a single report.

The nondirective approach places the control of the interview where it shouldn't be—in the hands of the source. An interviewer who uses the nondirective approach has little recourse when a subject is lying because a nondirective approach means by definition that the interviewer doesn't antagonize a source by asking tough questions. An interviewer using the nondirective approach must create an atmosphere of warmth and trust to lead a source to respond truthfully, but the potential for a source to intentionally mislead and misinform is greater in a nondirective interview.

This is not necessarily a disadvantage in public relations, where a writer should expect the interviewee will *not* lie. In a rare case, an internal source for text that will be posted on the company Web site may say that some information simply will *not* be released—and it is not, for that is not the writer's decision. The writer can make a case for disclosure—and even take the case to the highest organizational levels—but if he or she is told information will not be forthcoming, or must not be posted, it will not be. And the interview goes on. The real disadvantage of the nondirective interview for the public relations professional likely is time lost listening to rambling responses.

The greatest advantage of the nondirective approach is that it makes an interview seem informal, warm, friendly and less businesslike. A subject is encouraged to respond openly and freely and is less influenced by an interviewer (1) to provide only the information the interviewer wants or (2) to discuss only those areas (areas that may be less important than others) in which the writer appears interested.

An interviewer often obtains more and better information by simply listening than by forcing the interview in a single direction. This is nearly always the best way to get those compelling, interesting direct quotations that help the good writer or producer *show* someone's personality.

The nondirective approach is perfect for Web and public relations writers, who often can devote considerable time to interviews. While journalists, particularly broadcast reporters, have to discard much of their information, Web and public relations writers often do not. They can put the most compelling, important and interesting quotations on a main page and then use hyperlinks to direct the audience to pages that report more of the interview. And in fact, as more news organizations are finding ways to use Web sites, and as video streaming becomes more common, even print journalists are finding more of their material is used.

Combining Approaches

A writer rarely uses only a directive or a nondirective interview technique. It is best to combine the two, to get the straight, unadorned facts and then some general statements and opinions.

In preparing for an interview, media professionals typically plan both general and specific questions. They begin with the broad, nondirective questions that can be used to put the source at ease and to elicit complete responses. Such questions often turn up unanticipated, fruitful information (and sometimes ideas for other stories).

Writers proceed from the broad questions to specific questions designed to clear up any ambiguous or superficial responses to the nondirective questions. Journalists (but not public relations professionals) may ask "explosive" questions at this point.

The most effective mix of general and specific questions depends on the topic and on the medium. A Web writer who is assigned to write a personality sketch about a local celebrity or a high corporate official may use a mix of questions that is different from that of the broadcast journalist who is assigned to the same story.

Both writers seek interesting, but rather subjective, information about the source's attitudes, opinions and general outlook on life to make the subject appealing. But the Web writer is likely to ask more general questions than specific questions to motivate the source to talk freely and openly, simply because he or she has more space (or links)—and possibly more time to devote to an interview.

JAMES KILPATRICK ON WATCHING *INTENTLY*

This is the first secret of good writing: We must look *intently*, and hear *intently*, and taste *intently*. ... [We] must look at everything *very hard*. Is it the task at hand to describe a snowfall? Very well. We begin by observing that the snow is white. Is it as white as bond paper? White as whipped cream? Is the snow daisy white, or eggwhite white, or whitewash white? Let us look very hard. We will see that snow comes in different textures. The light snow that looks like powered sugar is not the heavy snow that clings like wet cotton. When we write matter-of-factly that *Last night it snowed and this morning the fields were white*, we haven't said much. We have not looked *intently*.

Source: James J. Kilpatrick, *The Writer's Art* (Kansas City, Kan.: Andrews, McMeel & Parker, 1984): 43.

A writer who merely tells *what happens will say, "It snowed last night at Rockefeller Center in New York." A writer who* shows *what happens will describe the look, feel and consistency of the snow.*

James J. Kilpatrick, author of several books and a popular opinion column, was, like many journalists, devoted to excellent writing.

The broadcast journalist, who has far less time and little space, will ask significantly fewer general questions. The broadcast journalist simply cannot use much of the material gathered from responses to broad questions, and he or she seldom has time for long interviews. This situation is changing rapidly, of course, as broadcast journalists start to post information on Web sites.

WRITTEN QUESTIONS

If a student were to ask professional communicators whether an interviewer should take written questions to interviews, he or she would probably get a split vote. Half probably would say yes, and half would say no. Even those who say yes likely are not suggesting that *every* question be written down, however, for the reasons listed below. Professional writers, with their experience and extensive background knowledge, have less need for written questions. A novice is well-advised to take a comprehensive list of questions to interviews—at least until he or she is comfortable with the process.

Advantages

The best reason for taking written questions to an interview is that they help ensure that all important questions are asked and that responses are obtained. Many interviewees skip from topic to topic, and questions can be checked off as they are answered. Writing questions also forces interviewers to think about the best ways to phrase queries and to identify potential follow-up questions.

Written questions also can impress the source; they make it clear that the writer has thought about the interview and considers it important. A source might give more time to the interview and respond more openly and completely to all questions.

Disadvantages

Sometimes an interviewer concentrates too hard on getting answers to prepared questions and fails to recognize the importance of off-the-cuff comments, which sometimes provide more productive information than answers to the prepared questions. A chief executive officer might mention plans to open a new branch in London, for example, and that information could make a report much more interesting to a Web site's visitors.

Prepared questions also can distract a source or make it difficult to establish the rapport that is so important to most interviews. A news source might begin staring at a list of prepared questions to determine how many questions remain or be insulted that an interviewer has to consult a list before asking a question. A source might get the impression that a writer seems more interested in obtaining answers to prepared questions than in listening carefully. A good interview flows smoothly and naturally; prepared questions can get in the way of this process.

Writers can get around these problems, to some extent, by writing questions on the last pages of their notebooks. They can locate them quickly during interviews and, since they are constantly writing or doodling anyway, the subject is unlikely to notice when they refer to them.

ELUSIVE QUESTIONS

Even an experienced interviewer occasionally is stuck for questions when an information source is particularly difficult or when he or she has been forced by time pressures to go to an interview without adequate preparation. A writer caught in a difficult situation can rely on two formulas for asking questions. One is the five W's and H; the other is the GOSS formula.

Five W's and H

A good interviewer always asks who, what, where, when, why and how. A broadcast journalist who knows only that bids for a highway construction project have been opened might ask the following questions, for example:

- Who submitted the lowest bid? Who was awarded the construction contract? Who else submitted bids? Who established specifications for the project? Who opened the bids? Who decided which bid to accept? Who was in a position to exert influence to help the winner get the bid? Who will benefit financially from this project? Who has to pay for faulty design or construction?

- What is the exact nature of the project for which bids were requested? What was the amount of the accepted bid? What were the amounts of all other bids? What were the specifications for the project? What bidders met the *exact* specifications, and were the specifications drawn so that only one bidder could meet them? What penalties will be imposed if deadlines are not met?

- Where will the highway be located? Where were bids opened? Where were the alternative routes?

- When will construction begin? When will construction be completed? When were bids opened?

- Why is the construction needed? Why won't existing highways handle the traffic volume? Why does the highway follow the route planned and not some other route? Why did some companies fail to bid? Why was there wide variation among bid amounts?

- How will the road be constructed (anything unusual)? How was the contractor able to underbid everyone else (what will be left out of the project that others would have put in)? How will officials ensure the project is completed on time?

GOSS Formula

The GOSS formula is not a prescription for all interview situations.[10] It is, instead, a formula that an interviewer might use when stumped for questions (Figure 10.1).

A Web writer who learned of the bid opening but knew nothing about the proposed highway construction project might use the GOSS formula to ask such questions as these:

- What is the *goal* of the construction project? What is to be accomplished? Is the *goal* to have a better traffic flow? Is the goal to provide public works jobs? Is the *goal* to enrich someone's friend or sister-in-law?

- Did any *obstacles* have to be overcome before this project could be gotten under way? Were funds short? Were there condemnation proceedings? Was there opposition from any group? What were the group's objections? Will any *obstacles* need to be overcome by the contractor before the highway can be completed?

FIGURE 10.1   THE GOSS FORMULA

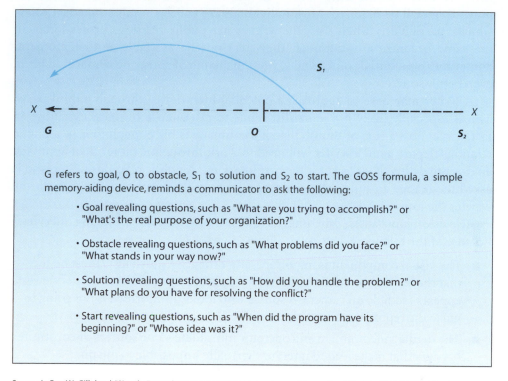

G refers to goal, O to obstacle, S_1 to solution and S_2 to start. The GOSS formula, a simple memory-aiding device, reminds a communicator to ask the following:

- Goal revealing questions, such as "What are you trying to accomplish?" or "What's the real purpose of your organization?"

- Obstacle revealing questions, such as "What problems did you face?" or "What stands in your way now?"

- Solution revealing questions, such as "How did you handle the problem?" or "What plans do you have for resolving the conflict?"

- Start revealing questions, such as "When did the program have its beginning?" or "Whose idea was it?"

Source: LaRue W. Gilleland, "Simple Formula Proves Helpful to Interviewers," *Journalism Educator,* 26:2 (1971): 19–20.

■ What was the *solution* to the problem that arose before bids were requested? What was the *solution* to the fund shortage, to the condemnation proceedings or the opposition by the organized group? How will the contractor *solve* the problem that could delay construction? Does the contractor already have a *solution* in mind?

■ Who *started* the idea that the construction project was needed in the first place? Who *started* the idea that the project might be a bad thing? When will construction get *started*?

Neither formula is a substitute for adequate pre-interview preparation, and neither should be used as a crutch. Writers who use either the five W's and H or the GOSS formula to help them prepare questions for all their stories write formula stories that sound alike and that may be shallow and full of unanswered questions. Formulas should not be used as substitutes for thought.

THE INTERVIEW

After a writer is familiar with the source and the topic and has prepared appropriate questions, it is time to arrange for an interview. Typically, one asks personally, writes to or telephones the potential interviewee. The source needs to know who the writer is, the interview topic, why he or she was contacted and how much time will be required. Most individuals are willing to talk to media professionals, particularly when they, the writers, are public relations professionals in the same organization, although they may not be available at that moment. Sometimes a potential source will suggest the name of someone who would be an even better source.

A writer may have to approach a potential interviewee through a third party. This is especially likely if a journalist wants to interview a business executive. In fact, it is almost a rule of thumb that, if a company is big enough to have a public relations department, a writer will need to work through it rather than approach an executive directly, at least for the first interview. A public relations writer who is asked to arrange an interview would be wise to make every effort to smooth the way for the journalist.

Television journalists sometimes have a bit more difficulty arranging interviews because of the following factors:

- The visual component is important, and broadcast journalists must be sure that the background for an interview is appropriate and that the interviewee appears credible on camera. A source who looks uninformed is not going to make the report seem credible.

- The digital video camera and operator intimidate some sources or constitute barriers that make a good interview virtually impossible to obtain.

Getting Started

Interpersonal relationships are most successful when conducted informally, even in interviews. It often is a good idea to open an interview with a brief discussion of a subject in which the source is particularly interested. If the source is interested in sports and the local team has won a big game, a mention of that might break the ice. A writer who is interviewing a college student who has a huge picture of the school's mascot on the wall might talk *briefly* about that. The initial connection often is critical.

Interviewers must remember, however, that busy schedules dictate that they get to business as quickly as courtesy allows. Idle chatter should be quickly replaced with general questions. Public relations writers are unlikely to impress their chief executive officers if they spend an inordinate amount of time talking about his or her view from the 51st floor. And an overworked government bureaucrat may become impatient with a journalist who doesn't get to the point fairly quickly.

Conversation and general questions serve two purposes: They put an interviewee at ease, and they give an interviewer time to analyze the source to determine whether the approach should be altered in any way. A source who is nervous, preoccupied or seems reluctant to talk might be hiding something. Or the source might simply be unsure, inarticulate or in a hurry. Different behavior patterns can demand entirely different approaches to interviews.

One way to determine whether a source is telling the truth is to ask a question to which the writer knows the answer. If the interviewee tries to mislead, the interviewer can cite a document, prior statements or information from other sources that contradict what the source is saying. That approach can cause a source to answer truthfully or to simply issue a damaging "no comment."

A media professional typically must avoid intimidating or offensive questions at the beginning of an interview. If such questions are asked immediately, he or she risks being thrown from the source's office (a good story in itself) and obtaining none of the information needed for the original story. Tough questions usually are deferred until near the end of the interview.

An exception is the elephant in the middle of the room, which cannot be ignored for long. This is the huge question that everyone knows is coming. If the mayor is charged with beating her husband that morning, a journalist's first question is not going to be about the city's traffic problems. The journalist knows it and the mayor knows it. Get to it.

A public relations writer needs to ask that intimidating or offensive question so that the executive is prepared when he or she is asked the same question by a journalist. But it's a good idea to ask tactfully and at the end of the interview—and to explain why it's necessary to ask the question.

Listening Carefully

A good interviewer listens carefully to everything the source says and makes every effort to understand the meaning of every statement. As one learns to listen attentively, one almost always has to break firmly entrenched, bad habits. Most people simply do not hear or understand what their friends, colleagues, acquaintances and families are saying. The reasons why human beings don't listen are exceptionally complex and have been studied extensively. Theorists offer three reasons:[11]

- Selective exposure, which means one listens only to messages that are of interest and importance and that are consistent with one's preconceptions and fundamental beliefs
- Selective perception, which means one perceives only those parts of a message that one approves or that one can use
- Selective retention, which means one is likely to retain only that information that supports one's views

Individuals who think binge drinking is not a problem on college campuses, for example, likely will not expose themselves to the evidence suggesting binge drinking is a major, dangerous problem. If they hear a debate that presents both sides of the problem, they may selectively perceive only those parts that support their views. And they may remember only those arguments that support their views.

Similarly, in conversations with friends, family, acquaintances and colleagues, many people ignore much of what other people say because they find most of it to be unimportant or uninteresting. They may also ignore others because they are thinking about what they will say to their friends—to make themselves look good or to get people to do things that they want them to do.

All of these things hinder good listening, and writers who want to be successful must overcome entire lifetimes of bad listening habits. This means interviewers must focus carefully on what their subjects say and not focus so much on taking notes that they miss the gist of the conversation. Nor should they try to think of dazzling questions that will make them look good to the interviewees or try to think of arguments to refute what interviewees say.

An interviewer must learn to observe nonverbal clues to a source's hidden thoughts, reactions and feelings. While this is exceptionally difficult and requires considerable experience, a writer can learn to recognize the frown, groan, wink or nod that belies the spoken word, that indicates a source's words don't necessarily correspond to his or her true feelings or that suggests the subject is trying to manipulate words or behavior so the interviewer will reach a false conclusion.[12]

Blatant deception is not very common in media interviews, for most interviewees would gain nothing from deceit. But a good interviewer is alert for deception—frequently manifested by nonverbal cues—particularly when a source could benefit from the dissemination of information he or she gives. A suspicious interviewer must ask more probing, pointed questions when a source appears to be lying or hiding something.

Good listening technique requires that an interviewer be willing to depart from prepared questions to explore ground not considered important before the interview. It's always possible to return to that prepared question, but a lost opportunity to explore potentially fruitful ground might not be regained.

Finally, a successful interviewer avoids the natural inclination to decide what a source has said *before the source says it*. Anticipating an answer can lead to poor comprehension, because people respond to what they *think* they hear or *expect* to hear, and not to what they *do* hear. Expectations about what an individual will say are based on all sorts of factors: dress, age, diction, gender, education, race, what "similar" people say, what the source said in the past, family ties, occupation and many other real or imagined attributes. Individuals may think they know a source after they have classified and stereotyped him or her and then they stop listening carefully. This is a mistake. This is a mark of a poor interviewer.[13]

This is not the same as anticipating responses as one prepares questions for an interview. In that instance, an interviewer may anticipate two or four or six possible responses, for example, and will have a question prepared for each possibility. Further, he or she will be alert during the interview to the unexpected response.

Requesting Information

An interviewer must be prepared at any point to ask clarifying questions when a subject makes ambiguous or questionable statements; to request correct spellings of all names; and to request verification by the source of important numbers and

A CAVEAT FOR BROADCAST INTERVIEWERS

The interviewing principles discussed in this chapter apply to all media professionals under most circumstances. Exceptions to these principles typically are found in broadcast interviews. We have tried to highlight some of these exceptions in the text, but we will repeat a few of them here so they will not be missed. Broadcast writers are prepared for an interview when they do the following:[14]

- Make sure their batteries are charged and their equipment is functioning well.

- Prepare their questions with greater care than most writers because they seldom have time for the kinds of long, rambling interviews their print colleagues conduct.

- Make sure they have a firm handle on the story. They need to think carefully about the message they wish to convey to their audience, for they may have only one shot at an interview.

- Make sure they get accurate, relevant, interesting, important sound bites—or actualities (verbal direct quotes that are aired)—that will add to the quality and credibility of a story. The criteria for good sound bites on television and radio are the same as for effective direct quotes in print—except that the visual dimension can be more important in broadcast news.

- Think about the backdrop. A writer should not interview someone in front of an ugly stone wall if a beautiful forest is available. Public relations professionals sometimes can suggest good locations for broadcast interviews with their bosses.

- Ensure that no irritating noises will interfere with the sound quality. Some noises may add to the story, as in the barking of dogs at a pet show, but most don't.

other facts. Accuracy is paramount, and a writer must not be too timid to ask questions, even when they seem trivial.

An interviewer sometimes can spend a great deal of time with a source and realize near the end of the interview that there isn't sufficient information for a story. Some communicators simply report back to their editors that they have nothing to write, a cardinal sin. Others ask the source to suggest areas or topics that are more interesting or important than those areas already discussed. Sometimes such questions, particularly by public relations writers, reveal topics that are more important and interesting than the original topic.

Again, of course, such a question cannot be put to all sources. Some might take the opportunity to use the writer for selfish purposes. Interviewers soon learn to make that judgment.

RECORDING INFORMATION

One of the more difficult tasks confronting inexperienced interviewers is the recording of information obtained during interviews. Each of the three means of recording information—memory, note taking and tape recording—presents its own problems.

Memory

An interviewer who is gifted with a photographic memory is safe in trusting to memory much of the information obtained during an interview. But most individuals don't have photographic memories. Someone with a poor memory who tries to remember the important details of an interview is increasing the probability of error.

An advantage of memorizing information is that those who don't take notes are able to concentrate more carefully on what a speaker says and almost certainly are less prone to distortion. However, those who don't take notes are more likely to omit useful facts than are those who take notes.

In some cases, an interviewer cannot take notes. If, for example, a subject is nervous and is likely to stop the interview the moment a notepad appears, notes should not be taken. It is better to trust the information to memory than not to get it at all. In such cases, an interviewer should sit down immediately after leaving the source and write down all the important facts and statements obtained.

Note Taking

Most interviewers take copious notes, and most of the rest take at least some notes because they cannot remember important facts and statements as they write their reports—sometimes hours after interviews. Many professionals also write several reports a day, and it would be easy to intermingle facts, figures and statements from one report to another. The taking of good notes clearly enhances accuracy.

One problem is that the appearance of a notebook may cause some sources to become uncomfortable, particularly if they are not accustomed to being interviewed. This problem is rare, but it is important to recognize the possibility.

A more serious problem is that note-takers can distort information because they concentrate *too* hard on their notes and miss the larger context of the topic they are researching, or they miss a critical detail as they are writing down other information. A good interviewer avoids concentrating too much on note taking and too little on content.

Finally, interviewers who leave virtually nothing to memory and attempt to write down essentially everything said in an interview sometimes face the problem of searching frantically through their notes, often under severe deadline pressure, for important information.

Solutions

One solution to the note-taker's dilemma is differential note taking. That is, an interviewer writes only the most crucial information and trusts to memory material that is less important.[15] Only key words, key phrases and all names, addresses and figures are written down during the interview to jog the interviewer's memory later. An interviewer who uses this selective method, however, should recognize two possible difficulties:

- Those who don't take any notes tend to omit more information than do those who do take notes; this problem could apply as well to those who take notes selectively.

- A writer who takes only a few notes is, in effect, telling a source, in nonverbal language, what he or she thinks is important. Differential note taking could influence a source to elaborate on an unimportant point (because an interviewer wrote it down) and de-emphasize a relatively important point (because the interviewer didn't write it down).

Another realistic solution to the problem of note taking is shorthand or speed writing.

Tape Recorders

Recorders are routinely used during interviews, although some interviewers cite some disadvantages:

- They can make interviewers less attentive because they don't have to be actively involved in the interview through note taking. Writers who know they can listen to the conversation later might be less attentive the first time.

- A recorder can interrupt a subject's train of thought if the interviewer is constantly fiddling with the machine or if the tape runs out at the wrong time (see the box "Get the Right Tape Recorder").

- Recorders may fail, leaving media writers without the information they thought they had.

- The very presence of a tape recorder can make some subjects uncomfortable, which is usually, but not always, a bad thing.

Tape recorders, however, can be quite beneficial if used skillfully:

- The interviewer who doesn't have to devote a great deal of energy and attention to note taking can maintain eye contact with a subject and listen attentively to what the person says.

- Questions about the accuracy of quotations and other information seldom are raised when an interview is recorded. A source can't complain that the interviewer used incorrect or incomplete quotations when they are on tape (unless of course the source was inaccurately quoted).

GET THE RIGHT TAPE RECORDER

Interviewers can use tape recorders effectively, if the recorders have the right features. The recorder should be a small cassette type that can run on either batteries or household current and that has a built-in microphone, digital counter and remote microphone. The tape also should be clearly visible (the door should not be too dark or too small), and the control buttons should be located near the door.

A small recorder is unobtrusive in an interview, and it isn't too heavy to lug around all day. A microphone built into the tape recorder is important so that an interviewer doesn't have to cram a remote microphone into sources' faces, making people uncomfortable. A writer really doesn't want to make his or her chief executive officer or crucial source uncomfortable.

The remote microphone is important when the room in which an interview is conducted is so crowded and noisy that it is difficult for a built-in microphone to pick up conversation clearly. A digital counter helps a user keep track during an interview of those points at which important information is discussed. When writing a report or seeking actualities later, the interviewer simply checks the notebook, uses "fast forward" or "reverse" and has the relevant information available in a few moments. The difficult task of searching an entire tape for information is eliminated.

Finally, the tape must be clearly visible at a distance of six to eight feet so the interviewer will know if the tape stops.

It is important to know if and when the tape stops so that the writer can take more notes.

An interviewer should not ask whether the source objects to having an interview recorded. A tape recorder is like a notebook; no writer would ask permission to use a notebook. If the subject objects, the writer can give good reasons for recording the interview, but if the source insists that the interview not be recorded, an interviewer has little alternative but to respect those wishes.

A tape recorder must be sufficiently sophisticated that it isn't necessary to place a microphone in a subject's mouth to obtain a clear, fully audible tape. A source can rightly feel offended by a writer who jams a microphone too close and persists in leaving it there.

Interviewers should avoid flipping tapes when that would interrupt a source. When approximately three-fourths of the first side is used, an interviewer should watch for a natural break in the conversation and flip the tape before the reel runs out. Nothing is lost by this procedure, and a source's concentration is not broken.

Recorders are electronic devices and as such are subject to breakdown. Interviewers should note important figures, names, addresses and similar material mentioned by a source, in the event the machine does falter.

TELEPHONES, ELECTRONIC MAIL

This chapter has dealt primarily with face-to-face interviews, although much of what has been said is applied by media writers who collect information by telephone and electronic mail, both of which have advantages and disadvantages.

Telephone Interviews

The telephone interview is useful, for it can save a journalist or public relations professional an enormous amount of time, which is extremely important for anyone working under deadline pressure. No time is wasted traveling to a source's office or home or waiting until the interviewee is able to talk. A writer rarely is kept waiting for long periods on the telephone.

Furthermore, a source tends to be more attentive on the telephone. Person-to-person interviews may be constantly interrupted by telephone calls, events occurring in an outer office or a dozen other activities. If someone is conducting business (or an interview) in an office and the telephone rings, he or she almost certainly is going to be left waiting while the office worker (or interviewee) tends to the needs of the caller. Interviewers can take advantage of this cultural phenomenon to conduct highly focused telephone interviews in little time.

Also, a news source often is available for a telephone interview, particularly when the interviewer needs a limited amount of very specific information, but not for a face-to-face interview. Personal interviews require more time, and some sources simply don't have it, although they may have the time for telephone interviews.

Disadvantages

It is fairly easy to reach most official or quasi-official sources, people who work in offices, but unofficial sources sometimes are difficult to track and are unwilling to talk by telephone. An interviewer who relies too much on the telephone may produce too many stories that are incomplete, or worse, because he or she doesn't talk to many unofficial sources.

It is difficult to establish rapport, to make a connection, during a telephone interview. The writer has the source's attention, but not for long—certainly not long enough to establish the rapport that is critical for a successful interview. The telephone interview is particularly ineffective for those stories in which information about a source's personality and general outlook on life is important (for example, a feature or personality sketch).

Bob Woodward (left) and Carl Bernstein of The Washington Post *use the telephone during their investigation of the Watergate scandal. Journalists rely heavily on telephones to get information because the process is fast, but they can miss important factual and contextual information when they don't interview sources face to face.*

A media writer also is unable to see on the telephone the important facial expressions and body movements that can provide a clue that a source is embarrassed or nervous or isn't telling the entire truth—or is lying. Nonverbal cues, so important in an interview, are missing in the telephone interview.

Another serious disadvantage of the telephone interview is the possibility that a source will simply hang up if an interviewer (in the source's opinion) has been offensive, if the source is unable to answer a difficult or embarrassing question or if the source decides the interview really isn't worth the time.

An interviewer can take steps to avoid some of these problems:

■ Don't use the telephone when it is important to establish rapport, to connect, with the source. The telephone should not be used by an interviewer who desires more from a source than a set of facts and short, formal statements. A writer who thinks the source may lie about an important aspect of the story, or suspects there is more to the story than other sources indicate, must interview the source in person.

■ Don't ignore unofficial sources simply because they cannot be contacted by telephone.

- Save difficult, offensive or embarrassing questions for last, when the story won't suffer much even if the interviewee hangs up. An interviewer obviously asks the offensive question right away if the interviewee expects the question (and would think it strange if it were not asked immediately).

- Don't attempt to obtain too much information in a telephone interview and don't ask irrelevant or insignificant questions.

Caveats

Writers must be careful in recording telephone interviews, for the practice is illegal in some states (Chapter 13), and it is unethical—even if it's not illegal—if he or she does not have the source's permission.

Another problem is associated with the ubiquitous cell phones, which make it possible to call anybody from any location at any time. The cell phone is a good tool for media professionals, but an interviewer has to think about the process. If a thought pops into a writer's head, he or she shouldn't just seize the telephone and make the call. An interviewer needs to think about what he or she needs to know for a few minutes and consider whether other information is needed. A writer shouldn't call a source four or five times for a story just because it is easy to do so.

Electronic Mail

Electronic mail was discussed in Chapter 8, but the challenges of using electronic mail in interviews were not addressed in detail. In fact, most journalists do not use electronic mail for interviews. Bruce Garrison's study of newspaper journalists suggests that 51.3 percent of interviews are conducted by telephone and 41.7 percent are conducted in person. Only 6.5 percent of newspaper interviews are conducted using electronic mail.[16]

Disadvantages

Garrison's findings obviously reflect the disadvantages of interviewing by electronic mail:

- It's difficult for a media professional (whether a Web, broadcast, magazine or newspaper journalist or a public relations writer) to establish the rapport that is needed for an excellent interview. A writer just doesn't get to know the source. It is difficult to collect more than superficial facts and stilted reactions to very specific questions.

- It is nearly impossible to get spontaneous reactions to questions and comments. It is far easier to sit in front of a computer and think of a response than it is to sit in the presence of an interviewer who is demanding an immediate answer. Any pressure on a source is gone.

- A writer can't know for certain that the person who is at the other end of the link is the person he or she is supposed to be. An electronic mail message can be answered by anyone who has access to an individual's electronic mailbox. A journalist may think he or she is citing the president of an organization, when the source really is a secretary.

- It is difficult to communicate electronically with unofficial sources, for many do not have access to electronic mail and it might be hard to find their addresses when they do (see the box "Find an Electronic Mail Address").

- A source's answers are right there in black and white, which is good; but many people don't worry about errors in their messages, and they may expect them to be "cleaned up." While a writer quotes accurately, the sentences themselves might contain errors. The errors should not be corrected, for then the source's words are changed. But does a writer really want to use them as they are?

- Broadcast journalists face a special difficulty in using electronic mail: There is no interesting visual image to accompany the information, unless a writer shows the message as it appears on the monitor. But that would get boring in a hurry. Broadcast journalists cannot even play the source's voice, as they can if it's a telephone interview, and show an interesting graphic at the same time. The problem is severe if the journalist needs to report more than a few sentences from a source.

Advantages

The advantage of electronic mail is that it is convenient, fast and accurate (writers have a person's exact words, for he or she wrote them); writers can reach some sources to whom they could *never* talk; and they can copy a source's responses to a word processing document. No typing required.

To realize these advantages, however, a media professional should use electronic mail only to get a quick reaction to a single question from a source he or she already knows well; to obtain technical information like budget numbers; or to verify information already collected.

A writer also must conduct the interview in real time, so that questions are answered almost instantly; new questions are formulated in response; they are sent; the source responds; and so on. This simulates the telephone, or even the person-to-person, interview, although with virtually none of the advantages of the person-to-person interview.

Public Relations

Public relations professionals are more likely than journalists to deal with cooperative sources because they (interviewers) often work in the same organization with their sources. Consequently, they may find electronic mail far more valuable than do other communicators. They should remember that they can help journalists enormously if they answer their queries, where appropriate, through electronic mail. This helps a writer build a good relationship.

FIND AN ELECTRONIC MAIL ADDRESS

Finding addresses can be a bother, but many addresses are published in easily accessible documents and databases. Internet service providers (the companies that provide links to the Web) frequently have address books in which many subscribers (and their electronic addresses) are listed. Individuals sometimes are listed in special directories. Many public relations professionals' addresses, for instance, are listed in the directory of the Public Relations Society of America, and many journalism and public relations teachers' addresses are listed in the directory of the Association for Education in Journalism & Mass Communication.

The Web is another good source for electronic mail addresses. Most organizations have Web sites, and most list the electronic mail addresses of their employees. Use a search service to find the Web site and then look for "Contact us" buttons. Unfortunately, those buttons sometimes just take a user to a generic address that is not targeted to any individual. (Public relations writers need to make sure their sites do not do this.) Sometimes the address is listed under "Site map" or under "Departments." Some sites are so poor a writer can burn an hour just trying to find an address. Before leaving such a site, a writer needs to send a message of complaint to the site's webmaster.

Many electronic mail addresses also are available from online directories. Here are a few possibilities: Bigfoot at <www.Bigfoot.com>, Infospace at <www.infospace.com>, Switchboard at <www.switchboard.com> or Telephone Directories on the Web at <www.contractjobs.com/tel>.

Public relations professionals have far more control of a journalist's interview when it is conducted by electronic mail than when it is conducted in person. They or their bosses can consider the questions outside the interview situation, when a journalist is expecting an immediate response. This means that a public relations person has more time to frame an answer; that he or she can tactfully "edit" the response of someone in his or her organization; and that others in the organization can be consulted about the appropriate response. This is not necessarily a good situation, from a journalist's viewpoint.

SPECIAL PROBLEMS

Four of the most common problems that arise in interviews are off-the-record comments, confidential sources, denials and source review of copy. Public relations professionals seldom face these problems, but they must understand them so they can behave accordingly when they are interviewed and so they can counsel their clients effectively. They should, for example, discourage their clients from ever seeking off-the-record or not-for-attribution agreements.

Off-the-record Comments

An interviewee occasionally will tell a journalist, "I have some information for you that I think is important, but I can't tell you what it is for the record." The journalist must decide whether to listen to what the source has to say or tell the source that off-the-record comments can't be accepted, which is an acceptable and frequently recommended response.

A writer who accepts the information cannot use the material in any way— except possibly to help get information from another source. Publication would violate the journalist's own ethical standards, lose for all journalists a potentially useful information source, make all sources suspicious of journalists and diminish the practice of journalism.

On the other hand, if a source gives the information and *then* says the material cannot be used, a writer is under no obligation to respect the source's wishes. The journalist must weigh the value of the information against the value of the source in making a decision. If the source is exceptionally valuable, the interviewer might accept the deal, but he or she must state clearly such an agreement will not be made in the future.

Advantages

Interviewers may accept off-the-record comments because they believe information nobody knows about will benefit no one. Some argue that off-the-record information can be helpful in structuring a story, suggesting sources and collecting other information. Off-the-record comments can be useful in suggesting the way a person thinks, an essential factor in writing about a news personality or source.

A news source, for instance, may tell a Web writer off the record that a discount store is going to ask the local zoning board for a variance so it can construct a new store in a residential area—an area that the residents want to keep free of commercial enterprise. The writer can watch closely the activities of the zoning board and check the history of the area before the variance is requested to find out whether the local residents have fought such requests in the past. That background information might help the writer produce a better report when the story breaks.

Off-the-record information also may give an interviewer something to pry out of someone else. In the zoning story, the Web writer might ask the chief executive officer of the discount store chain whether the rumor is accurate. The confidence of the original source would have to be carefully protected, however; the writer could not tell the chief executive officer where the rumor originated. The interviewer certainly could not approach the chief executive officer if the CEO would know—just by virtue of being asked the question—the identity of the Web writer's source. But an interviewer sometimes can obtain information from a second source without violating the confidence of a first source.

Disadvantages

Many interviewers refuse to accept off-the-record information under any circumstances. Some argue that a writer's job is to disseminate information, not to gather facts simply for the sake of gathering facts. Others argue that sources who request off-the-record agreements often are simply using writers for self-serving purposes.

The acceptance of off-the-record information is risky because a writer may forget that certain information was accepted off the record and use it anyway, which is inexcusable. Or the writer may simply use the information in a future story inadvertently because it was confused with other information. Either way, the interviewer has violated a confidence.

An unscrupulous source can effectively kill a story by providing off-the-record information to a willing interviewer. If the story can't be verified through other sources or if word of the story never leaks out through other sources, the story is dead and the public knows nothing of it.

Confidential Sources

A media writer sometimes agrees to publish information provided by a news source without identifying the source. Such agreements must be made *before* information is given, and the writer must know the policy of his or her news organization. Most organizations will honor not-for-attribution agreements, but the reasons must be compelling. Also, an interviewer must tell the source that he or she must be identified to the editor. Three potential problems are associated with this practice.

Legal Problems

A journalist who accepts information from confidential sources risks jail if the story reports illegal activities. A magazine writer, for example, who publishes information from two unnamed drug dealers should not be surprised by a call from the local district attorney, who will demand the sources' names. The district attorney could ask a judge to hold the journalist in contempt (and in jail) until he or she reveals the names. The magazine writer goes to the slammer, for it is unethical to reveal the names. (See also the box "Jail Is a Possibility.")

Attorneys in civil cases occasionally subpoena journalists and demand that they identify sources who have information that could help their clients. The attorneys obviously want to grill those sources in court. This happens infrequently, but journalists who will not reveal their sources risk going to jail. The bottom line is, journalists who are unwilling to risk jail to protect their sources shouldn't use confidential sources.

JAIL IS A POSSIBILITY

Writer Vanessa Leggett, jailed for five and one-half months for refusing to identify confidential sources to federal officials, holds the record for jail time in the wars over unnamed sources. Leggett, who was writing a book about the 1997 murder of a socialite, refused to turn over notes and recordings to a federal grand jury. U.S. District Judge Melinda Harmon held Leggett in contempt and locked her up in 2000–2001. The judge let Leggett go only because the grand jury's term had ended.[17]

Government lawyers argued that Leggett was not really a journalist because she did not work for a news outlet and she did not have a contract for her proposed book. U.S. Rep. Sheila Jackson Lee, D-Houston, who argued for a law that would shield journalists from government lawyers, said "intent to publish" should be the only criterion for determining who is a journalist.

Journalists must be ready to go to jail to protect sources, because that is ethical and because they must prevent government from controlling journalists, Leggett said on her release.

The Justice Department, according to the Reporters Committee for Freedom of the Press, violated its own 40-year-old standards, which say government investigators may subpoena journalists only for *specific* information they *cannot get from any other sources*. These two criteria are specified in most guidelines and shield laws.

Freelance writer Vanessa Leggett speaks to reporters after her release from prison. She holds the record for the longest time spent in jail (five and one-half months) for refusing to turn over information to a federal grand jury. She was released only after the grand jury's term expired.

While this is primarily an ethical issue, journalists might face legal difficulties if they reveal their sources. A Minnesota jury awarded $700,000 to a public relations consultant who was identified in stories by the Minneapolis *Star Tribune* and the *St. Paul* (Minn.) *Pioneer Press and Dispatch*. The two reporters had pledged to Dan Cohen, a spokesman for a 1982 gubernatorial candidate, that his name would not be used in their stories, agreements that both reporters' editors refused to honor. Jurors found the newspapers had violated verbal agreements.[18]

Credibility Problems

Many readers and viewers do not believe pseudo attributions ("Sources close to the mayor said today that ..." or "A usually reliable source said that ...") because they don't really know who is responsible for the information. They have only the writer's word that the information came from a reliable source, and that, to some readers and listeners, is not good enough.

Some members of the audience may suspect the interviewer made up the information to "improve" the story or to attack an unpopular individual or institution. In fact, some are convinced that all unattributed statements are nothing more than some writer's opinion.

False Information

Confidential sources sometimes abuse the privileges journalists accord them. A self-serving politician, for instance, can seize the opportunity to send up a trial balloon—that is, to test the impact of a position to determine whether the public would accept it. If public opinion were unfavorable, the politician could later deny that the policy ever was considered, blame the media for even mentioning the matter or, incredibly, accuse the media of making up the story for their own purposes.

Sources who are not identified are essentially given a soapbox from which to make all sorts of statements—for which they cannot be held accountable. Writers must be exceptionally careful in using information that cannot be attributed; the accuracy of such information must be verified by at least one other source. It is important to remember, too, that an interviewer is legally responsible for what an unnamed source says. If a writer attributes potentially libelous statements to an unnamed source, it is exceptionally difficult for the news organization to defend itself in court since the source will not be available to testify.

Denials

A writer has little defense against a news source who claims he or she was misquoted or quoted out of context. A source sometimes makes a statement and then, after the interview, has second thoughts, particularly after seeing the comments on the air or in type or receiving telephone calls from friends, an employer or associates who don't approve of the source's statements. The temptation is strong to deny the words, and some sources do.

Denials also may stem from deviousness on the part of a source. An interviewee may actually give a writer information, fully intending to deny the story, or parts of it, later. In this way, a dishonest person releases information without bearing responsibility for it.

If the disputed conversation has been tape-recorded, a journalist has no need to fear denials; the relevant material can be aired or published to document its accuracy. Magazines and newspapers sometimes merely assert that the report was correct, but without presenting hard evidence that the writer did record the information accurately. This is not an effective way to counter a denial.

The best defense against denials, aside from the tape recorder, is to do the best possible reporting job, which sometimes is difficult under deadline pressure. A journalist or news medium that has a reputation for fairness and accuracy often finds that reputation is the best defense.

A writer must verify through documents, records and other persons any controversial material. A source rarely denies information contained in documents and records, and rarely do two sources deny a story about which they have given the same information.

Source Review of Copy

News sources sometimes request permission to read a writer's copy before it is published. Indeed, sources sometimes demand permission to review an article before submitting to an interview. Other times, an interviewer simply chooses to let a source review an article (particularly when very complex or technical information is included) as a means of improving accuracy.

The primary advantage of source review of copy, certainly, is that accuracy—at least as the source perceives it—is increased. And it sometimes is advantageous to grant a source a right of review, because a writer might miss a critical point by refusing to let him or her read the story before publication.

Many writers oppose source review of copy, for the following reasons:

- There often is not time to allow a source to review an article before a deadline, particularly in broadcast and Web journalism. This argument applies principally to news stories and less to magazine articles or newspaper features.

- A source may not be able to rise above his or her own self-interest enough to comment only on factual errors. A source, influenced by his or her self-involvement, can drift easily into criticism of the writer's news judgment and style.

- A journalist cannot always guarantee that changes suggested by a source will be made. Articles go through a complex editorial process, and the writer usually does not have the final authority.

- The source may be responsible for only a part of an article, while the writer is responsible for all of it. If there are inaccuracies, the writer is the one who ultimately must take the blame. Therefore, the source should not be given special consideration.

- Any kind of source review is censorship and a threat to freedom of the press, some critics argue. If a right of review is extended to a Nobel Prize–winning scientist, the argument goes, it could then be demanded by any newsmaker, such as a party to an automobile accident.

- A source who doesn't like an article may take steps to keep it from being posted, published or aired. A source could go to a publisher or station manager, for example.

A Compromise

There is room for compromise between a source who argues for complete control over a journalist's copy and a journalist who argues that a source should never be allowed to review copy before publication. There are at least two ways a right of review can be successfully extended, on those occasions when time permits:

- The source is given access only to selected material, such as quotations, figures or analogies, and is asked to verify its accuracy. It is relatively easy to cut relevant material from a word processing program, paste it into an electronic mail message and send it to a source. The source never gets to see the entire article.

- The source is given access to the entire article and is asked to point out factual errors and suggest other changes, but the understanding is that the news organization has the final word.

This compromise combines the advantages of improving accuracy of reporting and keeping the final editorial decision with the writer and editors.

Public relations writers who work in highly technical or scientific organizations may offer to review factual information for a journalist or have a scientist or technical expert review that information. In some cases, journalists themselves might request reviews. Nothing is wrong with this, but public relations writers and their employers must understand the decision is the journalist's. And they should never grant an interview on the condition that the source gets to review the story. This makes for bad relations and likely will mean no story is aired or published. Worse, it might mean a negative story is published or aired, but *without* the organization's input.

Public relations persons must recognize, too, that their own work will be reviewed by the original source and, sometimes it seems, by everyone else in the organization—or in the world. This process may assure accuracy, but it can be frustrating, for few of those who sign off on a news release, for example, understand the needs and demands of the news editors who will receive or download the release.

A well-written release may turn into an unreadable Frankenstein-like monster after it has made its way through the approval process. Those releases are too often disseminated, only to pollute the communication environment and reduce the writer's credibility. Part of a public relations professional's job is education. It is important to teach the boss (or bosses) to recognize excellent writing—and to accept nothing less.

YOUR RESPONSIBILITY IS . . .

- To practice interviewing strangers every chance that you get, for the more you interview, the better you get at it.

- To place a high priority on acquiring a body of knowledge about economics, government, the sciences, culture, society, education and other matters so you will be an effective interviewer.

- To gain an appreciation for the importance of pre-interview research and to learn how to collect the necessary information.

- To know how to write good directive and nondirective questions, how to anticipate responses before an interview even begins and how to be flexible and to adjust follow-up questions according to what a source actually says.

- To learn how to establish rapport with a source and how to truly "hear" what he or she says.

- To learn that excessive reliance on the telephone for interviewing is not a good strategy.

- To understand the problems with using electronic mail for interviewing news sources and personalities.

- To understand the options when sources demand agreements that their information is confidential or off the record or that you will show them your story before publication.

- To understand that you can, if you want to be a public relations professional, help your organization a great deal if you will assist journalists who need to interview people in your company, agency or not-for-profit organization.

- To understand, if you want to be a public relations professional, that you need to learn *all* aspects of the interviewing process (even those you may never use) so you can help those in your organization who deal with the media understand journalists' needs and responsibilities.

NOTES

1. George Turnbull, "Some Notes on the History of the Interview," *Journalism Quarterly,* 13:3 (1936): 272–279; and Nils Gunnar Nilsson, "The Origin of the Interview," *Journalism Quarterly,* 48:4 (1971): 707–713.

2. "Meade and Titus: Theories as to Their Knowledge of the Murder at Hackettstown," *The New York Herald,* May 3, 1886: 6.

3. Les Switzer, John McNamara and Michael Ryan, "Critical-cultural Studies in Research and Instruction," *Journalism & Mass Communication Educator,* 54:3 (1999): 23–42.

4. Tom Koch, *The News as Myth: Fact and Context in Journalism* (New York: Greenwood, 1990); Meenakshi Gigi Durham, "On the Relevance of Standpoint Epistemology to the Practice of Journalism: The Case for 'Strong Objectivity,'" *Communication Theory,* 8:2 (1998): 117–140; Ted Friedman, "From Heroic Objectivity to the News Stream: The Newseum's Strategies for Relegitimizing Journalism in the Information Age," *Critical Studies in Mass Communication,* 15:3 (1998): 325–335; and Robert A. Hackett, "Decline of a Paradigm? Bias and Objectivity in News Media Studies," *Critical Studies in Mass Communication,* 1:3 (1984): 229–259.

5. Michael Ryan, "Journalistic Ethics, Objectivity, Existential Journalism, Standpoint Epistemology, and Public Journalism," *Journal of Mass Media Ethics,* 16:1 (2001): 3–22.

6. Hugh Pearson, "Enough of Al Sharpton's Masquerading as Leader," *Houston Chronicle,* Feb. 29, 2000: A-21; and Jack E. White, "Big Al's Finest Hour: Sharpton Emerges as the Voice of Black Outrage," *Time,* March 6, 2000: 28.

7. Shirley Biagi, *Interviews That Work: A Practical Guide for Journalists,* 2nd ed. (Belmont, Calif: Wadsworth, 1992): Chapter 8.

8. Robert L. Kahn and Charles F. Cannell, *The Dynamics of Interviewing: Theory, Technique, and Cases* (New York: John Wiley, 1957): 8.

9. Stanley E. Jones, "Directivity vs. Nondirectivity: Implications of the Examination of Witnesses in Law for the Fact-finding Interview," *Journal of Communication,* 19:1 (March 1969): 64–75.

10. LaRue W. Gilleland, "Simple Formula Proves Helpful to Interviewers," *Journalism Educator,* 26:2 (1971): 19–20; and Kenneth M. Jackson, "GOSS Formula May Handicap Reporter if Misapplied," *Journalism Educator,* 29:1 (1974): 31–32.

11. Leon Festinger, *A Theory of Cognitive Dissonance* (Stanford, Calif.: Stanford University Press, 1957); Werner J. Severin and James W. Tankard Jr., *Communication Theories: Origins, Methods, and Uses in the Mass Media,* 5th ed. (New York: Longman, 2001): chapters 4, 7.

12. David B. Buller and Judee K. Burgoon, "Interpersonal Deception Theory," *Communication Theory,* 6:3 (1996): 203–242; and Judee K. Burgoon, David B. Buller, Laura K. Guerrero, Walid A. Afifi and Clyde M. Feldman, "Interpersonal Deception: XII. Information Management Dimensions Underlying Deceptive and Truthful Messages," *Communication Monographs,* 63:1 (1996): 50–69.

13. Kahn and Cannell, *Dynamics of Interviewing:* 6.

14. Bruce Garrison, *Professional News Reporting* (Hillsdale, N.J.: Erlbaum, 1992): Chapter 7.

15. Eugene J. Webb and Jerry R. Salancik, "The Interview or The Only Wheel in Town," *Journalism Monographs,* No. 2 (1966).

16. Bruce Garrison, "The Use of Electronic Mail as a Newsgathering Resource," paper presented to the Newspaper Division's Southeast Colloquium, Association for Education in Journalism & Mass Communication, Gulfport, Miss., March 7–9, 2002.

17. Alan Bernstein, "Leggett Free—for Now: Feds Mum on Whether Case Will Go to New Grand Jury," *Houston Chronicle,* Jan. 5, 2002: A-1,18.

18. Andrew Radolf, "Anonymous Sources: Newspaper Issues New Guidelines After Losing Court Case," *Editor & Publisher,* Aug. 27, 1988: 17, 19, 33.

C H A P T E R 11

EVENTS

Meetings, Speeches and News Conferences

Societies could not function without their meetings, speeches and news conferences. Millions of decisions are made and discussed every single day by school boards, legislatures, political campaign committees, transportation boards, corporations, zoning boards, community associations, government commissions, courts, activist groups, government agencies, hospital boards and other groups and organizations.

Millions of people across the planet are affected by what happens (or doesn't happen) during these public events. It is in these forums that citizens learn (1) what problems and potential solutions are being discussed, (2) what decisions have been reached and what they mean and (3) why some decisions are problematic—or even bad.

Media professionals, as part of their responsibility to give their audiences daily accounts of what's going on in the world, try to cover many public events. They provide reports to the citizens who can't attend them, but who need to know about them. By one estimate, nearly 30 percent of all newspaper stories and 10–20 percent of all broadcast news stories cite public meetings or records.[1]

Covering public events is a function primarily of journalists, but public relations writers occasionally report about events for internal and external publications that have limited circulations or distribute releases about events the media haven't covered. They also have to ensure that upcoming events are adequately publicized and that the public and media have information they need to understand what's going on when they attend. They frequently distribute complete texts of speeches to guarantee that they are reported accurately, for example.

Professionals use the news values (Chapter 2) to determine which events to cover and which to ignore. Meetings of homeowners' associations, parent-teacher associations, church groups, photography and computer clubs, student groups, garden clubs, civic organizations or book and music clubs typically are not considered of interest and importance to large audiences. Meetings of Congress and its committees, state legislatures, city councils, county commissions, opponents of major government initiatives, zoning boards, taxing authorities, school boards and other prominent groups generally are covered.

A vast number of meetings are on the bubble. That is, they may or may not be considered newsworthy. Some meetings of consumer groups, city and county agencies and departments, transportation system boards, activist organizations and the courts are covered; some are not.

Speeches by little-known authors, professors, ministers or politicians seldom get covered, unless their topics are compelling, but speeches by prominent individuals are reported. No matter where they go, speeches by Jesse Jackson, Bill Moyers, Laura Bush, Al Sharpton, Bill Clinton, Jane Fonda, Christopher Reeve, Louis Farrakhan, George W. Bush, Maya Angelou, Hillary Clinton, Tony Blair, Lance Armstrong and Billy Graham are going to be covered.

Just about any news conference is covered, or it would not be scheduled in the first place.

Journalists need to be careful that they don't focus so much on "official" events that they ignore those organized and sponsored by the less powerful, wealthy and influential. Just as journalists can rely too much on official sources, they can focus too much on official events (city council meetings, Congress, Pentagon news conferences). If journalists simply refuse to cover "unofficial" meetings of ordinary people, it is difficult for citizens to make their views known, and society suffers.

Broadcast journalists are always pressed for time, so they are likely to cover far fewer events than are print and Web journalists, and those they do cover are not going to be described in much detail. Television journalists have the additional problem of identifying potentially interesting and relevant video and of getting sources to speak on camera. Potential sources frequently are participating in meetings or delivering speeches as broadcast deadlines loom—or even pass.

Collecting information from public events is similar in many ways to getting information from interviews, but there are some differences:

- There is substantially less face-to-face interaction between a news source and a writer who is covering a public event.
- A public event is physically more difficult to cover, particularly for broadcast journalists, because access might be limited, the room might be noisy or chaotic and sources might be difficult to corner.
- Many meetings, news conferences and speeches are scheduled at night, so journalists must work under extreme pressure when their deadlines also are at night.

Millions of meetings and news conferences, like this one, are held each day around the world. Public relations professionals often organize them and journalists cover those they think are newsworthy, like the one pictured here. Former Mississippi Gov. Ronnie Musgrove is explaining to Margaret Gibbs and other nursing home residents that they will lose no Medicaid benefits.

- Most public events are covered by more than one journalist, so the pressure to do an excellent job and to get a fresh angle is greater.
- Covering public events is enormously time-consuming.

Still, the fundamentals of writing are the same, and many of the information-collection techniques discussed in previous chapters are useful in covering public events. Some of the prerequisites for adequately handling stories about meetings, speeches and news conferences—and for doing a better job than the competition—are discussed in this chapter.

ADVANCE STORIES

Advance stories—announcements of upcoming meetings, speeches or news conferences—tell audiences about important events they might want to attend, and they help editors decide which events deserve coverage. The goal is not to hype the event so people will attend, but to give them enough information so they can make informed decisions. Advances are written by journalists and public relations persons in the same styles and formats as all other news reports.

Public relations professionals who think only a small group might be interested in their event can send an advance by fax, mail or electronic mail to the people who have been targeted as potentially interested. Or they might send it to publications that appeal to narrow interests. An announcement of a retirement seminar, for instance, might be sent to a small financial service's newsletter or distributed through an investment company's electronic mailing list.

If meetings, news conferences or speeches should appeal to broader audiences, public relations writers will send releases to local newspapers, magazines, broadcast outlets and Web sites. They might also write and record public service announcements about their events and forward those to local Web sites or broadcast outlets. If an event is particularly important, the organization might pay to have the PSA aired or an advertisement published.

In either case, public relations writers automatically post advance stories on their Web sites, with links to agendas, speakers' Web sites and background information.

Advance stories also are prepared by staff writers for Web sites, newspapers, magazines and broadcast outlets. The "preparation" might be simply to run as written a good public relations release, to rewrite and then run a poor release or to write an advance from information independently collected.

To write an advance, a journalist or public relations professional must have the following information:

- The time, day (or date) and place of the meeting, speech or news conference
- The exact name of the group that is meeting or sponsoring the speech or news conference
- The most important business to be discussed at the meeting or news conference or the complete identification of the speaker and the topic of the speech

A story that doesn't contain this information is incomplete and unacceptable. Compare the following versions of a news release. The version at the right contains all the relevant information and is a good advance, while the one at the left is unacceptable because the public relations writer failed to collect all the important information:

A meeting of the Reading City Council will be held at 8 p.m. Thursday in Room 503 at City Hall. A complete agenda is available at www.readinggovernment.gov. [site is fictitious]	Plans for a $1.5 million addition to Reading's municipal services building will be discussed by the Reading City Council at 8 p.m. Thursday in Room 503 at City Hall. A property tax increase to pay for the addition also will be discussed, Mayor Ashley George said today. A complete agenda is available at www.readinggovernment.gov. [site is fictitious]

Anyone only marginally interested in city business and taxes might not attend the Reading City Council meeting after reading the release at the left because it doesn't indicate what will be discussed. Notice also that the most important information is in the first part of the sentence in the version at the right (1-A) and the less important information is in the second part (1-B).

The public relations writer who was too lazy to find out what the City Council would be discussing was cheating the audience. It's a good bet, too, that the release would not be published or aired by anyone in that form. A journalist might contact the mayor for more details, but that would not be necessary if the public relations professional had done the job right. And if journalists simply discard the release, no story at all will be published or aired by the media they work for—and taxpayers are the losers.

It is not necessary to list *all* items on an agenda—just the most important ones will do. To create this list, the writer needs to comb carefully through the agenda for news, using the news values as guides. News media typically do not publish complete agendas because they can be quite long, as is the city council agenda in Appendix F.

The problem in the Reading release is evident again in the leads for two advance stories about an upcoming speech:

Richard Dray, a professional photographer from New York City, will speak at 7:30 p.m. Monday at the Fleming Hotel. The Fleming Photography Club is sponsoring the talk, "Digitalizing Nature."	Innovative ways to use digital cameras and equipment in nature photography will be discussed by Richard Dray, a professional photographer from New York City, at 7:30 p.m. Monday at the Fleming Hotel. The Fleming Photography Club is sponsoring the talk, "Digitalizing Nature."

The writer of the version at the left de-emphasized the crucial element—the subject of the talk. Unless the speaker is prominent, the *topic* should go into the first part of the sentence (1-A) and the speaker's *name* should go into the second part (1-B). Someone interested in innovative nature photography might pass up the speech because the version at the left doesn't specify the topic. The reader could call the president or secretary of the photography club and find out more about the talk, but that's the advance writer's job.

Notice, too, that the writer of the version on the right did not begin with the title of the speech. Since the title didn't tell much, it was better to go with a more complete description and then report the exact title later. That made the lead more interesting and informative.

COLLECTING INFORMATION

Information about sources and topics is as important in covering events as it is in conducting interviews (Chapter 10). This is illustrated in an account by the *Houston Chronicle* of a "state of the campus" speech by Arthur Smith, then president of the University of Houston.[2] Prior to the speech, a survey of faculty members showed that the UH provost received a 73 percent disapproval rating from the faculty who responded (51 percent) and that Smith got 43 percent approval and 44 percent disapproval ratings. Many of the reasons for the disapproval ratings were outlined in the report. The *Chronicle's* lead read:

> University of Houston President Arthur Smith painted a glowing picture of the school Wednesday in an annual speech to the faculty, but ducked most of the gripes leveled by professors in a recent survey.

The background information in 1-B got as much attention as the points Smith made in his speech. Paragraph two was a direct quotation, an upbeat appraisal of the state of the campus. But paragraphs three and four summarized the results of the survey, which were quite negative, and the two paragraphs after that reported what Smith did say about the complaints:

> Smith never mentioned the survey in his one-hour speech, but, toward the end, he alluded to the concerns by saying university administrators must make "difficult choices" in allocating funds and resources.
>
> "Whenever these choices are made, and by whatever process of governance we utilize to arrive at them, some members of the university community will be pleased, and some others will be disappointed, sometimes even to the point of alienation and long-term, simmering anger," he said.

Had the writer not gotten the background information from the *Chronicle's* archives, the story would have been incomplete and misleading.

Information Sources

The information required for advance stories and for covering meetings, speeches and news conferences is available from a variety of sources (chapters 8 and 9).

A public relations professional who is assigned to write an advance about a routine meeting of his or her organization should find out who is organizing the event (probably the secretary or clerk of the board, court or group) and then get a complete agenda from that person. If an agenda is unavailable, the public relations writer needs to help pull it together. Helping journalists cover meetings is important because that helps the writer establish good relationships with the media and ensure that stories are accurate—and *that* means the public relations writer communicates more effectively (if indirectly) with the public.

Speeches and special events (such as news conferences, symposia, panels and conferences) frequently are organized by a public relations department or agency.[3] The public relations person needs to contact speakers or participants (or their representatives) for information. For a speech, the writer needs material about the speaker, the speech title and a few sentences about the speech content.

It's not always enough simply to know the title. It's important to learn, too, about the subject matter of a speech. If information is not available from the sources themselves, it is likely to be available on the Web (Chapter 8) or from written documents (Chapter 9).

A Web, broadcast or journalism professional often obtains information for an advance for an upcoming meeting at the one that precedes it, particularly if an organization has a standard meeting time and date (for example, 8 p.m. on the third Monday of every month). After the writer has obtained an agenda and other necessary information, he or she needs only to verify the facts (to make sure nothing has changed) before writing the advance story a few weeks later.

If a group meets irregularly, the writer must contact the president, secretary or public relations professional to obtain the necessary information. Details may be sent to the newsroom in the form of a publicity release, or a representative of the group may give the writer the information by telephone, electronic mail or fax. It's important to get on the list to receive such information. Organizations increasingly use electronic mailing lists to announce meetings, agendas and other useful information to journalists and other interested individuals. A journalist who frequently covers a group, agency or organization needs to get on its list. That saves time and reduces the chances for error, assuming the journalist checks his or her electronic mail frequently.

Journalists can't rely exclusively on announcements, so they need contacts in the groups and organizations they cover. A public relations professional usually is the best source of information about an event, but if an organization does not have one, the secretary is a particularly good second choice because that person prepares the agenda and other materials and is in a good position to know what's going on. An added advantage of contacting a secretary is that the president of the group need not be bothered for routine information.

The court clerk is the best source of information about an upcoming trial or hearing. The clerk has the information, and the judge, plaintiff's attorney, district attorney or defense attorney needn't be bothered. If a journalist wants to write a more complete advance, he or she might need to contact a plaintiff's attorney, a prosecuting attorney or a defense attorney for comments about motions or charges. Journalists must avoid being used by court officers who want to gain some legal or political advantage and must avoid producing unbalanced reports (if, for example, the prosecutor comments on charges, but the defense does not).

Sometimes, an organization's chairperson, public relations person or secretary can provide little information about a speaker or topic. In such circumstances, information may be found by contacting the source or the source's agent or publicist or by checking media or other archives. A journalist covering a speech by Michel Brunet might use the same technique to find information for a story that a public relations writer uses to find information for a news release (Chapter 8).

Spontaneous Events

Many news conferences—and some meetings and speeches—are announced with essentially no warning at all. A spontaneous news conference was called when a sniper killed six people in October 2002 in Montgomery County, Md. Police Chief Charles Moose was pressed into an unaccustomed communications role as journalists swarmed the area in search of information. As the number of attacks increased, more spontaneous news conferences and speeches by government officials were scheduled.

Public relations professionals worked overtime during these critical, hectic days to try to keep the public informed through the news media, to help journalists do their jobs and to stifle or verify the many rumors that arose. There is little time in moments of crisis for media professionals to prepare for statements (issued during speeches or news conferences) by sources close to the events. If the event is big enough, most media organizations will assign several writers to get the information, with some trying to get the background that will help everyone do their jobs better.

COVERING A MEETING OR SPEECH

A meeting or speech can be covered in one of three ways: (1) A writer who knows a meeting or speech is over can call an informed source who attended the event to find out what was said or done. (2) A writer can attend part of the event and then talk to someone who attended the entire event to find out what happened. (3) A writer can attend the entire meeting or speech.

The first two approaches offer one advantage: They save time. Information about an hour-long speech or a seven-hour meeting can be obtained in moments. But there are three major disadvantages in allowing someone else to decide what was and was not important at a meeting or speech:

- A media professional is trained to decide what is important and what isn't. A writer who surrenders the right to select information may find that a nonprofessional provides unimportant facts (from the reporter's perspective) and fails to supply important information.

- Most individuals are inclined to select information that supports their side of an issue or that damages the side with which they disagree. A writer who uses an objective approach typically has nothing to gain or lose no matter which side prevails. Relying on a nonprofessional for information can be dangerous because a story based on facts selected by someone closely associated with one side of an issue can be distorted.

- A story based on information obtained from someone not trained in journalism might be inaccurate. A good media writer is dedicated to accuracy, knows what to look for and where to find the facts, and has sufficient background to put what is said or done into proper context. A nonprofessional may have none of these attributes.

A writer who uses either of the first two methods of information collection takes a risk. The report can be misleading, inadequate or blatantly inaccurate. It helps to

GET THE RIGHT INFORMATION

It is important during a meeting or speech for journalists to obtain at least the following information, and good public relations professionals understand what journalists need and, if asked, they help them get it.

MEETINGS	SPEECHES
Most important actions taken	Most important points made (in direct quotations)
Exact name of the group that is meeting	Exact name of the group that is sponsoring the speech
Exact names and titles of persons who make important statements (with statements in direct quotations)	Exact name, title and identification of the speaker
Exact wording of resolutions and motions passed	Title of the speech
Results of significant votes	Time, day (or date), place and subject of the next speech, if it is part of a series
Important arguments on all sides of a controversial issue	Responses to important or controversial questions
Time, day (or date), place and subject of the next meeting	Number who attend
Number who attend	Information about any group or individual who tries to disrupt the speech
Information about any group or individual who tries to disrupt the meeting	Relevant background material
Relevant background material	

get information from a public relations professional, because he or she likely has some journalistic training and understands the consequences of giving a journalist misleading or false information. Journalists and public relations writers also seem to hold similar news values. (See also the box "Get the Right Information.")

Of the three alternatives, the third is by far the best, although it is sometimes impossible for a writer to attend a meeting or speech about which he or she must write. This is particularly true for journalists who work for broadcast outlets or news services. They typically don't have the time to sit for hours in meetings—or even to sit for an hour listening to a speech.

The Right Facts

A report of a meeting or speech typically is written in inverted pyramid style, with the most important information at the beginning. Information that isn't newsworthy should be omitted altogether. To write a good story and to make the judgments about what is important and what isn't, however, a writer must have all the relevant information. The first thing is to get an agenda or a copy of the speech, as that makes the job much easier. A sample agenda is shown in Appendix F.

The potential for embarrassment about missed information is much greater during a public event than during a person-to-person interview because the competition probably has the information and will use it. Imagine a radio editor who has aired a story with this lead:

> THE OAK CLIFF LIONS CLUB DECIDED LAST NIGHT TO DONATE $500 TO THE ST. LUKE'S CHILDREN'S HOSPITAL.
>
> THE MONEY WILL BE USED TO BUY MUCH-NEEDED CHILDREN'S BOOKS.

The writer who produced that lead will avoid serious trouble as long as the editor does not hear the competition's lead:

> THE OAK CLIFF LIONS CLUB DECIDED LAST NIGHT TO DONATE $20,000 TO CONSTRUCT A NEW LITTLE LEAGUE BASEBALL STADIUM.
>
> THE NEW FACILITY WILL BE LOCATED NEAR STATE STREET AND SHEFFIELD AVENUE. IT SHOULD BE COMPLETE BY THE TIME THE SEASON BEGINS IN APRIL.

Oops! Somebody's going to need a good explanation, particularly if the new stadium is not mentioned at all in the first story. If it is mentioned, the editor shares the blame for not highlighting the right facts in the lead. It's not that the St. Luke's facility is less deserving than Little League. It's just that $20,000 (magnitude) is considerably more money than $500. Note that the first sentences would be put together differently if these were print or Web reports. Print and Web writers would start the sentences (1-A) with the donations.

Complete information also is needed about a speaker and the occasion for the speech. Background needs to be worked in carefully, so as not to detract from the content. These paragraphs based on testimony to a congressional committee show how background is handled:[4]

> Science writers can play a critical role in helping to increase scientific literacy among Americans who have dropped out of science, Wisconsin professor Deborah Blum said Friday in testimony before the House Committee on Science.
>
> "My point is that science journalism becomes an essential point of outreach and of translation," said Blum, a professor of journalism at the University of Wisconsin–Madison.
>
> Science writers can also help scientists learn how to communicate more effectively with the general public, said Blum, who won a Pulitzer Prize for science writing while working for *The Sacramento* (Calif.) *Bee*.

Poet-author Maya Angelou is one of the many prominent people whose speeches are covered wherever they go. Here she speaks to an audience at the University of Northern Iowa.

"I would argue that we should eventually require every person majoring in science to take a science communication course, to be taught that communicating with the public is part of the job description," said Blum, who has written for *Psychology Today*, *Health* magazine, *The New York Times* and *The Washington Post*.

Readers learn exactly who Blum is and the occasion for her remarks—and they learn it early in the story. Writers have got to get such information and work it in carefully.

News Values Help

It helps to keep the news values (Chapter 2) in mind as a meeting or speech rolls along. The mayor is going to be prominent in any city, so what she or he says is likely to carry more weight than what others say, although minority viewpoints must not be ignored. If a council member calls another council member a name, that confrontation should be in the story. Conflict shouldn't be invented, but if it is there—and it often is—it should be reported. If a citizen has been somehow oppressed or ignored by city government, that information must be collected, for it is human interest. And it says something about how city government does or does not work.

Most writers think ahead during an event to the story they will write. It's important to consider how different things said and done will appear in the story.

MR. ROBERT'S RULES

Meetings that just "happen" usually are incredibly boring and ultimately useless. They have little focus because they are disorganized and poorly run. This is not a profound observation, for groups have searched for centuries for rules and procedures that will help them reach consensus. Majorities must be allowed to take action and not be intimidated or manipulated by vocal, organized and relentless minorities. Minorities, on the other hand, must have legitimate opportunities to have their views heard. Meeting chairs must have the power to maintain order, but they must not be allowed to influence proceedings unfairly.

Some of the first rules for running meetings were developed and used by the British Parliament. They were brought to the United States by the early colonists and were used in town meetings in New England. Thomas Jefferson's book about parliamentary procedure, which was used for years by Congress, was published in 1801.

But a U.S. army engineer and general, Henry Martin Robert, wrote the procedures that are used by most groups today. *Robert's Rules of Order,* first published in 1876, is a compilation of rules and procedures that any group can use to ensure that meetings are orderly, efficient and fair (although Robert's rules are not always scrupulously followed).

Professional communicators should purchase *Robert's Rules of Order,* become familiar with the terminology and some of the more important rules and take the book to meetings. Decisions sometimes turn on points of order, and a professional who does not understand the rules will not have a clue about what's happening.

It's important to know, for example, what it means to table a motion, how a motion that has been defeated can be reconsidered, under what circumstances an assembly can punish one of its members or how debate can be cut off. It's not necessary to know all the intricacies of *Robert's Rules of Orders*—almost nobody does—but it is necessary to be familiar with them and to know how to look up rules.

This helps ensure that the writer, who is almost certainly under deadline pressure, gets the "right" information.

Some writers also find it helpful to write their "leads" in their notes as a meeting or speech progresses. This helps them to order their facts and to know what to look for as the event goes on. The technique also makes it easier to cope with deadline pressures and helps writers produce better stories.

Most speeches and meetings are organized in formats that are virtually opposite to that of a news report; that is, the best information is at the end. Most organizations and speakers address less important points and issues early and the more important points and issues later. (See also the box, "Mr. Robert's Rules.") It is not unusual to write three or four leads for a story about a long and complex meeting or speech, only to use the last one for the first sentence. This is not a problem. Having those "leads" helps a writer organize a story; they can be used easily somewhere else. They also help provide smooth transitions.

Writers must listen carefully for good quotations—statements that are interesting, controversial or unexpected—so they will have the direct quotes they need to add interest, insight and credibility to their reports. As they observe the meeting or speech, they evaluate what is said and decide what is worth getting down word for word as direct quotations.

Media professionals must trust their own judgments about what is interesting and important; the more writing they do, the better that judgment becomes. But even the news judgment of beginners typically is good. They have many of the same values, drives, attitudes, interests and needs as their audiences. If something truly interests a beginning writer, chances are it will interest other people, too.

Nonverbal Cues

Unspoken communication is as important to note in covering meetings and speeches as it is in interviews (Chapter 10). Sometimes an idle gesture or raised eyebrow is a cue that what someone says is not precisely true or that it is controversial.[5] However, nonverbal cues are used primarily as guides for questions that need to be asked later. They should be included in a story only with great care because they are not always what they seem. Someone who leans back noisily in a chair at the precise moment someone makes a statement, for instance, may not be disgusted. The person may just be tired of sitting. A person might cough loudly when something is said not to show displeasure at the comment, but because of a need to cough.

It is important to note such nonverbal cues, however, and to ask the person who communicated nonverbally if he or she was making a statement. A speaker might smile faintly while saying, "The crime commission's report is going to exonerate this administration of all wrongdoing." That may be an important clue that the report is merely a whitewash and that everyone (except the public) knows it.

Taking Names

It's not necessary to use the name of each participant in a meeting or speech, but it is necessary to use some names. The problem is, writers don't always know which names they will use until near the end of an event—or even until they are preparing a story afterward. It's important, therefore, to get as many names as possible as the event progresses. One often can get the names of some officials (city council members, for example) just before a meeting starts or from the organization's Web site. A

FIGURE 11.1   SAMPLE SKETCH OF MEETING PARTICIPANTS

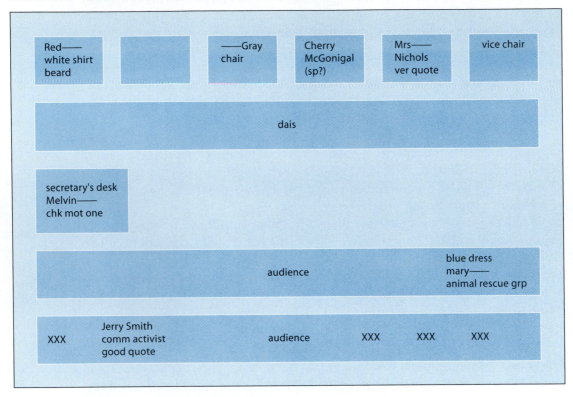

writer covering the Cedar Rapids, Iowa, City Council, for example, can type *cedar rapids city council* in the appropriate slot on the Google search page and then click on the City of Cedar Rapids Web site. From the home page, one can click on the "City Council for 2004–2006" button. Up pops a list of the city council members *with* photographs. Telephone numbers and electronic mail addresses also are available.

A group sometimes is gathered around a table or members sit looking at the audience from behind a dais. In either case, writers look for nameplates and write down each name. It helps to make an outline of the room, with a sketch of the dais or table, showing where each participant is sitting. If there are no nameplates, the journalist needs to write down names as they are mentioned during the meeting. If someone refers to a participant as "Red," that needs to go into the notes. A sketch like that in Figure 11.1 can be helpful. Note in the sketch that "Red" is printed at his "spot."

If an audience watching a meeting or speech is given the opportunity to make comments or to ask questions, the writer needs to write down as much as possible about those whose comments are noteworthy. It's not unusual for a writer to attribute a direct quotation to "Jerry——, black hair, red shirt, city employee, third row." Again, a sketch of the room can be helpful.

A writer uses the sketch to keep track of possible sources and questions that must be answered later. Some of the information can be filled in before the meeting. As a meeting progresses, a writer is likely to find out Mrs. Nichols' first name. If not, the writer can get the name as the quote is verified. At the end of the meeting or during a break, the writer will ask the secretary to verify the spelling of Cherry McGonigal's name. If "Mary in the blue dress" says something quotable during the meeting, the writer might catch her afterward to get more information (including her last name and its proper spelling). The XXXs represent audience members who haven't said much to this point.

After an Event

There usually is time at the end of a meeting or speech to gather additional information or to clarify points made. A writer doesn't interrupt a meeting or speech with questions (although it often is possible to discuss an issue with an informed source outside the meeting room), so unanswered questions must be clarified afterward or during a break.

The first step is to sit as close as possible to the individuals participating in the meeting or speech (an end seat on the front row is best). A writer can hear and see what is going on and is in a good position at the end of the meeting or speech to get to the person he or she most needs to talk to. Writers who sit in the back end up (1) waiting (as the deadline looms) while everyone in town talks to the source, or (2) plowing over everyone else to get to the source first. Neither option is pleasant.

Questions that arise during a meeting or speech should be carefully noted, perhaps on a separate page in a notebook. When the writer approaches a source later, the questions will be ready. Sources understandably are put off by such statements as, "Just give me a moment to think of my question."

A writer who needs to speak to more than one source must decide which one to catch first. Typically, a writer tries to corral the source who can answer the most questions, but if he or she knows that source will hang around for a while after the meeting and another one won't, the writer might try to catch the second source first. Jerry (of "Jerry——, black hair, red shirt, city employee, third row"), for instance, is unlikely to hang around, but the chair of the meeting probably will—a writer is smart to go for Jerry first if he or she wants to quote Jerry directly.

Recording Information

Writers use the same techniques in recording information from meetings and speeches that they use in interviews (Chapter 10). Most public events can be tape-recorded, a technique that works well when it is properly used. Television journalists can have special problems because they need to get video of at least part of a meeting or speech, a considerable chore when rooms are crowded or access is limited. This is why television journalists frequently are shown interviewing sources outside speech or meeting rooms. Sometimes news sources are savvy enough to do something visually interesting just to attract the attention of television cameras and still photographers. For instance, a representative of a taxpayer's association in North Carolina attending a county commissioners' meeting took out a leather punch and dramatically poked a hole in his belt as he talked about the need for local government to "tighten its belt." A television camera operator in the room made sure he captured this action.

Care must be exercised in taping legal proceedings because journalists do not enjoy a universal privilege to record electronically what goes on in court. While most appellate courts no longer accept excessive publicity (such as allowing cameras in a courtroom) as an *automatic* basis for appeal, the decision in most jurisdictions is in the hands of the individual judges. If a judge says recording devices are not allowed, he or she will hold in contempt a journalist who tries to record the proceedings (Chapter 13).

Writing It Up

A writer must identify the most important or interesting statement made during a speech or the most interesting or important action taken during a meeting; summarize that point clearly, succinctly and accurately; and put that phrase into Part 1-A of the first paragraph. The day the speech was given or the meeting was held (today or Wednesday, for example) also needs to be in the first paragraph. Here is an example from The Associated Press of a lead for a speech story:

> NAACP board Chairman Julian Bond criticized the Bush administration Sunday, saying it had failed to enforce civil rights laws, and he denounced the FBI's use of increased surveillance powers in fighting terrorism.

Here is an example from The Associated Press of a lead for a meeting story:

> NEWARK, N.J.—The City Council approved a lease extension for Newark Liberty International Airport on Wednesday night and authorized Mayor Sharpe James to move ahead with the development of an 18,500-seat sports arena using some of the lease money.

Meetings

One of the hardest meetings to cover is the one about a budget—any budget, anywhere (see the box "Coping With Budgets"). Writers need to have reasonable math skills and some knowledge of obscure and confusing rules governing zoning, accounting, property appraisals and other esoterica. But even a novice would know better than to return to a newsroom with the lead at the left, below. It says absolutely nothing. Any audience would be justified in demanding an apology for a story that began with this lead.

The Alvin City Council got its first look at the proposed budget for the next fiscal year Monday during its regular monthly meeting in the council chambers.	Alvin residents may have to pay higher utility rates next fiscal year if the city's proposed budget, unveiled Monday by the city manager, is approved by City Council. Property taxes would drop under the plan, but the tax decrease could mean a strike by city employees.

COPING WITH BUDGETS

Budgets are estimates of money coming in (revenue) and money going out (expenditures) for a period ahead, usually a year. Budgets are prepared by small business owners, corporations, public and private organizations, school districts, colleges, cities, towns, states—and at least a few students. The property tax is an essential component of many governmental budgets.

Budget stories and presentations should focus on what those figures mean for individuals (often payers of taxes and fees) and for the organization or government.

Formal budgets seldom show all the figures people need to make much sense of them. Sometimes those preparing budgets just don't think to put them in. Many times, they want to avoid unfavorable comparisons. Good public relations practitioners who are helping to prepare budget presentations will do their best to ensure that budgets are complete, accurate and meaningful; to hide or to mislead courts disaster. Broadcast and newspaper journalists must ensure that the necessary budget figures are available.

In making sense of, say, a 2005 budget, it would be ideal to have (1) a 2004 proposed budget—anticipated revenues and expenditures; (2) actual 2004 revenues and expenditures; and (3) proposed and actual budget figures for 2003 and earlier years. It is useful to compare actual and proposed figures in prior budgets to determine how well an organization predicted its budget needs in the past, and what changes it made later.

With these budgets, a writer can determine whether the figures, including tax rates and total taxes, are going up or down or staying the same. Besides overall increases or decreases, it's equally important to report changes in the many components of a budget. Writers need to note which units are getting more money and which less, and to ask officials why. They must always find out the reasons for changes.

Tracking the changes can provide a clear picture of the direction an agency or institution is traveling and its governing philosophy. That suggests more questions, such as whether the figures, and the picture the figures represent, are accurate. A writer must remember always that budget makers often strive to paint the most favorable picture. He or she must seek reactions from those who are affected by budget decisions made by others—particularly the powerless and the disadvantaged.

The budgets that writers deal with are primarily for governmental units such as a city, school district, university or county, state or federal agency. All the money comes from taxpayers, usually as taxes, sometimes as fees or bonds. It's important to find out whether taxes or fees are going up or down. They rarely go down. Remember, too,

(continued)

COPING WITH BUDGETS   *(continued)*

that some taxes hit the affluent harder than the poor (property and estate taxes), while some taxes hit the poor harder (sales taxes and fees).

It's critical in dealing with budgets to figure percentage increases and decreases, and then work out the percentage changes for the major items (Chapter 12). Writers can't ignore the raw numbers, but the percentages can help an audience understand the broad picture.

There's no formula for writing budget stories. However, it's important to report early in the story or news release what's up and what's down; by how much and why; and the impact on individuals. For example, it's important to tell specifically what a fee or tax change will cost a dorm student or the owner of a $50,000 house (or $100,000 house if that is the average price).

It helps to spread numbers out, rather than bunching them into just one or two paragraphs. Broadcast budget stories typically are pretty shallow, while print and Web writers can go into considerably more detail.

Graphics such as pie charts and tables are helpful visual elements that are often published with budget stories. These graphics are usually prepared by a graphic artist, but the writer who gathers the budget data should be on the lookout for information that could be used to create effective charts, and read the graphs and charts carefully before they're published to ensure accuracy and clarity.

Source: Based on handouts prepared by Ted Stanton, professor of communication at the University of Houston.

The lead at the right is decent, but a writer who is fearless in using numbers might produce a lead like this one:

> Alvin residents may pay 71 percent more next fiscal year to have their garbage picked up, if the budget unveiled last night by the city manager is passed by City Council, but property taxes would drop by almost 17 percent.
>
> Residents could see a strike by city workers, however, as their customary blanket pay increase would be eliminated to help pay for the property tax reduction, Freddy Jones, police union chief, said after the meeting.

This lead shows clearly that the burden for reducing property taxes will fall on the poorer citizens and public employees of Alvin. This is not a biased report. It simply reports the numbers in a way that makes the human consequences clear. Notice that the writer, using commendable initiative, got additional information (from the police union chief) following the meeting. The union chief might have been at the meeting, or the writer might have called him while driving back to the newsroom.

The writer of this version produced a two-paragraph "unit" lead—rather than cram several interesting and important elements into one first sentence. It's not unusual in writing a story about a meeting to discover that two or more elements are of equal importance, so a writer essentially produces two Part 1 paragraphs.

The third paragraph often is a direct quotation that follows up on the material in 1-A. But the model needs to be used with flexibility. In this case, the third paragraph follows up on the material in the second paragraph:

> "We would protest strongly any budget that doesn't include a pay increase for city workers," Jones said. "I'd certainly consider calling a strike if the council didn't move on the question eventually."

Yes, it can get confusing. A different writer might choose to emphasize in paragraph 3 the numbers mentioned in the first paragraph:

> The owner of a $50,000 home would save $76 a year in property taxes and would pay an additional $43 a year in sanitation fees, a savings of $33, City Manager Frank James told City Council during its regular monthly meeting. The owner of a $26,000 home would pay an additional $3 a year to support the city.

Clearly, Alvin's less affluent residents would bear the burden of the property tax cut. It would be important following the meeting to find out what properties City Council members own—to determine whether any would benefit from the proposed changes.

Here is the rest of the story:

> The budget calls for an increase of 17.9 percent in spending, to $4.29 million next year from $3.64 million this fiscal year, which ends Sept. 30. The budget projects a 17.2 percent increase in revenues, to $4.27 million.
>
> The deficit would be offset partially by the increased sanitation rates and by an overall increase in city property values, James said. Rates for residences and small businesses would rise to $8.55 from $5 monthly.
>
> The property tax rate this year is $1.07 per $100 of property valuation. James proposes a drop in that rate to 91.7 cents because of the increased property values. If the assessed value hasn't changed, the owner of a $50,000 home would pay approximately $459 next year, compared with $535 this year.
>
> All assessments are still tentative because the Board of Equalization has not set hearings for property owners who want to protest their assessments.
>
> The budget calls for an increase in water and sewer rates because of a projected shortfall in the utility fund, which is separate from the general fund. Water and sewer rates are each $5.50, and they'd go up $1 a month each, James said.
>
> Council had not seen the proposed budget before Monday.

Obviously, it would be most difficult for television and radio journalists to report specifics of the budget. It's not easy to follow the money even when figures are reported in print. Broadcast journalists could, however, air the first four paragraphs above and record reactions of City Council members and those who attended the meeting. Broadcast journalists often can link to the entire budget from a Web site, although that must be done with care.[6]

Speeches

A story about a speech differs somewhat from other stories. For one thing, speech stories often have more direct quotations because writers want to capture the personalities of the speakers. It is easy to become little more than a stenographer, however, writing down everything a speaker says in the speaker's exact words. This is not *writing,* so professionals need to exercise care. If more than half of a speech report is composed of direct quotations, a writer needs to take a critical look at his or her wording: The report might sound like a stenographer wrote it. Speech stories also tend to have more background information than many other kinds of stories, so care must be exercised in working in background information.

Still, speech stories are like all others in that they must capture the heart of the speech and report that in an accurate, complete and compelling way. Consider the two leads below:

A Colorado congresswoman talked today about the value of a liberal arts education in a speech to students, faculty and staff at Colorado College.	A liberal arts education is critical to those who want to make sense of and to use technical and scientific advances in this increasingly complex world, Rep. Diana DeGette, D-Colo., told students, faculty and staff today at Colorado College.

The lead at the left, which is deserving of an F, tells what the speech is about; it does not tell what DeGette said specifically about a liberal arts education, as does the lead at the right.[7] The lead at the right also puts the most important information in Part 1-A, while the lead at the left does not.

A writer typically will follow a good lead with a direct quotation that amplifies the points made in the lead, as in this example:

"In a world of advancing technology, exponential increases in scientific and medical discoveries and instant communication, a liberal arts education teaches us how to understand and to use the opportunities created by our fluid, complex world," DeGette said during Colorado College's opening convocation address of the year.

Note the background material is at the end of the sentence (Part 2-B), rather than at the beginning. The next two sentences are used to amplify the main theme:

> A liberal arts education—which teaches values, compassion and empathy—opens students' eyes to new possibilities and new choices, said DeGette, who was awarded an honorary degree during the convocation marking the start of the academic year.
>
> "It gives us the tools for life and insight into life itself."

The last sentence is a strong direct quote and occupies a paragraph by itself even though it is quite short. It's not a bad idea to highlight a strong quote in this way. Note, too, the lack of attribution. There will likely be only one source in a speech story, so excessive attribution is not necessary.

One theme of the speech was the attack on liberal arts education from many quarters. Here is how a writer might handle that in a block, or chunk, as a follow-up to statements about the value of the liberal arts education:

> The liberal arts education is attacked by many critics, DeGrette said, including those who argue that the liberal arts distract people from the "real world" of money, status, jobs and media popularity.
>
> Then there are those who see the liberal arts as dangerous, as "the road to misguided thinking, to paradox, to sin, to the collapse of the polity or to worldwide catastrophe."
>
> These critics see liberal arts students as troublemakers who will not follow the party line or dogmas, and who are not willing to have their thinking directed by others.
>
> "The attack against liberal arts is nothing less than an attack on rationality, on individual autonomy and on cultural diversity," she said. But compassion, mutual respect, responsibility and tolerance must prevail.

A third major theme is the relationship of the liberal arts to public policy. Here is how that might be handled in another block:

> A liberal arts education is critical to the making of sound public policy, but policymakers too often are concerned too much about polls, she said.
>
> A liberal arts education helps individuals develop "a breadth of experience and openness of mind to understand the people we encounter and the effect of legislation on the people we serve.
>
> "We cannot view people as stereotypical, predictable or flotsam on the tide of history's progress."

More could be written about this long, complex speech, but this example suggests how that writing might progress. Each major theme (liberal arts education is important; it is under attack; and it is especially useful in public policy-making) must be described in its own block before the writer moves on to the next major theme.

NEWS CONFERENCES

In a traditional news conference, a news source or personality calls together a group of journalists, usually makes a statement relating to the topic and answers questions. In the high-technology world, news conferences can be more complex. When a Boston children's hospital wanted to tell the public about a study of substance abuse in adolescents and a new tool for intervention, public relations professionals organized a news conference that could be "attended" via the Web. The event featured live audio coupled with a photograph of the main speaker; journalists could ask questions, hear all that was going on even if they weren't there and view supporting materials. The news conference was billed as "groundbreaking," but such events are increasingly common.[8]

Advantages

When it works well, the traditional or high-technology news conference is one of the most effective and efficient methods of information collection; when it works poorly, it is one of the worst. Public relations professionals can have an important role in determining which a news conference will be.

A news conference is a popular for two good reasons:

- A news source or personality—particularly one who is very busy—may not have the time to see several journalists individually. Even a popular news source with ample time is foolish to grant individual interviews because there are always charges that the source gives one writer better information than another. A news conference gives everyone the same opportunity and it saves time.

- A single writer can miss important information, but the chance that a group will miss an important question is fairly remote. That's not to say important questions are never missed in a news conference, however.

Disadvantages

There are also disadvantages to news conferences. Here are four:

- The source controls the news conference by deciding when a conference should be held and who should ask questions. This means he or she can evade questions more easily than in private interviews. If a source skirts the issue in a private interview, the interviewer can ask follow-up questions until the source either answers the question or refuses to answer (a response that should be reported). A writer doesn't always get a chance in a news conference to ask enough follow-up questions to elicit either an adequate response or a clear refusal to answer.

  If a question from one journalist is too hot, a news source can call on someone else. The source need never go back to the tough questioner, unless that writer shouts and screams for attention. There are those who ask extraordinarily easy questions in every news conference, and a source can call on them when the going gets rough.

News conferences, such as this one organized by an anti-abortion group in Buffalo, N.Y., often generate real news, but they sometimes generate only pseudo news.

■ There is little continuity in some news conferences. Media professionals too often skip from topic to topic in their questions, and no continuity for any one topic is established through follow-up questions. A writer might introduce a topic (for example, the university president's $10 million house), but before the subject can be fully explored, someone else is asking questions about the growth of the university library.

For the news conference to work, journalists must establish continuity through the use of tough follow-up questions. The news conference can hardly be effective when follow-up questions aren't asked—because the source who controls the situation doesn't allow them, because writers are afraid to ask questions they haven't rehearsed beforehand or because editors tell their writers to "ask that question if you get the chance, no matter what else happens."

■ Some writers might not ask their best questions simply because they don't want to tip off the competition to a good story, particularly when there is a chance to catch the source alone later. If most journalists at a news conference take that approach, there is little point in even having a news conference.

■ The potential for blatant manipulation (as opposed to simply avoiding questions) is extraordinarily great. When the Russian submarine *Kursk* sank in the Barents Sea, international journalists tried to get information about the fate of the 118 sailors on board—with no luck. Russian authorities controlled news conferences and controlled other news outlets to such an extent journalists felt they were being manipulated. "There was no sure-fire way to separate truth from falsehood, especially in the early stages of coverage. Reporters had to find ways to circumvent the official prattle and move beyond the big lie."[9]

A similar pattern emerges as one analyzes Pentagon briefings during recent wars. The Vietnam War was largely free of media censorship, but control has returned in all wars since. During the Persian Gulf War, the Pentagon released only "appropriate" information. Pool reporters complained they were not allowed to file timely reports and that they were isolated.[10]

The situation worsened during the bombing of Afghanistan, when "the challenge [was] not just in getting unfettered and uncensored access to U.S. troops and the battlefield—a long and mostly losing struggle in the past—but in discerning between information and disinformation."[11] The disturbing new element is that the government actually lies to its own citizens in part through news conferences. This is a concern for journalists who must find the truth, for public relations professionals whose credibility is at stake and for Americans who want to make sound decisions about war and peace.

Question Carefully

Preparation of questions is important, but a writer must feel free in a news conference to scrap prepared questions if necessary and to pursue an important line opened by a colleague. If an important question is asked and the source evades the question, no writer should ask a prepared question if a response to the earlier question might produce more productive information.

This assumes the writer isn't afraid to ask a question that is inspired by previous questions or answers; is sufficiently well prepared to recognize the genuine importance of a colleague's question; and is sufficiently open-minded to follow up the competition's lead.

As in meetings, speeches and interviews, a good writer always is alert for nonverbal cues that signal that a source's private thoughts don't necessarily correspond to public statements.

SPECIAL PROBLEMS

Several problems can arise for writers as they cover meetings, news conferences or speeches, and the writer's options often are limited when they do. Some of the more common are closed meetings, denials, off-the-record comments, asking questions when a news conference is over and estimating crowd sizes. These are not often problems for public relations professionals, but they need to understand them because they sometimes are problems and because an understanding of these issues will help public relations professionals work with their colleagues in journalism.

Closed Meetings

Virtually all government departments and agencies—federal, state and local—are required by open meetings laws to remain open when they discuss public money, public officials or public facilities (Chapter 13). But some groups try to close meetings anyway. When the Fulton, Mo., City Council closed 13 real estate–planning meetings, for example, a city resident took the city to court and argued the agreements reached in the meetings were illegal. The Missouri Supreme Court agreed.[12] Media writers must know how to react when groups try to close their meetings, and that means knowing the options:

- A good writer knows the provisions of state laws regarding public meetings and understands the conditions under which public meetings can (and cannot) be closed (Chapter 13). A writer who knows a meeting cannot be closed legally can respond more effectively if someone challenges his or her right to cover the meeting.

- A professional who is asked to leave a meeting that should not be closed has three choices: to leave quietly, to leave loudly or to refuse to leave at all. A journalist who quietly leaves a meeting that can't legally be closed has failed to represent the public interest properly.

A writer who wants to go loudly should not leave until a clear, unambiguous demand to leave—preferably a demand heard by others—has been made (see the box "Being Thrown Out Loudly"). Sometimes it is necessary to engage in an unpleasant or embarrassing exchange with the meeting chairperson to get that clear statement, but it's worth it.

Suppose, for instance, a committee chairperson simply said, "I wish you wouldn't cover this meeting." That isn't a clear statement that a media writer must not cover the meeting. If a writer said that he or she was ejected from the meeting, the source probably would deny the charge saying, "Well, I said 'I wish you wouldn't cover this meeting,' but I didn't say you couldn't." The writer would look rather foolish.

A journalist can refuse to leave a public meeting even after the person in charge says, "Okay, I'm throwing you out. I don't want you covering this meeting." Such an action could have one of three results: The meeting could continue; it could be called off and scheduled for another time and place; or police could be called to remove the journalist from the premises.

The last two results don't prove much, although the sight of the police dragging a journalist from the meeting would make a good story, particularly when cameras are around—and that would be a strong statement against closed meetings. It would not help the writer's relationship with the sources, however, and forced removal might take the spotlight off the issue of the closed meeting and put it on the question of the writer's conduct.

Finally, a writer who is forced to leave a meeting should remember always that his or her job is to get a story about the meeting. A journalist must get the names of people attending the meeting and interview them at meeting's end to find out what

BEING THROWN OUT LOUDLY

A journalist who is asked to leave a meeting that should be open to the public should not submit quietly to the request. This exchange took place between a reporter and the chairman of a state agency who wanted to have a closed meeting:

Chairman:	"Are you a reporter?"
Reporter:	"Yes."
Chairman:	"Who do you work for?"
Reporter:	"For the ——."
Chairman:	"I don't think your paper would be interested in this meeting."
Reporter:	"Well, I'll listen to what's said and then decide for myself whether it's interesting."
Chairman:	"These are just preliminary discussions. You wouldn't be interested in what we'll be talking about."
Reporter:	"Are you asking me to leave?"
Chairman:	"No."
Reporter:	"Then I'll stay."
Chairman:	"I think you'd better go."
Reporter:	"You're throwing me out of the meeting then?"
Chairman:	"I wouldn't put it that way."
Reporter:	"Then I'll stay here."
Chairman:	"Okay, I'm throwing you out."

The exchange was heard by everyone who attended the meeting, and they all knew that the reporter had been thrown out. The writer returned to his office, informed his editor and then wrote a story describing in detail what happened. That's leaving loudly. The journalist later interviewed some of those at the meeting to find out what happened—and wrote a story.

happened. But a writer should avoid using information obtained in this manner unless it is confirmed by at least two sources. If the information is controversial, it should be confirmed by at least one person on each side of the controversy.

After piecing together a story, the writer might call the head of the organization to confirm the accuracy of the report. If the accuracy is verified, the story can be printed as is. If the report is denied, the denial should be published along with the story. The writer will have done the best job possible to ensure the accuracy and fairness of the report.

Some meetings fall into a gray area and journalists aren't sure how they should react to an attempt to close a meeting. Madison, Wis., Mayor Sue Bauman, for example, asked journalists to leave a meeting she had with activist groups about the activists' intentions during the U.S. Conference of Mayors in Madison. The meeting was held on public property and it involved public officials, public events and public funds—and yet the journalists acceded to the mayor's request.

Norm Stockwell of radio station WORT was not happy. He was quoted as saying Madison's media are "responsible enough to cover the facts of the story and provide important information about how the city and demonstrators will be able to interact during the mayors conference." And Matt Stoner, an activist who was part of the meeting, was quoted as complaining: "I think it [a closed meeting] is problematic because it's symptomatic of a larger trend in city government. ... The public citizenry needs to know what goes on."[13]

Bauman did brief the media following the two-hour meeting, but for the journalists that most certainly was not the same as being there, for mayors typically are about the least objective people in town.

Denials

A denial is more unusual in a public event than in a personal interview, primarily because there are witnesses at public events to verify the accuracy of a story. It's difficult to deny a statement if 10 people heard it. It also is difficult to stand by the accuracy of a news report if 10 people know the writer misquoted or misrepresented a speaker or group.

If someone denies saying something or taking a certain action at a public event, a journalist should attempt to confirm the accuracy of the report through interviews with people who attended or by obtaining tapes made at the event. If the writer was wrong, the correct facts should be reported and an apology written. If the writer was right, the news medium should stand by its story. It should quote by name the people who verified the accuracy of the report or publish key portions of taped conversations.

It isn't necessary or desirable to get involved in a shouting match with a news source, but it is necessary to defend the credibility and fairness of the medium.

Off-the-record Comments

Anything said to an audience in an open meeting or speech may be reported, even if the source of the statement (or anyone else) strongly objects. A writer, however, must recognize the nonlegal consequences of reporting statements made at a public meeting when the source objects. A writer may lose an important source by reporting information the source doesn't want reported. If the source heads an important commission or group, the writer may be unwelcome at future meetings. No one can be barred from the public meeting, but other writers may receive more favorable treatment—usually in the form of newsbreaks and exclusive interviews.

A journalist who reports information a source doesn't want reported also may find other sources "unavailable." If a city council president says something uncomplimentary about the city's mayor and asks that the statement not be reported, a journalist who uses the statement may be cast in the role of villain. Other council members and the council staff may rally behind the president against the reporter. The writer's "grievous act" will be forgotten in time, but meanwhile his or her task is made much more difficult.

This is not to say, certainly, that a writer should be cowed by any source. But he or she should consider the possible consequences of reporting public statements that sources of the statements think shouldn't be reported. A writer in this situation has a few options:

- Interrupt a meeting or speech when a speaker says something like, "I'd like to tell you people something about that situation, if it's not going in the media." The journalist can say publicly that nothing said in a public meeting can be off the record. The source at that point can decide to forget the comment (to the irritation of some members of the audience) or go ahead and make the statement (for the record).
- Leave the meeting while the off-the-record material is discussed—and then write a story about it based on interviews with those who heard the comments. Some sources see this as "cheating," but few journalists do, as long as no agreements were made.
- Keep quiet, thereby making a tacit agreement with the source.

Questions After a News Conference

Substantive questions should be asked during a news conference, not afterward, when other journalists can't hear the questions or the responses. It is considered unethical by many professionals for a writer to sit through an entire news conference—perhaps without asking a single question—and then interview the news source confidentially immediately after the news conference has ended.

An experienced source might simply ignore a question asked after the news conference on the correct assumption that the question should have been asked earlier. Or a source might speak loudly enough for everyone present to hear the response. An inexperienced news source might simply answer the question, but after-the-event questions place the source in an awkward position.

Estimating Crowd Sizes

Getting a good estimate of a crowd's size often is important because of the way the information is used: Those who organize a demonstration, for example, want the crowd to be seen as huge because that supports the cause, while those who oppose the cause want people to see the crowd size as small.

It's easy enough to know the size of a crowd of only a few dozen—a writer can (and should) count the audience. When the crowd is large, particularly at an outdoor

THE JOY OF ESTIMATING CROWD SIZE

The difficulty of estimating crowds is evident in an experiment conducted by the *San Francisco Chronicle* after the newspaper reported that 200,000 persons attended a San Francisco anti-war demonstration in 2003. The *Chronicle* relied on estimates by the police and by demonstration organizers.

But the *Chronicle* hired an air photography firm to photograph the crowd from 2,000 feet as part of its experiment. The images "provide a perspective that allows a discrete count of individuals and a view of the spaces between them, a view that is impossible from ground-level."[14]

The air photography firm and the *Chronicle* studied the photographs separately and estimated the crowd at 65,000. Public transportation system estimates supported the lower number, and the air photography firm said its estimate was accurate within 10 percentage points either way.

The *Chronicle*'s report was controversial, for some police and march organizers stuck by the original estimate. So why did the *Chronicle* go to such lengths? "This innovative approach,

This aerial photograph of a 2003 anti-war march through San Francisco casts doubt on official estimates of the crowd's size. Journalists and public officials frequently are pressured to inflate or to deflate their estimates.

however controversial its conclusions, is nonetheless a far more exact way to provide readers with critically important information," executive editor Phil Bronstein was quoted as saying.[15]

event, the task becomes more difficult (see the box "The Joy of Estimating Crowd Size"). A writer has several alternatives. He or she can quote an "official source." A police department or other agency often estimates the size of a crowd it has been assigned to oversee. But police officers aren't necessarily the best judges of crowd sizes; they may have no special training, and they may give biased estimates.

A police estimate of the size of a crowd demonstrating *against* a mayor popular with the police, for instance, might be much lower than the actual figure. A police estimate of the size of a crowd demonstrating *for* the popular mayor might be considerably higher than the actual size.

A writer also can report a vague estimate of crowd size. Such words as *handful, hundreds, thousands, many, few* and *relatively large number* are so vague a writer won't be inaccurate when using them, but the phrases don't really say much. A handful could be anything from two to 10 or more; hundreds could range from 200 to 999; thousands could range from 2,000 to 999,000. Such estimates do not help the reader understand the magnitude of an event; it is little better to use "thousands," for example, than to say nothing at all of a crowd's size. Vague estimates also are easily challenged.

To get a more accurate estimate of crowd size, a writer can make a careful approximation and then balance that estimate against those of official sources and other media professionals. If all estimates agree, they probably are accurate. If they don't, the writer must use the one that seems most accurate. Before reaching the decision, it's necessary to learn how each estimate was determined. A police officer might say, "Well, I've seen a lot of crowds and this one looks like it's about 10,000." Such an estimate is questionable and should be discounted.

It's relatively easy to estimate a crowd's size indoors. If a minister is speaking in the Louisiana Superdome (or any other facility), a writer should count the number of persons in one section and multiply that figure by the number of sections. If some sections are less crowded than others, a writer should count the crowded sections and multiply that figure by the number of crowded sections; then he or she should count the less crowded sections and multiply that figure by the number of less crowded sections, and so on.

If the Superdome or other facility is full, the writer should ask the manager how many people the stadium seats. If tickets were sold for the event, it's necessary only to ask how many tickets were sold and how many were given away. All these figures should be available.

A SUGGESTION FOR PUBLIC RELATIONS

Public relations writers don't cover many meetings, speeches or news conferences, but the guidelines outlined in this chapter are helpful when they do. Some do write news releases based on speeches given by members of the organization they work for or by invited speakers. Many public relations professionals write the speeches that are delivered by corporate executives or government leaders. Knowing how journalists report speeches can help these professionals to do a better job of writing them. In addition, public relations people who don't know how events are covered miss an important opportunity to establish and maintain good relationships with news professionals and to help ensure that stories about their events are accurate.

It should be evident from this chapter that actions can be taken, or avoided, to make journalists' tasks easier. Journalists appreciate the help they get from the mayor's media secretary or the public relations professional who handles a special event.

Public relations professionals can help overworked journalists by, for example, ensuring that they are supplied with well-written and complete stories about upcoming events, complete meeting agendas, copies of speeches and biographies of speakers. They can make sure that journalists have good seats and that photographers have photo opportunities that are not disruptive to the proceedings. And they can help journalists talk briefly to sources or clarify issues as meetings progress.

When a journalist needs a story about an event but is unable to attend, a public relations person can provide a fair and accurate summary of what happened or what was said so the journalist can produce a story. This is not a perfect situation for either party, but it is helpful when both individuals try to make the situation work—and the journalist will be grateful.

Finally, public relations writers can educate others in their organizations (including their bosses, although this can be scary) about journalistic practices. Some organization chairs and heads try to close their meetings when that action is not appropriate or even legal—a practice that is guaranteed to create bad feelings. It is important for professionals to argue against closed meetings at every opportunity. When meetings must be closed, they need to know and to explain the conditions under which meetings may be closed. And they must ensure that any business conducted during a closed meeting is reported to the public.

Public relations professionals must explain that off-the-record comments and denials of statements made during public events must be avoided. They simply call attention to the problems the organization would like to minimize; they muddy the discussion to the point that nobody knows what was said or done; they lead to poor media relationships; and they might be embarrassing. A member of the audience, for example, might have a tape that proves the denied statement was, in fact, accurately reported.

Public relations professionals who try to help journalists nearly always reap large benefits later.

YOUR RESPONSIBILITY IS . . .

- To recognize how important meetings, speeches and news conferences are to any group, organization or society that seeks to function democratically and effectively.

- To recognize that covering (or helping others cover) meetings, speeches and news conferences is not easy, but that those stories are among the most important ones that media writers produce.

■ To understand that thousands of events cannot be covered and to learn to recognize those that should be.

■ To learn the importance of advance stories and to learn how to write good ones.

■ To learn that covering news events is considerably easier when you are well-informed about the topic of the meeting, news conference or speech and about the major participants or speaker. You need to try your hand at budget stories every chance you get, for they are difficult for journalists and public relations professionals to write.

■ To recognize that many of the special problems addressed in this chapter (closed meetings, denials and off-the-record comments) rarely occur, but to know what to do when one does.

■ To understand that, if you seek a career in public relations, you will incur enormous good will if you help journalists do their jobs as they cover events.

■ To learn, if you seek a career in public relations, the importance of trying to convince those for whom you work that they should avoid creating special problems for journalists. Your organization suffers if a journalist is tossed out of a meeting that is supposed to be open, for example.

NOTES

1. Ian Marquand, "Collecting Information: Share the Importance of Open Government," *Quill*, July/August 2002: 38.

2. Ron Nissimov, "Chancellor's Speech Ignores Criticism From Faculty at UH," *Houston Chronicle*, Oct. 17, 2002: A-27.

3. Event planning is described in Judy Allen, *Event Planning: The Ultimate Guide to Successful Meetings, Corporate Events, Fundraising Galas, Conferences, Conventions, Incentives and Other Special Events* (Toronto: John Wiley, 2000); and James S. Armstrong, *Planning Special Events* (San Francisco: Jossey-Bass, 2001).

4. Deborah Blum, "Communicating Science and Engineering in a Sound Bite World," *Gifts of Speech*, May 14, 1998. Downloaded on Oct. 10, 2002, from <gos.sbc.edu/b/blum.html>.

5. Mark L. Knapp and Judith A. Hall, *Nonverbal Communication in Human Interaction*, 4th ed. (Fort Worth, Texas: Harcourt Brace, 1997); and Ullica Segerstrale and Peter Molnar, *Nonverbal Communication: Where Nature Meets Culture* (Mahwah, N.J.: Erlbaum, 1997).

6. Karen Vargo, Carl Schierhorn, Stanley T. Wearden, Ann B. Schierhorn, Fred F. Endres and Pamela S. Tabar, "How Readers Respond to Digital News Stories in Layers and Links," *Newspaper Research Journal*, 21:2 (2000): 40–54.

7. Diana DeGette, "The Value of a Liberal Arts Education," *Gifts of Speech*, Aug. 31, 1998. Downloaded on Oct. 8, 2002, from <gos.sbc.edu/d/degette.html>.

8. "Groundbreaking Press Conference Will Unveil Troubling New Statistics on Teen Substance Abuse: Internet-Enabled Audio Webcast Will Allow Media to Interact From Around the World," news release, Children's Hospital Boston, *PR Newswire*, June 11, 2002.

9. Sherry Ricchiardi, "Smoke Screen: Reporters Covering the Sinking of the Russian Submarine *Kursk* Struggled to Penetrate a Barrage of Disinformation that Hearkened Back to the Unlamented Soviet Era," *American Journalism Review,* December 2000: 54–57, p. 54.

10. Stanley W. Cloud, "The Pentagon and the Press: Several 'Principles' of Coverage Became Victims of the War Against Terrorism," *Nieman Reports,* Winter 2001: 13–16.

11. Maud S. Beelman, "The Dangers of Disinformation in the War on Terrorism: 'We Actually Put Out a False Message to Mislead People,'" *Nieman Reports,* Winter 2001: 16–18.

12. "Closed Meetings on Golf Course Development Violate Law," *The News Media & the Law,* Winter 1999: 25–26.

13. Samara Kalk, "Bauman Excludes Media From Meeting With Activists," Madison, Wis., *Capital Times,* May 20, 2002: A-2.

14. Wyatt Buchanan, "Photos Show 65,000 at Peak of S.F. Rally: Aerial Study Casts Doubt on Estimates of 200,000," *San Francisco Chronicle,* Feb. 21, 2003: A-1,6, p. A-6. Available at <www.sfgate.com/rallycount>.

15. Ibid.

CHAPTER 12

NUMBERS

Statistics and Social Science Techniques

Numeracy is no less important than literacy to the 21st-century communication professional, and yet many writers are aggressively antagonistic toward numbers, while others are passively aggressive in refusing to acknowledge their existence. Many good writers would ridicule the professional who doesn't know the difference between a noun and a pronoun, and yet they see nothing particularly amiss if a writer doesn't know the difference between a mean and a median.

The lack of numerical competency can weaken the effectiveness of mass communication. A study of 2,000 stories published by one local newspaper shows nearly half required mathematical calculations, and many of the stories with numbers were published on the front page or the front pages of sections. Mathematical errors were identified and a new kind of numerical error was discovered nearly every other day. "Unquestioning use of figures, resulting in news stories with dubious and unsupported claims, also was documented."[1] Another study showed that news sources thought numerical errors were almost as severe as getting a name wrong, and numerical errors were seen as more severe than misquoting a source.[2]

One consequence of innumeracy is that errors of any kind (including numerical errors) can cause an audience to perceive a medium or organization as less credible. When credibility is all you really have to sell, that hurts. Another consequence is that writers and the public "become prey to commercial chicanery, financial foolery, medical quackery, and numerical terrorism from pressure groups, all because [they] are unable (or unwilling) to think clearly for a few moments."[3]

Innumeracy also can create hardships for innocent groups and organizations. When the Facility Needs Committee of an independent school district discussed plans for a $322 million bond issue, a local newspaper said the committee proposed an 11

This photograph captures the agony many media professionals feel when they have to deal with numbers. Modern media professionals must be well-versed in the use of numbers and social science methods, however.

percent increase in the property tax rate. That was a pretty big chunk at a time when many taxpayers were complaining about their property taxes. The newspaper noted in the next issue, after tempers flared following the initial report, that the group was recommending an 11 cent increase, which was *considerably* less than 11 percent.[4]

Numeracy requires much more than an ability to add, subtract, multiply and divide, although these skills are important. Professionals "need knowledge of survey research, field experiments, programming, a heavy dose of statistics, and how to apply scientific reasoning to investigative projects," says Philip Meyer, who is frequently described as the father of precision journalism (or less accurately, computer-assisted reporting. "Some minimum level of competency in quantitative methods ought to be an entry-level requirement."[5]

Meyer was referring to journalists, but public relations professionals also need to hone their mathematical skills and to understand the fundamentals of statistics and research. The Commission on Public Relations Education completed at the end of the 20th century one of the most comprehensive studies of public relations education ever attempted. The commission said public relations writers need to have knowledge about marketing, finance, research and forecasting, and they need to know how to conduct research, analyze data and manage information.[6]

It's not enough to sharpen arithmetic skills and to learn some of the basics of social science research. Writers must understand the contexts in which numbers are used. Communication professionals need to ask the same kinds of contextual questions statisticians ask as they evaluate surveys and other research, according to John Allen Paulos, mathematician and media critic. It is important to know the percentages and other numbers certainly:

> But we also want to know whether the numbers on homelessness or child abuse, say, come from police blotter reports (in which case they are likely to be low) or whether they come from scientifically controlled studies (in which case they are likely to be somewhat higher) or whether they come from the press releases of groups with an ideological axe to grind (in which case they are liable to be extremely high—or extremely low, depending on the ideology).
>
> Without an ambient story, background knowledge, and some indication of the provenance of the statistics, it is impossible to evaluate their validity.[7]

This chapter helps students understand the importance of numeracy, how to make some basic computations, how to put numbers in context and how to use and to understand a few basics of social science. Stay calm. Anyone can do this.

FUNDAMENTAL CONCEPTS

Books have been written about statistical testing and research design and how media professionals can use research techniques. Readers of this chapter will not get a complete course in the application of research methods to mass communication problems. However, they will be exposed to concepts they must understand if they are to deal successfully with numbers. Knowledge of these fundamentals will save readers from potential embarrassment, and it will be a good foundation for studies of more complex material. The concepts are random samples, percentages, per capita ratios, measures of central tendency, dispersion, relationships and significance testing.

Sample Versus Census

Anyone who hopes to understand and to evaluate statistics must first understand sampling, for that underpins everything. A sample may consist of individuals (registered voters, online shoppers, Web site users) or objects (records in a database, television programs, plots of land in a field in an agricultural study).

A good sample represents all of the persons or objects in the target group (called a population or universe). In an election poll, for example, the population is registered voters who are likely to cast ballots. In a study of a court's sentencing practices in murder cases, the population is all records in murder cases during the past, say, five years.

WHAT IS "RANDOM"?

The word *random* is frequently misused. It does not mean haphazard, careless or catch-as-catch-can. *Random* means objects or persons are selected from a larger group (called a population or universe) in such a way that every object or person has an equal chance of being selected. Selecting a random sample is difficult and requires careful procedures.

The word *random* should not be used when appropriate procedures have not been followed in selecting a sample. A better phrase for describing a nonrandom (or non-probability) sample, if one must be used, is *spot check.* John Allen Paulos recommends describing such samples this way: "Here are some abbreviated, quite minor variations on our story recounted by the indiscriminate collection of neighborhood residents."[8]

We recommend they not be used at all. Ever.

A researcher who studies *all* objects or persons in a universe is conducting a census, much as the U.S. Census Bureau conducts a census every decade. The Census is called a census because every American is counted, although there is considerable controversy about whether everyone really is contacted. Journalists who do systematic studies of records (such as researching court sentencing practices) almost always examine all of the cases, but they don't always need to (Chapter 9). They may feel, however, that a story based on census data carries more credibility than does one based on sampling data. They may be right.

The random sample is essential to almost any kind of research, but many media professionals (and some social science researchers) overlook its importance. Simply stated, a random sample means that every person or object in a population (the target group) has an equal chance of being selected. If it is large enough, the sample should represent the target group reasonably well. (See the box "What is 'Random.'")

Researchers follow several steps in drawing a random sample:

- The population must be defined precisely. In a study of Web site usage, for example, the population might consist of everyone who visits an organization's home page, but it might consist of everyone who visits at least one page in addition to the home page. The exact definition depends on the purpose of the study.

- A researcher must obtain a list (with electronic mail addresses or telephone numbers, depending on the project) of all those in the population. This can be extraordinarily difficult, particularly in public opinion polls where lists are not available (alternatives are discussed in a later section).

- A procedure for random selection must be used to guarantee that every case in the population has an equal chance of being chosen. In its simplest form, a random sample is drawn by numbering the members of the population from 1 to *N* and then randomly selecting names or records from the list. If one has a population of 5,000 names, one might pick 500 numbers between 1 and 5,000 using a random numbers table (found in most statistics books) or a calculator or computer that generates random numbers. A technique in which a researcher picks cases arbitrarily from a list, or draws names from a hat, is not random and should never be used.

A random sample is important for two reasons:

- It is the best assurance a researcher or media writer can have that a sample is representative of the population being studied. This can be demonstrated through probability theory,[9] but it is also intuitively true. If every case in the population has an equal chance of being selected, there is no bias or favoritism in the selection and the sample should represent the population—as long as the sample is sufficiently large.

- A researcher who uses a random sample is able to compute useful statistics. These include the margin of error, or the degree of inaccuracy that is likely in a poll; the standard deviation, which is a measure of score dispersion; and statistical significance. Each of these is discussed in the following pages.

It is difficult to overstate the importance of random sampling, particularly when a writer or researcher wants to generalize to a larger population or to calculate statistics. Nonprobability samples are those drawn in haphazard ways, although the methods may seem sophisticated and reasonable. A Web site, for instance, that conducts a "poll" might report data based on 250,000 strikes. But those data are worthless, at least in terms of suggesting what a larger population is thinking.

The first question *always* is: Did you use a random sample?

Percentage

Simple frequencies are the numbers of objects or people who fall into different categories. They often are sufficient when media professionals need to report numerical results. It's not necessary to compute a percentage or other statistic to report that 11 taxpayers complained to the mayor's office about shoddy sidewalk repair; 10 complained about police brutality; and 14 complained about the property tax rate.

Frequencies are not always enough, however, and percentages need to be computed. A percentage is essentially an index—one of the simplest and most useful of indices. Its main purpose is to make comparisons easier. The percentage is a ratio with a base of 100. When a polling organization says 75 percent of a group falls into a certain category, it is saying 75 of 100 people (or 750 of 1,000 people) fall into that category.

A percentage can be a media professional's best friend, if he or she calculates and uses it right (see the box "Using Percentages Wisely"). Journalists usually report in poll stories that 53 percent of likely voters favor candidate X and 47 percent favor candidate Y. That is much more enlightening than reporting that 901 support candidate X and 799 support candidate Y.

A public school public relations writer assigned to write a release about high school dropouts might report that 980 students of 3,220 who start high school in the district end up dropping out. These are meaningful numbers, but a lead might focus more on the percentage because it makes the data more compelling, as in this example:

> Thirty percent of students in Plain Valley schools who start high school drop out before they graduate, Superintendent Rhonda Johansen said today.

The 30 percent figure doesn't make the school district look good, but it is an accurate, fair summary of the results. The other numbers can be reported in the second paragraph.

It's not difficult to compute a percentage (or to check someone else's math) if one always remembers to divide by the base number (the denominator). For instance, a writer who wants to know the percentages of females (37) and males (43) in a group divides each number by the base number (80). That leaves 46 percent females and 54 percent males (numbers are rounded off as everyone was taught to do in fifth grade).[10]

Things get a little trickier in calculating a percentage difference, but it's still easy for writers who follow a few simple steps. Say they want to calculate the percentage difference when a bus fare is increased to $1 from 80 cents. Here's how to do it:

- Find the base number (the denominator), which always is the *original* number (this time, it's 80).
- Calculate the difference (20 cents).
- *Always* divide the little number (20) by the big number (80).

Twenty divided by 80 results in a 25 percent increase. If the original fare is $1 and it is reduced to 80 cents, the base number has changed: It is $1. The fare *decrease* is 20 percent. For a story about a fare increase, a good lead is:

> Bus riders in Colgate County will pay 25 percent more to ride starting on Nov. 1, the County Transportation Board decided today.

Per Capita Ratio

The per capita ratio is a good tool for social scientists and media writers who want to convert raw data (about numbers of crimes in three locales, for example) to formats that help people understand what the numbers mean. A ratio is the numerical relationship between two objects or individuals, and per capita is the number of times an event occurs per person in a population. The ratio of men to women in a

USING PERCENTAGES WISELY

Percentages are extremely useful, when they are used properly, because they are so specific. Some writers sacrifice that specificity, however, when they convert "65 percent" to "a huge majority," or "15 percent" to "a small minority." Why use a vague term when a specific percentage is available?

A writer who begins a report with "A huge majority of residents say ..." seems to think it's necessary to tell readers how to interpret a given percentage, which usually is given lower in the story. That isn't necessary. The exact percentage should be reported immediately so the audience can decide how huge the majority is. It doesn't solve the problem to write "A huge majority of residents (65 percent) say. ... " That still tells the audience how to interpret the percentage.

Most writers would do well simply to eliminate from their vocabularies such words as *overwhelming, huge, small, insignificant, large, vast, tremendous, enormous* and *immense* in describing majorities and minorities based on percentages. For one thing, these are judgmental words, and writers should not report their own judgments. Also, it's not easy to decide when a majority becomes "enormous." Is 56 percent "enormous"? Some readers might think so, but others might think an "enormous" percentage is one larger than 75 percent. Is 25 percent an "insignificant" minority? Some viewers would say yes, while others would say no.

Just report the percentages.

class, for instance, might be 4 to 3, meaning that 40 students are male and 30 are female. The number of female students per capita is 0.42 (40 divided by 70).

All this may seem mysterious and useless, but it's not. Assume a Web writer wants to compare the number of murders in Chicago, New Orleans and New York City. According to the FBI, the Chicago Police Department reported 648 murders in 2002; the New Orleans Police Department reported 258; and the New York City Police Department reported 590. The writer might produce this lead:

> Chicago, with 648 murders reported in 2002, is more dangerous than New Orleans and New York City.

This lead is poor for several reasons, but the worst problem is that it is inaccurate because it is based on raw numbers and faulty comparisons.

The situation is clearer if the writer brings in three more numbers: population of each city. The population of Chicago is 2.89 million; New Orleans, 473,681;

and New York City, 8.08 million. Chicago's 648 looks a little better now, but the comparison still is unclear, so the writer divides the number of murders by the population for each city to get a per capita ratio. Chicago is looking even better at 0.00022 (compared to 0.00007 for New York City and 0.00054 for New Orleans), but the numbers are so small, they are hard to comprehend.

To find the rate per 100,000 residents, the Web writer just multiplies 100,000 by the number of murders per person. For Chicago, that's 100,000 times 0.00022, or 22 murders per 100,000 residents. The result for New Orleans is 54 and the result for New York City is 7.

An individual's chance of getting murdered in the city with the most murders (Chicago) is lower than the chance of getting murdered in the city with the fewest murders (New Orleans). A Web writer who does not compute the per capita ratio is doing readers a disservice, for they are unlikely to understand the significance of the raw numbers. Here is a better lead for the story:

> Your chance for getting murdered in Chicago is higher than it would be if you lived in New York City, but lower than if you lived in New Orleans.

This lead is better because it is accurate (Chicago does not have more murders); it doesn't highlight an essentially meaningless statistic (648); and it focuses on murders (and not on the less specific "more dangerous").

Central Tendency

It often is sufficient for writers to report simple frequencies or percentages, but they sometimes need to use measures of central tendency. This seems a frightening term, but it doesn't have to be. A measure of central tendency (or of central value) refers to a single score that is typical of or represents a group of scores. The mean, median and mode are three widely used measures of central tendency.[11]

Mean

A mean is essentially an average, and an average is the sum of all measures (a test, for example) divided by the number of measures. If an instructor wants to compute a class average (mean) for 11 students, this is how he or she would do it. The grades are 80, 73, 64, 97, 56, 79, 83, 77, 92, 61 and 78. The total is 840. Divide by 11 and the mean is 76.

If the owner of a real estate company asks a public relations professional for the average sale price of homes in the community, she or he would get a listing of homes sold, say, in the past year, sum the prices and divide by the total number of homes. This mean, by the way, is well known in most communities.

The Wall Street Journal published an interesting story about the incentives manufacturers offered in 2003 to get people to buy their cars and trucks. The focus was on the problems manufacturers might have in subsequent years in getting people to buy vehicles when there were no incentives. *The Journal* needed a meaningful number that reflected rebates because incentives fluctuated throughout the year. It got meaningful numbers from the Power Information Network, which reported mean (average) rebates offered by manufacturers. The average cash rebate for Chevrolet in 2003 was $3,231, for example, and *The Journal* compared that average to the $1,654 average in 2001. The story would not have been meaningful without these means.[12]

Median

A median is the midpoint of all scores when they are ranked in order from smallest to largest. A writer who ranks the scores in the previous example finds 56, 61, 64, 73, 77, 78, 79, 80, 83, 92 and 97. The median score is 78. If the writer had only 10 numbers, he or she would average the two middle scores, as in 56, 61, 64, 73, *77, 79,* 80, 83, 92 and 97. In this case, the number would be the same: 78.

A median typically is used when there are extreme numbers in a set. For instance, if one student in the example made 6, rather than 56, and one made 1, rather than 61, the *mean* would be 67 rather than 76. The *median* would be a better reflection of the class scores. Recall the public relations writer who needed the mean sale price of homes in the community: In fact, the median might be the better indicator of a community's home values if 90 percent of the homes are valued at $150,000–$250,000 and 10 percent are valued below $50,000.

Mode

A mode is the value that appears most frequently in a series of numbers. Eighty is the value that appears most frequently in this series, for example: 80, 73, 64, 97, 56, 79, 83, 80, 77, 92, 61 and 78. The mode is not often used by media writers for a couple of reasons.

First, the mode can be misleading because attention is on one score (the one occurring most frequently) when other scores might be more important. Take this series of numbers, for example: 24, 80, 73, 64, 97, 56, 24, 79, 24, 83, 81, 77, 92, 61 and 78. Twenty-four occurs most frequently, but it obviously is not an accurate reflection of the group. Second, a distribution of numbers might have more than one mode, making interpretation difficult.

Dispersion

Measures of central tendency tell writers a great deal, but problems arise when data sets include extreme scores. A Web writer who is analyzing standardized test scores from a local school district might find a mean score of 80, but that mean score might hide some important differences among students.

Say the writer is analyzing 100 test scores and finds that 10 students score below 25 and 10 students score above 95. Those are significant numbers, which suggest that some students need special help to pass the tests and that some students need to move on to more challenging work. That important finding might be overlooked if the writer fails to account for score dispersion.

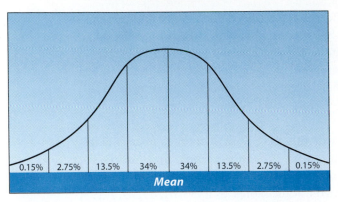

0.15% | 2.75% | 13.5% | 34% | 34% | 13.5% | 2.75% | 0.15%

Mean

FIGURE 12.1 THE NORMAL DISTRIBUTION

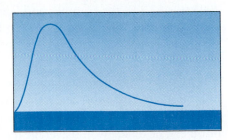

FIGURE 12.2 A SKEWED DISTRIBUTION

The difficulty can be overcome by finding the standard deviation, which is used to measure distance along the baseline of a normal distribution of numbers. The distribution is "normal" when scores or numbers are evenly distributed along a gently sloping bell curve, as shown in Figure 12.1. The folks at the ends of the curve express extreme opinions, have very high or very low intelligence or score very high or very low on tests. The scores need to be evenly distributed if the standard deviation is to have any meaning.

Computing the standard deviation is not difficult, but that is beyond the scope of this chapter. However, writers should understand the importance of the standard deviation. If the data are not evenly distributed, they are positively or negatively skewed and a writer needs to find out why. A skewed distribution, by the way, looks a bit like Figure 12.2. This most definitely is *not* the kind of curve that any researcher or media professional wants to see. One certainly cannot assume a normal distribution.

Relationships

Statisticians and media writers want to find relationships between and among variables (see the box "Correlation and Causality"). We all want to know whether variable *X* changes when variable *Y* changes. If that happens, there is a relationship between those two variables. A writer might want to know, for instance, whether there is some relationship between scores on standardized tests and home environment. This relationship is not difficult to compute if one understands measures of central tendency and the normal curve.

The New York Times relied on a simple relationship in a story about an attempt by New York City's mayor to reduce overtime spending for city employees. Writer Mike McIntire found that police officers worked 357,000 fewer overtime hours in 2003 than in 2001. But when he looked at the relationship between hours and dollars, he found that overtime spending had actually increased: The city reduced the hours by 4 percent, but increased spending by 3 percent. Senior employees, who

CORRELATION AND CAUSALITY

Many Americans are absolutely convinced that sex and violence on television and the Web have caused a decline in moral values. The Catholic Bishops of the United States, for example, argued that "Pornography, excessive violence, and other irresponsible uses of sex and violence in the media gravely harm the moral and psychological health of both society as a whole and its individual members—children and adults."[13]

While the bishops may be right, their evidence for stating such a strong cause-and-effect relationship is thin. Some of the "evidence" is anecdotal. When pornographic magazines are found in the home of a mass murderer, for instance, the pornography often is said to have "caused" the murders. Some of the evidence is stronger. Researchers test variables to find out whether some variables are correlated with (are related to) others. Some have reported relationships between antisocial behavior and pornography.

Journalists and public relations writers must avoid inferring cause-and-effect relationships as they write about studies that report correlations, for there may be other, unidentified variables accounting for the cause-and-effect relationship. For instance, a third variable (he was beaten as a child) may account for the mass murderer's violent behavior *and* for his taste for pornography.

A relationship may be well-documented, but that does not mean the researcher has found a cause-and-effect relationship, no matter how much he or she wants to.

---

earn more and therefore get more overtime pay, were working more overtime. Here is McIntire's lead:

> Despite a successful campaign by the Bloomberg administration to cut the number of overtime hours worked by city employees, overtime spending continues to rise, an analysis of budget figures shows.[14]

Researchers frequently compute correlation coefficients to determine the extent to which two variables are related, and results often are presented in scatterplots, which depict relationships visually. The writer who wants to correlate scores on standardized tests with measures of home environment could make a scatterplot: The standardized test score for each student is plotted along the Y axis (the vertical line), and the measure (score) for each student's home environment is plotted along the X axis.

Note in Figure 12.3 the line running from the bottom left to the top right. The line is called a regression line (or line of best fit), but the name is not critical here. It

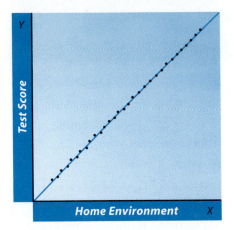

FIGURE 12.3 SCATTERPLOT SHOWING A PERFECT LINEAR RELATIONSHIP BETWEEN VARIABLES

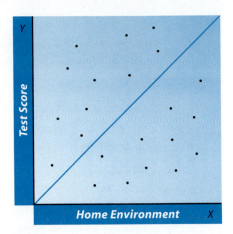

FIGURE 12.4 SCATTERPLOT SHOWING NO RELATIONSHIP BETWEEN VARIABLES

is critical to understand that each dot on the scatterplot represents a pair of numbers (test score and home environment) for each student and that the more scores cluster near that line, the higher the correlation is going to be.

Perfect linear relationships never occur in real life, but if they did, they would look like Figure 12.3 (where *r*, the relationship, equals 1.0). The scatterplot shows that all points fall onto the straight line. You would see this only if standardized test scores were perfectly correlated with home environment. Scores might be low for students whose parents do not encourage education and high for students whose parents do encourage education.

If there were no relationship, the results would look like Figure 12.4 (*r* may equal, say, .18).

Writers are most likely to see scatterplots suggesting some relationships but not perfect ones. That would look like Figure 12.5 (*r* might equal .82). Results in this scatterplot clearly suggest a relationship (but *not* necessarily a cause-and-effect relationship) between test score and home environment.

While all this may look overwhelming, it shouldn't be. Writers who understand the concept of correlation, along with measures of central tendency and standard deviations, can find the formulas in any statistics book and compute results themselves.[15] At the very least, writers armed with this information can ask the right questions and evaluate the data others report.

Cross-tabulation

Cross-tabulation is particularly useful for finding a relationship between two variables. Assume a broadcast journalist learns from a source that motorists who appear to be of Arab descent (because of their clothing or skin color) are stopped more frequently for speeding than other motorists. Suppose the journalist learns

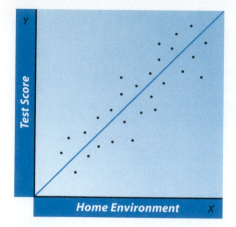

FIGURE 12.5 SCATTERPLOT SHOWING
A RELATIONSHIP (NOT PERFECT)
BETWEEN VARIABLES

		Arab Motorist	White Motorist
Fined for speeding?	Yes	67	48
	No	33	52

FIGURE 12.6 A SAMPLE CROSS-TABULATION TABLE

further that those who *are* determined to be of Arab descent are found guilty and fined more frequently than other motorists charged with the same offense. The journalist gathers data and arranges them in a simple cross-tabulation table that makes the findings clear and compelling (Figure 12.6).

Clearly, the Arab motorists who show up in court are more likely than white motorists to have to pay fines. It's useful to go an additional step and find out whether the differences are statistically significant. Not all listeners will fully understand what the broadcast reporter did, but many will and that should add credibility to the story. In any case, a statistical test will give the journalist a little more information as he or she tries to determine whether the difference is important. Following is one possible lead for a story based on this information:

> Arab motorists who are stopped for speeding are more likely than white motorists to
> be fined by Justice of the Peace Sally Strictland, an analysis of traffic records for the past
> three years shows.

Questions, Hypotheses

The first step in research is to ask a precise, useful question. The next step usually is to develop precise, useful hypotheses, which are declarative sentences that predict relationships among or between variables. In the social sciences, hypotheses are based on earlier work described in books, articles, convention papers and the like. Professional communicators may base hypotheses on previous scientific studies or on knowledge gained in the process of, for example, reporting the news. If anecdotal evidence suggests that binge drinking is related to school enthusiasm (students might tell a journalist this is the case), that could be the basis for a good hypothesis.

A corporation might find it useful for its public relations department to test this hypothesis: The attitudes of Internet users will be significantly more positive toward a site that loads in less than 20 seconds than toward a site that loads in more than 20 seconds. Attitudes might be reflected in responses to the statement "I will return to this site in the future" or "On a scale of 1 to 5, I rank this site is as a (1) (2) (3) (4) (5)."

Statistical significance can be tested after the hypothesis is specified and data are collected. Researchers have the option of using many statistical tests, but a user needs to "know" the test, not just how to calculate the numbers. A researcher or a communication professional should not use any test simply because it is convenient or familiar.

INTERPRETING NUMBERS

Data analysis gets easier with practice, but as writers become one with numbers and statistics, they usually learn that the real difficulty lies not in applying statistical tests, but in figuring out what the results mean. "Mathematics is not primarily a matter of plugging numbers into formulas and performing rote computations," Paulos argues. "It is a way of thinking and questioning that may be unfamiliar to many of us, but it is available to almost all of us."[16]

If writers don't think and question in new ways, their mechanical skills will be essentially useless. Statistical significance testing is a good example. A writer may find statistical significance, but the differences he or she has identified may not be terribly important. It is necessary to understand the difference. Writers who want to deal effectively and accurately with numbers must do two things. First, they need to ask the fundamental question (one that Nicole Bailey found many writers do not ask): "Does this make sense?"[17] Second, they need to understand the context surrounding the numbers they use, as Paulos suggests.

Sense Test

The Kansas City (Mo.) *Star* used social science techniques to produce a controversial series about the prevalence of AIDS among Roman Catholic priests. The research took four years and involved several writers. The journalists pored over church records and death certificates and interviewed hundreds of AIDS experts, priests and religious leaders. Among many other findings, they reported that priests seemed to be dying of AIDS at a higher rate than were members of the general population.[18]

The journalists, unfortunately, were comparing zebras to gazelles when they compared the rate of priests' deaths to the rate for the general population. Philip Meyer noted correctly that all Catholic priests are men and that men have higher mortality rates from AIDS than women do. *The Star* did report the more appropriate male-to-male comparison, but it was deep in the series. According to Meyer:

> Sure, it's a journalistic tradition to give scary but misleading information in the lead and then backpedal, but the backpedal was way too late, and the spurious comparison was beyond the range of reasonable exaggeration. The computer is a wonderful tool but it greatly increases the need to start thinking like a social scientist in approaching a topic.[19]

Context

Individuals can and do disagree about the meanings of some words. Sentences and passages from the Bible and from *Macbeth* are debated, sometimes hotly, from generation to generation to generation. Fortunately, numbers give us something solid to hold to in this chaotic world, for the meaning of numbers is certain and invariable. A number means only one thing, and everybody agrees about that meaning. Or do they?

In fact, numbers are not unlike words. The definition of 2 is pretty clear, and everyone essentially agrees about what 2 represents. But the meaning of 2 in some contexts is far less clear. Perceptions of numbers, like those of words, are influenced by each human being's worldview. How one interprets a number in a given context depends on one's political, social, economic and cultural values. Some Americans oppose war because one death is unacceptable, but others accept 500 deaths or 10,000 deaths as the inevitable price of war. We agree about what one, 500 and 10,000 represent, but our interpretations of those numbers may be vastly different.

Media writers who think numbers are as solid as the monolith in Stanley Kubrick's epic film *2001: A Space Odyssey* do not question numbers or their interpretations. This is because they do not have the confidence to do so or because a number is, well, a number and therefore is beyond question. It is a mistake and it is dangerous to hold this view.

The size of a number, for example, can be perceived in different ways depending on how the number is represented. An organization that wants to make a number look large might use a linear analogy, while a group that is driven by a different ideology might focus on volume. A writer who wants to represent the number of human beings on Earth might note that "Spacious cubical apartments (20 feet on a side) for every human being on Earth could fit comfortably into the Grand Canyon. By contrast, if all living humans were placed end to end, they would extend to the moon and back more than eight times."[20] Someone who thinks Earth is too crowded might use the linear analogy, while someone who thinks there's plenty of room might stress volume.

The ways in which writers represent numbers relating to tragedies and diseases also can affect perceptions. Someone who is concerned about the spread of a disease, for instance, might stress the number of people affected nationally, while someone who is not as concerned might stress the incidence rate.

> Hence, if 1 out of 100,000 people suffers from some malady, there will be 2,500 cases nationwide. The latter figure seems more alarming and will be stressed by maximizers. Dramatizing the situations of a few of these 2,500 people by publishing or televising interviews of their families and friends will further underscore the problem. Minimizers, on the other hand, might invoke the image of a crowded baseball stadium [seating roughly 50,000] during a World Series game and then point out that only one person in *two* such stadiums suffers from the misfortune in question.[21]

NARROWING THE GAP

HPD stopped more people in 2003 than in 2002, and searched and arrested more of those who were stopped. But the racial disparity in searches and arrests between whites and minorities decreased slightly.

How many more times likely to be searched than whites:

	2002	2003
Blacks	3.0	2.4
Hispanics	1.9	1.8

Source: Houston Police Department

Writers and editors often use photographs, tables, charts and other graphics to help readers and viewers understand numerical relationships. This table-photograph combination is from the Houston Chronicle.

While it's important for writers to help their audiences understand numbers, they must use analogies and comparisons carefully. And they must be very careful about passing on the analogies and comparisons given them by groups and individuals who are driven by ideology and self-interest.

A writer must also ask tough questions about how numbers are generated and analyzed. Some researchers use the same statistical tests over and over again without truly understanding them. The scholarly literature, for instance, is crowded with articles and books reporting the results of statistical tests that assume a random sample, and yet many of those samples were not randomly drawn. Statistical tests also are applied on occasion to inappropriate data. A mean score based on "yes" and "no" responses, for instance, would make little sense, and yet some researchers blithely and ignorantly compute that statistic.[22]

Operational definitions also are critical to understanding the relevance and significance of numbers. A common definition of binge drinking is five drinks in an hour for a man and four drinks for a woman. This definition is critical to anyone who conducts research or who wants to understand someone else's work, and a good writer questions the origin of the definition. Why not four and three drinks per hour, or six and five?

Communication writers have an advantage over statisticians, researchers and many others who work with numbers. They have the ability to incorporate numbers into stories that resonate with human beings. Statisticians tend to focus on correlations, relationships, statistical significance and the like; many have a rather narrow view of what the numbers mean for people. Writers focus on what the numbers mean. To the extent that they understand those numbers themselves, they will succeed.

John Allen Paulos is an advocate for the integration of numbers and stories. "The drama and humanity of stories enhance scientific and statistical studies, while the rigor and disinterested perspective of the latter keep stories from degenerating into maudlin trifles or pompous puffery."[23] That is a challenge worth accepting.

SOCIAL SCIENCE TECHNIQUES

- Do adults living in Nebraska approve or disapprove of using human genetic code to treat inherited diseases and disabilities, to screen people for life insurance coverage, to enhance intelligence or to improve physical characteristics?[24]

- Are Americans and others from around the world honest enough to return cash-stuffed billfolds they find on the ground?[25]

- What goes on behind the gates of Sing Sing, a high-security prison; how are guards and inmates affected by the prison environment; and how did the prison come to be what it is?[26]

Writers could answer these questions by interviewing sources, but the answers would be nearly useless because they would focus on *opinions* about behaviors or attitudes. Behaviors and attitudes must be measured directly if these kinds of questions—which are posed by sociologists, psychologists, anthropologists and other social scientists—are to be answered adequately. Systematic procedures and precise observations are required in every case.

The first question is about public opinion, and it can only be answered accurately by a carefully constructed public opinion poll or survey. The second question can be answered by a field experiment. The third question can be answered by participant observation research, in which the writer gets a job as a prison guard. A fourth useful social science technique—the systematic study of records—was described in Chapter 9.

Writers have been using variations of these techniques for a hundred years or more, but they do not always use them as carefully as they should. The approaches are discussed here to help students understand the value and relevance of these techniques and to help them avoid some of their pitfalls. Advanced textbooks devoted to social science methods describe these techniques in greater detail.[27]

Public Opinion Polls

The first public opinion polls appear to have been rough tallies of candidate preferences published by newspapers during the presidential election of 1824. In the presidential elections before that one, the leading candidates were hand-picked by a congressional caucus. Often they were heroes of the Revolution, whom no one wanted to oppose. All this changed during the election of 1824.[28]

The election was wide open: William H. Crawford, the caucus candidate, was opposed by Gen. Andrew Jackson, the hero of the War of 1812; John Quincy Adams, secretary of state; and Henry Clay, speaker of the House of Representatives. With this many candidates and a more competitive election, some newspapers were naturally drawn to try public opinion polling.

The (Raleigh, N.C.) *Star* began running a feature called the "Voice of North Carolina," made up mostly of votes taken at militia meetings but also including a preferential poll conducted in one county simultaneously with a state legislature election. The *American Watchman and Delaware Advertiser* of Wilmington, Del., also conducted a poll that appears to have been an impartial count, since it indicated Jackson would win, whereas the *Watchman* was for Adams. Compared to modern public opinion polling techniques, these early attempts were primitive.

Public opinion surveying originated in election polling, but that is only one of its important functions today. Commercial pollsters George Gallup, Louis Harris and other pioneers have been joined by many other commercial, academic, corporate, media and government pollsters, and they all have moved well beyond election forecasting to explore many current and controversial issues and problems (see the box "Topics for Public Opinion Polls").

Standards for Reporting Polls

Several polling and communication organizations have issued guidelines to help communication professionals report polls. The following list of questions that should be asked about any poll is based on guidelines issued by the National Council on Public Polls.[29] The questions also need to be answered in any report of results, whether they are summarized in print, on the air or online.[30]

- *Who paid for the poll?* A survey sponsored by a politician is more likely to be biased than a poll by a commercial or academic polling organization. Writers should tell their audiences who sponsored polls so readers can evaluate the potential for bias. Certainly, however, a poll that appears biased should not be published or aired at all.

- *Who conducted the poll?* Politicians, news media, nonprofit organizations, corporations and others interested in public opinion often hire professional polling organizations. This organization should be identified. If a politician's campaign staff conducted a poll, questions must be asked about its validity. A public relations professional who is trying to find a firm to conduct a poll must be extraordinarily careful, because some polling organizations have no idea what they're doing. Basing a campaign on bad information is one of the worst things a public relations person can do.

- *When was the poll conducted?* While some public attitudes can remain fairly stable over years or even decades, public opinion can be volatile. It can change rapidly as situations change. A poll that might have been accurate three days ago might not be today.

TOPICS FOR PUBLIC OPINION POLLS

The following polls illustrate the wide variety of topics explored by modern public opinion pollsters. Public relations writers had an important part in all of these polls, and all were reported in the news media.

- The American Medical Association surveyed parents to find out how concerned they are about binge drinking on college campuses. Ninety-five percent of U.S. parents said they are concerned about excessive drinking on campus. Ninety-two percent of the 801 parents surveyed said underage drinking laws need to be enforced. The margin of error was ±3.5 percent.[31]

- ICM and *The* (London) *Guardian* asked a random sample of 1,004 British adults to indicate whether they support, oppose or don't know about "the use of animals in the scientific testing of new medicines for human consumption." Many readers would be interested because this has long been a hot-button issue in the United Kingdom. The margin of error was ±3.1 percent.[32]

- The American Council on Education surveyed Americans to find out their attitudes toward international education, study-abroad programs and language training following the terrorist attacks of Sept. 11, 2001. Seventy-seven percent of the 1,000 respondents expressed support for international course requirements and nearly 75 percent agreed that colleges should help educate the public about international cultures, events and issues. The margin of error was ±3.1 percent.[33]

- *How were the interviews obtained?* The audience should be told that interviews were conducted by telephone, personal interview or mail questionnaire. The response rate—or the percentage contacted who actually submit their opinions—should also be reported, particularly in the case of mail questionnaires, which invariably have low response rates.

- *How were the questions worded?* Questions used in public opinion surveys have to be worded extremely carefully. They must be clear and unambiguous, and they must not suggest a "best" or "preferred" answer. A question asked by Blue Cross and Blue Shield of Massachusetts posed the question, "Do you think violence in the media contributes to violent acts?" Clearly, the question suggests an answer: Yes. The response might have been quite different had the writer asked, "Do you think violence in the media has no impact on the incidence of violence in society?" The question also is ambiguous in that there are many kinds of media content (from news to entertainment) and many kinds of violent acts (from cartoon violence to dismembered bodies).[34]

- *Who was interviewed?* Was the population carefully defined, and was the population appropriate to the question?

- *Were respondents randomly selected from an appropriate population?* If a random sample was not used, or if a pollster refuses to tell how respondents were selected, the poll should be taken less seriously.

- *What was the sample size?* Some critics of polls seem to think it would require a sample of 10,000 or 20,000 or 40,000 to draw accurate conclusions about the opinions of all adult Americans. This criticism makes intuitive sense, but it is not true. Reasonably accurate results can be obtained from surveys based on samples of between 1,400 and 1,600 persons. Samples of only a few hundred are sometimes adequate, depending on what the research question is. Sample size is not the most important consideration (although it is important). The important thing is that the sample is randomly drawn. A random sample of 1,000 may well be more accurate than a nonprobability sample of 100,000. In any case, the accuracy of the former can be assessed, while the accuracy of the latter cannot be.

- *What was the margin of error?* Public opinion polls are accurate only within a specified margin of error (margin of error cannot be computed if a sample is not randomly selected). One of the strengths of using scientific polling procedures is that they allow a pollster to compute the probable margin of error for a poll even before the poll is conducted.

  A pollster who reports a margin of error of ±3 percentage points is saying the results can be off by 3 percentage points in either direction. Consider a pollster who finds that 49 percent of a sample supports candidate A and 51 percent supports candidate B. The election would be too close to call because (assuming a margin of error of ±3 percentage points) the final figures could range from 46 to 52 percent for candidate A and from 48 to 54 percent for candidate B. Candidate A might win the election by 52 percent to 48 percent or candidate B might win by 54 percent to 46 percent.

  The margin of error is computed statistically and depends partly on the sample size and partly on the amount of confidence that is desired in the results (several other factors have been left out to simplify the discussion). Most national public opinion polls use a sample size of about 1,600. For this sample size and a confidence level of 95 percent, the margin of error is ±2.45 percent.

  The 95 percent confidence level means that in 95 percent (or 19 out of 20) of the samples of this size, the sample percentage estimated will be within ±2.45 of the true value of that percentage for the population. If the sample size were decreased to 400, the margin of error would increase to ±4.9 (again, at the 95 percent confidence level). It is possible to increase the accuracy of a poll by increasing the sample size, but this obviously increases the expense.

The Gallup Poll says the margin of error for a sample of 1,000 is ±3 percentage points. For a sample of 2,000 it is ±2. Doubling the sample size would double the cost, but would produce only a 1 percentage point gain in accuracy.[35] A commercial polling organization might want to pay that cost for the last poll of an election campaign. Since it sells its services, it want its results to be as accurate as possible to impress potential buyers. That extra 1 percentage point of accuracy might be worth some money.

■ *What was the margin of error for sample subgroups?* Most polls break numbers down by subgroups. In a poll about abortion, for example, a researcher might break the data down by religious preference. The margin of error for each subgroup is higher than the margin of error for the group as a whole. The margin of error for a sample of 1,600 is ±2.45 percent, but the margin of error for a subgroup of 400 is closer to ±4.9 percent.

The Gallup Organization employs hundreds of people to collect, analyze, interpret and report poll results. Media writers, in turn, must report those results accurately and in context.

Random Sampling Technique

Random sampling would be comparatively easy if one were interested only in selecting marbles from a barrel, but selecting people from a city, state or nation is infinitely more difficult. Pollsters such as George Gallup go through elaborate steps to construct a national random sample.

The Gallup Poll tried for decades to reach potential respondents in their homes. For half a century, that meant sending interviewers to U.S. cities and towns to knock on doors. From 1935 until 1985, potential respondents could not be reliably reached by telephone because many Americans did not have telephones or their numbers were unlisted. And a neat little technique called random-digit dialing was neither widely used nor trusted.[36]

Everything changed in 1986, when Gallup started conducting interviews by telephone—at substantially lower cost. Just about every poll conducted in America by every organization is done by telephone, which is feasible because roughly 95 percent of homes have telephones.

Gallup uses random samples selected from carefully defined populations. "If we were doing a poll about baseball fans on behalf of the sports page of a major newspaper, the target population might simply be all Americans aged 18 and older who say they are fans of the sport of baseball."[37] The population for Gallup's election polls includes individuals who are at least 18 and who live in U.S. homes with telephones. Hospital patients, college students who live on campus, military personnel who live on bases and other institutionalized persons are not part of the population. Gallup researchers don't particularly like this compromise, but they typically have to make it.

Gallup next compiles a computerized list of every telephone exchange in the United States and the numbers of home telephones within these exchanges. Using the random-digit dialing technique, telephone numbers are created from the exchanges. Telephone samples are selected from these lists.

Samples are not drawn from actual lists because nearly a third of U.S. telephone numbers are unlisted; individuals owning these telephones would be missed in a sample drawn from a telephone book. "In essence, this procedure creates a list of all possible household phone numbers in America and then selects a subset of numbers from that list for Gallup to call."[38]

Interviewers try to reach an adult in each household where a telephone is selected. If nobody answers on the first try or if the line is busy, interviewers try again a few hours later. If there is still no answer, the number is tried again on other nights during the polling period. Interviewers will not give up easily because poll accuracy can be reduced if Gallup interviewers give up after one try (since older people tend to stay at home more and talk less frequently on the telephone, they could be oversampled if interviewers tried only once).

When the telephone interviewer does get through, he or she tries to randomly select an individual living within the household, if more than one adult lives there. Sometimes interviewers will ask the person answering the telephone for the adult having the most recent birthday. Sometimes they ask the individual to list all adults in the household by age and gender; the interviewer selects one to interview. If that person is not home, the interviewer calls back.

A media organization that wants to conduct an accurate telephone poll will use procedures similar to Gallup's. Samples based on telephone directories are accurate enough for some purposes, however. A corporation that wants to do an image study, for instance, might sample from a telephone directory. The data would not be as accurate, but they likely are accurate enough for the corporation's purposes. A television news department should not use this technique for a campaign poll, however, for inaccurate results could be quite harmful to both a candidate and to the democratic process.

Polls That Aren't

The media and other organizations sometimes report poll results that appear to be reasonable indicators of public opinion, but that are not. Some news consumers may think on-the-street interviews, mood-of-the-state polls, magazine or newspaper ballot polls, Web polls, broadcast station call-ins and legislative newsletter polls are real surveys. They aren't. In fact, it is a mistake to even call them surveys or polls. (See the box "What's the Point?")

Interviews The problem with on-the-street and mood-of-the-state "polls" is that journalists interview whomever they can catch and whoever is willing to talk. One

WHAT'S THE POINT?

CNN ran on its Web site in 2003 a feature called the "QuickVote." One question was "Are you worried about the new virus known as Severe Acute Respiratory Syndrome?" What is most interesting about the feature, however, is the disclaimer at the bottom: "This QuickVote is not scientific and reflects the opinions of only those Internet users who have chosen to participate. The results cannot be assumed to represent the opinions of Internet users in general, nor the public as a whole. The QuickVote sponsor is not responsible for content, functionality or the opinions expressed therein."[39]

Any thinking reader of the QuickVote feature would wonder what the point is. Why report information that is so questionable? Would CNN put such a disclaimer on any other content that it distributed?

This kind of information is worse than useless, for it pollutes the information stream that is so important to a successful democracy.

radio station likes to send writers to a popular park before daylight to get the views of inner-city joggers about topics in the news. Runners are always out there, and many are happy to talk. Unfortunately, their views do not represent the views of the rest of the population. Poor people, for instance, tend not to drive to a park to jog, and they often are at work before dawn. Suburban runners aren't going to drive an hour to find a place to get in their miles.

These kinds of stories do have a place because many readers, listeners and viewers find them interesting, but they must reflect a wide range of views and a wide variety of people. On-the-street interviews following the attacks of Sept. 11, 2001, did not elicit any new information, but many people were interested to hear how others were coping with the awful events of that day.

A "poll" goes too far when it attempts to indicate the percentages of the public holding different opinions. ANARAC, an environmental advocacy group from Vancouver, British Columbia, for example, posts questions online and invites visitors to cast their "votes." Many groups and news sites post such questions and nothing is particularly wrong with the practice, unless they call them "polls" or "surveys" and report percentages.

ANARAC posted the question, "Do you agree with the Kyoto Protocol?" The group then reported that 48 percent said yes, they did agree with the recommendations to control global warming; 36 percent said no; and 4 percent said they didn't know. The sample is poor; the question suggests an answer; results are reported as percentages. This common practice is not good.[40]

Ballots and Call-ins In a legitimate poll, respondents are selected by the polling organization, but when individuals have to call a broadcast station, cast a ballot online or clip a ballot for a magazine or newspaper, they are selecting themselves to participate. No one knows whether the sample is representative.[41]

Congressional representatives and state legislators sometimes include questionnaires about public issues in newsletters to their constituents. These questionnaires might be helpful to the lawmakers, but, as reflections of public opinion, they share the same faults as the newspaper ballot poll and the broadcast call-in poll. The response rates are usually low, and people who respond are unlikely to be a fair representation of the population.

Some legislative and Web polls have the additional problem of being driven by self-serving or ideological interests. A representative who favors war with Iraq, for instance, might direct his or her public relations staff to ask this question in a poll: "Do you favor war with Iraq?" The result might be quite different if the question focused on peace: "Do you favor peace with Iraq?" Each question is bad, but each might be used by an ideologue to support a position.

A reasonable question about Iraq might be "Do you favor or oppose: (1) military intervention in Iraq to remove weapons of mass destruction; (2) continuation of the blockade of Iraq to keep military materiel from getting in or out; (3) a diplomatic solution to the current impasse or (4) some other option?" Respondents could choose any one of the four.

Field Experiments

The experiment is the best method scientists have invented for identifying causes and for measuring behavior directly. It is a procedure for studying reality not just by waiting for changes to occur but also by manipulating reality to produce changes. The scientist interested in whether the bite of a certain kind of mosquito causes malaria does not wait for that kind of mosquito to bite someone, but captures a mosquito and applies it to a volunteer subject's skin under controlled conditions. Then the scientist, after introducing the change, carefully observes the effects of that change.

The field experiment takes the experiment out of the laboratory setting and applies it to people in the day-to-day world (see the box "A Classic Field Experiment"). The central element—manipulation of some variable—still takes place, however.

The *Daily News'* investigation of the postal service illustrates the potential of field experiments for reporting about consumer services. Journalists have conducted similar experiments to determine whether automobile repair shops and television service centers are honest. They take automobiles or television sets that have nothing seriously wrong with them to repair shops and report what happens. Journalists also have conducted field experiments on prejudice and stereotyping.

Experiments also are used to measure behaviors that might not be confessed to in interviews. Eric Felten of the *Reader's Digest,* for example, started a story with

A CLASSIC FIELD EXPERIMENT

The *Chicago Daily News'* analysis of mail service is a classic in journalism. Several parts of it, such as a comparison of first-class and special-delivery mail and a comparison of mail that had zip codes and mail that did not, were genuine experiments.

The *Daily News* sent 588 pieces of mail to and from Chicago; Bath, Maine; Seattle; Columbia, Mo.; Phoenix; Palm Harbor, Fla.; and Kalamazoo, Mich. A variable was manipulated (either a zip code was used or not) and then the effect was observed (how fast did the letter arrive?).

The *Daily News* learned that "The average delivery time for intercity first-class, zip-coded mail in our sample was 2.7 days vs. 2.76 days for mail without zip codes." Special-delivery letters, which then cost 60 cents more than first-class, were delivered faster in 77.8 percent of the cases, but special-delivery was no better than first-class in 12.7 percent of the cases, and it was worse in 9.5 percent of cases.[42]

The *Daily News* compared its results with the U.S. Postal Service's service standards, one of which called for three-day delivery of first-class mail between Chicago and Phoenix. Delivery of intercity first-class mail failed to meet the standard in 12.5 percent of cases.

this lead: "Walking along, minding your own business, you see a billfold on the ground. You pick it up. Some photos inside, a card or two with ID. Hmm, and a nice wad of bills too. So what do you do? The right thing, or ... ?"[43]

Felton wanted to know how many people would do the "right thing," so he conducted an international study to find out. *Reader's Digest* editors dropped more than 1,100 wallets in the paths of unsuspecting individuals in the United States, Asia, Latin America, Australia, Europe and New Zealand. Each wallet contained the name and phone number of the billfold's "owner" and up to $50 in cash.

Fifty-six percent of the billfolds were returned—but 44 percent were not. Every wallet was returned in Norway and Denmark, and 90 percent were returned in Singapore. At the bottom were Mexico (21 percent returned), China (30 percent) and Italy (35 percent). In the United States, 67 percent of the wallets were returned.

The magazine reported the comments of several people who returned the wallets. These made the report more interesting and helped to explain the findings. A student in Greensboro, N.C., said she returned the billfold after she saw a baby's photograph inside. A student working three jobs, she said she thought someone else probably needed the money more than she did.

Random sampling is not as critical in field experiments as it is in opinion polling. Ideally, one might wish that the subjects in a field experiment would be a random sample of a larger population, but usually in a field experiment this kind of selection is not possible or even necessary. Researchers typically are not interested in generalizing to larger populations. Their goal is to document whether certain behavior occurs in the real world and to try to explain or understand it. A random sample is not always essential.

Random sampling is desired sometimes, however. In a study of the service given to black and white people in restaurants, for example, the establishments to be visited could and should be randomly selected from a list of restaurants in town.

Few field experiments require complicated statistical analyses. Sometimes it may be desirable to compute a statistical test to determine the significance level of a difference, but often the difference between conditions is dramatic enough to speak for itself.[44]

Social psychologists are concerned about the ethics of field experiments. One problem is that the subject in a field experiment usually has not given personal consent to be included in the experiment (consent is required for participation in a laboratory experiment). One rule some social psychologists have suggested is that the field experiment should not be more than a "simple acceleration of natural events." And, of course, no experiment should cause physical harm or mental stress.

Participant Observation

Scientific observation is the process of observing people or animals in their natural environments, but without participating in their lives.[45] Participant observation is a method of studying people by joining them in their activities or daily lives (see the box "'Just Listening' from *Street Corner Society*" on page 351). The method has been used by scientists and journalists for more than 100 years. An early participant-observer in journalism was Nellie Bly of *The* (New York) *World*.

Bly worked in the late 19th century, when women found it exceptionally difficult to land newspaper jobs. A first assignment for the extraordinarily persistent Bly was to get herself committed to the Women's Lunatic Asylum (yes, that was the not-so-subtle name) on Blackwell's Island in the East River.[46] Bly and her editor, Col. John Cockerill, knew there was a story there because every newspaper in town had written about the problem—from the outside.

Bly sought and received immunity from prosecution from an assistant district attorney before getting herself committed to the institution, where she remained for 10 days. Bly practiced before a mirror to look "deranged" (Figure 12.7), but it was not easy: "I remembered all I had read of the doings of crazy people, how first of all they must have staring eyes, and so I opened mine as wide as possible and stared unblinkingly at my own reflection. I assure you the sight was not reassuring, even to myself, especially in the dead of night. I tried to turn the gas up higher in hopes that it would raise my courage."[47]

FIGURE 12.7   A SAMPLE OF THE ART THAT ACCOMPANIED NELLIE BLY'S SERIES

NELLIE PRACTISES INSANITY AT HOME.

Bly's articles, which documented many of the findings reported later in scientific studies, was exceptionally detailed—and telling. This passage is typical:

> Mrs. Louise Schanz was taken next into the presence of Dr. Kinier, the medical man [possibly for the sole reason that she could not speak English and the authorities therefore judged her "crazy"]. "Your name?" he asked, loudly. She answered in German, saying she did not speak English nor could she understand it. However, when he said Mrs. Louis [sic] Schanz she said "Yah, yah." Then he tried other questions, and when he found she could not understand one word of English he said to Miss Grupe: "You are German: speak to her for me." Miss Grupe proved to be one of those people who are ashamed of their nationality and she refused, saying she could understand but a few words of her mother tongue. "You know you speak German. Ask this woman what her husband does," and they both laughed as if they were enjoying a joke. "I can't speak but a few words," she protested, but at last she managed to ascertain the occupation of Mr. Schanz. "Now, what was the use of lying to me?" asked the doctor, with a laugh which dispelled the rudeness. "I can't speak any more," she said, and she did not.
>
> Thus was Mrs. Louise Schanz consigned to the asylum without a chance to make herself understood. Can such carelessness be excused, I wondered, when it is so easy to get an interpreter? If the confinement was for but a few days one might question the necessity. But here was a woman taken without her own consent from a free world to

an asylum and there given no chance to prove her sanity. Confined most probably for life behind asylum bars, without even being told in her language the why and wherefore.[48]

Plans were being made to increase the budgets for mental health even before Bly's series was published, but her stories helped to ensure that the promises were not empty.

Ted Conover used the same technique more than 100 years later in a study of Sing Sing prison. But he stayed longer (a year) and assumed a different role (he was a prison guard). Conover could have interviewed experts about prison conditions, but he would not have been able to produce such a compelling, accurate description of what goes on behind bars. For one thing, prison authorities would not grant complete access. The training academy for new corrections officers, for example, was off-limits to writers. So Conover decided to work inside a prison and not tell anyone he was writing a book.[49]

A good participant-observer gathers considerable information about the people, facilities and institutions he or she intends to observe, and Conover did this. Conover reports that inmates were dispatched from Auburn prison in 1826 to build Sing Sing's first cellblock, remnants of which still stand; that inmates once traveled 30 miles by boat ("up the river") from New York City to get to "the big house"; that New York state operates 71 prisons and that 50 were built in the past 25 years, a time during which the number of prisoners grew to 70,000 from 12,500; that the number of correction officers increased roughly 400 percent from 1982 until 1998; and that Sing Sing got its name from the Sint Sinck Indians who lived at the site.[50]

Although Sing Sing's history is integrated at appropriate places throughout the book, an entire chapter is devoted to the prison's past. This kind of detail gives a writer an important structure on which to hang a story. And it tends to make the story more interesting and compelling.

Conover also kept meticulous notes about people and what they said—both prisoners and guards. An instructor at the jailers' school, for example, captured the essence of the system when he described a prison as a storage unit, not a rehabilitation center. "The truth of it is that we are warehousers of human beings," he told Conover.[51]

The first time Conover worked a night shift, the officer in charge told him that those on the night shift just wanted to make sure the inmates weren't dead. "'If they're dead and hard, you're gone' was the way the white-shirts put it. Dead and warm, on the other hand, showed you were doing your job."[52]

Conover found inmates would lie to him about any number of things, including why they were locked up. An inmate who used felt-tip pens to make greeting cards told Conover he had been convicted of murder. Conover looked him up at home on a victims' rights Web site and discovered he was in prison for burglary and larceny. "Everyone, I suppose, wanted to be known as a murderer in prison," Conover said.[53]

"JUST LISTENING" FROM *STREET CORNER SOCIETY*

Sociologist William F. Whyte used participant observation to study slum life for his book *Street Corner Society*. Whyte moved into the Italian community he was studying and became so accepted he was elected secretary of the Italian Community Club. He learned the value of keeping quiet and watching, however, when he asked a source about gamblers who bribed the police. That shut down that part of the conversation, and Whyte felt uncomfortable for the remainder of the night.

> The next day Doc explained the lesson of the previous evening. "Go easy on that 'who,' 'what,' 'why,' 'when,' 'where' stuff, Bill. You ask those questions, and people will clam up on you. If people accept you, you can just hang around, and you'll learn the answers in the long run without even having to ask the questions.
>
> I found that this was true. As I sat and listened, I learned the answers to questions that I would not even have had the sense to ask if I had been getting my information solely on an interviewing basis. I did not abandon questioning altogether, of course. I simply learned to judge the sensitiveness of the question and my relationship to the people so that I only asked a question in a sensitive area when I was sure that my relationship to the people involved was very solid.[54]

Another inmate told Conover he was in prison because of an argument, but Conover discovered he was there for sodomy. When he checked the statute, he found that someone convicted of first-degree sodomy had sexually abused someone against his or her will or someone who was less than 11 years old. "I wished, then, that I hadn't checked, because, thinking of my own kids, I couldn't talk to Van Essen after that."[55]

One of the more interesting aspects of Conover's book *Newjack* is the author's personal experiences and perceptions. Conover describes the stress of the work and its impact on his personal life, the desire to succeed in a job that had so many uncontrollable and unpredictable facets. "Sing Sing was a world of adrenaline and aggression to us new officers. It was an experience of living with fear—fear of inmates, as individuals and as a mob, and fear of our own capacity to fuck up."[56] Correction officers were caught between the inmates who could cause injury or death and the prison bosses, who could cause unemployment.

The main advantage of participant observation is that it makes a writer less dependent on interviews. Certain kinds of people, such as administrators of prisons or mental health institutions, might be unwilling to talk in detail about what they are doing. Certainly they are not going to volunteer information in an interview about deplorable conditions in their facilities. Participant observation also makes a writer less dependent on the observations of others. The best way to do a story about hang gliding might be not to interview a hang-gliding expert, but to try hang gliding.

A participant-observer must decide whether to reveal his or her identity and purpose to the people involved. The fairest procedure is to be completely honest. This is possible for some stories, but it would make other stories—the prison and mental health institution investigations—impossible.

A participant-observer also must decide the degree to which he or she will become involved. If a writer becomes too involved in or friendly with a group, it may limit objectivity. Conover reported that he sometimes felt he was too close to the prison personalities to remain objective, for example.

Another decision involves when and how to take notes. It is best to take them at the time of observation or as soon afterward as possible. Unless a participant-observer is with a group full time, it typically is feasible to type notes at night or at some other time when members of the group are not around.[57]

YOUR RESPONSIBILITY IS . . .

- To get over any apprehension you have about using numbers and about research, for both are indispensable parts of the writing process.

- To learn how to use and, even more important, how to interpret complex numerical and research information. You just won't be able to get your job done if you can't make sense of research studies that relate to stories you need to write or public relations campaigns you need to develop.

- To learn the fundamentals of mathematics and statistics so you will not make terrible mistakes or be manipulated by unscrupulous, ideological or ignorant sources. You should know, for example, how to calculate percentages, medians, means and per capita ratios.

- To learn strategies for making numbers interesting and comprehensible, without distorting what they say.

- To become familiar with the fundamentals of public opinion polls, field experiments and participant observation, for you may have to use one or all of these techniques, and you almost certainly will have to evaluate how well someone else has used them.

- To realize that quantitative research that is based on a nonrandom sample is worthless and should not be publicized or used in developing a public relations campaign.

- To understand that cause-and-effect relationships are exceptionally hard to document and that they often are not real.

NOTES

1. Scott R. Maier, "Numbers in the News: A Mathematics Audit of a Daily Newspaper," *Journalism Studies,* 3:4 (2002): 507–519, p. 507.

2. Scott Maier, "Getting It Right? Not in 59 Percent of Stories," *Newspaper Research Journal,* 23:1 (2002): 10–24.

3. A.K. Dewdney, *200% of Nothing: An Eye-opening Tour Through the Twists and Turns of Math Abuse and Innumeracy* (New York: John Wiley, 1993): v.

4. Jennifer Thomas, "$322 Million Proposal: New School Bond Issue Touted," *The* (Houston) *Citizen,* Jan. 22, 2003: A-1, B-3.

5. "Q&A: Reporting With Computers: Some Doubts From a Founder," *Columbia Journalism Review,* May/June 2001: 39.

6. Report of the Commission on Public Relations Education, *A Port of Entry: Public Relations Education for the 21st Century* (New York: Public Relations Society of America, October 1999). Available at <lamar.colostate.edu/~aejmcpr/commissionreport99.htm>. See also Bonita Dostal Neff, Gael Walker, Michael F. Smith and Pam J. Creedon, "Outcomes Desired by Practitioners and Academics," *Public Relations Review,* 25:1 (1999): 29–44; and Don W. Stacks, Carl Botan and Judy VanSlyke Turk, "Perceptions of Public Relations Education," *Public Relations Review,* 25:1 (1999): 9–28.

7. John Allen Paulos, *Once Upon a Number: The Hidden Mathematical Logic of Stories* (New York: Basic Books, 1998): 13–14.

8. John Allen Paulos, *A Mathematician Reads the Newspaper* (New York: Basic Books, 1995): 95.

9. Bart K. Holland, *What Are the Chances? Voodoo Deaths, Office Gossip, and Other Adventures in Probability* (Baltimore: Johns Hopkins University Press, 2002); and Deborah J. Bennett, *Randomness* (Cambridge, Mass.: Harvard University Press, 1998).

10. Proportions are more appropriately reported than percentages when a denominator is less than 100, as in this case. However, percentages are conventionally reported because more people are familiar with percentages and can understand them better.

11. Helpful books include Philip Meyer, *The New Precision Journalism* (Bloomington: Indiana University Press, 1991); Dewdney, *200% of Nothing;* Victor Cohn and Lewis Cope, *News & Numbers: A Guide to Reporting Statistical Claims and Controversies in Health and Other Fields,* 2nd ed. (Ames: Iowa State Press, 2001); Susan E. Morgan, Tom Reichert and Tyler R. Harrison, *From Numbers to Words: Reporting Statistical Results for the Social Sciences* (Boston: Allyn and Bacon, 2002); Kathleen Woodruff Wickham, *Math Tools for Journalists* (Oak Park, Ill.: Marion Street Press, 2002). Online help is available from Robert Niles at <robertniles.com/stats>; Power Reporting at <powerreporting.com/category/Newsroom_training/Training_courses>; Data Crunching 101 for Journalists at <www.quadrant.net/bdoskoch/numbers.html>; and Steve Doig, "Math Test for Journalists," Investigative Reporters and Editors, undated, at <www.ire.org.education/math_test.html>.

12. Karen Lundegaard and Sholnn Freeman, "Hitting the Breaks: Detroit's Challenge: Weaning Buyers from Years of Deals," *The Wall Street Journal,* Jan. 6, 2004: A-1, 12.

13. "Bishops Issue Statement on Overcoming Violence and Sex in Media," U.S. Catholic Bishops, news release, June 19, 1998. Downloaded on Jan. 24, 2003, from <www.nccbuscc.org/comm/archives/98–141xhtm>.

14. Mike McIntire, "Despite Fewer Hours, City's Overtime Costs Rise," *The New York Times,* Dec. 9, 2003: A-1, B-8, p. A-1.

15. Mary John Smith, *Contemporary Communication Research Methods* (Belmont, Calif.: Wadsworth, 1988); and Roger D. Wimmer and Joseph R. Dominick, *Mass Media Research: An Introduction,* 7th ed. (Belmont, Calif.: Thomson/Wadsworth, 2003).

16. Paulos, *A Mathematician Reads the Newspaper:* 3.

17. Nicole Bailey, "No Numbers Please—We're Journalists," *Thunderbird Online Magazine: UBC* (University of British Columbia) *Journalism Review,* April 2001. Downloaded on Jan. 23, 2003, from <www.journalism.ubc.ca/thunderbird/2000–01/april/numbers.html>.

18. The first article in the series is Judy L. Thomas, "A Church's Challenge: Catholic Priests Are Dying of AIDS, Often in Silence," *The Kansas City* (Mo.) *Star,* Jan. 30, 2000: A-1, 16–17.

19. "Q&A: Reporting with Computers": 39.

20. Paulos, *A Mathematician Reads the Newspaper:* 79.

21. Ibid., pp. 79–80.

22. Michael Ryan, "Pitfalls to Avoid in Conducting and Describing Scholarly Research: Authors Can Maximize Chances for Success," *Journalism & Mass Communication Educator,* 52:4 (1998): 72–79.

23. Paulos, *Once Upon a Number:* 179.

24. Martha Stoddard, "Poll: Nebraskans Think Gene Research OK for Some Uses," *Lincoln* (Neb.) *Journal Star,* Jan. 7, 2001: A-5. Downloaded on Jan. 28, 2003, from <net.uni.edu/newsFeat/med_eth/me_polls2.html>.

25. Eric Felten, "Finders Keepers?" *Reader's Digest,* April 2001: 103–107.

26. Ted Conover, *Newjack: Guarding Sing Sing* (New York: Random House, 2000).

27. Chris Mann and Fiona Stewart, *Internet Communication and Qualitative Research: A Handbook for Researching Online* (London: Sage, 2000); Smith, *Contemporary Communication Research Methods,* and Wimmer and Dominick, *Mass Media Research.*

28. James W. Tankard Jr., "Public Opinion Polling by Newspapers in the Presidential Election Campaign of 1824," *Journalism Quarterly,* 49:2 (1972): 361–365.

29. Sheldon R. Gawiser and G. Evans Witt, "20 Questions a Journalist Should Ask About Poll Results," National Council on Public Polls, undated. Downloaded on Jan. 30, 2003, from <www.ncpp.org/qajsa.htm>.

30. Sung Tae Kim and David Weaver, "Traditional, Online Polls Reported Differently," *Newspaper Research Journal,* 22:3 (2001): 71–85.

31. Melinda Deslatte, "Battle of the Binge: Officials, Parents Want Alcohol to Fade From College Life," *Houston Chronicle,* Aug. 30, 2001: A-14.

32. "The Guardian/ICM Monthly Poll—January 2001," *ICM Polls,* January 2001. Downloaded on Feb. 3, 2003, from <www.icmresearch.co.uk/reviews/2001/guardian-poll-jan-2001.htm>.

33. Laura Siaya, Maura Porcelli and Madeleine Green, "One Year Later: Attitudes About International Education Since September 11," *Public Opinion Poll,* American Council on Education, September 2002. Available at <www.acenet.edu/programs/international/pubs.cfm?pubID=266>.

34. *A Healthy Me!* Blue Cross Blue Shield of Massachusetts, undated. Downloaded on Jan. 29, 2003 from <www.ahealthyme.com/topic/violencepoll>.

35. Frank Newport, Lydia Saad and David Moore, "Frequently Asked Questions: Question: How Polls Are Conducted," The Gallup Organization, 2003. Downloaded on Jan. 30, 2003, from <www.gallup.com/help/FAQs/poll1.asp>. Excerpt based on Newport, Saad and Moore, *Where America Stands* (New York: John Wiley, 1997).

36. Ibid.

37. Ibid.

38. Ibid.

39. "CNN.com Quick Vote," CNN, March 31, 2003. Downloaded on March 31, 2003, from <www.cnn.com/POLLSERVER/results/2733.html>.

40. "ANARAC POLL," *ANARAC*, Dec. 26, 2003. Downloaded on Feb. 2, 2003, from <www .ANARAC.com>.

41. Nick Sparrow and John Curtice, "Internet Surveys Are Increasingly Popular as a Way of Testing Opinion, But New Evidence Suggests That on Some Issues They Can Be a Misleading Tool," *The* (London) *Guardian,* Jan. 9, 2003: 15; and Alan Travis, "Accuracy of Internet Polling Questioned," *The* (London) *Guardian,* Jan. 9, 2003: 7. Available at <media.guardian .co.uk/newmedia/story/0,7496,871296,00.html>.

42. Rob Warden, "Pony Express? A Gallop Poll on the Nation's Mailmen," *Chicago Daily News,* Dec. 14–15, 1974: A-1, 44, p. A-1.

43. Felten, "Finders Keepers?": 103.

44. Earl R. Babbie, *The Practice of Social Research,* 10th ed. (Belmont, Calif.: Thomson/Wadsworth, 2004).

45. Robert M. Sapolsky, *A Primate's Memoir* (New York: Scribner, 2001).

46. Brooke Kroeger, *Nellie Bly: Daredevil, Reporter, Feminist* (New York: Times Books, 1994): 79–99.

47. Nellie Bly, "Behind Asylum Bars: The Mystery of the Unknown Insane Girl," *The* (New York) *World,* Oct. 9, 1887: 25–26, p. 25.

48. Nellie Bly, "Inside the Madhouse: Nellie Bly's Experience in the Blackwell's Island Asylum," *The* (New York) *World,* Oct. 16, 1887: 25–26, p. 25.

49. Conover, *Newjack.*

50. Readers probably have read and heard "up the river" and "the big house" in countless gangster books and movies. They are tied directly to the Sing Sing experience.

51. Conover, *Newjack:* 41.

52. Ibid., p. 304.

53. Ibid., p. 224.

54. William Foote Whyte, *Street Corner Society: The Social Structure of an Italian Slum* (Chicago: University of Chicago Press, 1955): 303.

55. Conover, *Newjack.*

56. Ibid., p. 95.

57. Paul Atkinson and Amanda Coffey, "Revising the Relationship Between Participant Observation and Interviewing," in Jaber F. Gubrium and James A. Holstein (eds.), *Handbook of Interview Research: Context & Method* (Thousand Oaks, Calif.: Sage, 2002): 801–814.

PART IV

PERSPECTIVES

C H A P T E R 13

LAW

Pitfalls and Opportunities

Freelance writer Vanessa Leggett spent nearly half a year in jail for running afoul of a federal district court judge who wanted her to turn over her notes and audiotapes for a book about a sensational murder. She refused to cooperate, was held in contempt of court and didn't get out until the term of the grand jury investigating the case ended. She holds the record for the most days spent by a journalist in a U.S. jail.[1]

The Wall Street Journal alleged that an Illinois businessman had paid leaders of foreign governments to help his firm, G.D. Searle and Co., obtain business in their countries. Robert Crinkley, according to *The Journal*, resigned when the payments were made public. An Illinois court awarded Crinkley a $2.25 million judgment against *The Journal* because the report was inaccurate.[2]

Media professionals need to know the law if they are to do their jobs most effectively—and if they are to avoid going to jail or paying huge libel judgments. They need to know how the First Amendment, the 14th Amendment and freedom of information (open meetings and open records) laws protect freedom of expression. And, because bad things do happen to good people, professionals need to know how laws restrict what they do. Problem areas discussed in this chapter are libel, privacy, the free press–fair trial dilemma, source confidentiality, copyright and administrative regulations.

This is merely an introduction to an extraordinarily complex and confusing subject. Students need to know considerably more about mass communication law than is covered here. Several excellent books are available.[3]

THE FIRST AND 14TH AMENDMENTS

Americans enjoy substantial freedom to express themselves primarily because of the First and 14th Amendments to the U.S. Constitution. Because they were so committed to freedom of expression, the nation's founders adopted the following words in 1791 as their first addition to the Constitution:

> Congress shall make no law respecting an establishment of religion, or prohibiting the free exercise thereof; or abridging the freedom of speech, or of the press; or the right of the people peaceably to assemble, and to petition the Government for a redress of grievances.

The First Amendment is important to all Americans for a number of reasons:

- A democracy simply cannot exist without guaranteed freedom of expression.
- The best solutions to problems and the best ideas are more likely to emerge from societies in which free expression is guaranteed than from those in which expression is limited.
- Government tyranny, secrecy and incompetence cannot flourish in a society in which its activities are freely monitored, criticized and publicized.
- A city, state or nation's social and political system, culture and economy are likely to be more stable when freedom of expression is protected.
- Individuals have a fundamental right to express themselves freely.[4]

The First Amendment is particularly important to print, broadcast, public relations and Web professionals, for it guarantees freedom to disseminate (but not necessarily to gather) information. The freedom is not absolute, however, as will be discussed later.

The 14th Amendment—adopted in 1868 primarily to ensure that rights enjoyed by all citizens were not denied by the states to former slaves—says, in part:

> No State shall make or enforce any law which shall abridge the privileges or immunities of citizens of the United States; nor shall any State deprive any person of life, liberty, or property, without due process of law; or deny to any person within its jurisdiction the equal protection of the laws.

The U.S. Supreme Court said in 1925 that it assumed the First Amendment protections against federal attempts to limit individual freedoms also applied to the states. The court, in *Gitlow v. New York,* decided: "For present purposes we may and do assume that freedom of speech and of the press ... are among the fundamental personal rights and 'liberties' protected by the due process clause of the 14th

Amendment from impairment by the states."[5] Curiously, the court did not find unconstitutional the state law that was used to convict New York socialist Benjamin Gitlow for publishing a pamphlet calling for government overthrow.

Six years later, in *Near v. Minnesota,* the U.S. Supreme Court did overturn a state law that permitted prior restraint against the publication of "malicious, scandalous and defamatory" material.[6] Since 1931, the U.S. Supreme Court has applied most clauses of the Bill of Rights to the states.

Together, the First and 14th Amendments protect a wide array of expression, not all of which all Americans approve. Media professionals are for the most part protected against prior restraint, for example. Government officials who want to stop the publication or broadcast of materials before the fact have an exceptionally hard time convincing courts that such action is legal. This does not mean the media have an absolute protection against prior restraint, but courts have not approved such efforts.[7]

The amendments also protect (1) individuals who burn their own U.S. flags to emphasize their points (*United States v. Eichman*) and (2) journalists who are subjected to licensing schemes by government officials. When Lakewood, Ohio, required a license to install newsracks on sidewalks and gave the mayor the power to deny or approve applications, the U.S. Supreme Court ruled the ordinance unconstitutional in *City of Lakewood v. Plain Dealer Publishing Co.* because the law constituted prior restraint.[8]

Governments typically are prohibited from forcing citizens to speak or to express others' views against their will. When *The Miami Herald* criticized a candidate for Florida's House of Representatives, the politician demanded space to respond. His demand was based on a Florida law requiring the media to provide free space for candidates to respond to stories criticizing them. The U.S. Supreme Court, in *Miami Herald Co. v. Tornillo,* found the statute unconstitutional.[9]

Public relations professionals, however, can be forced indirectly by federal agencies and laws to disclose any information that could affect the price of a public corporation's stock, and officials of those companies (including public relations personnel) might be punished when they fail to do so.[10] And broadcasters may be required to provide time to individuals subjected to personal attacks, although the law is somewhat murky on this point.[11] The First Amendment does not automatically shield professionals in these circumstances.

First and 14th Amendment protections are not constant. The courts frequently interpret and reinterpret these amendments. All media professionals must dedicate themselves to the preservation of the rights guaranteed in these and other amendments, not only because it is in their self-interest to do so, but also because it is in the best interests of all Americans that they do so. (See also the box "The USA Patriot Act.")

THE USA PATRIOT ACT

The USA Patriot Act was passed by Congress and signed by President George W. Bush shortly after the terrorist attacks of Sept. 11, 2001. The act supposedly would help the government track down and punish potential terrorists, but media professionals and others are concerned that the law does not specify how it will be enforced or how its provisions might be used against media professionals—or private citizens.

The law gives the FBI broad authority to collect information through secret court orders. This includes enhanced authority to monitor telephone and electronic mail messages.

The FBI still has to get authorization to tap telephones, intercept electronic mail and eavesdrop on citizens, but the court that grants that authority—the Foreign Intelligence Surveillance Court—meets in secret and issues secret warrants. Nobody really knew, as of 2004, how many orders had been issued. Nor could an individual know whether he or she was under surveillance or challenge a surveillance order.

Under the law, "the FBI can seek an order requiring the production of 'any tangible thing'—which the law says includes books, records, papers, documents and other items—from anyone for investigations involving foreign intelligence or international terrorism. The person or business receiving the order cannot tell anyone that the FBI sought or obtained the 'tangible things.'"[12]

This means the government can ask the nation's librarians who is reading what and who is visiting which Web sites. Many libraries have posted signs warning patrons about the law, and some librarians have defied government requests to supply information in secret. The American Library Association said the act was a threat to privacy and a violation of the First Amendment.

Newsrooms could be searched under the terms of the act, although another law—the Privacy Protection Act—provides a measure of protection. A more likely possibility is that journalists may find their conversations with foreign nationals are intercepted. The act does not make it easier for journalists to be placed under surveillance, but it does make it easier to monitor "agents of a foreign power." A journalist who talks to an agent of a foreign power might become part of a surveillance effort.

FREEDOM OF INFORMATION

Writers, activists, foundations, private citizens and others frequently seek government records and documents, and they often demand that official meetings and trials be open to the public. They invariably argue that the public has a "right to know" what is in government documents and what is discussed in court and in official meetings. The U.S. Constitution does not guarantee access to information, but many federal and state laws do, although not all records, court proceedings and meetings are open. Media professionals have the same access rights—no more, no less—that every other American enjoys.

Public relations professionals can be affected in a couple of ways by laws that mandate that meetings and records be open:

- Those who work for advocacy and consumer groups can use the laws to pry information out of governments, groups and companies on the "other side" of the issue.

- They can represent organizations that are compelled to open their meetings or to release information under freedom of information laws and they must recognize the risks imposed by such laws. Public relations professionals must understand these laws.

Freedom of Information Act

The Freedom of Information Act, passed in 1966, made many federal records available to the public upon request. Federal agencies, Congress said, should release information whenever feasible and withhold information only when necessary.[13] Some federal agencies found ways around the FOIA, so it was amended in 1974 to close the loopholes. The amendments shortened the time an agency can take to reply to a request to 10 working days, and they stipulated that an appeal (sent to the same agency) of a rejected request must be answered in 20 working days. After that time, a writer or citizen may file a lawsuit with the nearest U.S. district court requesting the information.[14]

The law was amended by the Electronic Freedom of Information Act in 1996 to include digital information. Records are to be made available, when technically possible, in the electronic format requested, and the law extended to 20 days the time permitted for responses to FOIA requests. But the act also required agencies to develop ways to expedite requests from journalists and others who seek to inform the public.[15]

Some media professionals and citizens don't use the FOIA because it can take years and incredible persistence to get the records—and agencies sometimes end up withholding the information anyway. The process, which requires a formal letter, is made easier by the Reporters Committee for Freedom of the Press, which makes a form letter available at <www.rcfp.org/foi_letter/generate.php>.

Records subject to the FOIA generally include all those that an agency ordered, wrote or commissioned—and that it has in its physical possession. "Records" is defined to include films, recordings, databases, photographs and papers. The FOIA is specific about what kinds of information can be withheld by government:[16]

- Information specifically exempted by an executive order to protect national security or foreign policy secrets. Agencies can and sometimes do hide behind national security to withhold information that has little to do with keeping the country safe. But President Clinton issued in 1995 an executive order making it more difficult to withhold information on this ground. The order specifies that information cannot be classified to hide government inefficiency or violations of law and that employees can be fired or disciplined for concealing information that should be released.[17]

- Information relating solely to the internal practices and personnel rules of an agency. Records may be withheld only when they are of little concern to the public (for example, information about employee sick leave, parking, instruction manuals, hiring criteria and cafeteria use).

- Information exempted from disclosure by federal law. Congress has exempted tax returns, patent applications, the names and salaries of CIA employees, some Census Bureau records and similar materials.

- Commercial or financial information and trade secrets obtained in confidence from a person or business. Broadcast stations, pharmaceutical companies and businesses seeking government contracts must file substantial amounts of information, and much of that is exempted from disclosure.

- Internal interagency or intra-agency letters, policy discussions or memoranda. The exemption protects the policy-making process in the executive branch. Working documents, recommendations, opinions, proposals, studies and reports usually are protected.

- Personnel records, medical files and similar documents, the disclosure of which would constitute an unwarranted invasion of privacy. "Similar" documents are those containing employee financial records, Social Security number, marital status and the like. Such information might be released, however, if it sheds light on government activities.

- Investigatory records compiled for law enforcement purposes. Documents are protected only to the extent that release of the records would interfere with an ongoing investigation, deprive an individual of a fair trial or impartial hearing, invade personal privacy, expose a confidential source, reveal investigation procedures or endanger the lives or safety of law enforcement officers.

- Financial institutions regulated by the federal government. Records of banks, investment banking firms and trusts are protected.

■ Information about private companies' wells. This rather obscure exemption protects companies from speculators who want to know where oil, gas and water wells are located.

The federal FOIA does not apply to information produced by state, county and local governments, but the states have laws that give the public access to records of these bodies. All 50 states have adopted open records laws, but their provisions vary widely (see the box "Using an Open Records Law"). Most include provisions that most records in any form (film, paper, electronic) should be disclosed. Florida even encourages government agencies to make electronic records available to anyone who has access to a computer. A useful resource is maintained by the Marion Brechner Project at the University of Florida <www.citizenaccess.org>. All state freedom of information laws are listed and evaluated. Another excellent resource is the University of Missouri's "FOI Statutes by State" at <www.missouri.edu/~foiwww/citelist.html>.

Most state laws have restrictions similar to those in the federal FOIA: Law enforcement investigations, personal employee records, business information and trade secrets are exempt. In addition, most states do not allow disclosure of most personal records, such as welfare and adoption records, student files and library borrower records.

States give agencies varying amounts of time to respond to requests. Texas says that response time must be reasonable; Maryland allows 30 days for an agency to respond; Arkansas, Colorado, Georgia, Kansas, Kentucky, Louisiana and Missouri require agencies to respond within three business days; and 20 states mandate no specific response times.[18]

All states are prohibited from providing driving records under the federal Driver's Privacy Protection Act of 1994. States, for example, cannot release a driver's name, medical information, telephone number, Social Security number or address without the driver's consent. The DPPA does not preclude the release of details about motor vehicle violations, accidents or legal driving status.[19] States challenged the constitutionality of the act, but the U.S. Supreme Court ruled in *Condon v. Reno* that it is constitutional.[20]

The *Houston Chronicle* and one of its sources violated the DPPA when it covered an auction at which items belonging to Enron were sold.[21] One man bought an impressive Enron sign for $33,000, but he did not reveal his name publicly. The enterprising *Chronicle* reporter got the license plate number of the car he drove away in, however, and discovered the car was registered to Richard Bowman, who may or may not have been the buyer. The reporter discovered several facts about Bowman and reported them. The *Chronicle* might have been liable under the DPPA, and the source might have been fined or fired. If the source's information had been given in confidence, the reporter might have gone to jail if a judge demanded to know who gave him Bowman's name.

USING AN OPEN RECORDS LAW

Dave Umhoefer, an investigative reporter for the *Milwaukee Journal Sentinel*, used Wisconsin's open records law to get information for an influential series about Milwaukee's attempt to make streets safer. Under its "quality of life" policing program, the city dramatically increased the number of tickets written for jaywalking and other minor crimes in hopes of discouraging major crimes (Chapter 9).[22]

The records were maintained by Municipal Court, which adjudicated the "quality of life" citations. The *Journal Sentinel* wanted access to a computerized database containing information about 1 million cases. Municipal Court had never authorized access to the database, and court officials said there would be technical challenges to making the data available. Given this situation, the newspaper used the open records law to facilitate access. Umhoefer outlined in detail the information needed.

Municipal Court officials initially balked at giving access to the database, arguing that it would take a great deal of time and money to make the records available. A supervisor of the *Journal Sentinel*'s technology department ended up negotiating successfully to get the data: The newspaper simply copied the court's nightly backup file.

The official records request facilitated the process, for records custodians in Wisconsin must make data available without delay after a request is submitted. Had the official request not been filed, the process might have dragged on as court officials and the newspaper negotiated.

Public relations professionals, too, must know what records their organizations must file with government agencies and what records might be obtained under state or federal open records laws. And they need to anticipate any problems that might arise if they must release information because of an FOIA request. Those who work for consumer or advocacy organizations have to understand the laws so they know how to request relevant documents.[23]

Open Meetings Laws

The federal Sunshine Act of 1976 opened to the public the meetings of most federal agencies and their subdivisions.[24] Any meeting at which a quorum is present should be open to the public, and the public should be allowed to hear full discussion about pending actions.[25]

Congress included 10 exemptions to the Sunshine Act, and seven are similar to those contained in the Freedom of Information Act: National security, agency rules, matters exempted by other laws, information from companies, personal privacy matters, records of ongoing investigations and financial reports are exempt. Closed meetings also are allowed when participants discuss court or legal proceedings, reprimands, charges of criminal behavior or the regulation of financial institutions.

Agencies must publish meeting notices in the *Federal Register* at least a week in advance, give reasons why meetings will be closed, close meetings only by formal vote and keep a record (recording or transcript) of closed meetings. A federal judge can be asked later to review the transcript to determine whether the meeting was properly closed.

Although not bound by the Sunshine Act, most congressional meetings are open. The House and the Senate permit coverage by broadcast media, and committee meetings are open unless majorities of the committees vote to exclude the public. Under House rules, meetings can be closed to protect national security and law enforcement information or to avoid defaming or harming an individual.[26]

Each state also has an open meetings law. While states mandate that meetings of all agencies that receive public money or conduct public business are open, they all list exceptions. Many statutes exempt proceedings of parole and pardon boards and of jury proceedings. Legislatures typically are required to hold open meetings.

Many states have laws similar to that of West Virginia, which requires that written notice of the date, hour, place and subject of a meeting of a government body must be published at least five days before the day of the meeting (except for emergency meetings, which can be announced "at any time prior to the meeting"). A meeting is defined as any deliberation between a quorum of members of a governmental body attempting to arrive at a decision about any public business. Meetings conducted by telephone conference calls or other electronic devices fall under the law. A simple majority constitutes a quorum in West Virginia, although that is not the case in all states.[27]

The West Virginia law applies to meetings of state, county and city governments (but not to courts). It provides that the public may be excluded from the portions of meetings that deal with civil insurrections or riots, acts of war or attacks by foreign powers, purchases of land by government bodies when this could hurt their negotiating positions, discussions of individual personnel matters (a complaint against a public official, for instance) or with the disciplining of individual public school or college students. These exceptions are common in state open meetings laws.

The West Virginia law, as do most state laws, says specifically that tape recorders and cameras are allowed, although their placement may be decided by the group or agency meeting.

Open meetings laws do not work when violations are not challenged. If a government agency meets in closed session and is not challenged, it may well continue to meet in private until someone sues under state law. Since most state laws provide for jail terms and fines for officials who violate the law, most prefer to comply with the open meetings statutes. But media professionals and concerned citizens must be willing to sue when meetings are illegally closed.

Those who work in public relations for public or quasi-public groups need to know when it is appropriate to close a meeting—and to ensure that a meeting is not closed improperly. A public relations professional who arrived late to a meeting discovered that a journalist had been told to leave by the group's chair. When she found out the meeting had been closed improperly, she talked to the chair and then stopped the meeting. She called the journalist, who was at that moment writing a damaging story about the improper closure of a public meeting, and told him the meeting would not start until he got there. It didn't.

Right of Access

Journalists and other citizens do not have a constitutional right to go anywhere they wish, although court decisions and state and federal statutes do address the issue. The U.S. Supreme Court, for example, ruled in *Richmond Newspapers v. Virginia* that citizens and journalists have a right to attend trials.[28] But the court denied journalists free access to prison inmates in *Pell v. Procunier* and in *Saxbe v. Washington Post*.[29]

Journalists, like all citizens, generally have access to public places, although access can be denied during a disaster or public disturbance. Nobody is allowed to trample a crime scene, for example, or to hinder rescue efforts, and most writers would not want to do either. Those who do challenge an official order or refuse to move may be charged with obstruction of justice, resisting arrest, assault or trespassing. When photographer Harvey Lashinsky of *The* (Newark, N.J.) *Star-Ledger* was told by a police officer to move away from an accident scene, he argued and was arrested for arguing, refusing to leave and attracting a crowd (*State v. Lachinsky*).[30] He was convicted.

Lower courts have held that officials must not deny access to news events arbitrarily or to discriminate against any medium or writer. The National Transportation Safety Board, a court said, violated the First Amendment when it unreasonably limited access to Logan International Airport when an airplane slid off the runway (*Westinghouse Broadcasting Co. v. National Transportation Safety Board*).[31] Another federal court ruled unconstitutional (in *Daily Herald v. Munro*) Washington's law keeping journalists from interviewing voters within 300 feet of the polling place.[32]

Journalists have little right of access to quasi-public property—property that is owned by the public but is not used by the public. Nuclear power plants and military bases are good examples. Nine reporters covering a demonstration at a nuclear power plant in Oklahoma were charged with trespassing when they followed protestors through a hole in the plant's fence. The U.S. Supreme Court allowed the lower court's decision to stand in *Stahl v. State*.[33]

Nor do journalists have an automatic right of access to war zones. Most journalists, who are subject during war to the president's authority, recognize the danger of reporting information about troop movements. But they are upset when

Journalists, who sometimes stake out private homes to give readers and viewers a glimpse of a news personality, must not go onto private property without permission. Journalists shown here wait to photograph Michael Jackson.

the Pentagon unreasonably restricts their movements as officials did during military action in Afghanistan and Iraq. Their only real recourse is to negotiate with the Pentagon for better access.[34]

Juvenile court proceedings, in which children under 18 are prosecuted, traditionally are closed, unlike the proceedings in almost every other kind of court. Most journalists and legal experts accept that young offenders need rehabilitation more than punishment and that the glare of publicity does not contribute much to rehabilitation efforts. The U.S. Supreme Court has not addressed the matter of juvenile offenders, but other courts have supported closing those proceedings.[35]

In high-profile cases, such as the Washington, D.C.–area sniper attacks—in which one of the defendants was 17—proceedings are far less likely to be closed. And such cases have, in fact, encouraged some states to open juvenile proceedings—when, for instance, a minor commits an especially violent felony and is older than 12. Media professionals sometimes can use information from closed documents.

A writer for the Greenville, Miss., *Delta Democrat Times* heard a prosecutor refer in open court to an adult defendant's juvenile record. The writer was sentenced to three days in jail for publishing the information, but the Mississippi Supreme Court held in *Jeffries v. State of Mississippi* that anyone who heard confidential information cited in court had the right to disseminate that information.[36]

LIBEL

The fear of a potential libel action paralyzes some media professionals to the point that they don't write or produce stories that might have a positive impact. This paralysis can be avoided by writers who know what libel is and how the law is applied.

While libel is a problem primarily for journalists, public relations professionals need to understand the law, too. For example, those who practice the relatively new technique of de-positioning may find themselves at the wrong end of a libel action. De-positioning is a euphemism for bashing—as in attacking a competitor's product, idea or service simply to gain a competitive advantage. The practice is questionable at best, and it can lead to messy legal entanglements.[37]

Newspapers, magazines and broadcast outlets have lost costly libel suits over the years, and some have had severe financial problems because of libel actions filed against them. It can be exceptionally expensive to defend against a libel suit and a publication can be damaged financially even when it wins a case.

The Saturday Evening Post was required to pay one of the largest libel awards in history (at that time) in a case that probably contributed to the downfall of the magazine. *The Post* had printed a story accusing Wallace Butts, former athletic director of the University of Georgia, of conspiring to fix a football game between Georgia and the University of Alabama. Butts sued the Curtis Publishing Co. for $5 million in compensatory damages (which compensate an individual for injured feelings, loss of reputation or mental anguish) and $5 million in punitive damages (which punish a medium or individual for libeling someone). The trial jury awarded him $60,000 in general damages and $3 million in punitive damages.

The U.S. Supreme Court—which upheld the lower court in *Curtis Publishing Co. v. Butts*—found that *The Post* had shown "highly unreasonable conduct constituting an extreme departure from the standards of investigation and reporting ordinarily adhered to by responsible publishers."[38] Butts finally settled for $460,000.

The (Alton, Ill.) *Telegraph* declared bankruptcy after it lost a libel decision based on statements that were never published in the newspaper.[39] Two reporters thought they had found evidence that mafia cash was going into a savings and loan association that was lending money to a developer. The reporters wrote a memorandum, in which they named the developer, to a federal strike force investigating the financial activities. The strike force never found anything, but the memorandum found its way into the developer's hands. He was awarded $9.2 million and

HEED THE RED FLAG

Writers who know little about complex libel laws must know, at the very least, what defamation is, for that knowledge will help them avoid blundering blindly into a lawsuit.

Defamation, the basis for any libel (or slander) action, is a message that harms the reputation of organizations (unions, businesses, nonprofit organizations), products or individuals by challenging, for instance, their ethics, morality, professional abilities, safety, business practices, sanity or financial solvency. More specifically, defamation (1) exposes an individual to ridicule, contempt or hatred; (2) causes the individual's friends, customers or colleagues to hold him or her in lower regard; (3) injures the individual in a career, business or profession; or (4) causes the individual to be avoided or shunned.[40]

Writers who are sensitive and think critically about their work know when they have defamed a person or organization. This knowledge is a red flag that must not be ignored. Writers must be particularly careful (but not paralyzed) when their reports make readers, listeners or viewers think worse of an individual, product or organization.

settled for $1.4 million. *The Telegraph* spent approximately $400,000 of its own money just to defend itself, with insurance kicking in another $200,000.[41]

ABC News also has lost a good deal of money in libel actions. ABC argued that Lundell Manufacturing Co. was a public figure when a reporter for *World News Tonight With Peter Jennings* said Lundell's garbage recycling machine would not work. ABC argued unsuccessfully that the company should be regarded as a public figure because it tried to sell its product to local communities to solve a recycling controversy. The U.S. Supreme Court, saying Lundell was a private figure because it did not engage in the controversy, allowed the lower court's $1 million judgment to stand.[42]

An organization of cattle ranchers sued the *Oprah Winfrey Show* because, the ranchers said, comments made on the show defamed Texas beef. Beef sales dropped dramatically when a guest compared AIDS to mad cow disease and another said the disease could get to the United States quickly from the United Kingdom. The ranchers claimed in *Engler v. Winfrey* that the comments violated the state's food disparagement law. Several states have laws against questioning the value, safety or usefulness of products, food or trade, and groups and individuals can sue for libel under these statutes. Winfrey won in federal court when judges ruled that opinions expressed by Winfrey's guests were protected.[43]

Pieces of a Puzzle

The burden of proof in any legal action rests with the plaintiff—the individual, group or organization that files the action. It is difficult to win a libel case because the plaintiff must prove the following:[44]

- Defamation. If the defendant did not defame the plaintiff under the accepted definition, the libel action should die quickly. (See also the box "Heed the Red Flag" on the previous page.)

- Injury. Plaintiffs generally must prove that the defamation harms their business or profession—that they have lost money or the ability to perform their jobs—or that a publication has caused anguish and mental suffering. However, plaintiffs can and do win libel judgments without ever showing a financial loss.

- Publication. The defamation must be communicated to a third party. This could be publication in a news release, a news report, an annual report, a memorandum or even a letter.

- Identification. The person or organization defamed must be identified. This does not mean that a name is required. If a public relations person distributes a news release containing defamatory material about an unnamed person, he or she is not safe from a libel action. If anyone who reads that release can identify that person, the requirement for identification is satisfied.

- Falsity. Libel plaintiffs must prove the defamatory information was false when the information pertains to a matter of public concern (as most content does). This does not mean a plaintiff wins if he or she can find minor errors in media content. The errors must be substantial, and they must be directly related to the claimed defamation.

- Fault. Most libel plaintiffs must prove only that a defendant was reckless or negligent in publishing a defamatory statement. Public officials and public figures also must prove actual malice, however, which means a writer publishes material he or she knows is false. If a defendant can demonstrate that the defamatory statement was published in good faith and that generally accepted news and information processing procedures were followed, he or she should win the case.

Most libel suits are civil cases, in which a private citizen brings an action. Prosecuting attorneys can also bring charges of criminal libel, but these are rare. The concept of libel is essentially the same, whether a case is civil or criminal. Governments established criminal libel laws to punish those who would criticize the government or disturb the peace, such as demonstrators carrying racist signs while picketing a theater. Criminal libel charges have seldom been brought against journalists.[45]

Many pitfalls await the journalist who reports police and crime news. It's difficult to win a case when a journalist states that a person has been charged with a crime when the person has not (identifying a suspect as Richard Green of 211 Lakeview Drive when the suspect really is Richard Green of 419 Oak Hill Drive, for instance). The following corrections printed in newspapers describe errors that could have led to libel suits. The names have been changed to avoid repeating the potential libel.

> An error in typesetting in a story on the San Marcos school board in the Thursday edition of the —— resulted in the word "not" being left out of a paragraph near the end of the article.
>
> The paragraph should have read, "Five San Marcos trustees were found not guilty, repeat 'not guilty,' of open meetings law violations in justice of the peace court in January."

This correction resulted from a typesetting error. The phrase "not guilty" was intended, but the "not" was dropped somewhere in the editorial process.

> A story in the —— of last Saturday about a drug raid and the arrest of four men on holdup charges incorrectly said that Ed Street, 31, of Clarion Street near Reed, was one of those arrested and charged with aggravated robbery and other offenses. Street was not arrested and not charged. He was one of 20 persons at the location, 3700 Brown Lane, South Philadelphia, questioned by the police.

The mistake described in this correction seems to be a writer's error. How else but through a writer's carelessness could a person questioned by police be mistaken for a person arrested and charged with robbery? Reporting that a person was charged with or convicted of a crime when the person was not is dangerous business.

Many cases have been taken to court. *The* (Syracuse, N.Y.) *Post-Standard* was sued for libel after it reported that Hazel Robart was charged with driving an uninsured vehicle. Robart had been ticketed, but not charged, for failure to provide proof of insurance. When she did provide proof to the court, the ticket was dismissed. A New York appeals court said in *Robart v. Post-Standard* that the newspaper's report was defamatory and false because Robart was never charged with a crime.[46]

Writers need to be especially careful, too, when they talk about the professions and occupations of those about whom they write. Writers are walking on thin ice when they suggest that professionals, businesspeople, public employees, law enforcement officers, laborers, teachers and others are not smart enough or are not qualified enough to do their jobs. The *Louisville* (Ky.) *Times* got into trouble when it quoted Hattie Rose Ludwig's assertion that she became addicted to drugs while under a doctor's care. A Kentucky court held in *Pearce v. Courier-Journal and Louisville Times Co.* that the story probably would expose the doctor to disgrace or contempt in the minds of lay readers.[47]

Defenses

Professionals want to avoid libel actions, but sometimes that is impossible. When a suit is filed, an organization can use any of several defenses, including truth, qualified privilege, *The New York Times* rule, opinion and fair comment and retraction.

Truth

Truth alone is a strong defense in a libel suit, although the truth is not always easy to find, particularly in a courtroom in which plaintiff and defense attorneys argue about what is and is not true. In general, the plaintiff must prove statements are false. The U.S. Supreme Court held in *Philadelphia Newspapers Inc. v. Hepps* that libel plaintiffs must prove information is false when the "offending" passage relates to an issue of concern to the public—which media content nearly always does."[48]

Truth is elusive (Chapter 1). It is difficult for writers to respond to a plaintiff's assertion that statements are false when they have cited unnamed sources for their information, for those sources are under no legal obligation to testify about what they said. Even when sources do testify, they may have little credibility with juries.

It is also difficult for writers to defend themselves when they have omitted facts and statements to give a false impression—to make a news figure look bad. (See also the box "Trash on Talk Radio.") *The Memphis Press-Scimitar* ran into difficulty when it reported that Mrs. Newton shot Mrs. Nichols after she found Mrs. Nichols and Mr. Newton in the Nichols' home. *The Press-Scimitar* did not report that Mrs. Nichols, Mr. Newton and two friends were talking when Mrs. Newton shot Mrs. Nichols. The Tennessee Supreme Court said in *Memphis Publishing Co. v. Nichols* that the failure to do a complete report created a false impression that Mrs. Nichols and Mr. Newton were having an affair and that a journalist is not protected when an article that is literally true conveys defamatory meaning.[49]

A plaintiff usually will not win a libel judgment simply because she or he finds a trivial error in a report. The report must be substantially incorrect and the error must be closely tied to the alleged defamation. If a criminal robs a bank at 112 W. Elm St. and is said in a news report to have been charged with robbery, he or she will not win a libel suit if the report is correct in every way *except* for the street number. An editor won't be pleased if the writer says the bank is located at 114 W. Elm St., but that error alone will not cause the news medium to lose a libel case.

Qualified Privilege

The media generally have the right to print damaging statements made in government and court proceedings that are public and official. Witnesses in these proceedings must be given absolute privilege to protect them from libel suits, or courts and other public bodies could not conduct their business. Not many people would be willing to testify in murder trials if they could be sued later. The absolute privilege given to witnesses carries over to citizens (and media professionals) in the form of qualified privilege.[50]

TRASH ON TALK RADIO

Many radio talk show hosts make honest, genuine efforts to come to grips with intractable social, cultural, economic and political problems. They don't stand for inaccuracy and dishonesty. Some, however, are like Rush Limbaugh, who is a symbol of the worst of talk radio, where disinformation is common and binary thinking (where a war rages between "us" and "them") is the rule.[51]

Limbaugh says his talk radio network, Excellence in Broadcasting, purports to expose the lies and innuendos spread by the elite media. The conservative Limbaugh announced that nobody was indicted in the Iran-Contra affair and that Congress had opposed the Persian Gulf War. In fact, 14 were indicted during the Iran-Contra affair and both houses of Congress authorized the use of force in the Gulf War. These are just two of Limbaugh's many factual errors.

The rules of libel, privacy and copyright are not suspended for talk radio,

Rush Limbaugh, through his Excellence in Broadcasting network, sometimes misleads his audience as he advances conservative causes.

although it sometimes seems they must be. It is important for anyone considering a career in talk radio to understand that the rules still apply.[52]

The courts have long recognized this qualified privilege because of society's need to know what goes on in government meetings and how government functions. The privilege also helps ensure that parties to civil and criminal disputes get fair trials. The privilege typically applies to congressional and legislative proceedings (including committee meetings and investigations); municipal council meetings; official reports; acts of state, local or national government officials;

and civil and criminal courts. The privilege does not extend to a meeting of any private group, such as the stockholders of a corporation, unless the meeting is open to the public.

The privilege is qualified because writers must play by the rules, which means they cannot, for example, select facts and statements to construct one-sided accounts that make someone look bad. Accounts must be accurate, fair and balanced summaries of the original sources. They must not be malicious or vengeful. A writer who produces a report that is not an accurate, fair and balanced summary of what was said in an official meeting might well be sued successfully for libel.

Comments made in court by a defense attorney are privileged and may be used, but the same comments made on the courthouse steps may not carry this protection. A writer who quotes a police chief about someone's guilt or innocence must be exceptionally careful if the information is not part of an official document or investigation. If the same information is contained in a court document, it is protected in most states.

The New York Times Rule

A 1964 case in which *The New York Times* was the defendant makes it exceedingly difficult for a public official to win a libel suit, even when inaccurate or defamatory statements are reported. A public official might sue successfully only when he or she can *prove* a writer knew a statement was false or published with reckless disregard for the truth.[53]

The Times was sued for libel by L.B. Sullivan, commissioner of public affairs for the city of Montgomery, Ala. *The Times* had printed an advertisement by a civil rights group that told of demonstrations at Alabama State College in Montgomery. The advertisement did not name Sullivan, but it said police armed with shotguns and tear gas "ringed" the campus and that the demonstrations were met with an unprecedented wave of terror. The advertisement contained a number of errors. For one, police had not actually "ringed" the campus. And nine students were expelled for asking to be served at a courthouse lunch counter, not for singing at the Alabama capitol, as the advertisement reported. Sullivan, who was in charge of the police, sued *The Times* and four black clergymen who were among the people signing the advertisement.

The lower court found in favor of Sullivan and awarded him $500,000. The Alabama State Supreme Court upheld the decision in *New York Times v. Sullivan*, but it was overturned by the U.S. Supreme Court, which said a rule requiring a critic of official conduct to guarantee the truth of all factual statements would be too restrictive on public discourse. The case established *The New York Times* rule, which defined actual malice as publishing something defamatory about a public official with knowledge that it was false or with reckless disregard for its truth. Even inaccurate statements about a public official could not be found libelous, the court said, as long as the statements were not made with actual malice.

The U.S. Supreme Court extended *The New York Times* rule to public figures when it required two public figures to demonstrate that defamatory statements about them were published with malice, as defined in *The New York Times v. Sullivan.* The Court, in *Curtis Publishing Co. v. Butts,* defined public figures as individuals who are "intimately involved in the resolution of important public questions or, by reason of their fame, shape events in areas of concern to society at large."[54]

The U.S. Supreme Court seemed to reverse a trend of growing protection for seemingly libelous statements in *Gertz v. Robert Welch Inc.* This case grew out of the fatal shooting of a youth by a Chicago policeman named Richard Nuccio. Elmer Gertz, a Chicago trial lawyer, had been hired by the victim's family to represent it in civil litigation against Nuccio. *American Opinion,* the monthly magazine of the John Birch Society, published an article titled "FRAME-UP: Richard Nuccio and the War on Police." The article attempted to show that the prosecution of Nuccio was part of a communist campaign against police. The article portrayed Gertz as the architect of the frame-up, even though he played no part in the criminal proceeding. Gertz was said to have a police file so extensive it took "a big, Irish cop to lift." He was also reported to belong to certain Marxist groups. These statements were incorrect.

The Supreme Court ruled that Gertz was a private citizen and not a public figure, since he did not have "general fame or notoriety in the community" and did not "thrust himself into the vortex of this public issue, nor did he engage the public's attention in an attempt to influence its outcome." The Supreme Court said that private individuals are both more vulnerable to injury than public officials or public figures and more deserving of compensation. It held that a private individual should be able to recover for libel without having to show malice as defined by *The New York Times* rule.[55]

Opinion and Fair Comment

U.S. courts have long given the media great freedom to comment on matters of public interest. The fair comment defense protects the expression of opinion on a variety of public matters, including theatrical and musical performances, books, movies, plays, advertising and public relations campaigns, sports activities, political activities and behavior of government officials.

Such commentary is protected also by more recent rulings that distinguish fact from opinion (Chapter 7). Opinions include judgments (evaluations of goodness and badness) and inferences (statements about the unknown made on the basis of the known). The accuracy of opinions cannot be verified, although the accuracy of an assertion that a specific individual uttered an opinion may be. The accuracy of facts (reports), on the other hand, can be verified.[56] Since opinion cannot be proved false, libel plaintiffs find it difficult to win cases in which opinion is allegedly defamatory. To state that a singer is not good for a part because his voice is weak is opinion. The aggrieved singer may feel he was defamed, but any libel action would surely fail.[57]

It is important to keep this distinction in mind, for a libel decision can turn on a court's determination about what is a "fact" and what is an "opinion." A writer for *The* (Lorain, Ohio) *Morning Journal* expressed the opinion in his column that a high school wrestling coach had lied in a legal hearing about a brawl in which his team was involved. The coach sued and the U.S. Supreme Court upheld his position in *Milkovich v. Lorain Journal Co.* The court said the writer's column did not make the assertion in jest and that the writer's allegation was factual enough to be proved accurate or inaccurate.[58]

Retraction

A retraction—the withdrawal of a statement—usually is a correction of an error accompanied by an apology. A retraction typically is a limited defense serving mainly to reduce damages. It can be presented as evidence that a defamatory statement was not made with ill will.

Retractions must be good-faith attempts to correct false, defamatory statements. Publishing a retraction in seven-point type in the classifieds or in a news release that is not sent to the recipients of the original message is not a good-faith effort. The best retractions are complete, sincere, fair and accompanied by genuine apologies for error. If they are sincere, retractions are handled in roughly the same way as the original defamatory statement.

More than 30 states have adopted laws that protect news media that retract false and defamatory information, but the protection varies widely. In some states, punitive damages are prohibited when a news medium retracts defamatory and false statements. Plaintiffs in Wisconsin must allow a publication to correct an error before suing, and the state prohibits punitive damages when a retraction is published. But when an electronic bulletin board allegedly published false and defamatory information, an appeals court ruled that a plaintiff could sue without seeking the retraction that would preclude punitive damages. The court said in *It's in the Cards Inc. v. Fuschetto* that a bulletin board publishes randomly, not regularly, as do newspapers, magazines and periodicals.[59]

Other Warnings

All of the parties that help disseminate a libelous statement can be held accountable. This includes a news source who makes a libelous remark, a writer who reports it and a newspaper that publishes it. Even the news carrier who throws the newspaper on lawns can be held liable, although this would be unusual.

The law about Internet service providers is unclear. Under the Telecommunications Act of 1996, ISPs should not be viewed as the speaker or publisher of content supplied by someone other than the ISP. The intent was to give ISPs the authority to screen information posted on their sites.[60] A federal district court allowed to stand a lower court's decision throwing out a suit against AOL for failing to remove libelous statements immediately (*Zeran v. America Online Inc.*). Some observers argue, however, that an ISP might still be held liable for material that it reviewed and failed to recognize as defamatory.[61]

Using actualities, streaming video or quotation marks or attributing a libelous statement to a news source does not relieve a writer or medium of responsibility for libel (unless it is a situation covered by qualified privilege or one of the other defenses). A medium or Web site can be held responsible for libel contained in advertisements, promotional materials, news releases, annual reports, news service copy and letters to the editor. The reasoning is that the medium, Web site or communication professional contributed to the libel by spreading it.

The use of the word "alleged," as in the phrase "the alleged killer of three," does little to relieve a journalist or publication of the responsibility for libel. The important point is whether the person has been charged or convicted of a crime, and this should be brought out clearly. If a person has not yet been charged with a crime, the use of the word "alleged" will not prevent a libel suit. The safest course is not to write anything about a person who has not been charged, although that is not always feasible, particularly when individuals, events or groups are prominent.

PRIVACY

Privacy law is designed primarily to protect every American's right to be left alone. The Constitution does not mention this right, but the Fourth Amendment, which prohibits unreasonable government searches, has been used to protect privacy.

The (Cleveland) *Plain Dealer* learned about privacy the hard way when it published a story about the impact of a man's death on his family. Melvin Cantrell died when a bridge collapsed on the Ohio River. A writer and photographer visited the family's home while Mrs. Cantrell was at work and interviewed and photographed her children. The story contained inaccuracies and implied that the woman had been interviewed, when she had not. The story also emphasized the family's poverty. Mrs. Cantrell sued and was awarded $60,000 in damages. The U.S. Supreme Court ruled in *Cantrell v. Forest City Publishing Co.* that the newspaper published reckless falsehoods and portrayed the family in a false light (see discussion below).[62]

Concerns

Almost all the states have privacy laws that guarantee more than the right to be left alone: Many statutes also recognize the right of an individual to be portrayed accurately in the news media; to be free from snooping, trespass and electronic surveillance; and to keep media professionals from appropriating a person's name or image in promotional or news material. (See also the box "Samuel Warren and Louis Brandeis on Privacy.") A media professional must study the statutes of his or her own state because the laws vary widely. Some states recognize "false light," for instance, while others are backing off.

False Light

False light means disseminating offensive and false information about someone with reckless disregard for its truth. A writer who portrays an individual as something other than what he or she really is has cast the individual in a "false light." The plaintiff in a false-light case must prove the information was substantially

SAMUEL WARREN AND LOUIS BRANDEIS ON PRIVACY

Of the desirability—Indeed of the necessity—of some such [privacy] protection, there can, it is believed, be no doubt. The press is overstepping in every direction the obvious bounds of propriety and of decency. Gossip is no longer the resource of the idle and of the vicious, but has become a trade, which is pursued with industry as well as effrontery. To satisfy a prurient taste the details of sexual relations are spread broadcast [sic] in the columns of the daily papers. To occupy the indolent, column upon column is filled with idle gossip, which can only be procured by intrusion upon the domestic circle. The intensity and complexity of life, attendant upon advancing civilization, have rendered necessary some retreat from the world, and man, under the refining influence of culture, has become more sensitive to publicity, so that solitude and privacy have become more essential to the individual; but modern enterprise and invention have, through invasions upon his privacy, subjected him to mental pain and distress, far greater than could be inflicted by mere bodily injury. Nor is the harm wrought by such invasions confined to the suffering of those who may be the subjects of journalistic or other enterprise. In this, as in other branches of commerce, the supply creates the demand. Each crop of unseemly gossip, thus harvested, becomes the seed of more, and, in direct proportion to its circulation, results in a lowering of social standards and of morality. Even gossip apparently harmless, when widely and persistently circulated, is potent for evil. It both belittles and perverts. It belittles by inverting the relative importance of things, thus dwarfing the thoughts and aspirations of a people. When personal gossip attains the dignity of print, and crowds the space available for matters of real interest to the community, what wonder that the ignorant and thoughtless mistake its relative importance. ... Triviality destroys at once robustness of thought and delicacy of feeling.

Source: Samuel D. Warren and Louis D. Brandeis, "The Right to Privacy," *Harvard Law Review* 4:5 (Dec. 15, 1890): 193–200, p. 196.

Samuel D. Warren and Louis D. Brandeis helped establish the foundation for privacy law in their classic article in the *Harvard Law Review*.

false, that it was published, that it was about the plaintiff and that the information was highly offensive to a reasonable person.

One of the more famous false-light cases is that of John Gill, who was photographed with his arm around his wife and his cheek to her cheek at the counter of their ice cream parlor in Los Angeles. The *Ladies' Home Journal* used the photograph to illustrate a story about love at first sight, which the Gills supposedly represented. The *Journal* said that kind of love was bad because it was based entirely on sexual attraction. The California Supreme Court upheld the Gills' privacy action in *Gill v. Curtis Publishing Co.*[63]

False light in privacy cases is one of the more difficult legal concepts in part because legal scholars tend to disagree about the relationship of false light to libel and other privacy issues. "While false light shares similarities with libel, the false-light plaintiff does not sue for lost reputation but, like someone suing over publication of embarrassing facts, is seeking recompense, as the Gills were, for the psychic harms of mental distress and humiliation."[64] A false-light invasion of privacy is sometimes described as a libel action without defamation.[65]

False-light invasion of privacy also is difficult to understand because scholars (and state legislators) disagree about how much protection the First Amendment provides writers in the face of those who sue for mental anguish and about the kind of publication that should be considered highly offensive. Information may upset a news source or personality, but it is not necessarily highly offensive to a reasonable person.

Because of the difficulties, some states do not recognize false light as invasion of privacy.

Private Information

Writers run a risk when they publish private information over a source's objection. This does not mean that news sources and personalities can censor any information about them. If a dispute goes to court, the news personality must prove that the information would be considered by reasonable individuals to be offensive, that it had not been available previously and that it was not of interest to the public.

Time magazine fell into a legal quagmire when it ran a story about Dorothy Barber, a Missouri woman who had an odd eating disorder. *Time* published without her permission a photograph of her in a hospital bed and called her a starving glutton because she lost weight even as she ate large quantities of food. The Missouri Supreme Court ruled in *Barber v. Time Inc.* that *Time* had invaded her privacy unnecessarily. *Time*'s story was accurate, but truth is not a defense when private information is published in this way.[66]

Private information must indeed be *private*. A writer who disseminates information that is already generally available to the public should have little to fear in court. Defining "generally available" can be problematic, however. A plaintiff who discloses the information to a few friends or family members has not made the disputed information "generally available."[67]

Intrusion and Trespass

Intrusion and trespass can get writers and their media into considerable trouble. Though often used synonymously, intrusion usually refers to gathering information by secretly using electronic surveillance equipment or cameras, and trespass typically means entering uninvited onto someone's private property.[68]

All Americans have a right to solitude and seclusion, and media professionals have no constitutional right to invade their private space physically or with electronic equipment. Courts have long held that journalists intrude when they, for instance, record conversations secretly or intercept electronic mail.

Intrusion was the problem when *Inside Edition* was ordered by a federal judge in Pennsylvania to stop its aggressive surveillance of a prominent family. Paul Lewis and Stephen Wilson used sophisticated electronic equipment to monitor the family's activities from a van parked on public streets near the family's home. The judge in *Wolfson v. Lewis* said the tactics "altered the Wolfsons' physical and emotional sense of seclusion."[69]

Journalists may enter private property when they are given permission, but they must leave when they are asked to do so. If they do not have permission or do not leave when asked, they may be charged with trespass. Courts are not consistent in their rulings on trespass when journalists misrepresent themselves to get information about public companies.

A federal jury in Greensboro, N.C., found in 1997 that ABC News and *Prime Time Live* personnel trespassed and committed fraud and breach of loyalty in obtaining information and film for a story about the Food Lion supermarket chain. ABC producers Lynn Dale and Susan Barnett lied about their backgrounds to get jobs at Food Lion and took hidden cameras and microphones to work. They reported Food Lion was selling tainted food, a charge Food Lion did not challenge specifically.[70] Jurors and the judge emphasized in *Food Lion Inc. v. Capitol Cities/ABC Inc.* that the deception used to obtain information for the story was not the issue. The ABC staffers had broken the law to get the information. The 4th U.S. Circuit Court of Appeals ultimately overturned the lower court decision and ordered ABC to pay Food Lion only $2 for trespass and breach of loyalty to an employer.

But another federal court dismissed trespass and fraud charges against ABC when its reporters posed as clients of the Desnick Eye Centers in Indiana and Wisconsin and used hidden cameras to collect facts about supposedly unnecessary operations (*Desnick v. ABC*).[71]

Commercialization

The appropriation of an individual's likeness or name can constitute an invasion of privacy. Donald Manville won his suit when a photograph that he thought was going to be used in a news report was used in an advertisement in which he said Norge self-service laundries were good investments (*Manville v. Borg-Warner*

Corp.).[72] Bette Midler won a privacy judgment when a woman imitated Midler's voice in an advertisement for Ford Motor Co. (*Midler v. Young & Rubicam*).[73]

Public relations professionals must be careful when they use photographs in brochures, annual reports, newsletters and other documents. Subjects of photographs may not even know their pictures are taken, and they might object to their use. Even photographs of employees must be used with care. They must pertain to the employees' jobs, and they should be used only while the individuals remain employed with the company.[74]

Defenses

Newsworthiness is a good defense in many privacy cases. (It is not a good defense in false-light, intrusion and trespass cases.) Media professionals are on reasonably safe ground when information they disseminate would be judged by a reasonable person to be important (Chapter 2). But news does not necessarily have to be important. Information that is merely odd or curious can be newsworthy because readers, listeners and viewers find it interesting. Journalists must be most careful when they write about illness and trivial public embarrassments.[75]

Writers typically can use information contained in court records. A Georgia father sued under that state's privacy statute when his daughter was identified as the victim in a particularly vicious rape and murder. The Georgia law made identification of a rape victim a misdemeanor. The U.S. Supreme Court ruled in *Cox Broadcasting Corp. v. Cohn* that the father could not bring the suit. That ruling provides nearly complete protection for news media to report information in court records.[76] Protection was extended to information obtained outside a courtroom when a journalist got the name of a rape victim from the local sheriff's department and published it (*Florida Star v. B.J.F.*).[77]

Writers typically have to worry little about privacy actions when they base reports on information contained in public records. Courts have ruled that they simply provide additional publicity for information that already is public. An Iowa state court said Robin Howard could not sue a newspaper that reported her sterilization when she was a patient in a government facility because the information already was public (*Howard v. Des Moines Register*). The facts were contained in a report sent earlier to the governor's office.[78]

Professionals who have the implied or stated consent of the persons about whom they write also are unlikely to lose privacy cases. Courts usually find that anyone who participates voluntarily or involuntarily in a news event has consented to be photographed, videotaped, recorded, filmed or written about.[79] A person who knowingly talks to a journalist also has given implied consent to be named in any report, although consent is not implied if the individual does not know he or she is speaking to a journalist or that the information might be aired or published.

Public relations professionals should obtain written permission to use the information when they write about medical conditions, use private information about minors (who cannot give consent), describe psychological states and disseminate similar sensitive information.

When a department store's public relations department ran a photograph of a woman before and after she had plastic surgery, the woman sued because she had not given her consent (*Vassiliades v. Garfinckel*).[80] The public relations department got off the hook because the department store's lawyers argued that store officials thought the surgeon had gotten Vassiliades' consent. The surgeon did not get off.

The U.S. Supreme Court ruled in *Time Inc. v. Hill* that news media may not be sued successfully for false light if the plaintiff is unable to prove actual malice. Journalists who use good journalistic practices and who do not write with malicious intent are reasonably safe from false-light actions, even when news figures and sources are thrust against their will into a public event or issue.[81]

The First Amendment can be a defense against commercialization charges if someone is disseminating information and news that is of interest to the public. A U.S. Senator who published photographs of constituents in campaign material was exonerated by the Utah Supreme Court, which said the material was newsworthy (*Cox v. Hatch*).[82] Public relations professionals should get releases from the subjects of all photographs used, even when the subjects are employees.

FREE PRESS–FAIR TRIAL

Media coverage of state and federal courts often is marked by the collision between two constitutional amendments: the First Amendment guarantees of free speech and the Sixth Amendment guarantees of fair and speedy trials. To assure a fair trial, juries must be impartial and unprejudiced when trials begin, and they must be influenced during trials only by the evidence presented. While the Sixth Amendment applies to criminal proceedings, states have established similar standards for civil cases.

Pretrial Publicity

Media coverage of trials can pose problems during criminal and civil investigations, pretrial proceedings and trials. Pretrial publicity, which can focus on details of police investigations and on legal maneuvers, is problematic because potential jurors can be influenced by information reported in the media. If a criminal confesses to a crime, for instance, and then recants, jurors might know about a confession that is not even admissible at trial. Similarly, jurors might hear on the radio during a trial information that is not admitted by a judge.

Excessive pretrial publicity was one of the reasons the U.S. Supreme Court overturned the conviction in Ohio of Dr. Sam Sheppard, who was tried for the murder of his wife. Newspapers covering the landmark case (*State v. Sheppard*) had printed front-page stories that said Sheppard had refused to take a lie detector test, and newspaper editorials asked why Sheppard wasn't in jail.[83] Sheppard was convicted, spent 10 years in prison, lost his license to practice and then saw his case reviewed by the U.S. Supreme Court, which ruled Sheppard had not had a fair trial because of excessive publicity. Sheppard was acquitted the second time around.

Only certain kinds of pretrial publicity generally are considered to be prejudicial to a defendant. A set of standards approved a few years after the Sheppard trial by the American Bar Association—and reaffirmed over many years—warns attorneys not to release for publication or broadcast certain kinds of information:[84]

- A prior criminal record (including indictments, arrests or other criminal charges), or information about the character or reputation of an accused person. A lawyer may make a factual statement about the person's name, age, residence, occupation and family status. If the individual has not been apprehended, a lawyer associated with the prosecution may release information necessary to her or his apprehension or warn the public of any dangers the person may present.

- Contents (or even the existence) of any admission, confession or statement made by the individual or the failure or refusal of the person to make any statements.

- The results of any tests (for example, DNA or lie detector tests) or the individual's refusal or failure to submit to tests.

- The identity, testimony, credibility or criminal records of potential witnesses. The lawyer may announce the identity of the victim if the identity is not protected by law.

- The prospect for a plea of guilty to the charge or to a lesser charge.

- Any opinion about the person's guilt or innocence, about the merits of the case or about the evidence.

The guidelines have never been legally binding; if writers could get the information from attorneys, they could use it. But the guidelines did focus attention on major areas of disagreement and conflict in judicial coverage, and many journalists met with attorneys and judges to seek solutions to the dilemma. (See also the box "Statements Judged Not Prejudicial by the ABA.")

Gag Orders

Some judges became a bit too eager many years ago to control publicity about cases before the bar. They imposed on the media gag orders that amounted to prior restraint. More than three dozen such orders were issued from 1967 to 1975. In one of the more famous cases—*Nebraska Press Association v. Stuart*—a Nebraska handyman allegedly murdered six family members in a town of 850 people.[85] The judge ordered the media not to publish or broadcast information about the man's confession or any other information that might implicate him in the crime.

The U.S. Supreme Court ruled the gag order unconstitutional, effectively ending the reign of gag orders in criminal trials. The court, however, did not ban gag orders entirely, saying that such orders could be valid in exceptionally rare circumstances.

STATEMENTS JUDGED NOT PREJUDICIAL BY THE ABA

■ The general nature of the charges against the accused, provided that there is included therein a statement explaining that the charge is merely an accusation and that the defendant is presumed innocent unless proven guilty

■ The general nature of the defense to the charges or to other public accusations against the accused, including that the accused has no prior criminal record

■ The name, age, residence, occupation and family status of the accused

■ Information necessary to aid in the apprehension of the accused or to warn the public of any dangers that may exist

■ A request for assistance in obtaining evidence

■ The existence of an investigation in progress, including the general length and scope of the investigation, the charge or [offense] involved, and the identity of the investigating officer or agency

■ The facts and circumstances of an arrest, including the time and place, and the identity of the arresting officer or agency

■ The identity of the victim, where the release of that information is not otherwise prohibited by law or would not be harmful to the victim

■ Information contained within a public record, without further comment …

■ The scheduling or result of any stage in the judicial process

Source: American Bar Association, *The Reporter's Key: Access to the Judicial Process,* 3rd ed. (Chicago: Author, 2003): Standard 8-1.1(c) Downloaded on May 23, 2003, from <www.abanet.org/ftp/pub/media/reporter.pdf>.

Some judges have attempted from time to time to impose gag orders in civil cases. When Procter & Gamble Co. sued Bankers Trust Co. for fraud, the two sides drafted an agreement that many documents collected during discovery would be classified as trade secrets and sealed. The judge approved the agreement, but a federal Court of Appeals ruled the gag order unconstitutional, stating that "the private litigants' interest in protecting their vanity or their commercial self-interest simply does not qualify as grounds for imposing a prior restraint."[86]

Most court proceedings are open, and court officials generally do not have the authority to control what the media publish and air. But judges can take other steps to shield a jury from news coverage of a trial and related developments. A judge has the power to take the following actions:[87]

- Sequester a jury, or isolate members from personal contacts and exposure to the mass media. This is not uncommon when a case is particularly sensational.

- Change the venue, or move the trial to another location in which prejudicial news coverage might not be so extensive. The murder trial of David Wayne Henley was moved from Houston to San Antonio after there was extensive publicity about the "homosexual mass murders."

- Issue a gag order, not on the media, but on lawyers and other court officers. This usually means journalists find it more difficult to get information, for a court officer who defies a court order can be held in contempt.

- Ensure that potential jurors are questioned carefully before they are selected to determine that they have not been prejudiced by media coverage.

- Admonish the jury to avoid reading or viewing media reports about the trial.

- Control the media's behavior in the courtroom. The "carnival atmosphere" during the trial of Dr. Sam Sheppard was another factor leading the U.S. Supreme Court to overturn his conviction in *Sheppard v. Maxwell.* The Court emphasized that the presence of the media should have been limited, news media representatives should not have been placed inside the bar in the courtroom and the judge should have more carefully regulated the conduct of journalists.[88] A judge who finds that journalists are not behaving properly in a courtroom has the power to find them in contempt.

Judges can exercise some authority over public relations professionals who write about pending court cases involving their own organizations. A business that is party to a lawsuit is not supposed to take its case to the public, so a public relations writer might be held in contempt for producing a news release that a judge sees as an attempt to sway jurors or potential jurors.

Cameras in Court

Broadcast journalists and photographers are generally adamant that cameras should be allowed in court, but many lawyers and judges have argued that cameras should be barred—allegedly because they distract jurors; intimidate witnesses; encourage lawyers, judges and witnesses to grandstand; and disrupt the decorum of the court. The U.S. Supreme Court reversed a Texas conviction in 1965 on grounds that a defendant in a fraud case had not gotten a fair trial because of television cameras in the courtroom (*Estes v. Texas*).[89] This had a chilling effect for more than a decade.

Photographers were allowed to run amok during the 1962 trial of Billy Sol Estes, who is seated at the right in this photo of a conference with his attorneys. Cameras were banned for years from courtrooms across America in large part because of the excessive coverage of the Estes trial.

The Court reversed itself in 1981 in *Chandler v. Florida* when two police officers were convicted of conspiracy. The defendants objected to cameras in the courtroom, but the judge allowed them anyway. The justices ruled that cameras in court do not automatically make a trial unfair, but they did not grant the media a First Amendment right to photograph court proceedings.[90]

Most states permit cameras in court during criminal trials and appellate proceedings. However, approval is not automatic. Judges typically decide whether cameras will be allowed and how filming will be done. Motor drives, special lighting and close-up shots of witnesses and jurors are prohibited in some jurisdictions. Some states also require that all parties to a proceeding approve.

The *Federal Rules of Criminal Procedure* prohibit photography and filming of federal legal proceedings. The federal system tried a three-year experiment with cameras in selected trial and appellate courts, but the U.S. Judicial Conference voted in 1994 to discontinue the experiment and to reimpose the camera ban. The Conference decided in 1996 to allow each circuit to establish its own rules in civil cases.

CONFIDENTIAL SOURCES

The right (or not) of journalists to protect confidential sources is one of the most controversial issues in mass communication (Chapter 10). Should a journalist who has been writing about criminal activity be protected from having to identify news sources in court? Should a journalist who has information that could help one company in its civil suit against another company be compelled to reveal that information or its source? The Sixth Amendment, after all, guarantees speedy and fair trials.

Prosecutors argue that journalists sometimes have information that they, prosecutors, see as necessary to a criminal trial. Writers argue that they have to promise confidentiality to sources who know about criminal activity if they are going to get any information and that they will no longer have access to such sources if they name any of them in court. Defense attorneys obviously will stop at nothing to get information that will help their clients.

Simply naming the information source is not an option for a journalist who has been subpoenaed. A writer who promises confidentiality to a source in exchange for information is ethically and legally bound by that promise. A source might voluntarily come forth, but that decision is not the journalist's.

In *Cohen v. Cowles Media Co.,* writers for two Minnesota newspapers promised anonymity to Dan Cohen, a political consultant in the gubernatorial race. Cohen provided court documents showing that his campaign's opponent had been convicted of shoplifting. The editors of the two newspapers decided independently to publish Cohen's name. He sued for breach of contract and won. The U.S. Supreme Court upheld the lower court decision.[91]

Media professionals have no absolute privilege to protect confidential sources when a court demands they be identified, but some protection is accorded under state and federal constitutions, statutes and case laws.

Constitutional Privilege

Journalists argued for years that they had a privilege under the First Amendment to protect their confidential sources. The issue came to a head in 1972 when the U.S. Supreme Court considered several high-profile cases that were consolidated under a single name, *Branzburg.*[92]

One of the cases concerned Earl Caldwell, a reporter for *The New York Times* who used confidential sources in stories about the activities of the Black Panthers on the West Coast. Caldwell was ordered to appear, with his notes and tape recordings, before a grand jury investigating the Panthers. Caldwell refused even to appear, arguing that his appearance alone would cost him the trust of his sources. A federal district court ordered Caldwell to appear before the grand jury, but the appeals court overruled the district court, stating the lower court's decision did not adequately protect Caldwell's First Amendment rights.[93]

The Caldwell case, with the others under *Branzburg,* was decided by the U.S. Supreme Court, which failed to recognize a First Amendment privilege for journalists to protect their sources. The Court noted that journalists have no special rights not accorded other citizens and that the *Branzburg* cases did not turn on government efforts to influence media content.[94] The court did, however, leave the door ajar for at least a qualified privilege (see next section).

Some state constitutions contain provisions similar to the First Amendment, but they too have been interpreted over the years to exclude an absolute privilege.

Shield Laws

One exception to the general rule that media professionals do not have special privileges is the shield law legislation enacted by many state governments and considered by the federal government. A comprehensive shield law protects a journalist from government subpoenas demanding (1) identification of news sources or (2) journalists' notes, unused photographs and negatives, tape recordings, electronic files and outtakes (unused film or digital images) from television newscasts.[95]

When the U.S. Supreme Court rejected an absolute privilege, justices indicated that a qualified privilege might be acceptable under some circumstances. Lower courts typically consider four elements in such cases:

- Information-collection techniques. The need for protection is greater when information *must* be gathered from confidential sources.

- Importance and relevance of information. Trial judges consider whether information from journalists is directly relevant to the case and whether the information could affect the outcome.

- Availability of information from other sources. Journalists argue they are not investigative arms of government or defense attorneys and that any information they collect should be obtainable also by those who have greater resources than they do. Judges frequently require evidence that information could not be obtained elsewhere.

- The nature of the conflict. Protection is more likely to be upheld in a civil case, in which the public interest in resolving private disputes is less compelling, than in criminal cases, in which the public interest is great.[96]

The publicity of the *Branzburg* cases and others stimulated Congress to consider whether there should be a federal shield law giving journalists immunity from having to testify in cases that would compromise source confidentiality. Progress toward a national shield law was slow, however, because even journalists could not agree on terms.

Some journalists wanted an absolute shield law stating that no writer can be compelled to disclose a source or any other information (or how it was obtained) to any court, grand jury or other investigative body. Other journalists argued that a shield law was not necessary because the First Amendment gave them the right not to divulge sources. They argued that legislation might be a precedent for other actions detrimental to the news media. The attempts at compromise usually satisfied neither side. After three decades of debate, there is no federal shield law.

States are free to pass shield laws and 30 have done so. They are Alabama, Alaska, Arizona, Arkansas, California, Colorado, Delaware, Florida, Georgia, Illinois, Indiana, Kentucky, Louisiana, Maryland, Michigan, Minnesota, Montana, Nebraska, Nevada, New Jersey, New Mexico, New York, North Dakota, Ohio, Oklahoma, Oregon, Pennsylvania, Rhode Island, South Carolina and Tennessee.[97]

These laws differ widely, however, in the kind and strength of protection they provide. Most of the state laws have substantial qualifications. Restrictions include taking away a journalist's immunity when information is relevant to a criminal charge, when information cannot be obtained by other means and when it is of "compelling and overriding" interest for justice to be served. These are broad exceptions that can be and are abused.

State laws vary in other ways. A few states protect journalists only from grand jury probes, while others protect them from all government demands. Some laws apply only to information obtained from confidential sources, while others apply to any information journalists collect. Some states do not protect employees of nontraditional media such as the Web, while others do protect them. And some protect only information sources, while others protect the information collected.

Case Law

Several states give media professionals the privilege to keep sources confidential through case law, meaning that precedents established in individual cases are used in subsequent cases. Each state is different, so a writer needs to know the law in his or her state. Here are a couple of examples:

- Journalism students at the University of New Hampshire were ordered to turn over documents relating to a story about the supposed drug dealings of a murder victim. The students' sources were named in the documents, and so they refused to turn them over. A New Hampshire court ruled in *New Hampshire v. Siel* that the students did not have to release the documents because they had no bearing on the outcome of the case. The New Hampshire Supreme Court affirmed that ruling.[98]

- When the *Point Reyes* (Calif.) *Light* published an exposé of the Synanon Foundation's drug rehabilitation program, Synanon demanded the names of the *Light*'s sources as part of its libel suit. The paper refused. The *Light*'s circumstances were not covered by California's shield law, but California courts decided in *Mitchell v. Superior Court* that journalists can have a privilege when a libel suit is without merit (as was Synanon's) or when the importance of maintaining source confidentiality outweighs the plaintiff's need for information.[99]

Realize, of course, that case law also can work against journalists, for some courts restrict privilege rather than extend it.

COPYRIGHT LAW

Writers, artists, musicians, filmmakers, photographers, software writers and other creative individuals have a right to profit from their efforts, and copyright law is designed to protect that right. Congress and the courts have consistently held that a copyright owner may reproduce a copyrighted work, produce derivative works based on the original and perform the work, distribute it or display it. The ideas are not copyrighted. The news is not copyrighted. But the form of expression is—the U.S. Supreme Court ruled in *Feist Publications v. Rural Telephone Service Co.*—and anyone who uses copyrighted material without permission might be charged with copyright infringement.[100]

Anyone who copies a book, movie or song without permission and then sells it to others has infringed someone's copyright. A student who copies large amounts of text from a scholarly article and then includes that text in a term paper has infringed copyright. (See also the box "Copyright Violation Is Theft.")

All published and unpublished work is essentially protected under federal law the moment it is completed. Anyone who produces a unique work can put a notice of copyright on that work. The copyright can be registered for $30 with the U.S. Copyright Office in the Library of Congress, but registration is not necessary unless a copyright holder decides to sue a copyright infringer. If a copyright is not registered, the work's creator cannot sue for attorney's fees and statutory damages (an arbitrary amount a judge may award when a copyright violator's profits are difficult to document or are small). The work's creator still can sue for actual damages (the infringer's profits), however. Copyright extends for an individual copyright holder's life plus 70 years.[101]

To win a case, a copyright holder must prove that an infringer had access to the original work, that the two versions are substantially the same and that the copyright covers a unique work. It is most difficult, of course, to prove the two versions are substantially the same, for infringers usually try to revise the original to some degree.

Some creative individuals sell their rights to their works rather than retain copyright themselves. Few writers can afford to publish and promote books themselves, for example, so they sell their rights to publishing houses. And writers who work for others (newspaper writers, for example) also give up the rights to their work. These agreements fall under the "works made for hire" provision of the copyright law. Many public relations professionals work as freelance writers, producing work as needed and under contract. These professionals do not own the works they produce as "works made for hire." Copyright is held by those who hire them.

The copyright law does not prohibit all use of copyrighted materials. Under the fair use doctrine, students, media professionals and others can use protected materials. The guidelines for fair use, outlined in the Copyright Act of 1976, are vague and difficult to apply, but they are helpful. Four elements must be considered:[102]

- The impact on the original work of any subsequent use. If the subsequent use does not decrease the value or profit-earning potential of the original work, it likely will be allowed.

COPYRIGHT VIOLATION IS THEFT

Suppose you've honed your writing skills (in small part because you read this book and took the class for which it is required) to the point that editors are breaking down your door to acquire your services.

But you decide to write a novel based on your college experience, a novel that is highly entertaining and that is important because it exposes some of the warts in higher education. Publishing houses bid on your book and you take the offer with the best advance (you'll be paid before you begin writing, but the money has to be paid back automatically when the royalties start flooding in).

The book comes out. It is well reviewed. You're the latest "big thing." Cash is rolling in. But wait!

You discover your book is being posted on Web sites around the world and that people are downloading and reading it. You're losing all that money!

You could take the altruistic approach and just be glad the book is being so widely read. That's why you wrote it, right, because its message is important?

Or you could get mad as hell because you sacrificed so much and worked so hard to produce that book. Nobody should steal the fruits of your labor.

Most artists whose work is stolen (by surfers who illegally download music, for example) get mad as hell because their art is their livelihood.

Copyright laws are on the books for a reason (to protect society's creative individuals). All media professionals need to understand that.

- The nature of the original work. Short poems and books, for example, are treated somewhat differently. Using 10 lines from a book, for example, is probably trivial, while using 10 lines from a 20-line poem probably is not.
- The amount of the original work that is used.
- The purpose for using the original work. Courts are more likely to approve the use of original material for educational purposes than for commercial purposes.

The popularity of the Internet has made copyright law particularly difficult to enforce. It is so easy to download original work, many users don't give it a second thought. An entire article in a professional journal, for example, turned up on the Web as part of a college faculty member's course. And large chunks of newspaper and magazine articles frequently are incorporated into other newspaper and magazine articles. Some Web sites "import" entire documents and post them without permission, rather than supplying links to those works, a practice that is not a violation.

The Digital Millennium Copyright Act of 1998 was intended to resolve some of the copyright issues on the Web. The act extended more protection to digital copies of videos, recordings, movies, graphics and photographs, and it banned some technologies that could circumvent copy-prevention and encryption software. The act also exempted Internet service providers from liability for their users' postings—as long as the ISPs immediately shut down sites on which copyright-infringing materials are posted. A copyright owner can shut down a site simply by asserting copyright infringement—without having to prove a case in court.[103]

Writers still can use copyrighted material with permission, and they do not always have to pay for that use—particularly when the material is not part of a profit-making venture. Nonprofit organizations and educators, for example, often can get permission to use copyrighted materials at no cost. They must specify what material will be used, how it will be used and for how long.

ADMINISTRATIVE REGULATIONS

Media professionals must be cautious as they process and disseminate information that is regulated by government agencies. The Securities and Exchange Commission, Federal Trade Commission, Federal Communications Commission, National Labor Relations Board, Food and Drug Administration and others enforce rules and regulations that must be observed.

R. Foster Winans, a writer for *The Wall Street Journal,* was fired and served time in jail when he sold insider information to his friends in violation of SEC regulations. The SEC also charged R.F. Hengen Inc., a public relations agency, with using inside information after its client, Puritan Fashions, issued an earnings estimate that the company and the public relations firm knew could not be met. The head of the agency, Ronald Hengen, passed the word to two stockbrokers, who profited from the information.[104]

A public relations person can get into trouble even when he or she writes a news release in good faith. The writer might later discover he or she violated SEC regulations, an error that could cause trading in a company's stock to be suspended and result in legal actions against the company. The release might report information prematurely or fail to report information mandated by law. Or a writer might get into trouble with the National Labor Relations Board for publishing in a company newsletter an article that summarizes management's views about union organizers, particularly if the piece sounds coercive.

The National Securities Act mandates the release of information about public corporations so that investors can base decisions on facts and not rumors. This means all corporate employees, including public relations persons, must know their legal obligations to individual investors, to financial analysts and to brokerage firms. The guiding principle is that no important information may be released to analysts (or to any other individuals or groups) before it is released to the public. Preferential treatment almost certainly will lead to trouble. Even when important information will be disclosed during a meeting, speech or interview, a writer should prepare a news release detailing the information and release that before or during the meeting, speech or interview.

Public relations professionals must know, too, that they are insiders who have special obligations to the investment community. The U.S. Supreme Court let stand a lower court decision in *SEC v. Texas Gulf Sulphur* that anyone who has access to information that could influence a stock price is an insider. Texas Gulf Sulphur issued a belated release that minimized a mineral discovery so that it could purchase land near the discovery at good prices. Delaying the release was okay, courts found, but minimizing the discovery was misleading.[105]

Public relations professionals are not alone in interpreting and abiding by financial regulations. They are part of management teams that include accountants, attorneys and analysts. But public relations writers typically are responsible for information dissemination, and they need to establish procedures that include everyone who is part of the team. This means annual reports, speeches, news releases and public service announcements, for example, must be carefully reviewed by everyone in light of financial regulations.[106]

The human tendency to delay or to hide bad news must not be allowed to affect the disclosure of important information, for companies are required to disclose good or bad news that could affect a stock price. Some news can be withheld, but that typically includes only trade secrets and competitive information. And even then, management must be able to justify withholding facts.

Federal Trade Commission regulations, which are designed primarily to protect consumers, can be a minefield for public relations writers. If a company asks an agency to develop a campaign promoting a "miracle" medication, for example, the writers need to be sure the miracle drug works as intended. When Monsanto introduced NutraSweet, a sugar substitute, company executives said the product did not need FDA approval because it was made with natural ingredients. It was, but it still needed FDA approval. Public relations writers can get into considerable trouble when a product is not what it is claimed to be.[107]

Broadcast journalists are subject to the laws and regulations that apply to newspaper, magazine, Web and public relations professionals—but they also must deal with the Federal Communications Commission. Broadcasters are unique because they use a finite number of frequencies (or channels), as opposed to, say, newspaper or Web writers, who can start newspapers or Web sites literally anywhere. There is no limit to the number of newspapers or Web sites that can be created, if profitability is not an issue, but there is a limit to the number of available broadcast frequencies.

Most of the FCC regulations do not apply to broadcast news content, and, in fact, the Communications Act of 1934 prohibits the FCC from censoring broadcasters. Broadcasters may be required, however, under the personal attack rule to provide free time to those who have been personally attacked, although the law is unclear.[108] And they are required under the equal time rule to sell comparable time to political opponents for similar prices.[109]

YOUR RESPONSIBILITY IS . . .

- To understand that mass communication law is complex, subject to change and frequently perplexing, and to know communication law well enough to avoid legal pitfalls while doing your job effectively and responsibly.

- To be exceptionally careful when your information makes products, individuals or organizations look bad. But don't be intimidated, for society needs courageous media professionals.

- To remember that you have almost complete access to state and federal court proceedings (excluding juvenile court and discovery), but that you must be extraordinarily careful when you write about legal proceedings and police investigations.

- To recognize that while government meetings and records typically are open, you and other citizens must sometimes be extraordinarily persistent to make officials obey the law. Sometimes a legal action is required if public officials are obstinate.

- To understand that access to public property and facilities is generally guaranteed, except when the property is quasi-public or has been designated a crime scene or disaster area. Access to private property is severely limited.

- To understand and appreciate that private citizens have a right to be left alone unless their actions are newsworthy.

- To assume that you enjoy no legal protection when you are asked to reveal confidential sources or information. You may have no protection or qualified protection. You must learn the law of your state.

- To know, if you want to be a public relations professional, that copyright laws and administrative regulations are of particular importance to you. You need to know how the provisions of copyright law apply to and affect your work and your organization; which government regulations apply to your organization; and what information must be released to the public and at what times.

- To know, if you want to be a broadcast journalist, how policies and regulations of the Federal Communications Commission apply to you.

NOTES

1. Alan Bernstein, "Leggett Free—for Now: Feds Mum on Whether Case Will Go to New Grand Jury," *Houston Chronicle,* Jan. 5, 2002: A-1, 18.

2. *Crinkley v. Dow Jones & Co.,* 456 N.E. 2d 138 (Ill. App. Ct. 1983); "Wall Street Journal Loses $2.25 Million Libel Judgment," *Editor & Publisher,* June 1, 1991: 19.

3. Kent R. Middleton, Robert Trager and Bill F. Chamberlin, *The Law of Public Communication,* 5th ed. (New York: Longman, 2001); Roy L. Moore, *Mass Communication Law and Ethics,* 2nd ed. (Mahway, N.J.: Erlbaum, 1999); Wayne Overbeck, *Major Principles of Media Law,* 12th ed. (Fort Worth, Texas: Harcourt, 2001); Dwight L. Teeter and Bill Loving, *Law of Mass Communications: Freedom and Control of Print and Broadcast Media,* 10th ed. (New York: Foundation Press, 2001); and John D. Zelezny, *Communications Law: Liberties, Restraints and the Modern Media,* 3rd ed. (Belmont, Calif.: Wadsworth/Thomson Learning, 2001).

4. Daniel A. Farber, *The First Amendment* (New York: Foundation Press, 1998).

5. *Gitlow v. New York,* 268 U.S. 652 (1925).

6. *Near v. Minnesota,* 283 U.S. 697, 718–719 (1931).

7. Zelezny, *Communications Law:* 42–43.

8. *City of Lakewood v. Plain Dealer Publishing Co.,* 486 U.S. 750, 757 (1988); *Barnes v. Glen Theater,* 501 U.S. 560 (1991); *United States v. Eichman,* 496 U.S. 310 (1998).

9. *Miami Herald Publishing Co. v. Tornillo,* 418 U.S. 241, 256, 258 (1974).

10. Moore, *Mass Communication Law and Ethics:* 222–238.

11. 47 C. F. R. 73.1920. Ibid., pp. 283–284.

12. "The USA PATRIOT Act and Beyond," *Homefront Confidential,* Reporters Committee for Freedom of the Press, March 2003. Downloaded on May 23, 2003, from <www.rcfp.org/homefrontconfidential/usapatriot.html>.

13. 5 U.S. Code sec. 552. See also Middleton, Trager and Chamberlin, *The Law of Public Communication:* 481–503.

14. 5 U.S. Code sec. 552a. Overbeck, *Major Principles of Media Law:* 333–335.

15. Pub. Law No. 104-231, 110 Stat. 3048, 1–12 (1996). Teeter and Loving, *Law of Mass Communications:* 455.

16. Middleton, Trager and Chamberlin, *The Law of Public Communication:* 490–503.

17. Exec. Order No. 12,958, 60 Fed. Reg. 19,825 (April 20, 1995). Ibid., pp. 490–492.

18. Zelezny, *Communications Law:* 225.

19. 18 U.S. Code secs. 2721–25.

20. *Condon v. Reno,* 155 F. 3d 453 (4th Cir. 1998); rev. 120 S. Ct. 666 (1999).

21. Bill Murphy, "$33,000 Bid for Enron E Letter-perfect," *Houston Chronicle,* Dec. 5, 2002: A-33.

22. Dave Umhoefer, personal communication with the authors, Aug. 12, 2003.

23. Doug Newsom, Alan Scott and Judy VanSlyke Turk, *This Is PR: The Realities of Public Relations* (Belmont, CA: Wadsworth, 1993): 299–300.

24. 5 U.S. Code 552b.

25. Zelezny, *Communications Law:* 210–212.

26. House Information Resources, 104th Cong., 1st Sess., House Rules X1-2(g)(1)(Sept. 29, 1995); Middleton, Trager and Chamberlin, *The Law of Public Communication:* 512.

27. West Virginia Open Governmental Proceedings Act, 1999. Downloaded on Aug. 8, 2003, from <www.wvsos.com/adlaw/register/meetings/OpenMeetingsHandbook.pdf>.

28. *Richmond Newspapers Inc. v. Virginia,* 448 U.S. 555, 561 (1980).

29. *Pell v. Procunier,* 417 U.S. 817; *Saxbe v. Washington Post,* 417 U.S. 843.

30. *State v. Lashinsky,* 404 A.2d 1121 (N.J. 1979).

31. *Westinghouse Broadcasting Co. v. National Transportation Safety Board,* 670 F.2d 4 (D. Mass. 1982).

32. *Daily Herald v. Munro,* 838 F.2d 380 (9th Cir. 1988).

33. *Stahl v. State,* 665 P.2d 839 (Okla. Crim. App. 1983); cert. denied, 464 U.S. 1069 (1984).

34. Natalie Cortes, "Panel: Media-Military Tension Intensifying During War on Terrorism," The Freedom Forum, April 10, 2002. Downloaded on Dec. 16, 2002, from <freedomforum.org/templates/document.asp?documentID=16047>.

35. In re J.S., 438 A.2d 1125 (Vt. Sup. Ct. 1981).

36. *Jeffries v. State of Mississippi,* 724 So.2d 897 (Miss. Sup. Ct. 1998).

37. Alan Kelly, "Know the Power of De-positioning," *Public Relations Quarterly,* Summer 2001: 27–28; and Michael Ryan, "Letter to the Editor," *Public Relations Quarterly,* Fall 2001: 12.

38. *Curtis Publishing Co. v. Butts,* 388 U.S. 130 (1967).

39. *Green v. Alton Telegraph,* 438 N.E.2d 203 (1982).

40. Zelezny, *Communications Law:* 103–111.

41. Thomas B. Littlewood, *Coals of Fire: The* Alton Telegraph *Libel Case* (Carbondale, Ill.: Southern Illinois University Press, 1988).

42. *Lundell Manufacturing Co. v. ABC,* 98 F.3d 351 (8th Cir. 1996); cert. denied, 520 U.S. 1186 (1997).

43. *Engler v. Winfrey,* 201 F.3d 680 (2000).

44. Moore, *Mass Communication Law and Ethics:* 329–363.

45. Teeter and Loving, *Law of Mass Communications,* 79–87.

46. *Robart v. Post-Standard,* 425 N.Y.S.2d 891 (N.Y. App. Div. 1980); aff'd, 52 N.Y.2d 843 (N.Y. 1981).

47. *Pearce v. Courier-Journal & Louisville Times Co.,* 683 S.W.2d. 633 (Ky. Ct. App. 1985).

48. *Philadelphia Newspapers Inc. v. Hepps,* 475 U.S. 767 (1986).

49. *Memphis Publishing Co. v. Nichols,* 569 S.W.2d 412 (Tenn. 1978).

50. Teeter and Loving, *Law of Mass Communications:* 296–309.

51. David Brock, *Blinded by the Right: The Conscience of an Ex-conservative* (New York: Crown, 2002): 56.

52. *Media Law Handbook for Talk Radio* (Washington, D.C.: National Association of Broadcasters, 2000).

53. *New York Times v. Sullivan,* 376 U.S. 254.

54. *Curtis Publishing Co. v. Butts,* 388 U.S. 130 (1967).

55. *Gertz v. Robert Welch Inc.,* 418 U.S. 323, 325 (1974).

56. S.I. Hayakawa, *Language in Thought and Action,* 4th ed. (New York: Harcourt Brace Jovanovich, 1978).

57. Teeter and Loving, *Law of Mass Communications:* 316–334.

58. *Milkovich v. Lorain Journal Co.,* 497 U.S. 1 (1990). See *Moldea v. New York Times Co.,* 22 F.3d 310 (D.C. Cir. 1994); cert. denied, 513 U.S. 875 (1994).

59. *It's in the Cards Inc. v. Fuschetto,* 535 N.W.2d 11 (Wis. App. 1995).

60. Pub. L. No. 104-104, sec. 502, 110 Stat. 56 (1996).

61. *Zeran v. America Online Inc.,* 129 F.3d 327 (4th Cir. 1997); cert. denied, 118 S. Ct. 2341 (1998); Zelezny, *Communications Law:* 494–495.

62. *Cantrell v. Forest City Publishing Co.,* 419 U.S. 245, 248 (1974).

63. *Gill v. Curtis Publishing Co.,* 239 P.2d 630 (Cal. 1952).

64. Middleton, Trager and Chamberlin, *The Law of Public Communication:* 187.

65. Overbeck, *Major Principles of Media Law:* 190.

66. *Barber v. Time Inc.,* 159 S.W.2d 291 (Mo. 1942).

67. Overbeck, *Major Principles of Media Law:* 182–190.

68. Zelezny, *Communications Law:* 178–185 and 199–207.

69. *Wolfson v. Lewis,* 924 F. Supp. 1413 (E.D. Pa. 1996); Middleton, Trager and Chamberlin, *The Law of Public Communication:* 175.

70. *Food Lion Inc. v. Capital Cities/ABC Inc.,* 984 F. Supp. 923 (M.D.N.C. 1997).

71. *Desnick v. ABC,* 44 F.3d 1345 (7th Cir. 1995).

72. *Manville v. Borg-Warner Corp.,* 418 F.2d 434 (10th Cir. 1969).

73. *Midler v. Young & Rubicam,* 944 F.2d 909 (9th Cir 1991); cert. denied, 503 U.S. 951 (1992).

74. Newsom, Scott and VanSlyke Turk, *This Is PR:* 307–310.

75. Moore, *Mass Communication Law and Ethics:* 428–431.

76. *Cox Broadcasting Corp. v. Cohn,* 420 U.S. 469 (1975).

77. *Florida Star v. B.J.F.,* 491 U.S. 524 (1989).

78. *Howard v. Des Moines Register,* 283 N.W.2d 289 (Iowa 1979); cert. denied, 445 U.S. 904 (1980).

79. *Neff v. Time Inc.,* 406 F. Supp. 858 (W. D. Pa. 1976); *Prahl v. Brosamle,* 295 N. W.2nd, 774; *Bisbee v. Conover,* 9 Media L. Rep. 1298, 1299 (N.J. Super. Ct. App. Div. 1982); Moore, *Mass Communication Law and Ethics:* 400–404.

80. *Vassiliades v. Garfinckel's,* 492 A.2d 580, 11 Media L. Rep. 2057 (D. C. 1985).

81. *Time Inc. v. Hill,* 385 U.S. 374 (1967).

82. *Cox v. Hatch,* 761 P.2d 556 (Utah 1988).

83. *State v. Sheppard,* 128 N.E.2d, 471, 484, 485, 494 (Ohio Ct. App. 1955).

84. American Bar Association, *ABA Standards for Criminal Justice: Fair Trial and Free Press,* 3rd ed. (Chicago: Author, 1991).

85. *Nebraska Press Association v. Stuart,* 427 U.S. 539 (1976).

86. *Procter & Gamble v. Bankers Trust Co.,* 78 F.3d 219, 225 (6th Cir. 1996).

87. Middleton, Trager and Chamberlin, *The Law of Public Communication:* 392–398.

88. *Sheppard v. Maxwell,* 384 U.S. 333, 356 (1996).

89. *Estes v. Texas,* 381 U.S. 540 (1965).

90. *Chandler v. Florida,* 449 U.S. 568–69 (1981).

91. *Cohen v. Cowles Media Co.,* 501 U.S. 663 (1991).

92. *Branzburg v. Hayes* and *United States v. Caldwell,* 408 U.S. 665 (1972).

93. Teeter and Loving, *Law of Mass Communications:* 583–590.

94. Ibid.

95. Overbeck, *Major Principles of Media Law:* 316–317.

96. Zelezny, *Communications Law:* 266–267.

97. Middleton, Trager and Chamberlin, *The Law of Public Communication:* 454.

98. *New Hampshire v. Siel,* 8 Media L. Rep. 1265.

99. *Mitchell v. Superior Court,* 37 C.3d 268 (1984).

100. *Feist Publications Inc. v. Telephone Service Co.,* 499 U.S. 340 (1991).

101. 17 U.S. Code, secs. 101–810. Overbeck, *Major Principles of Media Law:* 209–223.

102. Middleton, Trager and Chamberlin, *The Law of Public Communication:* 235–245.

103. Pub. L. No. 105–304, 112 Stat. 2860. Overbeck, *Major Principles of Media Law:* 245–248.

104. Newsom, Scott and VanSlyke Turk, *This Is PR:* 291.

105. *SEC v. Texas Gulf Sulphur Co.,* 401 F.2d 833, 845 (1968); cert. denied, 394 U.S. 976 (1969).

106. Newsom, Scott and VanSlyke Turk, *This Is PR:* 279.

107. Ibid., p. 293.

108. 47 C. F. R. 73.1920. Moore, *Mass Communication Law and Ethics:* 283–284.

109. 47 U. S. Code 315. Overbeck, *Major Principles of Media Law:* 422–428.

CHAPTER 14

ETHICS

Navigating Rough Moral Seas

Chicago newspaper editor Walter Burns had the chance of a lifetime: His ace reporter, Hildy Johnson, could get him an exclusive interview with Earl Williams, a convicted cop killer who managed to escape only hours before his scheduled execution. Johnson discovered the killer in the press room of Chicago's Criminal Courts Building and hid him in a huge roll-top desk. Burns sent a crew to move the desk from the press room to his newspaper, where he intended to hide the escaped murderer until Johnson's exclusive hit the streets.

Burns' unethical behavior was more than matched by that of Conrad Brean, a public relations practitioner who created a war to get his boss, the president of the United States, re-elected. The president was in trouble just weeks before the election because he had lured a girl into the Oval Office and did what used to be unthinkable. When the opposition used the song *Thank Heaven for Little Girls* in their ads, the president knew he was in trouble. To distract voters, Brean created a "war" with Albania—in a studio.

Both of these accounts are fictional. Burns and Johnson are characters in *The Front Page,* a play by Chicago crime reporters Ben Hecht and Charles MacArthur. Produced in 1928, the play portrayed journalists as heavy-drinking, unscrupulous louts who make up facts for their stories.[1] The play was produced as two movies with the same name. Brean was a character in *Wag the Dog,* a satirical film based on Larry Beinhart's book, *American Hero.*[2] Brean, a symbol representing the worst in public relations practice, was portrayed as a manipulator who wouldn't know an ethic if it hit him in the ear.

Many Americans seem to think that real media professionals mirror the characters they encounter in popular films and literature. A few of those characters are,

Many public relations practitioners resent the portrayal of their industry in films like The Sweet Smell of Success *starring Tony Curtis and Burt Lancaster. Lancaster's character, Sidney Falco, is still viewed by many professionals as a symbolic albatross.*

for the most part, real, and some are even ethical. *All the President's Men* (the book and movie), for instance, portrayed journalists as ethical.[3] Other portrayals are mixed, as in *The Insider* (the movie), in which some broadcast journalists were ethical and some were not. For the most part, however, media professionals are portrayed as unethical, or at least amoral, and these portrayals may contribute to negative stereotypes.[4]

Public perceptions about the behavior of media professionals are important, certainly, but the real-life behavior is more important. In fact, media professionals are predominantly ethical. They are men and women of integrity whose goal is to collect, package and distribute news and information that is accurate, clear, compelling and concise. They know the difference between right and wrong, and they usually do the right thing. Their insights—achieved through hard work and rigorous, honest contemplation of the facts—are not sanitized to spare their own feelings or those of an audience or of powerful interests.[5]

This does not mean that it's easy for them to resolve difficult ethical problems and issues or that ethical professionals never reach different conclusions about the same ethical questions. Sometimes the options are not binary—right versus wrong. Sometimes the options are right versus right. Suppose, for example, that a newspaper's editors and writers learn that corrupt health department inspectors are taking payoffs to give bars clean bills of health. The journalists know they can document the payoffs if they buy and operate a bar and install hidden cameras. Some ethical journalists would say go ahead with the deception and some would say no. Such dilemmas are not uncommon. This chapter is intended to help students meet the following objectives:

- Understand that ethics are important
- Recognize those practices that are almost always seen by professionals as unethical
- Recognize the potential consequences of unethical behavior
- Recognize some of the ethical quagmires that await them
- Develop strategies and find information that will help them avoid unethical behavior
- Understand how ethical decisions may be linked to the nature of communication

Since this is an introduction, a starting point for the lifelong study of ethical communication, considerable emphasis is placed on identifying those ethical behaviors that should be avoided. Knowing what most professionals would consider unethical should help readers begin to establish an ethical baseline for themselves, although this is a kind of binary approach that readers should avoid as they explore ethics more deeply.

POLLUTION FROM UNETHICAL BEHAVIOR

Mass communication is littered with a few inferior and unethical "professionals" whose work appears in newspapers, public relations materials, books and films, and on television, the Web and radio. They produce a clutter of deceptive or false information that pollutes the information stream and makes the job of ethical professionals much harder. One example was the proposed plan by public affairs officers in the Pentagon to plant news reports, some false or misleading, in foreign news media. The plan, later dropped, was part of the war against terrorism. The goal was to promote U.S. values and to discredit unfriendly governments.[6]

Why It Happens

A small group of broadcast, newspaper, Web, magazine and public relations writers continues to pollute the communication stream for several reasons:

- The best media professionals continuously examine their own ethical behavior and participate in the ethical debate that is so common in media organizations and that is reflected in books, scholarly journals, documentary films, seminars, Web sites and professional publications. However, the ethical

WHAT'S LEGAL AND WHAT'S ETHICAL

Some kinds of media writing are prohibited by state and federal laws (Chapter 13). Professionals must understand, however, that some behavior judged by the judicial system to be illegal is not considered unethical.

A source, for instance, may give a journalist information on condition that his or her name is not reported (Chapter 10). A judge who demands in court that the writer reveal the name may jail the individual who refuses to do so. The writer's behavior might be judged illegal, but it is not unethical.

Similarly, behavior that is legal is not necessarily ethical. It is legal, for example, to report the name of an adult woman who has been raped. However, most news outlets have policies against publicizing the names of rape victims, usually on grounds that (1) publicity for many women seems to constitute a second rape, and (2) publicity may well discourage other women from reporting to the police when they have been raped.

This is not to say the names are *never* published. Some women, for example, are so prominent, their names may be reported, and some women acknowledge they were victims as part of their efforts to combat this crime or to seek justice. Even in these instances, writers are reluctant to name rape victims.

"Legal" and "ethical" are not synonymous.

debate itself, which is important and must continue, provides cover for some who would behave unethically. They frame the debate to obscure, rather than to clarify; to justify their own unethical actions, rather than to examine critically the ethical dimensions of those actions.

Some who supported the Pentagon's disinformation campaign argued, for example, that it is ethical to lie to protect national security and that no other issues or concerns matter. This is a specious argument because they merely asserted without evidence that national security would be protected by lying, and they refused to acknowledge that government-sanctioned lying is contrary to American tradition and law and that lying to friends leads to alienation and distrust. The false, incomplete argument provided a kind of smoke screen to hide unethical behavior.

■ Writers who use ethical debate as a smoke screen are abetted in their lack of integrity by those individuals, some quite sincere, who argue that (1) ethical decisions are intensely personal and should not be questioned or debated[7] and that (2) since ethics are based on socially constructed realities, there can be no universal standards for ethical behavior.[8]

JAY BLACK ON THE COMPLEXITY OF ETHICS STUDY

What's really interesting and important in the study of ethics is the right/right, or not-quite-right/not-quite-wrong ethical dilemma. Many realities of journalism and public relations are quite vexing and should be framed that way.

For instance, if you look at the SPJ Code of Ethics, you'll note that it asks journalists to seek out and report the truth, while at the same time asking them to minimize the harm that is inherent in truth-telling. It also asks them to be both independent and accountable.

Just how does a writer accomplish this task? He or she does it by carefully sifting and sorting through the variables, by recognizing the difficulty of telling truth, by coming to grips with the inevitability of offending someone or causing real or perceived harm, by not knuckling under to vested interests—but still recognizing the need to be accountable—and by being really competent in his/her work.

Source: Jay Black, personal communication with the authors, Aug. 12, 2003.

Jay Black, editor of the *Journal of Mass Media Ethics*, teaches media ethics at the University of South Florida St. Petersburg.

Some teachers and professionals are loath to suggest what behavior is or is not ethical. The problem with having role models—teachers and mentors—who stick their heads in the sand is that the ethical lapses continue. If nobody is willing to debate the ethics of questionable behavior, the view is strengthened that ethics are not important—or at least not as important as building audiences.

- The First Amendment guarantees freedoms that are absolutely essential to a free society, and all communication professionals must dedicate themselves to its preservation.[9] A downside of that freedom is that media writers and others can behave unethically with impunity—as long as they don't run afoul of criminal, libel, slander, copyright and privacy laws.

Unfortunately, some media professionals seem to think that any action that is legal is okay (see the box "What's Legal and What's Ethical?"). This can mean, for example, that a local television news team considers it quite all right to cram its newscasts with as much blood and gore as it can,[10] or that the webmaster of an anti-abortion site sees nothing wrong with publishing photographs of women entering abortion clinics.[11]

Consequences

It is important in debating media ethics to distinguish between (1) the individuals who produce, package and distribute media content and (2) the institutions for which the individuals work. While it is true that individuals *are* institutions, the distinction is important, for an institution's priorities can be quite different from an individual's, and individuals cannot simply ignore institutional priorities that conflict with their own.

It is evident to even a casual consumer of mass media content that some media professionals and institutions lack integrity and any sort of ethical foundation or training. Examples are legion of the unethical and improper behavior in which some mass communicators engage (Chapter 1). Most of the consequences for such behavior are quite negative for the communicator and for the medium for which he or she works:

- The impact of unethical behavior on a writer can be devastating. Even accurate, well-intentioned information gathered through ethical means can damage or destroy lives: "We are capable of sinking the Titanic for some people, leading them astray financially, disrupting their careers, spooking their children."[12] How much worse that distress is for an individual who has acted unethically in producing a message that results in great harm. Any individual is likely to find it quite difficult to reconcile the harmful consequences of unethical behavior with notions about what is right.

  An unethical mass communicator may also find that friends, relatives or neighbors no longer trust him or her after the unethical behavior is exposed.

- Professionally, a writer who is caught behaving unethically is like a teenager who is caught stealing: The transgressor won't be trusted again by colleagues (writers, editors, news directors, publishers), particularly if those colleagues are among those deceived. It is difficult for a writer who has behaved unethically to convince sources that such behavior was an aberration and that she or he now can be trusted, and it is difficult to convince readers, listeners or viewers that a story, book, advertisement or public relations release the person has produced has not been tainted by unethical behavior.

  A reputation that is compromised is difficult to rehabilitate. If the transgression is too great, a writer can lose his or her job. In fact, promising careers have been destroyed before they have gotten fully under way. The publicity that surrounds cases of plagiarism, for instance, can make it difficult for cheaters to get new jobs in any field.

  Plagiarism, long a problem in mass communication, has gotten worse with the advent of the World Wide Web. "Some who commit the unoriginal sin are charlatans. Others resort to it in moments of pressure or personal crisis. Others slide into it out of naivete or ignorance."[13] Plagiarism can damage or destroy careers. *Boston Globe* columnist Mike Barnicle resigned as questions were raised about the sources of information for some of his columns. A weekly newspaper had charged that Barnicle had lifted parts of an A.J. Liebling book for a column, and that he had used jokes from a George Carlin book without attribution.[14]

Historian Stephen Ambrose, accused of plagiarizing parts of another book in *The Wild Blue,* denied the plagiarism but promised to be more careful in future work. Doris Kearns Goodwin, a Pulitzer–Prize winning historian, was accused of plagiarizing parts of *The Fitzgeralds and the Kennedys.* She denied the charge but said she would correct mistakes in the book.[15] The reputations of all of these writers have been diminished.

■ The impact of unethical behavior on the media is undeniable. Survey after survey suggests the media are not believed by vast numbers of communication consumers. Perceptions are not always good reflections of professional and ethical practice, and some results of credibility surveys undoubtedly are unfair; but many people are turning away from the media because they cannot credit what they report or condone the techniques they sometimes use to get information.[16] The media are caught in an unfortunate downward spiral. The more they try to attract listeners, readers or viewers using unacceptable techniques, the more they are disliked and the more ammunition they give to their harshest critics.

Unethical communication behavior also undermines the communication process by contributing to the growth of an environment in which good communication practice is viewed as too slow or too much work. Some communicators abandon good practice because it is easier to use unethical and inappropriate techniques. Writers, for example, who make up an 8-year-old heroin addict to hype a story, as Janet Cooke did, or who "borrow" from the stories of other writers, as Jayson Blair did, are trying to find an easy path to career advancement.[17] Better that such a writer do the legwork and investigation necessary to get the story.

■ Society suffers when the communication process on which everyone relies is corrupted by unscrupulous media professionals. A free and just society cannot flourish in the absence of a free communication environment, one in which media professionals are trusted, valued and respected. One observer wrote a half century ago: "The news is the 'raw material of opinion' but it should not be manipulated with an eye to the finished product. ... The news that is good, bad, and indifferent must be held up to scrutiny so that newspaper readers are enabled to see life and see it whole—not just that part of it some editor thinks the public ought to see." The news is so important, media writers, editors and owners must be held strictly accountable for its handling.[18]

When a journalist lies for a story, everyone suffers. Wendy Bergen, a reporter for Denver's Channel 4, violated her commitment to society and to her profession in a report about dog fighting. "According to the grand jury, instead of

In October 2002, journalists covering the Washington, D.C.–area sniper shootings, like those shown here at a news briefing from police Chief Charles Moose, had to select carefully what information to present. They had to balance helping and informing the public against not aiding the snipers or hindering law enforcement.

merely attending a dog fight as a news reporter, Bergen actually arranged for the fight, paid for the event, lied to the TV audience about its circumstances and then lied to the grand jury about the entire episode."[19] Reports like Bergen's can suggest to some viewers that society is much more violent than it really is, and they might make public officials take actions that are not warranted by the facts.

AVOIDING UNETHICAL BEHAVIOR

Excellent books have been written about ethics in public relations and journalism, and a single book chapter cannot equip a communication student or professional to make the right ethical decision in every case.[20] Some ethical knots would challenge a professional who has read every ethics and moral philosophy treatise ever written. Journalists covering the Washington, D.C.–area snipers in 2002, for example, had to weigh giving residents information they might use to protect themselves against the possibility that the information could help the snipers. St. Thomas More would have trouble with that one. (See also the box "Olive Talley on Tough Ethical Quandaries.") The situation is not hopeless, however, because help is available.

OLIVE TALLEY ON TOUGH ETHICAL QUANDARIES

While I believe hidden cameras have been overused and improperly used by various local and network news shows, when used wisely they can provide the ultimate level of verification. Seeing is believing. It's compelling TV and good journalism when hidden cameras let viewers see and hear the misleading sales pitch, the abusive child-care worker, the dishonest employee.

In a report on the illegal trade of exotic animals and the serious dangers they pose as pets, I used a hidden camera to show the availability of baby tiger cubs in Texas. I went to a roadside zoo advertising them for sale on the Internet. I used my real name and my real phone number when I responded to the ad and when I showed up. Yet I did not tell the sellers that I worked for *Dateline NBC* and had cameras rolling. ...

[W]as I deceptive? I don't think so, nor did the senior producers and lawyers who reviewed the material and my script. In the two years I've worked for NBC, there has been a rigorous approval process involving senior producers and legal and standards attorneys before hidden cameras can be used. And the network publishes a 70-page policy manual that spells out its policies and standards on reporting, use of anonymous sources, and a variety of other news practices. I'm no shill for NBC, but I was heartened during my second week on the job to attend mandatory meetings to discuss and debate ways to raise standards in our reporting process.

Source: In this selection from "Determining the Line Between Fact and Fiction: In Broadcast News, Compelling TV and Good Journalism Can Coexist," *Nieman Reports,* Summer 2001: 15, Talley is responding to Bill Kovach and Tom Rosenstiel, *The Elements of Journalism: What Newspeople Should Know and the Public Should Expect* (New York: Crown, 2001).

Olive Talley, a producer for *Dateline NBC*, has worked for *20/20* and *Primetime Live.*

Codes of Ethics

Just about every professional organization has a code of ethics, a set of principles that helps members make good decisions. Communication is no exception, for codes designed primarily to enforce social responsibility have proliferated dramatically in recent decades.[21] The Public Relations Society of America, Society of Professional Journalists, Broadcast Educators Association, Associated Press Managing Editors Association, American Newspaper Publishers Association, Radio-Television News Directors Association and many other groups have developed standards for ethical behavior. Codes adopted by PRSA, SPJ and RTNDA are reproduced in this chapter.

Codes of ethics are far from perfect, and for a number of reasons. The main complaint about ethics codes is that they are not enforced. The Public Relations Society of America, which struggled for years with enforcement, finally threw in the towel in part because practitioners accused of code violations typically refused to submit evidence, making it virtually impossible for PRSA to investigate. The group simply eliminated enforcement provisions at the turn of the new century. The latest version "was designed to be aspirational and educational, such that prohibitions were replaced with positive, affirmative obligations." Instead of enforcement, the 2000 code "emphasized the need for 'responsible advocacy,' stressing loyalty to clients and employers."[22]

PRSA has adopted this position at a time when many critics argue that enforcement is more important than ever. As one observer put it, "What is needed are more 'public relations watchers,' monitoring the publicity and communication channels and blowing whistles when necessary. News media and trade journals should expose and bring shame to bear on unscrupulous PR practitioners."[23]

Codes are difficult to enforce because media professionals are not licensed to practice, as are doctors and lawyers, and because neither a college degree nor mastery of an identified, specialized body of knowledge is required. Some successful writers majored in disciplines other than communication and learned on the job.

At least one study suggests that some newspapers do not even have ethics codes, that staff members are not familiar with their publication's codes, that some staff writers find the codes irrelevant and that some editors are ambivalent about codes. Codes are not embraced by some organizations because they do not see them as expressions of useful values.[24] Codes drafted by some media organizations are not inspiring, focusing as they do on minimal standards that writers must follow to avoid getting fired or reprimanded. Many organizations, for example, proclaim that stereotyping by gender, religion or race is unacceptable. That is a minimal standard. Organizations might establish a higher ideal: that writers treat all sources and news personalities with respect and as individuals with their own stories to tell.

Codes are not always enforced also because they "lack intellectual precision over such issues as internal vis a vis external controls, ethics vis a vis First Amendment freedoms, and different forms and degrees of accountability to government, to fellow professionals, and to the general public."[25] Most codes stress responsibility to the public, but they are vague about what is and is not "responsible." They are simply too fuzzy.

One of many potential examples is from PRSA's Member Statement of Professional Values (see the box on the next page). Under "Advocacy," the code states: "We serve the public interest by acting as responsible advocates for those we represent. We provide a voice in the marketplace of ideas, facts, and viewpoints to aid informed public debate."[26] How a practitioner would interpret this statement depends on how he or she would define "public interest," "responsible advocates" and "voice in the marketplace."

MEMBER STATEMENT OF PROFESSIONAL VALUES, PUBLIC RELATIONS SOCIETY OF AMERICA

This statement presents the core values of PRSA members and, more broadly, of the public relations profession. These values provide the foundation for the Member Code of Ethics and set the industry standard for the professional practice of public relations.[27] These values are the fundamental beliefs that guide our behaviors and decision-making process. We believe our professional values are vital to the integrity of the profession as a whole.

ADVOCACY

We serve the public interest by acting as responsible advocates for those we represent. We provide a voice in the marketplace of ideas, facts, and viewpoints to aid informed public debate.

HONESTY

We adhere to the highest standards of accuracy and truth in advancing the interests of those we represent and in communicating with the public.

EXPERTISE

We acquire and responsibly use specialized knowledge and experience. We advance the profession through continued professional development, research, and education. We build mutual understanding, credibility, and relationships among a wide array of institutions and audiences.

INDEPENDENCE

We provide objective counsel to those we represent. We are accountable for our actions.

LOYALTY

We are faithful to those we represent, while honoring our obligation to serve the public interest.

FAIRNESS

We deal fairly with clients, employers, competitors, peers, vendors, the media, and the general public. We respect all opinions and support the right of free expression.

Source: "PRSA Member Statement of Professional Values," Public Relations Society of America, undated. Downloaded on Oct. 28, 2002, from <www.prsa.org/_About/ethics/values.asp?ident=eth4>.

A single example illustrates the difficulty with such a fuzzy guideline. Suppose a university learns the state's environmental protection agency soon will approve permits allowing its medical research laboratory to start a profitable program. But the university learns the same day that the toxic waste dump the laboratory was going to use will close within three months, that the dump operator doesn't want to announce the closing, that it will be impossible to find a new dump in less than a year and that the EPA's approval will be withheld if no dump site is available. The laboratory director tells a public relations officer to sit on the story.[28] The practitioner cannot honor the PRSA code, for the public interest (the state EPA's need to know about the dump closing if it is to make an informed decision) is not consistent with the university's interest (to open the laboratory and then deal with the dump problem).

Professional news organizations also seem unwilling to address some ethical issues directly. The Society of Professional Journalists' code (see the box on page 413) says writers should refuse favors, special treatment and gifts "if they compromise journalistic integrity," and the Radio-Television News Directors Association's code (see the box on page 419) says broadcasters should refuse gifts that could "influence or appear to influence their judgments." These definitions obviously allow a great deal of wiggle room.

Although they are criticized, and for good reasons, codes of ethics are useful to beginning professionals if only because they identify many of the problems and issues communicators face and can suggest what actions are appropriate.

Decision-making Strategies

Codes of ethics cause more harm than good, some critics argue, because they just moralize—they simply give advice. Critics worry that codes are based on inadequate philosophical constructs, that they could mislead young writers and that they do not provide the conceptual tools professionals need to make good ethical decisions. They argue that moral philosophy requires one to think about ethics and that communicators should learn that process.[29]

These critics may assign less value to codes than is appropriate, but they are right to suggest that practitioners must know how to think about ethics. Philosophers in communication and beyond have developed several principles, or models, that can be used by writers to judge what behavior is ethical and what behavior is not. Some are extremely rigid and unforgiving, allowing little or no deviation from ethical principles, while others permit considerable latitude. The strategies discussed here do not begin to exhaust the list, but they are illustrative.

Deontological Approach

Deontology, the study of duty, rejects the idea of *selective ethics* or of *ends justifying means*. Deontologists evaluate the ethics of actions strictly in terms of right and wrong, and they argue that human beings are obligated to treat other human beings with dignity and to respect their rights. The Declaration of Independence is

CODE OF ETHICS, SOCIETY OF PROFESSIONAL JOURNALISTS

PREAMBLE

Members of the Society of Professional Journalists believe that public enlightenment is the forerunner of justice and the foundation of democracy. The duty of the journalist is to further those ends by seeking truth and providing a fair and comprehensive account of events and issues. Conscientious journalists from all media and specialties strive to serve the public with thoroughness and honesty. Professional integrity is the cornerstone of a journalist's credibility. Members of the Society share a dedication to ethical behavior and adopt this code to declare the Society's principles and standards of practice.

SEEK TRUTH AND REPORT IT

Journalists should be honest, fair and courageous in gathering, reporting and interpreting information.

Journalists should:

Test the accuracy of information from all sources and exercise care to avoid inadvertent error. Deliberate distortion is never permissible.

Diligently seek out subjects of news stories to give them the opportunity to respond to allegations of wrongdoing.

Identify sources whenever feasible. The public is entitled to as much information as possible on sources' reliability.

Always question sources' motives before promising anonymity. Clarify conditions attached to any promise made in exchange for information. Keep promises.

Make certain that headlines, news teases and promotional material, photos, video, audio, graphics, sound bites and quotations do not misrepresent. They should not oversimplify or highlight incidents out of context.

Never distort the content of news photos or video. Image enhancement for technical clarity is always permissible. Label montages and photo illustrations.

Avoid misleading re-enactments or staged news events. If re-enactment is necessary to tell a story, label it.

Avoid undercover or other surreptitious methods of gathering information except when traditional open methods will not yield information vital to the public. Use of such methods should be explained as part of the story.

Never plagiarize.

(continued)

CODE OF ETHICS, SOCIETY OF PROFESSIONAL JOURNALISTS

(continued)

Tell the story of the diversity and magnitude of the human experience boldly, even when it is unpopular to do so.

Examine their own cultural values and avoid imposing those values on others.

Avoid stereotyping by race, gender, age, religion, ethnicity, geography, sexual orientation, disability, physical appearance or social status.

Support the open exchange of views, even views they find repugnant.

Give voice to the voiceless; official and unofficial sources of information can be equally valid.

Distinguish between advocacy and news reporting. Analysis and commentary should be labeled and not misrepresent fact or context.

Distinguish news from advertising and shun hybrids that blur the lines between the two.

Recognize a special obligation to ensure that the public's business is conducted in the open and that government records are open to inspection.

MINIMIZE HARM

Ethical journalists treat sources, subjects and colleagues as human beings deserving of respect.

Journalists should:

Show compassion for those who may be affected adversely by news coverage. Use special sensitivity when dealing with children and inexperienced sources or subjects.

Be sensitive when seeking or using interviews or photographs of those affected by tragedy or grief.

Recognize that gathering and reporting information may cause harm or discomfort. Pursuit of the news is not a license for arrogance.

Recognize that private people have a greater right to control information about themselves than do public officials and others who seek power, influence or attention. Only an overriding public need can justify intrusion into anyone's privacy.

Show good taste. Avoid pandering to lurid curiosity.

Be cautious about identifying juvenile suspects or victims of sex crimes.

Be judicious about naming criminal suspects before the formal filing of charges.

Balance a criminal suspect's fair trial rights with the public's right to be informed.

ACT INDEPENDENTLY

Journalists should be free of obligation to any interest other than the public's right to know.

Journalists should:

Avoid conflicts of interest, real or perceived.

Remain free of associations and activities that may compromise integrity or damage credibility.

Refuse gifts, favors, fees, free travel and special treatment, and shun secondary employment, political involvement, public office and service in community organizations if they compromise journalistic integrity.

Disclose unavoidable conflicts.

Be vigilant and courageous about holding those with power accountable.

Deny favored treatment to advertisers and special interests and resist their pressure to influence news coverage.

Be wary of sources offering information for favors or money; avoid bidding for news.

BE ACCOUNTABLE

Journalists are accountable to their readers, listeners, viewers and each other.

Journalists should:

Clarify and explain news coverage and invite dialogue with the public over journalistic conduct.

Encourage the public to voice grievances against the news media.

Admit mistakes and correct them promptly.

Expose unethical practices of journalists and the news media.

Abide by the same high standards to which they hold others.

Source: "Code of Ethics." From Society of Professional Journalists, 3909 N. Meridian St., Indianapolis, Ind. 46208, <www.spj.org>. Copyright © 2003 by Society of Professional Journalists. Reprinted by permission.

one reflection of deontological thinking. "This document guarantees human beings certain rights that cannot be violated by another. Actions that respect those rights are viewed as conforming to a basic concept of humanity."[30]

Immanuel Kant, who established much of the foundation for deontological thought, took an absolute position against lying. A lie, he said, even one that has a good result or that helps someone avoid disaster, always harms humanity because any lie violates the source of law. Kant's categorical imperative, which applies not only to lying, but to all sorts of human behavior, suggests that behavior must be evaluated by whether it is consistent with a higher moral law. Kant would consider an action appropriate if it could be applied to everyone who faces the same set of circumstances—that is, if the behavior could be translated into a universal law.[31]

Deontological thought is reflected in parts of the ethics codes of the Society of Professional Journalists and the Radio-Television News Directors Association. SPJ, for instance, states simply, "Never plagiarize," "Keep promises" to sources and "Disclose unavoidable conflicts." The RTNDA code states that professional electronic journalists should not "Report anything known to be false" or "Plagiarize" and that they should "Clearly label opinion and commentary."

A difficulty with deontological thought, as reflected in Kant's work, is that someone must decide what behavior can be translated into a universal law. Individuals can argue about what someone should do in a given situation, and that makes it difficult—though not impossible—to establish a universal law. A second difficulty is that Kant's strictures—the one against lying, for example—would prohibit behavior in which many individuals would like to engage without considering themselves unethical.

The *Chicago Sun-Times* published a widely discussed series of articles based on information from the Mirage bar, a tavern run by *Sun-Times* staffers who wanted to document the illegal payoffs that were being solicited regularly by inspectors and other city officials. The bar was a joint project of the *Sun-Times* and the Better Government Association of Chicago. Crimes documented by the *Sun-Times* were reported to an agent of the Illinois Department of Law Enforcement, but the *Sun-Times* stressed before opening the tavern that newspaper personnel were not arms of law enforcement. Other legal and ethical issues were debated extensively before the tavern was opened. The staffers used hidden cameras and microphones to document the illegal behavior.[32]

Kant and other deontologists almost certainly would condemn the Mirage bar stories on the grounds that one wrong (the dishonest solicitation of bribes) does not justify another (using deception to gather information). It often is difficult for human beings to live up to the strict standards that would be imposed by the deontologists.

Teleological Approach

Media professionals who endorse the teleological approach might see nothing wrong with the *Sun-Times'* Mirage bar story. Whereas deontology focuses on duties, teleology, the foundation for the utilitarian approach to ethics, focuses on consequences.

Teleologists evaluate the ethics of human behavior in terms of what is best for the greatest number. Jeremy Bentham, Henry Sidgwick and John Stuart Mill are three early proponents of the idea that the consequences must be considered as one decides whether an action is ethical. In discussing deception, for example, Sidgwick said that deception might be acceptable when it benefits the individuals deceived; that expediency must be considered as the admissibility of deception is judged; and that ethicists must weigh the benefit of any deception against the mutual confidence lost when truth is violated.[33]

Ethics codes frequently reflect teleological thinking. The Public Relations Society of America's code, for instance, states that "We serve the public interest by acting as responsible advocates for those we represent." The SPJ code says journalists should "Avoid undercover or other surreptitious methods of gathering information except when traditional open methods will not yield information vital to the public."

Many ethicists have condemned the utilitarians' acceptance of expediency, pointing out that no general rules or guidelines can be developed because each circumstance is different. The problem is compounded because *someone* must decide what is best for the greatest number and because that person has no guidelines and no real qualifications for decision making. The problems are reflected in most codes of ethics. Advice is not always concrete because circumstances vary widely.

The utilitarian, in reacting to the Mirage bar stories, probably would say it is unfortunate that deception had to be used to collect the facts for the 29 articles published by the *Sun-Times,* and then he or she would have to decide whether the good that resulted (dishonest inspectors lost their jobs and the system supposedly was purified) would justify the deception (which could pollute the communication and social process in Chicago). The *Sun-Times* staffers and the Better Government Association people obviously decided the ends justified the means. The series was nominated for a Pulitzer Prize, but some of the judges were uncomfortable with what they saw as questionable ethical behavior.

Bok's Framework

Moral philosopher Sissela Bok argues that a framework for ethical decision making must recognize two underlying principles: A primary goal must be the maintenance of social trust, and decision-makers must have some empathy for those affected by ethical choices. She then suggests that ethical decisions must be made in three steps:[34]

- The person making the choice must consult his or her own conscience, a step that some media professionals fail to take as they make moral decisions. This requires a writer to recognize an ethical dilemma and to decide what an appropriate response is. For a Web writer, that might mean reporting all facts regardless of consequences; for a public relations professional, that might mean doing what the organization mandates.

- A professional must evaluate all alternatives in the second stage. For a practitioner who must weigh the public interest versus the university's interest in the toxic dump case, an alternative might be to meet with university officials, the dump site owner and the medical school faculty. Working together, they might find a good alternative, one of which could be to meet with state EPA officials to discuss a new dump site or even to take over the old one. This might require persuading those who would resist full disclosure, but that could be a feasible option.

- Discuss the issues with the parties involved in the dispute to learn how each potential response would affect their lives. A real discussion would be best, certainly, but the dialogue might also be imaginary. An imagined discussion would force a media professional to consider the impact of a decision on all parties.

A 10-step Approach

The Poynter Institute for Media Studies in Florida, long a leader in the study of media ethics, has generated many ideas that help writers cope with ethical decision making. Bob Steele, the director of the ethics program, for example, has put together a 10-step, process approach for reaching ethical decisions.[35] The process depends upon the media writer's ability to ask 10 questions:

- What is happening? A writer must gather facts that are complete, clear, specific and accurate.

- What are the writer's goals? One must never lose sight of one's obligation to provide information that is clear, concise, accurate, to the point, relevant and meaningful. A writer must be socially responsible and independent, for example.

- What are the media writer's ethical concerns? One must balance information-dissemination goals with the need to tell the truth, to keep promises and to minimize harm.

- Are other points of view required? One must consider a diversity of views in reaching an ethical decision. It may be insufficient to discuss a situation with professionals who hold similar values.

- Who are the interested parties? Many groups and individuals (including the writer) may be affected by publication of sensitive information. The impact of that publication on each group should be carefully weighed as an ethical decision is considered.

- What are the consequences of an action? One must consider the long- and short-term consequences of a decision for various individuals and groups.

- What if roles were reversed? One should consider how he or she would feel if he or she were in the position of an individual who would be affected by an action.

CODE OF ETHICS AND PROFESSIONAL CONDUCT, RADIO-TELEVISION NEWS DIRECTORS ASSOCIATION

PREAMBLE

Professional electronic journalists should operate as trustees of the public, seek the truth, report it fairly and with integrity and independence, and stand accountable for their actions.

PUBLIC TRUST

Professional electronic journalists should recognize that their first obligation is to the public.

Professional electronic journalists should:

Understand that any commitment other than service to the public undermines trust and credibility.

Recognize that service in the public interest creates an obligation to reflect the diversity of the community and guard against oversimplification of issues or events.

Provide a full range of information to enable the public to make enlightened decisions.

Fight to ensure that the public's business is conducted in public.

TRUTH

Professional electronic journalists should pursue truth aggressively and present the news accurately, in context, and as completely as possible.

Professional electronic journalists should:

Continuously seek the truth.

Resist distortions that obscure the importance of events.

Clearly disclose the origin of information and label all material provided by outsiders.

Professional electronic journalists should not:

Report anything known to be false.

Manipulate images or sounds in any way that is misleading.

Plagiarize.

Present images or sounds that are reenacted without informing the public.

(continued)

CODE OF ETHICS AND PROFESSIONAL CONDUCT, RADIO-TELEVISION NEWS DIRECTORS ASSOCIATION *(continued)*

FAIRNESS

Professional electronic journalists should present the news fairly and impartially, placing primary value on significance and relevance.

Professional electronic journalists should:

Treat all subjects of news coverage with respect and dignity, showing particular compassion to victims of crime or tragedy.

Exercise special care when children are involved in a story and give children greater privacy protection than adults.

Seek to understand the diversity of their community and inform the public without bias or stereotype.

Present a diversity of expressions, opinions, and ideas in context.

Present analytical reporting based on professional perspective, not personal bias.

Respect the right to a fair trial.

INTEGRITY

Professional electronic journalists should present the news with integrity and decency, avoiding real or perceived conflicts of interest, and respect the dignity and intelligence of the audience as well as the subjects of news.

Professional electronic journalists should:

Identify sources whenever possible. Confidential sources should be used only when it is clearly in the public interest to gather or convey important information or when a person providing information might be harmed. Journalists should keep all commitments to protect a confidential source.

Clearly label opinion and commentary.

Guard against extended coverage of events or individuals that fails to significantly advance a story, place the event in context, or add to the public knowledge.

Refrain from contacting participants in violent situations while the situation is in progress.

Use technological tools with skill and thoughtfulness, avoiding techniques that skew facts, distort reality, or sensationalize events.

Use surreptitious newsgathering techniques, including hidden cameras or microphones, only if there is no other way to obtain stories of significant public importance and only if the technique is explained to the audience.

Disseminate the private transmissions of other news organizations only with permission.

Professional electronic journalists should not:

Pay news sources who have a vested interest in a story.

Accept gifts, favors, or compensation from those who might seek to influence coverage.

Engage in activities that may compromise their integrity or independence.

INDEPENDENCE

Professional electronic journalists should defend the independence of all journalists from those seeking influence or control over news content.

Professional electronic journalists should:

Gather and report news without fear or favor, and vigorously resist undue influence from any outside forces, including advertisers, sources, story subjects, powerful individuals, and special interest groups.

Resist those who would seek to buy or politically influence news content or who would seek to intimidate those who gather and disseminate the news.

Determine news content solely through editorial judgment and not as the result of outside influence.

Resist any self-interest or peer pressure that might erode journalistic duty and service to the public.

Recognize that sponsorship of the news will not be used in any way to determine, restrict, or manipulate content.

Refuse to allow the interests of ownership or management to influence news judgment or content inappropriately.

Defend the rights of the free press for all journalists, recognizing that any professional or government licensing of journalists is a violation of that freedom.

(continued)

CODE OF ETHICS AND PROFESSIONAL CONDUCT, RADIO-TELEVISION NEWS DIRECTORS ASSOCIATION *(continued)*

ACCOUNTABILITY

Professional electronic journalists should recognize that they are accountable for their actions to the public, the profession, and themselves.

Professional electronic journalists should:

Actively encourage adherence to these standards by all journalists and their employers.

Respond to public concerns, investigate complaints, and correct errors promptly and with as much prominence as the original report.

Explain journalistic processes to the public, especially when practices spark questions or controversy.

Recognize that professional electronic journalists are duty-bound to conduct themselves ethically.

Refrain from ordering or encouraging courses of action that would force employees to commit an unethical act.

Carefully listen to employees who raise ethical objections and create environments in which such objections and discussions are encouraged.

Seek support for and provide opportunities to train employees in ethical decision-making.

Source: "Code of Ethics and Professional Conduct," Radio-Television News Directors Association, undated. Downloaded on Nov. 7, 2002, from <www.rtnda.org/ethics/coe.html>.

- Is the writer doing the right thing? An action must not conflict with a writer's personal ethics, and the writer must determine that he or she is not rationalizing an action.

- Are there any alternatives? Good ethical decisions frequently fall between the extremes of the ethics continuum. The polar oppositions must be identified and the alternatives carefully considered.

- Can a decision and action be justified? One must think about how one would feel if it were necessary to explain an action to colleagues, to friends, to relatives. Would the writer be embarrassed if the decision were described on the nightly news?

An Objective Approach

Ethical communicators would do well to use an objective approach as they collect, write and disseminate news and information (Chapter 1). The argument in Chapter 1 is not repeated here, except to reiterate that media professionals who use an objective approach are likely to do the following:

- Enjoy greater credibility than those who do not because they typically will be viewed as fair and impartial conveyers of news and information

- Bring credit to their organizations and enhance the credibility of those organizations

- Produce more accurate descriptions of reality because they do not allow their personal preferences and biases (which they recognize and acknowledge), or those of their organizations or powerful interests, to interfere with their jobs

- Avoid some of the more thorny ethical issues because their charge is simply to describe and analyze situations and to report facts as they find them, without regard to personal, professional, organizational or societal preferences and considerations

The techniques of an objective approach are useful as professionals produce stories, certainly, but they are also useful as they try to work through tough ethical dilemmas. They collect and analyze information systematically, for instance; they try to ensure their personal biases or the interests of their organizations do not cloud their judgments; and they do not base decisions on ideological considerations.

This is not to suggest that absolute objectivity is attainable, that writers who try to be objective can avoid all ethical dilemmas or that they need not study and understand codes of ethics or strategies for making ethical decisions. All of these things are important as writers work their way through ethics challenges.

ETHICS AND PERSONAL GAIN

Media professionals sometimes stumble into ethical quagmires in which they clearly are in violation of widely held standards of ethical behavior; even the communicators often admit, after the fact, that their behavior was at least inappropriate, if not unethical. A few of the particularly troubling problem areas media professionals face are described here. In some instances, the ethical lapses are quite clear—and generally, though not unanimously, condemned. Remember, too, that in this introduction to ethics, the focus is on worst cases to help students know what is generally considered "wrong." In other circumstances, the ethical answers are far from clear.

Conflicts of Interest

A news medium and its staff must be free of obligations to news sources and special interests. Journalists should accept nothing of value from news sources or others outside the profession, pay all expenses associated with information collection and avoid accepting special favors and treatment. Involvement in politics, community affairs, demonstrations and social causes, even those that support the most laudable activities, create conflicts of interest, or the appearance of such conflict, and should be avoided.

Syndicated columnist and television personality George Will attacked, in his column and on *This Week With David Brinkley,* President Bill Clinton's plan in 1995 to impose huge tariffs on Japanese luxury cars. Tariffs would not be legal, Will asserted, and they would constitute "a subsidy for Mercedes dealerships." Will never admitted on the air or in his column that his wife's company, a registered foreign agent, was paid approximately $200,000 by the Japan Automobile Manufacturers Association to mobilize, in the United States, criticism of the plan. "When Will was asked why he had said nothing, he replied that it was 'just too silly' to think that his views might have been affected by his wife's contract."[36] Perhaps Will's attitudes were not influenced by his wife and her needs, but critics argue that real influence is only part of the problem. The appearance of a conflict of interest was real and that is just as harmful.

Outside employment of media professionals by potential news sources is considered unethical. *The* (Stamford, Conn.) *Advocate* fired a reporter and editor for accepting pay from a city's park department for stories they wrote. Recreation department officials charged that the newspaper's sports editor had to be hired by the recreation department before it could get adequate coverage of recreation news. The reporter lost his job because he allegedly received $2,750 from the park department, which he was writing about.[37]

A journalist who goes into politics is creating another kind of conflict of interest. It is difficult for a news director or anchor for a local television station to become secretary of the chamber of commerce or a member of the school board without creating the appearance of a conflict of interest. Paul A. Poorman, former managing editor of *The Detroit News,* advocated complete non-involvement and discouraged professionals from joining even parent-teacher associations. Journalists who adopt this approach are better able than others to avoid the appearance of conflicts of interest.

Public relations practitioners also can become embroiled in controversy about real or imagined conflicts of interest. The Susan G. Komen Foundation sponsors the annual Race for the Cure to heighten awareness about breast cancer and to raise funds for research. Some critics say they are appalled that some foundation funds are used to support Planned Parenthood, the nation's largest supplier of abortions.[38] Others are critical of the foundation's attempt to raise funds through corporate sponsorships. Some corporations give the Komen Foundation percentages of their sales, and they stress this tie-in as they market their products and services. Critics argue that breast cancer is a tool that multinational corporations use to make money, and they are concerned about the potential influence corporations have over the distribution of money raised.[39]

No one can argue that breast cancer sufferers don't need help or that the cause is not important. But public relations practitioners, like their colleagues in journalism, must recognize real and potential conflicts of interest. After a problem is recognized, it can be addressed.

Refusing to Disclose Information

ABC News reporter and analyst Cokie Roberts speaks often and for large fees to officers, employees and guests of large corporations, which consider it a coup to land a speaker who is on the inside of the news business and who is a "personality." Were she not an ABC News employee, she would not be able to get those lucrative speaking engagements. It is a conflict of interest to use her position to speak to corporate America because she often reports about corporate America, critics argue. Worse, she also has refused to disclose the names of the groups to which she speaks and how much money she has made.

Roberts, like other professionals, criticizes public officials for secrecy—even in their personal affairs. She is outraged when the wife of a public official declines to detail her financial dealings. But her own refusal to reveal her potential conflicts makes such attacks appear hypocritical. Furthermore, "she refuses to acknowledge that secrecy about financial interests undermines journalism's credibility too."[40]

Berman & Co., a public relations firm that aggressively opposes consumer organizations and activists, has created several think tanks and foundations to counter the "anti-choice zealots" and "hypocrites" they oppose. One of Berman's Web sites, ActivistCash.com, seeks to show where "anti-consumer" and "anti-choice" groups get their money and to expose conflicts of interest. This is fair, but ActivistCash.com—which has been linked to the hotel, tobacco, restaurant and food industries, which aren't enamored of consumer groups—refuses to reveal the sources of its funding, which it can do as a private organization. The hypocrisy certainly doesn't enhance its credibility.[41]

Financial Gain

R. Foster Winans, a columnist for *The Wall Street Journal*, was fired in 1984 for reporting to some of his friends the information in some of his columns before they were published. The information in Winans' columns sometimes influenced the stock markets or specific companies or industries in positive or negative ways. The friends used the information to profit from the stock market and paid Winans for his help. Winans, found guilty of 59 counts of fraud and conspiracy, got into serious trouble primarily because he broke the securities laws governing financial institutions of the United States. But beyond that, his actions were unethical by any standard.[42]

The Salt Lake Tribune was embroiled in a less common, but no less serious, incident when two reporters sold information to another newspaper. The reporters received $20,000 for providing information to *The National Enquirer* about the Elizabeth Smart kidnapping case and for misleading *The Tribune* about the nature of their involvement.[43] Michael Vigh and Kevin Cantera, lead writers for *The Tribune's*

JOHN DEVENY ON RECOVERING LOST CREDIBILITY

Admittedly, it's an uphill battle. Regaining credibility after it has been lost demands candor. Offenders have to recognize the reality of the situation and be open and honest about it. That first step cannot be overstated. If it doesn't happen, then all the smoke and mirrors embattled CEOs may beg for are not going to make a considerable difference. First, you need to be open and honest about what happened, and ask yourself what the causal incident was that lost your credibility.

If an organization and its leadership can do that, then they can start on the path to regain credibility. That path is marked by candid and honest disclosure, an interest in the community around you as expressed through the individuals that make up that community, and a dedication to doing the right thing.

Source: "'Credibility Is King': A Conversation With Conference Co-chair, John Deveney, APR," *Public Relations Tactics*, August 2003: 12.

John Deveny is senior counsel for Deveny Communication.

Smart coverage, claimed they provided *The Enquirer* with a road map for a story. *Tribune* editor James E. Shelledy, who later resigned, said he discovered the reporters had supplied *The Enquirer* with much more than that.

Ethical communicators condemn those who would use inside information for personal gain or to advance an ideological cause, but the line sometimes is blurred. For example, Chris Nolan, who covered the technology industry for the *San Jose* (Calif.) *Mercury News,* was suspended after she earned a $9,000 profit from her participation in an initial public offering. AutoWeb's chief executive officer, an old friend, gave Nolan a good price. When the stock price soared, Nolan sold. There was no evidence that Nolan used her position to make a profit and she did not write about AutoWeb, but the appearance of impropriety was unacceptable to her editors and critics.[44]

Freebies

Anything of value that is offered to a media writer is a freebie: the free food at a public relations party or "news" event; free passes to a play or film or game; free transportation to an event; free lunches or drinks with sources or lobbyists.

Ethical communication organizations have policies against accepting freebies because of the potential influence freebies give sources and because of the appearance of impropriety. For example, the RTNDA code of ethics states that electronic journalists should not "Accept gifts, favors, or compensation from those who might seek to influence coverage." CBS News says media discounts, which most codes ignore, must not be accepted unless they are available to the general public.[45]

The danger of accepting freebies is that a writer might feel obligated to someone who has given him or her a gift; if that person is a news source, the writer's work might be influenced. The problem is, of course, that everyone is at least a potential news source. And even if a writer isn't influenced by a gift from a news source, acceptance of a gift can create a damaging appearance of impropriety.

The Sydney (Australia) Morning Herald reported—in an unusual story in which a newspaper criticized itself—that journalists had accepted in a single week eight meals paid for by companies they were covering and nine had attended a promotional ball with all expenses paid. Others were flown free to New York, Hong Kong, Amsterdam or France at the expense of those about whom they were writing.[46] This is not an isolated, Aussie problem; freebies are offered and accepted routinely throughout the world.

The problem is particularly acute for those covering the Internet and technology. Software manufacturers want the media to publicize their new products, and so they send reviewers $500 software packages, which most keep. If a hardware manufacturer wants the media to review a new PC, it will send reviewers new computers, which are not always returned as requested.

A freelance writer said he sent his mother a $300 Sony WebTV unit that Sony had sent for review, and he said Polk Audio set up in his home a $9,000 home theater system. He did not say whether he kept it. As a freelance writer, he was not always bound by the guidelines established for full-time employees.[47]

Freelance writers, like all other communication professionals, must make ethical decisions all the time, even when they are not bound by codes and guidelines that apply to the employees in organizations for which they write. It is a good idea, however, whether required to or not, for freelance writers to abide by the stated policies of the organizations to which they contribute and to be familiar with the ethics codes of the media these organizations are part of.

Freelance writer Robin Gregg learned the lesson the hard way when he sold to the New York Post a piece that was plagiarized from The National Enquirer. The first four paragraphs of his story about the decision of Wal-Mart Stores Inc. to drop Kathie Lee Gifford's clothing line were very much like those in The Enquirer. Post management said Gregg will never write for the Post again.[48]

Public relations professionals may be in uncomfortable circumstances with regard to freebies, primarily because distributing freebies to journalists is not considered unethical by many in the public relations industry. The PRSA code is somewhat vague about gifts when it suggests: "Preserve the free flow of unprejudiced information when giving or receiving gifts by ensuring that gifts are nominal, legal, and infrequent." The code defines as improper the giving of a gift (for example, an expensive set of skis) to a writer so he or she will produce a favorable article about the product).[49]

A CLASSIC JUNKET

A classic junket—one that focused considerable attention on the junket as an ethical issue—was arranged years ago by the International Telephone and Telegraph Co., which spent approximately $20,000 to sell Palm Coast, an ITT-owned residential development near Daytona Beach, Fla., to 65 writers. ITT paid the writers' expenses for the "Palm Coast Yacht Club Weekend Party." A reporter for the *St. Petersburg Times* attended the event at her newspaper's expense. This is part of what she said about the weekend (and junkets in general):

> This relaxed atmosphere was, of course, abetted by Bloody Marys, which seemed to appear in everybody's hands just automatically. We were having a free lunch, a free weekend and we were expected to sing for our suppers. ... You could not possibly do the job that needed to be done in that length of time—especially when you had to do so much partying. ... One thing that is most interesting that happens as a result of this publicity is that ... these news stories that emanate from these junkets ... become public relations vehicles. They become part of sales packets. ... This kind of thing definitely occurs, and it's, of course, the kind of advertising that is far better than a paid advertisement and is worth probably hundreds of thousands of dollars.[50]

> *Media & Consumer* magazine found that the trip led to at least 22 uncritical stories, more than half of which relied heavily or exclusively on ITT's press kit. Most articles about Palm Coast stressed the development's environmental strengths, which ITT pushed, but which were seriously questioned by several qualified sources. Only four writers acknowledged that ITT sponsored the trip.[51] ITT obviously got its money's worth, and the integrity of many writers and media organizations was bruised.

It is worth considering, too, that practitioners who give away free stuff are leading others into temptation. There is no good answer for this quandary, but it needs to be recognized.

Junkets

A junket, a free trip given to journalists, is a special kind of freebie (see the box "A Classic Junket"). One kind of junket is a free trip to a resort that is trying to promote itself to travelers. These trips typically include lavish entertainment, gifts and accommodations, and they raise a serious question about whether the reviewer is in a position after returning home to evaluate the resort objectively. Junkets also are sponsored by manufacturing companies, governments, the real estate industry and technology companies.

Journalists wait to photograph stars of the DreamWorks SKG film Shark Tale *at an event promoting the movie during the Cannes Film Festival.*

A Los Angeles–based public relations firm spent thousands to send writer Elizabeth Austin and some of her colleagues to a luxury resort in Bali. She stayed in a $500-a-day room and got free massages and facials. "Every evening, I returned to my room to find a beautifully wrapped gift lying on my bed, left by some Indonesian hotel version of the tooth fairy. One night, I unwrapped a beautiful batik sarong. On another night, I found a handwrought sterling silver key ring. (All the gifts, of course, were accompanied by press releases about their makers.)"[52]

The big problem with the junket, Austin said, isn't the implied quid pro quo. "It's the controlled and sanitized travel experience it presents to the writers. ... In our serene boudoirs, there was no indication of the country's political unrest, religious strife or economic turmoil."[53]

The movie industry also relies heavily on junkets to promote films. Disney Studios, often cited as a champion in the junket world, took writers to the expensive Four Seasons Hotel in Los Angeles to promote *Crazy/Beautiful*. Director John Stockwell spoke with television writers for five minutes each during a morning interview session and with print journalists for 20 minutes each during an afternoon session. Such events cost studios an estimated $300,000–400,000.[54]

Writers get free transportation, hotel rooms, liquor and food, and they sometimes get autographed media kits, some of which are eventually posted for sale on the Internet. If a well-known film personality autographs the media kit, it can sell for $25 or so.[55] Few writers ask tough questions because "There's always an army of publicists hovering over our shoulders, some from the studios, some employed by the stars, all making sure we don't ask anything impolite or embarrassing or anything that strays too far from the movie." A critic who asks the wrong questions might not be invited back.[56]

Junkets are seen by many in public relations as "editorial tours." They are good ways to educate a large group of journalists in a short time about a service or product, and they are not seen as unethical. As with freebies, public relations professionals need to recognize that they may be leading others into what some critics see as unethical behavior and that junkets are especially problematic when they are seen as bribes.

COLLECTING, DISSEMINATING INFORMATION

Writers sometimes ponder just how far they should go to obtain the facts for their reports. Some journalists believe any action is justified. For them, nothing is unethical, not even breaking the law. Others believe there are ethical boundaries over which they should not step. Problems can arise from a number of actions described here.

Deceptive Practices

Vivian Toy, a writer for the *Milwaukee* (Wisc.) *Journal Sentinel*, posed as a student at a public high school near Milwaukee for a story about the concerns and daily lives of young adults. Metropolitan editor Patrick Graham defended the deception on grounds that an accurate appraisal of students' views could not be gotten any other way. "If you want the truth, if you want candor on such subjects, the only way is to have a reporter in school who is accepted as a peer," Graham is quoted as saying.[57]

A few days after the Sept. 11, 2001, terrorist attacks, two electronic-mail newsletters—*Silicon Alley Daily* and *Digital Coast Daily*—published a first-person story by Robert Galinsky about what he saw when he visited the wreckage of the World Trade Center on Sept. 12. Galinsky got to the rescue scene after he dressed in workman's clothing and a hard hat and lied to get through police checkpoints. Reader response was immediate and negative. The editor apologized for publishing the piece and said that journalists should not hinder rescue operations in any way.[58]

Two questions about both the Toy and Galinsky stories are important: Could the information have been obtained any other way, and were the writers hoping to correct wrongful conditions? Ethicist Edmund Lambeth asserts that deception is moral only when a wrongful condition exists, is pervasive and cannot be corrected by truthful means (the utilitarian approach).[59] Neither story seems to meet these prerequisites. (See also the box "Undercover Journalism.")

UNDERCOVER JOURNALISM

Magazine writer Ted Conover wanted to do a story about the training program for guards in New York prisons (Chapter 12).[60] His original idea was to follow one individual who was going through the training. The New York Department of Correctional Services refused to give him permission to do this.

Conover decided to undergo the training himself without letting anyone know that he was a writer. After receiving the training, he became a "newjack," or rookie guard. He spent almost a year at Sing Sing prison working as a guard and then published an article in *The New Yorker* detailing his experience. He later expanded the article into a book titled *Newjack*, which won several awards.

Undercover journalism of the kind undertaken by Conover has been practiced before by some notable individuals in journalism, including George Orwell, Nellie Bly, Jack London and Stephen Crane. But the technique does raise questions of ethics. People are being deceived, often for long periods of time.[61]

In Conover's case, it appears that the information could not have been gathered in any other way. He did initially propose that he follow someone else going through the training to be a guard, but his request was turned down. This is a case in which an ethical decision had to be made. Was the value of the information gained by the covert reporting techniques great enough to make up for the lengthy deception? Most ethicists evidently think so, since there has been little criticism of Conover's approach.

Journalists who use deceptive practices can run afoul of the law. ABC News reporters, for instance, got jobs processing meat for a Food Lion supermarket in North Carolina (Chapter 13). ABC was sued after the writers misrepresented themselves and surreptitiously collected information for stories about Food Lion's low-quality meat. ABC lost. The court said the reporters trespassed into nonpublic areas of the supermarket under false pretenses; that they lied on their job applications; and that they violated their legal obligation of loyalty to their employer.[62]

Public relations practitioners don't need to use deceptive practices to get information, but they sometimes use deception as they disseminate it. Sterling Corp., a Michigan-based public relations firm, was retained to help Pakistan polish its image, in part by identifying negative stories and supplying journalists with "clarifications." But Sterling also trained American Pakistanis to use media techniques as part of its "grassroots" campaign. Sterling wanted the talking points it gave to its surrogate messengers (the trainees) to show up in letters to editors, electronic-mail messages, newsletters, conversations—essentially in any venue.

Sterling was using the deceptive third-party technique, in which a message about a client (Pakistan) is disseminated by a seemingly objective source. Practitioners hope the surrogates' messages will have more credibility and that they won't be traced back to them, for no practitioner wants to be discovered using a deceptive practice.[63]

Altering Information

A 1994 photograph of O.J. Simpson on the cover of *Time* magazine was altered to give Simpson a sinister look. The same photograph, originally provided by the Los Angeles Police Department to several news media, was used unaltered on the cover of *Newsweek*. The *Time* photograph was blurry and portrayed a darkened and unshaven Simpson. *Time*'s Simpson was sinister-looking, while *Newsweek*'s Simpson was not.[64]

Most Americans accept some of the old clichés about photographs: One picture is worth a thousand words, and seeing is believing. But *Time* magazine has polluted that well. Photographs obviously can be doctored, and at least some media professionals are willing to do that. *Time*'s behavior causes some media consumers, especially those who read *Time*, to question whether other information has been altered. It is not difficult for an unethical journalist, for example, to leave out a portion of a direct quotation that he or she does not agree with. It is not difficult to simply fail to interview a source who has information that does not conform to a communicator's preconceptions. If the media are willing to alter photographs, why would they not alter other information?

Creating the News

A sensational 1992 story by *Dateline NBC* purported to demonstrate the danger in driving a General Motors truck. *Dateline NBC* had information that the trucks' gas tanks could explode on impact. To demonstrate the safety hazard, NBC arranged for an independent company to create an accident, which was appropriate, but the company used spark igniters to cause the gas tank to explode.[65]

NBC employees apparently knew about the igniters, but they went ahead with the story, thus creating the news rather than simply reporting it. Lazy, unethical communicators—encouraged by an ethical climate in which many questionable acts are substantially unchallenged or for which there are no real consequences—sometimes create the news, or embellish it, to heighten interest. Such behavior is not ethical, although journalists with vested interests in the products of such behavior (sensational, audience-building stories) might well argue otherwise, and it pollutes the communication stream for everyone. Many writers could avoid the traps into which they fall if they simply remember the old bromide: Let the facts speak for themselves.

Breaking Promises

Reporters for the Minneapolis, Minn., *Star Tribune* and the *St. Paul* (Minn.) *Pioneer Press and Dispatch* accepted information from the public relations representative of an Independent–Republican Party candidate for governor. The reporters agreed not to use the man's name in their stories, which reported derogatory information about the Democratic-Farm-Labor candidate for lieutenant governor. Honoring an agreement with a source is probably as close to a universal standard as one will find in journalism. Such commitments simply are not broken.

When the reporters wrote their stories, however, editors at the two newspapers decided independently not to honor the agreements for confidentiality, and the source's name was published. The source lost his job, sued and won (Chapter 13). The U.S. Supreme Court upheld the lower court finding that a verbal contract had been broken and that the source was entitled to compensation.[66]

The behavior of the Minneapolis/St. Paul newspapers was seen by many media professionals and consumers as unethical, for most journalists will go to jail to protect their sources. Many condemned the editors for overruling the reporters and for making the reporters break their promises and the newspapers' promises.

Accurate information obtained and reported in ethical ways is the primary commodity of the mass communicator. A communicator who breaks a promise to a source may well find that source and other sources no longer will be cooperative. Even other writers may find their sources are less likely to talk following a highly publicized incident in which a writer has lied to a source.

False Identification

A journalist arrives at the scene of a late-night murder at a local nightspot; a man has just killed his wife in full view of a dozen witnesses. The reporter learns from the police that the woman's relatives are standing near the ambulance. The writer goes up to the relatives and begins asking questions; one person asks for identification after a couple of questions. The reporter ignores the question and continues the interview. The relative asks for identification two or three different times, but the question is ignored. Finally, after the writer has the information, he identifies himself. The relatives didn't know they were talking to a journalist, and after they find out they are angry. They thought he was a police officer.

Some observers would say the reporter acted unethically; others would disagree. However, few would argue that a journalist would be justified in giving false identification (identifying himself or herself as a police officer) to get the facts for the story. Such action carries with it the risk that a reporter will go to jail (for impersonating an officer) or pay a fine. Also, when a reporter gives false identification to get information, the public usually finds out about it. Then the writer's action becomes of more concern than the information obtained. The attention is off the story and on the writer.

Private Information

To what extent is it ethical for a writer to obtain and use information to which an ordinary citizen has no access and that typically is considered to be private? More specifically, how ethical is it for a media professional to obtain and use documents such as personal telephone records, driving records, credit card transactions and bank records, all of which are increasingly easy to obtain?

Carl Bernstein was able to get telephone records for individuals involved in the Watergate affair, but he doubted the ethics of the practice. "It was a problem he had never resolved in his mind," he and Woodward wrote. "Why, as a reporter, was he entitled to have access to personal and financial records when such disclosure would outrage him if he were subjected to a similar inquiry by investigators?"[67] The use of private telephone records was an invasion of privacy and, in the view of many journalists, a violation of the professional ethics of journalism.

It is helpful as one considers the ethics of using private information to ask whether that information is newsworthy (Chapter 13). If it is not, it might very well be considered unethical to use it. It is not unethical to use information that is generally known. If a news source or personality discusses the information with others, for example, it probably is not unethical to use it.

OTHER ETHICAL QUAGMIRES

Students must be aware of another group of ethical difficulties that can result in writers, media organizations and society getting false, misleading or trivial information.

Misleading Information

The Natural Resources Defense Council hired Fenton Communications to publicize its report, "Intolerable Risk: Pesticides in Our Children's Food," which purported to show that children were exposed to carcinogens in Alar, a pesticide used to preserve apples. The goal was to give the report as much publicity as possible so that the story would develop a life of its own, David Fenton said. The story was intended to continue for months and to influence policy and consumer habits.

The report was so widely circulated that the apple industry had to spend $2 million to refute the charges. The limitations of the original study were identified and publicized, and the industry noted that Alar was used on only a small percentage of the nation's apples. Three U.S. government agencies finally declared apples safe and the Alar scare groundless. Apple farms lost more than $100 million, and some farms closed.[68]

The dissemination by public relations writers, or anyone else, of information that is false or misleading is not ethical, regardless of the purpose. Such promotion frequently requires the cooperation of unethical, ignorant or dumb journalists, but that does not relieve the writer of responsibility. Just because one *can* disseminate misleading or false information does not mean one *should*. In fact, the public relations person's obligation to ensure that information is sound may be greater when he or she knows a journalist is not paying close attention than it is when the journalist is paying close attention.

News Versus Publicity

A 7-year-old Windham, Maine, girl was at the end-stage of liver disease and her family needed to raise money to help pay for a liver transplant. A volunteer contacted the news media about a fund-raising dinner, and that started a wave of publicity that helped the family raise more than $100,000. When the child was ready to return home from Pittsburgh following surgery, the family needed to raise another $900. A local television station agreed to donate the money if it could send a photographer and a reporter along on the trip. The family agreed.[69]

The cause undoubtedly was a good one, and any family, any community, would appreciate the efforts of the news media. This is the kind of story that media cover all the time, but are such stories newsworthy? Is this a good use of a medium's precious time and space? If the media are to preserve the distinction between news and publicity, should they cover these kinds of stories? Should they *participate* in such stories, as the television news department did?

News is information gathered by a medium's reporters according to their own professional standards. Publicity is information coming from an outside source designed to promote that source's interests. A medium blurs the distinction between the two every time it reprints a publicity release or news handout without taking a hard, critical look at it first. Some releases should be regarded as news tips and used as the basis for a journalist's own reporting. Other releases at least need to be rewritten because in the form in which they are received they shamelessly promote a product, service or company.

The real estate and food sections of many newspapers frequently blur the distinction between news and publicity. News releases written by the local real estate board are often printed just as they are received. In some newspapers and magazines, large amounts of space frequently are devoted to descriptions of new housing developments or apartment complexes, and genuine news of solar heating for homes or of local transportation problems is ignored.

Good public relations professionals understand that the line between news and publicity should not be blurred, and they do not produce content for the news media that is not newsworthy. They understand that sending to journalists news releases that contain no news damages their credibility and makes it harder to get newsworthy releases published. This is not to say it always is easy to know what journalists will find newsworthy, but a conscientious professional is able to make sound predictions.

Pseudo-events

Daniel Boorstin coined the term *pseudo-event* more than four decades ago to describe events that appear to be news, but that are not. Boorstin notes that journalists, until early in the 20th century, simply reported whatever happened; they

Writers in the U.S. Office of War Information frequently blurred the line between news and publicity as they promoted the U.S. role in World War II. This was one of the largest public relations campaigns of that era.

were not expected to report about that which did not exist. In the past 100 years, however, media audiences have changed: They expect the media to be full of interesting material. "Demanding more than the world can give us, we require that something be fabricated to make up for the world's deficiency. ... The new kind of synthetic novelty which has flooded our experience I will call 'pseudo-events.'"[70]

The pseudo-event is not at all spontaneous; it is carefully planned by the media manipulator, and it is designed to attract media coverage. The relationship of the event to reality is not clear; did a statement or an event really mean what it said, and what were the motives of those involved? Finally, the pseudo-event is designed by the media manipulator to be a self-fulfilling prophecy: If one says that a new model automobile is wonderful, it is.

Pseudo-events litter and pollute the communication process because so many individuals, corporations and groups want and need publicity to flourish. There is no real news in a company's celebration of its 50th anniversary, but the celebration, if reported by the media, could produce considerable good will and could result in increased sales or new clients. Several forests are consumed each year by the manufacturers who supply paper to public relations firms. Many releases, annual reports and newsletters describe pseudo-events, and many of those reports are aired and published by the media because they don't have to pay anything for that "news" content.

This is another ethical issue that is not always as clear as it may seem. Any event can be evaluated along a continuum from "no news value at all" to "exceptionally newsworthy." Sometimes the line between "unworthy" and "worthy" is quite thin. And sometimes an event that is seen as an unworthy pseudo-event one day might be seen as newsworthy the next. A public relations practitioner who organizes an event that some journalists see as unworthy is not necessarily an unethical manipulator. Other factors must be considered.

Working With the Law

Rollo Taylor, publisher of *The Welch* (W.Va.) *Daily News,* allowed a West Virginia State Police agent to work undercover as a *Daily News* reporter as he gathered evidence about drug trafficking in McDowell County. Only Taylor and his managing editor knew about the deception, which gave the agent substantial freedom to move about and to gather evidence. His work was a major reason for the arrest of approximately 15 people on drug charges. Taylor and others argued that the end justified the means.[71]

Journalists must not become arms of law enforcement, for such cooperation almost always entails deception or some other unethical behavior, and their claims to independence and objectivity are compromised when they do. Critics of Taylor's action also were concerned that journalist-source relationships throughout the state would be damaged and that the action would undermine media credibility. Critics pointed out that law enforcement agencies have far more resources than most communication organizations and that they should be able to generate information for themselves.

This is seldom an ethical issue for public relations practitioners unless they work for military or law enforcement agencies that are considering using journalists to gather evidence. It's important to understand the implications for those journalists and for the free flow of information.

Sacred Cows

A sacred cow is a person, group, institution or issue that a news medium treats as if it were beyond criticism. A dominant local industry that supports a city, town or state might be a sacred cow. Or a mayor may be a sacred cow and never be criticized. A television station that is unwilling to run a negative story about food cooperatives because some of its biggest advertisers are cooperatives is looking out for a sacred cow.

Micron Technology was for years a sacred cow in Boise, Idaho. *The Idaho Statesman* permitted Micron officials to review stories about the company before they were published, a practice almost universally condemned by ethical media practitioners because Micron was going further than simply checking the facts. Micron officials complained when business editor Paul Beebe changed the lead on a story about complaints by Taiwanese computer chip manufacturers that Micron was

RIGHT-RIGHT CHOICES ARE TOUGH

One of the most troublesome of the right-right choices media writers face is the one presented by an information source who threatens suicide if his or her privacy is invaded. Norman J. Rees told *Dallas Times Herald* reporter Hugh Aynesworth he would commit suicide if the *Times Herald* published a story about his sale of secrets to Russia during World War II and about his role as a double agent.[72]

Aynesworth and the newspaper had conflicting choices: to go with a good story or to protect a human life. The *Times Herald* went with the story, and Rees shot himself the day the article appeared.

The *Times Herald* might seem insensitive for publishing the story, but suicide threats are not all that uncommon. If a news medium bows to them, sources begin to gain control of content, and that's not good for anybody. On the other hand, media writers are as responsible as anyone else for preserving life.

The first question to ask when a source threatens suicide on grounds that a story is an unnecessary invasion of privacy is this: Is the story newsworthy? If it's not, the source is right. It should not be published. The story about Norman Rees was newsworthy.

Ethicist Deni Elliott recommends these additional questions, which are appropriate for other kinds of ethical dilemmas:

■ How should the newsworthy fact so worrisome to the source be played? A change of emphasis or the inclusion of clarifying information important to the source may prevent the loss of a job, or a reputation, or a life.

■ How quickly does the information need to get out? The audience may need a newsworthy fact, but often fear of competition rather than commitment to disclosure propels a story into the community *now*. It's rare that information can't be held long enough to give the source (or those close to the source) time to prepare for publication.

■ How can the troubled source feel less powerless? Threats of suicide are "extreme examples of what happens when sources feel that the newspaper isn't treating them fairly," said Laurence Jolidon, who as metro editor of the *Dallas Times Herald* was the last person from the newspaper to talk to Norman Rees. "It is up to those in the newsroom to let sources who threaten suicide know that their interests are being taken into account," he said. "You have to keep the dialogue going."[73]

dumping chips in Taiwan. Micron had lodged the same complaint earlier against competitors from Japan. The Gannett newspaper fired Beebe.[74]

A news medium should have no sacred cows. Nothing should be immune from coverage because of its influence or position. And an ethical public relations practitioner will argue forcefully against the kind of practice in which Micron was engaged.

Invasions of Privacy

Former U.S. Rep. Steve Stockman, R-Texas, asked that trespassing charges be filed against a newspaper reporter who, he claims, barged into his home and "battered" campaign workers. The journalist denied the charges and said he was admitted into the home/campaign headquarters by campaign workers and left when asked—three times. Stockman was in Washington at the time, but his wife was home and she was afraid of the reporter, Stockman said. "We said you shouldn't just bust into people's homes and he started screaming and talking in a loud voice," the *Houston Chronicle* quoted a campaign worker as saying, "He started yelling and screaming 'You're pathetic' and acting very unprofessional."[75]

The trespassing charges were dropped, but even if the writer and photographer could not be sent to the slammer, their behavior raises some troubling ethical questions. Journalists certainly must not misrepresent themselves to gain entry to a campaign headquarters—or a meeting or a speech. If the writer wore a campaign badge to make campaign workers assume he was there to work, that would be ethically questionable. So are yelling and calling campaign workers "pathetic" for not answering questions, as the writer admitted he did. Such behavior borders on the illegal and, under some conditions, might be considered unethical.

There are other situations in which the decision of whether to invade someone's privacy is an ethical one. Sometimes television shows a journalist interviewing someone in the midst of tragedy—a survivor of a plane crash or a relative of a person who has been murdered. The viewer probably can't help feeling sympathy for the interviewee and wondering whether an interview was really necessary—or ethical. The legal implications of invading someone's privacy are discussed in Chapter 13.

YOUR RESPONSIBILITY IS . . .

- To appreciate why it is important for a media professional to be ethical, and to work for an organization that values and encourages ethical behavior.

- To understand that information gained from unethical behavior pollutes the information stream and ultimately makes it difficult for media professionals and society to function.

- To dedicate yourself to finding the most ethical solution to the moral dilemmas you will inevitably face.

■ To avoid binary thinking. Sometimes one choice obviously is right and another obviously is wrong, but the choices often are not binary. Sometimes writers face five alternatives, not two, and sometimes one choice might be "right" from one perspective and "wrong" from another.

■ To develop a clear understanding of what is considered by most professionals as unacceptable in writing for print and digital media. This chapter is a good beginning, for many questionable practices are outlined here, although it does not begin to address or resolve all ethical issues.

■ To read with a critical eye the codes of ethics reprinted here, for there are many loopholes and exceptions in them. They are a good foundation for further thought and study, however.

■ To understand the strengths and weaknesses of different approaches (deontology and teleology, for instance) to the study of ethical issues and to learn how to use them effectively.

NOTES

1. Ben Hecht and Charles MacArthur, *The Front Page: A Play in Three Acts* (New York: Samuel French, 1928).
2. Larry Beinhart, *American Hero* (New York: Pantheon, 1993).
3. Carl Bernstein and Bob Woodward, *All the President's Men* (New York: Simon & Schuster, 1974).
4. Joe Saltzman, *Frank Capra and the Image of the Journalist in American Film* (Los Angeles: Image of the Journalist in Popular Culture, 2002); and Howard Good, *Outcasts: The Image of Journalists in Contemporary Film* (Metuchen, N.J.: Scarecrow, 1989).
5. Michael Ryan, "Journalistic Ethics, Objectivity, Existential Journalism, Standpoint Epistemology, and Public Journalism," *Journal of Mass Media Ethics*, 16:1 (2001): 3–22.
6. Michael Ryan, "Pentagon Shouldn't Add to Litter of Disinformation," *Houston Chronicle*, Feb. 21, 2002: A-29.
7. Meenakshi Gigi Durham, "On the Relevance of Standpoint Epistemology to the Practice of Journalism: The Case for 'Strong Objectivity,'" *Communication Theory*, 8:2 (1998): 117–140; and Sandra Harding, "Rethinking Standpoint Epistemology: What Is 'Strong Objectivity'?" in Linda Alcoff and Elizabeth Potter (eds.), *Feminist Epistemologies* (New York: Routledge, 1993): 49–82.
8. Helen E. Longino, *Science as Social Knowledge: Values and Objectivity in Scientific Inquiry* (Princeton, N.J.: Princeton University Press, 1990); and John B. Harms and David R. Dickens, "Postmodern Media Studies: Analysis or Symptom?" *Critical Studies in Mass Communication*, 13:3 (1996): 210–227. For a different view, see John R. Searle, *The Construction of Social Reality* (New York: Simon & Schuster, 1995).
9. Daniel A. Farber, *The First Amendment* (New York: Foundation Press, 1998): chapters 1, 11.
10. Matthew R. Kerbel, *If It Bleeds, It Leads: An Anatomy of Television News* (Boulder, Colo.: Westview, 2001), and Paul D. Klite, Robert A. Bardwell and Jason Salzman, *Not in the Public Interest: A Snapshot of Local TV News in America*, report of the Rocky Mountain Media Watch, Denver, 1998.

11. Yochi J. Dreazen, "In the Shadows: Photos of Women Who Get Abortions Go Up on Internet," *The Wall Street Journal,* May 28, 2002: A-1, 8.

12. Peter P. Jacobi, "Produce, Produce, Produce; Abuse, Abuse, Abuse," *Quill,* January 1979: 9–10, 27–30, p. 10.

13. Roy Peter Clark, "The Unoriginal Sin: How Plagiarism Poisons the Press," *Washington Journalism Review,* March 1983: 42–47, p. 43.

14. "Boston Columnist Resigns Amid New Plagiarism Charges," CNN, Aug. 19, 1998. Downloaded on Nov. 6, 2002 from <www.cnn.com/US/9808/19/barnicle>.

15. "A Scholarly Crime Wave," *The Wilson Quarterly,* 26:2 (2002): 83–84.

16. American Society of Newspaper Editors, *Newspaper Credibility: Building Reader Trust: A National Study* (Washington, D.C.: Author, April 1985); American Society of Newspaper Editors, *Examining Our Credibility* (Washington, D.C.: Author, 1999); "Recent Journalistic Lapses Little Noted by Most Americans," The Freedom Forum's Media Studies Center, Oct. 16, 1998. Downloaded on Dec. 27, 2000, from <www.freedomforum.org/templates/document.asp?documentid=6401>; *The People, the Press, & Their Leaders 1995* (Washington, D.C.: Times Mirror Center for the People & the Press, 1995); and "PR Pros Are Among Least Believable Public Figures," *O'Dwyer's PR Services Report,* August 1999: 1, 24.

17. Ben Bradlee, *A Good Life: Newspapering and Other Adventures* (New York: Simon & Schuster, 1995): Chapter 17; "Times Reporter Who Resigned Leaves Long Trail of Deception," *The New York Times,* May 11, 2003: A-1, 20–23; and Richard Cohen, "Blind Spot at the N.Y. Times," *The Washington Post,* May 13, 2003: A-19.

18. James Russell Wiggons, "The News Is the First Concern of the Press," *Journalism Quarterly,* 23:1 (1946): 20–29, p. 21.

19. "'Blood Sport' of TV Ratings," *The Denver Post,* Sept. 24, 1990: B-7. See also Renate Robey, "'Blood Sport' Indictments: Bergen, 2 Others at KCNC Named in Pit-bull Case," *The Denver Post,* Sept. 22, 1990: A-1, 14; and Joanne Ostrow, "Entire System Fell Apart at Channel 4," *The Denver Post,* Sept. 22, 1990: A-1, 14.

20. Louis A. Day, *Ethics in Media Communications: Cases and Controversies,* 3rd ed. (Belmont, Calif.: Wadsworth, 2000); James A. Jaksa and Michael S. Pritchard, *Communication Ethics: Methods of Analysis,* 2nd ed. (Belmont, Calif.: Wadsworth, 1994); Philip Seib and Kathy Fitzpatrick, *Public Relations Ethics* (Fort Worth: Harcourt Brace, 1995); Philip Patterson and Lee Wilkins, *Media Ethics: Issues and Cases,* 4th ed. (Boston: McGraw-Hill, 2002); Clifford G. Christians, Mark Fackler, Kim B. Rotzoll and Kathy Brittain McKee, *Media Ethics: Cases and Moral Reasoning,* 6th ed. (New York: Longman, 2001); Jay Black, Bob Steele and Ralph Barney, *Doing Ethics in Journalism: A Handbook With Case Studies,* 3rd ed. (Boston: Allyn and Bacon, 1999); Richard Keeble, *Ethics for Journalists* (London: Routledge, 2001); and Larry Z. Leslie, *Mass Communication Ethics: Decision Making in Postmodern Culture,* 2nd ed. (Boston: Houghton Mifflin, 2004).

21. David E. Boeyink, "How Effective Are Codes of Ethics? A Look at Three Newsrooms," *Journalism Quarterly,* 71:4 (1994): 893–904.

22. Kathy R. Fitzpatrick, "Evolving Standards in Public Relations: A Historical Examination of PRSA's Codes of Ethics," *Journal of Mass Media Ethics,* 17:2 (2002): 89–110, p. 109.

23. Marvin N. Olasky, "Ministers or Panderers: Issues Raised by the Public Relations Society Code of Standards," *Journal of Mass Media Ethics,* 1:1 (1985–86): 43–49, p. 43.

24. Boeyink, "How Effective Are Codes of Ethics?"

25. Clifford Christians, "Enforcing Media Codes," *Journal of Mass Media Ethics,* 1:1 (1985–86): 14–21.

26. "PRSA Member Statement of Professional Values," Public Relations Society of America, undated. Available at <www.prsa.org/-About/ethics/values.asp?ident=eth4>.

27. The member statement is only a part of the PRSA code. See "Member Code of Ethics 2000," October 2000. Available at <www.prsa.org/_About/ethics/polf/codeofethics.pdf?/inden>.

28. Michael Ryan and David L. Martinson, "Public Relations Practitioners, Journalists View Lying Similarly," *Journalism Quarterly,* 71:1 (1994): 199–211.

29. Jay Black and Ralph D. Barney, "The Case Against Mass Media Codes of Ethics," *Journal of Mass Media Ethics,* 1:1 (1985–86): 27–36

30. Seib and Fitzpatrick, *Public Relations Ethics:* 32.

31. Immanuel Kant, "On a Supposed Right to Lie from Altruistic Motives," in *Critique of Practical Reason and Other Writings in Moral Philosophy* (ed. and trans. by Lewis White Beck) (Chicago: University of Chicago Press, 1949): 346–350.

32. Zay N. Smith and Pamela Zekman, "The Mirage Takes Shape," *Columbia Journalism Review,* September/October 1979: 51–53, 56–57. See also Zay N. Smith and Pamela Zekman, *The Mirage* (New York: Random House, 1979).

33. Henry Sidgwick, *The Methods of Ethics,* 5th ed. (London: Macmillan, 1893).

34. Sissela Bok, *Lying: Moral Choice in Public and Private Life* (New York: Pantheon, 1978).

35. Bob Steele, "Ethics Clinic: A 10-step Approach to Good Decision-making," *Quill,* March 1991: 36.

36. James Fallows, *Breaking the News: How the Media Undermine American Democracy* (New York: Vintage, 1997): 38.

37. "Two Newsmen Fired for Breach of Ethics," *Editor & Publisher,* Aug. 23, 1975: 20.

38. Karen Malec, "Susan G. Komen Foundation: Putting Ideology Ahead of Women's Lives," Coalition on Abortion/Breast Cancer, news release dated July 18, 2001. Downloaded on Jan. 28, 2004, from <abortionbreastcancer.com/news071801.htm.com/press_release_71801.htm>.

39. Andy Steiner, "Cause or Cure?" *womenspress.com,* Minnesota Women's Press Inc., Feb. 12, 2003. Downloaded on Jan. 20, 2004, from <www.womenspress.com/newspaper/2003/1824canc.html>.

40. Fallows, *Breaking the News:* 38.

41. "Impropaganda Review: A Rogues Gallery of Industry Front Groups and Anti-environmental Think Tanks," *PR Watch,* undated. Downloaded on Nov. 7, 2002, from <www.prwatch.org/improp/ddam.html>.

42. "Scandals: Cashing In on an Inside Story," *Time,* Sept. 29, 1986: 59.

43. "Smart Case Reporters Fired," *CBS News,* April 29, 2003. Downloaded on Jan. 28, 2004, from <www.cbsnews.com/stories/2003/04/29/national/printable551425.shtml>.

44. Scott Rosenberg, "Should Journalists and IPOs Mix?" *Salon.com,* July 27, 1999. Downloaded on Nov. 7, 2002, from <www.salon.com/tech/col/rose/1999/07/27/ipo_journalists>.

45. Trudy Lieberman, "Gimme! Freebies for Newsfolk in the World of High-tech," *Columbia Journalism Review,* January/February 1998: 45–49.

46. Robert Bolton, "Newspaper Journalists and Free Travel, and the Journalism of George Orwell," *The Media Report, ABC* (Australian Broadcasting Corp.) *Online,* July 29, 1999. Downloaded on Nov. 8, 2002, from <www.abc.net.au/rn/talks/8.30/mediarpt/stories/s40781.htm>.

47. Lieberman, "Gimme!"

48. The Associated Press, "Tabloid Writer Admits Copying Enquirer Story," *Houston Chronicle,* May 22, 2003: A-7.

49. "Member Code of Ethics 2000": 9.

50. *Behind the Lines,* WNET, Feb. 13, 1974.

51. Ellen Szita, "How ITT Purchased the Press: Background: A Weekend in Florida," *Media & Consumer,* October 1973: 8–11.

52. Elizabeth Austin, "All Expenses Paid: Exploring the Ethical Swamp of Travel Writing," *The Washington Monthly Online,* July/August 1999. Downloaded on Nov. 8, 2002, from <www.washingtonmonthly.com/features/1999/9907.austin.expenses.html>.

53. Ibid.

54. Tad Friend, "They Love You!" *The* (London) *Observer,* Dec. 8, 2002: OM-34, 37, 39–40, 42, 45. Available at <www.observer.co.uk/Print/0,3858,4563091,00.html>.

55. Ibid.

56. Gary Susman, "Tales of the Junket," *The* (London) *Guardian,* Oct. 5, 2001: Film-2–4, p. 4. Available at <film.guardian.co.uk/features/freaturepages/0,4120,563282,00.html>.

57. Richard P. Cunningham, "Using Deception to Get at the Truth," *Quill,* January 1987: 8–11, p. 8.

58. J.D. Lasica, "A Scorecard for Net News Ethics," *Online Journalism Review,* April 4, 2002. Downloaded on Nov. 9, 2002, from <www.ojr.org/ojr/ethics/1017782140.php>.

59. Edmund B. Lambeth, *Committed Journalism: An Ethic for the Profession,* 2nd ed. (Bloomington: Indiana University Press, 1992).

60. Ted Conover, *Newjack: Guarding Sing Sing* (New York: Random House, 2000). See Conover's Web site at <www.tedconover.com/newjackreviews.html>.

61. See Veronica Rusnak, "Participatory Reporting—Trusting Guts," *Poynteronline,* Nov. 20, 2002. Downloaded on June 19, 2003, from <www.poynter.org/content/content_view.asp?id=10673>.

62. Kent R. Middleton, Robert Trager and Bill F. Chamberlin, *The Law of Public Communication,* 5th ed. (New York: Longman, 2001): 182.

63. Bill Berkowitz, "Partnering With Pakistan," *WorkingForChange,* Nov. 5, 2002. Downloaded on Nov. 7, 2002, from <www.workingforchange.com/printitem.cfm?itemid=14031>.

64. "Ethics in the Age of Digital Photography," National Press Photographers Association, undated. Downloaded on Nov. 7, 2002, from <www.nppa.org/services/bizpract/eadp/eadp2.html>.

65. Elizabeth Jensen, "NBC-sponsored Inquiry Calls GM Crash on News Program a Lapse in Judgment," *The Wall Street Journal,* March 23, 1993: B-10.

66. Mitchell Zuckoff, "Thou Shalt Not Break Thy Promise: Supreme Court Rules on Betraying Sources' Anonymity," *Fineline: The Newsletter on Journalism Ethics,* July/August 1991: 2, 4.

67. Bernstein and Woodward, *All the President's Men:* 36.

68. Philip Patterson, "Public Relations' Role in the Alar Scare," in Patterson and Wilkins, *Media Ethics:* 67–71.

69. Deni Elliott, "A Case of Need," in Patterson and Wilkins, *Media Ethics:* 72–74.

70. Daniel J. Boorstin, *The Image: A Guide to Pseudo-events in America* (New York: Vintage, 1992): 9.

71. Michael Ryan, "A Publisher Employs a Cop," in Patterson and Wilkins, *Media Ethics:* 95–96.

72. Deni Elliott, "How to Handle Suicide Threats," *FineLine: The Newsletter on Journalism Ethics,* October 1989: 1, 8. Available at <www.journalism.Indiana.edu/Ethics/threatsu.html>.

73. Ibid.

74. Jim Fisher, "A Once-proud Newspaper Becomes the Micron Statesman," *Lewiston* (Idaho) *Morning Tribune,* Feb. 13, 2000: F-3.

75. Stephen Johnson, "Charges Sought Against Reporter: Trespassing Alleged at Stockman's House," *Houston Chronicle,* June 7, 1996: A-43.

C H A P T E R   1 5

CAREERS

Evaluations, Expectations and Goals

If you've ever bought a new car, you know it's hard to cope with all the choices in styles, colors, models, options, prices and financing. It would be easier if dealers sold a one-size-fits-all model. The same is true when you try to choose and prepare for a writing career. As with cars, there is no one-size-fits-all educational model. Educators and professional communicators have tried for nearly 140 years to find that singular model, and the debate, argument and discussion have produced considerable rancor—and some progress—over the years.

The seeds of journalism education were planted in 1869 when Washington and Lee University offered a "rather meager course of journalism instruction."[1] The first newspaper printing class was established in 1873 at Kansas State University,[2] and the first journalism "school" was established for women in 1886 by Martha Louise Rayne in Detroit.[3] The first university journalism school was created in 1908 at the University of Missouri.[4]

The push to segment journalism programs into public relations, advertising, broadcast journalism, telecommunication, media studies and other subspecialties gained momentum after World War II, when universities moved aggressively to emphasize professional education.[5]

During all that time, educators, students and professionals argued about how students should be educated. One observer said more than 80 years ago that "Of all subjects that have recently found a place in the college curriculum, probably none is more intensely concerned in working out a pedagogical [teaching] method than journalism."[6]

The wise student will learn at least two things from the confusion: (1) It's important for you to take a hands-on approach to college so you are ready for a

Potential journalists practiced their research and writing skills during a 1911–1912 class at Columbia University's School of Journalism. Early journalism schools established a foundation for modern media writing programs.

profession, citizenship and a life when you graduate, and (2) you need some knowledge to help you plan your college career. This chapter should help you get started.

SKILLS AND CONCEPTS, ARTS AND SCIENCES

You need to understand that journalism educators, students and professionals have argued almost from the beginning about the proper mix of skills, concepts and liberal arts and sciences coursework.

Skills and Concepts

Skills content refers to the practical, functional knowledge students need for entry-level jobs (Chapter 4). This includes, for instance, learning the fundamentals of editing videotape and news copy, producing computer-based, multimedia productions; writing for print and digital media; developing Web pages; designing advertisements; taking photographs; and conducting public relations campaigns (Figure 15.1).[7]

Conceptual courses (the sometimes dreaded "theory" courses) are organized around traditional academic themes (research, history, theory, literature, law, aesthetics, criticism and ethics) or around less-traditional academic themes (critical theory, gender issues, postcolonial studies, cultural studies, literary theory and

FIGURE 15.1 ENTRY-LEVEL WRITING AND EDITING TASKS

Magazines

- Captions for graphs and tables
- Copy reading
- Cutlines for photographs
- Feature stories
- Headlines
- Memoranda
- Proofreading
- Research reports
- Short blurbs and teasers

Radio

- Audio scripts
- Business news
- Community relations releases
- Copy-editing
- Feature stories
- Obituaries
- Public service announcements
- Spot news
- Weather reports

Television

- Copy-editing
- Captions for graphs and tables
- Feature stories
- Public service announcements
- Spot news
- Audio-video scripts

World Wide Web

- Captions for graphs and tables
- Cutlines for photographs
- Feature stories
- Spot news
- Audio-video scripts
- Copy-editing

Newspapers

- Captions for graphs and tables
- Copy-editing
- Cutlines for photographs
- Feature stories
- Headlines
- Obituaries
- Spot news

Public Relations

- Booklets and publicity materials
- Brochures
- Captions for graphs and tables
- Company publications
- Cutlines for photographs
- Employee newsletters
- Feature stories
- Fund-raising letters
- Headlines
- Memoranda
- News releases
- Proofread copy
- Public service announcements
- Research reports
- Speeches
- Stockholder reports
- Video scripts
- Web site copy

revisionist history). The ability to think critically is one of the key conceptual skills that many educators want you to learn, and they think you can learn them best in conceptual courses (Chapter 1).[8]

Some critics worry that the balance between skills and conceptual content is skewed toward skills content. They would like to see a different balance. They argue that faculty must reject a view that "would limit our priorities to that of entry-level media job prep schools designed to meet every passing need from supplying cheap labor to recruiting minorities."[9] They are concerned that programs stress skills too much when they establish new tracks and sequences to reflect new media delivery systems (the Web) and occupational subspecialties (Web writer).[10]

Other critics argue that some programs emphasize conceptual content too much. They criticize pressures that "promote removing journalism education as a separate academic discipline and merging it into communication courses designed not to prepare journalists—people with a mission to stimulate public discourse and serve the public interest—but to prepare generic communicators who could be hired to serve any interests."[11]

Many educators have moved beyond this argument. They are in fact integrating skills content and conceptual content. More than 90 percent of administrators in one study, for instance, agreed that teachers should try to ensure a balance between skills-based courses (e.g., writing releases, editing videotape, interviewing) and conceptual courses (e.g., literature, ethics, critical-cultural studies).[12] Most of the administrators also said educators must teach higher-order thinking skills, that critical thinkers are better professionals and that their programs manage to teach those skills.[13]

Still, the Columbia University Graduate School of Journalism, one of the most prestigious programs in the country, was described by one who should know, Michael Janeway, as a trade school. "They don't invite students to take part in other schools [within the University]. They don't ask them to read. It just replicates a newsroom. ... It should be more content-oriented," Janeway, director of the School's National Arts Journalism Program, was quoted as saying.[14]

Liberal Arts and Sciences

The exposure of journalism and public relations students to content outside their disciplines is critical for a couple of reasons:

- A broad background is essential if students (and professionals) are to perform ethically and effectively. "Information does not simply appear in the world, to be automatically transferred through media to readers. Reporters, magazine writers, and other media producers have to *learn* about their subjects and tell others what they have learned."[15] The liberal arts and sciences provide a good foundation for professionals who want and need to learn about the problems and issues they write about.

It's difficult to write a news release about an effort to clone a sheep if the writer has no science background or to write a news report about rising gasoline prices if the writer knows nothing about economics. It is difficult to work in a multinational, multicultural organization—as many public relations professionals do—if one knows little about other cultures and cannot speak other languages.[16] The foundation for this knowledge lies in the liberal arts and science classes on every college campus.

■ Students who possess higher-order skills (including critical thinking ability) and who have studied multiple disciplines (geography, politics, biology, psychology) are likely to be more effective and useful citizens than those who are narrowly educated. Obviously, media professionals can be responsible citizens in two ways: as professionals (when they produce stories that expose government corruption, for example) and as private citizens (when they cast votes).

A difficulty with requiring liberal arts and sciences classes is that some aren't worth a student's time. They contribute little or nothing to a student's personal or professional growth, and they are offered primarily because the faculty member offering the course is interested in the content. The assumption that just *any* liberal arts and sciences course is appropriate and valuable for students is, in fact, incorrect.[17] Unfortunately, research suggests that only half of the journalism/mass communication programs monitor their students' courses outside the field of communication.[18]

WHAT IT MEANS

How is all this relevant to what is, for you, the most important question: What do you want to do when you graduate, and how can you get there? Well, understanding the difference between skills and conceptual content and the importance of the liberal arts and sciences is useful as you decide which journalism/mass communication program is right for you and as you try to find ways to make your college experience the best it can be.

Select a Program

Some programs—appropriately, if they make their missions clear and public—are designed to educate newspaper journalists. While they give a nod to public relations, advertising, Web and broadcast students, that is not their primary mission. If you want to study public relations, you might find a better choice. If you want to learn to be a good newspaper journalist, you probably don't want to enroll in a media studies program, unless you have sound newspaper experience.

It's important also to analyze the details of a curriculum in a program you're considering. Some of the better programs offer a balance *between* skills and conceptual courses, a balance *within* courses between concepts and skills, a preponderance of courses within the liberal arts and sciences and a limited number of courses in journalism/mass communication. Most educators and professionals seem to agree that students must be numerate and literate and have a good understanding of history, law, aesthetics, research, ethics, theory and criticism. These elements should be evident in any curriculum.

Carve Out a Curriculum

You will likely have to take a certain number of required classes, but most programs afford students the opportunity to select courses and educational experiences that will help them make the most of their college experiences. You would be wise to take advantage of these opportunities.

Background Is Important

A student who has written stories for a news Web site or news releases for a corporation might not even major in journalism/mass communication—as long as the Web and corporate experiences were challenging and educational. Some experiences aren't worth much because some editors aren't worth much.

A student with sound professional experience might major in a discipline that he or she might like to cover one day as a journalist or public relations person. A student who wants to work in the public relations office at a genetics research laboratory, and who has a talent for science, might major in biology, for example. Or the student might major in journalism/mass communication and take the maximum number of conceptual courses and the minimum number of skills courses. This would make sense, even though it might not fit with a given program's definition of the ideal curriculum.

A student with no background in mass communication or journalism has to make some tough choices early on. Most programs offer specializations in public relations, advertising, magazine writing, journalism (broadcast, Web, print) and a few others, and students typically need to decide which area to study. This is not a life-or-death decision, particularly in a program that stresses cross-platform education with minimal specialization. Some students follow the newspaper sequence, graduate and then work in public relations, or they write newspaper reports and then broadcast them on camera. Still, it's a good idea to make the best decision you can.

Instructors in your classes can help you, and you can read newspapers and Web content, watch newscasts and read releases from corporations and nonprofit organizations. You can type *careers in* —— in Google's search box and find a great deal of good information from government sources, foundations and scholarly and professional organizations (see also the box "Web Sites for Career Information").

WEB SITES FOR CAREER INFORMATION

Here are some organizations, with Web addresses, that are good sources of information about media careers, internships and jobs. You should visit them often. And don't visit only the *one* that seems to fit your current career interest best. Even if you're interested in a career in broadcast news, you might find something at the American Society of Newspaper Editors' site that will change your life.

Accrediting Council on Education in Journalism and Mass Communications:
    <www.ku.edu/~acejmc/FULLINFO.HTML>

American Business Media: <www.americanbusinessmedia.com/education/bpef/
    scholarship.htm>

American Society of Newspaper Editors: <www.asne.org/kiosk/careers/index.htm>

Association of Women in Communications: <www.womcom.org/indexNS6.html>

Broadcast Education Association: <www.beaweb.org>

Broadcast Media and Journalism Career Guide: <www.khake.com/page43.html>

Dow Jones Newspaper Fund: <djnewspaperfund.dowjones.com/fund/default.asp>

Institute of Public Relations: <www.ipr.org.uk/About/aboutframeset.htm>

International Association of Business Communicators: <www.iabc.com>

Magazine Publishers of America: <www.magazine.org/jobfair/career_resources.html>

National Association of Broadcasters: <www.nab.org/bcc>

Newspaper Association of America: <www.naa.org/sectionpage.ctm?sid=84>

The Newspaper Guild: <www.newsguild.org>

New York New Media Association: <www.nynma.org>

Professional Development Workshops: <sunsite.stanford.org/SOLAR/saa/ProEd>

Public Relations Society of America:
    <www.prsa.org/_Resources/profession/careeroverview.asp?ident>

Radio-Television News Directors Association & Foundation:
    <www.rtnda.org/jobs/default.asp>

Society of Professional Journalists: <www.spj.org>

William Stanek's Internet Job Center: <www.tvpress.com/jobs>

Choose Courses Carefully

It's a good idea to seek a reasonable balance between skills and conceptual courses. If you take only skills courses, you might not develop fully the research and critical thinking skills that are essential to a good media professional. If you take only conceptual courses, you won't be able to get a job—or if you get one, you won't know how to do it. It is unlikely that you will run into a faculty member who will try to persuade you to take *only* skills or *only* conceptual courses, but if you do, politely decline the advice.

Exercise care in picking courses, for you probably should not take more than, say, a dozen courses (roughly 30 percent) in journalism/public relations. Don't waste any of them. Read course descriptions carefully and talk to instructors. If one course sounds a great deal like one you've already had, don't take it. You might get a good grade, but you're wasting precious hours.

Be careful also in picking liberal arts and science courses, some of which aren't very helpful to the novice media professional.[19] You want to seek a mix of courses that interest you and that help you become a good citizen and a good writer. Happily, the two usually go hand in hand. Given the nature of media writing, whatever interests you and makes you a good citizen is likely to make you a good professional.

If you are interested in science, for example, you might take four courses (a minor in many universities) in microbiology and some in general science. You would be well qualified on graduation for a public relations job in a health organization or for a reporting job covering science. You could do the same whether your interest is in computer science, education, anthropology, political science or anything else in your university.

SET GOALS

So when you get to the end of the road—when you graduate—what do you want to look like? And more important, what will you have to sell a potential employer? You have to answer that question yourself, but it helps to know what potential employers look for. If you've worked at all, you know that much of the employment game depends on luck. You interview for a job the day after someone else does, so you miss the opportunity. You've had an experience that another person hasn't had, so you get the job.

You can do some things as a student, however, that will tip the scale in your favor. Luck is still part of the mix, but it's a smaller part. Here are some things that can help.

Develop Writing Skill

Excellent writing ability is *the* skill that professionals in all facets of the media (Web, print and broadcast journalism, magazine writing and public relations) must have. This entire book is about developing writing skills, so we won't repeat that discussion. We will remind you, however, of the following essential points:

- The fundamentals of the English language (grammar, punctuation and spelling) and style are essential to good writing, but total familiarity with the basics is just the foundation for good writers.

- Critical thinking skill is essential. You have to know how to use the research skills outlined in this book. To reach your potential, you must know how to collect, analyze, interpret and report information so your readers, listeners and viewers can understand it.

- The objective approach is important. Writers who try to adopt the objective approach are skeptical of authority; dedicated to accuracy, completeness, precision and clarity; creative; consistent in making strategic decisions; fair and impartial; unwilling to support any political, social or economic interests; honest about their own preferences and idiosyncrasies; and willing and able to use analytic and interpretative skills where appropriate.

- You can't write insightfully and usefully if you don't understand the political, cultural, social, ethical, legal and economic context within which you work. You must understand your own environment and the topics you write about. This means, too, that you understand the importance of sound information in a democratic society and you appreciate the dangers of polluting the information stream.

- The communication context within which you work affects everything you do. Some elements of that context militate against excellence in communication, while other elements require only the very best. Understanding these elements can help you do better work.

- It's important to strive continuously to reach new levels of competence and creativity. This requires that you read constantly and that you write constantly. It takes practice, practice, practice.

Develop Sensitivity

Most power brokers in relatively open (democratic) and in relatively closed (authoritarian) societies have vested interests in supporting the status quo, for they want to continue exercising whatever power they have for as long as they can. They don't always see value in helping the disenfranchised and marginalized (the aged, the homeless, minorities, gays, lesbians, the disabled, the young) participate in cultural processes.[20] It would be unrealistic and untruthful to argue that media organizations never share these views, for the evidence is clear that they do.[21]

Media professionals have been an important part of an unprecedented push by many institutions during the past four decades to give voice to the marginalized and disenfranchised. The powerless simply did not appear much

Many media professionals are sensitive to the problems of the powerless. Lewis Hine, for instance, documented the horrors faced by child laborers, including this child spinner in 1909 North Carolina.

in mainstream media before the 1960s. Many newspapers refused to publish photographs of minority brides; a black or Hispanic man's picture was printed or broadcast only if he committed a crime; films featuring strong minority characters were the exception; all-white broadcast and print newsrooms were the norm; the marginalized essentially were not represented in corporate, not-for-profit and independent public relations departments and agencies; women were, with a few exceptions, consigned to a society page that fawned over the powerful or to doing grunt work for male public relations bosses; gays, lesbians and the disabled were off the screen.

Against this backdrop, today's society is wildly multicultural and the marginalized have been almost fully integrated. This is still not an accurate representation, of course, as much remains to be done. You can play an important role in bringing the marginalized into the mainstream—in making sure their voices are heard and they are treated with sensitivity and respect. (See also the box "Internalize Sensitivity.")

INTERNALIZE SENSITIVITY

Students and professionals need to ensure that their stories are based on information from a wide range of individuals—sources from varying races, religions, ethnic groups, social-economic backgrounds and cultures must be represented. Certainly the disabled must be included.

But diversity must be assured not because it is politically correct or because your editor expects you to be sensitive. Professionals who interview the disenfranchised and the marginalized just to fill quotas—to ensure that each powerless group has the "right" percentage of individuals represented—trivialize diversity.[22]

The best professionals make sure their sources are diverse because that is the right thing to do. Fairness demands that the news does not center exclusively on the privileged or the powerful, although their voices certainly must be heard.

Students and professionals must internalize sensitivity. They must talk and think critically about racism, privilege, sexism and powerlessness generally. A first step, according to Carol Liebler, a communications professor at Syracuse University, is for students and professionals to "look within, to better understand themselves before they try to understand others":

> As students explore their own identities, they can begin to recognize the filters and prejudices they bring to their own personal and professional interactions. Such introspection further enables them to explore the various layers or dimensions of diversity, to expand their consideration beyond race and gender.[23]

Diversity courses are offered at many universities, but they are not enough. You need to start early to develop genuine sensitivity. Here are some places to start:

- If Rigoberta Menchu comes to campus to talk about the plight of the Guatemalan Indians, go hear her speak. Make it a point to attend meetings, speeches and other events that are by and about the powerless.

- Try to write or produce for the campus media stories about those who are homeless, disabled, chemically dependent or otherwise powerless.

- Take courses that focus on the powerless—both now and in the past, in the United States and elsewhere, in inner city communities and in the suburbs.

(continued)

INTERNALIZE SENSITIVITY *(continued)*

- Try to listen to those among your friends and acquaintances who are members of marginalized groups. You might be surprised.

- Read books and watch movies about the experiences of the powerless. They can give you good information, and they can show you why the powerless feel as they do.

- Volunteer to tutor at a school for disadvantaged children, to distribute blankets to the homeless on a cold winter night, to help out at an animal rescue center (yes, animals are among society's least powerful members) or to ferry the powerless to and from the polls on election day.[24]

Get Some Experience

You may have run into the problem in an earlier job search: You need experience to get a job, but you need a job to get experience. Unless you know someone in the business, you're going to need to get some writing experience in college if you hope to land a decent entry-level job on graduation. Happily, there are many ways to get that experience. (See also the box "Theola Labbé on Internships" on page 458.)

Lyn Hunter, an editor for the *Berkeleyan* at the University of California, says she was surrounded by writers when she was a receptionist in the UC public affairs office. "I was really inspired by all the writing that was going on around me and asked the *Berkeleyan*'s managing editor if I could volunteer to write a story every now and then. I was able to contribute occasional stories and really enjoyed this type of work, but knew I would need more training to pursue a writing career."[25]

A college campus is a pretty good place to develop and to practice writing skills because a great deal of writing is done on a campus and not many people know how to do it well. The first stop is a campus newspaper, for every college has one. It doesn't matter if your ultimate goal is to write for Bill Gates at Microsoft or Peter Jennings at ABC News—or even to write the world's greatest novel. The campus newspaper is a good place to go first.

Every campus has a public relations (or public affairs) office, and they sometimes need help. If you want to work for *The* (London) *Times*, practice your skill at your campus public affairs office. Unless your editor is horrendous (in which case, quit), your writing will improve. Many campuses also have radio stations and Web sites that need volunteers. Check with them.

Students can learn a great deal about their chosen professions by listening to the professionals who frequently address university students. Here Sam Abell, a National Geographic photographer, mentors a graduate student at the University of Missouri School of Journalism.

Most mass communication professionals understand the importance of experience, as you'll learn if you listen to them talk for five minutes, and many are willing to help you get it. You can often land an internship through a professional or group. An internship is designed to give you experience. You might not be paid, but you might get academic credit. Or you might get paid, but not get academic credit (you really have a part-time job in this instance, not an internship—but it's just as good). If it's a good internship (or part-time job), take it even if you don't get paid or get credit. That's how important an internship is.

Check often with the Institute of Public Relations, American Society of Newspaper Editors, Public Relations Society of America, National Association of Broadcasters and other groups and organizations listed in Appendix G. They often can lead you to valuable internships. You can learn about internships through campus groups also as faculty, professionals and students meet to exchange information.

If you can do nothing more than write one article per semester for your campus newspaper, do it. Do whatever you can to get experience. You will take from the experience important skills that will impress a potential employer, and you will have a collection of stories (in a "string" book, portfolio, compact disc or videotape) that you have written. Research suggests this experience will help you find a job.[26]

THEOLA LABBÉ ON INTERNSHIPS

On the second day of my internship at the *Detroit Free Press*, I came in promptly at 10 a.m., read that day's newspaper, and the newspaper of our competitor (*The Detroit News*) at my desk, and tried to look busy. I knew I should have been asking for things to do—be aggressive!—but I still wasn't even sure where the bathroom was.

My editor, Bob Campbell, metro assignments editor, would soon solve my idleness. On his way to the 10:30 news meeting, he walked by my desk—Bob never ran—and uttered a few words about homeless people standing in line at the Joe to buy Wings tickets. Go down there, he said. I thought, The Joe ... Joe Louis Arena? Wings ... The Detroit Red Wings, the 1997 Stanley Cup champion hockey team currently in the Cup playoffs? I had never before set foot in Michigan, had been in Detroit for two days, and my editor expected me to piece it all together.

From late May to mid-August, I worked as a city desk intern at the *Detroit Free Press*, which is the city's leading daily, and has a daily circulation of about 375,000. I was one of three interns on the city desk in the downtown office, one of 12 interns total: two in features, one each at two of the suburban bureaus, and the rest in business, sports, photography, graphics, and web design. I wrote a story almost every day, about 50 stories total, and they were primarily hard news and breaking news stories. I once got paged early in the morning to cover a fire at a city landmark that was right around the corner from my apartment in downtown Detroit, a quiet city of high rises next to abandoned buildings. I spent a lot of time in district court following criminal cases. I helped out on big stories, like when the Wings won the Stanley Cup, and a really bad storm that ripped through the area in August, killing a young boy.

My internship experience solidified what I had learned in J-school, that I could report and write a story on a tight deadline. From my internship, I learned about news judgment—basically what constitutes a story. I was treated just like one of the staff, and for someone who had never worked at a newspaper before, I found the experience valuable and memorable.

So what happened at the sports arena? One of the homeless men asked me out, and I couldn't quite get a quote from the scalper.

Source: Theola S. Labbé, "Internship News: Life at the City Desk," *North Gate,* undated. Downloaded on April 24, 2003, from <journalism.Berkeley.edu/students/internlabbe.html>.

Theola S. Labbé was a journalism student at the University of California–Berkeley when she wrote this account of her internship at the *Detroit Free Press* for *North Gate*, a publication of the UCB Graduate School of Journalism. She works today at *The Washington Post*.

EXPECTATIONS

So why would any normal person seek a career in journalism or public relations? We all must answer that question for ourselves, and we need to have a realistic view of what a media career would be like. We discussed some of the upsides and downsides in this book, but here is a somewhat more formal statement of what you might expect.

It Feels Good

Many individuals seek media careers because they want to make a difference, and a media professional has a good chance to do that. It just feels good to get the right information to the right people at the right time—to help them cope with tragedy, uncertainty or disaster, as public relations professionals and journalists are sometimes called on to do. And it just feels good to right a wrong, as they also do from time to time.

There is no doubt that much of the world's population is better off than it was even 50 years ago. Freedom was extended in remarkable ways in many parts of the globe during the 20th century. Women; ethnic, religious and racial minorities; the disabled; nonconformists; and those who are just "different" were emancipated in many countries after centuries of oppression. Many societies moved to ensure that the fundamental human needs of the powerless were met. Media professionals had a large role in this movement.

But much remains to be done. More than 1 billion people have no access to clean water, and 2 billion have no access to sanitation facilities; 1.3 billion are breathing air that the World Health Organization considers unacceptable; hundreds of millions of farmers can't keep the soil fertile enough to support their crops; 20 percent of the globe's population consumes 85 percent of its income, while 80 percent lives on 15 percent. "The world's marine fisheries are grossly overexploited. Soils are eroding. Water is becoming scarcer. Deforestation is continuing."[27]

The opportunity to help solve some of these pressing problems through mass communication is extraordinary, for media professionals help collect and disseminate the facts, analyses and interpretations the world needs to confront its problems. Scientists, lawyers, politicians, educators and other professionals must be part of the process, but they need the help of journalists and public relations people if they are to overcome xenophobia, obscurity and self-interest—and if they are to promote tolerance and rational behavior successfully.[28]

It's Fun

Another reason for seeking a career in communication, of course, is that it's fun. It's fun to find information that nobody else has and to tell the world about it. It's fun to work in teams to solve problems and to help an organization you care about. It's fun to be good at what you do and to see reactions to what you produce. And it's fun to be part of a profession that offers so many different opportunities. If you get tired of writing news reports for a Web site, you have dozens of alternatives. If you can write well, the hard part will be deciding which option is best for you.

Jobs

Not all the news is good. Lee Becker's "Annual Survey of Journalism & Mass Communication Graduates" shows that graduates seeking media jobs did not have an easy time of it during the first three years of the 21st century. For example, 34.9 percent of bachelor's degree holders had no job offers on graduation in 2002, compared to 17.6 percent in 2000. "The average number of job offers held by graduates when they completed their studies in 2002 was 1.2, down from 1.6 a year earlier and down from 2.3 in 2000!"[29]

Only 63.3 percent of 2002 graduates held jobs within a year of graduation, compared to 66.3 percent in 2001 and 76.1 percent in 1999. Only half of the journalism and mass communication graduates in 2002 found work in communication. "Not since 1992 have so few of the graduates of the nation's journalism and mass communication programs found work in the field for which they studied and prepared."[30]

Job markets traditionally are fluid and can change from month to month. Students seeking careers in media writing need to monitor the economy and the job situation in mass communication. Current information is available at <www.grady.uga.edu/annualsurveys>.

Salaries

More bad news: Salaries in media writing are not the best on the planet—and they seldom are commensurate with the responsibility they entail. This is particularly true of entry-level salaries, which may pay less than some of the jobs students frequently get as waitresses and waiters (Figure 15.2).

Lee Becker's survey suggests that salaries and benefits for new media employees are not good and that they are better in some years than others. The median salary for all media jobs in 2001 and 2002, for example, was $26,000, which was nearly $1,000 less than the median salary in 2000.[31]

The median salary was progressively higher from 2000 to 2001 to 2002 for graduates seeking jobs in cable television news, but that was not the salary pattern for graduates seeking jobs in any other field. In fact, media salaries got progressively worse for graduates seeking jobs in daily newspapers and public relations. Graduates in only two fields—newsletters/trade publications and in Web writing—crashed the $30,000 barrier, but by 2002, graduates in both groups could expect median salaries of less than $30,000.

If you recall from Chapter 12 that median means half the numbers (in this case, salaries) are higher and half are lower than the median, you understand that some graduates make more than the median income. Those are the ones who learned how to write well and who managed to acquire media experience as students. Those earning less than the median possibly did not do either one.

Benefits also are important as graduates decide which jobs to seek. In 2002, 25.3 percent of employers paid the entire costs of medical coverage, compared to 30.4

FIGURE 15.2 MEDIAN ANNUAL SALARIES FOR BACHELOR'S DEGREE RECIPIENTS

	2000	2001	2002
All jobs	26,988	26,000	26,000
Daily newspapers	26,162	25,896	25,000
Weekly newspapers	22,880	24,000	22,000
Radio news	23,400	25,000	24,000
Television news	21,840	21,500	22,000
Cable television news	25,072	28,000	28,500
Advertising	26,988	26,500	27,000
Public relations	28,964	27,750	27,000
Consumer magazines	28,236	26,000	27,350
Newsletters, trade publications	27,976	30,000	28,665
World Wide Web	30,004	33,500	26,000

Source: Lee B. Becker, Tudor Vlad, Jisu Huh and Nancy R. Mace, "2002 Annual Survey of Journalism & Mass Communication Graduates: The Job Market Remains Bleak for Journalism and Mass Communication Graduates," *AEJMC News,* November 2003: 1, 4–6, p. 4; Lee B. Becker, Tudor Vlad, Jisu Huh and George L. Daniels, "200[1] Annual Survey of Journalism and Mass Communication Graduates: Job Market for Graduates Weakens Dramatically," *AEJMC News,* November 2002: 1, 4–6; and Lee B. Becker, Jisu Huh and Tudor Vlad, "2000 Annual Survey of Journalism and Mass Communication Graduates," *AEJMC News,* November 2001: 1, 6–7, 11. See also <www.grady.uga.edu/annualsurveys>.

percent in 2001; in 2002, 19.4 percent of employers paid for full dental coverage, compared to 22.3 percent in 2001; and 29.4 percent paid for maternity or paternity leaves, compared to 32.4 percent in 2001. The 2001 and 2002 percentages were lower overall than the 2000 figures.

Given the numbers, it's not surprising that many graduates said they wish they had majored in non-media careers. A total of 31.6 percent of 2002 graduates said they wish they had majored in something else, compared to 26.9 percent in 2001 and 22.7 percent in 2000. Overall job satisfaction dipped somewhat in the first years of the 21st century. In 2002, 30.2 percent said they were "very satisfied" with the jobs they got, compared to 28.9 percent in 2001 and 34.8 percent in 2000.

It's important to understand in making a career decision that entry-level media jobs don't pay much and that salaries (with benefits) can bounce all over the place from one year to the next. And it's important to understand that a first job is just that—a first job. If you are good and are prepared to move around, your salary will rise accordingly.

The focus in this book has been on entry-level positions. You will need good skills to get a first job and to succeed at it. However, there are many opportunities beyond those suggested here. Many professionals, for example, enter management, where they make more money as they develop additional skills.

An account executive in a consulting firm or someone working in a company's public relations department might earn $35,000 annually, for example. The public relations director for a medium or small organization can earn $25,000–$40,000, and the public relations director for a large organization can earn $40,000–$60,000. More experienced public relations persons can earn $75,000–$150,000, depending on responsibilities and organization size.[32]

A television news director in a medium-size market can earn roughly $68,000, while an assignment editor can earn roughly $32,000 and a news writer can earn $57,000. An assistant news director can earn $51,000; a news anchor can earn $62,000; and a correspondent can earn $30,000. A radio news director can earn $22,000 at a small station and $58,000 at a large station. The range for a radio news reporter is from $18,000 to $34,000.[33]

The editor of a small daily newspaper earns roughly $46,000–$49,000; the managing editor makes roughly $40,000–$48,000; the news editor earns roughly $32,000–$38,000; the city editor earns $34,000–$39,000; and a copy editor earns $23,000–$28,000. The editor of a magazine earns between $64,000 and $102,000. The range for a managing editor is $41,000 to $82,000, and the range for a copy editor is $27,000 to $37,000. The staff editor of a Web publication can earn roughly $25,000–$42,000; the managing editor can earn $39,000–$66,000; and a senior editor can earn $43,000 to $72,000.[34]

Salary estimates are not accurate, and they vary wildly by organization size. But the point is that you aren't stuck with an entry-level salary forever. How long it takes you to reach the higher levels depends on how good you are and how willing you are to work.

Stress

Stress is part of life and part of any job. But stress is more common and more intense in media work than in most other professions. A primary source of stress is the almost ever-present deadline. The audience that tunes in to the *CBS Evening News With Dan Rather* is not going to wait for a journalist who isn't ready to go. "Wait just a second!" is unacceptable.

A media professional often must rely on someone else as he or she tries to meet a crushing deadline. You've got to talk to a critical source before you can complete a story; a deadline is 30 minutes away; and the source is in a meeting. It's 9:50 p.m.; a television journalist has got to report an important decision by the city council on the 10 p.m. news; the vote is in progress; and some council members take time to explain their votes. A company has accidentally released a potentially dangerous chemical into the air; it's 5:25 p.m.; the local news ends at 5:30 p.m.; people are waiting for a public relations professional to report what the chemical is and what people must do to mitigate its damage; and the writer is waiting on the company chemist for a report. These are stressful situations.

The stress is worse because your "product" is out there for the world to evaluate. It's crude, but sometimes true: A surgeon buries his or her mistake, but a media professional's mistake is there for all to see. If the professional works for a print medium or the Web, the mistake might be distributed (by disgruntled readers) by electronic and traditional mail to half the planet. There is no hiding. And if the mistake is bad enough, you and your organization might get sued (Chapter 13).

A public relations professional who does not report all the facts about his or her company's role in an environmental accident might feel considerable stress, even when he or she has acted at the direction of the chief executive officer. This is a predicament for writers who work for organizations that define their interest as more important than the public interest, particularly when the two conflict. It is stressful to behave in ways that you think are unethical, and it's even more stressful when you know the odds are good that you will be caught.

There is a media job for you, even if you don't like extreme pressure. But there aren't many places where you can avoid stress altogether.

SOME JOB-HUNTING TIPS

One of the nice things about seeking a media job in the 21st century is that so much help is available. You'll want to take advantage of the many resources available, but here is a short list that will help get you started:

■ Be sure you have something to sell on graduation. The most important thing is writing, research and critical thinking ability—followed by professional experience and awareness of and sensitivity toward the world. Of course, a degree in journalism or public relations will help a good deal in the job search.

■ Understand why you want to have a career in communication and be able to articulate clearly and precisely what kind of work you want to devote your life to and why you want to do that. If you don't know what you want to do, you can't convince a potential employer to hire you.

■ Take advantage of the many job banks available (Appendix G). Spend a few hours from time to time browsing the job listings. That way you'll know what employers are looking for, and you can fill any gaps in your background before you graduate. If you note that advertisements for public relations writers are starting to suggest that applicants should know how to use Go Live, a program for creating Web pages, you have time to learn that software.

■ Be sure you tailor your "what I want to do in life" statement to the job for which you are applying. One statement seldom fits all opportunities, particularly if you graduate from a program that demanded cross-platform education. You might be able to handle a job in a newspaper, on the Web or in public relations, but one statement is unlikely to impress all three kinds of editors.

LAURA MERCER ON LETTERS, RESUMES

The following are tried-and-true reminders about how to write an effective cover letter and resume along with true-life examples I rescued from the recycling bin.

BE STRAIGHTFORWARD

"In an effort to be expeditious, I have enclosed my portfolio for your review." This writer clearly was not being expeditious; otherwise she would have eliminated the unnecessary introductory clause.

"I maintain the ability to speak Spanish at an educated level," was a convoluted way to say, "I am fluent in Spanish." Cover letters and resumes should get to the point quickly and avoid overblown claims and flowery language.

DON'T BE BLINDED BY TECHNOLOGY

I'm seeing more simple errors and typos than ever before, presumably because candidates are relying too much on technology to catch problems instead of good old-fashioned proofreading.

All the electronic spelling and grammar checkers in the world won't take the place of reading carefully yourself, and asking several other people to proof the document after you. Would you send out your company's press release without someone carefully reviewing it?

DON'T BE TOO CREATIVE

Creative approaches to your job search should be carefully considered. Sometimes demonstrating creativity can get out of hand, like the time a candidate arrived unannounced in my office to deliver a singing telegram. Unless you know the person who will receive the correspondence, it's better to look before you leap.

Finally, even if you are great, remember that humility goes a long way. One young woman forgot that when she wrote: "Attached is a copy of my resume for your viewing pleasure."

Source: Laura Mercer, "A Common-sense Guide to Letters and Resumes," *Public Relations Tactics,* May 2003: 11. Downloaded on May 23, 2003, from <www.prsa.org/_Publications/magazines/0503news.asp>.

Laura Mercer is a senior vice president–public relations director for PriceMcNabb, a large independent firm in the Southeast.

MARY CUSICK ON A FIRST JOB

After graduation, there will be pressure to get to work. Before you accept your first job, use your networking skills to get a feel for the environment. If a situation doesn't feel right, you don't connect with your future boss, or you can't find someone who sings his or her praises, don't take the job.

This will be hard. Your parents might not totally understand. But if you don't work for someone who is highly regarded and well-respected, you won't be able to learn the right things and it will be tough to earn respect for yourself. Ultimately, you won't be as competitive in the marketplace. You never get a second chance at a first job.

Source: Richard Weiner, "Advice for This Year's PR Graduates: Succinct Wisdom Useful to Novices and Everyone," *Public Relations Tactics,* May 2003: 10–11, p. 10. Downloaded on May 23, 2003, from <www.prsa.org/_Publications/magazines/0503news.asp>.

Mary L. Cusick is a senior vice president for Investor Relations and Corporate Communications for Bob Evans Farms Inc.

- Check with your career counseling center when you write your resume, for counselors will have many good suggestions. Above all, however, be sure your resume has *no* errors, that it is an honest account of what you've done and that it is clear, concise and to the point. If you fail on any one of these points, you'll not get past the first cut.

- Be flexible. Your goal might be to work for *Salon.com* or for Peter Jennings or for the largest public relations firm in Chicago. But you might need to take a detour as you move toward your professional goal. You might have to hone your skills on a medium-size daily newspaper before you even get a chance at *Salon.com*. Be prepared to do that. And be prepared to move on when the time comes.

YOUR RESPONSIBILITY IS . . .

- To think carefully and deeply about whether a career in broadcast, print or Web journalism or in public relations is right for you. Read as much as you can about the advantages and disadvantages of a media career, and talk to veterans who know what it's really like.

■ To think about what you can do as a media professional to contribute to society—to have a positive impact on political, cultural, social and economic processes.

■ To start preparing now if a media career seems right. You must read, write, think; you need to take the right classes and do well in them; and you must practice, practice, practice. If you don't prepare now, you won't be ready when the time comes and you won't be as successful as you might otherwise be.

■ To develop exceptional writing skill. This means that you can use the language, think critically, collect information effectively and efficiently from a wide variety of sources and present information accurately, compellingly, clearly and concisely.

■ To think about formal communication education in nonbinary terms. You should select classes that will give you the skills *and* the theoretical perspectives you need to succeed. It's a good idea to take as many classes in the liberal arts and sciences as you can. It helps to be able to use *all* the tools and *all* the approaches if you are to achieve maximum success.

■ To complete at least *one* internship successfully. Consider a part-time job in any medium (even if it's not the one you ultimately want to work in).

■ To learn how to be sensitive to the needs, problems and interests of the powerless and to include their views when you produce stories. You should take positive steps in college to internalize sensitivity.

■ To pick your first job with extreme care, for that will set the tone for the rest of your career.

■ To understand that your first job is not your last job. Salaries are better and the responsibility is greater as you gain experience in your field. Your opportunities are essentially unlimited.

NOTES

1. De Forest O'Dell, *The History of Journalism Education in the United States* (New York: Teachers College, Columbia University, 1935): 2.
2. Walter Wilcox, "Historical Trends in Journalism Education," *Journalism Educator*, 14:3 (1959): 2–7, 32, p. 5.
3. James Stanford Bradshaw, "Mrs. Rayne's School of Journalism," *Journalism Quarterly*, 60:3 (1983): 513–517, 579; and Linda Steiner, "Construction of Gender in Newsreporting Textbooks: 1890–1990, *Journalism Monographs*, 135 (October 1992): 7.
4. Tom Dickson, *Mass Media Education in Transition: Preparing for the 21st Century* (Mahwah, N.J.: Erlbaum, 2000): 12.
5. Burton J. Bledstein, *The Culture of Professionalism: The Middle Class and the Development of Higher Education in America* (New York: Norton, 1976), Chapter 3. See also James W. Carey, "A Plea for the University Tradition," *Journalism Quarterly*, 55:4 (1978): 846–855.

6. H.F. Harrington, "Teaching Journalism in a Natural Setting: An Application of the Project Method, *Educational Administration & Supervision,* 5:4 (1919): 197–206, p. 197.

7. Michael Ryan and Les Switzer, "Balancing Arts and Sciences, Skills, and Conceptual Content," *Journalism & Mass Communication Educator,* 56:2 (2001): 55–68.

8. Pamela J. Shoemaker, "Critical Thinking for Mass Communications Students," *Critical Studies in Mass Communication,* 10:1 (1993): 99–111; and Gerald Grow, "Higher-order Skills for Professional Practice and Self-direction," *Journalism Educator,* 45:4 (1991): 56–65.

9. Robert O. Blanchard, "Our Emerging Role in Liberal and Media Studies: How Do We Break the News to Media Professionals?" *Journalism Educator,* 43:3 (1988): 28–31, p. 28.

10. Ibid.

11. Betty Medsger, *Winds of Change: Challenges Confronting Journalism Education* (Arlington, Va.: The Freedom Forum, 1996): 5.

12. Ryan and Switzer, "Balancing Arts and Sciences."

13. Ibid.

14. Sharon Walsh and Piper Fogg, "Editing the Mission: Columbia's New President Wonders How a Journalism School Fits into a Research University," *The Chronicle of Higher Education,* Aug. 9, 2002: A-10, 11.

15. Grow, "Higher-order Skills for Professional Practice and Self-direction": 57.

16. Mark P. McElreath, *Managing Systematic and Ethical Public Relations* (Madison, Wis.: Brown & Benchmark, 1993), Chapter 11; Doug Newsom, Alan Scott and Judy VanSlyke Turk, *This Is PR: The Realities of Public Relations* (Belmont, Calif.: Wadsworth, 1993); Leonard Mogel, *Creating Your Career in Communications and Entertainment* (Sewickley, Penn.: GATF, 1998); Leonard Mogel, *Making It in Public Relations: An Insider's Guide to Career Opportunities,* 2nd ed. (Mahwah, N.J.: Erlbaum, 2002); "Careers in Public Relations: An Overview," Public Relations Society of America, February 2003. Downloaded on Feb. 17, 2003, from <www.prsa.org/_Resources/profession/careeroverview.asp?ident>.

17. Robert O. Blanchard and William G. Christ, *Media Education and the Liberal Arts: A Blueprint for the New Professionalism* (Hillsdale, N.J.: Erlbaum, 1993).

18. Ryan and Switzer, "Balancing Arts and Sciences."

19. Blanchard and Christ, *Media Education and the Liberal Arts.*

20. David Forgacs (ed.), *An Antonio Gramsci Reader: Selected Writings, 1916–1935* (New York: Schocken, 1988).

21. Ferdinand de Saussure, *Course in General Linguistics* (Charles Bally and Albert Sechehaye, eds.; Wade Baskin, trans.) (London: Philosophy Library, 1959).

22. Theodore L. Glasser, "Professionalism and the Derision of Diversity: The Case of the Education of Journalists," *Journal of Communication,* 42:2 (1992): 131–140.

23. Carol Liebler's comments are in "Has the Dream Stalled?" *Journalism & Mass Communication Educator,* 58:1 (2003): 20–23, p. 21.

24. Marie Hardin and Ann Preston, "Inclusion of Disability Issues in News Reporting Textbooks," *Journalism & Mass Communication Educator,* 56:2 (2001): 43–54; and Valerie Hyman, "Getting More Diversity in Content," The Poynter Institute for Media Studies, March 1996. Downloaded on Feb. 14, 2003, from <www.media-awareness.ca/eng/issues/minrep/journl/poynter.htm>.

25. Lyn Hunter, "Careers on Campus—Writing & Editing," University of California–Berkeley Career Center, April 12, 2002. Downloaded on Feb. 16, 2003, from <career.Berkeley.edu/Article/020412b/htm>.

26. Lee B. Becker, Gerald M. Kosicki, Thomas Engleman and K. Viswanath, "Finding Work and Getting Paid: Predictors of Success in the Mass Communications Job Market," *Journalism Quarterly,* 70:4 (1993): 919–933; Wilson Lowrey and Lee B. Becker, "The Impact of Technological Skill on Job-Finding Success in the Mass Communication Labor Market," *Journalism & Mass Communication Quarterly,* 78:4 (2001): 754–770.

27. Ismail Serageldin, "Perspectives: The Rice Genome: World Poverty and Hunger—the Challenge for Science," *Science,* April 5, 2002: 54–58, p. 54.

28. Ibid., p. 57.

29. Lee B. Becker, Tudor Vlad, Jisu Huh and Nancy R. Mace, "2002 Annual Survey of Journalism & Mass Communication Graduates: The Job Market Remains Bleak for Journalism and Mass Communication Graduates," *AEJMC News,* November 2003: 1, 4–6, p. 4. See also <www.grady.uga.edu/annualsurveys>.

30. Ibid., p. 5.

31. Ibid.

32. "Careers in Public Relations."

33. Mogel, *Creating Your Career in Communications and Entertainment.*

34. Ibid.

PART V

APPENDICES

APPENDIX A

SOME COMMON NEWS BEATS

Chances are good you'll be assigned to at least one beat when you get your first media job, and you're likely to cover a beat during your entire writing career. Beats typically are assigned on the basis of an organization's needs and the backgrounds of its writers. If you have a science background and you get a public relations job for a college, you may well cover biology, chemistry and other sciences, for example. If you have an economics background, a Web news site may have you cover labor.

The number of potential beats is quite large, for every organization in a reading or listening area could be a beat. Every department in a company is potentially a public relations person's beat. Some potential beats are more important than others, of course, and media writers tend to cover only the most important ones.

This list of potential beats is not comprehensive. National and international beats are not included, for example, because most organizations don't have the resources to staff faraway bureaus. Only the largest journalism and public relations organizations have such resources. Many of the potential beats that are listed could be divided. For example, professional sports could be divided into soccer, baseball, basketball and more.

The beats that journalism and public relations organizations create and cover depend on local needs, and these can vary widely. Many New England newspapers feature news from ski and winter sports beats, for example, while many Nevada newspapers feature reports from casino beats.

Business
Corporations
Criminal behavior
Economy
Finance, markets
Government regulation
Retail
Small business
Utilities

Civil Rights
Activist organizations
Affirmative action
Minority rights
Violations
Voting rights

Consumer Affairs
Better Business Bureau
Complaints
Credit counseling
Hot line

Courts
Appeals
  State
  Federal
Civil
  Municipal
  State
  Federal
Criminal
  Municipal
  State
  Federal

Education
Colleges, universities
Education boards
Finances
Public schools
School boards

Entertainment
Art
Books
Dining
Movies
Music
Television, radio
Theater
Travel

Government
City
  Agencies
  City council
  Departments
  Manager
  Mayor
County
  Agencies
  Commissioners
Federal
  Agencies
  Executive
  Congress
State
  Agencies
  Governor
  Legislature

Labor
Employment
Labor-management
Occupational safety
Salaries, benefits
Strikes
Unions

Military
Budget
Installations
Mortality
National Guard
U.S. Armed Services
Weapons

Politics
Campaigns
Candidates
Elections
Polls
Religion
Social issues
Voting

Public Safety
Attorneys general
City police
County sheriff
Highway patrol
Homeland security
Jails, prisons
Parole boards
Private security
Search, rescue

Recreation
Boating
Community sports
Facilities
Fishing programs
Fitness
Hunting
Parks
Running, walking, skiing
Youth programs

Religion
Churches
Education
Moral issues
Organizations
Personalities
Radio-television
Social, political activism
Theology

Science
Disease
Environment
Health
Hospitals, clinics
Medicine
Natural science
Physical science
Social science
Technology

Social Services
Adoptions
Agencies
Animal control
Animal rescue
Child abuse
Elder care
Housing
Spousal abuse
Substance abuse
Youth services

Sports
Community
Finances
Intercollegiate
Olympics
Professional
Public school
Senior leagues
Youth sports

Style
Decorating
Fashion
Furnishings
Products
Remodeling

Weather
Forecasts
Storms
Trends

A P P E N D I X B

SELECTED RULES
FOR ENGLISH USAGE

The most concise book of English usage is daunting. Some of the longer, more complex, guides seem impossible. But a communication professional simply *must* have a thorough knowledge of grammar, spelling and punctuation. This appendix is a good start if you want to learn these fundamentals, for it lists many of the more common mistakes in writing. The serious student should memorize all of these rules and then start learning—or relearning—the rules in any good text.

Adjective: 15, 17, 29, 40, 51

Adverb: 15, 16, 60

Affect-effect: 55

Agreement: 5, 9, 21

Appositive: 18

As-like: 25

Between-among: 59

Clause: 24–29, 53, 54

Collective nouns: 8, 9

Colon: 42, 50

Comma: 18, 26–28, 41, 44–46

Conjunction: 52

Contraction: 48, 60

Dash: 50

Farther-further: 56

Fragment: 1

Gender: 21, 23

Hyphen: 16, 49

Imply-infer: 58

Infinitive: 38

Less-fewer: 57

Lie-lay: 39

Modifier: 12–17

Noun: 4, 6–11, 14, 16–20, 25, 51, 55

Number: 4, 5, 21

Parallel construction: 51

Participle: 40

Period: 41, 50

Possessive: 11, 32, 33, 48, 60

Predicate: 1, 3, 5, 24, 46

Pronoun: 14, 19–22, 25, 29–33, 53

Question mark: 43

Quotation: 41–43

Referent (antecedent): 20, 21, 29

Run-on sentence: 46

Semicolon: 42, 47, 50

Sexism: 21, 22

Subject: 1–3, 5, 24, 46, 60

Tense: 35–37

That-which: 31, 53, 54

There-their-they're: 60

Verb: 4, 8, 9, 15, 34–40, 55, 60

Who-whom: 30

(1) Every sentence *must* have a subject and predicate, unless there is an *excellent* reason why not. A fragment is a phrase that has either no subject or no predicate, as in *full white box.*

(2) The subject of a sentence is what the sentence is about; it tells who or what performs the action of the verb, as in **The neighbor *brought the tools.*** Sometimes the subject is a compound, as in **Joy and Beth *were cleared of the charges.***

(3) The predicate tells what the subject is or is doing, as in **The *meeting* was *too long*** or **The *dog* growled *at the man.***

(4) Number indicates whether a noun or verb refers to one individual or object or to more than one.

(5) The subject and predicate must agree in number, as in **The *media are generally unbiased.* The *media is generally unbiased*** is wrong. This can be complicated in some usages, so writers must be careful. Compound subjects require plural predicates.

(6) A proper noun—the name of a specific person, animal, thing or place—is almost always capitalized, as in **The *car's name was* Destiny.** A noun may be a word or group of words, as in **United States of America.**

(7) A common noun is the name of a class of animals, persons, things or places, as in **The *car sped down the* highway.** Use lowercase.

(8) When a collective noun refers to a group or collection as a whole, it requires a singular verb, as in **The *school* band has won *its division.***

(9) When a collective noun refers to the individuals in a group, it requires a plural verb, as in **The *Cardinals* have *played well.***

(10) The plural of nouns ending in *ch, s, sh, ss, tch, x, z* or *zz* is created by adding *es,* as in **All the Henry Brookses *in the state were checked out.***

(11) The possessive case indicates ownership. Simply add an apostrophe and an *s* to a singular noun to indicate ownership, as in **Judy's *book.*** If the noun ends in *s,* or if it is plural, add only the apostrophe, as in **James' *house, the* boys' *baseball field.***

(12) A modifier is a word or group of words that describes or qualifies another word, as in **The *anchor performed* wonderfully.**

(13) Misplaced modifiers are words (modifiers) that are placed in ways that misdirect or obscure meaning, as does the sentence **Bobby *saw a car* in a showroom *he liked.*** The correct version is **Bobby *saw a car he liked* in a showroom.** He liked the car, not the showroom.

(14) A modifier must refer logically and clearly to a pronoun or noun that is modified. Dangling modifiers must be avoided: Write **Walking *along the highway,* we admired *the flowers,*** rather than **Walking *along the highway, the flowers were admired*** (probably because flowers can't walk along a street).

(15) An adverb—which usually modifies an adjective, verb or another adverb—typically specifies how much, when, where or how, as in **The *crook turned* slowly *and pointed the rifle.***

(16) Compound modifiers preceding nouns must be linked with hyphens except when using the adverb *very,* as in **know-it-all** *attitude* or *a* **very** *good time.* Do not use the hyphen when the adverb ends in *ly,* as in **an easily** *remembered rule.* Avoid using *very.*

(17) An adjective is a modifier that describes or limits a noun. They generally should be avoided, except in attribution, as in **President** *Sandra Smith spoke to the group.*

(18) An appositive is a word or phrase used to explain a noun, as in *John Dunn,* **director of the program,** *spoke today.* It is easy to forget that second comma and writers should always check.

(19) A pronoun is a word that replaces a noun, as in **He** *scored the goal.*

(20) The referent (or antecedent) of a pronoun is the word (a noun) the pronoun stands for, as in *John brought* **his** *car.*

(21) A pronoun agrees with its referent in gender and number, as in **Sally** *read* **her** *book* or **Fred and Samuel** *took* **their** *cars.* Avoid the common mistake of using the wrong *number* to avoid sexist language, as in **Each agent** *tries to make* **their** *deliveries on time.* Good thought; terrible grammar.

(22) In trying to avoid sexist language, good writers try to avoid *he* and *his* as generic pronouns: Don't write, *A pilot must be careful or* **he** *is likely to crash.* Instead, write, *Pilots must be careful or* **they** *are likely to crash.*

(23) *Chair* is appropriate when the gender of the head of an organization or group is to be determined, as in *The group will elect a chair Wednesday.* Use *chairman* or *chairwoman* when the gender is known, as in *Sally Richards was elected chairwoman.*

(24) A clause is a group of words having a predicate and subject, as in *John saw the boy who spoke.*

(25) *Like* refers to nouns and pronouns, as in *The coyotes looked* **like** *wolves.* **As** is used before clauses, as in *The team romped,* **as** *it did in the past.*

(26) A dependent clause does not make sense standing alone; an independent clause does. When a dependent clause comes before an independent clause, a comma is needed after the dependent clause, as in *Before she arrives, Sally studies hard.* Avoid this construction. The dependent clause usually goes last.

(27) A nonessential (or nonrestrictive) clause is not essential to a sentence; it can be omitted without changing the meaning. Nonessential clauses need to be set off with commas, as in *The woman,* **who teaches at my school,** *dodged the raging bull.*

(28) An essential (or restrictive) clause is essential to the sentence and should not be set off, as in *The woman* **who ran fast** *dodged the raging bull.*

(29) A relative pronoun (*who, whom, whose, which, that* and *what*) is a connecting word that joins a clause used as an adjective to its referent, as in *This is the car* **that I** *drove.*

(30) In using relative pronouns, *who* and *whom* typically refer to animals and individuals with names, as in *Fluffy is a cat* **who** *loves to sleep.*

(31) In using relative pronouns, *that* and *which* refer to unnamed animals and to inanimate objects, as in **The cat, which *is a demanding beast, is black,*** or **That *is the* car that *went into the lake.***

(32) Most personal pronouns used as possessives do not require an apostrophe: **The lion hurt *its* paw. The lion hurt it's *paw*** is always wrong. The pronouns are mine, my, their, theirs, its, yours, your, his, her, hers, ours, our.

(33) *One* is the only personal pronoun that requires an apostrophe to form the possessive, as in **One's *college diploma is worth a great deal.***

(34) A verb suggests action or state of being. A verb may be a word or a group of words.

(35) Present tense of a verb refers to an action happening now, as in **She writes *the speech.***

(36) Past tense refers to an action already completed, as in **She wrote *the speech.***

(37) Future tense refers to an action that will happen, as in **She will write *the speech.***

(38) An infinitive is a verb form that has *to* in front of it, as in **It's *time* to file *the* charges.** It is almost always a bad idea to split an infinitive, as in **The state police *moved* to quickly capture *the escapee.***

(39) *Lie,* an intransitive verb, means to rest, as in **The criminal went to lie *down. Lay,* a transitive verb, means to set something down, as in "Lay *the gun on the table and lie down on the floor," the policeman said.***

(40) A participle—which usually ends in *ed, en, ing* or *t*—is a verb form that is used as an adjective, as in **There sat two beaten *boxers.***

(41) In the United States, commas and periods always are placed inside quotation marks.

(42) Colons and semicolons generally go outside quotation marks.

(43) A question mark goes inside the quotation mark if the entire sentence is a question, but outside if the sentence is a question and the quote is not, as in **Did *the speaker say, "We've got to get there from here"?***

(44) Commas should be used before and after a state name that follows a city name, as in **Morgantown, W.Va., *is home to the West Virginia University Mountaineers.***

(45) Commas should be used before and after a year following a month and date, as in **April 15, 2005, *is the tax deadline.***

(46) A comma splice, which produces a run-on sentence—a grammatical error—occurs when a writer joins two complete sentences (that is, two sentences each having a subject and predicate) with a comma, as in **Jamie ruined the board, *however, it was old.***

(47) A semicolon is not dropped before the final *and* for items in a list, as in **One banner was red, white and blue; another was orange, yellow and red; and a third was black, blue and brown.**

(48) It is acceptable to use contractions in most writing, but only if the writer can spell them. Problems frequently arise with *it's* (it is) and *its* (possessive).

(49) Hyphens join numbers (as in telephone and Social Security numbers) and words, as in *e-mail message.* On a keyboard, this - is a hyphen. Use no spaces around the hyphen.

(50) Dashes may be thought of as punctuation marks (like colons, periods, semicolons, parentheses), usually used to show abrupt changes in thoughts, or to set off explanatory phrases in the middle of sentences, as in **The man bought the car—a Corvette—for a good price.** On a keyboard, this -- is a dash. Use spaces on both sides, or use no spaces.

(51) Parallel thoughts should be expressed in parallel construction, as in **The child is** beautiful **and** intelligent (both adjectives), rather than, **The child is** beautiful (adjective) **and** has intelligence (noun).

(52) A conjunction connects words or groups of words, as in **She wrote the release,** but *it was not sent.*

(53) *That* (a relative pronoun) usually is used to introduce a defining (essential) clause, as in **The book** that *changed my life is no longer in print.*

(54) *Which* introduces a nondefining (nonessential) clause, as in **The media, which** *were uninterested initially, jumped on the story.*

(55) *Effect* used as a noun means result; as a verb, it means to bring to pass, as in **Their training had a good** effect, or **She effected** *a compromise. Affect* as a verb means to pretend or to influence, as in **The confusion** affects *my study habits.*

(56) *Farther* refers to distance, as in **Billie ran** farther *than James. Further* refers to procedure, as in **She will consider this matter no** further.

(57) *Less* denotes amount, as in **We hope for** less *snow. Fewer* suggests number, as in **Fewer** *than 30 passed the exam.*

(58) *Imply* means to suggest in speech or writing, as in **The minister** implied *the end is near. Infer* means to draw a conclusion from someone's speech or manner, as in **The congregation** inferred *the minister is well educated.*

(59) *Between* suggests a choice between only two items, persons or alternatives, as in **He must choose** between *two options. Among* suggests a choice among more than two, as in **She must select** among *several players.*

(60) *They're* is the contraction for *they are,* as in **They're** heading home. *Their* is a possessive pronoun, as in **They fired** their *rifles. There,* an adverb, indicates direction, as in **Pauline went** there *to get the story. There* also may be used as an expletive in sentences in which the subject follows the verb, as in **There** *is little one can do.* Avoid this construction.

A P P E N D I X C

SELECTED STYLE RULES

Three people on the planet have memorized *The Associated Press Stylebook and Briefing on Media Law,* so students are not expected to do that. Readers should become acquainted with the AP style, however. Here are 35 rules that media writers should memorize to get them started. We recommend that students purchase *The Associated Press Stylebook and Briefing on Media Law* and start learning how to use it.

Academic degrees: 10	Day, date: 15, 33	Newspaper: 9
Academic departments: 7	Dictionary: 9, 19, 20	Numbers: 19, 28–35
Addresses: 19, 20, 30	Dimensions: 30	Organizations: 16, 17
Bible: 9	Direction: 5, 19, 20	Political parties: 13
Business name: 18	Encyclopedia: 9	Quotation marks: 8, 9, 33
Comma: 2–4, 18, 22, 33	Governing bodies: 6	Regions: 5
Committee: 11	Items in series: 4	State names: 21
Composition titles: 8, 27	Magazine: 9	Street names: 19, 20, 22, 31
Computer games: 8	Money: 34, 35	
Courtesy titles: 27	Month: 15	Time: 14, 33
Courts: 12	Name: 1–3, 7, 9–13, 15, 18, 21, 27, 32	Titles: 1–3, 23–26
Dateline: 22		Weekdays: 15

(1) Capitalize titles of authority before a name, but lowercase when standing alone or following a name. Lowercase occupational or false titles (day laborer,

attorney, professor), as in **Gov.** *Joan Williams and* **attorney** *Richard Morrison met with the* **attorney general.**

(2) Set a name off with commas and lowercase a title before a name when the title is preceded by *the*, as in **The provost** *of Western States University*, **Joan Goodwin, said. ...** It is usually best to put long titles (more than two words) after names. Lowercase *only* the title, not the name of the department or organization.

(3) Always set off titles and other identifications by commas when they follow names, as in **Beth Kelton, director of communications,** *said. ...*

(4) Drop the comma before the *and* when you list items in a series, as in **The flag is red, white and blue.**

(5) Capitalize the names of specific regions and areas, as in **Middle East, Oklahoma Panhandle, Southwest, West Houston.** Lowercase areas (north, west) when they represent compass directions, as in **They headed east.**

(6) Capitalize such words as *house, cabinet, city council* and *legislature* when preceded by the name of a town, state or nation. Lowercase when standing alone and used generically. Capitalize when the name of the town, state or nation is dropped, but reference is to that entity's governing body. Capitalize Congress in reference to the U.S. Congress.

(7) Lowercase the names of academic units, as in **department of English.** Proper names are always capitalized, as in **Spanish** *book,* or **French** *department.*

(8) Capitalize the titles of poems, films, books, songs, television programs, lectures, speeches, artworks, computer games and plays. Capitalize major words and prepositions and conjunctions of four letters or more. Put quotation marks around the titles, as in **"The Grapes of Wrath."**

(9) Capitalize Bible and the names of catalogs, encyclopedias, dictionaries, computer software, magazines and newspapers, but do not use quotation marks. Capitalize *the* only if it is part of the magazine or newspaper name, as in **The** *Seattle Times* or the *Detroit Free Press.*

(10) Capitalize the names of such academic degrees as *Master of Arts* and *Bachelor of Science,* as in **Bachelor of Science in Mass Communication.** Lowercase master's degree or master's, as in **She holds a master's.**

(11) Capitalize the exact name of a committee, as in **the Committee on the Future,** but lowercase *committee* when standing alone, even when *committee* refers to a previously named group.

(12) Capitalize and spell out the names of all courts, as in **the 32nd District Court** *of Harris County.*

(13) Capitalize the name of a political party and the word *party*, as in **The Democratic Party** *convention is scheduled for August.* Capitalize party names when they refer to parties or their members, as in **She was a Communist (or Republican, Democrat** *or* **Liberal,** *for example) at the time.*

(14) Capitalize *standard time* when it refers to a specific time zone, as in **Eastern Standard Time.** Lowercase when *standard time* stands alone.

(15) Abbreviate the names of months when used with specific dates, but spell out otherwise. Do not abbreviate *March, April, May, June* or *July* except in tabular or financial matter. Days of the week are abbreviated only in tabular material.

(16) First mentions of most organizations, firms or groups should be spelled out, as in **Association for Education in Journalism and Mass Communication.** Subsequent references can be to *AEJMC* or to *the association.* Do not follow an organization's name with an abbreviation or acronym in parentheses or set off by dashes.

(17) Abbreviations of well-known organization names (*FBI, CIA, AFL-CIO, AAA, AARP, ABC, IBM* and similar organizations) should not be spelled out. Check *The Associated Press Stylebook and Briefing on Media Law* when you're in doubt about whether an organization is well-known. Do not abbreviate *association* in an organization's name.

(18) Abbreviate *company, corporation* and *incorporated* at the end of a proper name, as in *John Smith Exterminators* **Inc.** Yes, do omit the comma before *incorporated.*

(19) In specific addresses, abbreviate *street, boulevard* and *avenue,* but spell out such designations as *road, drive* or *terrace.* All words are spelled out if a street number is not used. Abbreviate *north, south, east* and *west* when an address is mentioned, as in *12 S. Elm St.* Spell out directions when there is no address, as in **West Elm Street.** Capitalize and spell out *first* through *ninth* as street names; use numerals for *10th* and above, as in *129* **Fifth St.** or *1211* **11th** *Ave.*

(20) Spell out and capitalize when the street is named *North, South, East* or *West,* as in **11324 West Loop South.** The direction is spelled out and in lowercase when it follows the address, as in **2575 Interstate 45 south.**

(21) Abbreviate state names that follow town names, but do not abbreviate state names when they stand alone. Do not abbreviate Alaska, Hawaii, Idaho, Iowa, Maine, Ohio, Texas or Utah. Use abbreviations listed in the *The Associated Press Stylebook and Briefing on Media Law,* not U.S. Postal Service abbreviations:

Ala.	Kan.	Nev.	S.C.
Ariz.	Ky.	N.H.	S.D.
Ark.	La.	N.J.	Tenn.
Calif.	Md.	N.M.	Va.
Colo.	Mass.	N.Y.	Vt.
Conn.	Mich.	N.C.	Wash.
Del.	Minn.	N.D.	W. Va.
Fla.	Miss.	Okla.	Wis.
Ga.	Mo.	Ore.	Wyo.
Ill.	Mont.	Pa.	
Ind.	Neb.	R.I.	

(22) Datelines—which indicate where events happened—contain the names of cities, followed by the names of states, territories or counties. The city name is in all capital letters, followed by a comma, the state name and a dash, as in **NORMAN, Okla.—***Two people died here today when the car they were driving slid off the road and hit a rock wall.* Datelines are not used for local stories.

(23) Abbreviate *doctor* before a name in all uses and most professional and government titles (*Gov., Lt. Gov., Rep., Sen.*) when the name is used outside direct quotations, as in **Dr. Freda Jones,** or **Gov. Melvin Marks.** Do not abbreviate *president, vice president* or titles of cabinet officers.

(24) Military and police titles almost always are abbreviated, as in **Capt. Howard Hammond.**

(25) Academic titles are spelled out, as in *the visitor is* **professor Irma Jean Johnson.**

(26) Drop all government, personal and professional titles on second reference.

(27) Use a source's complete name the first time it appears in a story. Use only the last name on subsequent references. Do not use courtesy titles (*Miss, Mrs., Ms.* or *Mr.*), unless the title is part of an accepted pseudonym, such as Mister Rogers or a group with *mister* or *miss* as part of a member's name.

(28) Generally, spell numbers from zero to nine and use numerals for 10 and above. Numbers at the beginnings of sentences always are spelled out, but don't begin a sentence with 3,228.

(29) Specify the new amount first when you write about changes in numbers or rates (for example, tax rates, fares or prices), as in **The county raised the toll to 75 cents from 50 cents.**

(30) Use numerals with addresses, ages, distances, weights and percentages, as in **3 percent, 5 feet 8 inches** and **175 pounds.**

(31) Do not use *st, nd, rd* or *th,* as in **Let's go there 1st.** Spell out first through ninth to indicate sequence in time or location, as in **first base, Second Street** or **first in line.** Starting with 10th, use numerals, as in **42nd Street.**

(32) Use *1st, 2nd,* etc. when the sequence has been assigned in forming names, as in **1st Ward.**

(33) Use numerals, *a.m.* or *p.m.,* and day or date in specifying times, as in **9:15 a.m. Saturday.** Do not use *o'clock, :00, in the morning, at night, this afternoon.* Follow the form time, day or date and place, as in **4 p.m. Thursday at the administration building.** Do not separate these items with commas. Use *tomorrow* or *yesterday* only in direct quotations.

(34) In amounts of money of a million or more, round numbers take the dollar sign and million and billion are spelled out, as in **$1.35 million.** Decimalization is carried to two places only.

(35) Numerals are used in amounts less than a million, as in **$125,000.** Spell *cents* in amounts less than $1, as in **15 cents.**

APPENDIX D

COPY-EDITING SYMBOLS

New paragraph	①	⌐A man was killed
Capitalize		in the Idaho state bank
Lowercase		while talking to the Manager.
Insert apostrophe, letter, comma, word	②	Jon Johnson of Boise had his wifes picture,
		a letter and an envelope in pocket *his*
Delete word, letter		when he was ~~wrongfully~~ gunnmed down
Close space		at 9 a.m. Wednesday.
Join sentences	③	⌐The gunman, Mark Redd of Boise, ran. The police captured him in the mall.
Separate letters	⑥	⌐The gunman worked
Retain deleted material[1]		*previously* for ~~previously~~
Spell out, abbreviate word[2]		~~Tenn~~ Corp. at 16711 Gusher ~~Street~~ *Tenneco* *St.*
Use numerals		for ~~thirty-eight~~ years. *38*
Transpose words, letters[3]	④	He a had prison reocrd,
Add a period		Police Chief Joan Smith said⊗
Add a hyphen	⑤	⌐He served a two year term in
Add a dash		Greystone a state prison for theft.
Word is correct	⑦	⌐Johnson's friend, Geoff Hand, was not (cq)
		injured during the shooting.

To transpose paragraphs, number paragraphs to indicate the new order, as above.

[1] Some editors use the word "stet" to indicate that ~~deleted~~ material should be retained. (stet)

[2] Some (eds) circle abbreviated material to indicate that it should be spelled out or circle spelled out material to indicate that it should be abbreviated, although this increases the chances for inaccuracy.

[3] Some editors cross out the word that's in the ~~place~~ wrong and write it in above the line. *place*

A P P E N D I X   E

ONE STORY; MULTIPLE FORMATS

Writing fundamentals don't change from one medium to another or from one job to another, but formats and styles can vary. A script for a documentary film, for instance, doesn't look much like a public relations release. Some of the format differences are discussed here with examples. Students should use these formats in completing class assignments.

REASONS FOR FORMATS

Fewer pounds of paper pass through the hands of writers and editors each day as copy is increasingly processed electronically. When copy is processed electronically, some of the traditional format and editing rules do not apply. Copy-editing symbols, for example, are not useful to writers who never work with hard copy.

However, until all copy is processed electronically, print, Web, public relations and broadcast professionals need to know the rules for preparing hard copy. Within a communication organization, it is not unusual for professionals to process hundreds of pages of copy every day. A large newspaper like *The New York Times* publishes roughly 100,000 words each day, which represents a huge number of stories requiring considerable personal attention.

Standardized rules for copy preparation ensure that copy flows relatively smoothly and that little gets misplaced or lost. A writer who deviates from the established system can slow the production process, and that can mean an important deadline is missed.

Failure to put a slug on the second page of a newspaper story, for instance, can cause a long delay if a page is misplaced. An editor or a compositor who doesn't understand an editing symbol might simply guess at what the writer intended when he or she used that symbol. That's why most publications follow a set of standard editing symbols.

Regardless of medium or task, copy must be accurate and reasonably clean. Writers must not assume that editors will correct their mistakes. All facts must be verified; all words must be spelled correctly; all sentences must be well-structured and adequately attributed.

Format differences are discussed here in the context of a story about an airplane crash in Grand Canyon National Park, Ariz. Four passengers and two crew members are dead and 11 passengers are injured. The aircraft was landing following a sightseeing tour over the Grand Canyon. Sources are Juan Martinez, Coconino County sheriff; Ellen Cooke, National Park Service ranger; James W. Whitfield, Arizona Airlines' general manager; and Nakethia Johnson, FAA spokeswoman. Note that the facts are not ordered in the same ways in all versions and some facts are omitted altogether. All the stories are written in the inverted pyramid format, however, with the deaths and injuries displayed in the most prominent positions. Other facts are distributed throughout the stories according to interest and importance. (All Web sites and names mentioned in the stories are fictitious.)

PRINT (NEWSPAPER, PUBLIC RELATIONS, MAGAZINE)

Different print publications use slightly different formats, but the format on page A-19 is common; a notable exception is the format for public relations news releases, which is described later. All copy is double-spaced with the writer's name, telephone number and date in the top, left-hand corner. A one- or two-word slug (story description) is below the name, telephone number and date. The tab key is set to indent approximately five spaces for each paragraph with margins of an inch on all sides. *More* is written at the bottom of a page when a story is continued, and each new page begins with name, slug and add _ (*add 1* for page 2, *add 2* for page 3) in the top, left-hand corner. Any one of these symbols is used to indicate the end of the story: initials, endit, -30-, end or ###.

WORLD WIDE WEB

The format for a story that will be posted on a Web site (see page A-20) is essentially the same as that for a print story, although writing for the Web presents a few unique challenges and opportunities. The primary challenge, certainly, is to capture the interest of readers who are surfing so fast, they give the page virtually no time to make its case. This is not true of all readers all the time, but a Web writer is smart to assume that is the case. A writer can lose potential readers for a number of reasons:

- The page takes too long to load because of heavy concentrations of photographs, graphics or advertisements.
- The reader must search text to find news of interest and importance.

TYPICAL FORMAT FOR PRINT

Ashley Smith/888-8888/8-29-04
Grand Canyon crash

GRAND CANYON NATIONAL PARK, Ariz.–Four passengers and two crew members died Monday when a sightseeing aircraft slammed into a hillside while landing at the Grand Canyon National Park Airport.

Eleven others were injured when the twin-engine Arizona Airlines plane crashed into a grove of tall Ponderosa Pine trees, said Coconino County Sheriff Juan Martinez. They survived because the fuselage remained intact even as the wings were sheared off by the trees.

The dead are pilot Haley Martin, 36, of Flagstaff and co-pilot John Short, 29, of Grand Canyon, and passengers Cameron Rodriguez, 48, of San Diego; David Garman, 43, of San Francisco; Gina Mauer, 23, of Los Angeles; and Jeffrey Dobbs, 63, of El Paso.

Some of the passengers were walking around in the wreckage of the de Haviland DHC-6 Twin Otter when Ellen Cooke, a National Park Service ranger, arrived at the crash scene.

"They were shellshocked," she said. "They had that empty, dazed look."

The airplane was cleared to land following its Grand Canyon tour, touched down normally on the runway, became airborne again and veered to the east side of the airport, said James J. Whitfield, the airline's general manager and vice president.

The plane was approximately 1,500 feet down the 9,000-foot runway when it crashed and flipped over, said Nakethia Johnson, Federal Aviation Administration spokeswoman.

On its second tour of the day, the plane left the airport at 9 a.m. and was returning from its one-hour, 100-mile flight, Whitfield said. It crashed at 9:55 a.m.

Eight passengers are in critical condition at Flagstaff Medical Center and two are stable. One survivor did not go to the hospital.

endit

TYPICAL FORMAT FOR THE WEB

Ashley Smith/888-8888/8-29-04
Grand Canyon crash

GRAND CANYON NATIONAL PARK, Ariz.–Four passengers and two crew members died today when a sightseeing aircraft slammed into a hillside while landing at the Grand Canyon National Park Airport.

Click on www.arizonaairlines.com/crash/victims for information about the dead crew and passengers.

Eleven others were injured when the twin-engine Arizona Airlines plane crashed into a grove of tall Ponderosa Pine trees, said Coconino County Sheriff Juan Martinez. They survived because the fuselage remained intact even as the wings were sheared off by the trees.

Eight passengers are in critical condition at Flagstaff Medical Center and two are stable. One survivor did not go to the hospital. Click on www.arizonaairlines.com/crash/survivors for up-to-date information about survivors.

Some of the passengers were walking around in the wreckage of the de Haviland DHC-6 Twin Otter when Ellen Cooke, a National Park Service ranger, arrived at the crash scene.

"They were shellshocked," she said. "They had that empty, dazed look."

The airplane was cleared to land following its Grand Canyon tour, touched down normally on the runway, became airborne again and veered to the east side of the airport, said James J. Whitfield, the airline's general manager and vice president.

The plane was approximately 1,500 feet down the 9,000-foot runway when it crashed and flipped over, said Nakethia Johnson, Federal Aviation Administration spokeswoman.

On its second tour of the day, the plane left the airport at 9 a.m. and was returning from its one-hour, 100-mile flight, Whitfield said. It crashed at 9:55 a.m.

Photographs and video taken at the crash site are posted at www.southwestwebnews .com/crash.

endit

- Material simply is not interesting or important.
- The reader doesn't like the political, ideological, social or economic slant a particular page takes in reporting "news."

The inverted pyramid is well-suited to the needs of Web readers and writers, for reports written in this format show readers immediately what stories are about. Most readers are willing to devote a few moments to a page. If the writer has used the model effectively, the reader knows whether to stay or to surf on. The writer has met the challenge, regardless of the reader's ultimate decision. The reader is not turned off by the writer's slant because there isn't one—if the model is used properly (an objective approach is recommended).

The value of hyperlinks (or sidebars) for tailoring information to the interests and needs of individuals cannot be overstated. The primary story typically is only an electronic page long, since many readers refuse to scroll. But the writer may establish half a dozen hyperlinks to related content. Readers pick and choose which links to follow. Web writers have a power that other writers do not: Other media professionals can use sidebars, but none can use six or eight sidebars at a time, as a Web writer can.

Writers can establish hyperlinks to statistics, to agencies that can offer help (to abused children, for example) and additional information, to transcripts of interviews, to graphics, to streaming video or to photographs. A reader who has a dial-up modem, for example, can skip the photographs because they take too long to load.

A writer who works for an organization called, say, Southwest Web News might want to post on the site a story about the Arizona Airlines crash. He or she would write the story and establish appropriate links to other sites and pages in print format. Everything is set in Hypertext Markup Language, the language of the Web, but most writers never see their copy in HTML format.

PUBLIC RELATIONS RELEASES

Print

Public relations releases are written in essentially the format that other print stories are, except that the following information is given at the top of the page: date and release date; organization name, address and logo; telephone and fax numbers; electronic mail and Web addresses; contact person and numbers. See format on page A-22.

Radio

An Arizona Airlines news release might be written in the format on page A-23 (see more details about broadcast writing formats on page A-24). The biggest differences between this release and a print release include the use of all capital letters, shorter sentences and fewer details.

TYPICAL FORMAT FOR PUBLIC RELATIONS PRESS RELEASE

Arizona Airlines Inc.
www.arizonaairlines.com

1212 Ave. Q
Grand Canyon National Park, Ariz.
Main Number:(888) 888-8888
Fax:(888) 888-8888

Contact: Ashley Smith
Director, Public Affairs
(888) 888-8887
asmith@arizonaairlines.com

Aug. 24, 2004   For Immediate Release

Six die in air crash

GRAND CANYON NATIONAL PARK, Ariz.–Two crew members and four passengers aboard Arizona Airlines' Flight 201 died today when the aircraft crashed while landing at Grand Canyon National Park Airport, said James J. Whitfield, the airline's general manager and vice president.

Eight passengers are in critical condition at Flagstaff Medical Center and two are stable, Whitfield said. One passenger did not require hospitalization. The airline has established a hot line at (888) 888-8884. Additional information is available at www.arizonaairlines.com/crash.

The dead are pilot Haley Martin, 36, of Flagstaff and co-pilot John Short, 29, of Grand Canyon, and passengers Cameron Rodriguez, 48, of San Diego; David Garman, 43, of San Francisco; Gina Mauer, 23, of Los Angeles; and Jeffrey Dobbs, 63, of El Paso.

The airplane was cleared to land following its Grand Canyon tour, touched down normally on the runway, became airborne again and veered to the east side of the airport, Whitfield said.

The plane was approximately 1,500 feet down the 9,000-foot runway when it crashed and flipped over, said Nakethia Johnson, Federal Aviation Administration spokeswoman.

On its second tour of the day, the plane left the airport at 9 a.m. and was returning from its one-hour, 100-mile flight, Whitfield said. It crashed at 9:55 a.m.

end

TYPICAL FORMAT FOR PUBLIC RELATIONS RADIO RELEASE

Arizona Airlines Inc.
www.arizonaairlines.com

1212 Ave. Q
Grand Canyon National Park, Ariz.
General Number:(888) 888-8888
Fax:(888) 888-8888

Contact: Ashley Smith
Director, Public Affairs
(888) 888-8887
asmith@arizonaairlines.com

Aug. 24, 2004   For Immediate Release

Six die in air crash

GRAND CANYON NATIONAL PARK, ARIZ.–SIX PEOPLE ABOARD ARIZONA AIRLINES FLIGHT 201 DIED TODAY IN A CRASH NEAR GRAND CANYON NATIONAL PARK AIRPORT.

TWO OF THE DEAD WERE CREW MEMBERS AND FOUR WERE PASSENGERS.

ARIZONA AIRLINES' GENERAL MANAGER JAMES J. WHITFIELD SAYS EIGHT PASSENGERS ARE IN CRITICAL CONDITION AT FLAGSTAFF MEDICAL CENTER. TWO MORE ARE STABLE. A HOT LINE HAS BEEN ESTABLISHED AT (888) 888-8884.

THE PLANE WAS RETURNING FROM A SIGHTSEEING TOUR OF THE GRAND CANYON WHEN IT CRASHED WHILE LANDING.

THE CAUSE OF THE CRASH IS UNKNOWN.

ENDIT

BROADCAST FORMATS

Broadcast formats are all over the place; they seem to vary more widely than print formats do. Some writers use all capitals, and some use capital and lowercase letters; some string the name, slug, run time, and program time across the top, and others cluster that information in the corner. None of this is cause for concern. Most of the fundamentals are the same, and it's easy to learn a new format, after one has developed the discipline to write to a format and to a style. Some outlets use Associated Press style, incidentally, and some don't. To avoid confusion, AP style is used here.

Television

Television copy typically is triple-spaced with two-inch margins at the top and bottom. The page is divided in half vertically, with the story on the right and instructions for using video on the left. The length of the on-air reporter's story (with actualities) all must be timed precisely, for a reporter who has 20 seconds can't go 22 seconds or 18 seconds.

Writers use an average of six words per line. That means a line of roughly 40 characters. Most broadcast journalists read roughly 150 words per minute, which means roughly 25 lines per minute. The sample on page A-25 is not at all complex (many scripts are extraordinarily complicated), but it does suggest how they can look. (In the following story, PLANE CRASH is the slug; SMITH is the reporter's name; 10 P is the newscast; RUNS 1:20 is the story length; CU is close up; MS is medium shot; VOT is voice over tape.)

Radio

Radio format is quite similar to that of television, except that radio journalists obviously do not need to think about video. A writer follows all of the guidelines for television writing with one exception: Copy should be set at 70 characters per line, which means each line has roughly 10 words. A typical journalist will read approximately 150 words (15 lines) per minute. See the sample on page A-26.

TYPICAL FORMAT FOR TELEVISION NEWS

PLANE CRASH SMITH	12/12/04 10 P RUNS 1:20
MS: Smith at crash scene	FOUR PASSENGERS AND TWO CREW MEMBERS DIED TODAY WHEN A SIGHTSEEING AIRCRAFT SLAMMED INTO A HILLSIDE NEAR GRAND CANYON NATIONAL PARK, ARIZ.
VOT: Smith over crash footage	ELEVEN OTHERS WERE INJURED WHEN THE TWIN-ENGINE CRAFT CRASHED INTO A GROVE OF PINE TREES. COCONINO COUNTY SHERIFF JUAN MARTINEZ (WAHN MAHR-TEE'-NESS) SAYS THE SIGHTSEEING AIRCRAFT WAS ATTEMPTING TO LAND AT GRAND CANYON NATIONAL PARK AIRPORT.
CU: Martinez: 12 secs	"THE WINGS WERE SHEARED OFF WHEN THE PLANE PLOWED THROUGH THOSE PINES. BUT MOST OF THE FUSELAGE WAS INTACT. THAT'S WHY THOSE WHO DID SURVIVE MADE IT."
VOT: Smith over crash footage	NATIONAL PARK SERVICE RANGER ELLEN COOKE WAS AMONG THE FIRST ON THE SCENE. SHE FOUND SURVIVORS WALKING AROUND IN THE WRECKAGE.
CU: Cooke: 11 secs	"I'VE BEEN IN A COMBAT ZONE DURING WAR, AND THOSE PASSENGERS WERE SHELLSHOCKED THE WAY SOME SOLDIERS GET. THEY HAD THAT DAZED LOOK."
VOT: Smith over runway footage	THE AIRPLANE GIVES DAILY TOURS OF THE GRAND CANYON. IT HAD BEEN CLEARED TO LAND DURING ITS 9 A.M. FLIGHT. GENERAL MANAGER AND VICE PRESIDENT JAMES J. WHITFIELD SAYS THE PLANE TOUCHED DOWN ON THE RUNWAY. IT BECAME AIRBORNE AGAIN AND VEERED OFF INTO THE TREES,
CU: Smith	WHITFIELD SAYS EIGHT PASSENGERS ARE IN CRITICAL CONDITION AT FLAGSTAFF MEDICAL CENTER. TWO ARE STABLE. ONE PERSON DID NOT NEED HOSPITAL TREATMENT. THE FAA IS INVESTIGATING THE CRASH TONIGHT. THIS IS ASHLEY SMITH REPORTING FROM GRAND CANYON NATIONAL PARK, WHERE AN AIRLINE CRASH HAS KILLED SIX.

TYPICAL FORMAT FOR RADIO NEWS

PLANE CRASH   SMITH   12/12/04   5 P   RUNS 1:20

FOUR PASSENGERS AND TWO CREW MEMBERS DIED TODAY WHEN A SIGHTSEEING AIRCRAFT SLAMMED INTO A HILLSIDE NEAR GRAND CANYON NATIONAL PARK, ARIZ.

THE AIRCRAFT WAS ATTEMPTING TO LAND AT GRAND CANYON NATIONAL PARK AIRPORT.

ELEVEN OTHERS WERE INJURED WHEN THE TWIN-ENGINE CRAFT CRASHED INTO A GROVE OF PINE TREES.

COCONINO COUNTY SHERIFF JUAN MARTINEZ (WAHN MAHR-TEE'-NESS) WAS ONE OF THE FIRST ON THE SCENE:

Tape: Martinez . . . . . runs: 12 secs

"THE WINGS WERE SHEARED OFF WHEN THE PLANE PLOWED THROUGH THOSE PINES. BUT MOST OF THE FUSELAGE WAS INTACT. THAT'S WHY THOSE WHO DID SURVIVE MADE IT."

NATIONAL PARK SERVICE RANGER ELLEN COOKE WAS ON THE SCENE TO HELP WITH THE RESCUE OPERATION. SHE FOUND SURVIVORS WALKING AROUND IN THE WRECKAGE.

Tape: Cooke . . . . . runs: 11 secs

"I'VE BEEN IN A COMBAT ZONE DURING WAR, AND THOSE PASSENGERS WERE SHELLSHOCKED THE WAY SOME SOLDIERS GET. THEY HAD THAT DAZED LOOK."

GENERAL MANAGER AND VICE PRESIDENT JAMES J. WHITFIELD SAYS THE AIRPLANE GIVES DAILY TOURS OF THE GRAND CANYON. IT HAD BEEN CLEARED TO LAND DURING ITS 9 A.M. FLIGHT. IT TOUCHED DOWN ON THE RUNWAY, BECAME AIRBORNE AGAIN AND VEERED OFF INTO THE TREES,

WHITFIELD SAID EIGHT PATIENTS ARE IN CRITICAL CONDITION AT FLAGSTAFF MEDICAL CENTER. TWO ARE STABLE. ONE PERSON DID NOT NEED TREATMENT.

THE FEDERAL AVIATION ADMINISTRATION IS INVESTIGATING.

THIS IS ASHLEY SMITH REPORTING FROM THE GRAND CANYON NATIONAL PARK, WHERE SIX ARE DEAD IN AN AIRPLANE CRASH.

ENDIT

A P P E N D I X F

AGENDA, MANHATTAN, KAN., CITY COMMISSION

AGENDA, MANHATTAN, KAN., CITY COMMISSION

 This meeting is being held in the City Commission Room at City Hall, 1101 Poyntz Avenue. In accordance with provisions of the ADA, every attempt will be made to accommodate the needs of persons with disabilities. Please contact the Human Resources Department (587-2440) for assistance.

AGENDA
CITY COMMISSION MEETING
TUESDAY, AUGUST 19, 2003
7:00 P.M.
**The City Commission Meeting will be televised
live on local Cable Channel 3.**

PLEDGE OF ALLEGIANCE

COMMISSIONER COMMENTS

CONSENT AGENDA

[Items on the Consent Agenda are those of a routine and housekeeping nature or those items which have previously been reviewed by the City Commission. A Commissioner may request an item be moved to the end of the General Agenda.]

Approve the minutes of the Regular City Commission Meeting held Tuesday, August 5, 2003. Click Here to View Item.

Approve Claims Register No. 2487 authorizing and approving the payment of claims from July 23, 2003, to August 12, 2003, in the amount of $2,577,414.07.

Approve Ordinance No. 6353 amending the Final Development Plan of the Plaza West Planned Unit Development, located at 3003 Anderson Avenue, and Ordinance No. 4992, based on the findings in the Staff Report, with the one condition recommended by the Planning Board. Click Here to View Item.

Approve Ordinance No. 6354 rezoning Lot B and Lot C, Manko II Addition, generally located southeast of the intersection of Hayes Drive and McCall Road, from I-2, Industrial Park District, to C-5, Highway Service Commercial District, based on the findings in the Staff Report. Click Here to View Item.

Authorize the Mayor and City Clerk to execute an agreement in the amount of $192,959.00 with Insituform Technologies USA, Inc., of Blue Springs, Missouri, for a sanitary sewer rehabilitation project. *[CIP Item # UT03-1288P]* Click Here to View Item.

Award the purchase of a single axle four-wheel drive dump truck to Rusty Eck Ford, of Wichita, Kansas, with a net bid of $73,832.00, to replace Unit 31. *[CIP Item # PW03-0314E]* Click Here to View Item.

Authorize City Administration to purchase one 72" mower in the amount of $18,464.00 from Brooks Yamaha Inc., of Manhattan, Kansas, for the Parks and Recreation Department. *[page 193 in the Capital Improvements Program, CIP# PR03-0598E, budgeted $25,350.00, General Fund Budget.]* Click Here to View Item.

Accept the final report for the *Water Distribution System and Sanitary Sewer Collection System Master Plans Update*. Click Here to View Item.

Authorize the Mayor and City Clerk to accept and sign Federal Grant Offer 3-20-0052-25 in the amount of $100,000.00 for Airport Equipment Building–Phase 1 (Design). Click Here to View Item.

Authorize City Administration to purchase and install replacement name bricks in the Downtown Public Plaza. Click Here to View Item.

Approve Ordinance No. 6356 amending the *Code of Ordinances* to provide the authority for U.S.D. 383, the Riley County Police Department, and the City of Manhattan to designate persons to serve as crossing guards at any school zone. Click Here to View Item.

GENERAL AGENDA

A. **SECOND READING OF ORDINANCE NO. 6355 ADOPTING THE 2004 CITY BUDGET AND RESOLUTION NO. 081903-B APPROVING THE 2004-2009 CAPITAL IMPROVEMENTS PROGRAM** Click Here to View Item.

B. **PRESENTATION OF THE 2002 COMPREHENSIVE ANNUAL FINANCIAL REPORT (CAFR)** Click Here to View Item.

C. **MUNICIPAL FACILITY REVIEW FOR PROPOSED IMPROVEMENTS AT THE CITY OF MANHATTAN'S WATER TREATMENT PLANT LOCATED WEST OF THE INTERSECTION OF NORTH THIRD STREET AND TUTTLE CREEK BOULEVARD** Click Here to View Item.

1. Hold a public hearing; and
2. Approve first reading of an ordinance to permit the proposed Chemical Building, CO_2 Tank, and Future Chlorine Room/Building and Storage Garage at the City of Manhattan's Water Treatment Plant.

D. **REQUEST FOR PROPOSALS FOR FLINT HILLS PLACE REDEVELOPMENT** Click Here to View Item.
[Manhattan Housing Authority Board of Commissioners recommends approval]

E. **FIRST READING OF AN ORDINANCE AMENDING THE MANHATTAN URBAN AREA SUBDIVISION REGULATIONS AND ORDINANCE NO. 6163, CONCERNING SIDEWALK REQUIREMENTS AND SUBMITTAL REQUIREMENTS FOR DRAINAGE REPORTS AND PLANS, AND TRANSPORTATION IMPACT STUDIES** Click Here to View Item.

F. **FIRST READING OF AN ORDINANCE AMENDING THE FINAL DEVELOPMENT PLAN OF THE K-MART COMMERCIAL PLANNED UNIT DEVELOPMENT, GENERALLY LOCATED AT 401 EAST POYNTZ AVENUE, AND ORDINANCE NO. 4635** Click Here to View Item.
[Manhattan Urban Area Planning Board recommends approval]

G. **HOUSING REHABILITATION GRANT APPLICATION FOR 2003 HOME INVESTMENT PARTNERSHIPS PROGRAM** Click Here to View Item.

A P P E N D I X   G

HOT WEB SITES

Thousands of Web sites are useful to public relations practitioners, advertising professionals and broadcast, Web, magazine and newspaper journalists. No list can include all the useful sites, and this one doesn't either. The focus in this list is on sites that are highly reliable (no site is 100 percent reliable, so do not be misled) and that are good starting points for Web searches.

Information in 46 categories should get anyone off to a good start. All of the sites have links to other useful sites, most of which also are highly reliable. A few sites fit into two categories exceptionally well, so don't be surprised if you see a few twice. If you have a favorite site or if you find that one of the URLs here has changed, please send a message to mryan@uh.edu.

Academic, professional organizations	Environment
Aging	Ethics
Animals	Freedom of information
Arts, humanities	Government: City, county
Business, financial	Government: Executive
Colleges, universities	Government: Federal agencies
Computing	Government: Legislative
Crime	Health, medicine
Disability	Human rights
Disease	International
Education	Internet guides
Entertainment	Internet tutorials

Job search services	People, business directories
Labor relations	Polling
Law	Religion
Libraries, reference	Science
Maps	Search services
Mass media	Sports
Media information	Terrorism
Military	Travel
Minorities	Weather, disaster
Nonprofit organizations	Women
Numerical aids	Writing aids

ACADEMIC, PROFESSIONAL ORGANIZATIONS

American Advertising Federation <www.aaf.org>

American Association for Public Opinion Research <www.aapor.org>   Everything you want to know about public opinion surveys, ethics, standards, techniques.

Association for Education in Journalism and Mass Communication <www.aejmc.org>

Broadcast Education Association <www.beaweb.org>

California Journalism Online <www.csne.org>   Lists daily and weekly newspapers that are online, with brief descriptions.

Canadian Association of Journalists <www.eagle.ca/caj>

Freedom Forum <www.freedomforum.org>   Primary focus is on free speech, press, assembly.

Institute for Public Relations <www.instituteforpr.com>   Focus is on research and education in the United States; presentations, publications, articles, conferences, news, awards.

Institute of Public Relations <www.ipr.org.uk>   Almost anything you want to know about public relations in the United Kingdom, including training, careers, publications, events, news.

International Association of Business Communicators <www.iabc.com>

International Communication Association <www.icahdq.org>   Focus is on human communication; research, publications, directory.

Investigative Reporters and Editors Inc. <www.ire.org>   Provides legal help to journalists and news organizations; leads to outstanding broadcast and print news stories; good information for developing professional skills.

IPREX <www.iprex.com>   Maintained by the partnership for international public relations agencies, site provides information about member firms, describes specialties within firms and supplies public relations and marketing news.

Journalism.org (Research, Resources and Ideas to Improve Journalism) <www.journalism.org> Research and writing tools for print, online and broadcast writers; job links; news about the news; publications.

Public Relations Society of America <www.prsa.org>

Radio-Television News Directors Association <www.rtnda.org>

The Reporters Committee for Freedom of the Press <www.rcfp.org>   Reports, news, tips, guides about freedom of the press issues; free legal assistance to journalists.

Society of Professional Journalists <www.spj.org>

World Advertising Research Center <www.warc.com>   News, research, reports about advertising, marketing and mass communication; subscription required.

AGING

Administration on Aging <www.aoa.dhhs.gov>   Information for older people and their families and for those who provide services and information to and about older people; press center; good material for mass communicators.

American Association of Retired Persons <www.aarp.org>   Everything you want to know about AARP; lots of information about older and retired people; press center.

Growth House <www.growthhouse.org>   Information about all aspects of death and dying, from pain management to dealing with grief; also provides search engine for comprehensive list of other Web resources.

National Institute on Aging <www.nia.nih.gov>   Information about aging research, and consumer-oriented material about exercise, helpful organizations, diseases and disorders; links to federal Web sites of interest to the aging community.

Physician's Guide to Assessing and Counseling Older Drivers <www.ama-assn.org/ama/pub/ category/10791.html>   Good information from the American Medical Association about safety and the older driver.

ANIMALS

American Society for the Prevention of Cruelty to Animals <www.aspca.org>   Poison control center, legal information, pet care and nutrition, publications, adoption information, news.

Conservation Fund <www.swbg-conservationfund.org/projects_animal_rescue.html> Maintained by Sea World and Busch Gardens, site posts information about animal research, rescue, rehabilitation; habitat protection, conservation education; news.

The Endangered Species Program <http://endangered.fws.gov>   Maintained by the U.S. Fish & Wildlife Service, site has endangered species information, news, research, publications; details about the Endangered Species Act; recovery plans and programs.

Kyler Laird's Animal Rescue Resources <www.ecn.purdue.edu/~laird/animal_rescue>   Links to local animal rescue groups, shelters that have Web sites; links to other information sources.

Species Information <http://endangered.fws.gov/wildlife.html>   U.S. Fish & Wildlife Service site contains information about the Endangered Species Act; comprehensive data about each species in the United States and abroad; news.

ARTS, HUMANITIES

John F. Kennedy Center for the Performing Arts <www.artsedge.kennedy-center.org>   News and information about the Center, arts, education; links to other art Web sites.

Museumlink's Museum of Museums <www.museumlinks.com>   Links to many museums around the world; eventually hopes to link to them all.

National Endowment for the Arts <www.arts.endow.gov>   Interviews, news, works in the National Gallery of Art and the Writer's Corner, NEA information and publications; links to federal information about the arts.

National Endowment for the Humanities <www.neh.fed.us>   NEH news, information and publications; staff directory; links to information about NEH-funded activities in 56 states and territories.

World Wide Arts Resources <www.world-arts-resources.com>   Links to museums, galleries, artists, art history and education, antiques, dance, theater; links to related sites.

BUSINESS, FINANCIAL

AutoTrack Plus (Database Technologies) <www.llrx.com/features/dbt.htm>   Users can search nearly 4 billion business records purchased from more than 1,000 private and public sources. The per-minute fee discourages some potential users.

EDGAR (Electronic Data Gathering, Analysis, and Retrieval) Database of Corporate Information <www.sec.gov/edgar.shtml>   Compiles information companies are required to file with the Securities and Exchange Commission; reports information about SEC actions and rules; suggests related sites.

EDGAR Online <www.edgar-online.com>   Supplies the latest business news, links to useful Web sites, financial data and information about initial public offerings, customer support, corporate sales, international business and jobs. Specializes in collecting and distributing business information contained in filings with the Securities and Exchange Commission.

Europages <www.europages.com>   Data about European companies and business, including agriculture, energy, transportation, construction, public works, textiles, technology, telecommunications.

Hoover's Online <www.hoovers.com>   Initial public offerings, companies and industries, career development, newsletters.

Latin Focus <www.latin-focus.com>   Economic forecasts and statistics, political risk assessments, market information for seven Latin American countries and for the region; news articles and commentaries.

LexisNexis for the public relations industry <www.lexisnexis.com/prpo>   Business and public records; news and legal information about companies, products, services and people. Provides access to more than 200 million state and federal court records. Expensive, but available in many libraries.

PBS's *Nightly Business Report* <www.nightlybusiness.org>   U.S. and international business news summaries, market information, news headlines; links to other sites featuring financial information.

The Wall Street Journal <www.wsj.com>   Business, finance, company, small business and market news.

COLLEGES, UNIVERSITIES

Campus Tours <www.campustours.com>   Links to virtual tours offered by American colleges and universities, with links to Web cameras on several campuses.

University of Texas at Austin <www.utexas.edu/world/univ/state>   Complete list of Web sites established by American colleges and universities, sorted by state.

U.S. News & World Report <www.usnews.com/usnews/edu/eduhome.htm>   Information about American colleges and universities, with rankings of institutions and graduate programs.

COMPUTING

Computer Systems Policy Project <www.cspp.org>   Sponsored by the information technology industry; includes policy statements, press releases, links to relevant sites.

CyberLaw & CyberLex <www.cyberlaw.com>   Reports on legal issues relating to the computer industry.

Electronic Frontier Foundation <www.eff.org>   Maintained by the nonprofit EFF; provides information about privacy, free expression, access to online information.

Global Computing <www.globalcomputing.com>   Computer companies, publications, government regulation, search services, computers and universities; also links to each state's home page.

World Wide Web Consortium <www.w3.org>   Resources relating to technology and policy issues about the Web's development.

CRIME

Bureau of Justice Statistics <www.ojp.usdoj.gov/bjs>   Links to sites that report crime, punishment data.

Federal Bureau of Investigation <www.fbi.gov>   All you want to know about the FBI; most-wanted lists; reports, publications, news; counterterrorism activities; field offices.

International Centre for Criminal Law Reform and Criminal Justice Policy <www.icclr.law.ubc.ca>   Information about the reform of national and international criminal law, practice and policy; links to similar institutes.

National Criminal Justice Reference Service <www.ncjrs.org>   Substance abuse, crime victims, prisoner re-entry, courts, juvenile justice, hate crimes, forensic science, policy, law enforcement, crime statistics, public safety. Electronic mail addresses are supplied for experts who will answer questions.

Organized Crime: A Crime Statistics Site <www.crime.org>   Helps users to locate, understand and assess the credibility of international and national crime statistics; good tutorial about crime statistics.

DISABILITY

American Association of People with Disabilities <www.aapd.com>   Advocacy group seeks self-sufficiency for the disabled through enforcement of laws against discrimination. News, court cases, benefits, calendars, publications, research studies, legislative updates.

Americans with Disabilities Act <www.usdoj.gov/crt/ada>   Maintained by the Department of Justice, site lists ADA and general publications, business and nonprofit service providers, state and local government actions pertaining to the disabled, enforcement issues, employment policies and problems, frequently asked questions, guide to rights for the disabled.

Chartbook on Women and Disability in the United States <www.infouse.com/disabilitydata/womendisability>   Reference for technical and nontechnical users who need information about the relationship between women and disability. Format is topic question, explanatory text and graphic or table.

National Council on Disability <www.ncd.gov>   News, answers to frequently asked questions, links to other federal agencies, program and policy information, enforcement and implementation of the Americans with Disabilities Act.

National Dissemination Center for Children With Disabilities <www.nichcy.org>   News, publications, resources by state, frequently asked questions, good links to state and federal resources.

National Institute on Disability and Rehabilitation Research <www.ed.gov/about/offices/list/osers/nidrr/index.html>   Information about research related to the rehabilitation of the disabled. News, contacts, grants, funding, publications, products, statistics; links to other sites.

Office of Disability Employment Policy, Department of Labor <www.dol.gov/odep>   News, frequently asked questions, programs and initiatives, policy, state liaisons, procedures that ensure nondiscrimination.

Office of Special Education and Rehabilitative Services <www.ed.gov/about/offices/list/osers/index.html>   OSERS supports states, individuals and school districts in special education, vocational rehabilitation and research. News, products, publications, programs, frequently asked questions, legislation, policy, statistics; links to other sites.

World Institute on Disability <www.wid.org>   A nonprofit research, policy and training center, the WID maintains this site, which includes contact information, publications, calendars, reports, programs, benefits for the disabled, news.

DISEASE

AIDS.org <www.aids.org>   Frequently asked questions, news, fact sheets, publications; treatment programs; links to other sites.

American Diabetes Association <www.diabetes.org>   Everything users want to know about diabetes, including how to live with it.

American Sickle Cell Anemia Association <www.ascaa.org>   Mission statement, screening of newborns; programs, services, support groups, message board, educational material.

Centers for Disease Control and Prevention <www.cdc.gov>   News from and about the CDC, health information, statistics, training and employment, health funding.

Heart Information Network <www.heartinfo.org>   Current news and information about nutrition, heart disease, CPR; members are able to ask questions via electronic mail. The beating heart is worth the visit.

Medscape <www.medscape.com>   New medical research, medical definitions, a medical library, medical headlines; information about illnesses and diseases, such as AIDS and heart disease.

UNAIDS <www.unaids.org/en/default.asp>   Maintained as part of the Joint U.S. Programme on HIV/AIDS, site has an epidemic update; international AIDS campaigns; fact sheets, news releases, publications; AIDS breakdowns by regions, countries.

World Health Organization's Whosis (WHO Statistical Information System) <www.who.int/whosis>   Guide to statistical information available from WHO; descriptions of diseases and where they occur.

EDUCATION

American Federation of Teachers <www.aft.org>   Education news, human rights, information technology, legislation; publications, research reports, Web resources; links to other sites. Public school through college education.

International Bureau of Education <www.ibe.unesco.org>   Research, policy dialogues, conferences, contact persons, publications, world education data; links to related sites.

National Center for Education Statistics <www.nces.ed.gov>   NCES is the primary federal repository for education data from the United States and other nations. If you want to know something about education, you're likely to find it here.

National Education Association <www.nea.org>   NEA news and announcements, newsgroups.

National School Board Association <www.nsba.org>   Publications, reports, monographs; links to periodicals and newspapers online; technology in education; educational trends and tools.

Office of Special Education and Rehabilitative Services <www.ed.gov/about/offices/list/osers/index.html>   OSERS supports states, individuals and school districts in special education, vocational rehabilitation, research. News, products, publications, programs, frequently asked questions, legislation, policy, statistics; links to other sites.

U.S. Department of Education <www.ed.gov>   News releases and guides, grants and funding opportunities, staff directory, budgets, late news, research, programs, services, Title IV school codes; links to other sites.

U.S. Office of Non-Public Education <www.ed.gov/about/offices/list/oii/nonpublic/index.html>   State laws regarding nonpublic schools; participation in federal education programs; reports, publications, research, government policies, laws.

ENTERTAINMENT

American Film Institute <www.afi.com>   Seminars, workshops, awards, history, catalog of feature films, film preservation efforts, film news, contacts.

BBC News Entertainment <http://news.bbc.co.uk/1/hi/entertainment/default.stm>   Entertainment news mainly from Europe and the United Kingdom; television, film, music, show business.

Billboard <www.billboard.com>   News about artists, albums, home videos, concerts, products, digital downloads, television; directories; industry awards; music business news.

The British Film Institute <www.bfi.org.uk>   Film reviews and features, collections, archives, film facts, film links, books, video.

CNN Entertainment <www.cnn.com/SHOWBIZ>   New music, films, books, television programs; news about artists; reviews.

Entertainment Weekly <www.ew.com/ew>   News, features about artists, films, music, books, television.

The Greatest Films <www.filmsite.org>   Reviews, lists of top-grossing films, Academy Awards information, descriptions of the greatest films ever.

MSN Entertainment <www.entertainment.msn.com>   Celebrity chats; film, book, music; television news and reviews; free music.

MTV <www.mtv.com>   Bands, shows, news, features, downloads, MTV schedules and news.

National Film Board of Canada <www.nfb.ca>   News releases, television listings, features, resources.

Real Movies <http://movies.guide.real.com>   Box office watch, top artists' ratings, movies, music, radio, television, news, features.

Variety <www.variety.com>   All the news and information from the entertainment magazine. Subscription required. Reviews, hot topics, obituaries, calendar, box office charts, television, film, people.

ENVIRONMENT

Canadian Environmental Assessment Agency <www.ceaa.gc.ca>   Environmental assessment activities; Environmental Assessment Index; research and publications, legislation, five-year review, environmental protection projects.

The Ecological Society of America <www.esa.org>   Describes the ESA, an organization of scientists; ecological research and publications; analyses, explanations of ecological issues and problems.

Environmental Defense Fund <www.edf.org>   EDF lobbying activities; environmental news, reports, research; proposed environmental laws and administrative actions; interviews; developments in science, economics.

Environmental Protection Agency <www.epa.gov>   Environmental profiles; digital library, statistical reports, research, publications; environmental trends and status.

Los Alamos Environmental Science and Technology <www-emtd.lanl.gov/TD/Technology .html>   Research that addresses environmental needs; waste management, nuclear science, environmental restoration, pollution issues.

National Audubon Society <www.audubon.org>   Conservation, birds, science, Audubon resources, forest habitat, endangered species, activist guide.

National Resources Conservation Service <www.nrcs.usda.gov>   Maintained by the Department of Agriculture; droughts, watershed infrastructure, farm and ranch bills, animal feeding, backyard conservation, land and water conservation; National Resources Inventory; media information section.

National Response Team <www.nrt.org>   Oil and chemical spills; description of the National Response System; member agencies, research reports, statistics, preparedness, response; links to more than 100 sites about hazardous materials and oil.

Sierra Club <www.sierraclub.org>   Environmental reports, research, publications; legislation, voter information, environmental news; environmental threats; preservation, reclamation projects.

ETHICS

Media Ethics Resources on WWW <www.ethicsweb.ca>   Centre for Applied Ethics site focuses largely on Canada, but posts useful links to sites and articles about ethics in other parts of the planet.

Poynter Institute for Media Studies <www.poynter.org>   Essays about ethical issues; links to other resources.

Silha Center for the Study of Media Ethics and Law <www.silha.umn.edu>   University of Minnesota site features news about ethical problems and issues; links to other sites.

FREEDOM OF INFORMATION

College Freedom <www.collegefreedom.org>   Data about college press freedom, faculty and student freedom, current happenings.

Electronic Frontier Foundation <www.eff.org>   Maintained by the nonprofit EFF, site provides information about privacy, free expression, access to online information.

Freedom Forum <www.freedomforum.org>   Focus is on the First Amendment; free speech, press, assembly.

Reporters Committee for Freedom of the Press <www.rcfp.org>   Reports, news, tips, guides about freedom of the press issues; legal assistance to journalists.

GOVERNMENT: CITY, COUNTY

County and City Data Book <www.census.gov/prod/www/ccdb.html>   Published by the U.S. Census Bureau, contains hundreds of bits of data about all U.S. counties, metropolitan areas having more than 25,000 residents and places having more than 2,500 inhabitants. Latest edition at this site.

County and City Data Book <http://fisher.lib.virginia.edu/collections/stats/ccdb>   The 1998 and 1994 editions are available at this site.

National Association of Counties <www.naco.org>   News, daily updates about terrorism; announcements, information about counties, projects, programs, publications.

National City Government Resource Center <www.geocities.com/CapitolHill/1389>   Roger Kemp's site has general, functional and regional city links; national think tanks; city resources.

State & County QuickFacts <www.census.gov>   Located on the right side of the U.S. Census Bureau's home page; frequently requested national, state and county census data; interactive maps and menus.

State and Metropolitan Area Data Book <www.census.gov/statab/www/smadb.html>   Reports statistics about economic and social conditions in U.S. cities, states, counties; guide to other Census Bureau sources.

Statistical Abstract of the United States <www.census.gov/prod/www/statistical-abstract-us.html>   Guide to data about U.S. and international economic and social conditions; guide to other Census Bureau sources.

USA Counties <www.census.gov/statab/www/county.html>   More than 5,000 bits of data relating to 3,142 U.S. counties; data from the Census Bureau, government agencies, private organizations.

GOVERNMENT: EXECUTIVE

Campaign Finance Information Center <www.campaignfinance.org>   Maintained by Investigative Reporters and Editors, site helps writers find out who contributes to campaigns and who benefits.

Catalog of United States Government Publications <www.gpoaccess.gov/cgp/index.html>   Main source for locating U.S. government documents published since 1994.

FECInfo <www.tray.com/fecinfo>   Nonpartisan source for campaign funding information; provides data for all federal candidates; lists PACs and donors.

Federal Election Commission <www.fec.gov>   Financial reports filed by presidential and congressional campaigns, parties and PACs; guide to campaign contributions and law; information about elections and voting.

Federal Register <www.gpoaccess.gov/fr/index.html>   Orders, proclamations and regulations issued by the president and by bureaus and agencies within the executive branch. Local news about hospitals, military installations, waterways, corporations, power companies.

GovSpot <www.govspot.com>   Links to useful Web sites, useful lists (teacher salaries, safest cities); news, military updates, world affairs, politics, social services.

State and Local Government on the Net <www.statelocalgov.net>   A good start for information about the states; governors, energy, environment, public safety, revenue, libraries, corrections, criminal justice, education, legal opinions.

United States Government Manual <www.gpoaccess.gov/gmanual/index.html>   Information about all branches of the federal government, but focuses primarily on the executive branch. Describes the creation and function of important federal agencies and bureaus; lists the major officials in agencies and bureaus; information about committees and commissions that aren't part of formal departments and agencies (the Interstate Commerce Commission) and quasi-governmental organizations (the National Academy of Science).

Weekly Compilation of Presidential Documents <www.gpoaccess.gov/wcomp/index.html>   Verbatim transcripts of presidential messages, speeches, news conferences, public statements.

The White House <www.whitehouse.gov>   Information about the president and vice president; White House history and recent news, latest federal statistics and White House documents; includes an interactive guide to information about the federal government; provides direct access to federal services.

GOVERNMENT: FEDERAL AGENCIES

Aviation Safety Information <www.nasdac.faa.gov/internet>   Links to important aviation safety data and information sources used by the federal government; aviation glossary, aviation regulations.

Census Bureau <www.census.gov>   Start here to learn how to use the Bureau's raw data.

Census Bureau <www.census.gov/pubinfo/www/news.html>   The Bureau's news section. Useful news releases prepared by Census Bureau public relations personnel describe social, economic, cultural trends. Online releases take writers to local sites where raw data are stored (and can be re-analyzed).

Department of Agriculture <http://usda.mannlib.cornell.edu/usda/usda.html>   Economics and Statistics System contains nearly 300 reports and data sets about U.S. and international agriculture and related topics; includes land and water conservation, livestock, rural affairs, trade issues, field crops, farm economics.

Energy Information Administration <www.eia.doe.gov>   Prepared by EIA, an independent agency within the U.S. Department of Energy; news, statistics, information about all forms of energy.

Federal Citizen Information Center <www.pueblo.gsa.gov>   Publications and news about all sorts of consumer problems, issues, opportunities.

Federal Emergency Management Agency <www.fema.gov>   FEMA facts and news, flood insurance, preparedness, storm watch, disaster assistance, safety tips.

FedStats <www.fedstats.gov>   The Federal Interagency Council on Statistical Policy maintains this site; provides access to data compiled by more than 70 federal agencies; profiles for each state.

Immigration and Naturalization Service <www.ins.gov>   INS documents that are available to the public; statistics about undocumented immigrants; naturalization information, appropriations; description of INS.

Internet Nonprofit Center <www.nonprofits.org/library/gov.html>   Government information about every nonprofit organization in the United States. Information is from federal and state governments; nonprofit organization locator is useful.

National Aeronautics & Space Administration <www.nasa.gov>   News about NASA and links to other NASA sites; space, earth science and aeronautics.

Population Reference Bureau <www.prb.org>   Links to other PRB sites; resources for communicators; world and U.S. population statistics, population projections, research reports, publications, fertility rates, health statistics, projections.

Social Security Administration <www.ssa.gov>   Guide to understanding Social Security; financing, benefits, disability information; earnings, tax rates, laws, regulations, news releases, statistics, research results, business services.

Uniform Crime Reports <www.fbi.gov/ucr.ucr.htm>   The FBI receives and compiles crime reports from local law enforcement agencies; these data are reported at this site.

U.S. Postal Service <www.usps.com>   If you want to know about the Postal Service, this is the place.

GOVERNMENT: LEGISLATIVE

Catalog of United States Government Publications <www.gpoaccess.gov/cgp/index.html> Main source for locating U.S. government documents published since 1994.

Congressional Record <www.gpoaccess.gov/crecord/index.html>   Voting records of members of Congress; verbatim accounts of speeches and debates; texts of bills; links to useful databases.

FECInfo <www.tray.com/fecinfo>   Nonpartisan source for campaign money information; provides data for all federal candidates; lists PACs and donors.

Federal Election Commission <www.fec.gov>   Financial reports filed by presidential and congressional campaigns, parties, PACs; guide to campaign contributions and law; information about elections, voting.

General Accounting Office <www.gao.gov>   News from the audit, evaluation and investigative arm of Congress; reports updated daily; legal decisions, press releases, federal agency issues.

Official Congressional Directory <www.access.gpo.gov/congress/browse-cd-oct02.html> Organization of Congress and committee memberships; biographical sketches of senators, representatives, other public officials; terms of service; committee memberships; government contact information; data about the many organizations that work with Congress. Information about congressional districts, senators and representatives arranged by state.

THOMAS: Legislative Information on the Internet <www.thomas.loc.gov>   Text of congressional legislation, electronic mail addresses for members of Congress and staff members, committee assignments, congressional ethics manual, committee reports, status of bills, votes, Declaration of Independence, U.S. Constitution.

HEALTH, MEDICINE

Center for Drug Evaluation and Research <www.fda.gov/cder/drug/default.htm>   Prescription and over-the-counter drug information; drug side effects and safety; reports, publications, special projects, drug approvals; links to other sites.

Centers for Disease Control and Prevention <www.cdc.gov>   News from and about the CDC; health information, statistics, training, employment, health funding.

Child Health USA 2002 <www.mchb.hrsa.gov/chusa02>   Report from the Health Resources and Services Administration; data about dozens of children's health topics, including health insurance, low birth weights, adolescent birthrates, infant mortality, vaccinations, diseases; publications, resources; program information.

Department of Health and Human Services <www.os.dhhs.gov> Health topics, Medicare, government, disease prevention, consumer issues, families, minorities, fraud, complaints.

Food and Drug Administration <www.fda.gov> Maintained by the U.S. Department of Health and Human Services; FDA news, safety alerts, warnings, product approvals, research, publications, regulated products (e.g., animal drugs and feed, vaccines, cosmetics, medical devices, cell telephones, implants).

Harvard Medical School <www.hms.harvard.edu> Medical news, facts, publications, maps; includes access to Library of Medicine Web sources (sciences, heath care, society, education).

HealthComm Key <www.cdc.gov/od/oc/hcomm> Maintained by the Centers for Disease Control and Prevention, site is a search service for health communication topics.

Healthfinder <www.healthfinder.gov> A federal gateway to information about consumer health and human services; links to clearinghouses, health databases, publications, Web sites, support groups.

HealthGate <www.healthgate.com> Health, biomedical research, medicine, patient education, nursing, diseases, recent health news and developments; *New England Journal of Medicine* briefings.

Higher Education Center for Alcohol and Other Drug Prevention <www.edc.org/hec> Just about anything you need to know about alcohol and drug abuse treatment, prevention, statistics, research.

International Food Information Council Foundation <www.ific.org> Food and health research; suggests essential information to look for; defines key scientific terms; explains scientific methodology.

Merck <www.merck.com/pubs/mmanual> This is the old, wonderful (and latest) edition of *The Merck Manual of Diagnosis and Therapy*. Information about disease, drugs, illness; definitions; research.

National Academy for State Health Policy <www.nashp.org> Information on state health care policies; links to other useful sites.

National Center for Health Statistics <www.cdc.gov/nchs> A service of the Centers for Disease Control and Prevention, the site provides statistics about virtually every aspect of health; includes news releases, vital statistics, research and development, births, deaths, nursing homes, children, the aged.

National Institutes of Health <www.nih.gov> Overview and introduction to NIH, health information and NIH resources, online catalogs; links to other NIH organizations.

National Library of Medicine's MEDLINE <www.nlm.nih.gov/databases/databases_medline .html> A database of more than 9 million references to articles published in 3,800 biomedical journals.

National Library of Medicine's MEDLINEplus <www.nlm.nih.gov/medlineplus>   Material about diseases, wellness, generic and nongeneric drugs; locations and credentials of doctors and dentists; hospitals, consumer health libraries; includes a medical encyclopedia and dictionaries.

National Women's Health Information Center <www.4woman.gov>   Free, reliable health information for women; breast-feeding, body image, hormone therapy, minority health, smoking, violence, other issues.

National Women's Health Resource Center <www.healthywomen.org>   Extensive information and resources about women's health; includes a question-answer section.

Official U.S. Government Site for Medicare Information <www.medicare.gov>   Everything a user could want to know about Medicare services and policies and about health issues and problems; links to regional and state offices; useful nursing home data.

World Health Organization's Whosis (WHO Statistical Information System) <www3.who.int/whosis>   Guide to statistical information available from WHO; descriptions of diseases and where they occur.

HUMAN RIGHTS

American Civil Liberties Union <www.aclu.org>   Site contains all sorts of information relating to the Bill of Rights (which the ACLU pledges to defend); news and information about free speech, press freedom, national security, police practices, civil rights and more.

Amnesty International <www.amnesty.org>   One of the most famous human rights groups; essays, reports about global violations, breakdowns by countries, death penalty.

Anti-defamation League <www.adl.org>   Information about anti-Semitism around the world; civil rights, the Holocaust, religious freedom, terrorism; news.

Civil Rights Division, U.S. Department of Justice <www.usdoj.gov/crt/crt-home.html>   Overview and agency description, frequently asked questions, freedom of information, recent civil rights developments, news.

Human Rights Watch <www.hrw.org>   Commentary; news about violations worldwide; essays, news from international courts, global issues, information by country.

Office of the United Nations High Commissioner for Human Rights <www.unhchr.ch>   The United Nations' human rights activities; links to human rights bodies, children's rights; special reports from world trouble spots; programs; good databases and search mechanism.

United Nations <www.un.org/english>   Look here first for international reports, data, news, crises, human rights, laws; links to other U.N. agencies.

Urban Morgan Institute for Human Rights <www.law.uc.edu/morgan2>   Maintained by the University of Cincinnati, site contains information about human rights worldwide; includes DIANA, a huge human rights database.

U.S. Commission on Civil Rights <www.usccr.gov>   Overview of commission duties, reports, publications, news; regional offices.

INTERNATIONAL

Latin American Network Information Center <www.lanic.utexas.edu>   Maintained by the University of Texas at Austin, site reports information about Latin America, including economies, education, travel, libraries and reference sources, social and natural sciences, development, recreation, mass communication, media.

Statistics Canada <www.statcan.ca>   Reports any statistic you're likely to need about Canada, including the economy, trade, government, people; products, services, international statistical conferences and proceedings, research reports, analytical articles, employment opportunities, education, the census.

The World Factbook <www.odci.gov/cia/publications/factbook/index.html>   This Central Intelligence Agency site provides extensive information by country, including useful reference maps.

World Gazetteer <www.world-gazetteer.com>   Populations of towns, regions, cities from around the world; images of national flags.

INTERNET GUIDES

American Journalism Review <www.ajr.org>   Information about mass communication; claims 8,000 links to media around the world; useful search tools and starting points for journalists; a useful job link.

Blue Skyways' Train Stations <http://skyways.lib.ks.us/training>   Divided into six tracks, site is a good starting point for those who want to learn about the Internet and computers; includes discussions of ethics, censorship, copyright, filtering.

Campaign Finance Information Center <www.campaignfinance.org>   Maintained by Investigative Reporters and Editors, site helps users track campaign contributions nationally and by state; stories, tips, federal contracts database, resources, training opportunities. Some parts require registration.

Columbia Journalism Review <www.cjr.org>   Mass communication with links to archives, magazines, newspapers, academic and professional communication organizations; a useful job link.

Columbia Missourian, University of Missouri <www.columbiamissourian.com>   Stan Ketterer's list of Web resources and help; sources, electronic mail addresses, maps, government statistics, databases.

Educational Resources Information Center <www.eric.ed.gov>   The place to start a search for information about education issues; links to the ERIC database, a virtual library; research and development resources.

The Essential Guide to the Web <www.bbc.co.uk/webguide>   Maintained by the British Broadcasting Corp., site is devoted to the arts, culture, business and finance, nature, education, entertainment, science.

FACSNET <www.facsnet.org>   Helpful information in several categories, including Internet resources, reporting tools, major communication issues, sources online.

Federal Web Locator <www.infoctr.edu/fwl>   Maintained by the Center for Information Law and Policy, a cooperative effort by the Villanova School of Law and the Illinois Institute of Technology; a comprehensive, one-stop guide to federal government sites on the Web.

Finding Data on the Internet: A Journalist's Guide <www.nilesonline.com/data>   Maintained by Robert Niles; suggests useful Web sites in many categories (e.g., agriculture, education, military, politics); useful for all mass communication professionals.

Global Computing Inc. <www.globalcomputing.com/states.html>   Links to states and to sites providing data about businesses, government publications, search services for broadcasters, sports, travel, universities.

Internet Resources for Latin America <http://lib.nmsu.edu/subject/bord/laguia>   Maintained by New Mexico State University, this is a guide to online information about Latin America.

Investigative Reporters and Editors, Inc. <www.ire.org>   IRE site offers several good features, including a frequently updated list of tip sheets that help users learn to use the Web.

Kennedy School of Government, Harvard <www.ksg.harvard.edu/library/all_guides.htm>   Includes sections on how to get the most from the Web and how to evaluate Web information. Lists many sources for communicators, with links to newspapers, magazines.

Librarians' Index to the Internet <http://lii.org>   Maintained by the California State Library; Web sites in many, varied categories; search capability.

LITA <www.ala.org/ala/lita/litaresources/toolkitforexpert/toolkitexpert.htm>   The Library & Information Technology Association's "Toolkit for the Expert Web Searcher."

National Institute for Computer-Assisted Reporting <www.nicar.org>   Maintained by the Missouri School of Journalism and Investigative Reporters and Editors, site helps writers learn how to find, get and analyze electronic information.

Power Reporting <www.powerreporting.com>   Bill Dedman's site links to thousands of free research tools for writers. Search tips; annotated lists of good sites.

Search Systems <www.searchsystems.net>   Stores many state and local records; more than 21,000 searchable, public, free databases.

State Web Locator <www.infoctr.edu/swl>   Maintained by the Villanova Center for Information Law and Policy; links to sites maintained by state, city, county governments, departments, agencies.

Webgator <www.virtualgumshoe.com/wgator1.html>   Useful to investigative journalists for an impressive array of subjects, including cults, gangs, terrorists, military, vital records, bankruptcy, companies, parole boards, inmates, prison information, wanted lists.

INTERNET TUTORIALS

A Journalist's Guide to the Internet (the St. Louis Chapter of the Society of Professional Journalists) <www.stlouisspj.org/surf/surf.html>

Net Tour (the National Institute for Computer Assisted Reporting) <www.ire.org/training/nettour>

JOB SEARCH SERVICES

America's Career InfoNet <www.acinet.org/acinet/default.asp>   Job bank, job market trends, compensation trends, career advice, information by state.

America's Job Bank <www.ajb.dni.us>   Job listings in many fields; advice about job searches; job market information; news about employers.

Careerbuilder <www.careerbuilder.com>   Lists newspaper want ads; provides resume help and advice.

hotjobs <http://hotjobs.yahoo.com>   Lists jobs in many fields; helpful job search advice.

Internet Career Connection <www.iccweb.com>   Personal resumes posted online; lists 1 million want ads; information about government job opportunities.

JobBankUSA <www.jobbankusa.com>   Employment and resume services for job candidates, employers, recruitment firms; job search resources, company profiles, fairs; online job search.

JobOptions <www.joboptions.com>   Posts resumes; job alerts, career aids, employer profiles; online job search.

Monster <www.monster.com>   Lists a trillion jobs, including mass communication. Also provides helpful hints about the job search, resume construction. Comprehensive, easy to use.

The Riley Guide <www.rileyguide.com>   Introduction to job seeking; includes links to career planning and resume preparation, online job searches, student and alumni sources, internships, career fairs.

TrueCareers<www.careercity.com>   Helpful advice for resumes, dressing for interviews, successful job searches; lists job fairs; discusses salaries and negotiation tactics.

LABOR RELATIONS

AFL-CIO <www.aflcio.org>   Includes news releases, policy statements, boycott lists; links to related sites.

Bureau of Labor Statistics <www.bls.gov>   All sorts of labor statistics; information about the economy, occupational outlook, public education resources, publications, research papers, contact information; helps users identify and access huge volumes of time series statistics; links to other BLS Web pages.

Cornell University School of Industrial & Labor Relations <www.ilr.cornell.edu/library>   Federal commission reports about labor relations; important government documents and reports, policy position papers, statistics about employer-employee relationships.

Equal Employment Opportunity Commission <www.eeoc.gov>   Fact sheets, news releases, laws relating to employment discrimination.

LAW

Cornell University Legal Information Institute <www.supct.law.cornell.edu/supct/>   U.S. Supreme Court decisions since 1990 indexed and searchable.

CyberLaw & CyberLex <www.cyberlaw.com>   Reports on legal issues relating to the computer industry.

Electronic Privacy Information Center <www.epic.org>   Civil liberties issues, privacy, encryption, the First Amendment, the Constitution.

Electronic Privacy Information Center/Open Government <www.epic.org/open_gov>   Guide to the Freedom of Information Act of 1966; includes complete text, White House and Department of Justice memos; information about generating a request; other useful open government resources.

Emory University School of Law <www.law.emory.edu/FEDCTS>   Full text versions of the opinions of the 11 U.S. Circuit Courts of Appeal.

FedWorld <www.fedworld.gov/supcourt/index.htm>   U.S. Supreme Court decisions rendered before 1990.

FindLaw (West Publishing Co.) <www.directory.findlaw.com>   Perhaps the most complete directory of U.S. law firms and attorneys. Listing nearly 1 million firms and lawyers, FindLaw is searchable by name, legal specialization, state, city, college attended.

InterLaw <www.interlaw.org>   A huge, free legal resource; includes court rulings, state laws, law encyclopedia and dictionary, legal forms, consumer information, legal software.

LawGuru <www.lawguru.com>   From the law offices of Eslamboly & Barlavi; helps with legal research and questions; links to hundreds of pages and sites dealing with legal issues and problems.

Legal Information Institute at Cornell University <www.law.cornell.edu>   Maintained by the Cornell Law Library; contact information for law school faculties and others in the legal profession; extensive library resources, including information about federal court decisions, international treaties, newsworthy cases.

National Archives and Records Administration <www.gpoaccess.gov/nara/index.html>   Text of presidential orders, public laws, laws published in the Federal Register and the Code of Federal Regulations.

University of Pittsburgh School of Law <www.jurist.law.pitt.edu/dictionary.htm>   Dictionary of legal terminology, with emphasis on legal procedure; links to relevant sites.

U.S. Code <www4.law.cornell.edu/uscode>   Cornell University's archive of the U.S. Code, which contains all the laws passed by the federal government; easy to use when you get the hang of it.

Versuslaw <www.versuslaw.com>   Comprehensive database with information about malpractice, case law, opinions.

LIBRARIES, REFERENCE

American Library Association <www.ala.org>   Professional information services and access; professional tools, education, news.

Information Please <www.infoplease.com>   One of the best reference works, with useful facts about a wide variety of subjects; national and international data from almanacs, atlases, dictionaries, encyclopedias; highly reliable.

Internet Public Library Reference Center <www.ipl.org>   Education, science, technology, law, government, business, finance, social sciences.

LibraryHQ.com <www.libraryhq.com>   Lists dozens of library associations and organizations in several categories (academic, art and music, medical, religion, federal, technology, ethnic); news, information about new products and services.

Library of Congress <www.loc.gov> Every book, government document and article published in the United States, and many nongovernment research reports, are archived here; copyright information; access to LOC services, research tools, catalogs, digital collections; provides full text of legislation, global legal information, country studies; links to Internet resources.

Reference Desk <www.refdesk.com/expert.html> Ask questions of the refdesk experts, or link to other, similar sites; law, medicine; many subject categories.

Smithsonian Institution <www.si.edu> Smithsonian publications and photographs; *Encyclopedia Smithsonian*; history, museums, organizations of the Smithsonian; facilitates search of hundreds of topics in dozens of fields (history, culture, music, armed forces, anthropology, technology).

U.S. National Commission on Libraries and Information Science <www.nclis.gov/index.cfm> Government information policy, freedom of information, surveys, statistics, national libraries, news.

The Virtual Reference Desk by Thor (The Online Resource) <www.thorplus.lib.purdue.edu/eresources/readyref> Links to government documents, telephone books, maps, science data, dictionaries, archives.

MAPS

Maps and Cartographic Resources, U.S. Census Bureau <www.census.gov/geo/www/maps/> Links to free downloadable maps in PDF format; links to mapping applications based on Census Bureau base map data.

National Geographic Society <www.nationalgeographic.com/maps> Conservation maps, country profiles, atlas updates, reference maps, recreation maps, trails, street maps.

Old-Maps <www.old-maps.co.uk> A good archive of digitalized historical maps. Neighborhood maps from the 1800s. Searchable by place name, address or coordinate.

Perry-Castaneda Library Map Collection, The University of Texas <www.lib.utexas.edu/maps/index.html> Maps of the world, the continents, countries, states; historical maps; indexes; government information; wildfire-related maps; links to other sites.

TopoZone <www.topozone.com> Recreational and professional topographic maps; the Web's first interactive topographical map of the United States; news and information.

MASS MEDIA

ABC News <www.abcnews.go.com>

The Associated Press <www.ap.org>

British Broadcasting Corp <www.bbc.co.uk>

CBS News <www.cbsnews.com>

Chicago Tribune <www.chicagotribune.com>

CNN Interactive <www.cnn.com>

C-SPAN <www.c-span.org>

The (London) *Guardian* <www.guardian.co.uk/online>

Los Angeles Times <www.latimes.com>

National Public Radio <www.npr.org>

NBC News <www.msnbc.msn.com>

Newsweek <www.newsweek.com>

The New York Times <www.nytimes.com>

PR Wire <www.prnewswire.com>   Access news from thousands of organizations around the planet.

Public Broadcasting Service <www.pbs.org>

Reuters News Headlines <www.reuters.com>

Time <www.time.com>

Times of London <www.timesonline.co.uk>

USA Today <www.usatoday.com>

The Washington Post <www.washingtonpost.com>

MEDIA INFORMATION

Advertising Age <www.adage.com>   Maintained by the advertising magazine, site supplies information about advertisers, advertising agencies, jobs, industry statistics; links to related sites.

Ad Week <www.adweek.com>   News, information, statistics about the advertising industry.

J.P. Bowen in the United Kingdom <www.comlab.ox.ac.uk/archive/publishers/broadcast.html> Lists broadcasters and Web sites from around the world; satellites, museums, news groups, programming guides, organizations.

Broadcasting & Cable Online <www.broadcastingcable.com>   Broadcast and cable news, station sales, industry calendar, policy briefings, Nielson ratings, FCC actions; job bank.

Editor & Publisher Online <www.mediainfo.com>   Daily media news, directories, conferences, classifieds; links to media outlets.

Federal Communications Commission <www.fcc.gov>   FCC actions, meetings, agendas; digital and children's television, V-chip news, channel auctions, search tools, annual reports, industry statistics, economic information, offices, bureaus.

Image Technics Inc <www.imagetechnics.com/hmag.htm>   Links to electronic media magazines on the Web.

IPREX <www.iprex.com>   Maintained by IPREX, the partnership of independent public relations agencies worldwide; describes IPREX resources, capabilities; background about specialty areas within the organizations; member firms; marketing and public relations news.

Islandnet <www.islandnet.com>   Electronic mail addresses for worldwide media outlets (newspapers, magazines, radio and television stations and networks, services and associations) that accept electronic submissions.

Media Awareness Network in Canada <www.media-awareness.ca>   A springboard to information about media issues (privacy, media ownership, children, media).

Video Age <www.videoageinternational.com>   Online news and features about the international video industry; calendar of video events by city and state.

The Working Reporter: A Resource for Journalists <www.workingreporter.com>   Links to commercial and college newspapers, professional and trade journals, magazines, broadcasting; associations; ethics codes; freedom of information sites.

MILITARY

Federation of American Scientists <www.fas.org>   Analyses of science, technology and public policy issues about the military; emphasis on nuclear weapons and disarmament issues; data about arms sales, chemical and biological warfare, arms control, intelligence, space policy.

Jane's Defence Glossary <www.janes.com/defence/glossary>   Database contains more than 20,000 defense-related acronyms and abbreviations in easy-to-use format.

U.S. Department of Defense <www.defenselink.mil/sites/f.html#facts>   An interagency collection of information important to communicators; site helps military public affairs officers give access and information to civilian media.

MINORITIES

Administration for Native Americans <www.acf.dhhs.gov/programs/ana>   News and information about the ANA.

American-Arab Anti-Discrimination Committee <www.adc.org>   Lists experts on Arabs, Islam, Middle East; news; government affairs updates; hate crimes and discrimination information.

American Civil Liberties Union <www.aclu.org> Information about struggles of minorities (gays, persons of color, students, lesbians, women, immigrants) to retain their civil liberties.

Arab American Institute <www.aaiusa.org> News; AAI publications, position statements and contacts; discrimination and civil rights; census information center; helpful links.

Black and Minority Ethnic People <www.sosig.ac.uk/roads/subject-listing/World-cat/ethnic .html> Focuses on the social welfare and civil rights of racial groups; conferences, events, tutorials, papers, reports, books, databases, educational materials, government bodies, news; helpful links.

Black Information Link <www.blink.org.uk/pdescription.asp?key=1389&grp=30> BLINK posts information about black issues and people in the United Kingdom; includes health, jobs, immigration, politics, reparation, art and culture, law, civil rights, children, women.

Facts on the Asian/Pacific Islander Population, U.S. Census Bureau <www.census.gov/population/ www/socdemo/race/api.html> Data about Asians and Pacific Islanders; social and economic characteristics, profiles, news; tons of census data.

Facts on the Black/African Population, U.S. Census Bureau <www.census.gov/population/ www/socdemo/race/black.html> Data about blacks and Africans; social and economic characteristics, profiles, news; tons of census data.

Facts on the Hispanic/Latino Population, U.S. Census Bureau <www.census.gov/population/ www/socdemo/race/hispanic.html> Data about Hispanics; social and economic characteristics, profiles, news; tons of census data.

Human Rights Campaign <www.hrc.org> Maintained by the HRC—which works for gay, lesbian, bisexual and transgender rights—site provides news, legislative updates, facts.

Lesbian and Gay Rights, American Civil Liberties Union <www.aclu.org/LesbianGayRights/ LesbianGayRightsMain.cfm> Latest news, publications, position papers, legislative updates, fact sheets, resources, issues.

Native Americans—Internet Resources <http://falcon.jmu.edu/~ramseyil/native.htm> From the Internet School Library Media Center, site provides links to directories, bibliographies about tribes, historical documents, periodicals.

Status and Trends in the Education of Hispanics <http://nces.ed.gov/pubsearch/pubsinfo.asp? pubid=2003008> Draws on statistics published by the National Center for Education Statistics relating to the educational status of Hispanics.

U.S. Hispanic Chamber of Commerce <www.ushcc.com/hisp_today_tv.htm> A good source of information about legislative affairs, services, events, statistics, resources, programs and international business.

NONPROFIT ORGANIZATIONS

Charities Review Council <www.crcmn.org>   Designed primarily for the use of donors and nonprofit agencies, site is a good place to start for a writer analyzing any nonprofit organization.

General Accounting Office <www.gao.gov>   A good description of Form 990, which is required of nonprofit organizations.

Internet Nonprofit Center <www.nonprofits.org/library/gov.html>   Government information about every nonprofit organization in the United States. Information is from federal and state governments; nonprofit organization locator is useful.

Your Guide to IRS Form 990 <www.crcmn.org/donorinfo/form990/>   Form 990 is the place to start in any analysis of any nonprofit organization. Go here first.

NUMERICAL AIDS

Robertniles.com <www.nilesonline.com/stats>   Part of Niles' guide to the Web. Percentage, mean, median, mode, standard deviation and the rest; tips for data analyses, statistical tests; tips to avoid getting duped.

PEOPLE, BUSINESS DIRECTORIES

BigBook <www.bigbook.com>   A Yellow Pages-type directory that includes more than 16 million listings to help businesses and consumers research each other; lists product and service information, maps, directions, voting information.

Bigfoot <www.bigfoot.com>   Another good source of electronic mail addresses, telephone listings, Web pages. It's fairly simple, but powerful.

Infospace/The Ultimate Directory <www.infospace.com>   Yellow and white pages, shopping information, classifieds (real estate, cars, boats), government listings, business guides, chat rooms, news, sports, international sources.

Switchboard <www.switchboard.com>   More than 100 million residential and 11 million business listings; offers free home page, e-mail and links to more than 15,000 sites.

Telephone Directories on the Web <www.numberway.com>   Directories from around the world, including yellow and white pages, electronic mail addresses, government listings.

Yahoo! <www.people.yahoo.com>   Your best source for electronic mail addresses; but remember, there is no comprehensive list of addresses.

POLLING

American Association for Public Opinion Research <www.aapor.org>   Everything anyone needs to know about public opinion surveys, ethics, standards, techniques.

Gallup Poll <www.gallup.com>   Poll results and analyses; good explanations of polling procedures. Fee required to view some results.

The Pew Research Center for the People and the Press <www.people-press.org>   American and international poll results, commentaries.

Polling Organizations <www.library.yale.edu/socsci/opinion/pollingorganizations.html> Yale University's comprehensive list of U.S. and international polling organizations; links to each organization.

RELIGION

Ontario Consultants on Religious Tolerance <www.religioustolerance.org>   Information about many religions, including cults.

Religion Source, American Academy of Religion <www.religionsource.org>   "The Journalists' Shortcut to 5,000 Scholars"; search by topic to get expertise and contacts; free for journalists.

Religious Newswriters Association and Its Foundation <www.religionwriters.com>   Reference sources, speakers bureau, newsroom training resources, breaking news, hot sources, background information.

Religious Studies Web Guide <www.ucalgary.ca/~lipton>   Free Internet resources for writers and researchers; world religions, subjects and denominations; texts, indices, images.

Gene R. Thursby <www.clas.ufl.edu/users/gthursby/rel>   Maintained at the University of Florida; information and links for the study and interpretation of religions; religious traditions, research, teaching, reference sources.

World Lecture Hall/Religious Studies <www.utexas.edu/world/lecture>   Maintained at the University of Texas; links to sites about classic religious literature, comparative religion, myth, ethics, God in culture, history, magic, mystery; includes most religions.

SCIENCE

American Association for the Advancement of Science <www.eurekalert.org>   News releases; research in science, medicine, technology; links to scholarly journals, science media, contributing institutions.

International Atomic Energy Agency <www.iaea.org>   Research reports, news, periodicals, reference center; accounts of IAEA activities.

NASA/Global Change Master Directory <http://gcmd.gsfc.nasa.gov>   International climate change center; links to hundreds of domestic and international sites.

National Academy of Sciences <www.nationalacademies.org>   Directories and publications; news, projects, events; information about the National Academy of Engineering, Institute of Medicine and National Research Council.

National Science Foundation <www.nsf.gov>   Grants and awards in science and engineering, special notices and news about NSF; staff directory, science and engineering statistics; search help.

Rice University <http://conbio.net/vl>   A virtual library of resources, articles and links about ecology, the environment and biodiversity; Internet sources are evaluated for their educational value.

SEARCH SERVICES

Most search services have powerful search engines, but they also offer other features, including telephone and electronic mail directories.

Alltheweb <www.alltheweb.com>   Indexes billions of Web pages, hundreds of millions of FTP, multimedia and audio files, tens of millions of PDF files.

AltaVista <www.altavista.com>   Comprehensive services and an outstanding search engine.

Ask Jeeves <http://ask.com>   Type in a question and click Ask.

Dogpile <www.dogpile.com>   Meta-search engine that scans multiple search engines at one time.

Go <http://go.com>   A comprehensive service.

Google <www.google.com>   Google is a bit unusual in that it ranks selected sites by frequency of use.

Lycos <www.lycos.com>   A comprehensive service.

37.com <www.37.com>   Lists sites selected from a search of 37 search engines.

Yahoo! <www.yahoo.com>   A comprehensive service.

SPORTS

CBSSportsline.com <www.cbs.sportsline.com>

ESPN <www.espn.com>

Fox Sports <www.foxsports.com>

National Collegiate Athletic Association <www.ncaa.org>   The NCAA's administrative site; NCAA news, facts, polls, statistics, publications, governance, rules, grants, research, enforcement, reinstatement.

Sports Illustrated <www.sportsillustrated.cnn.com>

The Sports Network <www.sportsnetwork.com>

TERRORISM

Centre for the Study of Terrorism and Political Violence <www.st-andrews.ac.uk/academic/intrel/research/cstpv>   Based at the University of St. Andrews in the United Kingdom, site provides information about studies of the roots, impact and responses to political violence.

The International Policy Institute for Counter-Terrorism <www.ict.org.il>   Maintained by the Interdisciplinary Center, Herzliya, Israel, site features breaking news, counterterrorism activities, forum, Arab-Israeli conflict, essays.

Jurist Legal Intelligence <www.jurist.law.pitt.edu/terrorism.htm>   University of Pittsburgh site focuses mainly on legal implications of terrorism; terrorists and fight against terrorism; world and U.S. terrorism laws; civil liberties.

Office of Homeland Security <www.whitehouse.gov/homeland>   News briefings, fact sheets, updates, official government pronouncements; global communication, levels of terrorist threats; funding for anti-terrorist activity; breaking news.

Response to Terrorism <http://usinfo.state.gov/is/international_security/terrorism.html>   U.S. State Department site has official U.S. government views and news; links to other agencies.

Terrorism and Terrorists <www.homeoffice.gov.uk/terrorism>   Official reports, studies, commentaries and documents from the British government; links to other government offices; news of emergencies, immigration, nationality, passports.

U.N. Action Against Terrorism <www.un.org/terrorism>   What the United Nations is doing to combat terrorism; latest developments; disarmament.

TRAVEL

Bureau of Consular Affairs, Department of State <www.travel.state.gov>   Travel warnings and consular information sheets; embassy and consulate Web sites; crisis information from the Office of Homeland Security, citizenship, nationality, voting assistance abroad, children's issues, health warnings abroad, foreign consular offices in the United States; visa information.

CNN Travel <www.cnn.com/TRAVEL>   Travel features, warnings, cool destinations, travel industry, driving directions, travel resources.

Travelers' Health, National Center for Infectious Diseases <www.cdc.gov/travel>   Diseases in foreign countries; vaccinations, safe water and food, traveling with kids.

Travel Library <www.travel-library.com>   International tourist information; travel features, where to find information, what's popular and what's not, how to get there.

WEATHER, DISASTER

Disaster Relief <www.disasterrelief.org>   Maintained by IBM, CNN and the American Red Cross, this site tracks worldwide disasters and provides information about disaster preparedness.

Federal Emergency Management Agency <www.fema.gov>   Disasters, flood insurance, surviving disasters, storm watches, disaster declarations.

National Aeronautics & Space Administration: Global Change Master Directory <gcmd .gsfc.nasa.gov>   International climate change center; links to hundreds of domestic and international sites.

National Hurricane Center/Tropical Prediction Center <www.nhc.noaa/gov>   Warnings, watches, forecasts, analyses of hazardous tropical weather, preparedness information.

National Weather Service <www.nws.noaa.gov>   Local, national and international weather information; some historical data.

National Weather Service/Storm Watch <www.nws.noaa.gov>   Information sent to news organizations about tropical storms and depressions, hurricanes, waves.

Weather Channel <www.weather.com>   Major weather headlines and news, forecasts and current conditions for U.S. and international cities; maps, travel conditions, publications about weather, ski reports.

WOMEN

American Association of University Women <www.aauw.org>   News for and about women in higher education; research, events, political actions on college and university campuses.

Chartbook on Women and Disability in the United States <www.infouse.com/disabilitydata/ womendisability>   Reference for technical and nontechnical users who need information about the relationship between women and disability. Format is topic question, explanatory text and graphic or table.

League of Women Voters <www.lwv.org>   Site offers just about all the facts anyone (male or female) needs to know about voting in the United States, including news, the League's position on issues, voter information, electoral reform.

National Organization for Women <www.now.org>   Calendar of events; news of interest and importance to women; legislative updates, NOW positions on the issues.

National Women's Health Information Center <www.4woman.gov>   Free, reliable health information for women; breast-feeding, body image, hormone therapy, minority health, smoking, violence, other issues.

National Women's Health Resource Center <www.healthywomen.org>   Extensive information and resources about women's health; includes a question-and-answer section.

Office on Violence Against Women <www.ojp.usdoj.gov/vawo>   What local and state officials can do to help prevent violence against women; federal laws against violence against women; research, statistics, publications; news; links to hot lines, coalitions, advocacy groups.

Women Watch <www.un.org/womenwatch>   The United Nations' gateway to the advancement of women; statistics, research, publications; links to useful sites; calendar; information about women by country; conventions and declarations relating to women's rights.

WRITING AIDS

American Heritage Book of English Usage <www.bartleby.com/64>   An authoritative guide to diction, style, gender, grammar, word usage.

The American Language <www.bartleby.com/185>   H.L. Mencken's classic analysis of U.S. English usage defines the language.

The Columbia Guide to Standard American English <www.bartleby.com/68>   More than 6,500 prescriptive and descriptive entries; 4,300 links to other references.

The Columbia World of Quotations <www.bartleby.com/66>   Contains 65,000 quotations from more than 5,000 authors in 6,500 subjects.

The Elements of Style <www.bartleby.com/141>   The Strunk and White classic remains useful in this electronic age; other useful reference books are available here.

Merriam-Webster Online/Dictionary, Thesaurus <www.m-w.com>   Check spelling and find the word you *really* want.

On Line English Grammar <www.edunet.com/english>   Easy-to-use guide to grammar and style.

Roget's II: The New Thesaurus <www.bartleby.com/62>   More than 35,000 synonyms in user-friendly format.

Simpson's Contemporary Quotations <www.bartleby.com/63>   More than 10,000 quotations from more than 4,000 sources in 25 categories.

The Working Reporter: A Resource for Journalists <www.workingreporter.com>   A good resource for working writers; writing aids and ideas; links to commercial and college newspapers, professional and trade journals, magazines, broadcasting; career guide; ethics codes.

The Writer's Home <www.writershome.com/magazines/mag1.htm>   Writing aids, article ideas, critical thinking, word usage, writers' tools; links to 1,000 sites that can help writers of all types.

CREDITS

INDEX